The Ultimate Instant Pot

Cookbook for Beginners

1500 Easy & Delicious Instant Pot Recipes for Beginners and Advanced Users to Pressure Cooker, Slow Cooker, Rice/Grain Cooker, Sauté, and More

Martha Romero

Table of Contents

Chapter 5 Stew Recipes 51

Chapter 6 Bean, Pasta and Grain Recipes 65

Chapter 7 Fish and Seafood Recipes 81

Chapter 8 Chicken and Poultry Recipes 103

Introduction

You always hear everyone raving about Instant pot, but what are Instant Pots? Well, the popular Instant Pots are great for two obvious reasons. In short, they save time and space in the kitchen. They replace many other kitchen appliances and some can be even used as yogurt makers. After discovering the magic of Instant Pot, you will honestly say that it has made preparing Sunday breakfast a thousand times easier. Instant Pot lets you cook meals and dinners every week for about an hour, avoiding the sink with dirty pots and pans.

Instant Pots are a variety of cooking machines with a variety of functions including slow cooking, baking, steaming, reheating, and sautéing. Yes, all of these features in one device to speed up the cooking process. The first Instant Pots were announced in 2010. Fast forward to 2021, it has become the most popular kitchen appliance of the kitchen and has conquered its top space due to ease and time management during cooking. Instant Pots come in a variety of sizes from 3 quarts to 8 quarts. They all look good for a little different but approximately have the same functions in it.

Instant Pots are the best for most people, especially since they come in low and high-pressure cooking. You can cook your food in pressure cook mode which helps cook your food fast and reduce cooking time drastically. With the help of sautéing function, you can cook your food like any pot and get a magnificent result. With this function, you can sauté your food and then turn it on to another process like slow cook or pressure cooking. This aids in lowering the kitchen mess and cleaning countertops and sinks. Overall, Instant pot is a blessing for the cooks for making delicious meals without creating a mess in the kitchen.

This cookbook is the best option for using and cooking in an Instant Pot. This guide will help you to manage your instant pot with a variety of delicious recipes and its cleaning after cooking. In short in this book, you will get all you want about your Instant pot.

Fundamentals of Instant Pot

Like a microwave or an electric kettle, Instant Pots have become a kitchen essential. This versatile machine transforms countless countertop appliances, from rice cookers to slow cookers. It introduces a new generation of culinary delights and shows you how fast you can prepare healthy food.

Whether you're a new Instant Pot owner or have been on the shelf for a long time, this guide is for you. This guide helps you through the basics, including explaining the basics and the different buttons used to make delicious dishes.

What is Instant Pot

Instant Pot is a multi-purpose pressure cooker. It can also prepare sauces and light dishes, rice, steamed vegetables, and chicken-like any traditional cooking to other cooking appliances. It's an all-in-one dish, so you can braise your chicken and cook it all with just one Instant Pot. Typically, Instant Pot meals are prepped to work in less than an hour. The fast cooking time is due to the pressure generating techniques where even the juices from the meat and vegetables lock into the chamber and food is cooked in their liquid. But don't confuse it with the stove. Unlike a traditional pressure cooker, this Instant Pot eliminates dangerous issues with the lid closed and stays closed until the pressure is reduced.

With Instant Pot, you can cook a complete meal for the whole family can safely eat in 30 minutes. You can cook many dishes from 30 to 60 minutes such as rice, chicken, beef stew, peppers, and whole chicken. And yes, you can bake bread with the instant pot right away. Paleo and ketogenic dieters prefer Instant Pots, which allow you to "simmer" and "Sauté" meat in no time, also vegetarians and vegans can quickly cook up dishes like butternut squash soup, sweet potatoes, peppers, oats, and mac and cheese. You can cook food, like dried beans, which are always required overnight to cook and can be prepared for up to 30 minutes for many dishes such as chilies and hummus.

How to Cook Food with the Instant Pot

How you use Instant Pot depends on the recipe you cook. However, many recipes, especially meat, prefer to follow this process:

Set the instant pot to sauté mode. Add oil and brown proteins such as beef or chicken. Spices such as garlic and onion also brown during this time.

Click the Cancel button. Add broth or soup to scrape the browned bits off the pot.

Now close the lid to Sealing position and then set the Instant Pot on Pressure Cook.

Set cooking time and cooking temperature on the Instant Pot according to your cooking needs or the recipes.

Then release the pressure according to guidance and taste you prefer.

The steps above may vary slightly depending on the recipe, but most things you do in your Instant Pan will follow the order.

Benefits of Using It

Following are some of the benefits of using Instant pot for cooking. After this, you will proudly use it for your cooking.

1.Saves Energy

According to Instant Pot manufacturers, "The electric pressure cooker is the second-best electric appliance after microwave ovens. Compared to other cooking methods such as baking, boiling, or steaming, high cooking pressure can reduce cooking time and energy by up to 70%.

2.Saves Time

As mentioned earlier, it can save a lot of time in the kitchen by not only reducing cooking time but also reducing prep time. It saves time by eliminating the need for thawed meat or soaked beans.

3.Saves Money

Instant Pot can provide your family with home-cooked meals without having to skip meals or opt for groceries, which can save you a lot of money. You can also reduce expensive foods in your diet. For example; dried beans are about one-third the cost of canned beans.

4.Healthy Method of Cooking

Reduces Dining Out: Instant pot allows you a variety of dishes to cook at home with perfection. It will reduce your dining out because of fancy food you cooked at home with help of this appliance.

Non-toxic: The food you cooked in an instant pot is non-toxic because it is cooked by yourself and you know what ingredients are used in it and other the high pressure kills any possible harmful bacteria in the food.

Nutritious: Pressure Cooking is a more nutritious cooking method than many methods of cooking, retaining more water-soluble vitamins than boiling or even traditional steaming.

Main Functions of Instant Pot

An Instant Pot is the most popular multi-cooker. Several settings are depending on the model and cooking methods in this one appliance.

Pressure Cooking

Among the many functions that Instant Pot can perform, pressure cooking is the most popular and widely used function. High cooking pressure reduces cooking time, usually less than half the cooking time regularly. This is done by heating the cooking liquid usually water or broth in a closed, airtight environment. High-pressure cooking food is safe and fast. Many pressure cooking program settings is depending on the recipes you are making:

· High/Low Pressure	· Soup/Broth
· Rice	· Cake
· Bean/Chili	· Sterilize
· Poultry	· Steam
· Meat/Stew	· Egg
· Multigrain	· Manual or Pressure Cooking
· Porridge	

Slow Cooking

If you want to slow cook, this is the place for you. By using Instant Pot in a slow cooker setting, you can prepare your food like in a Crock-Pot type slow cooker with 100% perfection.

Sauté

The sauté function lets you sauté any way you like on the stovetop. If you want to brown the meat for a recipe or sauté the onion, this is a good choice. I like this for two reasons. First of all, there is no need to clean another pot. This is also the start of immediate preheating of the pan, so it comes to pressure faster.

Yogurt

Yes, you can make yogurt with Instant Pot. To make yogurt you need a low temperature for a long time. it is great that you can make yogurt at home and adapt it to many tastes as you want and that of your family.

Keep Warm

This setting allows you to maintain warm food at the desired temperature for serving for the desired period.

Pressure Cooking with the Instant Pot

Cooking with an instant pot is far easier than anyone thinks. You just have to manage some techniques for the perfect cooking. In the pot, pressure cooking uses steam pressure to raise the boiling point of the added liquid. This makes the food to cook fast and appliance an energy-efficient cooking product to cook your meals in the fastest way.

Instant pots go through 3 stages when pressure cooking; They are

Pre-heating and pressurization

Cooking

Depressurization

Preheating and Pressurization

The pot waits for 10 seconds until ensure you have adjusted all your settings and then display "On" on the control panel which indicates that it starts preheating. When the cooker is preheating it vaporizes the liquid into steam in the inner pot. Once required, steam is built to generate the pressure the float valve pops up and locks the cooker's lid in place to safe pressure cooking. When the float valve popped up the silicon cap attached to the bottom sealed the steam inside the cooking chamber and allow to raise the

pressure to higher. Higher pressure means a higher cooking temperature. It is normal to see some steam escaping through the float valve but it is normal. If you experience steam escaping from the sides of the lid cancel the cooking and call customer service for guidance.

Cooking

After the float valve pops up, the cooker needs little time to maintain pressure. When the required pressure is generated, the process of cooking starts. The display window shows a cooking timer instead of "On". The cooking time is displayed in HH: MM format.

In a smart program setting like cooking time, cooking temperature, pressure level, and whether Keep warm will come on automatically or not can adjust your cooking time during cooking.

Depressurization

After the pressure cooking completes, do follow the recipe instruction for depressurizing the cooker.

If you set the automatic setting of keep warm after cooking completes, the timer counts up from 00:00 to indicate the elapsed time up to 10 hours. If not, then the cooker return to standby mode and displays "END".

Difference between Natural Release and Quick Release

For releasing pressure two methods are established. One is natural release and the other is a quick release of pressure but always follow recipe instructions for depressurizing the cooker.

Natural Release

For naturally releasing pressure leave the steam release handle in the sealing position. As the temperature within the inner pot drops the cooker depressurizes naturally over time.

Depressurizing varies based on the volume and type of food. When the cooker depressurized completely the float valve drops into the lid.

Quick Release

Quickly and carefully turn the steam release valve to the venting position from the sealing position. A stream of heavy steam releases through the top of the steam release handle. If spatter occurs while venting, turn the steam release handle back to sealing position and try after some time. If spatter occurs continuously, go for natural release of pressure.

Buttons and User Guide of Instant Pot

The Instant pot is a multi-functional pressure cooker with a digital control system. It has touch buttons with a digital display screen that shows the time and temperature settings of the pot.

Enlisted the buttons and the function of the instant pot.

Time Display:
The digital time display is designed on the control panel of the instant pot that indicates cooking time and Delay Start time. The display timer is designed in an Hour format. If the timer displays 05:20 that means cooking time is 5 hours and 20 minutes.

Pressure Field:
LED indicators on the panel illuminate to indicate the pressure level. Like if pressure is low, the low-pressure indicator enlightens.

Less-Normal-More:
The indicator with the "Less-Normal-More" is the time options for the Pressure cooking with 3 preset time options. For non-pressure cooking, the "Less-Normal-More" is the three options of the temperature levels.

LED Indicators:
LED indicators displayed on the panel illuminate to indicate the active smart Program and setting selection during the cooking process.

Smart Program Setting:

The smart program setting has the following buttons in an Instant pot;

· Pressure level   · Delay Start
· Keep Warm   · Cancel
· -/+ button

Smart Program
The Instant pot may have the following smart feature button to maintain cooking. You can choose the cooking function button for your desired recipe.

Pressure Cooking Functions

· Pressure Cook   · Rice
· Soup/Broth   · Multigrain
· Meat/ Stew   · Porridge
· Bean/Chili   · Steam
· Poultry

Non Pressure Cooking Functions

· Slow Cook   · Yogurt
· Sauté   · Keep Warm

Each button indicates the cooking function along with default time and temperature settings. However, you can adjust time and temperature manually as per your recipe requirement.

Adjust and Save Pressure Cooking Temperature
For the pressure cooking temperature, select the pressure cooking program then press pressure level to toggle between HIGH - and LOW - pressure levels. When the cooking starts the pressure level you choose is saved in the smart program. The temperature can also be adjusted at any time during cooking by selecting a pressure level.

Adjust and Save Pressure Cooking Time
For the pressure cooking time, select the pressure cooking program then press the "Less-Normal-More" to adjust the cooking time. You can adjust time by using the -/+ buttons as per requirement. When the cooking starts the cooking time you choose is saved in the smart program. The time can also be adjusted at any time during cooking by selecting time.

Adjust and Save Non-Pressure Cooking Temperature
Select the Non-pressure cooking Smart Program then select the "Less-Normal-More" setting to adjust the cooking temperature. You can adjust the temperature manually by using the -/+ buttons as per the recipe requirement. It can also adjust at any time during cooking.

Adjust and Save Non-Pressure Cooking Time
Select the Non-Pressure Smart cooking and use the -/+ buttons to manage cooking time as per your recipe

requirement.

Cancel and Standby Mode
You can cancel the cooking process any time during cooking with the cancel button. If the instant pot is plugged in but not in operation, it indicates on standby mode.

Turn Sound ON/OFF
Sound On: When the pot is on standby press and hold the + buttons for a while until the display indicates "S On".
Sound Off: When the pot is on standby press and hold - the buttons for a while until the display indicates "SOff".

Set the Delay Start Timer
In the Instant Pot, the delay timer can be adjusted to min 10 minutes up to 24 hours. For the delay time selection one must follow these steps;
· Select the Smart Program to your desired setting and press "Delay Start".
· When the hour field flashes, select the time delay with help of -/+ buttons to adjust your delay time.
· Select the Delay start to toggle to the minute's field and follow the same step as the previous one.
· Delay start begins after 10 seconds and timer countdown starts.
· When the delay start ends, the Smart program activates by indicating "On".

Keep Warm Setting
Keep warm setting will keep food warm after cooking until you desire to eat. Keep warm setting will adjust on all programs except yogurt and Sauté mode.

Reheat Food or Keep Warm for a Long Time
When the instant pot is on standby mode, select the keep warm button. Press keep warm to cycle through a Less-Normal-More warming temperature setting. Use -/+ buttons to increase or decrease warming time up to 99 hours and 50 minutes.

Parts and Accessories of Instant Pot

If you are using an instant pot you must be familiar with its parts and which accessories come along the main unit.

Inner Pot: The inner pot is the essential part of an instant pot. This pot is mainly used for cooking.

Cooker base: The cooker base in the main unit is electrically designed to manage the cooking procedure of Instant pot cooking. It has the following parts;

· Outer pot   · Control Panel
· Condensation Rim   · Base power Socket
· Interior heating element · Stainless steel exterior
· Cooker handles

Accessories along with Instant Pot
Following accessories comes with the instant pot. They are;
· Sealing Ring: It is installed on the lid like a normal pressure cooker to secure the steam in

the cooker.
· Condensation collector: This small device allows collecting any possible water generates during the condensation process and saves the electric machine from any harm.
· Steam Rack: There is a steam rack with an instant pot to steam cooks your food.

Troubleshooting

The Instant Pot is an electric device to cook food. In some circumstances you that experience some troubles with the machine and it working.

The following guide will help you to manage all possible issues you may face during Instant pot usage.

Why am I experiencing difficulty in the closing lid?
Possible Reasons: Sealing Ring not properly installed or Float valve in the popped-up position or Content in the cooker is hot.
Solution: Try repositioning the sealing ring and ensure it is snug behind the sealing ring.

Why am I facing difficulty in the opening lid?
Possible Reasons: High pressure inside the cooker, float valve stuck at the popped-up position
Solution: Release pressure according to recipe direction. Make sure steam is completely vented out by quick-release pressure and the float valve is easily pressed with a long utensil.

The inner pot is stuck to the lid when the cooker is opened.
Possible Reasons: Inner pot cooling may create suction.
Solution: To release the suction, turn the steam release handle to the venting position.

Steam leaks from the sides of the pot.
Possible Reasons: No sealing ring in the lid, damage sealing ring, Food residual attached in sealing ring, sealing ring rack in warped or off-center, rim of inner pot may be misshapen.
Solution: Install sealing ring properly, replace sealing ring, remove the sealing ring and clean thoroughly, if sealing ring rack bend or wrap call customer care. Check for deformation and contact customer care.

Float Valve does not rise.
Possible Reasons: Food debris on float valve or in silicon cap, too little liquid in the pot, damage silicon cap, obstruction of float valve by lid locking, no heat in the inner pot, damage inner pot base.
Solution: Clean float valve thoroughly, check for scorching on the bottom of the inner pot. Add thin water base liquid to the inner pot. Replace float valve, call customer care for other issues.

Hissing from the steam released during the cooking cycle.
Possible Reasons: Steam release is not in sealing position; cooker is regulating extra pressure.
Solution: Maintain steam release in sealing position, extra pressure is normal no action required.

Steam gushes from release when steam release handle is in sealing position.
Possible Reasons: Not enough liquid in the inner pot, pressure sensor control failure, steam valve not sealed.
Solution: Add liquid to the inner pot. Contact customer care, maintain the steam valve in sealing position.

The display remains blank after connecting the power cord.
Possible Reasons: Bad power connection, electric fuse of the cooker is blown.
Solution: Inspect power cord damages, contact customer care.

Error codes appear.

Possible Reasons: Code may appear like (C1, C2, C6, C6H, C6L) it is faulty sensor indication, C5 is for high temperature and no water in the inner pot, C7 or NoPr is for heat element failure, not enough water, the steam valve in venting position, PrSE is for pressure accumulation for non-pressure cooking function.
Solution: For C errors call customer care, for other issues manage accordingly to the guideline.

Clicking or light cracking sound.
Possible Reasons: The sound of power switching during temperature changing, bottom of the inner pot is wet.
Solution: This is normal and wipes off water from the surface.

How to Clean & Maintain

It is mandatory to clean your Instant pot thoroughly before and after every use.

Cleaning before first use:
· Remove the inner pot from the base of the cooker and wash it with hot water and dish soap to get rid of dust and dirt. Rinse the pot with warm clean water and dry it with a clean soft cloth completely.
· Wipe the heating element to get it free from any packaging element.
· The inner pot is designed to integrated safety during the cooking process so the food must be placed in the inner pot not in the base cooker.
· Clean all the Instant pots with a damp clean cloth to avoid dust before cooking.

Cleaning after every use:
You must clean your instant pot after every use like any other pot. For cleaning, purposes follow these simple steps to get maximum cleanliness and long life of your appliance.
· Unplug the instant pot from the switch and place it in a dry place.
· Cool the pot at room temperature before cleaning.
· Wash your Steam rack after every use if you use it. Wash gently and never use harsh chemicals for cleaning these parts. If require soak in hot soapy water for a while for effective cleaning. Place them on the top rack of a dishwasher.
· Empty and rinse condensation collector before every use.
· Wash the anti-block shield well after use with soapy water and air dry it.
· Remove all small parts of the lid before washing it.
· The clean interior of the steam valve and steam release pipe to avoid clogging.
· Store sealing rings in a well-ventilated area to avoid any foul smell of the food.
· To get rid of odors, add 1 cup water and 1 cup vinegar in a pot and run pressure cook function for 5-10 minutes, and then quickly release pressure. Rinse off and pat dry.
· Clean the inner pot with soapy warm water or if require hard cleaning use vinegar with the sponge and scrub it gently to get rid of the residuals.
· For tough or burned food residue, soak in hot water for a few hours and clean it like a regular pot.
· Dry it well before placing it in the cooker base.
· There may be some discoloration occur due to heat effect and cleaning but it will not affect the Instant pot safety and performance.
· For detachable cord, cleaning uses a barely damp cloth and wipes off the dirt.
· To clean the cooker base, Wipe the pot well with a damp cloth and allow air to dry.
· Clean cooker base and control panel with soft barely damped cloth and allow air dry.

4-Week Meal Plan

Week-1

	Breakfast	Lunch	Snack	Dinner	Dessert
Day-1	Easy-to-Cook Sweet Potato Hash	Dill Black-Eyed Peas	Fresh Tomato Chutney	Simple and Delicious Halibut Fillets	Maple Pecan Pears
Day-2	Simple Almond Date Oatmeal	Beef Potato Stew	Savory Deviled Eggs	Tomato, Arugula and Feta Pasta Salad	Cinnamon Apples
Day-3	Peach Pecan Oatmeal	Saucy Red Snapper	Savory Cocktail Sausages	Tasty Indian-Style Spaghetti Squash	Cinnamon-Vanilla Rice Pudding
Day-4	Steamed Potatoes with Onions and Peppers	Teriyaki Chicken Rice Bowl	Sesame-Soy Frozen Pot Stickers	Shrimp and Lentil Stew with Spinach	Chocolate Lava Cakes
Day-5	Whole-Grain Vanilla Blueberry Muffins	Spiced Millet with Onion	Hot Cauliflower Bites	Catalan Shellfish Stew	Lemony Mixed Berry Jam
Day-6	Apple Cardamom Oatmeal	Turkey Carrot Taco Lettuce Boats	Garlicky Brussels Sprouts	Parmesan Cod with Basmati Rice	Coconut Mini Cheesecakes with Almond
Day-7	Simple Boiled Eggs	Fish Paprikash	Avocado Hummus	Steamed Garlic Edamame	Bread Pudding with Apricots

Week-2

	Breakfast	Lunch	Snack	Dinner	Dessert
Day-1	Spanish Vegetable Tortilla	Orange Sea Bass	Corn with Tofu Crema	Sweet Potato Black Bean Chili with Cinnamon	Rice Pudding with Raisin
Day-2	Cinnamon Fruit Steel-Cut Oatmeal	Brunswick Stew	Lentil Ball	Simple Zucchini Ratatouille	Maple Rice Pudding with Cranberry
Day-3	Dill Egg Salad with Low-Fat Yogurt	Sausage and Prawn Boil	Garlic Baby Potatoes	Italian Beef Stew	Creamy Carrot Soufflé
Day-4	Tomato Asparagus Frittata with Parmesan Cheese	Tuna Casserole with Noodles	Garlic White Bean Hummus	Hyderabadi- Lentil Stew	Chocolate Mini Crepes with Cinnamon
Day-5	Steamed Eggs with Feta and Spinach	Savory Mushroom Polenta	Broccoli Bites	Toasted Orzo Salad	Yummy Arroz Con Leche
Day-6	Coconut Oatmeal	Teriyaki Wing	Parmesan Stuffed Artichoke	Eggplant Caponata	Citrusy Cranberry Spritzer
Day-7	Creamy Pumpkin Yogurt	Bowtie Pesto Pasta Salad	Smoky Roasted Red Pepper Hummus	Tuna and Asparagus Casserole	Traditional Chewy Brownies

Week-3

	Breakfast	Lunch	Snack	Dinner	Dessert
Day-1	Almond Granola	Oregano Mussels Saganaki with Feta Cheese	Cilantro-Lime Brown Rice	Rich Chicken Purloo	Chocolate Peanut Butter Popcorn
Day-2	Blueberry Quinoa Porridge	Slumgullion Stew	Classic Hummus	Butter Mashed Potatoes	Lemon Bars
Day-3	Chocolate Oatmeal	Foil-Packet Fish with Aioli	Stuffed Egg White Halves	Ginger Chicken Porridge	Cherry Cheesecake Bites
Day-4	Berry Steel Cut Oats	Spiced Coconut Chicken	Homemade Yogurt	Seafood Vegetable Ragout	Apple Bundt Cake
Day-5	Strawberries Quinoa Porridge	Tuscan White Beans in Vegetable Broth	Deviled Eggs	Texas Beef Chili	Banana Pudding Cake
Day-6	Sausage Pancake Bites	Haddock Fillets with Steamed Green Beans	Cheesy Egg Bake with Turkey Bacon	Artichokes Provençal	Cinnamon Pineapple
Day-7	Avocado Toast with Boiled Egg	Tuscan Chicken with Tomatoes and Kale	Herbed Artichokes	Marinara Spaghetti with Mozzarella Cheese	Bread Pudding with Rum Sauce

Week-4

	Breakfast	Lunch	Snack	Dinner	Dessert
Day-1	Bacon-Cheddar Egg Bites	Italian Fish with Herbs	Garlic Hummus with Tahini	Corn on the Cob	Gooey Chocolate Chip Cookie Sundae
Day-2	Chocolate Chip Banana Bread	Greek-Style Fish	Greek Egg Dish	Chicken and Rice Bowl with Cilantro	White Chocolate Crème Brûlée
Day-3	Sausage Spinach Quiche	Simple Steamed Onion Clams	Luscious Baba Ghanoush	Chicken and Broccoli with Honey-Sesame Sauce	Apple Crisp
Day-4	Biscuit Dumplings and Gravy	Mulligan Stew	Marinated Balsamic Mushrooms and Pearl Onions	Homemade Three-Bean Salad	Orange Walnut Coffee Cake
Day-5	Pumpkin Quinoa	Citrus Fish Tacos	Cauliflower Hummus	Beef and Potato Stew	Zucchini Cake
Day-6	Breakfast Biscuits and Gravy	Garlic Shrimp with Parsley	Cinnamon Almonds	Peanut Butter Sweet Potato and Kale Stew	Blueberry Almond Cakes
Day-7	Ham and Hash	Long-Grain Rice in Tomato Sauce	Sweet Potato Hummus	Irish Lamb Stew	Walnut Brownies

Chapter 1 Breakfast Recipes

Gluten-free Banana Bread

Prep time: 15 minutes | Cook Time: 55 minutes | Serves: 6

Nonstick cooking spray
1 ripe banana, peeled
1 large egg, beaten
2 tablespoons honey
1 tablespoon coconut oil, melted
½ teaspoon vanilla extract
1 cup gluten-free oat flour
½ teaspoon baking powder
¼ teaspoon kosher salt

1. Mash the banana until it is smooth in a large-size bowl, then add the honey, coconut oil, vanilla in and whisk well. 2. Pour the mixture onto the sprayed 6-inch cake pan lined with aluminum foil, then also cover the pan with aluminum foil. 3. In the Inner Pot, pour in 1 cup of water and then place in the Steam Rack. Arrange the cake pan to the Steam Rack. 4. Insert the pot into the Cooker Base and then close the lid rightly. 5. Select the Pressure Cook mode. 6. Press the Pressure Cook button again and adjust the cooking time to 55 minutes; press Level button to choose High Pressure. 7. When the time is up, leave the steam release handle in the Sealing position. 8. Carefully remove the lid and lift out the pan. Remove the foil cover and let the banana bread cool for 10 minutes on the rack. 9. Lift the bread from the pan and cut it into six wedges. Serve warm or at room temperature.
Per Serving: Calories 99; Fat: 3.8g; Sodium 109mg; Carbs: 14.9g; Fiber 1g; Sugars: 8.3g; Protein 2.5g

Simple Boiled Eggs

Prep time: 15 minutes | Cook Time: 5-6 minutes | Serves: 6

6 large eggs
Prepare a bowl of ice water in
advance.

For Hard-boiled Eggs: 1. In the Inner Pot, add 1 cup of water and place the Steam Rack in. Arrange the eggs to the rack. 2. Insert the pot into the Cooker Base and then close the lid rightly. 3. Select Pressure Cook mode. Press Pressure Cook button again to adjust the cooking time to 5 minutes. Press Pressure Level to choose High Pressure. 4. When the time is up, leave the steam release handle in the Sealing position. 5. Remove the eggs to the ice water and set aside for 5 minutes. 6. Serve and enjoy.
For Soft-boiled Eggs: 1. In the Inner Pot, add 1 cup of water and place the Steam Rack in. Arrange the eggs to the rack. 2. Insert the pot into the Cooker Base and then close the lid rightly. 3. Select Pressure Cook mode. Press Pressure Cook button again to adjust the cooking time to 6 minutes. Press Pressure Level to choose Low Pressure. 4. When the time is up, to release the steam, quickly and carefully turn the steam release handle from the Sealing position to the Venting position. 5. Remove the eggs to the ice water and wait for 5 minutes. 6. Serve and enjoy.
Per Serving: Calories 72; Fat: 5g; Sodium 70mg; Carbs: 0.4g; Fiber 1g; Sugars: 0.4g; Protein 6.3g

Vanilla Honey Buckwheat Porridge

Prep time: 15 minutes | Cook Time: 6 minutes | Serves: 6

1 cup buckwheat groats
2 cups canned coconut milk
1 cup water
1 teaspoon kosher salt
½ teaspoon vanilla extract
2 teaspoons honey
1 cup peeled, chopped citrus fruit of choice

1. In the Inner Pot, add the buckwheat, coconut milk, water, salt, and vanilla in. Stir until the buckwheat is submerged and the coconut milk is smooth. 2. Insert the pot into the Cooker Base and then lock the lid in place. 3. Select the Pressure Cook mode. 4. Press the Pressure Cook

button again and adjust the cooking time to 6 minutes; press 5. Press Level button to choose High Pressure. 6. When the time is up, leave the steam release handle in the Sealing position. 7. Carefully remove the lid and stir in the honey and fruit. Serve warm.
Per Serving: Calories 268; Fat: 19.7g; Sodium 403mg; Carbs: 22.9g; Fiber 1g; Sugars: 7g; Protein 4.4g

Vanilla Blueberry Muffins

Prep time: 15 minutes | Cook Time: 9 minutes | Serves: 6

1 cup gluten-free flour blend
¼ cup gluten-free old-fashioned rolled oats
2 teaspoons baking powder
Pinch of salt
¼ cup maple syrup
¼ cup Simple Applesauce or no-
sugar-added store-bought
2 tablespoons milk
1 tablespoon chia seeds
1 teaspoon pure vanilla extract
½ cup blueberries
1 cup water

1. In a small bowl, thoroughly mix up the chia seeds, applesauce, vanilla and milk. 2. In another medium-sized bowl, mix up the flour, baking powder, oats and salt, then add in the milk mixture and stir until just moistened. 3. After folding in the blueberries, evenly distribute the batter among 6 suitable silicone bake pans or cups. 4. In the Inner Pot, add the water and place the Steam Rack in it, then arrange the bake pans to the rack. 5. Place and close the lid in right way. 6. Press Pressure Cook button to select the program, press it again to adjust the cooking time to 9 minutes; press Pressure Level to choose High Pressure. 7. When the time is up, quickly and carefully turn the steam release handle from the Sealing position to the Venting position. 8. When released, take out the pans and remove the muffins to a cooling rack to cool for at least 10 minutes before serving.
Per Serving: Calories 134; Fat: 0.8g; Sodium 33mg; Carbs: 29.8g; Sugars: 10.4g; Protein 2.7g

Spanish Vegetable Tortilla

Prep time: 15 minutes | Cook Time: 30 minutes | Serves: 6

Nonstick cooking spray
1 tablespoon olive oil
½ cup thinly sliced Yukon Gold potato
½ cup thinly sliced zucchini
½ cup thinly sliced yellow onion
6 large eggs, beaten
¼ teaspoon kosher salt
¼ teaspoon freshly ground black pepper

1. Insert the Inner Pot into the Cooker Base without the lid. 2. Select Sauté mode and then press the same button again and then adjust the cooking temperature to Normal. 3. When the display switches On to Hot, add the olive oil and heat the oil. 4. After heating the oil, add in the potato slices, onion slices and zucchini slices. Stir occasionally for 6 minutes or until the onion slices begin to brown and the potato slices crisp. 5. Press Cancel button to stop the program, then transfer the mixture to the sprayed 6-inch cake pan. 6. Whisk together the eggs, salt and pepper in a suitable bowl, then pour the egg mixture over the vegetable mixture. 7. In the Inner Pot, add 1 cup of water and place the Steam Rack in. Arrange the cake pan to the rack and cover it with aluminum foil. 8. Insert the pot into the Cooker Base and then close the lid rightly. 9. Select Pressure Cook mode. Press Pressure Cook button again to adjust the cooking time to 30 minutes. Press Pressure Level to choose High Pressure. 10. When the time is up, leave the steam release handle in the Sealing position for 10 minutes, then turn the steam release handle to the Venting position. 11. Carefully remove the lid and lift out the cake pan. Uncover the tortilla and let it cool for 10 minutes on the rack, then cut it into 6 wedges. 12. Serve warm.
Per Serving: Calories 105; Fat: 7.3g; Sodium 168mg; Carbs: 3.7g; Sugars: 1.1g; Protein 6.7g

Healthy and Nutritious Veggies Breakfast

Prep time: 15 minutes | Cook Time: 10 minutes | Serves: 4

1 tablespoon olive oil	1 tablespoon low-sodium soy sauce
1 small sweet onion, peeled and diced	¼ cup water
2 large carrots, peeled and diced	1 cup diced peeled zucchini or summer squash
2 medium potatoes, peeled and diced	2 medium tomatoes, peeled and diced
1 stalk celery, diced	2 cups cooked brown rice
1 large red bell pepper, seeded and diced	½ teaspoon ground black pepper

1. Insert the Inner Pot into the Cooker Base without the lid. 2. Select Sauté mode and then press the same button again and then adjust the cooking temperature to Normal. 3. When the display switches On to Hot, add and heat the oil; add onion and cook for 2 minutes or until just tender; add the bell pepper, carrots, potatoes and cook for another 2 minutes or until just tender; lastly, add the soy sauce and water. 4. Press the Cancel button to stop this cooking program. 5. Place and close the lid in right way. 6. Press Pressure Cook button to select the program, press it again to adjust the cooking time to 2 minutes; press Pressure Level to choose High Pressure. 7. When the time is up, quickly and carefully turn the steam release handle from the Sealing position to the Venting position; when the float valve drops, press Cancel button to stop this cooking program. 8. Open lid and then add squash, tomatoes and stir well; close the lid again. 9. Press Pressure Cook button to select the program, press it again to adjust the cooking time to 1 minutes; press Pressure Level to choose High Pressure. 10. When the time is up, quickly and carefully turn the steam release handle from the Sealing position to the Venting position; when the float valve drops, press Cancel to end this cooking program. 11. Sprinkle with black pepper and serve over rice.
Per Serving: Calories 498; Fat: 6.5g; Sodium 264mg; Carbs: 100.7g; Fiber 1g; Sugars: 8.3g; Protein 10.9g

Tasty Red Pepper and Feta Egg Rolls

Prep time: 15 minutes | Cook Time: 8 minutes | Serves: 6

1 tablespoon olive oil	6 large eggs, beaten
½ cup crumbled feta cheese	¼ teaspoon ground black pepper
¼ cup chopped roasted red peppers	1 cup water

1. In a suitable bowl which has an inverted spout, beat the eggs with the black pepper. 2. Oil the silicone muffin molds, then divide feta and roasted red peppers among the molds. 3. Insert the Inner Pot into the Cooker Base, add 1 cup of water and then place the Steam Rack in the pot; place and close the lid in right way. 4. Press Pressure Cook button to select the program and then press it again to set the cooking time to 8 minutes; press Pressure Level button to choose High Level. 5. When the time is up, quickly and carefully turn the steam release handle from Sealing position to the Venting position. 6. When the float valve drops, open the lid and take out the molds carefully. 7. Serve the food on plates.
Per Serving: Calories 127; Fat: 10g; Sodium 229mg; Carbs: 1.4g; Fiber 1g; Sugars: 1.2g; Protein 8.2g

Vanilla Banana Loaves

Prep time: 15 minutes | Cook Time: 50 minutes | Serves: 4

1 tablespoon ground flaxseed	1 very ripe banana, peeled
2½ tablespoons water, plus 1 cup	⅓ cup maple syrup
1¼ cups gluten-free oat flour	3 tablespoons simple applesauce or no-sugar-added store-bought
1½ teaspoons baking powder	
½ teaspoon baking soda	1 teaspoon pure vanilla extract
½ teaspoon ground cinnamon	Nonstick cooking spray
⅛ teaspoon salt	

1. Spray 2 mini suitable bake pan with the non-stick spray. 2. In a small bowl, thoroughly mix up the flaxseed and 2½ tablespoons of water. 3. In a medium-size bowl, mash the banana, then mix up with the maple syrup, applesauce, vanilla, and flaxseed mixture. 4. In a large-sized bowl, whisk together the oat flour, baking powder, baking soda, cinnamon, and salt, then add the mixture in the medium bowl. 5. Divide the final mixture in two and arrange them to the sprayed bake pan separately; cover them with a few layers of paper towels and then tightly wrap them with aluminum foil. 6. In the Inner Pot, add the remaining 1 cup of water and place the Steam Rack in it, then transfer the bake pans to the pot. 7. Place and close the lid in right way. 8. Press Pressure Cook button to select the program, press it again to adjust the cooking time to 50 minutes; press Pressure Level to choose High Pressure. 9. When the time is up, leave the steam release handle in the Sealing position for 10 minutes, then turn it to the Venting position. 10. When released, take out the bake pans, discard the covers and cool for 5 minutes. 11. Turn the bread out onto a cooling rack to cool for 10 more minutes before slicing. 12. Serve and enjoy.
Per Serving: Calories 224; Fat: 2.8g; Sodium 169mg; Carbs: 46.3g; Fiber 1g; Sugars: 19.4g; Protein 5.5g

Chickpea Breakfast Hash

Prep time: 15 minutes | Cook Time: 35 minutes | Serves: 4

1 cup dried chickpeas	and chopped
4 cups water	1 teaspoon minced garlic
2 tablespoons extra-virgin olive oil, divided	½ teaspoon ground cumin
	½ teaspoon ground black pepper
1 medium onion, peeled and chopped	¼ teaspoon salt
	4 large hard-cooked eggs, peeled and halved
1 medium zucchini, trimmed and sliced	½ teaspoon smoked paprika
1 large red bell pepper, seeded	

1. In the Inner Pot, add the water, chickpeas and 1 tablespoon of oil, then close the lid in right way. 2. Press Pressure Cook button to select the program, press it again to adjust the cooking time to 30 minutes; press Pressure Level to choose High Pressure. 3. When the time is up, quickly and carefully turn the steam release handle from the Sealing position to the Venting position. 4. When released, open the lid; drain the chickpeas well, set aside after transferring to a suitable bowl. 5. Press Cancel button to stop this cooking program. 6. After cleaning and drying the Inner Pot, insert it into the Cooker Base. 7. Press Sauté button and press it again to choose the Normal cooking temperature. 8. When the display switches On to Hot, add and heat the remaining 1 tablespoon of oil; add onion, bell pepper and zucchini and cook for 5 minutes until tender; add garlic, cumin, salt and bell pepper and cook for 30 seconds; lastly, add the cooked chickpeas and make them coated with the mixture evenly. 9. Arrange the food on a plate, top with eggs and paprika. 10. Serve and enjoy.
Per Serving: Calories 274; Fat: 10.3g; Sodium 174mg; Carbs: 37.5g; Fiber 1g; Sugars: 8.9g; Protein 11g

Feta Crustless Quiche with Spinach

Prep time: 15 minutes | Cook Time: 30 minutes | Serves: 4

Nonstick cooking spray	¼ teaspoon kosher salt
6 large eggs, beaten	¼ teaspoon freshly ground black pepper
¼ cup skim milk	
¼ cup crumbled feta	2 cups frozen chopped spinach
1 shallot, finely chopped	

1. Arrange the spinach to the sprayed 6-inch cake pan. 2. In a large-size bowl, crack in the eggs and whisk them with the milk until frothy, then add in the feta, shallot, salt, pepper and stir thoroughly. 3. Pour the egg mixture over the pan. 4. In the Inner Pot, add 1 cup of water and place the Steam Rack in. Arrange the cake pan to the rack. 5. Insert the pot into the Cooker Base and then close the lid rightly. 6. Select Pressure Cook mode. Press Pressure Cook button again to adjust the cooking time to 30 minutes. Press Pressure Level to choose High Pressure. 7. When the time is up, leave the steam release handle in the Sealing position for 10 minutes, then turn the steam release handle to the Venting position. 8. Carefully remove the lid and lift out the cake pan. Cut the quiche into 4 slices and serve.
Per Serving: Calories 141; Fat: 9.5g; Sodium 377mg; Carbs: 2.3g; Sugars: 1.8g; Protein 11.7g

Oatmeal Diced Apple

Prep time: 15 minutes | Cook Time: 4 minutes | Serves: 4

2 cups water	1 teaspoon vanilla extract
1 cup gluten-free steel cut oats	½ teaspoon kosher salt
2 apples, peeled and diced	¼ cup pure maple syrup
1 teaspoon ground cinnamon	

1. In the Inner Pot, mix up the oats, apples, cinnamon, vanilla, salt and water, then insert the pot into the Cooker Base and lock the lid in place. 2. Select the Pressure Cook mode. 3. Press the Pressure Cook button again and then adjust the cooking time to 4 minutes; press Level button to choose High Pressure. 4. When the time is up, let the pressure release naturally. 5. When done, carefully remove the lid and stir in the maple syrup. Serve warm.
Per Serving: Calories 284; Fat: 3.3g; Sodium 297mg; Carbs: 58.2g; Fiber 1g; Sugars: 23.5g; Protein 7.3g

Easy-to-Cook Sweet Potato Hash

Prep time: 15 minutes | Cook Time: 13 minutes | Serves: 4

1 tablespoon olive oil	½ teaspoon cayenne pepper
1½ pounds sweet potatoes, peeled and diced	½ teaspoon kosher salt
1 yellow onion, chopped	¼ teaspoon freshly ground black pepper
1 red bell pepper, seeded and chopped	½ cup Vegetable Broth or store-bought low-sodium vegetable broth
2 garlic cloves, minced	
1 teaspoon dried oregano	4 large eggs

1. Insert the Inner Pot into the Cooker Base without the lid. 2. Select Sauté mode and then press the same button again and then adjust the cooking temperature to Normal. 3. When the display switches On to Hot, add the olive oil and heat the oil, then add the sweet potatoes and stir occasionally for 10 minutes or until the sweet potatoes begin to brown and soften. 4. Add in the onion, bell pepper, oregano, garlic, cayenne pepper, salt and black pepper and resume stirring for a few minutes until well combined. 5. Press Cancel to stop this cooking program. 6. Pour in the broth and stir well, then beat in the eggs. 7. Close the lid rightly. 8. Select Pressure Cook mode and press the same button again to adjust the cooking time to 3 minutes. 9. Press Pressure Level button to choose High Pressure. 10. When the time is up, to release the steam, quickly and carefully turn the steam release handle from the Sealing position to the Venting position. 11. When done, serve and enjoy.
Per Serving: Calories 332; Fat: 9.1g; Sodium 474mg; Carbs: 53.7g; Fiber 1g; Sugars: 4.1g; Protein 10.3g

Baked Ham, Kale and Eggs

Prep time: 15 minutes | Cook Time: 10 minutes | Serves: 6

1 tablespoon olive oil	1 (8-ounce) package cream cheese
2 cups diced ham	¼ teaspoon salt
1 medium yellow onion, peeled and chopped	¼ teaspoon ground black pepper
2 pounds chopped kale	⅛ teaspoon ground nutmeg
½ cup heavy cream	6 large eggs
	1 cup water

1. Prepare an 8-inch round baking dish and spray it with the non-stick cooking spray. 2. Insert the Inner Pot into the Cooker Base without the lid. 3. Press the Sauté button to select the program and then press it again to adjust the cooking temperature to Normal. 4. When the display switches On to Hot, add and heat the oil. 5. When the oil heated, add ham and cook for 5 minutes or until the ham starts to brown; add the onion and resume cooking for another 5 minutes until tender, then add kale and cook for 5 minutes more or until wilted. 6. Add the nutmeg, cream, cream cheese, salt and pepper, stir for 5 minutes or until thickened. 7. Press Cancel to stop this cooking program and then transfer thickened mixture to the 8-inch sprayed baking dish. Spoon the mixture to press 6 indentations. 8. Clean the pot and then place in the Steam Rack; fold a long piece of aluminum

foil in half lengthwise and then lay it over rack to form a sling. 9. Arrange the dish to the foil sling and use another piece aluminum foil to cover the dish loosely. 10. Place and close the lid rightly. 11. Press Pressure Cook button to select the program and then press it again to adjust the cooking time to 5 minutes; press Pressure Level button to choose Low Pressure. 12. When the time is up, quickly and carefully turn the steam release handle from Sealing position to the Venting position. 13. Wait for 5 minutes before removing the dish from pot. 14. Serve and enjoy.
Per Serving: Calories 413; Fat: 28.1g; Sodium 937mg; Carbs: 21g; Sugars: 1.3g; Protein 21.5g

Dill Egg Salad with Low-Fat Yogurt

Prep time: 15 minutes | Cook Time: 5 minutes | Serves: 6

6 large eggs	¼ teaspoon salt
1 cup water	¼ teaspoon ground black pepper
1 tablespoon olive oil	½ cup low-fat plain Greek yogurt
1 medium red bell pepper, seeded and chopped	2 tablespoons chopped fresh dill

1. Prepare a large bowl of ice water in advance. 2. In the Inner Pot, add 1 cup of water, place in the Steam Rack and then arrange the eggs to it. 3. Select Pressure Cook mode. Press Pressure Cook button again to adjust the cooking time to 5 minutes. Press Pressure Level to choose Low Pressure. 4. When the time is up, leave the steam release handle in the Sealing position until the float valve drops. 5. Transfer the eggs to the prepared ice water and let them stand for 10 minutes, then place the peeled and chopped egg pieces on a medium-sized bowl. 6. Clean the Inner Pot and dry it well before inserting it into the Cooker Base. 7. Without the lid, select Sauté mode and then press the same button again and then adjust the cooking temperature to Normal. 8. When the display switches On to Hot, add and heat the bell pepper, salt and black pepper for 5 minutes or until the pepper is tender. 9. When cooked, transfer the food to the bowl with egg pieces, then add yogurt and dill, fold to combine; cover with lid and chill for 1 hour before serving.
Per Serving: Calories 112; Fat: 7.4g; Sodium 180mg; Carbs: 3.4g; Sugars: 2.1g; Protein 8.7g

Whole-Grain Vanilla Blueberry Muffins

Prep time: 15 minutes | Cook Time: 10 minutes | Serves: 6

Nonstick cooking spray	3 tablespoons nondairy milk
1 cup spelt flour	2 tablespoons coconut oil, melted
1 teaspoon baking powder	2 tablespoons honey
¼ teaspoon baking soda	1 teaspoon vanilla extract
⅛ teaspoon kosher salt	½ cup fresh or frozen blueberries
1 egg, beaten	

1. Use the non-stick cooking spray to oil the outer 6 wells of a 7-well silicone egg bite mold. 2. Combine and stir well the flour, salt, baking powder and baking soda in a medium-size bowl. 3. In another small-size bowl, crack the egg in and add the coconut oil, milk, honey and vanilla. Whisk well. 4. Add the egg mixture to the flour mixture and stir until combined into a thick batter. 5. Divide the batter between the prepared egg bite mold, filling each well about halfway. Gently press the blueberries into the top of each muffin. Place the lid on the mold. 6. In the Inner Pot, pour 1 cup of water and place the Steam Rack. Place the egg bite mold on top of the Steam Rack and then insert the pot into the Cooker Base. 7. Place the lid on the Instant Pot and lock it in place. 8. Select the Pressure Cook mode. 9. Press the Pressure Cook button again and adjust the cooking time to 10 minutes; press Level button to choose High Pressure. 10. When the time is up, leave the steam release handle in the Sealing position. 11. When done, carefully remove the lid and lift out the mold. 12. Uncover the muffins and let them cool for 3 to 5 minutes or until the mold is cool to the touch, then pop the muffins out. 13. Serve warm or store at room temperature in an airtight container for up to 3 days.
Per Serving: Calories 148; Fat: 5.7g; Sodium 64mg; Carbs: 22.6g; Sugars: 7.2g; Protein 3.8g

Cinnamon Fruit Steel-Cut Oatmeal

Prep time: 15 minutes | Cook Time: 5-10 minutes | Serves: 2

3 cups water, divided
1 cup toasted steel-cut oats
2 teaspoons unsalted butter
1 cup apple juice
1 tablespoon dried cranberries
1 tablespoon golden raisins
1 tablespoon snipped dried apricots
1 tablespoon maple syrup
¼ teaspoon ground cinnamon
⅛ teaspoon salt

1. In a suitable bowl, add 2-½ cups of water and the other ingredients and combine well. 2. In the Inner Pot, add the remaining ½ cup of water and then place the Steam Rack in. 3. Fold a long piece of aluminum foil in half lengthwise and then lay it over the rack to form a sling. Let the bowl rest on the foil sling. 4. Place and close the lid in right way. 5. Press Pressure Cook button to select the program; press it again to adjust the cooking time to 5 minutes for chewy oatmeal, or 8 minutes for creamy oatmeal. 6. Press Pressure Level to choose High Pressure. 7. When the time is up, to release steam, leave the steam release handle in the Sealing position. 8. Remove the bowl out of the pot carefully with the help of the foil sling. 9. Serve and enjoy.
Per Serving: Calories 218; Fat: 5.8g; Sodium 49mg; Carbs: 39.4g; Sugars: 21.5g; Protein 3.3g

Flavor Spinach Feta Frittata

Prep time: 15 minutes | Cook Time: 11-15 minutes | Serves: 4

1 tablespoon olive oil
½ medium onion, peeled and chopped
½ medium red bell pepper, seeded and chopped
2 cups chopped fresh baby spinach
1 cup water
1 cup crumbled feta cheese
6 large eggs, beaten
¼ cup low-fat plain Greek yogurt
½ teaspoon salt
½ teaspoon ground black pepper

1. Spray a 1.5-liter baking dish with the non-stick cooking spray. 2. Select Sauté mode and then press the same button again and then adjust the cooking temperature to Normal. 3. When the display switches On to Hot, add and heat the onion and bell pepper for 8 minutes or until tender; add spinach and resume cooking for 3 minutes or until wilted. 4. Press Cancel button to stop the cooking program and then transfer the food to a medium-sized bowl. 5. Drain excess liquid from spinach mixture, then add them and cheese to the prepared baking dish. 6. In another bowl, thoroughly mix up the eggs, yogurt, salt and black pepper, then also pour the mixture over the dish. Tightly cover the dish with foil. 7. In the wiped Inner Pot, place the Steam Rack in it and add 1 cup of water, then transfer the dish to the rack. 8. Select Pressure Cook mode. Press Pressure Cook button again to adjust the cooking time to 15 minutes. Press Pressure Level to choose High Pressure. 9. When the time is up, leave the steam release handle in the Sealing position until the float valve drops. 10. Wait for 10 to 15 minutes before removing the dish out of the pot. 11. Turning the frittata out onto a serving plate by running a thin knife around the edge is suggested. 12. Serve and enjoy.
Per Serving: Calories 173; Fat: 12.7g; Sodium 557mg; Carbs: 3.9g; Fiber 1g; Sugars: 2.7g; Protein 11.4g

Nuts Farro with Dried Fruit

Prep time: 15 minutes | Cook Time: 20 minutes | Serves: 8

16 ounces farro, rinsed and drained
4½ cups water
¼ cup maple syrup
¼ teaspoon salt
1 cup dried mixed fruit
½ cup chopped toasted mixed nuts
2 cups almond milk

1. In the Inner Pot, add and mix up the farro, water, salt and maple syrup, then close the lid in right way. 2. Press Multigrain button to select the program, press it again to adjust the cooking time to 20 minutes; press Pressure Level to choose High Pressure. 3. When the time is up, leave the steam release handle in the Sealing position. 4. When released, open the lid and add the dried fruit; close the lid again and Keep Warm for 20 minutes. 5. With nuts and almond milk, serve and enjoy.

Per Serving: Calories 346; Fat: 23.6g; Sodium 299mg; Carbs: 31.9g; Fiber 1g; Sugars: 9.6g; Protein 7.3g

Ham Swiss Egg Rolls

Prep time: 15 minutes | Cook Time: 12 minutes | Serves: 8

Nonstick cooking spray
8 large eggs, beaten
½ cup milk of choice
½ cup shredded Swiss cheese
½ cup finely diced red bell pepper
¼ cup diced uncured ham
½ teaspoon kosher salt
½ teaspoon freshly ground black pepper

1. Prepare a suitable bowl, after whisking the milk and eggs until frothy, add in the cheese, ham, bell pepper, salt and black pepper and stir thoroughly. 2. Spray the outer 6 wells of two 7-well silicone egg bite molds with nonstick cooking spray. 3. Fill each sprayed well about 3-quarter full after dividing the egg mixture between the prepared egg bite wells, filling each well about three-quarters full. Cover the molds with their lids or aluminum foil. 4. In the Inner Pot, add 1 cup of water and place the Steam Rack in. Arrange the mold to the rack. 5. Insert the pot into the Cooker Base and then close the lid rightly. 6. Select Pressure Cook mode. Press Pressure Cook button again to adjust the cooking time to 12 minutes. Press Pressure Level to choose High Pressure. 7. When the time is up, leave the steam release handle in the Sealing position for 10 minutes, then turn the steam release handle to the Venting position. 8. Carefully remove the lid and let the food cool for a minute or two minutes before releasing them from the molds. 9. Serve and enjoy.
Per Serving: Calories 114; Fat: 7.5g; Sodium 293mg; Carbs: 2.3g; Sugars: 1.6g; Protein 9.4g

Simple Almond Date Oatmeal

Prep time: 15 minutes | Cook Time: 12 minutes | Serves: 4

1 cup sliced almonds
4 cups water
2 cups rolled oats
1 tablespoon extra-virgin olive oil
¼ teaspoon salt
½ cup chopped pitted dates

1. Insert the Inner Pot into the Cooker Base without the lid. 2. Select Sauté mode and then press the same button again and then adjust the cooking temperature to Normal. 3. When the display switches On to Hot, add almonds. Stir constantly for 8 minutes or until the almonds are golden brown. 4. Press Cancel button to stop this cooking program, then add oil, oats, salt, dates and water in and stir well. 5. Place and close the lid in right way. 6. Press Pressure Cook button to select the program and then press it again to adjust the cooking time to 4 minutes; press Pressure Level to choose High Pressure. 7. When cooked, to release the pressure in short time, quickly and carefully turn the steam release handle from Sealing position to the Venting position. 8. When done, serve and enjoy.
Per Serving: Calories 385; Fat: 18.1g; Sodium 158mg; Carbs: 49.5g; Fiber 1g; Sugars: 15.5g; Protein 11g

Quinoa with Berries

Prep time: 15 minutes | Cook Time: 2 minutes | Serves: 4

1 cup white quinoa, rinsed
1¾ cups milk
½ cup frozen blueberries
½ cup frozen strawberries
½ cup frozen raspberries
¼ cup maple syrup
2 teaspoons pure vanilla extract
1 cup water

1. In the Inner Pot, add the water and place the Steam Rack in it. 2. Prepare a heatproof bowl, mix up the quinoa, milk, blueberries, strawberries, raspberries, maple syrup, and vanilla; arrange the bowl to the rack in the pot. 3. Place and close the lid in right way. 4. Press Pressure Cook button to select the program, press it again to adjust the cooking time to 2 minutes; press Pressure Level to choose High Pressure. 5. When the time is up, leave the steam release handle in the Sealing position. 6. When released, take out the bowl. 7. After stirring well, serve and enjoy. 8. Store in the fridge for up to 4 days in a covered container. Reheat in the microwave, adding a bit more milk, as the quinoa will thicken in the fridge.
Per Serving: Calories 297; Fat: 1.6g; Sodium 9mg; Carbs: 66.3g; Fiber 1g; Sugars: 43.4g; Protein 3.7g

Oatmeal Pumpkin Pie Bites

Prep time: 15 minutes | Cook Time: 10 minutes | Serves: 6

Nonstick cooking spray	¼ cup spelt flour or white whole-wheat flour
1 egg, beaten	
¾ cup pumpkin puree	1 teaspoon baking powder
3 tablespoons honey	1 teaspoon pumpkin pie spice
¾ cup gluten-free rolled oats	¼ teaspoon kosher salt

1. Spray the outer 6 wells of a 7-well silicone egg bite mold with nonstick cooking spray. 2. Prepare a suitable bowl, beat the egg in, add the honey, pumpkin puree and whisk well. 3. Continue adding the oats, flour, salt, baking powder, pumpkin pie spice and mix completely. 4. Fill each well about halfway after dividing the mixture between the prepared mold, then cover the mold with lid or aluminum foil. 5. In the Inner Pot, pour in 1 cup of water and then place in the Steam Rack. Arrange the mold to the Steam Rack. 6. Insert the pot into the Cooker Base and then close the lid rightly. 7. Select the Pressure Cook mode. 8. Press the Pressure Cook button again and adjust the cooking time to 10 minutes; press Level button to choose High Pressure. 9. When the time is up, leave the steam release handle in the Sealing position. 10. When done, carefully remove the lid and lift out the mold. Uncover the oatmeal bites and let them cool for 4 to 5 minutes before unmolding them. 11. Serve warm or at room temperature.
Per Serving: Calories 117; Fat: 1.8g; Sodium 110mg; Carbs: 23.4g; Fiber 1g; Sugars: 9.7g; Protein 3.8g

Low-Fat Greek Yogurt

Prep time: 15 minutes | Cook Time: 10 hrs. | Serves: 6

8 cups whole or 2% milk	yogurt with live active cultures
2 tablespoons plain low-; Fat	

1. To cook successfully, you should sterilize all equipment. 2. Add the milk in the clean Inner Pot and insert the pot into the Cooker Base. Place and close the lid rightly. 3. Press Yogurt to select the program and press it again to cycle to the More option. The display indicates boil. 4. When boiled, the display indicates End. 5. When done, use the sterilized thermometer to check if the milk has reach 180 degrees F. 6. After removing skin from milk, place the Inner Pot in an ice water bath, whisk occasionally for 5 to 7 minutes without scraping its bottom or sides. When the milk reaches 110 degrees F, remove the pot away and dry thoroughly. 7. In a suitable bowl, whisk 1 cup of heated milk and yogurt, then pour the mixture into the Inner Pot. 8. Insert the pot into the Cooker Base and then close the lid rightly. 9. Press Yogurt to select the cooking program and then press it again to cycle to the Normal option. Use the -/+ buttons to adjust the fermentation time to 10 hours. 10. When the cooker beeps and displays End, open lid and transfer yogurt to a storage container. Refrigerate the yogurt for at least 2 hours. 11. When refrigerated, take the yogurt out of the refrigerator and use a spoon to put it into a fine mesh filter lined with 3 layers of cheesecloth or a coffee filter. 12. Place the filter on a medium-sized bowl, cover with plastic wrap and refrigerate overnight. 13. When finished, transfer the thickened yogurt to an airtight container and discard the water and cheesecloth. 14. Serve and enjoy.
Per Serving: Calories 166; Fat: 6.7g; Sodium 157mg; Carbs: 16.4g; Fiber 1g; Sugars: 15g; Protein 11g

Quinoa Greek Yogurt with Blueberries

Prep time: 15 minutes | Cook Time: 12 minutes | Serves: 8

2 cups quinoa, rinsed and drained	yogurt
4 cups water	2 cups blueberries
1 teaspoon vanilla extract	1 cup toasted almonds
¼ teaspoon salt	½ cup pure maple syrup
2 cups low-; Fat plain Greek	

1. In the Inner Pot, add the quinoa, vanilla, salt and water, then close the lid in right way. 2. Press Rice button to select the program, press it again to choose Normal cooking time (12 minutes); press Pressure Level to choose High Pressure. 3. When the time is up, leave the steam release handle in the Sealing position. 4. When released, open the lid and use a fork to fluff the quinoa. 5. Add yogurt and stir well, top with the blueberries, almonds and maple syrup. 6. Serve and enjoy.
Per Serving: Calories 334; Fat: 8.8g; Sodium 110mg; Carbs: 50.9g; Fiber 1g; Sugars: 18.1g; Protein 14.8g

Peach Pecan Oatmeal

Prep time: 15 minutes | Cook Time: 4 minutes | Serves: 4

4 cups water	diced
2 cups rolled oats	¼ teaspoon salt
1 tablespoon light olive oil	½ cup toasted pecans
1 large peach, peeled, pitted, and	2 tablespoons maple syrup

1. In the inner pot, stir the oats, oil, peach, salt and water well, then insert the pot into the Cooker Base. 2. Place and close the lid in right way. 3. Select Pressure Cook mode. Press Pressure Cook button again to adjust the cooking time to 4 minutes. Press Pressure Level to choose Low Pressure. 4. When the time is up, quickly and carefully turn the steam release handle from Sealing position to the Venting position until the float valve drops. 5. Take out the food and stir well, then top with the pecans and maple syrup. 6. Serve and enjoy.
Per Serving: Calories 421; Fat: 26.3g; Sodium 158mg; Carbs: 41.9g; Fiber 1g; Sugars: 10.9g; Protein 8.7g

Apple Cardamom Oatmeal

Prep time: 15 minutes | Cook Time: 7 minutes | Serves: 4

1 tablespoon light olive oil	1 cup steel-cut oats
1 large apple, peeled, cored, and	3 cups water
diced	¼ cup maple syrup
½ teaspoon ground cardamom	½ teaspoon salt

1. Insert the Inner Pot into the Cooker Base without the lid. 2. Select Sauté mode and then press the same button again and then adjust the cooking temperature to Normal. 3. When the display switches On to Hot, add the apple and cardamom in the pot and cook for 2 minutes or until the apple is just softened. 4. Press Cancel button to stop this cooking program. 5. Add oats, maple syrup, salt and water in the pot and stir well. 6. Place and close the lid in right way. 7. Select Pressure Cook mode. Press Pressure Cook button again to adjust the cooking time to 5 minutes. Press Pressure Level to choose High Pressure. 8. When the time is up, leave the steam release handle in the Sealing position for 10 minutes, then turn the steam release handle to the Venting position to quick-release the remaining pressure. 9. Stir well after removing out and serve hot.
Per Serving: Calories 153; Fat: 4.6g; Sodium 301mg; Carbs: 28.1g; Fiber 1g; Sugars: 17.7g; Protein 1.7g

Fresh Fruit Buckwheat Porridge

Prep time: 15 minutes | Cook Time: 6 minutes | Serves: 4

1 cup buckwheat groats, rinsed and drained	½ teaspoon vanilla extract
	1 cup blueberries
3 cups water	1 cup raspberries
½ cup chopped pitted dates	1 cup hulled and quartered
1 tablespoon light olive oil	strawberries
¼ teaspoon ground cinnamon	2 tablespoons balsamic vinegar
¼ teaspoon salt	

1. In the inner pot, stir the buckwheat, water, dates, oil, cinnamon, and salt well, then insert the pot into the Cooker Base. 2. Select Pressure Cook mode. Press Pressure Cook button again to adjust the cooking time to 6 minutes. Press Pressure Level to choose Low Pressure. 3. While cooking, in a medium-sized bowl, thoroughly mix up the blueberries, raspberries, strawberries, and vinegar. 4. When the time is up, leave the steam release handle in the Sealing position until the float valve drops. Open lid and stir in vanilla. 5. Top porridge with berry mixture. 6. Serve and enjoy.
Per Serving: Calories 246; Fat: 5g; Sodium 158mg; Carbs: 50g; Fiber 1g; Sugars: 21.8g; Protein 5.3g

Boiled Eggs in Tomato Sauce

Prep time: 15 minutes | Cook Time: 10 minutes | Serves: 6

2 tablespoons olive oil	oregano
1 medium onion, peeled and chopped	½ teaspoon ground fennel
1 clove garlic, peeled and minced	¼ teaspoon salt
1 (15-ounce) can tomato purée	¼ teaspoon ground black pepper
2 medium tomatoes, seeded and diced	¼ teaspoon crushed red pepper flakes
2 tablespoons chopped fresh	6 large eggs

1. Insert the Inner Pot into the Cooker Base without the lid. 2. Select Sauté mode and then press the same button again and then adjust the cooking temperature to Normal. 3. When the display switches On to Hot, add and heat the oil. 4. Add onion and cook for 5 minutes until tender; add garlic and cook for 30 seconds until fragrant; add tomato purée, diced tomatoes, oregano, fennel, salt, black pepper, and crushed red pepper, stir and resume cooking for 3 minutes or until the mixture starts to bubble. 5. Press Cancel button to stop this cooking program. 6. Carefully crack eggs one at a time into a small ramekin and carefully turn out into sauce, making sure eggs are evenly distributed. 7. Select Pressure Cook mode. Press Pressure Cook button again to adjust the cooking time to 10 minutes. Press Pressure Level to choose Low Pressure. 8. When the time is up, quickly and carefully turn the steam release handle from the Sealing position to Venting position. 9. When done, serve and enjoy.
Per Serving: Calories 133; Fat: 9.9g; Sodium 170mg; Carbs: 5g; Fiber 1g; Sugars: 2.3g; Protein 7.1g

Apricots Quinoa Porridge

Prep time: 15 minutes | Cook Time: 12 minutes | Serves: 4

1½ cups quinoa, rinsed and drained	1 cup almond milk
1 cup chopped dried apricots	1 tablespoon rose water
2½ cups water	½ teaspoon cardamom
	¼ teaspoon salt

1. In the Inner Pot, add all of the ingredients, then close the lid in right way. 2. Press Rice button to select the program, press it again to choose Normal cooking time (12 minutes); press Pressure Level to choose High Pressure. 3. When the time is up, leave the steam release handle in the Sealing position. 4. When released, open the lid and use a fork to fluff the quinoa. 5. Serve and enjoy.
Per Serving: Calories 269; Fat: 4.8g; Sodium 205mg; Carbs: 47.3g; Fiber 1g; Sugars: 5g; Protein 9.8g

Steamed Eggs with Feta and Spinach

Prep time: 15 minutes | Cook Time: 5 minutes | Serves: 2

2 tablespoons olive oil, divided	2 tablespoons low-; Fat plain Greek yogurt
2 cups chopped baby spinach	2 tablespoons crumbled feta cheese
1 scallion, chopped	2 large eggs
1 clove garlic, peeled and minced	1 cup water
¼ teaspoon salt	
¼ teaspoon ground black pepper	

1. Insert the Inner Pot into the Cooker Base without the lid. 2. Select Sauté mode and then press the same button again and then adjust the cooking temperature to Normal. 3. When the display switches On to Hot, add and heat 1 tablespoon of oil; add spinach, scallion and cook for 3 minutes until the spinach wilts, then add garlic and cook for about 30 seconds or until fragrant. 4. Press Cancel button to stop this cooking program. 5. Brush two 4-ounce ramekins with the remaining oil, add the spinach mixture into them separately and season with salt and pepper, then spread yogurt over them and top each ramekin with feta and egg. 6. After cleaning and drying the Inner Pot, add in water and place in the Steam Rack, then arrange the ramekins to the rack. 7. Select Pressure Cook mode. Press Pressure Cook button again to adjust the cooking time to 2 minutes. Press Pressure Level to choose Low Pressure. 8. When the time is up, quickly and carefully turn the

steam release handle from Sealing position to the Venting position. 9. When done, transfer the ramekins to plate and enjoy.
Per Serving: Calories 368; Fat: 21.6g; Sodium 609mg; Carbs: 13.1g; Fiber 1g; Sugars: 10.1g; Protein 32.8g

Delicious Oatmeal with Nuts and Fruit

Prep time: 15 minutes | Cook Time: 7 minutes | Serves: 2

1 cup rolled oats	¼ cup chopped walnuts
1¼ cups water	1 tablespoon honey
¼ cup orange juice	¼ teaspoon ground ginger
1 medium pear, peeled, cored, and cubed	¼ teaspoon ground cinnamon
¼ cup dried cherries	⅛ teaspoon salt

1. In the Inner Pot, mix up the oats, water, orange juice, pear, cherries, walnuts, honey, ginger, cinnamon, and salt, then close the lid in right way. 2. Press Pressure Cook button to select the program, press it again to adjust the cooking time to 7 minutes; press Pressure Level to choose Low Pressure. 3. When the time is up, leave the steam release handle in the Sealing position. 4. When done, serve on a plate, stir well and enjoy.
Per Serving: Calories 357; Fat: 12.1g; Sodium 15mg; Carbs: 56.2g; Fiber 1g; Sugars: 20.9g; Protein 9.8g

Nutritious Banana Walnut Millet Porridge

Prep time: 15 minutes | Cook Time: 6 minutes | Serves: 4

½ cup millet	¼ teaspoon salt
½ cup rolled oats	½ teaspoon vanilla extract
2½ cups almond milk	1 cup toasted walnuts
2 tablespoons maple syrup	2 medium bananas, peeled and sliced
1 tablespoon unsalted butter	
½ teaspoon ground cinnamon	

1. In the Inner Pot, add the millet, oats, almond milk, maple syrup, butter, cinnamon, and salt, then close the lid in right way. 2. Press Pressure Cook button to select the program, press it again to adjust the cooking time to 6 minutes; press Pressure Level to choose High Pressure. 3. When the time is up, leave the steam release handle in the Sealing position. 4. When released, open lid and stir in vanilla. 5. Serve on a plate, top with walnuts and bananas and enjoy.
Per Serving: Calories 448; Fat: 23.9g; Sodium 207mg; Carbs: 50.7g; Fiber 1g; Sugars: 15.2g; Protein 12.6g

Tomato Asparagus Frittata with Parmesan Cheese

Prep time: 15 minutes | Cook Time: 15 minutes | Serves: 4

1 cup water	6 large eggs
1 teaspoon olive oil	¼ cup low-; Fat plain Greek yogurt
1 cup halved cherry tomatoes	½ teaspoon salt
1 cup cooked asparagus tips	½ teaspoon ground black pepper
¼ cup grated Parmesan cheese	

1. Oil a 1.5-liter baking dish, then add tomatoes, asparagus and cheese to it. 2. In the Inner Pot, place in the Steam Rack and add in the water, then transfer the dish to the rack and tightly cover it with a piece of aluminum foil. 3. Select Pressure Cook mode. Press Pressure Cook button again to adjust the cooking time to 15 minutes. Press Pressure Level to choose Low Pressure. 4. When the time is up, leave the steam release handle in the Sealing position until the float valve drops. 5. Wait for 10 to 15 minutes before removing the dish out of the pot. 6. Turning the frittata out onto a serving plate by running a thin knife around the edge is suggested. 7. Serve and enjoy.
Per Serving: Calories 151; Fat: 9g; Sodium 520mg; Carbs: 4.9g; Fiber 1g; Sugars: 2.9g; Protein 12.8g

Peanut Butter Oatmeal with Jelly

Prep time: 15 minutes | Cook Time: 5 minutes | Serves: 4

2 cups gluten-free old-fashioned rolled oats
2 cups milk
1 tablespoon ground flaxseed
3 cups water, divided
½ cup peanut butter
½ cup Strawberry Compote or no-sugar-added fruit preserves

1. Prepare a heatproof bowl, mix up the oats, flaxseed, milk and 2 cups of water. 2. In the Inner Pot, add the remaining 1 cup of water and place the Steam Rack in it, then transfer the bowl to the rack. 3. Place and close the lid in right way. 4. Press Pressure Cook button to select the program, press it again to adjust the cooking time to 3 minutes; press Pressure Level to choose High Pressure. 5. When the time is up, leave the steam release handle in the Sealing position for 10 minutes, then turn it to the Venting position. 6. When released, there may be some liquid on the top of the oatmeal. 7. Add he peanut butter and stir well to incorporate; top each serving with 2 tablespoons of the compote. 8. Serve and enjoy.
Per Serving: Calories 344; Fat: 20.8g; Sodium 211mg; Carbs: 28.4g; Fiber 1g; Sugars: 9.1g; Protein 14.9g

Steamed Potatoes with Onions and Peppers

Prep time: 15 minutes | Cook Time: 8 minutes | Serves: 4

1 cup water
2 pounds red or yellow potatoes, cubed into 1½-inch chunks
1 medium onion, diced
1 bell pepper, diced
1 teaspoon garlic powder
¾ teaspoon paprika
Freshly ground black pepper
Salt (optional)

1. In the Inner Pot, add the water and place the Steam Rack in it, then transfer the potato chunks to the rack. 2. Place and close the lid in right way. 3. Press Pressure Cook button to select the program, press it again to adjust the cooking time to 5 minutes; press Pressure Level to choose High Pressure. 4. When the time is up, leave the steam release handle in the Sealing position. 5. After removing out the rack and steamed potato chunks, dry the Inner Pot and insert it into the Cooker Base again. 6. Without closing the lid, select Sauté mode and then press the same button again and then adjust the cooking temperature to Normal. 7. When the display switches On to Hot, add the onion, pepper and sauté for 3 minutes; slowly add the water if them begin to stick, 1 tablespoon a time; add the steamed potato chunks, garlic powder, paprika, salt and black pepper, cook until they are done to your liking. 8. Serve and enjoy.
Per Serving: Calories 34; Fat: 0.2g; Sodium 43mg; Carbs: 7.8g; Fiber 1g; Sugars: 4.4g; Protein 1.1g

Tofu Scramble with Vegetables

Prep time: 15 minutes | Cook Time: 10 minutes | Serves: 4

1 medium onion, diced
1 medium red bell pepper, diced
2 tablespoons no-salt-added veggie broth or water, divided
1 garlic clove, minced
1 (14-ounce) package firm tofu, drained and crumbled
2 teaspoons ground turmeric
½ teaspoon garlic powder
½ teaspoon paprika
3 ounces' fresh baby spinach
Salt (optional)
Freshly ground black pepper

1. Insert the Inner Pot into the Cooker Base without the lid. 2. Select Sauté mode and then press the same button again and then adjust the cooking temperature to Normal. 3. When the display switches On to Hot, add 1 tablespoon of the broth, onion, bell pepper and sauté for 5 minutes or until the onion begins to brown and the bell pepper is soft. 4. To prevent sticking, add a teaspoon of broth more at a time. 5. Stir in the minced garlic; add in the tofu, turmeric, garlic powder, paprika and stir until the tofu is yellow, similar to scrambled eggs; add the spinach and cook for 5 minutes more or until the spinach is just wilted. 6. Season with salt and black pepper. 7. When done, serve and enjoy.
Per Serving: Calories 127; Fat: 4.4g; Sodium 173mg; Carbs: 15.4g; Fiber 1g; Sugars: 3.4g; Protein 10.5g

Soy Yogurt

Prep time: 15 minutes | Cook Time: 15 hours| Serves: 4

1 (32-ounce) carton unsweetened plain soy milk (containing only
soybeans and water)
12 billion CFU probiotics

1. Mix up the soy milk in the clean Inner Pot and empty the powder in the probiotic capsule into the milk; insert the pot into the Cooker Base, place and close the lid rightly. 2. Press Yogurt to select the program and press it again to cycle to the Normal option; use the -/+ buttons to set the cooking time to 15 hours. 3. When cooked, remove and lid carefully. 4. Use a large spoon to remove and discard any excess liquid on the top of the yogurt, then transfer the yogurt to a suitable container and let it chill in the fridge. When it cools, it will thicken further. 5. For thicker Greek-style yogurt, us a clean muslin cloth to strain it for 15 to 20 minutes. 6. Serve and enjoy.
Per Serving: Calories 132; Fat: 4.3g; Sodium 125mg; Carbs: 15.4g; Fiber 1g; Sugars: 9.8g; Protein 8g

Onion Sweet Potato Hash

Prep time: 15 minutes | Cook Time: 15 minutes | Serves: 4

1 cup water
4 medium sweet potatoes, peeled and diced
1 medium red onion, diced
1 medium red or green bell pepper, diced
1 teaspoon garlic powder
1 teaspoon smoked paprika
Freshly ground black pepper
Salt (optional)
4 to 6 leaves Swiss chard, woody stems removed and discarded, greens chopped
¼ cup milk

1. In the Inner Pot, add the water and place the Steam Rack in it, then arrange the sweet potatoes to the rack. 2. Place and close the lid in right way. 3. Press Pressure Cook button to select the program, press it again to adjust the cooking time to 6 minutes; press Pressure Level to choose High Pressure. 4. When the time is up, quickly and carefully turn the steam release handle from the Sealing position to the Venting position. 5. When the float valve drops, remove out sweet potatoes and the rack. 6. After drying the Inner Pot, insert it back into the Cooker Base. 7. Without the lid, select Sauté mode and then press the same button again and then adjust the cooking temperature to Normal. 8. When the display switches On to Hot, add the bell pepper, onion and cook for 3 to 5 minutes; to prevent sticking, add water as needed during the cooking. 9. After 5 minutes, add the sweet potatoes, garlic powder, paprika, black pepper, salt and cook for 1 to 2 minutes; add the Swiss chard and cook for 3 more minutes or until wilted; lastly, add the milk and stir to scrap the bottom of the pot. 10. When done, serve and enjoy.
Per Serving: Calories 211; Fat: 0.6g; Sodium 159mg; Carbs: 49.3g; Fiber 1g; Sugars: 4.2g; Protein 4g

Healthy Quinoa with Yogurt and Walnuts

Prep time: 15 minutes | Cook Time: 12 minutes | Serves: 6

1½ cups quinoa, rinsed and drained
2½ cups water
1 cup almond milk
2 tablespoons honey
1 teaspoon vanilla extract
½ teaspoon ground cinnamon
¼ teaspoon salt
½ cup low-; Fat plain Greek yogurt
8 fresh figs, quartered
1 cup chopped toasted walnuts

1. In the Inner Pot, add the quinoa, almond milk, honey, vanilla, cinnamon, salt and water, then close the lid in right way. 2. Press Rice button to select the program, press it again to choose the Normal cooking time (12 minutes); press Pressure Level to choose High Pressure. 3. When the time is up, leave the steam release handle in the Sealing position. 4. When released, open lid and use a fork to fluff the quinoa. 5. With the yogurt, figs and walnuts, serve and enjoy.
Per Serving: Calories 394; Fat: 15.6g; Sodium 148mg; Carbs: 53.7g; Fiber 1g; Sugars: 20g; Protein 14.1g

Breakfast Biscuits and Gravy

Prep time: 10 minutes | Cook time: 15 minutes | Serve: 1

1 slice uncooked thick-cut bacon, minced
¼ cup ground breakfast sausage
1 tablespoon all-purpose flour
1/16 teaspoon ground cayenne pepper
⅛ teaspoon salt
⅛ teaspoon black pepper
½ cup whole milk
2 cooked buttermilk biscuits, halved

1. Select Sauté smart program. 2. Press the "Sauté" button again to select "More" option. 3. Without the lid, add bacon to the Inner Pot, and stir-fry for about 4 minutes until crispy. 4. Remove bacon and set aside for later use, leaving the bacon grease in the pot. 5. Add sausage to the pot, and sauté for about 5 minutes until browned. 6. Add flour, cayenne pepper, salt, and black pepper to the pot, mix them with sausage, and then cook them for 1 minute. 7. Whisk in milk. Cook gravy, whisking continuously, for 3–5 minutes until thickened. 8. Press Cancel button and add bacon bits. 9. Lay biscuit halves on the serving plate and top with sausage mixture. 10. Enjoy.
Per Serving: Calories 371; Fat 17.91g; Sodium 1037mg; Carbs 40.04g; Fiber 1.8g; Sugar 11.93g; Protein 13.31g

Maple Steel-Cut Oats

Prep time: 5 minutes | Cook time: 15 minutes | Serve: 1

⅓ cup steel-cut oats
1 cup water
3 tablespoons maple syrup
3 tablespoons vanilla almond milk

1. Add the oats and water to the Inner Pot. 2. Select Pressure Cook mode, and then press the "Pressure Cook" button again to select "Less" time option. 3. Use the "-" key on the control panel to set the cooking time to 15 minutes. 4. Press the Pressure Level button to adjust the pressure to "Low Pressure." 5. When cooked, allow the steam to release naturally. 6. Stir oats, and add maple syrup and almond milk. Ladle the food into a bowl and serve immediately.
Per Serving: Calories 249; Fat 2.68g; Sodium 42mg; Carbs 63.72g; Fiber 5g; Sugar 39.54g; Protein 5.58g

Steel-Cut Oatmeal with Apple and Cinnamon

Prep time: 15 minutes | Cook Time: 10 minutes | Serves: 4

5 cups water
2 cups gluten-free steel-cut oats
1 apple, cored and diced
3 tablespoons maple syrup
1 teaspoon ground cinnamon

1. In the Inner Pot, add and mix up the oats, apple, cinnamon, maple syrup and water, then place and close the lid in right way. 2. Press Pressure Cook button to select the program, press it again to adjust the cooking time to 10 minutes; press Pressure Level to choose High Pressure. 3. When the time is up, leave the steam release handle in the Sealing position for 10 minutes, then turn it to the Venting position; when the float valve drops, open the lid carefully. 4. There will be some liquid on the top of the oatmeal, stir well to incorporate it. 5. Serve warm and enjoy.
Per Serving: Calories 410; Fat: 6.1g; Sodium 11mg; Carbs: 76.2g; Fiber 1g; Sugars: 14.7g; Protein 14.2g

Feta Frittata

Prep time: 10 minutes | Cook time: 10 minutes | Serve: 1

2 large eggs
½ tablespoon heavy cream
2 tablespoons chopped spinach
2 tablespoons crumbled feta cheese
½ tablespoon chopped kalamata olives
1 cup water
¼ teaspoon balsamic glaze
⅛ teaspoon salt

1. Prepare an 8-ounce ramekin, and grease it with cooking spray. 2.

Mix eggs, cream, spinach, fata, and olives in a bowl until thoroughly combined. 3. Transfer the mixture to the greased ramekin and cover with foil. 4. Pour water into Inner Pot, and place in the Steam Rack; put the ramekin on Steam Rack. 5. Select Pressure Cook mode, and then press the "Pressure Cook" button again to select "Less" time option. 6. Press the "-" button to set the cooking time to 10 minutes. 7. Press the Pressure Level button to adjust the pressure to "Low Pressure." 8. When the time is up, allow the steam to release naturally. Then, remove the pressure lid from the top carefully. 9. Drizzle the frittata with balsamic glaze and salt, and serve immediately.
Per Serving: Calories 268; Fat 19.28g; Sodium 991mg; Carbs 5.14g; Fiber 1.1g; Sugar 2.83g; Protein 18.17g

Banana Oatmeal with Walnuts

Prep time: 15 minutes | Cook Time: 7 minutes | Serves: 2

1 cup rolled oats
1 cup water
1 cup whole milk
2 ripe bananas, peeled and sliced
2 tablespoons pure maple syrup
2 teaspoons ground cinnamon
¼ teaspoon vanilla extract
2 tablespoons chopped walnuts
⅛ teaspoon salt

1. In the Inner Pot, add and mix up all of the ingredients, then close the lid in right way. 2. Press Pressure Cook button to select the program, press it again to adjust the cooking time to 7 minutes; press Pressure Level to choose High Pressure. 3. When the time is up, leave the steam release handle in the Sealing position. 4. When released, open the lid and stir well. 5. Serve and enjoy.
Per Serving: Calories 441; Fat: 11.7g; Sodium 58mg; Carbs: 76.3g; Fiber 1g; Sugars: 33.4g; Protein 12.6g

Ham and Hash

Prep time: 10 minutes | Cook time: 20 minutes | Serves: 1-2

2 large eggs
½ tablespoon butter, melted
¼ cup frozen hash browns or potatoes
2 tablespoons diced ham
½ tablespoon chopped pickled
jalapeño peppers
2 tablespoons shredded Cheddar cheese
⅛ teaspoon salt
1 cup water
1 tablespoon salsa

1. Grease an 8-ounce ramekin with oil or cooking spray. 2. Whisk together eggs and butter in a bowl. 3. Add potatoes, ham, jalapeños, Cheddar cheese, and salt to the bowl, and thoroughly combine them. 4. Transfer the mixture to the prepared ramekin, and cover with foil. 5. Pour water into Inner Pot and place the Steam Rack in it. Put the ramekin on the Steam Rack. 6. Select Pressure Cook mode, and then press the "Pressure Cook" button again to select "Less" time option (20 minutes). 7. Press the Pressure Level button to adjust the pressure to "Low Pressure." 8. When cooked, allow the steam to release naturally. 9. When released, carefully remove ramekin from the Inner Pot and remove the foil. 10. Top the food with salsa and enjoy.
Per Serving: Calories 160; Fat 11.68g; Sodium 593mg; Carbs 7.61g; Fiber 0.7g; Sugar 1.58g; Protein 6.22g

Brown Sugar Quinoa

Prep time: 10 minutes | Cook time: 2 minutes | Serves: 2

½ cup uncooked quinoa, rinsed
1 cup vanilla almond milk
1 tablespoon butter
1/16 teaspoon salt
2 tablespoons brown sugar
½ cup whole milk
¼ cup heavy cream

1. Add quinoa, almond milk, butter, and salt to the Inner Pot. 2. Select Pressure Cook mode, and then press the "Pressure Cook" button again to select "Less" time option. 3. Use the "-" key to set the cooking time to 2 minutes. 4. Press the Pressure Level button to adjust the pressure to "Low Pressure." 5. When cooked, allow the steam to release naturally. Then, carefully remove the lid and transfer the food to the serving plate. 6. Stir in brown sugar and milk, and scoop into a bowl. 7. Serve with whipped cream.
Per Serving: Calories 455; Fat 18.99g; Sodium 163mg; Carbs 59.68g; Fiber 3g; Sugar 32.24g; Protein 12.7g

Maple Polenta with Nut

Prep time: 15 minutes | Cook Time: 15 minutes | Serves: 4

3 cups water
2 cups milk
1 cup polenta

½ cup pecan or walnut pieces
¼ cup maple syrup

1. Insert the Inner Pot into the Cooker Base without the lid. 2. Select Sauté mode and then press the same button again and then adjust the cooking temperature to Normal. 3. When the display switches On to Hot, add water, milk and polenta in the Inner Pot, stir constantly for 5 minute or until the polenta reaches a simmer. 4. Press Cancel button to stop this cooking program. 5. Place and close the lid in right way. 6. Press Pressure Cook button to select the program, press it again to adjust the cooking time to 10 minutes; press Pressure Level to choose High Pressure. 7. When the time is up, quickly and carefully turn the steam release handle from the Sealing position to the Venting position. 8. When the float valve drops, open the lid and add the nuts, maple syrup and stir well. 9. Serve and enjoy.
Per Serving: Calories 397; Fat: 17.9g; Sodium 66mg; Carbs: 52.6g; Fiber 1g; Sugars: 18.4g; Protein 9.1g

Chocolate and Almonds Amaranth Breakfast Bowl

Prep time: 15 minutes | Cook Time: 6 minutes | Serves: 6

2 cups amaranth, rinsed and drained
2 cups almond milk
2 cups water
¼ cup maple syrup
3 tablespoons cocoa powder

1 teaspoon vanilla extract
¼ teaspoon salt
½ cup toasted sliced almonds
⅓ cup miniature semisweet chocolate chips

1. In the Inner Pot, place and mix up the amaranth, water, almond mild, vanilla, maple syrup, cocoa powder and salt, then close the lid in right way. 2. Press Rice button to select the program, press it again to adjust the cooking time to 6 minutes; press Pressure Level to choose High Pressure. 3. When the time is up, quickly and carefully turn the steam release handle from the Sealing position to the Venting position. 4. When released, open the lid and stir well. 5. Top with chocolate chips and almonds and enjoy!
Per Serving: Calories 401; Fat: 12.2g; Sodium 169mg; Carbs: 63.3g; Fiber 1g; Sugars: 16.2g; Protein 12.6g

Cheddar Egg Puff

Prep time: 10 minutes | Cook time: 20 minutes | Serve: 1

2 large eggs
½ tablespoon butter, melted
2 tablespoons cottage cheese
1 tablespoon chopped green chilies
2 tablespoons shredded Cheddar cheese

½ tablespoon all-purpose flour
⅛ teaspoon salt
1/16 teaspoon black pepper
1/16 teaspoon garlic powder
1/16 teaspoon ground cayenne pepper
1 cup water

1. Grease an 8-ounce ramekin with oil or cooking spray. 2. Beat eggs and butter in a small bowl. 3. Add cottage cheese, green chilies, Cheddar cheese, all-purpose flour, salt, black pepper, garlic powder, and cayenne pepper to the bowl, and combine them well. 4. Pour mixture into prepared ramekin and cover with foil. 5. Pour water into Inner Pot, and place the Steam Rack in the pot; put the ramekin on the rack. 6. Select Pressure Cook mode, and then press the "Pressure Cook" button again to select "Less" time option. 7. Use the "-" button on the control panel to adjust the cooking time to 15 minutes. 8. Press the Pressure Level button to choose "Low Pressure." 9. When cooked, allow the steam to release naturally. Then, carefully remove ramekin from Inner Pot and remove foil. 10. Serve immediately.
Per Serving: Calories 293; Fat 18.75g; Sodium 1045mg; Carbs 11.24g; Fiber 3.1g; Sugar 3.35g; Protein 20.71g

Bacon-Cheddar Egg Bites

Prep time: 10 minutes | Cook time: 8 minutes | Serves: 2

5 large eggs
¼ cup cottage cheese
⅛ teaspoon salt
1 tablespoon butter, melted

7 teaspoons crumbled bacon bits
7 tablespoons shredded Cheddar cheese
1 cup water

1. Add eggs, cottage cheese, salt, and butter to the blender, and blend them until smooth. 2. Spray a silicone egg-bite mold with cooking spray. 3. Into each cup of the mold, add 1 teaspoon bacon bits. 4. Divided the egg mixture among the cups of the mold, top each of them with 1 tablespoon Cheddar cheese, and then cover the mold with foil. 5. Pour water into Inner Pot, and place the Steam Rack in it. Put the mold on Steam Rack. 6. Select Pressure Cook mode, and then press the "Pressure Cook" button again to select "Less" time option. 7. Use the "-" key to set the cooking time to 8 minutes. 8. Press the Pressure Level button to adjust the pressure to "High Pressure." 9. When cooked, allow the steam to release naturally. Then, remove the pressure lid carefully. 10. Invert mold onto a plate and squeeze egg bites out. 11. Serve immediately.
Per Serving: Calories 339; Fat 23.15g; Sodium 856mg; Carbs 6.85g; Fiber 0.8g; Sugar 2.97g; Protein 24.71g

Steel-Cut Oatmeal with Date and Walnut

Prep time: 15 minutes | Cook Time: 5 minutes | Serves: 4

1 tablespoon light olive oil
1 cup steel-cut oats
3 cups water
⅓ cup chopped pitted dates

¼ cup ground flax
¼ teaspoon salt
½ cup toasted chopped walnuts

1. In the Inner Pot, add the oil, water, dates, flax and salt, then close the lid in right way. 2. Press Pressure Cook button to select the program, press it again to adjust the cooking time to 5 minutes; press Pressure Level to choose High Pressure. 3. When the time is up, leave the steam release handle in the Sealing position for 10 minutes, then turn the steam release handle to the Venting position. 4. When released, open the lid and stir in walnuts. 5. Serve and enjoy.
Per Serving: Calories 214; Fat: 14g; Sodium 156mg; Carbs: 20g; Fiber 1g; Sugars: 9.7g; Protein 5.8g

Raspberry Steel Cut Oatmeal Bars

Prep time: 10 minutes | Cook time: 15 minutes | Serves: 6

3 cups steel cut oats
3 large eggs
2 cups unsweetened vanilla almond milk

⅓ cup Erythritol
1 teaspoon pure vanilla extract
¼ teaspoon salt
1 cup frozen raspberries

1. Mix all ingredients except the raspberries in a medium bowl. 2. Fold the mixture in the raspberries. 3. Spray a 6" cake pan with cooking oil. 4. Transfer the oat mixture to the pan and cover the pan with aluminum foil. 5. Pour 1 cup water into the Inner Pot and place the Steam Rack inside. 6. Place the pan with the oat mixture on top of the rack. 7. Select Pressure Cook mode, and then press the "Pressure Cook" button again to select "Less" time option. 8. Use the "-" key on to set the cooking time to 15 minutes. 9. Press the Pressure Level button to adjust the pressure to "Low Pressure." 10. Once the cooking cycle is completed, quickly and carefully turn the steam release handle from Sealing position to the Venting position. 11. Carefully remove the pan from the Inner Pot and remove the foil. 12. Allow to cool completely before cutting into bars and serving.
Per Serving: Calories 287; Fat 8.13g; Sodium 207mg; Carbs 57.06g; Fiber 8.8g; Sugar 24.75g; Protein 14.48g

Blueberry French Toast Bake

Prep time: 10 minutes | Cook time: 35 minutes | Serves: 2

French Toast
1 large egg
¾ cup whole milk
2 tablespoons granulated sugar
¼ teaspoon vanilla extract
¼ teaspoon almond extract
4 slices stale Texas Toast bread, cubed into 1" pieces
¼ cup blueberries
¼ teaspoon ground cinnamon
½ tablespoon brown sugar
1 cup water
Cream Cheese Glaze
3 tablespoons confectioners' sugar
1 ½ tablespoons cream cheese, softened
⅛ teaspoon vanilla extract
¼ teaspoon whole milk

1. Grease a suitable cake pan. 2. Beat the egg with milk, granulated sugar, vanilla extract, and almond extract in a bowl. 3. Arrange bread cubes in the prepared cake pan, then pour milk mixture over the cubes and let them soak for 5 minutes. 4. Top the cubes with blueberries, cinnamon, and brown sugar. 5. Tightly cover the pan with foil. 6. Pour water into Inner Pot, place the Steam Rack in the pot, and then put the pan on Steam Rack. 7. Select Pressure Cook mode, and then press the "Pressure Cook" button again to select "Normal" time option (35 minutes). 8. Press the Pressure Level button to adjust the pressure to "Low Pressure." 9. Once the cooking cycle is completed, quickly and carefully turn the steam release handle from Sealing position to the Venting position. 10. Carefully remove pan from the Inner Pot, remove foil, and let the dish cool for 5 minutes. 11. Mix confectioners' sugar, softened cream cheese, vanilla extract, and whole milk in another bowl to make the cream cheese glaze. 12. Spread glaze evenly on bread and enjoy immediately.
Per Serving: Calories 441; Fat 10.37g; Sodium 395mg; Carbs 76.54g; Fiber 3g; Sugar 50.12g; Protein 11.37g

Sausage Pancake Bites

Prep time: 10 minutes | Cook time: 15 minutes | Serves: 4

1 cup pancake mix
¼ cup whole milk
1-½ cups water
3 tablespoons maple syrup
3 ½ fully cooked frozen sausage links, split in half

1. Grease a silicone egg bites mold. 2. Mix pancake mix, milk, ½ cup water, and maple syrup in a small bowl. 3. Spoon 1-½ tablespoons batter into each cup of prepared mold. 4. Place half of a sausage link in the middle of the batter in each cup, pressing down slightly. 5. Top each sausage link with an additional ½ tablespoon batter. 6. Cover the mold with a paper towel, then cover tightly with foil. 7. Pour remaining 1 cup water into Inner Pot and add the Steam Rack. Place mold on Steam Rack. 8. Select Pressure Cook mode, and then press the "Pressure Cook" button again to select "Less" time option. 9. Use the "-" key on the control panel to set the cooking time to 15 minutes. 10. Press the Pressure Level button to adjust the pressure to "Low Pressure." 11. Once the cooking cycle is completed, allow the steam to release naturally. 12. Carefully remove mold from Inner Pot, then invert pancake bites onto a plate. 13. Serve immediately.
Per Serving: Calories 249; Fat 8.69g; Sodium 688mg; Carbs 35.75g; Fiber 0g; Sugar 9.95g; Protein 7.74g

Avocado Toast with Boiled Egg

Prep time: 10 minutes | Cook time: 5 minutes | Serves: 2

1 cup water
1 large egg
½ medium avocado, peeled, pitted, and sliced
1 (1-ounce) slice sourdough bread, toasted
⅛ teaspoon salt
⅛ teaspoon black pepper
⅛ teaspoon crushed red pepper flakes
½ tablespoon roasted pepitas
½ teaspoon olive oil

1. Pour water into Inner Pot and place the Steam Rack in it. 2. Put the egg on Steam Rack. 3. Select Pressure Cook mode, and then press the "Pressure Cook" button again to select "Less" time option. 4. Use the "-" key to adjust the cooking time to 5 minutes. 5. Press the Pressure Level button to adjust the pressure to "Low Pressure." 6. When the time is up, quickly and carefully turn the steam release handle from Sealing position to the Venting position. 7. Spread avocado slices evenly over toast. 8. Carefully peel soft-boiled egg and place it on top of avocado. 9. Sprinkle salt, black pepper, red pepper flakes, pepitas, and oil over avocado. 10. Serve immediately.
Per Serving: Calories 328; Fat 13.5g; Sodium 620mg; Carbs 41.2g; Fiber 5.1g; Sugar 3.81g; Protein 12.25g

Creamy Oatmeal

Prep time: 10 minutes | Cook time: 2 minutes | Serve: 1

½ cup rolled oats
1 cup water
1/16 teaspoon salt
½ tablespoon butter
3 teaspoons brown sugar
⅛ teaspoon vanilla extract
⅛ teaspoon ground cinnamon
½ tablespoon heavy cream

1. Mix oats with water, and salt in the Inner Pot. 2. Select Pressure Cook mode, and then press the "Pressure Cook" button again to select "Less" time option. 3. Use the "-" key to set the cooking time to 2 minutes. 4. Press the Pressure Level button to adjust the pressure to "Low Pressure." 5. When the time is up, quickly and carefully turn the steam release handle from Sealing position to the Venting position. 6. Stir oats, and then add the remaining ingredients. 7. Scoop the meal into a bowl and enjoy.
Per Serving: Calories 224; Fat 11.84g; Sodium 49mg; Carbs 39.12g; Fiber 7.4g; Sugar 8.3g; Protein 8.36g

Coconut Oatmeal

Prep time: 10 minutes | Cook time: 15 minutes | Serve: 1

½ cup rolled oats
1 cup water
1/16 teaspoon salt
3 tablespoons cream of coconut
2 tablespoons whole milk
¼ cup raspberries
2 tablespoons toasted coconut

1. Mix oats with water, and salt in the Inner Pot. 2. Select Pressure Cook mode, and then press the "Pressure Cook" button again to select "Less" time option. 3. Use the "-" key to set the cooking time to 2 minutes. 4. Press the Pressure Level button to adjust the pressure to "Low Pressure." 5. Once the cooking cycle is completed, quickly and carefully turn the steam release handle from Sealing position to the Venting position. 6. Stir oats, then add cream of coconut and milk to the pot. 7. Scoop the meal into a bowl and top with raspberries and toasted coconut. 8. Enjoy.
Per Serving: Calories 337; Fat 23.44g; Sodium 61mg; Carbs 42.07g; Fiber 10.2g; Sugar 2.54g; Protein 10.91g

Blueberry- Oatmeal

Prep time: 10 minutes | Cook time: 2 minutes | Serve: 1

½ cup rolled oats
½ cup water
½ cup vanilla almond milk
1/16 teaspoon salt
3 tablespoons blueberries
3 teaspoons brown sugar
⅛ teaspoon almond extract
¼ teaspoon ground cinnamon
1 tablespoon heavy cream
1 tablespoon granola
2 teaspoons sliced almonds

1. Add oats, water, almond milk, salt, and blueberries to the Inner Pot, and lightly stir them well. 2. Select Pressure Cook mode, and then press the "Pressure Cook" button again to select "Less" time option. 3. Use the "-" key to set the cooking time to 2 minutes. 4. Press the Pressure Level button to adjust the pressure to "Low Pressure." 5. Once the cooking cycle is completed, quickly and carefully turn the steam release handle from Sealing position to the Venting position. 6. Remove the lid, stir the oats, and then add brown sugar, almond extract, and cinnamon. 7. Stir them well and scoop into a bowl. 8. Top the meal with cream, granola, and almonds, and enjoy.
Per Serving: Calories 313; Fat 10.49g; Sodium 149mg; Carbs 58.72g; Fiber 9.4g; Sugar 23.29g; Protein 10.49g

Breakfast Grits

Prep time: 10 minutes | Cook time: 10 minutes | Serves: 2

¼ cup grits
½ cup whole milk
1 ½ cups water

1 tablespoon butter
3 tablespoons brown sugar
2 tablespoons heavy cream

1. Mix grits, milk, and ½ cup water in a suitable cake pan. 2. Pour the remaining water into the Inner Pot, and place the Steam Rack in the pot. Put the cake pan on Steam Rack. 3. Select Pressure Cook mode, and then press the "Pressure Cook" button again to select "Less" time option. 4. Use the "-" key to set the cooking time to 10 minutes. 5. Press the Pressure Level button to adjust the pressure to "Low Pressure." 6. Once the cooking cycle is completed, quickly and carefully turn the steam release handle from Sealing position to the Venting position. 7. Carefully remove cake pan from Inner Pot, and mix in butter, brown sugar, and cream. 8. Scoop the food into a bowl and enjoy immediately.
Per Serving: Calories 235; Fat 14.65g; Sodium 143mg; Carbs 24.34g; Fiber 0.2g; Sugar 20.11g; Protein 2.65g

Banana Date Porridge

Prep time: 10 minutes | Cook time: 4 minutes | Serves: 4

1 cup buckwheat groats
1½ cups unsweetened vanilla almond milk
1 cup water

1 large banana, mashed
5 pitted dates, chopped
¾ teaspoon ground cinnamon
¾ teaspoon pure vanilla extract

1. Add all the ingredients to the Inner Pot, and stir them well. 2. Select Pressure Cook mode, and then press the "Pressure Cook" button again to select "Less" time option. 3. Use the "-" key to set the cooking time to 4 minutes. 4. Press the Pressure Level button to adjust the pressure to "Low Pressure." 5. Once the cooking cycle is completed, quickly and carefully turn the steam release handle from Sealing position to the Venting position. 6. Allow the porridge to cool slightly before spooning into bowls to serve.
Per Serving: Calories 132; Fat 1.35g; Sodium 60mg; Carbs 29.23g; Fiber 3.4g; Sugar 15.9g; Protein 2.41g

Vanilla Bean Yogurt

Prep time: 10 minutes | Cook time: 6 hours | Serves: 1

¾ cup ultra-pasteurized whole milk
¼ teaspoon yogurt starter, such as store-bought plain yogurt
1 tablespoon sweetened

condensed milk
¼ teaspoon vanilla extract
¼ teaspoon vanilla bean paste
1 cup water

1. In an 8-ounce ramekin, thoroughly mix all ingredients except water. 2. Cover the ramekin with foil. 3. Pour water into Inner Pot, place the Steam Rack in the pot, and then put the ramekin on Steam Rack. 4. Press the "Yogurt" button one time to select "Normal" option. 5. Use the "+/-" keys to set the cooking time to 6 hours. 6. Cover the jar with plastic wrap or the jar lid and then transfer to the refrigerator. 7. Chill overnight, then serve.
Per Serving: Calories 341; Fat 24.68g; Sodium 170mg; Carbs 7.42g; Fiber 0.1g; Sugar 2.04g; Protein 21.57g

Vegetable Egg White

Prep time: 10 minutes | Cook time: 15 minutes | Serve: 1

3 large egg whites
½ tablespoon butter, melted
2 tablespoons cottage cheese
1 tablespoon chopped and sautéed mushrooms
1 tablespoon chopped and sautéed

red bell pepper
1 tablespoon chopped and sautéed yellow onion
2 tablespoons chopped and sautéed spinach
2 tablespoons shredded Cheddar

cheese
½ tablespoon all-purpose flour
⅛ teaspoon salt
1/16 teaspoon black pepper

1/16 teaspoon garlic powder
1/16 teaspoon ground cayenne pepper
1 cup water

1. Grease an 8-ounce ramekin. Set aside. 2. Mix egg whites, butter, cottage cheese, mushrooms, bell pepper, onion, spinach, Cheddar, flour, salt, black pepper, garlic powder, and cayenne pepper. 3. Pour mixture into prepared ramekin and cover with foil. 4. Pour water into the Inner Pot, and then place the Steam Rack in it; put the ramekin on Steam Rack. 5. Select Pressure Cook mode, and then press the "Pressure Cook" button again to select "Less" time option. 6. Use the "-" key to set the cooking time to 15 minutes. 7. Press the Pressure Level button to adjust the pressure to "Low Pressure." 8. Once the cooking cycle is completed, allow the steam to release naturally. 9. Carefully remove ramekin from Inner Pot and remove the foil. 10. Serve immediately.
Per Serving: Calories 348; Fat 18g; Sodium 861mg; Carbs 26.85g; Fiber 4.3g; Sugar 11.6g; Protein 21.5g

Denver Omelet

Prep time: 10 minutes | Cook time: 15 minutes | Serve: 1

2 large eggs
½ tablespoon butter, melted
2 tablespoons cottage cheese
2 tablespoons diced ham
1 tablespoon diced and sautéed red onion

1 tablespoon diced green bell pepper
2 tablespoons shredded Cheddar cheese
⅛ teaspoon salt
1 cup water

1. Grease an 8-ounce ramekin. 2. Whisk eggs, butter, cottage cheese, ham, onion, bell pepper, Cheddar, and salt in the bowl. 3. Pour mixture into prepared ramekin and cover the ramekin with foil. 4. Pour water into Inner Pot and add the Steam Rack. Place ramekin on Steam Rack. 5. Select Pressure Cook mode, and then press the "Pressure Cook" button again to select "Less" time option. 6. Use the "-" key to set the cooking time to 15 minutes. 7. Press the Pressure Level button to adjust the pressure to "Low Pressure." 8. Once the cooking cycle is completed, allow the steam to release naturally. 9. Carefully remove ramekin from Inner Pot and remove foil. 10. Serve immediately.
Per Serving: Calories 300; Fat 18.44g; Sodium 1109mg; Carbs 9.48g; Fiber 1g; Sugar 5.43g; Protein 24.03g

Egg Kale Casserole

Prep time: 10 minutes | Cook time: 20 minutes | Serves: 6

1 tablespoon avocado oil
1 small yellow onion, peeled and chopped
5 large kale leaves, tough stems removed and finely chopped
1 clove garlic, diced
2 tablespoons lemon juice

½ teaspoon salt
9 large eggs
2 tablespoons water
1½ teaspoons dried rosemary
1 teaspoon dried oregano
¼ teaspoon black pepper
½ cup nutritional yeast

1. Select Sauté mode, press the "Sauté" button again and select "Normal". 2. Add the oil to the Inner Pot, and heat oil for 1 minute. 3. Add the onion, and sauté for 2 minutes until just softened. 4. Add the kale, garlic, lemon juice, and ¼ teaspoon salt, stir and allow to cook for 2 minutes more. Press the Cancel button. 5. Whisk eggs, water, rosemary, oregano, ¼ teaspoon salt, pepper, and nutritional yeast in a medium bowl, then add the onion and kale mixture to them, stir well. 6. Spray a 7" spring form pan with cooking spray. Transfer the egg mixture to the spring form pan. 7. Rinse the Inner Pot, add 2 cups water, and place a steam rack inside. 8. Place the pan on the steam rack and secure the lid. 9. Select Pressure Cook mode, and then press the "Pressure Cook" button again to select "Less" time option. 10. Use the "-" key to set the cooking time to 12 minutes. 11. Press the Pressure Level button to adjust the pressure to "Low Pressure." 12. Once the cooking cycle is completed, quickly and carefully turn the steam release handle from Sealing position to the Venting position. 13. Remove the pan from pot and allow to cool 5 minutes before slicing and serving.
Per Serving: Calories 185; Fat 9.83g; Sodium 1016mg; Carbs 8.25g; Fiber 2.3g; Sugar 1.55g; Protein 15.84g

Blueberry Quinoa Porridge

Prep time: 10 minutes | Cook time: 1 minute | Serves: 6

1½ cups dry quinoa
3 cups water
1 cup frozen wild blueberries

½ teaspoon pure stevia powder
1 teaspoon pure vanilla extract

1. Rinse the quinoa very well until the water runs clear. 2. Add the quinoa, water, blueberries, stevia, and vanilla to the Inner Pot. Stir to combine. 3. Select Pressure Cook mode, and then press the "Pressure Cook" button again to select "Less" time option. 4. Use the "-" key to set the cooking time to 1 minute. 5. Press the Pressure Level button to adjust the pressure to "Low Pressure." 6. Once the cooking cycle is completed, quickly and carefully turn the steam release handle from Sealing position to the Venting position. 7. Allow the quinoa to cool slightly before spooning into bowls to serve.
Per Serving: Calories 115; Fat 1.75g; Sodium 4mg; Carbs 20.42g; Fiber 2.7g; Sugar 1.17g; Protein 4.01g

Creamy Pumpkin Yogurt

Prep time: 10 minutes | Cook time: 6 hours | Serves: 2

¾ cup ultra-pasteurized whole milk
¼ teaspoon yogurt starter, such as store-bought plain yogurt
1 tablespoon sugar

⅛ teaspoon vanilla extract
1 ½ tablespoons pumpkin puree
1/16 teaspoon pumpkin pie spice
1 cup water

1. In an 8-ounce ramekin, thoroughly mix all ingredients except water. 2. Cover the ramekin with plastic wrap or foil. 3. Pour water into Inner Pot, place the Steam Rack in the pot, and then put the ramekin on Steam Rack. 4. Press the "Yogurt" button two times to select "Normal" option. 5. Use the "+/-" keys to set the cooking time to 6 hours. 6. Chill overnight in the refrigerator, then serve.
Per Serving: Calories 213; Fat 14.92g; Sodium 82mg; Carbs 8.29g; Fiber 0.5g; Sugar 4.36g; Protein 12.2g

Banana Oatmeal

Prep time: 10 minutes | Cook time: 7 minutes | Serves: 6

3 cups old fashioned rolled oats
¼ teaspoon salt
2 large bananas, mashed (1

heaping cup)
2 large eggs, lightly beaten
⅓ cup xylitol

1. Stir oats, salt, bananas, eggs, and xylitol in the bowl. 2. Lightly spray a suitable cake pan with cooking spray. Transfer the oat mixture to the pan. 3. Pour 1½ cups water into the Inner Pot. Place a Steam Rack in the Inner Pot and put the pan on the steam rack. 4. Select Pressure Cook mode, and then press the "Pressure Cook" button again to select "Less" time option. 5. Use the "-" key to set the cooking time to 7 minutes. 6. Press the Pressure Level button to adjust the pressure to "Low Pressure." 7. Once the cooking cycle is completed, allow the steam to release naturally. 8. Allow the oatmeal to cool 5 minutes before serving.
Per Serving: Calories 211; Fat 4.96g; Sodium 102mg; Carbs 51.12g; Fiber 8.4g; Sugar 15.67g; Protein 9.53g

Chocolate Oatmeal

Prep time: 10 minutes | Cook time: 6 minutes | Serves: 4

1 cup steel cut oats
1 (12.5-ounce) can full-fat unsweetened coconut milk
2 cups water

½ cup cacao powder
½ cup Erythritol
⅛ teaspoon sea salt

1. Place the oats, coconut milk, water, cacao powder, Erythritol, and salt in the Inner Pot, and stir to combine. 2. Select Pressure Cook mode, and then press the "Pressure Cook" button again to select "Less" time option. 3. Use the "-" key to set the cooking time to 6 minutes. 4. Press the Pressure Level button to adjust the pressure to "Low Pressure." 5. Once the

cooking cycle is completed, quickly and carefully turn the steam release handle from Sealing position to the Venting position. 6. Allow the oatmeal to cool slightly before spooning into bowls to serve.
Per Serving: Calories 395; Fat 24.18g; Sodium 96mg; Carbs 55.05g; Fiber 8.8g; Sugar 31.73g; Protein 8.05g

Banana Walnut Oats

Prep time: 10 minutes | Cook time: 4 minutes | Serves: 4

2 cups steel cut oats
2½ cups water
2½ cups unsweetened vanilla almond milk
3 medium bananas, thinly sliced

1½ teaspoons ground cinnamon
1 teaspoon pure vanilla extract
¼ teaspoon salt
4 tablespoons walnut pieces

1. Add the steel cut oats, water, almond milk, banana slices, cinnamon, vanilla, and salt to the Inner Pot and stir to combine. 2. Select Pressure Cook mode, and then press the "Pressure Cook" button again to select "Less" time option. 3. Use the "-" key to set the cooking time to 4 minutes. 4. Press the Pressure Level button to adjust the pressure to "Low Pressure." 5. Once the cooking cycle is completed, allow the steam to release naturally for 10 minutes, turn the steam release handle to the Venting position. 6. Divide the oatmeal among the serving bowls, and top each serving with 1 tablespoon walnut pieces.
Per Serving: Calories 305; Fat 9.8g; Sodium 246mg; Carbs 62.89g; Fiber 11.2g; Sugar 21.12g; Protein 11.64g

Almond Granola

Prep time: 10 minutes | Cook time: 7 minutes | Serves: 8

1½ cups old fashioned rolled oats
½ cup unsweetened shredded coconut
¼ cup monk fruit sweetener

⅛ teaspoon salt
¾ cup almond butter
¼ cup coconut oil

1. In a medium bowl, mix together the oats, coconut, sweetener, and salt. 2. Add the almond butter and oil and mix until well combined. 3. Spray a 6" cake pan with nonstick cooking oil. Transfer the oat mixture to the pan. 4. Add 1 cup water to the Inner Pot, place the Steam Rack in it, and then put the pan on the rack. 5. Select Pressure Cook mode, and then press the "Pressure Cook" button again to select "Less" time option. 6. Use the "-" key to set the cooking time to 7 minutes. 7. Press the Pressure Level button to adjust the pressure to "Low Pressure." 8. Once the cooking cycle is completed, quickly and carefully turn the steam release handle from Sealing position to the Venting position. 9. Remove the pan from the Inner Pot and transfer the granola to a baking sheet to cool completely. 10. Serve.
Per Serving: Calories 270; Fat 21.12g; Sodium 57mg; Carbs 21.89g; Fiber 5.3g; Sugar 6.36g; Protein 8.08g

Buckwheat Granola

Prep time: 10 minutes | Cook time: 10 minutes | Serves: 8

1½ cups raw buckwheat groats
1½ cups old fashioned rolled oats
⅓ cup walnuts, chopped
⅓ cup unsweetened shredded coconut
¼ cup coconut oil, melted

1" piece fresh ginger, peeled and grated
3 tablespoons date syrup
1 teaspoon ground cinnamon
¼ teaspoon salt

1. Mix the buckwheat groats, oats, walnuts, shredded coconut, coconut oil, ginger, date syrup, cinnamon, and salt until well combined. 2. Transfer this mixture to the 6" cake pan. 3. Pour 1 cup water into the Inner Pot and place a Steam Rack inside. Place the pan on the rack. 4. Select Pressure Cook mode, and then press the "Pressure Cook" button again to select "Less" time option. 5. Use the "-" key to set the cooking time to 10 minutes. 6. Press the Pressure Level button to adjust the pressure to "Low Pressure." 7. Once the cooking cycle is completed, quickly and carefully turn the steam release handle from Sealing position to the Venting position. 8. Spread the granola onto a large sheet pan and allow it to cool, undisturbed, for 1 hour. It will crisp as it cools.
Per Serving: Calories 179; Fat 10.44g; Sodium 90mg; Carbs 25.42g; Fiber 4.1g; Sugar 7.23g; Protein 4.71g

Artichoke Egg Casserole

Prep time: 10 minutes | Cook time: 18 minutes | Serves: 8

12 large eggs
¼ cup water
4 cups baby spinach, roughly chopped
1 (14-ounce) can baby artichoke hearts, drained and roughly
chopped
1 tablespoon chopped fresh chives
1 tablespoon fresh lemon juice
¾ teaspoon table salt
½ teaspoon black pepper
¼ teaspoon garlic salt

1. Spray a suitable round pan with cooking spray. 2. Whisk eggs and water in a medium bowl. 3. Stir in the spinach, artichokes, chives, lemon juice, table salt, pepper, and garlic salt. 4. Transfer the mixture to the prepared pan. 5. Place 2 cups water in the Inner Pot and place the Steam Rack inside. Place the pan on top of the Steam Rack. 6. Select Pressure Cook mode, and then press the "Pressure Cook" button again to select "Less" time option. 7. Use the "-" key to set the cooking time to 18 minutes. 8. Press the Pressure Level button to adjust the pressure to "Low Pressure." 9. Once the cooking cycle is completed, quickly and carefully turn the steam release handle from Sealing position to the Venting position. 10. Remove egg casserole from pot and allow to cool 5 minutes before slicing and serving.
Per Serving: Calories 164; Fat 7.35g; Sodium 351mg; Carbs 11.03g; Fiber 3.4g; Sugar 1.08g; Protein 13.19g

Cinnamon Oatmeal Muffins

Prep time: 10 minutes | Cook time: 15 minutes | Serves: 6

3 cups old fashioned rolled oats
1 teaspoon baking powder
¼ teaspoon salt
1 teaspoon ground cinnamon
¼ cup unsweetened vanilla
almond milk
¼ cup fresh orange juice
3⅓ cups mashed bananas
1 large egg
¼ cup Erythritol

1. Stir all of the ingredients in a medium bowl until well combined. 2. Place six silicone muffin cups inside of a suitable cake pan. 3. Spoon the oatmeal mixture into the muffin cups. Cover the pan with aluminum foil. 4. Pour 1 cup water into the Inner Pot and place the Steam Rack inside. 5. Place the cake pan with the muffins on the rack. 6. Select Pressure Cook mode, and then press the "Pressure Cook" button again to select "Less" time option. 7. Use the "-" key to set the cooking time to 15 minutes. 8. Press the Pressure Level button to adjust the pressure to "Low Pressure." 9. Once the cooking cycle is completed, quickly and carefully turn the steam release handle from Sealing position to the Venting position. 10. Carefully remove the pan from the Inner Pot and remove the foil from the top. 11. Serve.
Per Serving: Calories 286; Fat 4.63g; Sodium 119mg; Carbs 71.74g; Fiber 10.8g; Sugar 26.9g; Protein 10.67g

Pumpkin Quinoa

Prep time: 10 minutes | Cook time: 1 minute | Serves: 4

¾ cup dry quinoa
2 cups water
¾ cup pumpkin purée
¼ cup monk fruit sweetener
1½ teaspoons pumpkin pie spice
1 teaspoon pure vanilla extract
¼ teaspoon salt

1. Rinse the quinoa very well until the water runs clear. 2. Stir the quinoa, water, pumpkin purée, fruit sweetener, pumpkin pie spice, vanilla extract, and salt in the Inner Pot. 3. Select Pressure Cook mode, and then press the "Pressure Cook" button again to select "Less" time option. 4. Use the "-" key to set the cooking time to 1 minute. 5. Press the Pressure Level button to adjust the pressure to "Low Pressure." 6. Once the cooking cycle is completed, quickly and carefully turn the steam release handle from Sealing position to the Venting position. 7. Allow the quinoa to cool slightly before spooning into bowls to serve.
Per Serving: Calories 292; Fat 12.93g; Sodium 9mg; Carbs 34.79g; Fiber 3.8g; Sugar 9.82g; Protein 11.15g

Poppy Seed Oatmeal Cups

Prep time: 10 minutes | Cook time: 5 minutes | Serves: 4

2 cups old fashioned rolled oats
1 teaspoon baking powder
2 tablespoons Erythritol
1 tablespoon poppy seeds
¼ teaspoon salt
1 large egg
Juice and zest from 1 Meyer lemon
1 cup unsweetened vanilla almond milk

1. Lightly grease four (8-ounce) ramekin dishes. 2. Mix the oats, baking powder, Erythritol, poppy seeds, and salt in a medium bowl. 3. Add the egg, almond milk, juice and zest from the lemon to the oat bowl, and stir to combine. 4. Divide the oatmeal mixture into the four dishes. 5. Pour ½ cup water into the Inner Pot of the Instant Pot. 6. Place the Steam Rack inside the Inner Pot and place the ramekins on top of the rack. 7. Put on the pressure cooker's lid and turn the steam valve to "Sealing" position. 8. Select Pressure Cook mode, and then press the "Pressure Cook" button again to select "Less" time option. 9. Use the "-" key to set the cooking time to 5 minutes. 10. Press the Pressure Level button to adjust the pressure to "Low Pressure." 11. Once the cooking cycle is completed, quickly and carefully turn the steam release handle from Sealing position to the Venting position. 12. Serve.
Per Serving: Calories 224; Fat 7.1g; Sodium 205mg; Carbs 47.38g; Fiber 7.7g; Sugar 15.07g; Protein 11.44g

Apple Steel Cut Oats

Prep time: 10 minutes | Cook time: 4 minutes | Serves: 6

2 cups steel cut oats
3 cups unsweetened vanilla almond milk
3 cups water
3 small apples, peeled, cored, and
cut into 1"-thick chunks
2 teaspoons ground cinnamon
¼ cup date syrup
¼ teaspoon salt

1. Add the steel cut oats, almond milk, water, apple chunks, cinnamon, date syrup, and salt to the Inner Pot and stir to combine. 2. Put on the pressure cooker's lid and turn the steam valve to "Sealing" position. 3. Select Pressure Cook mode, and then press the "Pressure Cook" button again to select "Less" time option. 4. Use the "+/-" keys on the control panel to set the cooking time to 4 minutes. 5. Press the Pressure Level button to adjust the pressure to "Low Pressure." 6. Once the cooking cycle is completed, quickly and carefully turn the steam release handle from Sealing position to the Venting position. 7. When all the steam is released, remove the pressure lid from the top carefully. 8. Serve warm.
Per Serving: Calories 233; Fat 6.36g; Sodium 163mg; Carbs 48.48g; Fiber 7.1g; Sugar 25.29g; Protein 9.49g

Berry Steel Cut Oats

Prep time: 10 minutes | Cook time: 4 minutes | Serves: 6

2 cups steel cut oats
3 cups unsweetened almond milk
3 cups water
1 teaspoon pure vanilla extract
⅓ cup monk fruit sweetener
¼ teaspoon salt
1½ cups frozen berry blend with strawberries, blackberries, and raspberries

1. Add the steel cut oats, almond milk, water, vanilla, sweetener, and salt to the Inner Pot, and stir to combine. Place the frozen berries on top. 2. Select Pressure Cook mode, and then press the "Pressure Cook" button again to select "Less" time option. 3. Use the "-" key to set the cooking time to 4 minutes. 4. Press the Pressure Level button to adjust the pressure to "Low Pressure." 5. Once the cooking cycle is completed, allow the steam to release naturally for 10 minutes, then turn the steam release handle to the Venting position. 6. Serve warm.
Per Serving: Calories 219; Fat 6.25g; Sodium 156mg; Carbs 42.9g; Fiber 4.8g; Sugar 20.71g; Protein 9.28g

Banana Bites

Prep time: 10 minutes | Cook time: 6 minutes | Serves: 3

1¾ cups old fashioned rolled oats
3 small ripe bananas
3 large eggs
2 tablespoons Erythritol

1 teaspoon ground cinnamon
1 teaspoon pure vanilla extract
1 teaspoon baking powder

1. Blend the oats, bananas, eggs, Erythritol, cinnamon, vanilla extract, and baking powder in a large, powerful blender until very smooth, for 1 minute. 2. Pour the mixture into a silicone mold with seven wells. 3. Place a paper towel on top and then top with aluminum foil. 4. Tighten the edges to prevent extra moisture getting inside. 5. Place the mold on top of your steam rack with handles. 6. Pour 1 cup water into the Inner Pot. Place the Steam Rack and mold inside. 7. Select Pressure Cook mode, and then press the "Pressure Cook" button again to select "Less" time option. 8. Use the "-" key to set the cooking time to 6 minutes. 9. Press the Pressure Level button to adjust the pressure to "Low Pressure." 10. Once the cooking cycle is completed, quickly and carefully turn the steam release handle from Sealing position to the Venting position. 11. Pull the steam rack and mold out of the Inner Pot and remove the aluminum foil and paper towel. 12. Allow the pancake bites to cool completely, and then use a knife to pull the edges of the bites away from the mold. 13. Press on the bottom of the mold and the pancake bites will pop right out.
Per Serving: Calories 325; Fat 8.96g; Sodium 76mg; Carbs 66.72g; Fiber 11.6g; Sugar 18.74g; Protein 16.9g

Cinnamon Breakfast Loaf

Prep time: 10 minutes | Cook time: 30 minutes | Serves: 6

½ cup ground golden flaxseed meal
½ cup almond flour
1 tablespoon ground cinnamon
2 teaspoons baking powder

½ teaspoon salt
⅔ cup xylitol
4 large eggs
½ cup coconut oil, melted and cooled

1. Whisk the flaxseed meal, flour, cinnamon, baking powder, salt, and xylitol in a medium bowl. 2. Whisk the eggs and cooled coconut oil in another bowl. 3. Combine the wet ingredients and dry ingredients. 4. Grease a suitable cake pan well, pour the mixture into the pan, and then cover with aluminum foil. 5. Pour 1½ cups water into the Inner Pot and place the Steam Rack with handles in the pot. Place the cake pan on top of the Steam Rack. 6. Select Pressure Cook mode, and then press the "Pressure Cook" button again to select "Normal" time option. 7. Use the "-" key to set the cooking time to 30 minutes. 8. Press the Pressure Level button to adjust the pressure to "Low Pressure." 9. Once the cooking cycle is completed, quickly and carefully turn the steam release handle from Sealing position to the Venting position. 10. Slice and serve.
Per Serving: Calories 376; Fat 27.31g; Sodium 247mg; Carbs 29.74g; Fiber 4.6g; Sugar 23.91g; Protein 6.83g

Strawberries Quinoa Porridge

Prep time: 10 minutes | Cook time: 1 minute | Serves: 6

1½ cups dry quinoa
1½ cups water
1 can unsweetened full-fat coconut milk
½ teaspoon pure stevia powder

1 teaspoon pure vanilla extract
1 cup sliced strawberries
⅓ cup unsweetened shredded coconut

1. Rinse the quinoa very well until the water runs clear. 2. Add the quinoa, water, coconut milk, stevia powder, and vanilla extract to the Inner Pot. Stir to combine. 3. Select Pressure Cook mode, and then press the "Pressure Cook" button again to select "Less" time option. 4. Use the "-" keys to set the cooking time to 1 minute. 5. Press the Pressure Level button to adjust the pressure to "Low Pressure." 6. Once the cooking cycle is completed, quickly and carefully turn the steam release handle from Sealing position to the Venting position. 7. Remove the lid and stir in the sliced strawberries. 8. Allow the quinoa

to cool slightly before spooning into bowls to serve. 9. Top each bowl with a portion of the coconut.
Per Serving: Calories 343; Fat 20.7g; Sodium 29mg; Carbs 33.92g; Fiber 5.3g; Sugar 4.15g; Protein 8g

Vegetable Breakfast Bowls

Prep time: 10 minutes | Cook time: 20 minutes | Serves: 2

2 tablespoons avocado oil
3 leeks, white and light green portion thinly sliced
8 oz. sliced baby bella mushrooms
½ teaspoon salt

¼ teaspoon black pepper
2 large carrots, peeled and sliced
5 kale leaves, tough stems removed and finely chopped
Juice from ½ medium lemon

1. Add the oil to the Inner Pot and press the Sauté button tow times to choose "Normal." 2. Allow the oil to heat 2 minutes and then add the leeks, mushrooms, salt, and pepper. 3. Sauté the leeks and mushrooms 10 minutes. Press the Cancel button. 4. Add the carrots, kale, and lemon juice and stir to combine. 5. Put on the pressure cooker's lid and turn the steam valve to "Sealing" position. 6. Select Pressure Cook mode, and then press the "Pressure Cook" button again to select "Less" time option. 7. Use the "+/-" keys on the control panel to set the cooking time to 4 minutes. 8. Press the Pressure Level button to adjust the pressure to "Low Pressure." 9. Once the cooking cycle is completed, quickly and carefully turn the steam release handle from Sealing position to the Venting position. 10. When all the steam is released, remove the pressure lid from the top carefully. 11. Serve immediately.
Per Serving: Calories 254; Fat 15.21g; Sodium 631mg; Carbs 27.43g; Fiber 5.2g; Sugar 8.8g; Protein 7.32g

5-Ingredient Oatmeal

Prep time: 10 minutes | Cook time: 6 minutes | Serves: 2

2 cups water
1 cup old-fashioned oats
¾ cup milk

2 tablespoons brown sugar
½ teaspoon ground cinnamon

1. Pour 1 cup of water into the Inner Pot and place the Steam Rack in the pot. 2. Stir together the remaining 1 cup of water, oats, milk, brown sugar, and cinnamon in a heat-safe bowl. 3. Put the bowl on the Steam Rack. 4. Select Pressure Cook mode, and then press the "Pressure Cook" button again to select "Less" time option. 5. Use the "-" key to set the cooking time to 6 minutes. 6. Press the Pressure Level button to adjust the pressure to "High Pressure." 7. Once the cooking cycle is completed, allow the steam to release naturally for 10 minutes, then turn the steam release handle to the Venting position. 8. Remove the bowl from the pressure cooker and stir. 9. Serve.
Per Serving: Calories 227; Fat 6.3g; Sodium 50mg; Carbs 49.95g; Fiber 7.6g; Sugar 19.09g; Protein 11.06g

Eggs with Asparagus

Prep time: 10 minutes | Cook time: 3 minutes | Serve: 1

2 large eggs
5 large asparagus spears, woody

ends removed

1. Place the whole eggs and asparagus into the steamer basket. 2. Pour 1 cup water into the Inner Pot and place the Steam Rack inside. 3. Place the steamer basket on the rack. 4. Select Pressure Cook mode, and then press the "Pressure Cook" button again to select "Less" time option. 5. Use the "-" key to set the cooking time to 3 minutes. 6. Press the Pressure Level button to adjust the pressure to "Low Pressure." 7. Once the cooking cycle is completed, quickly and carefully turn the steam release handle from Sealing position to the Venting position. 8. Prepare an ice bath by filling a large bowl with cold water and ice. 9. Carefully remove the steamer basket from the Inner Pot. 10. Place the eggs into the ice bath until they have cooled enough to handle. 11. Peel the eggs and serve with the asparagus.
Per Serving: Calories 147; Fat 9.53g; Sodium 142mg; Carbs 1.4g; Fiber 0.4g; Sugar 0.7g; Protein 12.95g

Loaded Bacon Grits

Prep time: 10 minutes | Cook time: 15 minutes | Serves: 4

3 cups water	½ cup shredded cheddar cheese
1½ cups milk	¼ cup real bacon bits
1 cup quick grits (not instant grits)	2 tablespoons unsalted butter, at room temperature
¼ teaspoon salt	1 tablespoon chopped fresh chives

1. Pour 1 cup of water into the Inner Pot and place the Steam Rack in the pot. 2. Stir the remaining 2 cups of water, milk, grits, and salt in a ovenproof bowl. 3. Place the bowl on the Steam Rack. 4. Select Pressure Cook mode, and then press the "Pressure Cook" button again to select "Less" time option. 5. Use the "-" key to set the cooking time to 15 minutes. 6. Press the Pressure Level button to adjust the pressure to "High Pressure." 7. Once the cooking cycle is completed, allow the steam to release naturally. 8. Remove the bowl from the pressure cooker and stir. The grits will thicken as they cool. 9. Stir in the cheese, bacon bits, butter, and chives, and enjoy.
Per Serving: Calories 200; Fat 12.01g; Sodium 593mg; Carbs 15.17g; Fiber 1.2g; Sugar 5.68g; Protein 7.98g

Root Vegetable Casserole

Prep time: 10 minutes | Cook time: 30 minutes | Serves: 4

1 tablespoon avocado oil	2 small carrots, peeled and diced
1 small yellow onion, peeled and diced	1 teaspoon kosher salt
1 small turnip, peeled and diced	8 large eggs
1 medium parsnip, peeled and diced	1 tablespoon lemon juice
	1 tablespoon fresh thyme leaves

1. Add the oil to the Inner Pot and press the Sauté button tow times to choose "Normal." 2. Heat the oil for 1 minute; add the onion, turnip, parsnip, carrots, and salt, and sauté them for 10 minutes until the vegetables are softened. 3. Press the Cancel button. 4. Whisk the eggs and lemon juice in a medium bowl. 5. Add the thyme and vegetable mixture to the bowl, and stir them well to combine. 6. Spray the inside of a 7-cup glass bowl with cooking spray. Transfer the mixture to the glass bowl. 7. Add 1 cup water to the Inner Pot and place the steam rack inside. 8. Place the bowl on top of the steam rack. 9. Select Pressure Cook mode, and then press the "Pressure Cook" button again to select "Less" time option. 10. Use the "-" key to set the cooking time to 18 minutes. 11. Press the Pressure Level button to adjust the pressure to "Low Pressure." 12. Once the cooking cycle is completed, quickly and carefully turn the steam release handle from Sealing position to the Venting position. 13. Remove bowl from pot and allow to cool 5 minutes before slicing and serving.
Per Serving: Calories 247; Fat 13.32g; Sodium 758mg; Carbs 18.1g; Fiber 4.6g; Sugar 6.16g; Protein 13.97g

Ham Cheese Egg Bites

Prep time: 10 minutes | Cook time: 11 minutes | Serves: 7

Nonstick cooking spray	½ tablespoon chopped fresh parsley
1 cup water	¼ teaspoon garlic powder
4 large eggs	¼ teaspoon salt
½ cup chopped ham	¼ teaspoon black pepper
½ cup shredded cheddar cheese	
¼ cup cottage cheese	

1. Spray the cups of a silicone egg mold with nonstick cooking spray. 2. Pour the water into the Inner Pot and place the Steam Rack in the pot. 3. Whisk the eggs with ham, cheddar cheese, cottage cheese, parsley, garlic powder, salt, and pepper in a medium bowl. 4. Divide the egg mixture evenly into the seven egg-bite mold cups. Place the egg-bite mold on the Steam Rack. 5. Select Pressure Cook mode, and then press the "Pressure Cook" button again to select "Less" time option. 6. Use the "-" key to set the cooking time to 11 minutes. 7. Press the Pressure Level button to adjust the pressure to "High Pressure."

8. Once the cooking cycle is completed, allow the steam to release naturally. 9. Remove the mold from the pressure cooker and cool on a wire rack before using a spoon or butter knife to remove the egg bites from the mold.
Per Serving: Calories 76; Fat 4.21g; Sodium 397mg; Carbs 1.62g; Fiber 0g; Sugar 0.88g; Protein 7.6g

Sausage Spinach Quiche

Prep time: 10 minutes | Cook time: 30 minutes | Serves: 4

8-ounce ground sausage	¼ teaspoon garlic powder
¼ cup finely chopped onion	¼ teaspoon salt
6 large eggs	¼ teaspoon black pepper
½ cup heavy cream	½ cup chopped tomato
1½ cups chopped spinach	1 cup water
¼ cup Parmesan cheese	Nonstick cooking spray

1. Select Sauté mode and press the "Sauté" button two time to select "Normal" setting. 2. When the pot is hot, add the ground sausage and chopped onion, and sauté until the sausage is browned. 3. Press Cancel button. 4. Transfer the sausage and onion mixture to a paper towel–lined plate, and set aside to drain. 5. Wipe out the inside of the pressure cooker pot when it is cool enough to handle. 6. Whisk the eggs and heavy cream in a medium bowl; add the spinach, Parmesan cheese, garlic powder, salt, and pepper to the bowl, and stir them until well blended. 7. Add the sausage and onion mixture to the egg mixture, along with the tomato, and stir well. 8. Pour the water into the Inner Pot, and place the Steam Rack in it. 9. Spray a soufflé dish with nonstick cooking spray. 10. Pour the egg mixture into the prepared soufflé dish and cover loosely with aluminum foil. 11. Put the dish on the Steam Rack. 12. Select Pressure Cook mode, and then press the "Pressure Cook" button again to select "Normal" time option. 13. Use the "-" key to set the cooking time to 30 minutes. 14. Press the Pressure Level button to adjust the pressure to "High Pressure." 15. Once the cooking cycle is completed, allow the steam to release naturally. 16. Serve warm.
Per Serving: Calories 280; Fat 18.92g; Sodium 415mg; Carbs 3.91g; Fiber 0.7g; Sugar 1.55g; Protein 23.27g

Blueberry Coffee Cake

Prep time: 10 minutes | Cook time: 35 minutes | Serves: 8

Nonstick cooking spray	butter
2¼ cups all-purpose flour	1 large egg
1 teaspoon baking powder	1 cup blueberries
1 teaspoon baking soda	1 cup water
¼ teaspoon salt	¼ cup brown sugar
1 cup granulated sugar	¼ teaspoon ground cinnamon
1 cup plain unsweetened Greek yogurt	½ cup purchased cream cheese frosting, melted
8 tablespoons (1 stick) unsalted	

1. Spray a 6-cup Bundt pan with nonstick cooking spray. 2. Whisk 2 cups of flour, the baking powder, baking soda, and salt in a medium bowl. 3. Beat egg with the granulated sugar, yogurt, and unsalted butter in another bowl until smooth. 4. Add the dry ingredients to the wet ingredients, and mix with the hand mixer until completely combined. Fold in the blueberries. 5. Pour the batter into the prepared Bundt pan. 6. Lay a paper towel over the top of the pan, then cover the paper towel and pan loosely with aluminum foil. 7. Pour the water into the Inner Pot and place the Steam Rack in the pot. 8. Place the foil-covered Bundt pan on the Steam Rack. 9. Press the "Pressure Cook" button one time to select "Normal" option. 10. Press the Pressure Level button to adjust the pressure to "High Pressure." 11. Once the cooking cycle is completed, allow the steam to release naturally. 12. Mix the brown sugar, the remaining flour, 2 tablespoons melted butter, and cinnamon together in a small bowl until it forms a crumbly texture. 13. Carefully remove the Bundt pan from the pot and cool on a wire rack. 14. When cool enough to handle, invert the pan over a serving plate. 15. Drizzle the cake with the melted cream cheese frosting and top with the crumble mixture.
Per Serving: Calories 372; Fat 14.05g; Sodium 321mg; Carbs 55.51g; Fiber 1.5g; Sugar 27.5g; Protein 6.78g

Chocolate Chip Banana Bread

Prep time: 10 minutes | Cook time: 60 minutes | Serves: 8

Nonstick cooking spray
¾ cup brown sugar
8 tablespoons (1 stick) unsalted butter
2 large eggs, at room temperature
2 cups mashed overripe bananas
2 cups all-purpose flour
1½ teaspoons baking soda
¼ teaspoon salt
¾ cup chocolate chips
1½ cups water

1. Spray a 6-cup Bundt pan with nonstick cooking spray and lightly dust it with flour. 2. Beat the eggs with brown sugar, butter, and eggs with a hand mixer in a medium bowl until creamy. 3. Add the mashed bananas to the egg mixture, and stir them until evenly incorporated. 4. Add the flour, baking soda, and salt, and beat until well mixed; be careful not to overmix. 5. Fold in the chocolate chips. 6. Pour the batter into the prepared Bundt pan. Lay a paper towel over the top of the pan, then cover the paper towel and pan loosely with aluminum foil. 7. Pour the water into the Inner Pot and place the Steam Rack in the pot. 8. Place the foil-covered Bundt pan on the Steam Rack. 9. Press the "Pressure Cook" button one time to select "More" option. 10. Use the "+" key to set the cooking time to 55 minutes. 11. Press the Pressure Level button to adjust the pressure to "High Pressure." 12. Once the cooking cycle is completed, allow the steam to release naturally for 10 minutes, then turn the steam release handle to the Venting position. 13. Carefully remove the Bundt pan from the pot. If the bread still seems doughy, replace the paper towel and foil and return it to the pot to pressure cook for an additional 5 minutes. 14. Allow the banana bread to cool completely on a wire rack before removing the bread from the pan.
Per Serving: Calories 407; Fat 12.47g; Sodium 410mg; Carbs 68.5g; Fiber 2.8g; Sugar 32.61g; Protein 6.91g

Vanilla Yogurt with Granola

Prep time: 10 minutes | Cook time: 8 hours | Serves: 16

8 cups whole milk
2 tablespoons yogurt with active cultures
4 cups granola
1 cup honey

1. Add the milk with active cultures, and whisk together until the yogurt is completely blended into the milk. 2. Press the "Yogurt" button and then press it again to select "More" option. The display indicates "boiL". 3. Heat the milk until it reaches 180 degrees F, about 90 minutes. 4. When done, leave the milk in the pot until it cools to 115 degrees F, about 1 hour. 5. Gently skim off this layer with a skimmer or slotted spoon and discard the thin film. 6. Add the prepared yogurt with active cultures and whisk together until the yogurt is completely blended into the milk. 7. Press the "Yogurt" button one time to select "Normal" option. The display indicates 08:00. 8. Cook for 8 hours. 9. After 8 hours, the yogurt should be thickened and ready to serve or store in containers in the refrigerator. 10. Serve in ½-cup portions, each topped with ¼ cup granola and 1 tablespoon honey.
Per Serving: Calories 267; Fat 7.67g; Sodium 113mg; Carbs 45.85g; Fiber 1.1g; Sugar 38.72g; Protein 5.72g

Biscuit Dumplings and Gravy

Prep time: 10 minutes | Cook time: 15 minutes | Serves: 4

1 tablespoon unsalted butter
1-pound pork sausage
¼ cup all-purpose flour
2⅓ cups whole milk
2 teaspoons dried thyme
1 teaspoon salt
1½ teaspoons black pepper
¾ cup Bisquick or other baking mix

1. Melt the butter on the Sauté function at Normal cooking temperature. 2. When melted, add the sausage and cook until browned, for about 8 minutes. 3. Break up the sausage as it cooks, leaving some bigger pieces for better texture. 4. Do not drain the pot. Add the flour and stir well. 5. Continue to cook the flour and sausage mixture for 2 to 3 minutes until brown. Make sure to stir often. 6. When the mixture starts to brown, slowly add 2 cups of milk and mix; then add the thyme, salt, and ½ teaspoon of pepper. 7. Scrape the bottom of the pot well to release any browned bits. 8. Turn the pot off and allow it to cool for 3 to 4 minutes. 9. Stir the Bisquick, remaining ⅓ cup of milk, and remaining 1 teaspoon of pepper in a medium bowl until the dough just comes together. 10. Drop dollops of the dough into the sausage gravy. 11. Select Pressure Cook mode, and then press the "Pressure Cook" button again to select "Less" time option. 12. Use the "-" key to set the cooking time to 5 minutes. 13. Press the Pressure Level button to adjust the pressure to "High Pressure." 14. Once the cooking cycle is completed, quickly and carefully turn the steam release handle from Sealing position to the Venting position. 15. Serve
Per Serving: Calories 460; Fat 21.82g; Sodium 712mg; Carbs 32.16g; Fiber 4.7g; Sugar 18.5g; Protein 32.58g

Ham Cheese Omelet

Prep time: 10 minutes | Cook time: 6 minutes | Serves: 4

Nonstick cooking spray
5 large eggs
2 tablespoons whole milk
½ cup chopped deli ham
½ cup shredded cheddar cheese
¼ cup sliced or cubed red bell pepper
1 cup roughly chopped fresh baby spinach
¼ cup chopped fresh flat-leaf parsley
¼ teaspoon garlic powder
¼ teaspoon red pepper flakes
Salt
Black pepper

1. Grease a 7-inch Bundt pan with cooking spray. 2. Whisk the eggs and milk in a medium bowl. 3. Add all the remaining ingredients to the bowl, and stir to combine. 4. Pour the mixture into the prepared pan. Do not cover the pan. 5. Set the Steam Rack in the Inner Pot and pour in 1 cup of water. 6. Place the Bundt pan on the Steam Rack and lock the lid on the pressure cooker. 7. Press the "Pressure Cook" button. 8. Use the "+/-" keys on the control panel to set the cooking time to 6 minutes. 9. Press the Pressure Level button to adjust the pressure to "High Pressure." 10. Once the cooking cycle is completed, quickly and carefully turn the steam release handle from Sealing position to the Venting position. 11. When all the steam is released, remove the pressure lid from the top carefully.
Per Serving: Calories 140; Fat 8.14g; Sodium 385mg; Carbs 6.8g; Fiber 1.7g; Sugar 2.62g; Protein 10.83g

Egg Bites

Prep time: 10 minutes | Cook time: 12 minutes | Serves: 3

Nonstick cooking spray
4 large eggs
¼ cup cottage cheese
½ cup shredded cheddar cheese
4 cooked bacon slices, crumbled

1. Spray a 7-cup silicone egg bite mold with cooking spray. 2. Whisk the eggs in a medium bowl until they're fluffy. 3. Add the cottage cheese to the eggs and beat them until the mixture is fully incorporated. 4. Stir in the cheddar cheese and bacon. 5. Divide the egg mixture among the cups of the prepared egg mold, filling each cup about three-quarters full. 6. Cover the mold with the lid or with foil. 7. Set the Steam Rack in the Inner Pot and pour in 1 cup of water. 8. Place the egg bite mold on the Steam Rack and lock the lid on the pressure cooker. 9. Select Pressure Cook mode, and then press the "Pressure Cook" button again to select "Less" time option. 10. Use the "-" key to set the cooking time to 12 minutes. 11. Press the Pressure Level button to adjust the pressure to "Low Pressure." 12. Once the cooking cycle is completed, allow the steam to release naturally. 13. Remove the lid and let the egg bites cool for a minute or two before inverting them onto a plate.
Per Serving: Calories 288; Fat 22.46g; Sodium 530mg; Carbs 3.4g; Fiber 0g; Sugar 2.34g; Protein 17.2g

Broccoli Frittata with Ham

Prep time: 10 minutes | Cook Time: 20 minutes | Serves: 4

Vegetable oil or unsalted butter, for greasing the pan	1 cup half-and-half
1 cup sliced bell peppers	1 teaspoon salt
8 ounces ham, cubed	2 teaspoons freshly ground black pepper
2 cups frozen broccoli florets	1 cup grated Cheddar cheese
4 eggs	

1. Arrange the pepper slices to the suitable baking pan that has been oiled in advance; top with the cubed ham and cover with the frozen broccoli. 2. Thoroughly mix up the eggs, half-n-half, salt and pepper in a suitable bowl, then stir in the cheese; pour the cheese mixture over the vegetables and ham in the pan and then cover the pan with foil. 3. In the Inner Pot, add 2 cups of water and place the Steam Rack; transfer the baking pan to the rack. 4. Place and lock the lid. 5. Select Pressure Cook mode. Press Pressure Cook button again to adjust the cooking time to 20 minutes; press Pressure Level to choose High Pressure. 6. When the time is up, leave the steam release handle in the Sealing position for 10 minutes, then turn it to the Venting position. 7. Uncover the lid, carefully take out the pan and let the food stand for 5 to 10 minutes. 8. Gently loosen the sides of the frittata; place a plate on top of the pan and hold in place, then invert the frittata onto the plate. 9. Serve immediately or broil the frittata 3 to 4 minutes more to brown its top.
Per Serving: Calories: 396; Fat: 27g; Carbs: 9g; Sodium: 326mg; Fiber: 3g; Sugar: 3g; Protein: 30g

Simple Egg Loaf

Prep time: 5 minutes | Cook Time: 4 minutes | Serves: 6

Unsalted butter, for greasing the bowl	6 eggs
	2 cups water, for steaming

1. Oil a heatproof bowl with the butter and then crack in the eggs, keeping the yolks intact. 2. Use the aluminum foil to cover the bowl and set aside for later use. 3. In the Inner Pot, add the water and place the Steam Rack; transfer the bowl to the rack. 4. Place and lock the lid. 5. Select Pressure Cook mode. Press Pressure Cook button again to adjust the cooking time to 4 minutes; press Pressure Level to choose High Pressure. 6. When the time is up, quickly turn the steam release handle from the Sealing position to the Venting position. 7. Uncover the lid and carefully take out the bowl; pop out the egg loaf from the bowl. 8. Chop the egg loaf as you like. 9. You can mix the egg loaf with a little mayonnaise for egg salad, or stir with a little butter, salt and pepper for a quick snack or meal.
Per Serving: Calories: 74; Fat: 5g; Carbs: 0g; Sodium: 230mg; Fiber: 0g; Sugar: 0g; Protein: 6g

Tasty Egg Cups

Prep time: 10 minutes | Cook Time: 7 minutes | Serves: 4

Unsalted butter or vegetable oil, for greasing the jars	1 teaspoon salt
4 eggs	1 teaspoon freshly ground black pepper
1 cup diced vegetables, such as onions, bell peppers, mushrooms, or tomatoes	2 tablespoons chopped fresh cilantro or other herb of choice (optional)
½ cup grated sharp Cheddar cheese	½ cup shredded cheese of choice, for garnish
¼ cup half-and-half	

1. Prepare 4 half-pint wide-mouth, heatproof glass jars and use a brush to oil each jar into every crevice. 2. In a suitable bowl, thoroughly mix up the eggs, vegetables, cheese, half-and-half, salt, pepper and cilantro (if using); divide the mixture among the jars. 3. Place the lids on the top of the jars but do not tighten. 4. In the Inner Pot, add 2 cups of water and place the Steam Rack; transfer the jars to the rack. 5. Place and lock the lid. 6. Select Pressure Cook mode. Press Pressure Cook button again to adjust the cooking time to 5 minutes; press Pressure Level to choose High Pressure. 7. When the time is up, quickly turn the steam release handle from the Sealing position to the Venting position. 8. Uncover the lid and take out the jars carefully; top each jar with the cheese as you like. 9. Broil the jar in your oven for 2 to 3 minutes to melt the cheese until lightly browned. 10. Serve and enjoy.
Per Serving: Calories: 239; Fat: 17g; Carbs: 7g; Sodium: 235mg; Fiber: 2g; Sugar: 2g; Protein: 15g

Cream Cheese Egg Frittatas

Prep time: 10 minutes | Cook Time: 5 minutes | Serves: 3

6 eggs	Sea salt and ground black pepper, to taste
¼ cup milk	½ cup cream cheese
½ teaspoon cayenne pepper	

1. In a suitable bowl, mix up all of the ingredients and then divide the mixture into 3 molds. 2. In the Inner Pot, add 1 cup of water and place the Steam Rack; transfer the molds to the rack. 3. Place and lock the lid. 4. Select Pressure Cook mode. Press Pressure Cook button again to adjust the cooking time to 5 minutes; press Pressure Level to choose High Pressure. 5. When the time is up, quickly turn the steam release handle from the Sealing position to the Venting position. 6. Uncover the lid, serve and enjoy.
Per Serving: Calories 249; Fat 13g; Sodium 556mg; Carbs 10g; Sugar 1.1g; Fiber 0.7g; Protein 31g

Cheese Frittata

Prep time: 10 minutes | Cook Time: 20 minutes | Serves: 4

Vegetable oil or unsalted butter, for greasing the pan	1½ teaspoons salt
4 eggs	½ teaspoon ground cumin
1 cup half-and-half	1 cup Mexican blend shredded cheese, divided
1 (10-ounce) can chopped green chilies, drained	¼ cup chopped fresh cilantro

1. Oil a suitable baking pan in advance. 2. In a suitable bowl, combine the eggs, half-and-half, chilies, salt, cumin and ½ cup of cheese; pour the mixture into the oiled pan and the cover with foil. 3. In the Inner Pot, add 2 cups of water and place the Steam Rack; transfer the jars to the rack. 4. Place and lock the lid. 5. Select Pressure Cook mode. Press Pressure Cook button again to adjust the cooking time to 20 minutes; press Pressure Level to choose High Pressure. 6. When the time is up, leave the steam release handle in the Sealing position for 10 minutes, then turn it to the Venting position. 7. Uncover the lid and carefully take out the pan. 8. Top each frittata with the remaining cheese and then broil them in your preheated oven for 2 to 5 minutes, or until the cheese is bubbling and brown. 9. When done, let the frittata stand for 5 to 10 minutes and then gently loosen the sides from the pan with a knife; place a plate on top of the pan and hold in place, then invert the frittata onto the plate. 10. Enjoy.
Per Serving: Calories: 283; Fat: 22g; Carbs: 7g; Sodium: 326mg; Fiber: 1g; Sugar: 1g; Protein: 16g

Baked Cheesy Hash Brown with Eggs

Prep time: 30 minutes | Cook Time: 25 minutes | Serves: 3

3 ounces bacon, chopped
1 onion, chopped
1 cup frozen hash browns
5 eggs
¼ cup milk
⅓ cup Swiss cheese, shredded
1 teaspoon garlic powder
¼ teaspoon turmeric powder
Kosher salt and ground black pepper, to taste

1. Insert the Inner Pot into the Cooker Base without the lid. 2. Press the Sauté button to select the cooking mode and press it again to adjust the cooking temperature to Normal. 3. When the display switches On to Hot, add the bacon and cook until it is crisp and browned; add the onions and stir constantly for 3 to 4 minutes; stir in the frozen hash browns and cook until slightly thawed. 4. In a suitable bowl, mix up the eggs, milk, shredded cheese, garlic powder, turmeric powder, salt, black pepper and then add in the onion mixture. 5. Oil the oven-proof dish and then spoon the egg mixture into it. 6. In the Inner Pot, add 1 cup of water and place the Steam Rack; transfer the dish to the rack. 7. Place and lock the lid. 8. Select Pressure Cook mode. Press Pressure Cook button again to adjust the cooking time to 20 minutes; press Pressure Level to choose High Pressure. 9. When the time is up, quickly turn the steam release handle from the Sealing position to the Venting position. 10. Uncover the lid, serve and enjoy!
Per Serving: Calories 312; Fat 15g; Sodium 548mg; Carbs 12g; Sugar 1.2g; Fiber 0.7g; Protein 29g

Stuffed Egg White Halves

Prep time: 10 minutes | Cook Time: 5 minutes | Serves: 5

10 eggs
½ teaspoon coarse sea salt
¼ teaspoon black pepper, to taste
½ teaspoon turmeric powder
2 teaspoons balsamic vinegar
2 tablespoons Greek-style yogurt
4 tablespoons mayonnaise
1 teaspoon fresh dill, chopped

1. In the Inner Pot, add 1 cup of water and place the Steam Rack; transfer the eggs to the rack. 2. Place and lock the lid. 3. Select Pressure Cook mode. Press Pressure Cook button again to adjust the cooking time to 5 minutes; press Pressure Level to choose High Pressure. 4. When the time is up, quickly turn the steam release handle from the Sealing position to the Venting position. 5. Uncover the lid and take out the eggs; peel the eggs and slice them into halves. 6. In a suitable bowl, thoroughly mix up the turmeric powder, vinegar, yogurt, mayonnaise, sea salt and black pepper, and then stir in the eggs yolks. 7. Fill the egg white halves with a piping bag and garnish with the fresh dill, enjoy!
Per Serving: Calories 336; Fat 17.3g; Sodium 281mg; Carbs 8.1g; Fiber 5.3g; Sugars 17.7g; Protein 32.3g

Flavored Spanish Tortilla with Manchego Cheese

Prep time: 30 minutes | Cook Time: 20 minutes | Serves: 4

8 eggs
8 ounces hash browns
1 ½ tablespoons olive oil
1 onion, sliced
Sea salt and ground black pepper, or to taste
1 teaspoon taco seasoning mix
1 teaspoon fresh garlic, minced
⅓ cup milk
4 ounces Manchego cheese, grated

1. Except for the Manchego cheese, thoroughly mix up the other ingredients in a suitable bowl until well incorporated. 2. Oil a soufflé dish with the non-stick cooking oil and then scrape the mixture into it. 3. In the Inner Pot, add 1 cup of water and place the Steam Rack; transfer the dish to the rack. 4. Place and lock the lid. 5. Select Pressure Cook mode. Press Pressure Cook button again to adjust the cooking time to 17 minutes; press Pressure Level to choose High Pressure. 6. When the time is up, leave the steam release handle in the Sealing position. 7. Uncover the lid, top with the Manchego cheese and lock the lid again; let the food sit for a few minutes until the cheese melts. 8. When done, serve and enjoy.

Per Serving: Calories 272; Fat 19g; Sodium 389mg; Carbs 10.4g; Fiber 0.7g; Sugars 1.1g; Protein 15.6g

Jalapeño Pepper Omelet Cups

Prep time: 20 minutes | Cook Time 5 minutes | Serves: 2

½ tsp. olive oil
3 eggs, beaten
1 cup water
Salt and freshly ground black
pepper to taste
1 onion, chopped
1 jalapeño pepper, chopped

1. Rub two ramekins with a drop of olive oil. 2. In a suitable bowl, mix up the eggs, water, salt and black pepper until well combined; stir in the onion and jalapeño pepper. 3. Transfer the mixture to the ramekins. 4. In the Inner Pot, add the water and place the Steam Rack; transfer the ramekins to the rack. 5. Place and close the lid. 6. Select Pressure Cook mode. Press Pressure Cook button again to adjust the cooking time to 5 minutes; press Pressure Level to choose High Pressure. 7. When the time is up, quickly and carefully turn the steam release handle from the Sealing to Venting position. 8. Uncover the lid and serve warm.
Per Serving: Calories 344; Fat 14.9g; Sodium 227mg; Carbs 14g; Fiber 1g; Sugars 1.4g; Protein 25.7g

Tomato Spinach Quiche with Parmesan Cheese

Prep time: 15 minutes | Cook Time: 20 minutes | Serves: 4-6

10-12 large eggs, beaten
½ cup milk
½ teaspoon kosher salt
Ground black pepper to taste
2½ cups baby spinach, diced
1 cup tomato, deseeded and
roughly chopped
4 medium green onions, chopped
3 tomato slices
⅓ cup parmesan cheese, shredded
2 cups water

1. In a suitable bowl, mix up the eggs, milk, salt, and pepper until well-combined. 2. In the suitable baking dish, mix up the spinach, tomato and green onions; stir in the egg mixture and top with 3 tomato slices. 3. In the Inner Pot, add the water and place the Steam Rack; transfer the dish to the rack. 4. Place and close the lid. 5. Select Pressure Cook mode. Press Pressure Cook button again to adjust the cooking time to 20 minutes; press Pressure Level to choose High Pressure. 6. When the time is up, leave the steam release handle in the Sealing position for 5 minutes, then turn it to Venting position. 7. Uncover the lid and take out the dish. 8. Serve warm; you can also broil the dish in your broiler for a few minutes more if you want a browned top.
Per Serving: Calories 254; Fat 28 g; Sodium 346mg; Carbs 12.3 g; Sugar 1g; Fiber 0.7g; Protein 24.3 g

Cheesy Bacon Hash Brown

Prep time: 10 minutes | Cook Time: 10 minutes | Serves: 4

6 slices bacon, chopped
2 cups frozen hash browns
8 beaten eggs
1 cup shredded cheddar cheese
½ cup milk
½ tsp salt
½ tsp ground black pepper

1. In a bowl, mix up the eggs, cheese, milk, salt and pepper. 2. Insert the Inner Pot into the Cooker Base without the lid. 3. Press the Sauté button to select the cooking mode and press it again to adjust cooking temperature to Normal. 4. When the display switches On to Hot, add the bacon and cook until lightly crispy; add the hash brown and stir occasionally for 2 minutes until they start to thaw. 5. Press the Cancel button to stop the cooking program and pour in the egg mixture; place and lock the lid. 6. Select Pressure Cook mode. Press Pressure Cook button again to adjust the cooking time to 7 minutes; press Pressure Level to choose High Pressure. 7. When the time is up, quickly and carefully turn the steam release handle from the Sealing to Venting position. 8. Uncover the lid, slice and enjoy.
Per Serving: Calories 272; Fat 19g; Sodium 389mg; Carbs 10.4g; Fiber 0.7g; Sugars 1.1g; Protein 15.6g

Delightful Soft Eggs with Ham and Chives

Prep time: 5 minutes | Cook Time: 4 minutes | Serves: 3

3 eggs	1 cup water
1 tsp. salt	6 oz. ham
½ tsp. ground white pepper	2 tbsp. chives
1 tsp. paprika	¼ tsp. ground ginger

1. Prepare 3 small ramekins and crack one egg in each; season the eggs with the salt, pepper and paprika. 2. In the Inner Pot, add the water and place the Steam Rack; transfer the ramekins to the rack. 3. Place and lock the lid. 4. Select Steam mode. Press Pressure Cook button again to adjust the cooking time to 4 minutes; press Pressure Level to choose High Pressure. 5. While cooking, chop the chives, ham and combine them well in a bowl; add the ground ginger and stir well; transfer the mixture to the prepared plate. 6. When the time is up, quickly turn the steam release handle from the Sealing position to the Venting position. 7. Uncover the lid and take out the ramekins and place them on the plate. 8. Serve with the ham mixture.
Per Serving: Calories 344; Fat 14.9g; Sodium 227mg; Carbs 14g; Fiber 1g; Sugars 1.4g; Protein 25.7g

Mexican-Style Omelet

Prep time: 30 minutes | Cook Time: 11 minutes | Serves: 4

1 tablespoon olive oil	1 bell pepper, sliced
1 medium onion, chopped	1 Poblano pepper, seeded and
2 cloves garlic, minced	minced
1 cup Mexica cheese blend,	5 eggs
crumbled	4 ounces cream cheese
1 cup Chanterelle mushrooms,	Sea salt and ground black pepper,
chopped	to taste

1. In a suitable, mix up all of the ingredients. 2. Oil a soufflé dish and then scrape the mixture into it. 3. In the Inner Pot, add 1 cup of water and place the Steam Rack; transfer the dish to the rack. 4. Place and lock the lid. 5. Select Pressure Cook mode. Press Pressure Cook button again to adjust the cooking time to 11 minutes; press Pressure Level to choose High Pressure. 6. When the time is up, leave the steam release handle in the Sealing position. 7. Uncover the lid and serve; you can enjoy with the salsa.
Per Serving: Calories 344; Fat 14.9g; Sodium 227mg; Carbs 14g; Fiber 1g; Sugars 1.4g; Protein 25.7g

Homemade Yogurt

Prep time: 9 hours | Cook Time: 8 hours 5 minutes | Serves: 12

68-ounce milk	with cultures
2 tablespoons prepared yogurt	A pinch of salt

1. In the Inner Pot, add the milk. 2. Press Yogurt to select the program and press it again to cycle to the More option. The display indicates boil. 3. When boiled, the display indicates End; let the milk sit for 5 minutes and remove the Inner Pot. 4. When the milk cools to about 115 degrees F, stir in the prepared yogurt with the cultures, add a pinch of salt. 5. Insert the Inner Pot back to the Cooker Base and lock the lid. 6. Press Yogurt to select the program and press it again to cycle to the Normal option. The screen displays 8:00. 7. Uncover the lid and transfer the yogurt to the refrigerator. 8. When done, serve and enjoy.
Per Serving: Calories 285; Fat 9.8g; Sodium 639mg; Carbs 11.1g; Fiber 1.2g; Sugars 5.1g; Protein 27.8g

Hard-Boiled Eggs Ever

Prep time: 15 minutes | Cook Time: 5 minutes | Serves: 3

5 eggs	¼ teaspoon red pepper flakes,
½ teaspoon salt	crushed

2 tablespoons fresh chives,   chopped

1. In the Inner Pot, add 1 cup of water and place the Steam Rack; transfer the eggs to the rack. 2. Place and lock the lid. 3. Select Pressure Cook mode. Press Pressure Cook button again to adjust the cooking time to 5 minutes; press Pressure Level to choose High Pressure. 4. When the time is up, quickly turn the steam release handle from the Sealing position to the Venting position. 5. Uncover the lid and transfer the eggs to icy-cold water to cool for a few minutes. 6. Peel the eggs and season with the salt and pepper. 7. Garnish with the freshly chopped chives and enjoy.
Per Serving: Calories 336; Fat 17.3g; Sodium 281mg; Carbs 8.1g; Fiber 5.3g; Sugars 17.7g; Protein 32.3g

Eggs with Bacon and Chives

Prep time: 10 minutes | Cook Time: 8 minutes | Serves: 4

½ tsp. olive oil	Salt to taste
4 eggs	4 tbsp. chives, chopped
4 slices bacon	1 cup water

1. Oil four small ramekins and then crack one egg in each; top with one bacon slice, chives and season with the salt. 2. In the Inner Pot, add the water and place the Steam Rack; transfer the ramekins to the rack. 3. Place and lock the lid. 4. Select Pressure Cook mode. Press Pressure Cook button again to adjust the cooking time to 8 minutes; press Pressure Level to choose High Pressure. 5. When the time is up, quickly turn the steam release handle from the Sealing position to the Venting position. 6. Uncover the lid, serve and enjoy.
Per Serving: Calories 344; Fat 14.9g; Sodium 227mg; Carbs 14g; Fiber 1g; Sugars 1.4g; Protein 25.7g

Simple Spanish Dip de Queso

Prep time: 10 minutes | Cook Time: 10 minutes | Serves: 10

3 tablespoons butter	8 ounces Monterey Jack, shredded
3 tablespoons all-purpose flour	Kosher salt, to taste
1 cup whole milk	½ teaspoon hot sauce

1. Insert the Inner Pot into the Cooker Base without the lid. 2. Press the Sauté button to select the cooking mode and press it again to adjust the cooking temperature to Normal. 3. When the display switches On to Hot, add and melt the butter; add the flour and stir until well combined; gradually pour in the milk and stir constantly to avoid clumps. 4. When boiled, press the Cancel button to stop this cooking program. 5. Add the Monterey Jack cheese and stir until cheese melted; add the salt and hot sauce. 6. Serve warm; you can also serve with the tortilla chips.
Per Serving: Calories 272; Fat 19g; Sodium 389mg; Carbs 10.4g; Fiber 0.7g; Sugars 1.1g; Protein 15.6g

Egg Halves with Cottage Cheese

Prep time: 10 minutes | Cook Time: 5 minutes | Serves: 6

6 eggs	minced
¼ cup Cottage cheese, crumbled	1 teaspoon paprika
1 tablespoon butter, softened	Sea salt and ground black pepper,
2 tablespoons fresh parsley,	to taste

1. In the Inner Pot, add 1 cup of water and place the Steam Rack; transfer the eggs to the rack. 2. Place and lock the lid. 3. Select Pressure Cook mode. Press Pressure Cook button again to adjust the cooking time to 5 minutes; press Pressure Level to choose High Pressure. 4. When the time is up, quickly turn the steam release handle from the Sealing position to the Venting position. 5. Uncover the lid and take out the eggs; peel the eggs and slice them into halves after cooling them a few minutes. 6. In a suitable bowl, thoroughly mix up the Cottage cheese, butter, parsley, paprika, sea salt and black pepper, then stir in the eggs yolks. 7. Fill the egg white halves with a piping bag, then serve and enjoy.
Per Serving: Calories 344; Fat 14.9g; Sodium 227mg; Carbs 14g; Fiber 1g; Sugars 1.4g; Protein 25.7g

Mac and Cheese with Cauliflower Florets

Prep time: 15 minutes | Cook Time: 5 minutes | Serves: 4

1-pound cauliflower florets	to taste
1 cup heavy cream	½ teaspoon garlic powder
4 ounces Ricotta cheese	½ teaspoon shallot powder
1 ½ cups Cheddar cheese, shredded	½ teaspoon celery seeds
Sea salt and ground white pepper,	½ teaspoon red pepper flakes
	¼ cup Parmesan cheese

1. In the Inner Pot, add 1 cup of water and place the Steam Rack; transfer the cauliflower florets to the rack. 2. Place and lock the lid. 3. Select Pressure Cook mode. Press Pressure Cook button again to adjust the cooking time to 2 minutes; press Pressure Level to choose High Pressure. 4. When the time is up, quickly and carefully turn the steam release handle from the Sealing position to the Venting position. 5. Uncover the lid, drain the cauliflower florets and reserve. 6. Press the Cancel button and remove the lid. 7. Select the Sauté button to select the cooking mode and press it again to adjust the cooking temperature to Less. 8. When the display switches On to Hot, add the heavy cream, Ricotta cheese, Cheddar cheese, spices and let simmer until the cheese melted; add the cauliflower florets and lightly stir to combine; scatter the Parmesan cheese over the cauliflower and cheese. 9. Serve and enjoy!
Per Serving: Calories 249; Fat 13g; Sodium 556mg; Carbs 10g; Sugar 1.1g; Fiber 0.7g; Protein 31g

Tomato Spinach Stew with Parmesan Cheese

Prep time: 15 minutes | Cook Time: 20 minutes | Serves: 4-6

1½ cups water	1 cup tomato, diced
12 beaten eggs	3 cups baby spinach, chopped
Salt and ground black pepper to the taste	3 green onions, sliced
	4 tomatoes, sliced
½ cup milk	¼ cup parmesan, grated

1. Crack the eggs in a bowl, add the salt, pepper and milk and stir until well combined. 2. In a suitable baking dish, mix up the diced tomato, spinach and green onions; pour the egg mixture and then top with the tomato slices; sprinkle with the Parmesan cheese. 3. In the Inner Pot, add the water and place the Steam Rack; transfer the dish to the rack. 4. Place and lock the lid. 5. Select Pressure Cook mode. Press Pressure Cook button again to adjust the cooking time to 20 minutes; press Pressure Level to choose High Pressure. 6. When the time is up, quickly turn the steam release handle from the Sealing position to the Venting position. 7. Uncover the lid, serve and enjoy. 8. You can slide under the oven for a few minutes more if you want a crisp top.
Per Serving: Calories 336; Fat 17.3g; Sodium 281mg; Carbs 8.1g; Fiber 5.3g; Sugars 17.7g; Protein 32.3g

Mini Raisin Almond Pancakes

Prep time: 15 minutes | Cook Time: 8 minutes | Serves: 4

1 cup all-purpose flour	2 eggs, whisked
2 teaspoons baking powder	2 tablespoons maple syrup
1 teaspoon salt	½ cup raisins
¼ cup milk	2 tablespoons almonds, chopped

1. Thoroughly mix up the other ingredients in a suitable bowl until well incorporated. 2. Spray a muffin tin with the cooking spray and then pour the mixture into it. 3. In the Inner Pot, add 1 cup of water and place the Steam Rack; transfer the dish to the rack. 4. Place and lock the lid. 5. Select Pressure Cook mode. Press Pressure Cook button again to adjust the cooking time to 8 minutes; press Pressure Level to choose High Pressure. 6. When the time is up, leave the steam release handle in the Sealing position. 7. Uncover the lid, serve and enjoy!
Per Serving: Calories 307; Fat 11g; Sodium 477mg; Carbs 12g; Fiber 1.2g; Sugars 1g; Protein 27g

Spinach and Mushroom Frittata

Prep time: 15 minutes | Cook Time: 5 minutes | Serves: 4

6 eggs	1 yellow onion, finely chopped
¼ cup double cream	2 cloves garlic, minced
1 cup Asiago cheese, shredded	6 ounces Italian brown mushrooms, sliced
Sea salt and freshly ground black pepper, to taste	4 cups spinach, torn into pieces
1 teaspoon cayenne pepper	1 tablespoon Italian seasoning mix
2 tablespoons olive oil	

1. Thoroughly mix up the eggs, double cream, Asiago cheese, salt, black pepper and cayenne pepper, then add the remaining ingredients. 2. Spray a baking dish with the olive oil and then spoon the mixture into it. 3. In the Inner Pot, add 1 cup of water and place the Steam Rack; transfer the dish to the rack. 4. Place and lock the lid. 5. Select Pressure Cook mode. Press Pressure Cook button again to adjust the cooking time to 5 minutes; press Pressure Level to choose High Pressure. 6. When the time is up, quickly and carefully turn the steam release handle from the Sealing position to the Venting position. 7. Uncover the lid, serve and enjoy.
Per Serving: Calories 336; Fat 17.3g; Sodium 281mg; Carbs 8.1g; Fiber 5.3g; Sugars 17.7g; Protein 32.3g

Ham, Cheese and Egg Muffins

Prep time: 15 minutes | Cook Time: 6 minutes | Serves: 4

8 eggs	8 ounces ham, chopped
¼ teaspoon ground black pepper, or more to taste	½ cup sour cream
1 teaspoon paprika	½ cup Swiss cheese, shredded
Sea salt, to taste	2 tablespoons parsley, chopped
1 cup green peppers, seeded and chopped	2 tablespoons cilantro, chopped
	2 tablespoons scallions, chopped

1. Thoroughly mix up the other ingredients in a suitable bowl until well combined. 2. Spoon the mixture into the prepared silicone molds. 3. In the Inner Pot, add 1 cup of water and place the Steam Rack; transfer the molds to the rack. 4. Place and lock the lid. 5. Select Pressure Cook mode. Press Pressure Cook button again to adjust the cooking time to 6 minutes; press Pressure Level to choose High Pressure. 6. When the time is up, quickly and carefully turn the steam release handle from the Sealing position to the Venting position. 7. Uncover the lid, serve and enjoy.
Per Serving: Calories 336; Fat 17.3g; Sodium 281mg; Carbs 8.1g; Fiber 5.3g; Sugars 17.7g; Protein 32.3g

Egg Bacon Muffins

Prep time: 5 minutes | Cook Time: 10 minutes | Serves: 2

4 beaten eggs	1 green onion, chopped
4 bacon slices, cooked and crumbled	A pinch of salt
4 tablespoons cheddar cheese, shredded	1½ cups water
	Prepare 2 muffin cups.

1. In a suitable bowl, mix up the eggs, bacon, cheese, onion and salt until combined, then divide the mixture into the cups. 2. In the Inner Pot, add the water and place the Steam Rack; transfer the cups to the rack. 3. Place and close the lid. 4. Select Pressure Cook mode. Press Pressure Cook button again to adjust the cooking time to 8 minutes; press Pressure Level to choose High Pressure. 5. When the time is up, leave the steam release handle in the Sealing position for 2 minutes, then turn it to Venting position. 6. Uncover the lid, serve and enjoy.
Per Serving: Calories 254; Fat 28 g; Sodium 346mg; Carbs 12.3 g; Sugar 1g; Fiber 0.7g; Protein 24.3 g

Cheesy Egg Bake with Turkey Bacon

Prep time: 10 minutes | Cook Time: 10 minutes | Serves: 4

1 teaspoon olive oil
6 slices of turkey bacon, cubed
2 cups frozen hash browns
1 cup cheddar cheese, shredded

8 beaten eggs
½ cup half and half or milk
Salt to taste

1. Insert the Inner Pot into the Cooker Base without the lid. 2. Press the Sauté button to select the cooking mode and press it again to adjust the cooking temperature to Normal. 3. When the display switches On to Hot, add and heat the oil; add the turkey bacon slices and cook for 1 to 2 minutes until browned. 4. Press the Cancel button and then top the bacon with the hash brown potatoes; sprinkle half of the Cheddar cheese. 5. Place and close the lid. 6. Select Pressure Cook mode. Press Pressure Cook button again to adjust the cooking time to 7 minutes; press Pressure Level to choose High Pressure. 7. When the time is up, quickly and carefully turn the steam release handle from the Sealing to Venting position. 8. Uncover the lid, serve and enjoy.
Per Serving: Calories 285; Fat 9.8g; Sodium 639mg; Carbs 11.1g; Fiber 1.2g; Sugars 5.1g; Protein 27.8g

Bacon and Sausage Omelet

Prep time: 20 minutes | Cook Time: 30 minutes | Serves: 6

6-12 beaten eggs
½ cup milk
6 sausage links, sliced
1 onion, diced
Garlic powder
Salt and ground black pepper to taste

Olive oil cooking spray
2 cups water
6 bacon slices, cooked
Dried oregano, optional
Equipment:
1½-quart ceramic baking dish

1. In a bowl, beat the eggs and then pour in the milk, stir to combine well; add the sausages, onion and season with the garlic powder, salt and pepper, stir well. 2. Spray the baking dish with the cooking spray; pour the egg mixture into it and wrap tightly with the foil all over. 3. In the Inner Pot, add the water and place the Steam Rack; transfer the dish to the rack. 4. Place and close the lid. 5. Select Pressure Cook mode. Press Pressure Cook button again to adjust the cooking time to 25 minutes; press Pressure Level to choose High Pressure. 6. When the time is up, leave the steam release handle in the Sealing position. 7. Uncover the lid and remove the foil carefully; top with the cooked bacon and the shredded cheese. 8. Place and close the lid. 9. Select Pressure Cook mode. Press Pressure Cook button again to adjust the cooking time to 5 minutes; press Pressure Level to choose High Pressure. 10. When the time is up, quickly turn the steam release handle from the Sealing position to the Venting position. 11. Uncover the lid, serve and you can enjoy with the dried oregano.
Per Serving: Calories 344; Fat 14.9g; Sodium 227mg; Carbs 14g; Fiber 1g; Sugars 1.4g; Protein 25.7g

Egg and Potato Salad with Mayonnaise

Prep time: 15 minutes | Cook Time: 5 minutes | Serves: 2-4

1½ cups water
6 russet potatoes, peeled and diced
4 large eggs
1 cup mayonnaise
2 tablespoons fresh parsley,

chopped
¼ cup onion, chopped
1 tablespoon dill pickle juice
1 tablespoon mustard
Pinch of salt
Pinch of ground black pepper

1. In the Inner Pot, add the water and place the Steam Rack; transfer the eggs and potatoes to the rack. 2. Place and close the lid. 3. Select Pressure Cook mode. Press Pressure Cook button again to adjust the cooking time to 5 minutes; press Pressure Level to choose High Pressure. 4. While cooking, in a bowl, mix up the mayonnaise, parsley, onion, dill pickle juice, mustard, salt and pepper. 5. When the time is up, quickly and carefully turn the steam release handle from the Sealing to Venting position. 6. Uncover the lid and transfer the eggs to the bowl of cold water

to cool for 2 to 3 minutes. 7. Peel and slice the eggs; toss the potatoes and eggs in the bowl and stir with the mixture. 8. Enjoy.
Per Serving: Calories 336; Fat 17.3g; Sodium 281mg; Carbs 8.1g; Fiber 5.3g; Sugars 17.7g; Protein 32.3g

Sausage Frittata with Cheddar Cheese

Prep time: 15 minutes | Cook Time: 20 minutes | Serves: 2-4

1½ cups water
1 tablespoon butter
4 beaten eggs
2 tablespoons sour cream

¼ cup cheddar cheese, grated
½ cup cooked ground sausage
Salt and ground black pepper to taste

1. Oil a suitable soufflé dish (about 6-7 inches) with the butter. 2. In a bowl, mix up the eggs and sour cream until well combined; add the cheese, sausage, salt and pepper and stir well. 3. Pour the mixture into the oiled dish and wrap tightly with foil all over. 4. In the Inner Pot, add the water and place the Steam Rack; arrange the dish to the rack. 5. Select Pressure Cook mode. Press Pressure Cook button again to adjust the cooking time to 17 minutes; press Pressure Level to choose Low Pressure. 6. When the time is up, quickly turn the steam release handle from the Sealing position to the Venting position. 7. Uncover the lid, serve and enjoy.
Per Serving: Calories 285; Fat 9.8g; Sodium 639mg; Carbs 11.1g; Fiber 1.2g; Sugars 5.1g; Protein 27.8g

Mayo Eggs Dish

Prep time: 15 minutes | Cook Time 5 minutes | Serves: 4-6

1 cup water
8 eggs
¼ cup cream
1 teaspoon mayo sauce
1 tablespoon mustard

1 teaspoon ground white pepper
1 teaspoon minced garlic
½ teaspoon sea salt
¼ cup dill, chopped

1. In the Inner Pot, add the water and place the Steam Rack; transfer the eggs to the rack. 2. Place and close the lid. 3. Select Pressure Cook mode. Press Pressure Cook button again to adjust the cooking time to 5 minutes; press Pressure Level to choose High Pressure. 4. When the time is up, quickly and carefully turn the steam release handle from the Sealing to Venting position. 5. Uncover the lid and cool the eggs in the bowl of cold water for 2 to 3 minutes. 6. Peel the eggs, remove the egg yolks and mash them. 7. In a bowl, mix up the cream, mayo sauce, mustard, pepper, garlic, salt and mashed egg yolks; sprinkle the mixture with the dill and stir well. 8. Transfer the egg yolk mixture to the pastry bag; fill the egg whites with the yolk mixture. 9. Enjoy!
Per Serving: Calories 249; Fat 13g; Sodium 556mg; Carbs 10g; Sugar 1.1g; Fiber 0.7g; Protein 31g

Cheesy Tomato Egg Cups

Prep time: 10 minutes | Cook Time: 8 minutes | Serves: 4

1 cup water
1 cup chopped baby spinach
6 beaten eggs
1 chopped tomato
½ cup mozzarella cheese,

shredded
¼ cup feta cheese, cubed
1 tsp black pepper
½ tsp salt

1. In a bowl, mix up the eggs, mozzarella cheese, feta cheese, chopped tomato, salt and pepper until well-combined. 2. Prepare 2 heatproof cups and add the spinach in them, then pour in the egg mixture, leaving ¼-inch of head room. 3. In the Inner Pot, add the water and place the Steam Rack; transfer the cups to the rack. 4. Place and close the lid. 5. Select Pressure Cook mode. Press Pressure Cook button again to adjust the cooking time to 8 minutes; press Pressure Level to choose High Pressure. 6. When the time is up, quickly and carefully turn the steam release handle from the Sealing to Venting position. 7. Uncover the lid and serve warm.
Per Serving: Calories 305; Fat 15g; Sodium 548mg; Carbs 12g; Sugar 1.2g; Fiber 0.7g; Protein 29g

Egg Casserole with Red Onion

Prep time: 15 minutes | Cook Time: 25 minutes | Serves: 4-6

½ teaspoon olive oil
1 large red onion, chopped
1-pound mild sausages, ground
8 large eggs, beaten
½ cup flour
1 can black beans, rinsed
1 cup Cotija cheese (or any semi-

hard cheese)
1 cup mozzarella cheese
1 cup water
Sour cream, optional to garnish
Cilantro, optional to garnish
½ cup green onions

1. Insert the Inner Pot into the Cooker Base without the lid. 2. Press the Sauté button to select the cooking mode and press it again to adjust the cooking temperature to Normal. 3. When the display switches On to Hot, add and heat the oil; add the onion and cook for 2 to 3 minutes; add the sausages and cook until all sides start to brown. 4. Press the Cancel button to stop the cooking program. 5. In a suitable bowl, mix up the eggs and flour until well-combined; add the beans, Cotija cheese, mozzarella cheese and sausages, then pour the mixture to the heatproof round baking dish. 6. In the Inner Pot, add the water and place the Steam Rack; transfer the bowl to the rack. 7. Place and close the lid. 8. Select Pressure Cook mode. Press Pressure Cook button again to adjust the cooking time to 20 minutes; press Pressure Level to choose High Pressure. 9. When the time is up, leave the steam release handle in the Sealing position for 10 minutes, then turn it to Venting position. 10. Uncover the lid, top the dish with sour cream, green onion and cilantro. 11. Chill for a few minutes before serving.
Per Serving: Calories 336; Fat 17.3g; Sodium 281mg; Carbs 8.1g; Fiber 5.3g; Sugars 17.7g; Protein 32.3g

Homemade Cheese Dip

Prep time: 15 minutes | Cook Time: 10 minutes | Serves: 10

½ stick butter
½ teaspoon onion powder
½ teaspoon garlic powder
¼ teaspoon dried dill weed
Sea salt and ground black pepper,

to taste
2 tablespoons tapioca starch
1 ½ cups whole milk
1 ½ cups Swiss cheese, grated

1. Insert the Inner Pot into the Cooker Base without the lid. 2. Press the Sauté button to select the cooking mode and press it again to adjust the cooking temperature to Normal. 3. When the display switches On to Hot, add and melt the butter; add the onion powder, garlic powder, dill, salt, black pepper and stir in the tapioca starch until well combined; gradually pour in the milk and then stir constantly to avoid clumps. 4. When the mixture boiled, press the Cancel to stop this cooking program. 5. Add the Swiss cheese and stir until the cheese melted. 6. Serve warm with breadsticks or veggie sticks.
Per Serving: Calories 305; Fat 15g; Sodium 548mg; Carbs 12g; Sugar 1.2g; Fiber 0.7g; Protein 29g

Delicious Ham Egg Casserole

Prep time: 15 minutes | Cook Time: 20 minutes | Serves: 2-4

6 beaten eggs
½ cup plain Greek yogurt
1 cup cheddar cheese, shredded
1 cup ham, diced

¼ cup chives, chopped
½ teaspoon black pepper
1 cup water

1. In a heatproof bowl, mix up the eggs and yogurt until well-combined, then stir in the cheese, ham, chives and pepper. 2. In the Inner Pot, add the water and place the Steam Rack; transfer the bowl to the rack. 3. Place and close the lid. 4. Select Pressure Cook mode. Press Pressure Cook button again to adjust the cooking time to 20 minutes; press Pressure Level to choose High Pressure. 5. When the time is up, quickly and carefully turn the steam release handle from the Sealing to Venting position. 6. Uncover the lid and serve warm.
Per Serving: Calories 272; Fat 19g; Sodium 389mg; Carbs 10.4g; Fiber 0.7g; Sugars 1.1g; Protein 15.6g

Simple Soft-Boiled Eggs

Prep time: 5 minutes | Cook Time: 4 minutes | Serves: 2

4 eggs
1 cup water
2 English muffins, toasted

Salt and ground black pepper to taste

1. In the Inner Pot, add the water and place the Steam Rack; transfer the eggs to the rack. 2. Place and lock the lid. 3. Select Steam mode. Press Pressure Cook button again to adjust the cooking time to 4 minutes; press Pressure Level to choose High Pressure. 4. When the time is up, quickly turn the steam release handle from the Sealing position to the Venting position. 5. Uncover the lid and transfer the eggs to the bowl of cold water to cool for 2 to 3 minutes. 6. When cooled, peel each egg into 2 slices; serve one egg per half of toasted English muffin. 7. Season with the salt and pepper, enjoy.
Per Serving: Calories 285; Fat 9.8g; Sodium 639mg; Carbs 11.1g; Fiber 1.2g; Sugars 5.1g; Protein 27.8g

Homemade Fresh Cream Cheese

Prep time: 20 minutes | Cook Time: 5 minutes | Serves: 10

3 ½ cups whole milk
1 cup double cream

1 teaspoon kosher salt
2 tablespoons lemon juice

1. In the Inner Pot, stir in the milk, double cream and salt. 2. Place and lock the lid. 3. Select Pressure Cook mode. Press Pressure Cook button again to adjust the cooking time to 5 minutes; press Pressure Level to choose Low Pressure. 4. When the time is up, leave the steam release handle in the Sealing position. 5. Uncover the lid and stir in the lemon juice. 6. Prepare a strainer and line with cheesecloth, then pour the mixture into the cheesecloth; allow the curds to continue to drain in the strainer for about 1 hour. 7. Discard the whey. 8. Form your cheese into ball and remove from the cheesecloth. 9. The cheese balls can be refrigerated for a week. 10. Bon appétit!
Per Serving: Calories 351; Fat 22g; Sodium 502mg; Carbs 15.2g; Sugar 1.1g; Fiber 0.7g; Protein 26.4g

Bacon Cheese Quiche with Sausage

Prep time: 20 minutes | Cook Time: 30 minutes | Serves: 4

1 cup water
6 large eggs, beaten
½ cup almond or coconut milk
¼ teaspoon salt
⅛ teaspoon black pepper, ground
½ cup diced ham

1 cup ground sausage, cooked
4 slices cooked and crumbled bacon
1 cup parmesan Cheese
2 large green onions, chopped

1. In a heatproof round baking dish, mix up the eggs, milk, salt and pepper until combined; stir in the ham, sausage, bacon, cheese and green onion. 2. Cover the dish with foil. 3. In the Inner Pot, add the water and place the Steam Rack; transfer the dish to the rack. 4. Place and close the lid. 5. Select Pressure Cook mode. Press Pressure Cook button again to adjust the cooking time to 30 minutes; press Pressure Level to choose High Pressure. 6. When the time is up, leave the steam release handle in the Sealing position for 10 minutes, then turn it to Venting position. 7. Uncover the lid and remove the foil. 8. Serve immediately; you can sprinkle more cheese and broil the dish in the broiler for a few minutes if you want a crisp top.
Per Serving: Calories 344; Fat 14.9g; Sodium 227mg; Carbs 14g; Fiber 1g; Sugars 1.4g; Protein 25.7g

Easy Hard-Boiled Eggs

Prep time: 10 minutes | Cook Time: 5 minutes | Serves: 4-8

5-15 eggs   1 cup water

1. In the Inner Pot, add the water and place the Steam Rack; transfer the eggs to the rack. 2. Place and lock the lid. 3. Select Pressure Cook mode. Press Pressure Cook button again to adjust the cooking time to 5 minutes; press Pressure Level to choose High Pressure. 4. When the time is up, leave the steam release handle in the Sealing position for 5 minutes, then turn it to the Venting position. 5. Uncover the lid; cool the eggs in the bowl of cold water for 2 to 3 minutes. 6. Serve.
Per Serving: Calories 336; Fat 17.3g; Sodium 281mg; Carbs 8.1g; Fiber 5.3g; Sugars 17.7g; Protein 32.3g

Mushroom Frittata with Cheddar Cheese

Prep time: 15 minutes | Cook Time: 5 minutes | Serves: 2-4

4 beaten eggs   pepper to taste
1 cup fresh mushrooms, chopped   1 cup sharp cheddar cheese,
¼ cup half-and-half   shredded and divided
Salt and freshly ground black   1 cup water

1. In a suitable bowl, mix up the eggs, mushrooms, half-and-half, salt and pepper, and ½ cup of cheese. 2. Divide the mixture into ½-pint wide mouth jars evenly and sprinkle with the remaining cheese; place the lids on the top of the jars but do not tighten. 3. In the Inner Pot, add the water and place the Steam Rack; arrange the jars to the rack. 4. Select Pressure Cook mode. Press Pressure Cook button again to adjust the cooking time to 3 minutes; press Pressure Level to choose High Pressure. 5. When the time is up, quickly turn the steam release handle from the Sealing position to the Venting position. 6. Uncover the lid, serve and enjoy.
Per Serving: Calories 305; Fat 15g; Sodium 548mg; Carbs 12g; Sugar 1.2g; Fiber 0.7g; Protein 29g

Delectable Mac and Cheese

Prep time: 15 minutes | Cook Time: 5 minutes | Serves: 6

12 ounces elbow macaroni   4 ounces milk
2 tablespoons butter   2 ½ cups cheddar cheese,
½ teaspoon celery seeds   shredded
Kosher salt, to taste   1 cup Parmesan cheese, shredded
3 cups water

1. In the Inner Pot, add the elbow macaroni, butter, celery seeds, water and salt. 2. Place and lock the lid. 3. Select Pressure Cook mode. Press Pressure Cook button again to adjust the cooking time to 5 minutes; press Pressure Level to choose Low Pressure. 4. When the time is up, quickly and carefully turn the steam release handle from the Sealing position to the Venting position. 5. Uncover the lid, add the milk and half of the cheeses and stir until the cheeses are melted; add the remaining cheeses and stir until well combined. 6. When the sauce cools, it will be thickening. 7. Bon appétit!
Per Serving: Calories 254; Fat 28 g; Sodium 346mg; Carbs 12.3 g; Sugar 1g; Fiber 0.7g; Protein 24.3 g

Herbed Egg Cups

Prep time: 15 minutes | Cook Time: 4 minutes | Serves: 4

4 bell peppers   ⅔ cup water
4 eggs   2 tablespoons mozzarella cheese,
Salt and ground black pepper to   grated freshly
taste   Chopped fresh herbs

1. Cut the bell peppers ends to form about 1½-inch high cup and discard the seeds. 2. Crack one egg into each pepper, season with the salt and black pepper and cover each pepper with foil. 3. In the Inner Pot, add the water and place the Steam Rack; transfer the bell peppers to the rack. 4. Place and close the lid. 5. Select Pressure Cook mode. Press Pressure Cook button again to adjust the cooking time to 4 minutes; press Pressure Level to choose High Pressure. 6. When the time is up, quickly and carefully turn the steam release handle from the Sealing to Venting position. 7. Uncover the lid and serve the pepper on a plate; sprinkle with the mozzarella cheese and chopped fresh herbs as you like.
Per Serving: Calories 285; Fat 9.8g; Sodium 639mg; Carbs 11.1g; Fiber 1.2g; Sugars 5.1g; Protein 27.8g

Chapter 3 Rice Recipes

Simple Homemade Brown Rice

Prep time: 1 minutes | Cook Time: 22 minutes | Serves: 4

1 cup brown rice   1 cup chicken stock

1. In the Inner Pot, add the rice and chicken stock. 2. Place and close the lid rightly. 3. Select Pressure Cook mode. Press Pressure Cook button again to adjust the cooking time to 22 minutes; press Pressure Level to choose High Pressure. 4. When the time is up, leave the steam release handle in the Sealing position. 5. When done, use a fork to fluff the rice and serve.
Per Serving: Calories: 130; Fat: 1g; Sodium: 86mg; Carbs: 25g; Sugar: 1g; Protein: 4g

Tasty Jasmine Rice

Prep time: 1 minutes | Cook Time: 3 minutes | Serves: 4

1 cup jasmine rice   1 cup water

1. Rinse the rice well in a fine-mesh strainer. 2. In the Inner Pot, add the rice and water. 3. Place and close the lid rightly. 4. Select Pressure Cook mode. Press Pressure Cook button again to adjust the cooking time to 3 minutes; press Pressure Level to choose High Pressure. 5. When the time is up, leave the steam release handle in the Sealing position. 6. When done, use a fork to fluff the rice and serve.
Per Serving: Calories: 154; Fat: 0g; Sodium: 1mg; Carbs: 33g; Sugar: 0g; Protein: 3g

Lime Cilantro Brown Rice

Prep time: 5 minutes | Cook Time: 22 minutes | Serves: 4

1 cup brown rice   oil
1 cup water   2 tablespoons fresh lime juice
1 teaspoon salt   1 cup chopped fresh cilantro
2 tablespoons extra-virgin olive

1. In the Inner Pot, add the rice, salt and water. 2. Place and close the lid rightly. 3. Select Pressure Cook mode. Press Pressure Cook button again to adjust the cooking time to 22 minutes; press Pressure Level to choose High Pressure. 4. When the time is up, leave the steam release handle in the Sealing position. 5. When done, use a fork to fluff the rice and transfer to a large bowl. 6. Cool the rice for a few minutes, then combine the rice with the olive oil, lime juice and cilantro. 7. Enjoy.
Per Serving: Calories: 171; Fat: 7g; Sodium: 583mg; Carbs: 23g; Sugar: 0g; Protein: 2g

Turmeric Jasmine Rice

Prep time: 5 minutes | Cook Time: 5 minutes | Serves: 4

1 cup jasmine rice   ¼ teaspoon ground cumin
1 tablespoon avocado oil   ⅛ teaspoon ground cinnamon
2 cloves garlic, minced   1 cup chicken stock
1 tablespoon peeled and grated ½ cup chopped fresh cilantro
fresh turmeric

1. Rinse the rice in a fine-mesh strainer. 2. Insert the Inner Pot into the Cooker Base without the lid. 3. Press the Sauté button to select the cooking mode and press it again to adjust the cooking temperature

to Normal. 4. When the display switches On to Hot, add and heat the oil for 1 minutes; add the turmeric, garlic, cumin and cinnamon and stir constantly for 1 to 2 minutes. 5. Press Cancel button to stop this cooking program. 6. Still in the Inner Pot, add and combine the clean rice and stock; scrape any brown bits stuck to the bottom of the pot with a spoon. 7. Place and close the lid in right way. 8. Select Pressure Cook mode. Press Pressure Cook button again to adjust the cooking time to 3 minutes; press Pressure Level to choose High Pressure. 9. When the time is up, leave the steam release handle in the Sealing position. 10. When released, use a fork to fluff the rice. 11. With the fresh cilantro, serve and enjoy.
Per Serving: Calories: 216; Fat: 4g; Sodium: 88mg; Carbs: 38g; Sugar: 1g; Protein: 5g

Flavorful Forbidden Rice

Prep time: 15 minutes | Cook Time: 30 minutes | Serves: 4

1 cup forbidden rice   peeled, pitted, and cut into ½"
1 cup water   dice
⅛ cup fresh lime juice   ½ cup finely chopped red onion
⅛ cup fresh orange juice   ½ cup unsalted almond slices
2 tablespoons extra-virgin olive 3 scallions, thinly sliced
oil   1 medium jalapeño, seeded and
⅛ teaspoon salt   minced
1 medium just-ripe mango,   ½ cup fresh cilantro leaves

1. In the Inner Pot, add the rice and water. 2. Place and close the lid rightly. 3. Select the Pressure Cook and press the button again to adjust the cooking time to 30 minutes; press the Pressure Level button to choose High Pressure. 4. While cooking the rice, to make the dressing, mix up the lime juice, oil, orange juice and salt in a small bowl. 5. When the time is up, leave the steam release handle in the Sealing position. 6. When done, use a fork to fluff the rice and then transfer to a suitable bowl. 7. Toss the rice with the mango, onion, almond slices, scallions and jalapeño, then add the dressing and cilantro and coat well. 8. You can serve the rice cold or at room temperature.
Per Serving: Calories: 304; Fat: 14g; Sodium: 79mg; Carbs: 42g; Sugar: 15g; Protein: 7g

Jasmine Rice with Mushrooms

Prep time: 5 minutes | Cook Time: 15 minutes | Serves: 4

1 cup jasmine rice   mushrooms
1 tablespoon avocado oil   3 cloves garlic, minced
1 small yellow onion, peeled and ¼ teaspoon salt
chopped   1 cup vegetable broth
10 ounces sliced baby bella

1. Rinse the rice in a fine-mesh strainer. 2. Insert the pot into the Cooker Base without the lid. 3. Select Sauté mode and then press the same button again and then adjust the cooking temperature to Normal. 4. When the display switches On to Hot, add and heat the oil for 1 minute; add the garlic, onion, mushrooms and salt and cook for 5 minutes. 5. Press the Cancel button to stop this cooking program. 6. Stir in the clean rice and vegetable broth, then lock the lid in right way. 7. Select the Pressure Cook and press the button again to adjust the cooking time to 10 minutes; press the Pressure Level button to choose High Pressure. 8. When the time is up, leave the steam release handle in the Sealing position. 9. When done, serve and enjoy.
Per Serving: Calories: 229; Fat: 4g; Sodium: 287mg; Carbs: 43g; Sugar: 2g; Protein: 5g

Spanish-Style Rice

Prep time: 15 minutes | Cook Time: 4 minutes | Serves: 6

2 tablespoons vegetable oil
2 tablespoons finely chopped onion
2 cups long-grain white rice, rinsed until the water runs clear
1½ cups chicken broth, store-bought or homemade (here)

1 (10-ounce) can diced tomatoes with green chilies (such as Ro-Tel)
1 teaspoon seasoning salt
½ teaspoon chili powder
¼ teaspoon garlic powder

1. Insert the Inner Pot into the Cooker Base without the lid. 2. Select Sauté mode and then press the same button again and then adjust the cooking temperature to Normal. 3. When the display switches On to Hot, add and heat the vegetable oil; add the onion and cook for 1-2 minutes until soft; add the rice and cook for 2 minutes more. 4. Press the Cancel button to stop this cooking program. 5. Still in the Inner Pot, add the chicken broth, diced tomatoes with green chilies with their juices, seasoning salt, chili powder and garlic powder. 6. Lock the lid. Select the Pressure Cook mode and press the button again to adjust the cooking time to 3 minutes; press the Pressure Level to choose High Pressure. 7. When the time is up, leave the steam release handle in the Sealing position for 10 minutes, then turn the handle to the Venting position. 8. When released, use a fork to fluff the rice and serve.
Per Serving: Calories: 283; Fat: 9g; Sodium: 615mg; Carbs: 52g; Fiber: 1g; Protein: 6g

Risotto with Cheeses

Prep time: 15 minutes | Cook Time: 6 minutes | Serves: 6

3 tablespoons unsalted butter
1 cup finely chopped onion
2 garlic cloves, minced
1½ cups arborio rice
½ cup dry white wine
3 cups chicken broth, store-bought or homemade (here)
1 cup heavy cream

½ teaspoon salt
¼ teaspoon freshly ground black pepper
½ cup shredded fontina cheese
½ cup shredded mozzarella cheese
½ cup shredded Parmesan cheese

1. Insert the Inner Pot into the Cooker Base without the lid. 2. Select Sauté mode and then press the same button again and then adjust the cooking temperature to Normal. 3. When the display switches On to Hot, add and melt the butter; add the garlic and onion and cook for 2 minutes; add the rice and wine and stir for 2-½ minutes; stir in the chicken broth, heavy cream, salt and pepper. 4. Press the Cancel button to stop this cooking program. 5. Lock the lid. Select the Pressure Cook mode and press the button again to adjust the cooking time to 6 minutes; press the Pressure Level to choose High Pressure. 6. When the time is up, quickly and carefully turn the steam release handle from the Sealing position to the Venting position. 7. Open the lid, regularly stir in the cheeses until they are melted. 8. Without the lid, let the food sit in the pot for 3 to 4 minutes until thickened. 9. When done, serve and enjoy.
Per Serving: Calories: 464; Fat: 35g; Sodium: 539mg; Carbs: 43g; Fiber: 2g; Protein: 14g

Tasty White Basmati Rice

Prep time: 10 minutes | Cook Time: 6 minutes | Serves: 4

1 cup white basmati rice
1¼ cups water

¼ tsp. salt
Butter to taste, optional

1. Rinse the basmati rice in a fine-mesh strainer. 2. In the Inner Pot, add the rice and stir in the salt and water. 3. Select the Pressure Cook mode and press the button again to adjust the cooking time to 6 minutes; press the Pressure Level button to choose High Pressure. 4. When the time is up, leave the steam release handle from the Sealing position for 10 minutes, then turn it to the Venting position. 5. Uncover the lid when released and then use a fork to fluff the rice. 6. Serve and you can enjoy with the butter as you like.
Per Serving: Calories 336; Fat 17.3g; Sodium 281mg; Carbs 8.1g; Fiber 5.3g; Sugars 17.7g; Protein 32.3g

Basmati Rice in Beef Broth

Prep time: 20 minutes | Cook Time: 25 minutes | Serves: 4-6

1 tbsp. olive oil
2 cups basmati rice
3 oz. butter
1 tbsp. minced garlic
1 cup spinach

1 tsp. salt
1 tsp. dried oregano
1 cup dill
2½ cups beef broth

1. Rinse the spinach and dill carefully, then chop them. 2. Blend the chopped spinach and dill in a blender, set aside for later use. 3. Insert the Inner Pot into the Cooker Base without the lid. 4. Select Sauté mode and then press the same button again and then adjust the cooking temperature to Normal. 5. When the display switches On to Hot, add and heat the oil; add the garlic, butter and rice and sauté for 5 minutes; stir in the beef broth, the blended spinach and dill. 6. Press the Cancel button to stop this cooking program. 7. Still in the Inner Pot, add the salt and dried oregano, then lock the lid. 8. Select the Rice mode and press the button again to adjust the cooking time to 20 minutes; press the Pressure Level button to choose High Pressure. 9. When the time is up, quickly and carefully turn the steam release handle from the Sealing to the Venting position. 10. Uncover the lid, serve the rice in a prepared bowl and enjoy.
Per Serving: Calories 272; Fat 19g; Sodium 389mg; Carbs 10.4g; Fiber 0.7g; Sugars 1.1g; Protein 15.6g

Lime Long-Grain White Rice

Prep time: 15 minutes | Cook Time: 4 minutes | Serves: 4

1 cup long-grain white rice, rinsed until the water runs clear
1 cup water
½ teaspoon salt
1 tablespoon finely chopped fresh

cilantro
1 teaspoon grated lime zest
1 tablespoon fresh lime juice
1 teaspoon vegetable oil

1. In the Inner Pot, add the rice, water and salt, stir well. 2. Place and close the lid rightly. 3. Select Pressure Cook mode. Press Pressure Cook button again to adjust the cooking time to 4 minutes; press Pressure Level to choose High Pressure. 4. When the time is up, leave the steam release handle in the Sealing position for 10 minutes, then turn the steam release handle to the Venting position. 5. When released, stir in the oil, cilantro, lime zest and juice, then use a fork to fluff the rice. 6. Serve and enjoy.
Per Serving: Calories: 182; Fat: 2g; Sodium: 293mg; Carbs: 38g; Fiber: 1g; Protein: 3g

Parmesan Risotto with Peas

Prep time: 15 minutes | Cook Time: 15 minutes | Serves: 4

1 tbsp. extra-virgin olive oil
2 tbsp. butter
1 yellow onion, chopped
1½ cups Arborio rice
3 cups chicken stock
2 tbsp. lemon juice

1½ cups frozen peas, thawed
2 tbsp. parmesan, finely grated
2 tbsp. parsley, finely chopped
1 tsp lemon zest, grated
Salt and ground black pepper to taste

1. Insert the Inner Pot into the Cooker Base without the lid. 2. Select Sauté mode and then press the same button again and then adjust the cooking temperature to Normal. 3. When the display switches On to Hot, heat the oil and 1 tablespoon of butter; add the onion and cook for 5 minutes; add the rice and stir for 3 minutes. 4. Stir in the lemon juice and 3 cups of stock, then press the Cancel button to stop this cooking program and lock the lid. 5. Select the Pressure Cook mode and press the button again to adjust the cooking time to 5 minutes; press the Pressure Level button to choose High Pressure. 6. When the time is up, quickly and carefully turn the steam release handle from the Sealing position to the Venting position. 7. When released, remove the lid, add the peas and the remaining stock, then cook for 2 minutes more on Sauté mode at Less cooking temperature. 8. Stir in the parmesan, parsley, lemon zest, salt, pepper and the remaining butter. 9. Serve and enjoy.
Per Serving: Calories 305; Fat 15g; Sodium 548mg; Carbs 12g; Sugar 1.2g; Fiber 0.7g; Protein 29g

Wild Rice in Chicken Stock

Prep time: 1 minutes | Cook Time: 30 minutes | Serves: 4

1 cup wild rice	1 cup chicken stock

1. In the Inner Pot, add the wild rice and chicken stock. 2. Place and close the lid rightly. 3. Select the Pressure Cook and press the button again to adjust the cooking time to 30 minutes; press the Pressure Level button to choose High Pressure. 4. When the time is up, leave the steam release handle in the Sealing position. 5. When done, use a fork to fluff the rice and serve.

Per Serving: Calories: 164; Fat: 1g; Sodium: 88mg; Carbs: 32g; Sugar: 2g; Protein: 7g

Long Grain White Rice with Onion

Prep time: 10 minutes | Cook Time: 15 minutes | Serves: 4-6

1 tbsp. olive oil	2 cups chicken stock
¼ cup onion, diced	1 cup salsa
2 cups long grain white rice	1 tsp salt

1. Insert the Inner Pot into the Cooker Base without the lid. 2. Select Sauté mode and then press the same button again and then adjust the cooking temperature to Normal. 3. When the display switches On to Hot, add and heat the oil; add the onion and cook for 2 minutes or until translucent; add the rice and cook for 2 to 3 minutes. 4. Press the Cancel button to stop this cooking program. 5. Stir in the salt, salsa and chicken stock, then lock the lid. 6. Select the Pressure Cook mode and press the button again to adjust the cooking time to 10 minutes; press the Pressure Level button to choose High Pressure. 7. When the time is up, leave the steam release handle from the Sealing position for 10 minutes, then turn it to the Venting position. 8. Uncover the lid and then use a fork to fluff the rice. 9. Serve and enjoy.

Per Serving: Calories 285; Fat 9.8g; Sodium 639mg; Carbs 11.1g; Fiber 1.2g; Sugars 5.1g; Protein 27.8g

Delicious Risotto in Chicken Stock

Prep time: 20 minutes | Cook Time: 20 minutes | Serves: 4-6

1½ tbsp. olive oil	Salt and ground black pepper to taste
1 finely chopped medium onion	
1½ cups Arborio rice	3 tbsp. Romano or Parmesan cheese
2½ cups chicken stock	

1. Insert the Inner Pot into the Cooker Base without the lid. 2. Select Sauté mode and then press the same button again and then adjust the cooking temperature to Normal. 3. When the display switches On to Hot, add and heat the oil; add the onion and cook for a few minutes until translucent, then add the rice and chicken stock. 4. Press the Cancel button to stop this cooking program and then lock the lid in right way. 5. Select the Rice mode and press the button again to adjust the cooking time to 15 minutes; press the Pressure Level button to choose High Pressure. 6. When the time is up, leave the steam release handle in the Sealing position for 10 minutes, then turn it to the Venting position. 7. When released, carefully remove the lid. 8. Season with the salt and black pepper. 9. With the Romano or Parmesan cheese, enjoy.

Per Serving: Calories 285; Fat 9.8g; Sodium 639mg; Carbs 11.1g; Fiber 1.2g; Sugars 5.1g; Protein 27.8g

Mushroom Risotto with Parmesan Cheese

Prep time: 15 minutes | Cook Time: 15 minutes | Serves: 4

2 oz. olive oil	2 cups Arborio rice
2 cloves garlic, crushed	3 cups chicken stock
1 yellow onion, chopped	4 oz. sherry vinegar
8 oz. mushrooms, sliced	4 oz. heavy cream

2 tbsp. Parmesan cheese, grated	Salt to taste
1 oz. basil, finely chopped	

1. Insert the Inner Pot into the Cooker Base without the lid. 2. Select Sauté mode and then press the same button again and then adjust the cooking temperature to Normal. 3. When the display switches On to Hot, add and heat the oil; add the garlic, mushrooms and onion and cook for 3 minutes. 4. Stir in the rice, vinegar and chicken stock, then lock the lid in right way. 5. Select the Pressure Cook mode and press the button again to adjust the cooking time to 10 minutes; press the Pressure Level button to choose High Pressure. 6. When the time is up, quickly and carefully turn the steam release handle from the Sealing position to the Venting position. 7. Uncover the lid and stir in the Parmesan and heavy cream. 8. Sprinkle salt and top with basil, serve and enjoy.

Per Serving: Calories 249; Fat 13g; Sodium 556mg; Carbs 10g; Sugar 1.1g; Fiber 0.7g; Protein 31g

Homemade Risotto

Prep time: 20 minutes | Cook Time: 11 minutes | Serves: 4-6

2 tbsp. butter	1 cup milk
1½ cups Arborio rice	Salt to taste
⅓ cup brown sugar	1½ tsp cinnamon powder
2 apples, cored and sliced	½ cup cherries, dried
1 cup apple juice	

1. Insert the Inner Pot into the Cooker Base without the lid. 2. Select Sauté mode and then press the same button again and then adjust the cooking temperature to Normal. 3. When the display switches On to Hot, add and melt the butter; add the rice and stir for 5 minutes; stir in the cinnamon, sugar, apple juice, apple slices, milk and a pinch of salt. 4. Press the Cancel button to stop this cooking program and then lock the lid in right way. 5. Select the Pressure Cook and press the button again to adjust the cooking time to 6 minutes; press the Pressure Level button to choose High Pressure. 6. When the time is up, leave the steam release handle in the Sealing position. 7. When released, carefully remove the lid and add the cherries; stir well and close the lid, let the food sit in the pot for 5 minutes. 8. When done, serve and enjoy.

Per Serving: Calories 307; Fat 11g; Sodium 477mg; Carbs 14g; Fiber 1g; Sugars 1.4g; Protein 25.7g

Cheese Long Grain Rice with Chicken Breasts

Prep time: 15 minutes | Cook Time: 25 minutes | Serves: 4-6

2 tbsp. butter	taste
1½ lbs. boneless chicken breasts, sliced	1 and ⅓ cups long grain rice
	1 and ⅓ cups chicken broth
1 onion, chopped	½ cup milk
2 cloves garlic, minced	1 cup broccoli florets
Salt and ground black pepper to	½ cup cheddar cheese, grated

1. Insert the Inner Pot into the Cooker Base without the lid. 2. Select Sauté mode and then press the same button again and then adjust the cooking temperature to Normal. 3. When the display switches On to Hot, add and melt the butter; add the garlic, onion, chicken pieces, salt and pepper and cook for 5 minutes, until the chicken pieces have slightly browned. 4. Press the Cancel button to stop this cooking program. 5. Add the rice, broccoli florets, cheddar cheese and stir in the milk and chicken broth, then lock the lid. 6. Select the Pressure Cook mode and press the button again to adjust the cooking time to 15 minutes; press the Pressure Level button to choose High Pressure. 7. When the time is up, leave the steam release handle from the Sealing position for 10 minutes, then turn it to the Venting position. 8. Uncover the lid and serve.

Per Serving: Calories 336; Fat 17.3g; Sodium 281mg; Carbs 8.1g; Fiber 5.3g; Sugars 17.7g; Protein 32.3g

Brown Rice with Black Beans

Prep time: 10 minutes | Cook Time: 28 minutes | Serves: 4-6

2 cups uncooked brown rice	1 tsp garlic
1 cup soaked black beans	2 tsp onion powder
5 cups water	2 tsp chili powder
6 oz. tomato paste	1 tsp salt

1. In a suitable bowl, add the beans and pour in enough water to cover them, let the beans soak for at least 2 hours. 2. Rinse and drain the beans. 3. In the Inner Pot, add the soaked beans and the remaining ingredients. 4. Place and lock the lid. 5. Select the Rice mode and press the button again to adjust the cooking time to 28 minutes; press the Pressure Level button to choose High Pressure. 6. When the time is up, quickly and carefully turn the steam release handle from the Sealing to the Venting position. 7. Uncover the lid and serve the rice in a prepared bowl. 8. Enjoy.
Per Serving: Calories 272; Fat 19g; Sodium 389mg; Carbs 10.4g; Fiber 0.7g; Sugars 1.1g; Protein 15.6g

Thai Sweet Rice with Coconut Milk

Prep time: 20 minutes | Cook Time: 3 minutes | Serves: 2-4

1 cup Thai sweet rice	2 tbsp. sugar
1½ cups water	½ tsp. salt
½ can full-; Fat coconut milk	

1. In the Inner Pot, add the rice and stir in water. 2. Place and lock the lid in right way. 3. Select the Pressure Cook mode and press the button again to adjust the cooking time to 3 minutes; press the Pressure Level button to choose High Pressure. 4. While cooking the rice, heat the sugar, salt and coconut milk in a saucepan, until the sugar has melted. 5. When the time is up, leave the steam release handle from the Sealing position for 10 minutes, then turn it to the Venting position. 6. Uncover the lid and stir in the coconut milk mixture. 7. Close the lid again and wait for 5 to 10 minutes before serving.
Per Serving: Calories 344; Fat 14.9g; Sodium 227mg; Carbs 14g; Fiber 1g; Sugars 1.4g; Protein 25.7g

Rice Bowl with Maple Syrup

Prep time: 15 minutes | Cook Time: 20 minutes | Serves: 4

1 cup brown rice	¼ cup raisins
1 cup water	Salt to taste
1 cup coconut milk	A pinch of cinnamon powder
½ cup coconut chips	½ cup maple syrup
¼ cup almonds	

1. In the Inner Pot, add the rice and chicken stock. 2. Place and close the lid rightly. 3. Select Pressure Cook mode. Press Pressure Cook button again to adjust the cooking time to 15 minutes; press Pressure Level to choose High Pressure. 4. When the time is up, quickly and carefully turn the steam release handle from the Sealing position to the Venting position. 5. Open the lid, stir in the milk, coconut chips, almonds, raisins, maple syrup, salt and cinnamon. 6. Continue to cook for 5 minutes more on Pressure Cook mode at High Pressure. 7. When cooked, quickly and carefully release the pressure by turning the steam release handle from the Sealing position to the Venting position. 8. When done, serve and enjoy.
Per Serving: Calories 336; Fat 17.3g; Sodium 281mg; Carbs 8.1g; Fiber 5.3g; Sugars 17.7g; Protein 32.3g

Rice in Vegetable Stock

Prep time: 2 minutes | Cook Time: 30 minutes | Serves: 4

1 cup rice	1 cup vegetable stock

1. In the Inner Pot, add the forbidden rice and vegetable stock. 2. Place and close the lid rightly. 3. Select the Pressure Cook and press the button again to adjust the cooking time to 30 minutes; press the Pressure Level button to choose High Pressure. 4. When the time is up, leave the steam release handle in the Sealing position. 5. When done, use a fork to fluff the rice and enjoy.
Per Serving: Calories: 114; Fat: 1g; Sodium: 218mg; Carbs: 22g; Sugar: 1g; Protein: 4g

Simple-Cooked Pink Rice

Prep time: 15 minutes | Cook Time: 5 minutes | Serves: 2-4

1 cup pink rice	½ tsp salt
1 cup water	

1. Rinse the pink rice in a fine-mesh strainer. 2. In the Inner Pot, add the rice and stir in the salt and water. 3. Select the Pressure Cook mode and press the button again to adjust the cooking time to 5 minutes; press the Pressure Level button to choose High Pressure. 4. When the time is up, leave the steam release handle from the Sealing position for 10 minutes, then turn it to the Venting position. 5. Uncover the lid and then use a fork to fluff the rice. 6. Serve and enjoy.
Per Serving: Calories 344; Fat 14.9g; Sodium 227mg; Carbs 14g; Fiber 1g; Sugars 1.4g; Protein 25.7g

Turmeric Basmati Rice with Sweet Corn

Prep time: 10 minutes | Cook Time: 10 minutes | Serves: 6-8

3 tbsp. olive oil	1 cup garden peas, frozen
1 large onion, finely chopped	¼ tsp. salt
3 cloves garlic, minced	1 tsp. turmeric powder
3 tbsp. cilantro stalks, chopped	3 cups chicken stock
2 cups basmati rice	2 tbsp. butter, optional
1 cup sweet corn, frozen	

1. Rinse the basmati rice well in a fine-mesh strainer. 2. Insert the Inner Pot into the Cooker Base without the lid. 3. Select Sauté mode and then press the same button again and then adjust the cooking temperature to Normal. 4. When the display switches On to Hot, add and heat the oil; add the garlic, onion and cilantro and cook for 5 to 6 minutes until the onion is translucent. 5. Add the rice, peas and sweet corn, stir in the salt, turmeric and chicken stock. 6. Press the Cancel button to stop this cooking program and then lock the lid in right way. 7. Select the Pressure Cook mode and press the button again to adjust the cooking time to 4 minutes; press the Pressure Level button to choose High Pressure. 8. When the time is up, quickly and carefully turn the steam release handle from the Sealing to the Venting position. 9. Uncover the lid, serve and you can enjoy with the butter as you like.
Per Serving: Calories 344; Fat 14.9g; Sodium 227mg; Carbs 14g; Fiber 1g; Sugars 1.4g; Protein 25.7g

Butter Brown Rice in Vegetable Stock

Prep time: 20 minutes | Cook Time: 22 minutes | Serves: 4-6

1 stick (½ cup) butter	1 cups vegetable stock
2 cups brown rice	1½ cups French onion soup

1. Insert the Inner Pot into the Cooker Base without the lid. 2. Select Sauté mode and then press the same button again and then adjust the cooking temperature to Normal. 3. When the display switches On to Hot, add and melt the butter; add the rice and stir in the vegetable stock and onion soup. 4. Press the Cancel button to stop this cooking program and then lock the lid. 5. Select the Pressure Cook mode and press the button again to adjust the cooking time to 22 minutes; press the Pressure Level button to choose High Pressure. 6. When the time is up, leave the steam release handle from the Sealing position for 10 minutes, then turn it to the Venting position. 7. Uncover the lid and serve, you can enjoy with the fresh parsley.
Per Serving: Calories 344; Fat 14.9g; Sodium 227mg; Carbs 14g; Fiber 1g; Sugars 1.4g; Protein 25.7g

Wild Rice Blend in Chicken Stock

Prep time: 1 minutes | Cook Time: 28 minutes | Serves: 4

1 cup wild rice blend   1 cup chicken stock

1. In the Inner Pot, add the wild rice blend and chicken stock. 2. Place and close the lid rightly. 3. Select the Pressure Cook and press the button again to adjust the cooking time to 28 minutes; press the Pressure Level button to choose High Pressure. 4. When the time is up, leave the steam release handle in the Sealing position. 5. When done, use a fork to fluff the rice and enjoy.
Per Serving: Calories: 164; Fat: 1g; Sodium: 88mg; Carbs: 32g; Sugar: 2g; Protein: 7g

Brown Rice and Wild Rice

Prep time: 15 minutes | Cook Time: 25 minutes | Serves: 4

3-4 tbsp. red, wild or black rice   ¼ tsp. sea salt
¾ cup (or more) short grain   1½ cups water
brown rice

1. Rinse the rice in a fine-mesh strainer. 2. In the Inner Pot, add the rice and stir in the salt and water. 3. Select the Multigrain mode and press the button again to adjust the cooking time to 23 minutes; press the Pressure Level button to choose High Pressure. 4. When the time is up, leave the steam release handle from the Sealing position for 10 minutes, then turn it to the Venting position. 5. Uncover the lid and then use a fork to fluff the rice. 6. Serve and enjoy.
Per Serving: Calories 336; Fat 17.3g; Sodium 281mg; Carbs 8.1g; Fiber 5.3g; Sugars 17.7g; Protein 32.3g

White Jasmine Rice with Chicken Thighs

Prep time: 30 minutes | Cook Time: 20 minutes | Serves: 4-6

1 tbsp. olive oil   3 carrots, diced
3 small shallots, diced   1½ cups white jasmine rice,
2 cloves garlic, minced   rinsed and drained
1 lb. boneless chicken thighs   1½ cups chicken stock
Salt and ground black pepper to   2 tbsp. thyme leaves
taste

1. Insert the Inner Pot into the Cooker Base without the lid. 2. Select Sauté mode and then press the same button again and then adjust the cooking temperature to Normal. 3. When the display switches On to Hot, add and heat the oil; add the chicken thighs, salt, pepper and stir regularly for 5 minutes, until the chicken meat starts to brown; stir in the carrots, rice, thyme leaves and chicken stock. 4. Press the Cancel button to stop this cooking program and then lock the lid. 5. Select the Pressure Cook mode and press the button again to adjust the cooking time to 10 minutes; press the Pressure Level button to choose High Pressure. 6. When the time is up, leave the steam release handle from the Sealing position for 10 minutes, then turn it to the Venting position. 7. Uncover the lid and then use a fork to fluff the rice. 8. Serve and enjoy.
Per Serving: Calories 254; Fat 28 g; Sodium 346mg; Carbs 12.3 g; Sugar 1g; Fiber 0.7g; Protein 24.3 g

Basmati Rice with Carrot Dice

Prep time: 15 minutes | Cook Time: 20 minutes | Serves: 4-6

1 tbsp. olive oil   2 tsp curry powder
1 clove garlic, minced   1½ cups chicken broth
¼ cup shallots, chopped   1 cup frozen peas
1½ cups basmati rice   Salt and ground black pepper to
½ cup carrots, chopped   taste

1. Rinse the basmati rice in a fine-mesh strainer. 2. Insert the Inner Pot into the Cooker Base without the lid. 3. Select Sauté mode and then press the same button again and then adjust the cooking temperature to Normal. 4. When the display switches On to Hot, add and heat the oil; add the shallots and garlic until fragrant; add the rice, peas, carrots and stir in chicken broth, then sprinkle the curry powder, salt and pepper. 5. Press the Cancel button to stop this cooking program and then lock the lid. 6. Select the Rice mode and press the button again to adjust the cooking time to 20 minutes; press the Pressure Level button to choose High Pressure. 7. When the time is up, leave the steam release handle from the Sealing position for 10 minutes, then turn it to the Venting position. 8. Uncover the lid and then use a fork to fluff the rice. 9. Serve and enjoy.
Per Serving: Calories 312; Fat 15g; Sodium 548mg; Carbs 12g; Sugar 1.2g; Fiber 0.7g; Protein 29g

Brown Rice with Chopped Cilantro

Prep time: 15 minutes | Cook Time: 12 minutes | Serves: 4-6

2 cups brown rice, rinsed   1½ tbsp. olive oil
2¾ cups water   1 lime, juiced
4 small bay leaves   1 tsp. salt
½ cup chopped cilantro

1. In the Inner Pot, add the rice, bay leaves and water. 2. Place and lock the lid. 3. Select the Rice mode and press the button again to adjust the cooking time to 12 minutes; press the Pressure Level button to choose High Pressure. 4. When the time is up, leave the steam release handle from the Sealing position for 10 minutes, then turn it to the Venting position. 5. Uncover the lid and mix the rice with the oil, lime juice, salt and cilantro. 6. Serve and enjoy.
Per Serving: Calories 307; Fat 11g; Sodium 477mg; Carbs 14g; Fiber 1g; Sugars 1.4g; Protein 25.7g

Brown Rice in Vegetable Broth

Prep time: 10 minutes | Cook Time: 21 minutes | Serves: 4-6

2 cups brown rice   ½ tsp. salt
2 cups vegetable broth or water

1. In the Inner Pot, add the rice and stir in the salt and vegetable broth (or water). 2. Select the Pressure Cook mode and press the button again to adjust the cooking time to 21 minutes; press the Pressure Level button to choose High Pressure. 3. When the time is up, leave the steam release handle from the Sealing position for 10 minutes, then turn it to the Venting position. 4. Uncover the lid and then use a fork to fluff the rice. 5. Serve and enjoy.
Per Serving: Calories 351; Fat 22g; Sodium 502mg; Carbs 15.2g; Sugar 1.1g; Fiber 0.7g; Protein 26.4g

Simple Jasmine Rice

Prep time: 15 minutes | Cook Time: 5 minutes | Serves: 4-6

2 cups jasmine rice   2 tsp. olive oil
2 cups water   ½ tsp. salt

1. Rinse the jasmine rice in a fine-mesh strainer. 2. In the Inner Pot, add the rice and stir in the oil, salt and water. 3. Select the Pressure Cook mode and press the button again to adjust the cooking time to 4 minutes; press the Pressure Level button to choose High Pressure. 4. When the time is up, leave the steam release handle from the Sealing position for 10 minutes, then turn it to the Venting position. 5. Uncover the lid when released and then use a fork to fluff the rice. 6. Serve and enjoy.
Per Serving: Calories 344; Fat 14.9g; Sodium 227mg; Carbs 12g; Fiber 1.2g; Sugars 1g; Protein 27g

Ginger Pumpkin Risotto

Prep time: 10 minutes | Cook Time: 12 minutes | Serves: 4-6

2 oz. extra virgin olive oil	1 tsp thyme, chopped
2 cloves garlic, minced	½ tsp nutmeg
1 small yellow onion, chopped	½ tsp ginger, grated
2 cups Arborio rice	½ tsp cinnamon
3 cups chicken stock	½ cup heavy cream
¾ cup pumpkin puree	Salt to taste

1. Insert the Inner Pot into the Cooker Base without the lid. 2. Select Sauté mode and then press the same button again and then adjust the cooking temperature to Normal. 3. When the display switches On to Hot, add and heat the oil; add the garlic and onion and cook for 1-2 minutes. 4. Press the Cancel button to stop this cooking program. 5. Stir in the rice, cinnamon, pumpkin puree, thyme, nutmeg, ginger and chicken stock, then lock the lid in right way. 6. Select the Pressure Cook mode and press the button again to adjust the cooking time to 10 minutes; press the Pressure Level button to choose High Pressure. 7. When the time is up, quickly and carefully turn the steam release handle from the Sealing position to the Venting position. 8. Uncover the lid and stir in the heavy cream. 9. Serve and enjoy.
Per Serving: Calories 272; Fat 19g; Sodium 389mg; Carbs 10.4g; Fiber 0.7g; Sugars 1.1g; Protein 15.6g

Long Grain Rice in Tomato Sauce

Prep time: 20 minutes | Cook Time: 15 minutes | Serves: 4-6

2 tbsp. butter	1 tsp. chili powder
2 cups long grain rice	½ tsp. garlic powder
1½ cups chicken stock or water	½ tsp. onion powder
8 oz. tomato sauce	½ tsp. salt
1 tsp. cumin	

1. Insert the Inner Pot into the Cooker Base without the lid. 2. Select Sauté mode and then press the same button again and then adjust the cooking temperature to Normal. 3. When the display switches On to Hot, add and melt the butter; add the rice and stir regularly for 4 minutes. 4. Press the Cancel button to stop this cooking program. 5. Add the cumin, chili powder, garlic powder, onion powder, salt and stir in the chicken stock and tomato sauce, then lock the lid. 6. Select the Pressure Cook mode and press the button again to adjust the cooking time to 10 minutes; press the Pressure Level button to choose High Pressure. 7. When the time is up, leave the steam release handle from the Sealing position for 10 minutes, then turn it to the Venting position. 8. Uncover the lid and use a fork to fluff the rice. 9. Serve and enjoy.
Per Serving: Calories 272; Fat 19g; Sodium 389mg; Carbs 10.4g; Fiber 0.7g; Sugars 1.1g; Protein 15.6g

Rice and Millet

Prep time: 5 minutes | Cook Time: 10 minutes | Serves: 4-6

2 cups jasmine rice or long-grain white rice	3¼ cups water
½ cup millet	1 tsp. salt

1. In the Inner Pot, add the rice, millet, salt and stir in the water. 2. Select the Rice mode and press the button again to adjust the cooking time to 10 minutes; press the Pressure Level button to choose Low Pressure. 3. When the time is up, quickly and carefully turn the steam release handle from the Sealing to the Venting position. 4. Uncover the lid and then use a fork to fluff the rice. 5. Serve and enjoy.
Per Serving: Calories 336; Fat 17.3g; Sodium 281mg; Carbs 8.1g; Fiber 5.3g; Sugars 17.7g; Protein 32.3g

Cauliflower and Pineapple Rice

Prep time: 20 minutes | Cook Time: 20 minutes | Serves: 4-6

2 tsp. extra virgin olive oil	and chopped
2½ cups water	½ pineapple, peeled and chopped
2 cups jasmine rice	Salt and ground black pepper to
1 cauliflower, florets separated	taste

1. In the Inner Pot, add all of the ingredients and mix well. 2. Place and lock the lid in right way. 3. Select the Pressure Cook and press the button again to adjust the cooking time to 20 minutes; press the Pressure Level button to choose Low Pressure. 4. When the time is up, leave the steam release handle from the Sealing position for 10 minutes, then turn it to the Venting position. 5. Uncover the lid and then use a fork to fluff the rice. 6. Serve and enjoy.
Per Serving: Calories 249; Fat 13g; Sodium 556mg; Carbs 10g; Sugar 1.1g; Fiber 0.7g; Protein 31g

Beef Rice Porridge with Onion Dice

Prep time: 15 minutes | Cook Time: 6 minutes | Serves: 4

1 tbsp. olive oil	1½ cups basmati rice, rinsed
5 cloves garlic, minced	1½ cups water (chicken or
1 cup onion, diced	vegetable stock)
1 lb. ground beef	Salt to taste

1. Insert the Inner Pot into the Cooker Base without the lid. 2. Select Sauté mode and then press the same button again and then adjust the cooking temperature to Normal. 3. When the display switches On to Hot, add and heat the oil; add the garlic and cook for 30 seconds; add the onion and ground beef, stir regularly until the onion start to brown. 4. Add the rice, salt and stir in the water. 5. Press the Cancel button to stop this cooking program and then lock the lid. 6. Select the Pressure Cook mode and press the button again to adjust the cooking time to 5 minutes; press the Pressure Level button to choose High Pressure. 7. When the time is up, leave the steam release handle from the Sealing position. 8. When released, carefully remove the lid and serve.
Per Serving: Calories: 254; Fat: 14.2 g; Sodium 345g; Fiber 1.2g; Sugar 1.1g; Carbs: 5.7 g; Protein: 39.1 g

Shawarma Rice with Ground Beef

Prep time: 20 minutes | Cook Time: 15 minutes | Serves: 6-8

1½ cups basmati rice, rinsed and drained	1 tbsp. olive oil
1 lb. ground beef (chicken, fish, pork, etc. optional), cooked	5 cloves garlic, minced
	1 cup onion, chopped
1½ cups water	3 tbsp. shawarma spice
4 cups cabbage, shredded	1 tsp. salt
	¼ cup cilantro, chopped

1. In the Inner Pot, add the clean basmati rice, ground beef, cabbage, olive oil, garlic, onion, shawarma spice and salt, stir well to mix. 2. Place and lock the lid in right way. 3. Select the Pressure Cook mode and press the button again to adjust the cooking time to 15 minutes; press the Pressure Level button to choose High Pressure. 4. When the time is up, leave the steam release handle from the Sealing position for 10 minutes, then turn it to the Venting position. 5. Uncover the lid and stir in the cilantro. 6. Serve and enjoy.
Per Serving: Calories 285; Fat 9.8g; Sodium 639mg; Carbs 11.1g; Fiber 1.2g; Sugars 5.1g; Protein 27.8g

Sesame-Soy Frozen Pot Stickers

Prep time: 5 minutes | Cook Time: 3 minutes | Serves: 5

Pot Stickers
1 cup water
5 frozen pot stickers
1 teaspoon chopped green onion
½ tablespoon sesame seeds
Sesame-Soy Dipping Sauce
1 tablespoon soy sauce
1 tablespoon rice wine vinegar
1 teaspoon sesame oil
⅛ teaspoon grated fresh ginger
⅛ teaspoon minced garlic
¼ teaspoon chopped green onion
1/16 teaspoon crushed red pepper flakes
⅛ teaspoon chili oil

1. In the inner pot, pour water and the pot sticks. 2. Close the lid and turn the steam release handle to Sealing position. 3. Set the Instant Pot on Pressure Cook at High and adjust time to 3 minutes. 4. While cooking, mix all the Sesame-Soy Dipping Sauce ingredients in a small bowl. 5. When cooked, turn the handle from Sealing to Venting to release the pressure and then remove the lid carefully. 6. Transfer carefully the pot stickers onto a serving plate. 7. Add chopped green onion and sesame seeds to garnish. 8. Serve with Sesame-Soy Dipping Sauce. Enjoy!
Per Serving: Calories 346; Fat: 10.5g; Sodium 977mg; Carbs: 49.4g; Fiber 1g; Sugars: 5.1g; Protein 15.5g

Green Sauce

Prep time: 10 minutes | Cook Time: 2 minutes | Serves: 8

1-pound tomatillos, outer husks removed and cut into halves
2 small jalapeño peppers, seeded and chopped
1 small onion, peeled and diced
½ cup chopped fresh cilantro
1 teaspoon ground coriander
1 teaspoon sea salt
1½ cups water

1. Place the tomatillo halves in the inner pot and then pour water to cover. 2. Close the lid and turn the steam release handle to Sealing position. 3. Set the Instant Pot on Pressure Cook at High and adjust time to 2 minutes. 4. When cooked, naturally release the pressure about 20 minutes. Turn off the heat and carefully open the lid. 5. Drain excess water off the tomatillos and transfer to a food processor. Add onion, cilantro, salt, water, coriander, and jalapeno and pulse to combine well. 6. Chill in a serving dish in the refrigerator for at least 2 hours.
Per Serving: Calories: 22; Fat: 0.6g; Sodium 240mg; Carbs: 4.2g; Fiber 1g; Sugars: 0.4g; Protein 0.7g

Deviled Eggs

Prep time: 5 minutes | Cook Time: 16 minutes | Serves: 1

1 cup water
2 large eggs
1 tablespoon mayonnaise
⅛ teaspoon yellow mustard
1/16 teaspoon salt
1/16 teaspoon ground black pepper
1/16 teaspoon smoked paprika

1. In the inner pot, pour water and place the trivet at the bottom. Place the eggs onto the trivet. 2. Close the lid and turn the steam release handle to Sealing. 3. Set the Instant Pot on Pressure Cook at High and adjust time to 2 minutes. 4. When cooked, naturally release pressure about 14 minutes and then remove the lid carefully. 5. Place the eggs in an ice bath about 10 minutes. Peel and cut lengthwise in half, then remove the egg yolks in a small bowl and egg white halves in a small plate. 6. Break up egg yolks with a fork until crumbly. 7. Add in mayonnaise, salt, mustard, and pepper and mix well. 8. Stuff the egg white halves with the whisked egg yolks and sprinkle paprika on the top. 9. Serve in a serving plate and enjoy!
Per Serving: Calories 201; Fat: 14.9g; Sodium 399mg; Carbs: 4.4g;

Fiber 1g; Sugars: 1.7g; Protein 12.7g

Hearty Sausage Dip

Prep time: 10 minutes | Cook Time: 25 minutes | Serves: 4

2 ounces cream cheese, softened
3 tablespoons Rotel Diced Tomatoes and Green Chilies
½ cup cooked and crumbled
Italian sausage
3 tablespoons shredded Cheddar cheese, divided
1 cup water

1. Prepare an 8-ounce ramekin and grease. Set it aside. 2. Add tomatoes, chilies, 2 tablespoons Cheddar, sausage, and cream cheese in a small bowl and combine well. Then spoon into the greased ramekin and use foil to cover. 3. In the inner pot, pour water and place the trivet at the bottom. 4. Close the lid and turn the steam release handle to Sealing position. 5. Set the Instant Pot on Pressure Cook at High and adjust time to 20 minutes. 6. When cooked, release the pressure by turn the handle from Sealing to Venting and then carefully remove the lid, transfer the ramekin to an ovenproof plate. 7. Remove the foil from the dip and top with the remaining Cheddar. 8. Preheat your air fryer to high heat. 9. Then broil in the air fryer for 3 to 5 minutes or until brown. Serve and enjoy!
Per Serving: Calories: 122; Fat: 9.5g; Sodium 592mg; Carbs: 3.9g; Fiber 1g; Sugars: 2.4g; Protein 5.1g

Spicy Salsa

Prep time: 10 minutes | Cook Time: 20 minutes | Serves: 12

12 cups seeded diced tomatoes
6 ounces tomato paste
2 medium yellow onions, peeled and diced
6 small jalapeño peppers, seeded and minced
4 cloves garlic, peeled and
minced
¼ cup white vinegar
¼ cup lime juice
2 tablespoons granulated sugar
2 teaspoons salt
¼ cup chopped fresh cilantro

1. In the inner pot, add tomato paste, jalapeno, garlic, salt, sugar, lime juice, vinegar, onions, and tomatoes and stir well. 2. Close the lid and turn the steam release handle to Sealing. 3. Set the Instant Pot on Pressure Cook at High and adjust time to 20 minutes. 4. When cooked, quick-release the pressure and open the lid carefully. 5. Stir in cilantro and then turn off the heat. Cool the salsa to room temperature. 6. Transfer to a storage container and chill in the refrigerator overnight.
Per Serving: Calories: 32; Fat: 0.2g; Sodium 587mg; Carbs: 7.4g; Fiber 1g; Sugars: 4.8g; Protein 1g

Traditional Applesauce

Prep time: 5 minutes | Cook Time: 10 minutes | Serves: 4

1 medium Granny Smith apple, peeled, cored, and sliced
1 medium honey-crisp apple, peeled, cored, and sliced
½ tablespoon lemon juice
¼ teaspoon ground cinnamon
½ cup water
1 tablespoon sugar

1. In the inner pot, add lemon juice, cinnamon, water, and apples. 2. Close the lid and turn the steam release handle to Sealing position. 3. Set the Instant Pot on Pressure Cook at High and adjust time to 10 minutes. 4. When cooked, naturally release the pressure about 15 minutes and then remove the lid carefully. 5. Stir in applesauce to combine well and then taste to season with 1 tablespoon of sugar or more as you like. 6. Serve in a bowl and enjoy!
Per Serving: Calories: 61; Fat: 0.1g; Sodium 2mg; Carbs: 16.4g; Fiber 1g; Sugars: 13.1g; Protein 0.2g

Spiced Vanilla-Pear Sauce

Prep time: 5 minutes | Cook Time: 10 minutes | Serves: 6

3 medium ripe pears, peeled, cored, and diced
⅛ teaspoon ground cinnamon
1/16 teaspoon ground ginger
1/16 teaspoon ground cloves
1/16 teaspoon ground nutmeg
⅓ cup apple juice
½ teaspoon vanilla extract

1. Combine pears, gingers, nutmeg, cloves, apple juice, and cinnamon in the inner pot. 2. Close the lid and turn the steam release handle to Sealing position. 3. Set the Instant Pot on Pressure Cook at High and adjust time to 10 minutes. 4. When cooked, release the pressure by turn the handle from Sealing to Venting and then remove the lid carefully. 5. Stir in the pear sauce with a whisk or potato masher until all the pears are broken up and smooth. 6. Add vanilla and stir well. Then transfer to a bowl. 7. Serve warm or chill in the refrigerator until ready to serve.
Per Serving: Calories 56; Fat: 0.2g; Sodium 2mg; Carbs: 14.3g; Fiber 1g; Sugars: 9.5g; Protein 0.3g

Lemony Shrimp with Cocktail Sauce

Prep time: 5 minutes | Cook Time: 10 minutes | Serves: 4

1 cup water
½ teaspoon salt
2 cups frozen peeled and deveined
jumbo shrimp
2 tablespoons cocktail sauce
½ medium lemon

1. Add salt, shrimp, and water in the inner pot. 2. Close the lid and turn the steam release handle to Sealing position. 3. Set the Instant Pot on Pressure Cook at High and adjust time to 10 minutes. 4. When cooked, release the pressure by turning the handle from Sealing to Venting and then remove the lid carefully. 5. Drain the shrimp and soak in icy water 5 minutes. 6. Serve with the cocktail sauce and lemon. Enjoy!
Per Serving: Calories 113; Fat: 1.1g; Sodium 929mg; Carbs: 9.5g; Fiber 1g; Sugars: 6.5g; Protein 15g

Garlic White Bean Hummus

Prep time: 10 minutes | Cook Time: 30 minutes | Serves: 10

⅔ cup dried white beans, rinsed and drained
3 cloves garlic, peeled and crushed
¼ cup olive oil
1 tablespoon lemon juice
½ teaspoon salt

1. In the inner pot, stir in beans and garlic. Pour cold water until the mixture is covered. 2. Close the lid and turn the steam release handle to Sealing position. 3. Set the Instant Pot on Pressure Cook at High and adjust time to 30 minutes. 4. When cooked, naturally release about 20 minutes. Turn off the heat and carefully open the lid. 5. Drain the beans and transfer to a food processor and add in lemon juice, salt, and oil. Process until it is smooth with little chunks. 6. Transfer into a storage container and chill in the refrigerator for at least 4 hours and up to 7 days. 7. Serve and enjoy!
Per Serving: Calories 90; Fat: 5.2g; Sodium 119mg; Carbs: 8.5g; Fiber 1g; Sugars: 0.3g; Protein 3.2g

Savory Cocktail Sausages

Prep time: 3 minutes | Cook Time: 15 minutes | Serves: 4

1 cup water
½ (14-ounce) package cocktail sausages
2 tablespoons barbecue sauce
¼ cup grape jelly

1. In the inner pot, pour water and place the trivet. 2. In a suitable cake pan, add the cocktail sausages, barbecue sauce, and the grape jelly and then use foil sheet to cover. Transfer onto the trivet. 3. Close the lid and turn the steam release handle to Sealing. 4. Set the Instant Pot on Pressure Cook at High and adjust time to 15 minutes. 5. When cooked, release the pressure by turning the handle from Sealing to Venting and then remove the lid carefully. 6. Transfer the sausages to a serving plate. Enjoy!
Per Serving: Calories 88; Fat: 1.4g; Sodium 129mg; Carbs: 17.6g; Fiber 1g; Sugars: 11.7g; Protein 1g

Deviled Eggs with Jalapeno

Prep time: 5 minutes | Cook Time: 16 minutes | Serves: 1

1 cup water
2 large eggs
1 tablespoon ranch dressing
1/16 teaspoon salt
1/16 teaspoon ground black pepper
4 slices pickled jalapeño pepper
4 small potato chips

1. In the inner pot, pour the water and place the trivet. 2. Close the lid and turn the steam release handle to Sealing position. 3. Set the Instant Pot on Pressure Cook at High and adjust time to 2 minutes. 4. When cooked, naturally release the pressure for 14 minutes and then remove the lid carefully. 5. Soak the eggs in an ice bath about 10 minutes. Peel and cut lengthwise half. Remove the yolks to a small bowl and the egg white halves on a small plate. 6. Mash the egg yolks with a fork until crumbly. Then add ranch, pepper, and salt, and mix well until smooth. 7. Stuff the egg white halves with egg yolk mixture. Sprinkle a jalapeno slice and potato chip on the top. 8. Serve in a serving plate.
Per Serving: Calories 326; Fat: 21.4g; Sodium 1998mg; Carbs: 19.9g; Fiber 3.6g; Sugars: 3.2g; Protein 15.5g

Bacon-Chive Deviled Eggs

Prep time: 5 minutes | Cook Time: 16 minutes | Serves: 2

1 cup water
2 large eggs
1 tablespoon mayonnaise
1 teaspoon bacon bits
⅛ teaspoon dried chives
1/16 teaspoon salt
1/16 teaspoon ground black pepper

1. In the inner pot, pour the water and place the trivet. 2. Close the lid and turn the steam release handle to Sealing position. 3. Set the Instant Pot on Pressure Cook at High and adjust time to 2 minutes. 4. When cooked, naturally release the pressure for 14 minutes and then remove the lid carefully. 5. Soak the eggs in an ice bath about 10 minutes. Peel and cut lengthwise half. Remove the yolks to a small bowl and the egg white halves on a small plate. 6. Mash the egg yolks with a fork until crumbly. Then add bacon bits, salt, chives, pepper, and mayonnaise and mix well until smooth. 7. Stuff the egg white halves with egg yolk mixture. 8. Serve in a serving plate.
Per Serving: Calories 152; Fat: 11.4g; Sodium 419mg; Carbs: 2.3g; Fiber 1g; Sugars: 0.9g; Protein 9.9g

Parmesan Stuffed Artichoke

Prep time: 5 minutes | Cook Time: 45 minutes | Serves: 6

1 cup water
1 large (over 1-pound) artichoke
2 tablespoons panko bread crumbs
½ teaspoon Italian seasoning
½ teaspoon minced garlic
2 tablespoons grated Parmesan cheese
1 tablespoon lemon juice
3 tablespoons butter, melted, divided

1. In the inner pot, pour water and place the trivet. 2. Remove the bottom stem off the artichoke and then discard the ¼ top off the artichoke. Trim the tips of the outer leaves. 3. Then spread the leaves to leave gaps among leaves. 4. Add the bread crumbs, Parmesan, Italian seasoning, and garlic in a small bowl and toss well. 5. Then sprinkle over the artichoke and press down to spread evenly among the leaves. Transfer the artichoke onto the trivet. 6. Close the lid and turn the steam release handle to Sealing. 7. Set the Instant Pot on Pressure Cook at High and adjust time to 45 minutes. 8. When cooked, release the handle by turning the handle from Sealing to Venting and then remove the lid carefully. 9. Transfer the artichoke onto a serving plate. Pour lemon juice and 1 tablespoon of butter on the top. Leave the 2 tablespoons of butter for dipping. 10. Serve and enjoy!
Per Serving: Calories 102; Fat: 8.1g; Sodium 166mg; Carbs: 4.4g; Fiber 1g; Sugars: 0.4g; Protein 4.1g

Savory Chili-Cheese Dip

Prep time: 10 minutes | Cook Time: 25 minutes | Serves: 4

3 ounces cream cheese, softened
½ cup chili (any kind)
4 tablespoons shredded Cheddar
cheese, divided
1 cup water

1. Prepare an 8-ounce ramekin and grease. Set it aside. 2. Add chili, 3 tablespoons of Cheddar, and cream cheese in a small bowl and combine well. Then use a spoon to transfer the mixture into the greased ramekin and use a piece of foil to cover. 3. In the inner pot, pour water and place the trivet at the bottom. Transfer ramekin onto the trivet. 4. Close the lid and turn the steam release handle to Sealing position. 5. Set the Instant Pot on Pressure Cook at High and adjust time to 20 minutes. 6. When cooked, quick-release the pressure and then remove the lid carefully. Transfer the ramekin onto an ovenproof plate. 7. Preheat your air fryer to high heat. 8. Remove the foil from the dip and then top with the remaining Cheddar cheese. 9. Broil in the air fryer until browned about 3 to 5 minutes. 10. Serve and enjoy!
Per Serving: Calories 138; Fat: 11.5g; Sodium 276mg; Carbs: 4.5g; Fiber 1g; Sugars: 0.5g; Protein 5.2g

Black Bean Dip with Bacon

Prep time: 10 minutes | Cook Time: 35 minutes | Serves: 16

1 tablespoon olive oil
2 slices bacon, finely diced
1 small onion, peeled and diced
3 cloves garlic, peeled and minced
1 cup low-sodium chicken broth
1 cup dried black beans, soaked overnight and drained
1 (14.5-ounce) can diced

tomatoes, including juice
1 small jalapeño pepper, seeded and minced
1 teaspoon ground cumin
½ teaspoon smoked paprika
1 tablespoon lime juice
½ teaspoon dried oregano
¼ cup minced fresh cilantro
¼ teaspoon sea salt

1. Set the Instant Pot on Sauté at More and heat the oil. 2. Add onion and bacon and cook until the onion is just transparent about 5 minutes. 3. Then add garlic and cook about 30 seconds or until fragrant. 4. Pour broth and scrape all the browned bits off the pot. 5. Place tomatoes, jalapeno, paprika, cumin cilantro, salt, oregano, beans, and lime juice. Turn off the heat. 6. Close the lid and turn the steam release handle to Sealing position. 7. Set the Instant Pot on Bean at More and adjust time to 30 minutes. 8. When cooked, naturally release the pressure about 10 minutes and quick-release the rest pressure. Turn off the heat and carefully open the lid. 9. Blend the ingredients in a blender until smooth. 10. Serve and enjoy!
Per Serving: Calories 71; Fat: 2.2g; Sodium 93mg; Carbs: 9.4g; Fiber 1g; Sugars: 1.2g; Protein 4g

Greek Eggplant Dip

Prep time: 10 minutes | Cook Time: 3 minutes | Serves: 8

1 cup water
1 large eggplant, peeled and chopped
1 clove garlic, peeled
½ teaspoon salt

1 tablespoon red wine vinegar
½ cup extra-virgin olive oil
2 tablespoons minced fresh parsley

1. In the inner pot, pour water and place the rack. Place the steamer basket on the rack. 2. Spread eggplant onto the steamer basket. 3. Close the lid and set the steam release handle to Sealing position. 4. Set the Instant Pot on Pressure Cook at High and adjust time to 3 minutes. 5. When cooked, quick-release the pressure and turn off the heat. Open the lid carefully and transfer the eggplant to a food processor. 6. Add salt, garlic, and vinegar and pulse until smooth. 7. Add oil and stir until well incorporated. 8. Sprinkle with the chopped parsley. 9. Serve and enjoy!
Per Serving: Calories 124; Fat: 12.7g; Sodium 150mg; Carbs: 3.6g; Fiber 1g; Sugars: 1.7g; Protein 0.6g

Cheddar Jalapeño Popper Dip

Prep time: 10 minutes | Cook Time: 20 minutes | Serves: 4

2 ounces cream cheese, softened
4 tablespoons shredded Cheddar cheese, divided
2 tablespoons minced pickled jalapeño peppers
1 tablespoon sour cream

4 teaspoons bacon bits
1/16 teaspoon salt
1/16 teaspoon garlic powder
3 slices pickled jalapeño peppers
1 cup water

1. Prepare an 8-ounce ramekin and grease. Set aside. 2. Add 3 tablespoons Cheddar, sour cream, bacon bits, garlic powder, salt, and cream cheese in a small bowl. Then spoon into the greased ramekin and sprinkle the jalapeno slices on the top and use a piece of foil to cover. 3. In the inner pot, pour water and place the trivet. Transfer the ramekin onto the trivet. 4. Close the lid and turn the steam release handle to Sealing. 5. Set the Instant Pot on Pressure Cook at High and adjust time to 15 minutes. 6. When cooked, release the pressure by turn the handle from Sealing to Venting and then carefully remove the ramekin onto an ovenproof plate. 7. Preheat your air fryer to a high heat. 8. Uncover the foil and top the dip with the remaining Cheddar. 9. Broil in the air fryer about 3 to 5 minutes. Serve and enjoy!
Per Serving: Calories 188; Fat: 15.9g; Sodium 619mg; Carbs: 1.1g; Fiber 1g; Sugars: 0.2g; Protein 10g

Plant-Based Hummus

Prep time: 10 minutes | Cook Time: 30 minutes | Serves: 6

1 cup dried chickpeas
4 cups water
1 tablespoon plus ¼ cup extra-virgin olive oil, divided
⅓ cup tahini
1½ teaspoons ground cumin

¾ teaspoon salt
½ teaspoon ground black pepper
½ teaspoon ground coriander
⅓ cup lemon juice
1 teaspoon minced garlic

1. In the inner pot, add water, chickpeas, and 1 tablespoon of oil. 2. Close the lid and turn the steam release handle to Sealing. 3. Set the Instant Pot on Pressure Cook at High and then adjust time to 30 minutes. 4. When cooked, quick-release the pressure and then carefully open the lid. Turn off heat. Reserve the cooking liquid. 5. In a food processor, add the remaining oil, cumin, tahini, pepper, salt, garlic, lemon juice, coriander, and chickpeas and process until creamy. 6. If hummus is too thick, add reserved cooking liquid 1 tablespoon at a time until it reaches desired consistency. 7. Serve at room temperature.
Per Serving: Calories 212; Fat: 9.7g; Sodium 325mg; Carbs: 24.4g; Fiber 1g; Sugars: 4g; Protein 9.2g

Garlic Hummus with Tahini

Prep time: 10 minutes | Cook Time: 30 minutes | Serves: 8

1 cup dried chickpeas
4 cups water
1 tablespoon plus ¼ cup extra-virgin olive oil, divided
⅓ cup tahini
1 teaspoon ground cumin
½ teaspoon onion powder

¾ teaspoon salt
½ teaspoon ground black pepper
⅓ cup lemon juice
3 tablespoons mashed roasted garlic
2 tablespoons chopped fresh parsley

1. In the inner pot, add water, 1 tablespoon of oil, and chickpea. 2. Close the lid and turn the steam release handle to Sealing. 3. Set the Instant Pot on Pressure Cook at High and adjust time to 30 minutes. 4. When cooked, quick-release the pressure and then turn off the heat. Open the lid and drain. Reserve the cooking liquid. 5. In a food processor, add the remaining ¼ cup oil, cumin, tahini, salt, onion powder, lemon juice, roasted garlic, pepper, and the chickpeas and process until creamy. 6. If hummus is too thick, add reserved cooking liquid 1 tablespoon at a time until it reaches desired consistency. 7. Then sprinkle the chopped parsley on the top. Serve and enjoy!
Per Serving: Calories 155; Fat: 7g; Sodium 241mg; Carbs: 17.9g; Fiber 1g; Sugars: 3g; Protein 6.7g

Tasty Buffalo Chicken Dip

Prep time: 8 minutes | Cook Time: 20 minutes | Serves: 6

1 (8-ounce) boneless, skinless chicken breast	2 ounces cream cheese, softened
1 cup water	2 tablespoons buffalo sauce
1/16 teaspoon salt	1 teaspoon dry ranch seasoning
1/16 teaspoon ground black pepper	1 ½ tablespoons shredded Cheddar cheese
	1 tablespoon chopped green onion

1. Add chicken and water in the inner pot and then add salt and pepper to season. 2. Close the lid and turn the steam release handle to Sealing position. 3. Set the Instant Pot on Pressure Cook at High and adjust time to 20 minutes. 4. When cooked, naturally release the pressure about 10 minutes and then carefully remove the lid. 5. Transfer the chicken to a small bowl and then pour in the 1 tablespoon cooking liquid. Shred the chicken with 2 forks. 6. Mix in the remaining ingredients thoroughly. 7. Serve in a serving bowl and enjoy!
Per Serving: Calories 88; Fat: 4.8g; Sodium 403mg; Carbs: 1g; Fiber 1g; Sugars: 0.1g; Protein 9.2g

Tasty Sun-Dried Tomato Cheesecake

Prep time: 10 minutes | Cook Time: 20 minutes | Serves: 12

3 tablespoons unsalted butter, melted	3 large eggs
⅓ cup bread crumbs	3 tablespoons all-purpose flour
½ cup sun-dried tomatoes in oil, drained, leaving 1 tablespoon oil	2 (8-ounce) packages cream cheese
6 cloves garlic, peeled and minced	¾ cup sour cream, divided
1 teaspoon dried oregano	½ cup diced scallions
	2 cups hot water

1. Brush butter inside ta suitable spring-form pan. Then arrange bread crumbs at the bottom and sides of the pan. 2. Put the pan in the center of a piece of plastic wrap and then form and crimp an equal-sized aluminum foil to seal. 3. In a food processor, add tomatoes, garlic, oregano, flour, eggs, cream cheese, and ¼ cup sour cream. Puree until smooth. Add scallions and stir well. 4. Pour into prepared pan. Cover with foil; crimp to seal. 5. In the inner pot, place a rack and then pour in water. 6. Fold a long piece of foil in half lengthwise and lay over rack to form a sling. Place pan in the pot so it rests on the sling. 7. Close the lid and then turn the steam release handle to Sealing position. 8. Set the Instant Pot on Pressure Cook at High and adjust time to 20 minutes. 9. When cooked, naturally release the pressure about 10 minutes and then quick-release the remaining pressure. Then open the lid carefully and allow it to cool until all the steam has dissipated. 10. Lift the pan from pot with sling. Remove foil lid and use a paper towel to dab away any accumulated moisture. Cool cheesecake completely. 11. Top the cheesecake with the remaining sour cream. Serve at room temperature or chill at least 4 hours in the refrigerator.
Per Serving: Calories 229; Fat: 20.5g; Sodium 182mg; Carbs: 6.3g; Fiber 1g; Sugars: 0.5g; Protein 5.7g

Mayonnaise Spinach-Artichoke Dip

Prep time: 10 minutes | Cook Time: 25 minutes | Serves: 6

4 ounces cream cheese, softened	cheese
2 tablespoons mayonnaise	2 tablespoons shredded Parmesan cheese, divided
2 tablespoons sautéed spinach	⅛ teaspoon salt
2 tablespoons finely minced artichoke hearts	⅛ teaspoon crushed red pepper flakes
1 tablespoon chopped green chilies	1 cup water
½ cup shredded mozzarella	

1. Prepare an 8-ounce ramekin and grease inside. Set aside. 2. Add cream cheese, mayonnaise, spinach, artichokes, chilies, mozzarella, 1 tablespoon Parmesan, salt, and red pepper flakes in a small bowl. 3. Spoon the mixture into prepared the greased ramekin and use a piece of foil to cover. 4. In the inner pot, pour water and place the trivet at the bottom. Then transfer the greased ramekin onto the trivet. 5. Close the lid and turn the steam release handle to Sealing position. 6. Set the Instant Pot on Pressure Cook at High and adjust time to 20 minutes. 7. When cooked, release the pressure by turning the handle from Sealing to Venting and then remove the ramekin to an oven-proof plate. 8. Preheat your air fryer to high heat. 9. Remove the foil from the dip and top with the remaining Parmesan. 10. Broil until the top is browned about 3 to 5 minutes. Serve and enjoy!
Per Serving: Calories 143; Fat: 10.7g; Sodium 233mg; Carbs: 6.8g; Fiber 1g; Sugars: 0.9g; Protein 6.6g

White Bean Soup with Dandelion

Prep time: 10 minutes | Cook Time: 30 minutes | Serves: 6

1 tablespoon olive oil	2 teaspoons fresh thyme leaves
2 medium onions, peeled and chopped	1 teaspoon salt
3 medium carrots, peeled and chopped	½ teaspoon ground black pepper
3 stalks celery, chopped	8 cups vegetable stock
4 cloves garlic, peeled and minced	2 cups fresh dandelion greens, steamed until wilted
1 bay leaf	1 (15-ounce) can cannellini beans, drained and rinsed
¼ cup chopped fresh parsley	¼ cup grated Parmesan cheese

1. Set the Instant Pot on Sauté at Normal and add oil to heat. 2. Cook onion, celery, carrots, and garlic in the inner pot until soften. Then add parsley, thyme, pepper, salt, and bay leaf and cook until fragrant about 5 minutes. Turn off the heat. 3. Stir in stock. Close the lid and turn the steam release handle to Sealing. 4. Set the Instant Pot on Soup at High and adjust time to 20 minutes. 5. When cooked, quick-release the pressure and then turn off the heat. 6. Carefully open the lid and mix in beans and dandelion greens. 7. Close the lid and turn the steam release handle to Sealing position. 8. Set the Instant Pot on Pressure Cook at High and adjust time to 1 minute. 9. When cooked, quick-release the pressure and then turn off the heat. 10. Carefully open the lid and remove. Give away bay leaf. 11. Sprinkle cheese on the top to serve.
Per Serving: Calories 233; Fat: 2.7g; Sodium 396mg; Carbs: 40g; Sugars: 4.4g; Protein 14.3g

Savory Deviled Eggs

Prep time: 10 minutes | Cook Time: 18 minutes | Serves: 6

6 large eggs	2 tablespoons chopped fresh dill
1 cup water	1 tablespoon chopped capers
2 tablespoons olive oil mayonnaise	1 tablespoon minced Kalamata olives
½ teaspoon Dijon mustard	¼ teaspoon ground black pepper

1. Prepare a large bowl of ice water. In the inner pot, place a rack at the bottom. 2. Place the eggs on the rack and then pour water. 3. Close the lid and turn the steam release handle to Sealing position. 4. Set the Instant Pot on Pressure Cook at High and adjust time to 8 minutes. 5. When cooked, naturally release the pressure about 10 minutes and then quick-release the remaining pressure. 6. Turn off the heat and carefully open the lid. Remove eggs into ice water. Let it stand for 10 minutes. Remove shells. 7. Slice the eggs into halves and remove the yolks. In a medium bowl, place the yolks. Mash the yolks until crumbled and add mayonnaise and mustard. 8. Fold in dill, olives, capers, and pepper. 9. Fill egg whites with yolk mixture, then chill for at least 2 hours before serving.
Per Serving: Calories 77; Fat: 5.2g; Sodium 133mg; Carbs: 1.2g; Fiber 1g; Sugars: 0.4g; Protein 6.6g

Simple Hard-Boiled Eggs

Prep time: 1 minutes | Cook Time: 15 minutes | Serves: 1

1 cup water	⅛ teaspoon salt
2 large eggs	

1. In the inner pot, pour water and place the trivet at the bottom. 2. Add the eggs onto the trivet. 3. Close the lid and turn the steam release handle to Sealing position. 4. Set the Instant Pot on Pressure Cook at High and adjust time to 2 minutes. 5. When cooked, naturally release the pressure and then remove the lid carefully. 6. Soak the eggs in an ice bath about 10 minutes. Peel the eggs and transfer into a serving bowl. 7. Add salt to season. Serve and enjoy!
Per Serving: Calories 143; Fat: 9.9g; Sodium 147mg; Carbs: 0.8g; Fiber 1g; Sugars: 0.8g; Protein 12.6g

Herbed Artichokes

Prep time: 10 minutes | Cook Time: 10 minutes | Serves: 6

3 medium artichokes with stems cut off
1 medium lemon, halved
1 cup water
¼ cup lemon juice
⅓ cup extra-virgin olive oil
1 clove garlic, peeled and minced
¼ teaspoon salt
1 teaspoon chopped fresh oregano
1 teaspoon chopped fresh rosemary
1 teaspoon chopped fresh flat-leaf parsley
1 teaspoon fresh thyme leaves
Clean and rinse completely the artichokes.

1. Slice off top ⅓ of artichoke and discard any tough outer leaves. Rub lemon over the cut surfaces. 2. In the inner pot, pour together lemon juice and water and place a rack. 3. Arrange artichokes upside down on the rack. 4. Close the lid and turn the steam release handle to Sealing position. 5. Set the Instant Pot on Pressure Cook at High and adjust time to 10 minutes. 6. When cooked, naturally release the pressure about 20 minutes. 7. Turn off the heat and carefully open the lid. Transfer the artichoke onto a cutting board and slice in half. Transfer onto a serving plate. 8. Combine garlic, oregano, parsley, thyme, rosemary, salt, and oil in a small bowl. Add half the mixture over the artichokes. 9. Serve with the remaining mixture as a dipping.
Per Serving: Calories 153; Fat: 11.5g; Sodium 206mg; Carbs: 12.2g; Fiber 1g; Sugars: 1.4g; Protein 3.8g

Flavorful Black-Eyed Pea "Caviar"

Prep time: 10 minutes | Cook Time: 30 minutes | Serves: 10

1 cup dried black-eyed peas
4 cups water
1-pound cooked corn kernels
½ medium red onion, peeled and diced
½ medium green bell pepper, seeded and diced
2 tablespoons minced pickled jalapeño pepper
1 medium tomato, diced
2 tablespoons chopped fresh cilantro
¼ cup red wine vinegar
2 tablespoons extra-virgin olive oil
1 teaspoon salt
½ teaspoon ground black pepper
½ teaspoon ground cumin

1. In the inner pot, pour water and add black-eyed peas. 2. Close the lid and turn the stream release handle to Sealing. 3. Set the Instant Pot on Pressure Cook at High and adjust time to 30 minutes. 4. When cooked, naturally release the pressure about 25 minutes and then open the lid carefully. 5. Drain the peas and place into a large mixing bowl. 6. Stir in all the remaining ingredients in the bowl until well combined. 7. Cover and chill in the refrigerator about 2 hours before serving.
Per Serving: Calories 64; Fat: 3.3g; Sodium 266mg; Carbs: 7.8g; Fiber 1g; Sugars: 1.4g; Protein 2g

Herbed White Bean Dip

Prep time: 10 minutes | Cook Time: 30 minutes | Serves: 16

1 cup dried white beans, rinsed and drained
3 cloves garlic, peeled and crushed
8 cups water
¼ cup extra-virgin olive oil
¼ cup chopped fresh flat-leaf parsley
1 tablespoon chopped fresh
oregano
1 tablespoon chopped fresh tarragon
1 teaspoon chopped fresh thyme leaves
1 teaspoon grated lemon zest
¼ teaspoon salt
¼ teaspoon ground black pepper

1. In the inner pot, add garlic and beans and stir well. 2. Then pour water and place the trivet in the inner pot. 3. Set the Instant Pot on Pressure Cook at High and adjust time to 30 minutes. 4. When cooked, naturally release the pressure about 20 minutes. Turn off the heat and open the lid carefully. Drain the beans and transfer the beans and garlic to a food processor. 5. Mix in pepper, parsley, tarragon, thyme, salt, lemon zest, oregano, and thyme. Pulse 3 to 5 times. 6. Store in a container and chill in a refrigerator for 4 hours or overnight. 7. Serve and enjoy!

Per Serving: Calories 72; Fat: 3.3g; Sodium 41mg; Carbs: 8.2g; Fiber 1g; Sugars: 0.3g; Protein 3.1g

Marinated Balsamic Mushrooms and Pearl Onions

Prep time: 10 minutes | Cook Time: 4 minutes | Serves: 10

3 pounds button mushrooms, trimmed
1 (15-ounce) bag frozen pearl onions, thawed
3 cloves garlic, peeled and minced
1 cup vegetable broth
¼ cup balsamic vinegar
¼ cup red wine
2 tablespoons olive oil
2 sprigs fresh thyme
½ teaspoon ground black pepper
¼ teaspoon crushed red pepper flakes

1. In the inner pot, add all the ingredients and mix well. 2. Close the lid and turn the steam release handle to Sealing. 3. Set the Instant Pot on Pressure Cook at High and adjust time to 4 minutes. 4. When cooked, quick-release the pressure and carefully open the lid. 5. Serve on a bowl and enjoy!
Per Serving: Calories 65; Fat: 3.3g; Sodium 85mg; Carbs: 5.2g; Fiber 1g; Sugars: 2.5g; Protein 4.8g

Greek Egg Dish

Prep time: 10 minutes | Cook Time: 8 minutes | Serves: 4

½ cup crumbled feta cheese
¼ cup bread crumbs
1 medium onion, peeled and minced
4 tablespoons all-purpose flour
2 tablespoons minced fresh mint
½ teaspoon salt
½ teaspoon ground black pepper
1 tablespoon dried thyme
6 large eggs, beaten
1 cup water

1. Add bread crumbs, onion, mint, flour, pepper, salt, thyme, and cheese in a medium bowl and then whisk in the eggs. 2. Spritz nonstick cooking spray over a suitable round baking dish. Then pour the egg mixture into dish. 3. In the inner pot, pour water and place rack at the bottom. 4. Fold a long piece of foil in half lengthwise. Lay foil over rack to form a sling and top with dish. Cover loosely with foil. 5. Close the lid and turn the steam release handle to Sealing position. 6. Set the Instant Pot on Pressure Cook at High and adjust time to 8 minutes. 7. When cooked, quick-release the pressure and then open the lid carefully. Let it stand for 5 minutes. 8. Serve and enjoy!
Per Serving: Calories 227; Fat: 12g; Sodium 659mg; Carbs: 15.6g; Sugars: 3g; Protein 14.3g

Creamy Corn Dip

Prep time: 10 minutes | Cook Time: 20 minutes | Serves: 6

2 ounces cream cheese, softened
3 tablespoons shredded Cheddar cheese
1 tablespoon minced pickled jalapeño peppers
½ cup corn
1 tablespoon bacon bits
1/16 teaspoon salt
1/16 teaspoon ground black pepper
1 cup water
1 tablespoon shredded Parmesan cheese

1. Lightly grease an 8-ounce ramekin and set it aside. 2. Add Cheddar, corn, salt, bacon bits, pepper, cream cheese, and jalapeños in a small bowl. Then use a spoon to transfer the mixture into the greased ramekin and use foil to cover. 3. In the inner pot, pour water and place the trivet. Transfer the ramekin onto the trivet. 4. Close the lid and turn the steam release handle to Sealing position. 5. Set the Instant Pot on Pressure Cook at High and adjust time to 15 minutes. 6. When cooked, release the pressure by turning the handle from Sealing to Venting and then remove the lid carefully. 7. Transfer the ramekin onto an oven-proof plate. 8. Preheat your air fryer to high heat. 9. Remove the foil from the dip and then top with Parmesan. 10. Broil in the air fryer until brown about 3 to 5 minutes. 11. Serve and enjoy!
Per Serving: Calories 91; Fat: 7g; Sodium 211mg; Carbs: 3g; Fiber 1g; Sugars: 0.5g; Protein 4.7g

Smoky Roasted Red Pepper Hummus

Prep time: 10 minutes | Cook Time: 30 minutes | Serves: 12

1 cup dried chickpeas
4 cups water
1 tablespoon plus ¼ cup extra-virgin olive oil, divided
½ cup chopped roasted red pepper, divided
⅓ cup tahini

1 teaspoon ground cumin
¾ teaspoon salt
½ teaspoon ground black pepper
¼ teaspoon smoked paprika
⅓ cup lemon juice
½ teaspoon minced garlic

1. In the inner pot, add water, 1 tablespoon of oil, and chickpeas. 2. Close the lid and turn the steam release handle to Sealing position. 3. Set the Instant Pot on Pressure Cook at High and adjust time to 30 minutes. 4. When cooked, quick-release the pressure. Turn off the heat and open the lid carefully. 5. Drain and reserve the cooking liquid. 6. In a food processor, add ⅓ cup roasted red pepper, cumin, tahini, paprika, lemon juice, salt, garlic, the remaining oil, black pepper, and chickpeas and process until creamy. 7. If hummus is too thick, add reserved cooking liquid 1 tablespoon at a time until it reaches desired consistency. 8. Sprinkle the reserve roasted red pepper on the top to garnish. Serve and enjoy!
Per Serving: Calories 105; Fat: 4.7g; Sodium 181mg; Carbs: 12.3g; Fiber 1g; Sugars: 2.3g; Protein 4.5g

Herbed Chickpea, Parsley, and Dill Dip

Prep time: 10 minutes | Cook Time: 21 minutes | Serves: 12

8 cups 2 tablespoons water, divided
1 cup dried chickpeas
3 tablespoons olive oil, divided
2 garlic cloves, peeled and minced

2 tablespoons chopped fresh parsley
2 tablespoons chopped fresh dill
1 tablespoon lemon juice
¼ teaspoon salt

1. In the inner pot, pour 4 cups of water. 2. Close the lid and turn the steam release handle to Sealing position. 3. Set the Instant Pot on Pressure Cook at High and adjust time to 1 minute. 4. When cooked, quick-release the pressure and turn off the heat. Open the lid carefully. 5. Add water and the chickpeas to the pot. Soak for 1 hour. 6. Add 1 tablespoon of oil in the pot. Close the lid and then turn the steam release handle to Sealing position. 7. Set the Instant Pot on Pressure Cook at High and adjust time to 20 minutes. 8. When cooked, naturally release the pressure about 20 minutes. 9. Turn off the heat and carefully open the lid. Drain the beans and transfer to a blender. Add garlic, dill, lemon juice, the remaining water, and parsley and blend for about 30 seconds. 10. Add the remaining oil slowly and blend. Then add salt to season. 11. Serve and enjoy!
Per Serving: Calories 93; Fat: 4.5g; Sodium 56mg; Carbs: 10.6g; Fiber 1g; Sugars: 1.8g; Protein 3.4g

Fresh Tomato Chutney

Prep time: 10 minutes | Cook Time: 10 minutes | Serves: 12

4 pounds ripe tomatoes, peeled
1 (1") piece fresh ginger, peeled
3 cloves garlic, peeled and chopped
1¾ cups sugar
1 cup red wine vinegar
2 medium onions, peeled and diced
¼ cup golden raisins

¾ teaspoon ground cinnamon
½ teaspoon ground coriander
¼ teaspoon ground cloves
¼ teaspoon ground nutmeg
¼ teaspoon ground ginger
1 teaspoon chili powder
⅛ teaspoon paprika
1 tablespoon curry paste

1. In a blender, add tomatoes and fresh ginger to puree. 2. In the inner pot, pour the tomato mixture and then add the remaining ingredients. Stir well. 3. Close the lid and turn the steam release handle to Sealing position. 4. Set the Instant Pot on Pressure Cook at Low and adjust time to 10 minutes. 5. When cooked, naturally release the pressure about 25 minutes and then carefully release the pressure. Stir well. 6. Store in a storage container and chill in the refrigerator. Serve at room temperature or chilled.
Per Serving: Calories 262; Fat: 1.1g; Sodium 12mg; Carbs: 65.2g; Fiber 1g; Sugars: 60.8g; Protein 1.8g

Greek-style Garlic Dip

Prep time: 10 minutes | Cook Time: 10 minutes | Serves: 16

1-pound russet potatoes, peeled and quartered
3 cups plus ¼ cup water, divided
2 teaspoons salt, divided
8 cloves garlic, peeled and minced

¾ cup blanched almonds
½ cup extra-virgin olive oil
2 tablespoons lemon juice
2 tablespoons white wine vinegar
½ teaspoon ground black pepper

1. In the inner pot, add 3 cups of water, 1 teaspoon salt, and potatoes and stir well. 2. Close the lid and turn the steam release handle to Sealing position. 3. Set the Instant Pot on Pressure Cook at High and adjust time to 10 minutes. 4. Meanwhile, spread the remaining salt and garlic on a cutting board. Press the garlic and salt to make a paste with a side of a knife. 5. Transfer into a food processor and add in the olive oil and almonds. 6. Purée into a paste. Set aside. 7. When cooked, quick-release the pressure and then turn off the heat. Open the lid carefully. Drain the potatoes and then place in a medium bowl. 8. Mash the garlic mixture with a potato masher until smooth. 9. Add lemon juice, pepper, and vinegar and stir well. 10. Then Stir in ¼ cup water a little at a time until mixture is thin enough for dipping. 11. Serve and enjoy!
Per Serving: Calories 103; Fat: 8.6g; Sodium 293mg; Carbs: 6g; Fiber 1g; Sugars: 0.6g; Protein 1.6g

Avocado Pinto Bean Dip

Prep time: 10 minutes | Cook Time: 30 minutes | Serves: 16

1 cup dried pinto beans, soaked overnight and drained
4 cups water
4 tablespoons roughly chopped cilantro, divided
3 tablespoons extra-virgin olive oil
1 teaspoon ground cumin
1 clove garlic, peeled and minced
½ teaspoon salt

1 medium avocado, peeled, pitted, and diced
1 large ripe tomato, seeded and diced
1 small jalapeño pepper, seeded and minced
½ medium white onion, peeled and chopped
2 teaspoons lime juice

1. In the inner pot, add water, 2 tablespoons cilantro, and beans 2. Close the lid and turn the steam release handle to Sealing position. 3. Set the Instant Pot on Bean at High and adjust time to 30 minutes. 4. When cooked, naturally release the pressure about 20 minutes. Then carefully open the lid. 5. Drain off water from the beans and transfer to a medium bowl. Mash the beans until chunky. 6. Mix in oil, garlic, salt, and cumin. 7. In a separate bowl, add the remaining cilantro, avocado, tomato, jalapeno, lime juice, and onion and toss well. 8. Spoon topping over bean dip in a serving bowl. Serve and enjoy!
Per Serving: Calories 94; Fat: 5.3g; Sodium 79mg; Carbs: 9.5g; Fiber 1g; Sugars: 0.8g; Protein 3g

Kidney Bean Dip

Prep time: 10 minutes | Cook Time: 30 minutes | Serves: 16

1 cup dried kidney beans, soaked overnight and drained
4 cups water
3 cloves garlic, peeled and crushed
¼ cup roughly chopped cilantro,

divided
¼ cup extra-virgin olive oil
1 tablespoon lime juice
2 teaspoons grated lime zest
1 teaspoon ground cumin
½ teaspoon salt

1. In the inner pot, add water, 2 tablespoons cilantro, garlic, and beans. 2. Close the lid and turn the steam release handle to Sealing position. 3. Set the Instant Pot on Bean at Normal and adjust time to 30 minutes. 4. When cooked, naturally release the pressure about 20 minutes. Turn off the heat and then carefully open the lid. 5. Drain off the excess water from the beans and transfer to a medium bowl. Mash beans until chunky. 6. Stir in lime juice, lime zest, salt, cumin, and remaining 2 tablespoons of cilantro and combine well. 7. Serve and enjoy!
Per Serving: Calories 67; Fat: 3.3g; Sodium 77mg; Carbs: 7.3g; Fiber 1g; Sugars: 0.3g; Protein 2.7g

Luscious Baba Ghanoush

Prep time: 10 minutes | Cook Time: 6 minutes | Serves: 8

2 tablespoons extra-virgin olive oil, divided
1 large eggplant, peeled and diced
3 cloves garlic, peeled and minced
½ cup water
3 tablespoons chopped fresh flat-leaf parsley
½ teaspoon salt
¼ teaspoon smoked paprika
2 tablespoons lemon juice
2 tablespoons tahini

1. Set the Instant Pot on Sauté at Normal and heat 1 tablespoon of oil. 2. Cook eggplant until soft about 5 minutes. Add in garlic and cook about 30 seconds or until fragrant. 3. In the inner pot, pour water. Close the lid and turn the steam release handle to Sealing. 4. Set the Instant Pot on Pressure Cook at High and adjust time to 6 minutes. 5. When cooked, quick-release the pressure and turn off the heat. Open the lid carefully. 6. Strain the cooked eggplant and garlic and transfer into a food processor. Then add salt, smoked paprika, tahini, lemon juice, and parsley. Scrape off the browned bits from the blender. 7. Add the remaining oil and process until smooth. 8. Serve and enjoy!
Per Serving: Calories 70; Fat: 5.7g; Sodium 155mg; Carbs: 4.7g; Fiber 1g; Sugars: 1.9g; Protein 1.4g

Unique Pepperoni Pizza Dip

Prep time: 10 minutes | Cook Time: 20 minutes | Serves: 6

2 ounces cream cheese, softened
3 tablespoons shredded mozzarella cheese, divided
⅛ teaspoon garlic powder
⅛ teaspoon plus 1/16 teaspoon Italian seasoning, divided
⅛ teaspoon salt
3 tablespoons marinara sauce
1 tablespoon diced pepperoni
1 teaspoon shredded Parmesan cheese
1 cup water

1. Prepare an 8-ounce ramekin and grease. Set it aside. 2. Add salt, garlic powder, cream cheese, 2 tablespoons mozzarella, and ⅛ teaspoon Italian seasoning. Use a spoon to transfer onto the greased ramekin. 3. Sprinkle the remaining 1 tablespoon of mozzarella, Parmesan, peperoni, marinara, and the remaining 1/16 teaspoon Italian seasoning. Cover with foil. 4. In the inner pot, pour water and place the trivet at the bottom. Transfer the ramekin on the trivet. 5. Close the lid and turn the steam release handle to Sealing position. 6. Set the Instant Pot on Pressure Cook at High and adjust time to 15 minutes. 7. When cooked, release the pressure by turning the handle from Sealing to Venting and then carefully remove the lid. 8. Transfer the ramekin to an ovenproof plate. 9. Preheat your air fryer to high heat. Remove the foil from the dip and then broil in the air fryer until browned about 3 to 5 minutes. 10. Serve and enjoy!
Per Serving: Calories 301; Fat: 25.4g; Sodium 881mg; Carbs: 2g; Fiber 1g; Sugars: 0.7g; Protein 15.8g

Garlic Lentil Dip

Prep time: 10 minutes | Cook Time: 30 minutes | Serves: 16

2 tablespoons olive oil
½ medium yellow onion, peeled and diced
3 cloves garlic, peeled and minced
2 cups dried red lentils, rinsed
and drained
4 cups water
1 teaspoon salt
¼ teaspoon ground black pepper
2 tablespoons minced fresh flat-leaf parsley

1. Set the Instant Pot on Sauté at Normal and add oil in the inner pot. Cook the onion in the inner pot for about 2 to 3 minutes. Then add garlic and cook about 30 seconds. 2. Add in water, salt, and beans in the pot and stir well. 3. Close the lid and turn the steam release handle to Sealing position. 4. Set the Instant Pot on Bean at High and adjust time to 30 minutes. 5. When cooked, naturally release the pressure about 10 minutes and quick-release the remaining pressure. 6. In a food processor, add the lentil mixture and blend until smoke. 7. Add pepper and parsley. Serve and enjoy!
Per Serving: Calories 102; Fat: 2g; Sodium 151mg; Carbs: 15g; Fiber 1g; Sugars: 0.7g; Protein 6.3g

Unsweetened Applesauce

Prep time: 10 minutes | Cook time: 8 minutes | Serves: 6

6 apples (about 1½-pound)
¼ cup water
¼ teaspoon ground cinnamon

1. Peel and core the apples. Cut each apple into roughly eight large chunks. 2. Combine the apples, water, and cinnamon in the Inner Pot. 3. Select Pressure Cook mode, and then press the "Pressure Cook" button again to select "Less" time option. 4. Use the "-" key to set the cooking time to 8 minutes. 5. Press the Pressure Level button to adjust the pressure to "High Pressure." 6. Once the cooking cycle is completed, allow the steam to release naturally for 10 minutes, then turn the steam release handle to the Venting position. 7. Gently mash the apples into applesauce. 8. Serve warm or refrigerate in an airtight container for up to 10 days.
Per Serving: Calories 95; Fat 0.31g; Sodium 2mg; Carbs 25.23g; Fiber 4.4g; Sugar 18.91g; Protein 0.48g

Cauliflower Hummus

Prep time: 15 minutes | Cook time: 15 minutes | Serves: 10

1 tablespoon avocado oil
1 small yellow onion, chopped
3 cloves garlic, minced
1 small head cauliflower, cut into florets
¾ cup water
½ teaspoon salt
Juice from 1 large lemon
1 (15-ounce) can cooked chickpeas
¼ cup tahini
1 teaspoon ground cumin

1. Select Sauté mode and press the "Sauté" button again to select "Normal" setting. 2. Add the oil to the Inner Pot, and heat it for 1 minute. 3. Add the onion, and sauté for 7 minutes until softened. 4. Add the garlic, and sauté for 30 seconds. 5. Press the Cancel button, and add the cauliflower and water to the pot. 6. Select Pressure Cook mode, and then press the "Pressure Cook" button again to select "Less" time option. 7. Use the "+/-" keys on the control panel to set the cooking time to 5 minutes. 8. Press the Pressure Level button to adjust the pressure to "Low Pressure." 9. Once the cooking cycle is completed, quickly and carefully turn the steam release handle from Sealing position to the Venting position. 10. Transfer the food to a large food processor, leaving the liquid in the pot. 11. Add the salt, lemon juice, chickpeas, tahini, and cumin to the processor, and process them until you have a smooth mixture. 12. If the mixture is too thick, add some of the liquid in the Inner Pot. 13. Allow the hummus to chill in the refrigerator at least 30 minutes before serving.
Per Serving: Calories 96; Fat 5.47g; Sodium 195mg; Carbs 9.66g; Fiber 2.9g; Sugar 1.98g; Protein 3.5g

Coconut Brown Rice

Prep time: 10 minutes | Cook time: 15 minutes | Serves: 6

2 tablespoons unsweetened shredded coconut
1½ cups long-grain brown rice, rinsed
1 (14-ounce) can light coconut milk
½ cup water
¼ teaspoon kosher salt

1. Cook the shredded coconut in the Inner Pot on Sauté mode at Normal cooking temperature, for 2 to 3 minutes. 2. Press the Cancel button to stop this cooking program. 3. Transfer the toasted coconut to a small dish, and set aside for later use. 4. Combine the rice, light coconut milk, water, and salt in the Inner Pot. 5. Select Pressure Cook mode, and then press the "Pressure Cook" button again to select "Less" time option. 6. Use the "-" key to set the cooking time to 15 minutes. 7. Press the Pressure Level button to adjust the pressure to "High Pressure." 8. Once the cooking cycle is completed, allow the steam to release naturally for 10 minutes, then turn the steam release handle to the Venting position. 9. Remove the lid and stir in the toasted coconut before serving.
Per Serving: Calories 324; Fat 17.13g; Sodium 116mg; Carbs 39.57g; Fiber 3.1g; Sugar 2.73g; Protein 5.22g

Refried Beans

Prep time: 10 minutes | Cook time: 60 minutes | Serves: 6

6 cups homemade chicken stock or store-bought chicken stock
3 cups dried pinto beans
1 yellow onion, diced

1 tablespoon apple cider vinegar
2 teaspoons ground cumin
½ teaspoon kosher salt

1. Combine the stock, beans, onion, vinegar, cumin, and salt in the Inner Pot. 2. Select Pressure Cook mode, and then press the "Pressure Cook" button again to select "More" time option. 3. Use the "+" key to set the cooking time to 60 minutes. 4. Press the Pressure Level button to adjust the pressure to "High Pressure." 5. Once the cooking cycle is completed, allow the steam to release naturally for 10 minutes, then turn the steam release handle to the Venting position. 6. Carefully remove the lid. 7. Reserve ½ cup of the bean cooking liquid, then drain the beans. 8. Return the beans to the pot and use an immersion blender to blend them to your desired consistency. 9. Serve.
Per Serving: Calories 432; Fat 4.24g; Sodium 551mg; Carbs 70.88g; Fiber 15.3g; Sugar 6.63g; Protein 27.04g

Classic Hummus

Prep time: 10 minutes | Cook time: 60 minutes | Serves: 2

¾ cup dried chickpeas
1½ cups water
4 garlic cloves
½ teaspoon baking soda

2 tablespoons tahini
1 tablespoon lemon juice
¼ teaspoon kosher salt
¼ teaspoon ground cumin

1. Combine the chickpeas, water, garlic, and baking soda in the Inner Pot. 2. Select Pressure Cook mode, and then press the "Pressure Cook" button again to select "More" time option. 3. Use the "+" key to set the cooking time to 60 minutes. 4. Press the Pressure Level button to adjust the pressure to "High Pressure." 5. Once the cooking cycle is completed, quickly and carefully turn the steam release handle from Sealing position to the Venting position. 6. Add the tahini and lemon juice to the pot, and stir them well. 7. Use an immersion blender to puree the hummus into a smooth paste. 8. Season with salt and cumin. 9. Serve warm or chilled.
Per Serving: Calories 384; Fat 12.7g; Sodium 646mg; Carbs 53.01g; Fiber 10.7g; Sugar 8.36g; Protein 18.36g

Mediterranean Stuffed Grape Leaves

Prep time: 10 minutes | Cook Time: 15 minutes | Serves: 16

⅓ cup extra-virgin olive oil
½ medium onion, peeled and diced
¼ cup minced fresh mint
¼ cup minced fresh dill
3 cloves garlic, peeled and minced
1 cup long-grain white rice

2 cups vegetable broth
½ teaspoon salt
¼ teaspoon ground black pepper
½ teaspoon grated lemon zest
1 (16-ounce) jar grape leaves
2 cups water
½ cup lemon juice

1. Set the Instant Pot on Sauté at Normal and add oil to heat in the inner pot. 2. Cook the onion, dill, and mint about 4 minutes or until tender. Then add garlic and cook about 30 seconds or until fragrant. 3. Add rice to coat and then the broth, salt, pepper, and lemon zest to stir together. 4. Close the lid and turn the steam release handle to Sealing position. 5. Set the Instant Pot on Pressure Cook at High and adjust time to 8 minutes. 6. When cooked, quick-release the pressure and then turn off the heat. Carefully open the lid and transfer the rice mixture into a medium bowl. 7. Drain grape leaves and rinse with warm water. With leave rib side up. spoon about 2 teaspoons of rice mixture for each. Roll the leave and arrange the stuffed leaves with seam side down. Lay onto the steamer basket. 8. In the inner pot, pour water and place the steamer basket inside. Pour lemon juice over the stuffed leaves. 9. Close the lid and turn the steam release handle to Sealing position. 10. Set the Instant Pot on Pressure Cook at High and adjust time to 10 minutes. 11. When cooked, quick-release the pressure and carefully open the lid. Remove from the pot and sit for 5 minutes. 12. Serve and enjoy!
Per Serving: Calories 109; Fat: 4.7g; Sodium 175mg; Carbs: 15.5g; Fiber 1g; Sugars: 5g; Protein 2g

Classic Black Beans

Prep time: 10 minutes | Cook time: 40 minutes | Serves: 4

2 tablespoons olive oil
1 yellow onion, diced
1 green bell pepper, seeded and diced
1 jalapeño pepper, seeded and minced
2 garlic cloves, minced

1 teaspoon dried oregano
1 teaspoon ground cumin
1 cup dried black beans
1 tablespoon apple cider vinegar
½ teaspoon kosher salt
1½ cups water

1. Heat the olive oil in the Inner Pot on Sauté mode at Normal cooking temperature. 2. When the oil is hot, add the onion, bell pepper, jalapeño, and garlic, and sauté them for 3 to 5 minutes until softened. 3. Press the Cancel button. 4. Add the oregano and cumin to the pot and stir well, then add the beans, vinegar, salt, and water. 5. Select Pressure Cook mode, and then press the "Pressure Cook" button again to select "Normal" time option. 6. Use the "+" key to set the cooking time to 40 minutes. 7. Press the Pressure Level button to adjust the pressure to "High Pressure." 8. Once the cooking cycle is completed, allow the steam to release naturally for 10 minutes, then turn the steam release handle to the Venting position. 9. Serve directly.
Per Serving: Calories 251; Fat 7.65g; Sodium 299mg; Carbs 35.88g; Fiber 8.5g; Sugar 3.39g; Protein 11.44g

Cilantro-Lime Brown Rice

Prep time: 10 minutes | Cook time: 15 minutes | Serves: 4

1 cup long-grain brown rice, rinsed
1¼ cups water

Zest and juice of 1 lime
¼ cup freshly chopped cilantro
1 teaspoon kosher salt

1. Combine the rice and water in the Inner Pot. 2. Select Pressure Cook mode, and then press the "Pressure Cook" button again to select "Less" time option. 3. Use the "-" key to set the cooking time to 15 minutes. 4. Press the Pressure Level button to adjust the pressure to "High Pressure." 5. Once the cooking cycle is completed, allow the steam to release naturally for 10 minutes, then turn the steam release handle to the Venting position. 6. Add the lime zest, lime juice, cilantro, and salt to the pot, and stir them well. 7. Serve and enjoy.
Per Serving: Calories 334; Fat 7.9g; Sodium 704mg; Carbs 6g; Fiber 3.6g; Sugar 6g; Protein 18g

Cinnamon Acorn Squash

Prep time: 10 minutes | Cook time: 5 minutes | Serves: 4

2 acorn squash
4 teaspoons coconut oil
4 teaspoons pure maple syrup

¼ teaspoon ground cinnamon
¼ teaspoon kosher salt

1. Cut the squash in half through the root, then scoop out and discard the seeds. 2. Divide the coconut oil, maple syrup, cinnamon, and salt evenly between the centers of each squash half. 3. Pour 1 cup of water into the Inner Pot and insert the Steam Rack. 4. Stack the squash, cut-side up, on top of the Steam Rack. 5. Put on the pressure cooker's lid and turn the steam valve to "Sealing" position. 6. Press the "Pressure Cook" button three times to select "Less" option. 7. Use the "+/-" keys on the control panel to set the cooking time to 5 minutes. 8. Press the Pressure Level button to adjust the pressure to "High Pressure." 9. Once the cooking cycle is completed, allow the steam to release naturally for 10 minutes, then turn the steam release handle to the Venting position. 10. When all the steam is released, remove the pressure lid from the top carefully. 11. Serve.
Per Serving: Calories 184; Fat 5g; Sodium 441mg; Carbs 17g; Fiber 4.6g; Sugar 5g; Protein 9g

Feta Chickpea Salad

Prep time: 10 minutes | Cook time: 15 minutes | Serves: 4

2 tablespoons olive oil, plus ¼ cup
1 red onion, diced
1 red bell pepper, seeded and diced
1 zucchini, diced
1 cup dried chickpeas, soaked overnight
3 cups water
1 cup baby spinach
3 tablespoons lemon juice
¼ teaspoon kosher salt
¼ teaspoon black pepper
¼ cup crumbled feta cheese
1 teaspoon dried oregano

1. Heat 2 tablespoons of olive oil in the Inner Pot on Sauté mode at Normal cooking temperature. 2. When the oil is hot, add the onion, bell pepper, and zucchini, and sauté them for 4 to 5 minutes until softened. 3. Press the Cancel button to stop this cooking program. 4. Add the chickpeas and water to the Inner Pot. 5. Select Pressure Cook mode, and then press the "Pressure Cook" button again to select "Less" time option. 6. Use the "-" key to set the cooking time to 15 minutes. 7. Press the Pressure Level button to adjust the pressure to "High Pressure." 8. Once the cooking cycle is completed, allow the steam to release naturally for 10 minutes, then turn the steam release handle to the Venting position. 9. Add the remaining ¼ cup of olive oil, the spinach, lemon juice, salt, and black pepper to the pot, and stir well. 10. Top this dish with the feta and oregano, and enjoy.
Per Serving: Calories 221; Fat 7.9g; Sodium 704mg; Carbs 6g; Fiber 3.6g; Sugar 6g; Protein 18g

Potato Pea Salad

Prep time: 10 minutes | Cook time: 4 minutes | Serves: 6

1½-pound (4 or 5) yellow potatoes
1 shallot, finely chopped
¼ cup apple cider vinegar
¼ cup olive oil
1 teaspoon Dijon mustard
½ teaspoon kosher salt
4-ounce sugar snap peas, halved lengthwise

1. Cut each potato into 12 pieces. 2. Whisk the shallot, vinegar, olive oil, mustard, and salt in a bowl. Set the dressing aside for later use. 3. Pour 2 cups of water into the Inner Pot and place the Steam Rack in the pot. 4. Put the potatoes on the rack. 5. Select Pressure Cook mode, and then press the "Pressure Cook" button again to select "Less" time option. 6. Use the "-" key to set the cooking time to 4 minutes. 7. Press the Pressure Level button to adjust the pressure to "High Pressure." 8. Once the cooking cycle is completed, quickly and carefully turn the steam release handle from Sealing position to the Venting position. 9. Transfer the cooked potatoes to the bowl of dressing, and then stir in the peas. 10. Enjoy this salad warm or chilled.
Per Serving: Calories 182; Fat 9.18g; Sodium 212mg; Carbs 23.01g; Fiber 3.1g; Sugar 2.9g; Protein 2.94g

Cider Collard Greens

Prep time: 10 minutes | Cook time: 12 minutes | Serves: 6

6 no-sugar-added uncured bacon slices, diced
1 yellow onion, diced
16-ounce frozen chopped collard greens
1 tablespoon apple cider vinegar
¼ teaspoon kosher salt
¼ teaspoon garlic powder

1. Select Sauté mode and Normal setting. 2. Add the bacon to the Inner Pot, and sauté for 3 minutes until the fat renders. 3. Add the onion and sauté for 3 minutes until soft. 4. Press the Cancel button to stop Sauté program. 5. Add the collard greens, vinegar, salt, and garlic powder to the pot, and stir well. 6. Use your spoon to scrape up anything that's stuck to the bottom of the pot. 7. Cover the pot with lid. 8. Select Pressure Cook mode, and then press the "Pressure Cook" button again to select "Less" time option. 9. Use the "-" key to set the cooking time to 12 minutes. 10. Press the Pressure Level button to adjust the pressure to "High Pressure." 11. Once the cooking cycle is completed, quickly and carefully turn the steam release handle from Sealing position to the Venting position. 12. Carefully remove the lid, stir, and serve.
Per Serving: Calories 139; Fat 10.51g; Sodium 256mg; Carbs 6.93g; Fiber 3g; Sugar 1.01g; Protein 5.52g

Garlicky Brussels Sprouts

Prep time: 10 minutes | Cook time: 2 minutes | Serves: 6

1 tablespoon olive oil
1 pound Brussels sprouts, bottoms trimmed
½ cup Vegetable Broth or store-bought low-sodium vegetable
broth
5 garlic cloves, minced
¼ teaspoon kosher salt
¼ teaspoon black pepper

1. Heat the oil on Sauté mode at Normal cooking temperature. 2. When the oil is hot, add the Brussels sprouts, and cook undisturbed for 3 to 4 minutes until lightly browned. 3. Press the Cancel button to stop this cooking program. 4. Add the broth, garlic, salt and black pepper to the pot, and then cover the pot. 5. Select Pressure Cook mode, and then press the "Pressure Cook" button again to select "Less" time option. 6. Use the "-" key to set the cooking time to 2 minutes. 7. Press the Pressure Level button to adjust the pressure to "High Pressure." 8. Once the cooking cycle is completed, quickly and carefully turn the steam release handle from Sealing position to the Venting position. 9. Serve.
Per Serving: Calories 60; Fat 2.56g; Sodium 128mg; Carbs 8.48g; Fiber 3.1g; Sugar 2.28g; Protein 2.92g

Mashed Potato and Cauliflower

Prep time: 10 minutes | Cook time: 8 minutes | Serves: 6

1 pound potatoes, peeled and cubed
2 cups fresh or frozen cauliflower florets
4 garlic cloves
¼ cup unsweetened nondairy milk, such as almond or coconut
¼ teaspoon kosher salt
½ teaspoon black pepper

1. Pour 2 cups of water into the Inner Pot, and add the potatoes, cauliflower, and garlic. 2. Select Pressure Cook mode, and then press the "Pressure Cook" button again to select "Less" time option. 3. Use the "-" key to set the cooking time to 8 minutes. 4. Press the Pressure Level button to adjust the pressure to "High Pressure." 5. Once the cooking cycle is completed, quickly and carefully turn the steam release handle from Sealing position to the Venting position. 6. Drain the water. 7. Return the vegetables to the pot, and add the milk, salt, and pepper. 8. Use a potato masher to mash the potatoes and cauliflower to your desired consistency, and then serve.
Per Serving: Calories 77; Fat 0.41g; Sodium 117mg; Carbs 16.58g; Fiber 2.8g; Sugar 2.1g; Protein 2.9g

Honey Sweet Potatoes

Prep time: 15 minutes | Cook time: 7 minutes | Serves: 4

1 pound sweet potatoes (about 2 medium potatoes), cut into ½-inch rounds
2 teaspoons coconut oil
1 teaspoon honey
1 teaspoon chili powder
¼ teaspoon smoked paprika
¼ teaspoon kosher salt

1. Pour ½ cup of water into the Inner Pot, then add the potato rounds. 2. Put on the pressure cooker's lid and turn the steam valve to "Sealing" position. 3. Select Pressure Cook mode, and then press the "Pressure Cook" button again to select "Less" time option. 4. Use the "-" key to set the cooking time to 4 minutes. 5. Press the Pressure Level button to adjust the pressure to "High Pressure." 6. Once the cooking cycle is completed, quickly and carefully turn the steam release handle from Sealing position to the Venting position. 7. Press Cancel to stop this cooking program. 8. Add the coconut oil, honey, chili powder, paprika, and salt to the pot, and stir well. 9. Press the "Sauté" button two times to select "Normal" mode and cook for 2 to 3 minutes, until the potatoes are coated with a thick glaze. 10. Serve warm.
Per Serving: Calories 113; Fat 2.52g; Sodium 195mg; Carbs 21.97g; Fiber 3.1g; Sugar 8.03g; Protein 1.67g

Cinnamon Raisin Granola Bars

Prep time: 15 minutes | Cook time: 10 minutes | Serves: 10

2 cups quick-cooking oats
⅓ cup date syrup
⅓ cup avocado oil
⅓ cup monk fruit sweetener
⅓ cup almond butter
⅓ cup raisins
½ teaspoon ground cinnamon

1. Combine the oats, date syrup, oil, fruit sweetener, almond butter, raisins, and cinnamon in a medium bowl. 2. Spray a suitable baking dish with cooking spray. Press the oat mixture firmly into the pan. 3. Add 1 cup water to the Inner Pot and place the Steam Rack inside. 4. Put the baking dish on the Steam Rack. 5. Select Pressure Cook mode, and then press the "Pressure Cook" button again to select "Less" time option. 6. Use the "-" key to set the cooking time to 10 minutes. 7. Press the Pressure Level button to adjust the pressure to "High Pressure." 8. Once the cooking cycle is completed, quickly and carefully turn the steam release handle from Sealing position to the Venting position. 9. Once completely cooled, turn the pan upside down onto a cutting board to remove the granola from the pan. 10. Cut into ten bars and serve.
Per Serving: Calories 186; Fat 12.2g; Sodium 8mg; Carbs 20.87g; Fiber 2.1g; Sugar 14.06g; Protein 3.15g

Almond Butter Chocolate Chip Granola Bars

Prep time: 15 minutes | Cook time: 10 minutes | Serves: 10

2 cups quick-cooking oats
⅔ cup almond butter
⅓ cup avocado oil
⅓ cup monk fruit sweetener
⅓ cup stevia-sweetened dark chocolate chips
¼ teaspoon salt

1. Combine the oats, almond butter, oil, sweetener, chocolate chips, and salt in a medium bowl. 2. Spray a suitable baking dish with cooking spray. Press the oat mixture firmly into the pan. 3. Add 1 cup water to the Inner Pot and place the steam rack inside. 4. Put the baking dish on the steam rack. 5. Select Pressure Cook mode, and then press the "Pressure Cook" button again to select "Less" time option. 6. Use the "-" key to set the cooking time to 10 minutes. 7. Press the Pressure Level button to adjust the pressure to "Low Pressure." 8. Once the cooking cycle is completed, quickly and carefully turn the steam release handle from Sealing position to the Venting position. 9. Carefully remove the pan from the Inner Pot and place it on a baking rack to cool completely. 10. Once completely cooled, turn the pan upside down onto a cutting board to remove the granola from the pan. 11. Cut into ten bars and serve.
Per Serving: Calories 232; Fat 17.91g; Sodium 84mg; Carbs 17.53g; Fiber 3g; Sugar 7.65g; Protein 5.26g

Lemon Eggplant in Vegetable Broth

Prep time: 5 minutes | Cook time: 15 minutes | Serves: 2

¼ to ½ cup vegetable broth
1 medium eggplant, peeled and sliced
1 cup water
3 garlic cloves, unpeeled
2 tablespoons lemon juice
2 tablespoons tahini
1 tablespoon white miso paste
½ teaspoon ground cumin, plus more for garnish

1. Select Sauté mode and press the "Sauté" button again to select "Normal" setting. 2. Pour 2 tablespoons of broth in the Inner Pot. 3. Arrange as many slices of eggplant as possible in one layer on the bottom of the pot. 4. Cook the eggplant slices for 2 minutes, then flip, adding more of the broth as needed, and cook for another 2 minutes. 5. After another 2 minutes, pile the first batch of eggplant on one side of the Inner Pot and add the remaining eggplant. 6. Cook them for 2 minutes on each side, adding broth as needed. 7. Press the Cancel button, and add the water and garlic. 8. Select Pressure Cook mode, and then press the "Pressure Cook" button again to select "Less" time option. 9. Use the "-" key to set the cooking time to 3 minutes. 10. Press the Pressure Level button to adjust the pressure to "High

Pressure." 11. Once the cooking cycle is completed, quickly and carefully turn the steam release handle from Sealing position to the Venting position. 12. Remove the garlic and take off the outer peel. 13. Blend the garlic, eggplant, lemon juice, tahini, miso, and cumin in the blender until smooth, then transfer the dish to the serving plate and enjoy. 14. You can also cover the plate and refrigerate this meal, and serve cold.
Per Serving: Calories 207; Fat 10.64g; Sodium 488mg; Carbs 24.46g; Fiber 10.2g; Sugar 10.95g; Protein 8.17g

White Bean Dip

Prep time: 5 minutes | Cook time: 8 minutes | Serves: 10

1 tablespoon avocado oil
1 medium yellow onion, peeled and chopped
2 cloves garlic, minced
2 (15-ounce) cans cannellini beans, drained
1 (15-ounce) can diced tomatoes, drained
½ teaspoon salt
¼ teaspoon black pepper
½ cup chopped fresh basil
1 tablespoon fresh lemon juice

1. Select Sauté mode and press the "Sauté" button again to select "Normal" setting. and add the oil to the Inner Pot. 2. Add the oil to the Inner Pot and heat for 1 minute; add the onion and sauté the onion for 3 minutes until softened. 3. Add the garlic, and sauté for 30 seconds. 4. Press the Cancel button. Add the beans, tomatoes, salt, and pepper to the pot, and stir well. 5. Select Pressure Cook mode, and then press the "Pressure Cook" button again to select "Less" time option. 6. Use the "-" key to set the cooking time to 3 minutes. 7. Press the Pressure Level button to adjust the pressure to "High Pressure." 8. Once the cooking cycle is completed, quickly and carefully turn the steam release handle from Sealing position to the Venting position. 9. Stir in the basil and lemon juice, and then use an immersion blender to blend to a chunky consistency. 10. Serve warm or cold.
Per Serving: Calories 35; Fat 1.74g; Sodium 169mg; Carbs 4.81g; Fiber 1.9g; Sugar 1.99g; Protein 1.04g

Hot Cauliflower Bites

Prep time: 15 minutes | Cook time: 2 minutes | Serves: 4

1 large head cauliflower, cut into large pieces
½ cup buffalo hot sauce

1. Pour 1 cup water into the Inner Pot and place the Steam Rack inside. 2. Place the cauliflower in a 7-cup glass bowl, and add the buffalo hot sauce. 3. Toss to evenly coat. Put the bowl on the steam rack. 4. Select Pressure Cook mode, and then press the "Pressure Cook" button again to select "Less" time option. 5. Use the "-" key to set the cooking time to 2 minutes. 6. Press the Pressure Level button to adjust the pressure to "High Pressure." 7. Once the cooking cycle is completed, quickly and carefully turn the steam release handle from Sealing position to the Venting position. 8. Transfer to a plate and serve with toothpicks.
Per Serving: Calories 62; Fat 0.64g; Sodium 292mg; Carbs 12.62g; Fiber 4.8g; Sugar 5.29g; Protein 4.53g

Nacho Cheese Sauce

Prep time: 5 minutes | Cook time: 10 minutes | Serves: 4

1¼ cups vegetable broth
1 cup plain nondairy yogurt
3 tablespoons oat flour
¼ teaspoon salt
¼ teaspoon garlic salt
½ teaspoon cumin
1 teaspoon chili powder
¼ teaspoon paprika
⅛ teaspoon cayenne powder

1. Mix the yogurt and flour in a bowl. 2. Select Sauté mode and press the "Sauté" button again to select "Normal" setting. 3. Add the broth to the Inner Pot and bring to a boil. 4. When boiled, add the yogurt mixture, salt, and spices to the pot; cook and stir them for 5 minutes until thick and bubbly. 5. Transfer to a bowl and serve.
Per Serving: Calories 65; Fat 2.62g; Sodium 366mg; Carbs 7.62g; Fiber 0.7g; Sugar 3.59g; Protein 3.02g

Tamari Edamame

Prep time: 5 minutes | Cook time: 1 minute | Serves: 4

1 (10-ounce) bag frozen edamame in pods
2 tablespoons reduced sodium tamari
¼ teaspoon kosher salt

1. Pour 1 cup water in the Inner Pot, and place a Steam Rack in the pot. 2. Place the edamame in a steamer basket and place basket on the steam rack. 3. Select Steam mode and press the "Steam" button again to select "Less" setting. 4. Use the "-" key to set the cooking time to 1 minutes. 5. Press the Pressure Level button to adjust the pressure to "Low Pressure." 6. Once the cooking cycle is completed, quickly and carefully turn the steam release handle from Sealing position to the Venting position. 7. Transfer the edamame to a medium bowl and top with the tamari and salt, and enjoy.
Per Serving: Calories 134; Fat 7.68g; Sodium 166mg; Carbs 8.79g; Fiber 4.2g; Sugar 2.29g; Protein 9.63g

Buffalo Chicken Dip

Prep time: 10 minutes | Cook time: 7 minutes | Serves: 10

2 cups cooked, shredded chicken
1 cup vegan nondairy blue cheese-style dressing
8-ounce nondairy cream cheese
½ cup buffalo hot sauce

1. In a 7" glass bowl, add the chicken, blue cheese dressing, cream cheese, and hot sauce. Mix. 2. Add 1 cup water to the Inner Pot and place the steam rack inside. Place the bowl on top of the steam rack. 3. Put on the pressure cooker's lid and turn the steam valve to "Sealing" position. 4. Select Pressure Cook mode, and then press the "Pressure Cook" button again to select "Less" time option. 5. Use the "+/-" keys on the control panel to set the cooking time to 7 minutes. 6. Press the Pressure Level button to adjust the pressure to "High Pressure." 7. Once the cooking cycle is completed, allow the steam to release naturally. 8. When all the steam is released, remove the pressure lid from the top carefully. 9. Stir the dip and then serve warm.
Per Serving: Calories 129; Fat 8.15g; Sodium 295mg; Carbs 3g; Fiber 0.3g; Sugar 2.45g; Protein 10.64g

Spinach Artichoke Dip

Prep time: 10 minutes | Cook time: 6 minutes | Serves: 10

½ cup vegetable stock
1 (10-ounce) package frozen, cut spinach
1 (14-ounce) can artichoke quarters, drained
8-ounce nondairy cream cheese
¾ cup nondairy Greek yogurt
¼ cup vegan mayonnaise
1 teaspoon onion powder
¼ teaspoon garlic salt
¼ teaspoon black pepper
1 cup nutritional yeast

1. Add all of the ingredients to the Inner Pot. 2. Select Pressure Cook mode, and then press the "Pressure Cook" button again to select "Less" time option. 3. Use the "-" key to set the cooking time to 6 minutes. 4. Press the Pressure Level button to adjust the pressure to "High Pressure." 5. Once the cooking cycle is completed, quickly and carefully turn the steam release handle from Sealing position to the Venting position. 6. Stir well, and then transfer the dip to a serving bowl. The dip will thicken as it sits.
Per Serving: Calories 167; Fat 9.39g; Sodium 1072mg; Carbs 10.85g; Fiber 3.5g; Sugar 2.56g; Protein 10.86g

Sweet Potato Hummus

Prep time: 10 minutes | Cook time: 10 minutes | Serves: 10

2 tablespoons avocado oil
1 large sweet potato, peeled and cut into cubes
½ teaspoon salt
3 cloves garlic, minced
Juice from 1 large lemon
1 (15-ounce) can cooked chickpeas
¼ cup tahini
1 teaspoon ground cumin

1. Select Sauté mode and press the "Sauté" button again to select "Normal" setting. 2. Add the oil to the Inner Pot, and heat the oil for 2 minutes. 3. Add the sweet potato and salt, and sauté for 2 minutes; add the garlic, and sauté for 30 seconds. 4. Press the Cancel button to stop this cooking program, and then add the lemon juice to the pot. 5. Select Pressure Cook mode, and then press the "Pressure Cook" button again to select "Less" time option. 6. Use the "-" key to set the cooking time to 2 minutes. 7. Press the Pressure Level button to adjust the pressure to "High Pressure." 8. Once the cooking cycle is completed, quickly and carefully turn the steam release handle from Sealing position to the Venting position. 9. Transfer the food to a large food processor. 10. Add the chickpeas, tahini, and cumin to the processor, and process them until smooth. 11. Allow the hummus to chill in the refrigerator at least 30 minutes before serving.
Per Serving: Calories 115; Fat 6.82g; Sodium 192mg; Carbs 11.42g; Fiber 2.8g; Sugar 2.35g; Protein 3.28g

Lentil Balls

Prep time: 40 minutes | Cook time: 15 minutes | Serves: 4

For the Lentil Balls
⅓ cup cooked black beans, drained
½ cup old fashioned rolled oats
1¼ cups cooked lentils
¼ cup unsweetened almond milk
¼ teaspoon coarse salt
¼ teaspoon ground ginger
⅛ teaspoon garlic powder
⅛ teaspoon black pepper
2 tablespoons avocado oil
2 tablespoons oat flour
For the Sauce
¾ cup tomato sauce
1 tablespoon tomato paste
¼ cup maple syrup
2 tablespoons cup coconut aminos
1 tablespoon apple cider vinegar
½ teaspoon ground ginger
¼ teaspoon crushed red pepper flakes

1. Partially mash the black beans in a bowl. 2. Pulse the oats a few times in a food processor; add the lentils and pulse again. 3. Add the milk, salt, ginger, garlic powder, and black pepper, and pulse. Do not over mix. 4. Combine the lentil mixture and black beans. 5. Form the mixture into tablespoon-sized balls and refrigerate for 30 minutes. 6. Mix all of the sauce ingredients together in a medium bowl. 7. Pour the oat flour into a shallow bowl, and coat the lentil balls with the flour. 8. Select Sauté mode and press the "Sauté" button again to select "More" setting. 9. Add the avocado oil to the Inner Pot and heat for 2 minutes. 10. Add the lentil balls to the oil, and carefully move them around to brown, for about 1 minute per side. 11. Remove the balls and place them in a suitable cake pan. 12. Mix all the sauce ingredients in a bowl. 13. Top the lentil balls with the sauce and cover with a paper towel, then tightly cover the pan with foil. 14. Add ½ cup water to Inner Pot and scrape up any brown bits from the bottom. 15. Place the Steam Rack in the pot, and put the pan on the rack. 16. Select Pressure Cook mode, and then press the "Pressure Cook" button again to select "Less" time option. 17. Use the "-" key to set the cooking time to 5 minutes. 18. Press the Pressure Level button to adjust the pressure to "Low Pressure." 19. Once the cooking cycle is completed, quickly and carefully turn the steam release handle from Sealing position to the Venting position. 20. Serve directly.
Per Serving: Calories 336; Fat 9.07g; Sodium 975mg; Carbs 56.38g; Fiber 12.8g; Sugar 23.72g; Protein 11.88g

Quinoa Energy Balls

Prep time: 15 minutes | Cook time: 5 minutes | Serves: 5

½ cup quinoa
1 cup water
¼ cup almond butter
2 teaspoons raw honey
½ teaspoon ground cinnamon
½ teaspoon blackstrap molasses
⅛ teaspoon fine sea salt

1. Place the quinoa in a fine-mesh strainer and rinse under water until the water runs clear. 2. Add the quinoa and water to the Inner Pot. 3. Select Pressure Cook mode, and then press the "Pressure Cook" button again to select "Less" time option. 4. Use the "-" key to set the cooking time to 5 minutes. 5. Press the Pressure Level button to adjust the pressure to "High Pressure." 6. Once the cooking cycle is completed, quickly and carefully turn the steam release handle from Sealing position to the Venting position. 7. Transfer the cooked quinoa to a medium bowl and allow it to cool. 8. Once it is cooled, add the rest of the ingredients to the bowl and stir to combine. 9. Form the mixture into 1" balls and place them onto a tray or plate. 10. Place them in the freezer about 30 minutes to firm. 11. Keep stored in the refrigerator.
Per Serving: Calories 151; Fat 7.97g; Sodium 93mg; Carbs 16.32g; Fiber 2.6g; Sugar 3.63g; Protein 5.04g

Black Bean Dip

Prep time: 10 minutes | Cook time: 7 minutes | Serves: 10

1 tablespoon avocado oil
1 medium yellow onion, peeled and chopped
2 (15-ounce) cans black beans, drained
1 teaspoon ground cumin

½ teaspoon chili powder
½ teaspoon smoked paprika
½ teaspoon salt
Juice from ½ medium lime
¼ cup nutritional yeast

1. Select Sauté mode and press the "Sauté" button again to select "Normal" setting. 2. Add the oil to the pot and heat for 1 minute; add the onion and sauté for 3 minutes until softened. 3. Press the Cancel button. 4. Add the beans, cumin, chili powder, paprika, and salt to the pot. 5. Select Pressure Cook mode, and then press the "Pressure Cook" button again to select "Less" time option. 6. Use the "-" key to set the cooking time to 3 minutes. 7. Press the Pressure Level button to adjust the pressure to "Low Pressure." 8. Once the cooking cycle is completed, quickly and carefully turn the steam release handle from Sealing position to the Venting position. 9. Add the lime juice and nutritional yeast and use an immersion blender to blend the dip. 10. Serve warm.
Per Serving: Calories 42; Fat 1.76g; Sodium 335mg; Carbs 4.75g; Fiber 1.6g; Sugar 0.98g; Protein 2.4g

Avocado Deviled Eggs

Prep time: 15 minutes | Cook time: 7 minutes | Serves: 12

6 large eggs
1 medium avocado, peeled, pitted, and diced
2½ tablespoons mayonnaise
2 teaspoons lime juice

1 clove garlic, crushed
⅛ teaspoon cayenne pepper
⅛ teaspoon salt
1 medium jalapeño pepper, sliced
12 dashes hot sauce

1. Pour 1 cup water into the Inner Pot and place the Steam Rack inside. 2. Carefully place the eggs directly onto the steam rack. 3. Put on the pressure cooker's lid and turn the steam valve to "Sealing" position. 4. Select Pressure Cook mode, and then press the "Steam" button again to select "Normal" option. 5. Use the "+/-" keys on the control panel to set the cooking time to 7 minutes. 6. Press the Pressure Level button to adjust the pressure to "Low Pressure." 7. Once the cooking cycle is completed, quickly and carefully turn the steam release handle from Sealing position to the Venting position. 8. Transfer the eggs to a bowl filled with iced water and let them sit 15 minutes. 9. Remove the eggs from the water and peel the shells away from the eggs. 10. Slice the eggs in half. 11. Scoop egg yolks into a medium bowl, and add the avocado, mayonnaise, lime juice, garlic, cayenne pepper, and salt. 12. Mash the egg yolk mixture until filling is evenly combined. 13. Spoon the filling into a piping bag and pipe filling into each egg white. 14. Top each with a jalapeño slice and a dash of hot sauce.
Per Serving: Calories 75; Fat 5.86g; Sodium 214mg; Carbs 2.31g; Fiber 1.2g; Sugar 0.5g; Protein 3.78g

Hard-Boiled Eggs

Prep time: 5 minutes | Cook time: 10 minutes | Serves: 6

6 large eggs

1. Pour 1 cup water into the Inner Pot and place the Steam Rack inside. 2. Carefully place the eggs directly onto the rack. 3. Select Pressure Cook mode, and then press the "Steam" button again to select "Normal" time option. 4. Use the "-" key to set the cooking time to 7 minutes. 5. Press the Pressure Level button to adjust the pressure to "High Pressure." 6. Once the cooking cycle is completed, quickly and carefully turn the steam release handle from Sealing position to the Venting position. 7. Immediately transfer the eggs to a bowl filled with iced water and let them sit 15 minutes. 8. Remove the eggs from the water and peel the shells away from the eggs. 9. Store in the refrigerator.
Per Serving: Calories 72; Fat 4.76g; Sodium 71mg; Carbs 0.36g; Fiber 0g; Sugar 0.19g; Protein 6.28g

Avocado Hummus

Prep time: 15 minutes | Cook time: 10 minutes | Serves: 8

¾ cup dry chickpeas
3 cups water
1 teaspoon salt
1 large avocado, peeled, pitted, and sliced

2 tablespoons olive oil plus ⅛ teaspoon for drizzling
2 tablespoons fresh lemon juice
½ teaspoon crushed red pepper flakes

1. Put the chickpeas in a bowl, and cover with 3" water. 2. Allow to soak 4–8 hours, and then drain them. 3. Add the soaked chickpeas, 3 cups water, and salt to the Inner Pot. 4. Select Pressure Cook mode, and then press the "Pressure Cook" button again to select "Less" time option. 5. Use the "-" key to set the cooking time to 10 minutes. 6. Press the Pressure Level button to adjust the pressure to "High Pressure." 7. Once the cooking cycle is completed, allow the steam to release naturally for 10 minutes, then turn the steam release handle to the Venting position. 8. Transfer the chickpeas to your food processor, and add the avocado, oil, and lemon juice. 9. Process until super smooth. 10. If the mixture is too thick, add water, 1 teaspoon at a time until desired consistency is reached. 11. Refrigerate until completely cooled and then sprinkle with crushed red pepper flakes and drizzle with the remaining ⅛ teaspoon olive oil before serving.
Per Serving: Calories 74; Fat 4.64g; Sodium 342mg; Carbs 7.28g; Fiber 3.1g; Sugar 1.22g; Protein 2.04g

Cauliflower Queso with Bell Pepper

Prep time: 5 minutes | Cook time: 5 minutes | Serves: 5

1 head cauliflower, cut into about 4 cups florets
2 cups water
1½ cups carrots, chopped into ½-inch-thick round pieces
½ cup raw cashews
1 (15-ounce) can no-salt-added diced tomatoes

½ cup nutritional yeast
1 tablespoon white miso paste
2 teaspoons gluten-free chili powder
1 red bell pepper, diced
4 scallions, white and green parts, diced

1. Combine the cauliflower, water, carrots, and cashews in the Inner Pot. 2. Select Pressure Cook mode, and then press the "Pressure Cook" button again to select "Less" time option. 3. Use the "-" key to set the cooking time to 5 minutes. 4. Press the Pressure Level button to adjust the pressure to "High Pressure." 5. Once the cooking cycle is completed, quickly and carefully turn the steam release handle from Sealing position to the Venting position. 6. Drain the water, then transfer the mixture to a blender. 7. Add the liquid from the can of tomatoes and set the drained tomatoes aside. 8. Add the nutritional yeast, miso, and chili powder, and blend until very smooth. 9. Transfer the mixture to a medium bowl and stir in the drained tomatoes, bell pepper, and scallions. 10. Enjoy.
Per Serving: Calories 268; Fat 14.71g; Sodium 1139mg; Carbs 25.67g; Fiber 7.3g; Sugar 8.7g; Protein 12.95g

Garlic Collard Greens in Vegetable Broth

Prep time: 10 minutes | Cook time: 10 minutes | Serves: 4-6

1½-pound collard greens, stems removed, leaves chopped
1½ cups no-salt-added vegetable broth

3 tablespoons rice vinegar
3 garlic cloves, minced
1 (2-inch) knob fresh ginger, grated

1. Mix the collard greens, vegetable broth, vinegar, garlic, and ginger in the Inner Pot. 2. Select Pressure Cook mode, and then press the "Pressure Cook" button again to select "Less" time option. 3. Use the "-" key to set the cooking time to 10 minutes. 4. Press the Pressure Level button to adjust the pressure to "High Pressure." 5. Once the cooking cycle is completed, quickly and carefully turn the steam release handle from Sealing position to the Venting position. 6. Serve and enjoy.
Per Serving: Calories 289; Fat 14g; Sodium 791mg; Carbs 18.9g; Fiber 4.6g; Sugar 8g; Protein 6g

Jalapeño Peppers with Cashews

Prep time: 10 minutes | Cook time: 30 minutes | Serves: 4-6

2 jalapeño peppers
½ pound dried great northern beans, rinsed and sorted
½ medium onion, roughly chopped
4 cups water
½ cup cashews

¼ cup unsweetened plant-based milk
2 garlic cloves, crushed
2 tablespoons nutritional yeast
1 tablespoon chickpea miso paste
1 tablespoon apple cider vinegar

1. Slice one jalapeños pepper in half lengthwise and remove the seeds. 2. Combine the halved pepper, beans, onion, and 3 cups of the water in the Inner Pot. 3. Select Pressure Cook mode, and then press the "Pressure Cook" button again to select "Normal" time option. 4. Use the "-" key to set the cooking time to 30 minutes. 5. Press the Pressure Level button to adjust the pressure to "High Pressure." 6. While cooking, boil the remaining 1 cup of water and, using a large bowl, pour it over the cashews; let soak for at least 30 minutes. 7. Drain and discard the soaking liquid before using the cashews. 8. Once the cooking cycle is completed, allow the steam to release naturally for 10 minutes, then turn the steam release handle to the Venting position. 9. Remove the jalapeño pepper from the pot, and finely chop it. 10. Finely chop another raw jalapeño pepper, removing the seeds if you prefer a milder dish. 11. Set both peppers aside. 12. Drain the beans and onion, then combine them in a blender with the cashews, milk, garlic, nutritional yeast, miso paste, and vinegar. 13. Blend them until creamy. 14. Spoon the mixture into a medium mixing bowl, and stir in the jalapeños. 15. Enjoy.
Per Serving: Calories 295; Fat 10.9g; Sodium 354mg; Carbs 20.5g; Fiber 4.1g; Sugar 8.2g; Protein 06g

Spiced Potatoes Dip

Prep time: 15 minutes | Cook time: 27 minutes | Serves: 4-6

1 cup unsweetened plant-based milk
½ cup vegetable broth
2 scallions, white and green parts, chopped
2 tablespoons nutritional yeast
1 tablespoon arrowroot powder
1 teaspoon garlic powder

1 teaspoon minced fresh rosemary
1 teaspoon mustard powder
Black pepper
Salt
1½-pound russet potatoes (4 or 5 medium), peeled
1 cup water

1. Whisk the milk, broth, scallions, nutritional yeast, arrowroot powder, garlic powder, rosemary, and mustard powder in a large bowl. 2. Season the milk mixture with pepper and salt. 3. Slice the potatoes very thinly. 4. Arrange a 1-inch layer of potatoes on a suitable ovenproof baking dish, followed by enough of the sauce to just cover the potatoes. 5. Continue layering until all the potatoes are submerged under the sauce. 6. Pour the water into your Inner Pot and insert the Steam Rack. Place the baking dish on the Steam Rack. 7. Select Pressure Cook mode, and then press the "Pressure Cook" button again to select "Less" time option. 8. Use the "+" key to set the cooking time to 27 minutes. 9. Press the Pressure Level button to adjust the pressure to "High Pressure." 10. Once the cooking cycle is completed, quickly and carefully turn the steam release handle from Sealing position to the Venting position. 11. Serve immediately.
Per Serving: Calories 361; Fat 10.9g; Sodium 454mg; Carbs 10g; Fiber 3.1g; Sugar 5.2g; Protein 10g

Creamed Spinach with Cashews

Prep time: 10 minutes | Cook time: 12 minutes | Serves: 4-6

½ medium onion, diced
4 garlic cloves, minced
1 (16-ounce) package frozen chopped spinach
1¾ cups unsweetened plant-based milk
1 cup water

¾ cup raw cashews
1 tablespoon lemon juice
1 teaspoon chickpea miso paste
½ teaspoon ground or freshly grated nutmeg
Black pepper

1. Select Sauté mode and press the "Sauté" button again to select "Normal" setting. Let the machine heat for 2 minutes. 2. Sauté the onion in the pot for 3 to 5 minutes until translucent, adding water as needed to prevent sticking. 3. Add the garlic and sauté for 30 seconds. 4. Cancel the Sauté function, then add the spinach and 1¼ cups of the milk. 5. Select Pressure Cook mode, and then press the "Pressure Cook" button again to select "Less" time option. 6. Use the "-" key to set the cooking time to 5 minutes. 7. Press the Pressure Level button to adjust the pressure to "High Pressure." 8. Once the cooking cycle is completed, allow the steam to release naturally. 9. Boil the water, then pour it over the cashews; let the cashews soak for at least 30 minutes before draining. 10. Add the drained cashews, the remaining milk, the lemon juice, miso paste, nutmeg, and black pepper to a blender, blend them until smooth. 11. Combine the sauce with the spinach. 12. Serve immediately.
Per Serving: Calories 372; Fat 20g; Sodium 891mg; Carbs 29g; Fiber 3g; Sugar 8g; Protein 7g

Corn with Tofu Crema

Prep time: 10 minutes | Cook time: 6 minutes | Serves: 4-6

1 cup water
4 to 6 frozen mini corncobs
1 (14-ounce) package silken tofu, drained
1 tablespoon lemon juice
1 tablespoon apple cider vinegar

1 teaspoon ground cumin
Salt
1 lime, cut into wedges
1 tablespoon no-salt-added gluten-free chili powder

1. Pour the water into the Inner Pot and place the Steam Rack inside. Put the corncobs on the Steam Rack. 2. Select Pressure Cook mode, and then press the "Pressure Cook" button again to select "Less" time option. 3. Use the "+/-" keys on the control panel to set the cooking time to 6 minutes. 4. Press the Pressure Level button to adjust the pressure to "High Pressure." 5. Once the cooking cycle is completed, quickly and carefully turn the steam release handle from Sealing position to the Venting position. 6. Add the tofu, lemon juice, vinegar, cumin, and salt to a blender, blend them well and set aside for later use. 7. Rub each cob with a lime wedge and then slather it with a generous amount of crema. 8. Sprinkle ¼ to ½ teaspoon chili powder on each. 9. Serve immediately.
Per Serving: Calories 334; Fat 7.9g; Sodium 704mg; Carbs 6g; Fiber 3.6g; Sugar 6g; Protein 18g

Garlic Baby Potatoes

Prep time: 10 minutes | Cook time: 7 minutes | Serves: 4-6

2-pound baby red-skinned potatoes
1 cup water
3 tablespoons plant-based butter, melted, or olive oil
1 teaspoon garlic powder

1 teaspoon dried thyme
1 teaspoon dried rosemary, crushed
1 teaspoon salt
Black pepper

1. Pierce the potatoes with a fork and slice any larger potatoes in half. 2. Combine the potatoes and water in the Inner Pot. 3. Select Pressure Cook mode, and then press the "Pressure Cook" button again to select "Less" time option. 4. Use the "+/-" keys on the control panel to set the cooking time to 7 minutes. 5. Press the Pressure Level button to adjust the pressure to "High Pressure." 6. Once the cooking cycle is completed, quickly and carefully turn the steam release handle from Sealing position to the Venting position. 7. Drain the water, select the Sauté function and Normal setting. 8. Add the butter or olive oil, garlic powder, thyme, rosemary, salt, and black pepper to taste. 9. Stir to combine and allow the potatoes to brown slightly for 3 to 4 minutes.
Per Serving: Calories 184; Fat 5g; Sodium 441mg; Carbs 17g; Fiber 4.6g; Sugar 5g; Protein 9g

Beet Hummus

Prep time: 10 minutes | Cook time: 45 minutes | Serves: 4-6

3 cups water
1 cup dried chickpeas, rinsed and sorted
1 medium beet, peeled and quartered

½ cup tahini
2 tablespoons lemon juice
4 garlic cloves, crushed
Salt

1. Combine the water, chickpeas, and beets in the Inner Pot. 2. Select Pressure Cook mode, and then press the "Pressure Cook" button again to select "More" time option (45 minutes). 3. Press the Pressure Level button to adjust the pressure to "High Pressure." 4. Once the cooking cycle is completed, allow the steam to release naturally for 10 minutes, then turn the steam release handle to the Venting position. 5. Using a slotted spoon, transfer the chickpeas and beets to a blender, leaving the liquid in the pot. 6. Add the tahini, lemon juice, garlic, and salt to the blender---blend them well, adding one tablespoon of the liquid at a time. 7. Serve.
Per Serving: Calories 382; Fat 7.9g; Sodium 704mg; Carbs 6g; Fiber 3.6g; Sugar 6g; Protein 18g

Cinnamon Almonds

Prep time: 5 minutes | Cook time: 2 minutes | Serves: 8

2 cups raw unsalted almonds
1 teaspoon ground cinnamon
2 tablespoons water
40 drops pure liquid stevia
½ teaspoon pure vanilla extract
¼ teaspoon coarse salt

1. Mix all the ingredients in a 7-cup glass bowl. 2. Pour ½ cup hot water into the Inner Pot and place the steam rack inside. 3. Put the glass bowl on the rack. 4. Select Pressure Cook mode, and then press the "Pressure Cook" button again to select "Less" time option. 5. Use the "-" key to set the cooking time to 2 minutes. 6. Press the Pressure Level button to adjust the pressure to "High Pressure." 7. Once the cooking cycle is completed, quickly and carefully turn the steam release handle from Sealing position to the Venting position. 8. Serve warm.
Per Serving: Calories 208; Fat 18.13g; Sodium 74mg; Carbs 8.04g; Fiber 3.9g; Sugar 1.72g; Protein 7.24g

Dijon Brussels Sprouts

Prep time: 10 minutes | Cook time: 1 minutes | Serves: 4-6

1 pound fresh Brussels sprouts
1 cup water
2 garlic cloves, smashed
3 tablespoons apple cider vinegar
2 tablespoons Dijon mustard
1 tablespoon maple syrup
Black pepper

1. Combine the Brussels sprouts, water, and garlic in the Inner Pot. 2. Select Pressure Cook mode, and then press the "Pressure Cook" button again to select "Less" time option. 3. Use the "-" key to set the cooking time to 1 minute. 4. Press the Pressure Level button to adjust the pressure to "High Pressure." 5. Once the cooking cycle is completed, quickly and carefully turn the steam release handle from Sealing position to the Venting position. 6. Whisk the vinegar, mustard, and maple syrup in a small bowl. 7. When the cook time is complete, quick-release the pressure and carefully remove the lid. 8. Drain the water and mince the garlic. Add the mustard dressing to the sprouts and garlic, and toss to coat. 9. Season the Brussels sprouts with pepper and enjoy.
Per Serving: Calories 122; Fat 7.9g; Sodium 704mg; Carbs 6g; Fiber 3.6g; Sugar 6g; Protein 18g

Broccoli Bites

Prep time: 10 minutes | Cook time: 1 minute | Serves: 4

1 large crown broccoli, cut into large pieces
2 tablespoons toasted sesame oil
½ teaspoon salt
¼ teaspoon ground ginger
⅛ teaspoon garlic powder
2 tablespoons sesame seeds

1. Place the broccoli pieces into a suitable cake pan. 2. In a small bowl, whisk together the sesame oil, salt, ginger, and garlic powder. 3. Add it to the broccoli and toss to coat. 4. Pour 1 cup water into the Inner Pot and place the Steam Rack inside. 5. Put the pan on the rack. 6. Select Pressure Cook mode, and then press the "Pressure Cook" button again to select "Less" time option. 7. Use the "-" key to set the cooking time to 1 minute. 8. Press the Pressure Level button to adjust the pressure to "High Pressure." 9. Once the cooking cycle is completed, quickly and carefully turn the steam release handle from Sealing position to the Venting position. 10. Carefully remove the pan from the Inner Pot. 11. Toss the broccoli pieces with sesame seeds. Transfer the food to a plate and enjoy.
Per Serving: Calories 94; Fat 9.35g; Sodium 300mg; Carbs 2.12g; Fiber 0.5g; Sugar 0.03g; Protein 1.7g

Sweet Potatoes with Maple Syrup

Prep time: 10 minutes | Cook time: 9 minutes | Serves:4-6

4 sweet potatoes (about 2 pounds), peeled and cut into 1-inch chunks
1 cup orange juice
2 garlic cloves, minced
1 (1-inch) knob fresh ginger, peeled and grated, or 1 teaspoon ground ginger
1 (1-inch) knob fresh turmeric, peeled and grated, or 1 teaspoon ground turmeric
½ teaspoon ground cinnamon
1 tablespoon maple syrup

1. Combine the sweet potatoes, orange juice, garlic, ginger, turmeric, and cinnamon in the Inner Pot. 2. Select Pressure Cook mode, and then press the "Pressure Cook" button again to select "Less" time option. 3. Use the "+/-" keys on the control panel to set the cooking time to 9 minutes. 4. Press the Pressure Level button to adjust the pressure to "High Pressure." 5. Once the cooking cycle is completed, quickly and carefully turn the steam release handle from Sealing position to the Venting position. 6. Add the maple syrup to the sweet potatoes, and mash the potatoes with a handheld potato masher or a large fork. 7. Stir well and serve immediately.
Per Serving: Calories 184; Fat 5g; Sodium 441mg; Carbs 17g; Fiber 4.6g; Sugar 5g; Protein 9g

Simple Lentil-Walnut Dip

Prep time: 10 minutes | Cook time: 10 minutes | Serves: 4-6

¾ cup walnuts
2 cups water
1 cup green or brown lentils
½ medium onion, roughly chopped
1 bay leaf
2 garlic cloves, minced
2 tablespoons lemon juice
1 tablespoon white miso paste
1 tablespoon apple cider vinegar
Black pepper

1. Select Sauté mode and press the "Sauté" button again to select "Normal" setting. Let the machine heat for 2 minutes. 2. Add walnuts to the Inner Pot, and sauté for 3 to 5 minutes until slightly darker in color and the oils begin to release. Transfer the walnuts to a bowl and set aside for later use. 3. Combine the water, lentils, onion, and bay leaf in the Inner Pot. 4. Select Pressure Cook mode, and then press the "Pressure Cook" button again to select "Less" time option. 5. Use the "+/-" keys on the control panel to set the cooking time to 10 minutes. 6. Press the Pressure Level button to adjust the pressure to "High Pressure." 7. Once the cooking cycle is completed, allow the steam to release naturally for 10 minutes, then turn the steam release handle to the Venting position. 8. Remove and discard the bay leaf. 9. Add the lentils, onion, garlic, lemon juice, miso paste, vinegar, and black pepper to the blender. Blend them until creamy. 10. Serve either immediately as a warm dip or chill.
Per Serving: Calories 282; Fat 7.9g; Sodium 704mg; Carbs 6g; Fiber 3.6g; Sugar 6g; Protein 18g

Polenta with Mushroom Ragù

Prep time: 10 minutes | Cook time: 30 minutes | Serves: 4-6

1 medium onion, diced
1⅓ cups Easy Vegetable Broth
2 garlic cloves, minced
8-ounce white button mushrooms, sliced
8-ounce cremini mushrooms, sliced
3 tablespoons tomato paste
2 teaspoons dried thyme
1 teaspoon balsamic vinegar
Black pepper
3 cups water
1 cup polenta or ground cornmeal
1 cup unsweetened plant-based milk

1. Select Sauté mode and press the "Sauté" button again to select "Normal" setting. Let the machine heat for 2 minutes. 2. Sauté the onion for 3 to 5 minutes until translucent, adding broth as needed to prevent it from sticking. 3. Add the garlic and sauté for 30 seconds; add the mushrooms and sauté for about 5 minutes until softened. 4. Stir in the tomato paste, thyme, vinegar, and pepper to taste. 5. Add ⅓ cup of the broth and scrape up any browned bits from the bottom of the pot. 6. Bring to a simmer and cook for 3 minutes. 7. Cancel the Sauté function and remove the mushroom mixture to a small bowl. 8. Rinse and dry the Inner Pot. 9. Add the water, polenta, milk, and the remaining 1 cup of broth to the Inner Pot, then cook them for 5 minutes on Sauté mode at Normal cooking temperature. 10. Press Cancel button to stop this cooking program. 11. Select Pressure Cook mode, and then press the "Pressure Cook" button again to select "Less" time option. 12. Use the "-" key to set the cooking time to 10 minutes. 13. Press the Pressure Level button to adjust the pressure to "High Pressure." 14. Once the cooking cycle is completed, allow the steam to release naturally. 15. Stir, then transfer to a serving bowl and top with the mushroom ragù. 16. Serve immediately.
Per Serving: Calories 295; Fat 12.9g; Sodium 414mg; Carbs 11g; Fiber 5g; Sugar 9g; Protein 11g

Chapter 5 Stew Recipes

Garlic Veggie Chili

Prep time: 10 minutes | Cook Time: 10 minutes | Serves: 4

1 tablespoon extra-virgin olive oil
3 garlic cloves, minced
12 scallions, whites and greens chopped, with 2 tablespoons chopped greens reserved
1 bell pepper, diced
1 jalapeño, finely diced (optional)
2 teaspoons chili powder
1 teaspoon ground cumin
½ teaspoon kosher salt
¼ teaspoon freshly ground black pepper

2 (15-ounce) cans black beans, rinsed and drained
1 (15-ounce) can pinto or kidney beans, rinsed and drained
1 (14.5-ounce) can diced tomatoes with juice, with or without chilies
1 cup frozen corn
½ cup beer (preferably lager) or water
Sour cream, for serving (optional)
Tortilla chips, for serving

1. Set the Instant Pot on Sauté and adjust the temperature setting to More. 2. After 30 seconds, add the oil and heat. Then add scallions (whites and greens chopped), jalapeno, scallions (2 tablespoons of greens reserved), and garlic and sauté about 3 minutes or until just soften, stirring from time to time. 3. Add cumin, chili powder, pepper, and salt in the pot and cook until fragrant, about 1 minute. Stir while cooking. 4. Place the pinto or kidney beans, tomatoes with juice, black beans, beer or water, and corn in the pot. 5. Then close the lid and turn the steam release handle to Sealing. 6. Set your Instant Pot on Pressure Cook at High and adjust the cooking time to 3 minutes. 7. When the cooking time is up, quick release the pressure. 8. Then carefully remove the lid. 9. If you desire a thicker chili, sauté again in the pot at More temperature setting for 3 to 5 minutes. Season as you like. 10. Transfer to serving bowls. Add a sprinkle of the remaining chopped scallion green, tortilla chips, and a dollop of sour cream(optional) to serve. 11. Enjoy!
Per Serving: Calories 595; Fat: 6.3g; Sodium 330mg; Carbs: 104.3g; Fiber 1g; Sugars: 7g; Protein 34.2g

Simple Beef and Veggies Stew

Prep time: 6 minutes | Cook Time: 43 minutes | Serves: 4

1 ½ tablespoons olive oil
1 cup beef stew meat
¼ teaspoon smoked paprika
¼ teaspoon dried thyme
⅛ teaspoon seasoned salt
1 tablespoon tomato paste

2 teaspoons dried onion flakes
½ teaspoon minced garlic
1 cup beef broth
⅓ cup sliced mushrooms
½ cup frozen diced potatoes
½ cup frozen mixed vegetables

1. Set your Instant Pot on Sauté and adjust the temperature to More. 2. Add in the inner pot and heat until hot and shiny. 3. Add beef, thyme, paprika, and salt in a small bowl. Toss well until evenly coated. 4. Then add the meat to the inner pot and sauté about 3 minutes or until both sides of meat are golden brown. Make sure not to stir while cooking. 5. Then stir the meat together with onion flakes, garlic, and tomato paste until completely coated. 6. Pour broth in the inner pot and scrape all the browned bits off the pot to deglaze. Turn off the heat and add the mixed vegetables, mushrooms, and potato. 7. Close the lid and turn the steam release handle to Sealing position. 8. Set your Instant Pot on Pressure Cook at High and adjust the cooking time to 30 minutes. 9. When the cooking time is up, naturally release the pressure about 10 minutes and carefully remove the lid. 10. Then serve the meal in a serving bowl. Enjoy!
Per Serving: Calories 258; Fat: 11g; Sodium 262mg; Carbs: 10.4g; Fiber 1g; Sugars: 2g; Protein 28.6g

Flavorful Three-Bean Chicken Chili

Prep time: 10 minutes | Cook Time: 21 minutes | Serves: 8

1 tablespoon avocado oil
1 large yellow onion, peeled and diced
2 medium carrots, peeled and diced
2 cloves garlic, minced
1 (15-ounce) can black beans, drained and rinsed
1 (15-ounce) can red kidney beans, drained and rinsed

1 (15-ounce) can pinto beans, drained and rinsed
1 tablespoon chili powder
1 teaspoon dried oregano
1 teaspoon salt
½ teaspoon black pepper
8 cups chicken stock
2 (5-ounce) boneless, skinless chicken breasts

1. Set your Instant Pot on Sauté and adjust the temperature setting to More. Then add oil to the inner pot and cook about 1 minute or until heated. 2. Add onion and carrots and cook about 5 minutes. Then add garlic and cook for 5 minutes. Turn off the heat. 3. In the inner pot, add chili powder, salt, oregano, stock, beans, salt, and pepper and stir well. Then add the chicken breasts. 4. Close the lid and turn the steam release handle to Sealing position. 5. Set your Instant Pot on Pressure Cook at High and adjust the cooking time to 10 minutes. 6. When the cooking time is up, naturally release the pressure. 7. Carefully remove the lid and shred the chicken with 2 forks. 8. Serve and enjoy!
Per Serving: Calories 643; Fat: 5.6g; Sodium 1121mg; Carbs: 104; Fiber 1g; Sugars: 5.7g; Protein 46.3g

Hearty Avocado Turkey Chili

Prep time: 15 minutes | Cook Time: 40 minutes | Serves: 8

½ pound dry black beans
10 ounces uncured turkey bacon, chopped
½ large yellow onion, peeled and diced
1-pound lean ground turkey
1 tablespoon minced garlic
½ large red bell pepper, seeded and diced
½ large orange bell pepper, seeded and diced

1 medium jalapeño, seeded and minced
2 cups chicken stock
1 tablespoon dried oregano
1 teaspoon ground cumin
2 teaspoons kosher salt
1 teaspoon black pepper
1 teaspoon smoked paprika
2 tablespoons chili powder
1 tablespoon Worcestershire sauce
1 medium avocado, sliced

1. In a large bowl, add the dry beans and pour over 5 cups of water. Soak the beans at room temperature about 4 to 8 hours. Then drain and set aside. 2. Set your Instant Pot on Sauté and adjust the temperature setting to More. Then add the bacon and cook about 6 to 8 minutes or until crispy, stirring often while cooking. Then place onto a paper towel lined plate. 3. Then add the onion and cook about 3 to 4 minutes or until just soften. Then add garlic and turkey in the pot and sauté about 7 minutes or until golden brown, stirring often while cooking. Turn off the heat. 4. Place jalapeno, stock, cumin, salt, black pepper, chili powder, the soaked beans, ¾ of the cooked bacon, oregano, bell pepper, and Worcestershire sauce in the pot and scrape all the browned bits off the pot to deglaze. 5. Close the lid and turn the steam release handle to Sealing. 6. Set your Instant Pot on Pressure Cook at High and adjust the cooking time to 25 minutes. 7. When cooked, naturally release the pressure. 8. Serve on serving bowls and sprinkle on the top with the remaining bacons and the avocado slices. 9. Enjoy!
Per Serving: Calories 288; Fat: 13.1g; Sodium 1022mg; Carbs: 24g; Fiber 1g; Sugars: 2.3g; Protein 21.1g

Irish Lamb Stew

Prep time: 10 minutes | Cook Time: 40 minutes | Serves: 4

2 tablespoons olive oil
2 pounds boneless leg of lamb, fat trimmed, cut into 1-inch pieces
Salt and freshly ground black pepper
1 medium yellow onion, thinly sliced through the root end
½ cup Guinness or Murphy's Irish stout
1½ cups store-bought beef broth, or homemade (page 228)
3 medium carrots, peeled and cut into 1-inch-thick coins
1 large (16-ounce) russet potato, peeled and cut into ½-inch slices
2 tablespoons cornstarch

1. Rub salt and pepper over the lamb to season. 2. Set the Instant Pot on Sauté at More heat. Add the oil in the inner pot. Heat. 3. Add 1 cup of the seasoned lamb pieces to the pot and cook about 8 minutes or until browned, stirring from time to time. Leave space among the meat. 4. Then add onion to the pot and sear about 5 minutes or until browned, stirring occasionally. 5. Add the stout in the pot and cook for 1 minute. To deglaze, scrape all the browned bits off the pot. Then turn off the heat. 6. Stir in the broth, carrots, and the remaining lamb in the pot until well combined. Arrange the potatoes on the top without stirring. 7. Close the lid and turn the steam release handle to Sealing position. 8. Set your Instant Pot on Pressure Cook at High and adjust the cooking time to 25 minutes. 9. When cooked, naturally release the pressure about 10 minutes and then quick release the remaining pressure. 10. Carefully remove the lid. 11. Mix cornstarch with 2 tablespoons of water. Gently stir to combine well and then pour into the stew. 12. Set the Instant Pot on Sauté at More heat. Simmer about 1 minute or until bubbly. 13. Season with salt and pepper and transfer onto serving bowls. Serve and enjoy!
Per Serving: Calories 516; Fat: 23.6g; Sodium 204mg; Carbs: 8.2g; Fiber 1g; Sugars: 2.3g; Protein 64.1g

One-Pot Beef Chili Mac

Prep time: 10 minutes | Cook Time: 20 minutes | Serves: 4

1 tablespoon olive oil
1 pound 95% lean ground beef
1 medium yellow onion, chopped
1 (28-ounce) can crushed fire-roasted tomatoes (such as Muir Glen)
1 (15-ounce) can kidney beans, drained
1 cup elbow macaroni (4 ounces)
1 cup store-bought beef broth, or
homemade
2 tablespoons plus 1½ teaspoons mild chili powder
Salt and freshly ground black pepper
Optional Garnishes
2 cups grated cheddar
1 cup sour cream or homemade yogurt

1. Set the Instant Pot on Sauté and adjust the temperature setting to Normal. 2. Then add oil in the inner pot and heat. Add the onion and beef and cook about 10 minutes or until brown. Stir from time to time while cooking. Leave the beef in 1-inch chunks for best cooking texture. Then turn off the heat. 3. Add beans, macaroni, chili powder, ½ teaspoon of salt, several grinds of pepper, and tomatoes. 4. Close the lid and turn the steam release handle to Sealing position. 5. Set the Instant Pot on Pressure Cook at High and adjust the cooking time to 5 minutes. 6. When cooked, naturally release the pressure about 5 minutes and then quick release the remaining pressure. 7. Add salt and pepper to season. Garnish with grated cheddar or sour cream and serve.
Per Serving: Calories 714; Fat: 13.9g; Sodium 409mg; Carbs: 85.9g; Fiber 1g; Sugars: 5.5g; Protein 60.9g

Hearty Turkey and Wild Rice Stew

Prep time: 10 minutes | Cook Time: 36 minutes | Serves: 4

1 tablespoon avocado oil
1 medium yellow onion, peeled and diced
2 medium carrots, peeled and chopped
2 medium stalks celery, ends
removed and sliced
8 ounces sliced white mushrooms
4 cloves garlic, minced
1 tablespoon Worcestershire sauce
1 teaspoon dried thyme
1 teaspoon dried rosemary
1 teaspoon salt
¼ teaspoon black pepper
1-pound lean ground turkey
4 cups chicken stock
1 cup wild rice blend
½ cup sliced almonds

1. Set your Instant Pot on Sauté and adjust the temperature setting to More. 2. Then add oil in the inner pot and cook about 1 minute to heat. 3. Add onion, celery, garlic, thyme, rosemary, pepper, salt, Worcestershire sauce, carrots, and mushrooms in the pot and sauté about 10 minutes. 4. When cooked, stir turkey and rice in the pot. 5. Close the lid and turn the steam release handle to Sealing. 6. Set your Instant Pot on Pressure Cook at High and adjust the cooking time to 20 minutes. 7. When the cooking time is up, naturally release the pressure about 10 minutes and then quick release the remaining pressure. 8. Carefully remove the lid. 9. Serve on a serving bowl and sprinkle with the sliced almond. Stir well. 10. Enjoy!
Per Serving: Calories 291; Fat: 15.3g; Sodium 1499mg; Carbs: 13.1g; Fiber 1g; Sugars: 5.6g; Protein 28.1g

Mexican Chicken Pozole Verde

Prep time: 10 minutes | Cook Time: 15 minutes | Serves: 4

3 cups store-bought chicken broth, or homemade
1¼ pounds boneless, skinless chicken breasts, cut in half crosswise
1 medium yellow onion, chopped
1 cup green tomatillo salsa
1 (15-ounce) can white hominy, drained and rinsed
1¼ teaspoons chili powder
Finely grated zest and juice of 1 lime
Salt and freshly ground black pepper
OPTIONAL GARNISHES
Sliced radishes
Sour cream
Diced avocado

1. In the inner pot, add chicken, onion, salsa, hominy, chili powder, and pour the broth. Combine well. 2. Close the lid and turn the steam release handle to Sealing position. 3. Set the Instant Pot on Pressure Cook at High and adjust the cooking time to 5 minutes. 4. When cooked, naturally release the pressure about 10 minutes and then quick release the remaining pressure. 5. Remove the chicken onto a clean cutting board and cool for a while. Then chop the chicken into bite-size pieces. 6. Place the chicken pieces back to the soup. Then add lime juice and zest in the inner pot and add salt and pepper to season. 7. Garnish with the above optional garnishes and serve!
Per Serving: Calories 718; Fat: 25.4g; Sodium 1140mg; Carbs: 20.1g; Fiber 1g; Sugars: 3.8g; Protein 96.2g

Chicken, Carrots, and Dumplings

Prep time: 10 minutes | Cook Time: 15 minutes | Serves: 4

1 tablespoon olive oil
1 medium yellow onion, chopped
2 medium carrots, chopped
2 celery ribs, sliced
1 pound boneless, skinless chicken breasts
Salt and freshly ground black pepper
3 cups store-bought chicken broth, or homemade
1 cup Bisquick
⅓ cup milk

1. Set your Instant Pot on Sauté and adjust the temperature setting to Normal. 2. Add oil in the inner pot and heat. Then add carrot, celery, and onion in the pot, stirring often, for 4 minutes or until the onion are softened. Turn off the heat. 3. To season, rub salt and pepper over the chicken. Then pour broth in the pot. 4. Close the lid and turn the steam release handle to Sealing. Set your Instant Pot on Pressure Cook at High and timer for 5 minutes. 5. When cooked, quick release the pressure. Then place the chicken onto a clean cutting board. Cool for a while and cut the chicken into bite-size pieces. Then return the chicken pieces back to the pot. 6. Mix together the milk with Bisquick until a sticky batter is formed. Using a tablespoon to drip the batter in the pot. 7. Set your Instant Pot on Sauté and adjust the temperature to Normal. Cook about 5 minutes or until the dumplings are fluffy and cooked through. If the dumplings are done, they should be dry in the center. 8. Serve and enjoy!
Per Serving: Calories 433; Fat: 17.8g; Sodium 1081mg; Carbs: 25.9g; Fiber 1g; Sugars: 7.7g; Protein 40.1g

Shrimp and Lentil Stew with Spinach

Prep time: 10 minutes | Cook Time: 25 minutes | Serves: 4

2 tablespoons extra-virgin olive oil
1 small onion, chopped
2 carrots, peeled and chopped
2 celery stalks, chopped
4 garlic cloves, minced
½ teaspoon ground cumin
¼ teaspoon ground turmeric
3 cups chicken broth (try the recipe here)
1 cup dried green lentils, rinsed and drained
1 bay leaf
Kosher salt
Freshly ground black pepper
16 uncooked large shrimp, peeled and deveined
5 ounces fresh spinach, roughly chopped
Juice of ½ lemon

1. Set your Instant Pot on Sauté and adjust the temperature setting to More. 2. After 10 seconds, add onion, carrots, garlic, celery, and oil in the inner pot. Cook until the onion just softened, about 3 minutes. 3. Stir in the turmeric and cumin. Then add lentils, bay leaf, and broth in the pot. To season, add salt and pepper. 4. Close the lid and turn the steam release handle to Sealing position. 5. Set your Instant Pot on Pressure Cook at High and adjust the cooking time to 20 minutes. 6. When the cooking time is up, naturally release the pressure for 10 minutes and then quick release the remaining pressure. Carefully remove the lid. 7. Set your Instant Pot on Sauté and adjust the temperature setting to More. 8. Then add spinach and shrimp in the inner pot and stir. When the soup begins boiling, turn off the heat. 9. Then let it sit for a few minutes or until the shrimps are opaque. 10. Carefully remove and discard the bay leaf. 11. Drizzle with lemon juice. Serve and enjoy!
Per Serving: Calories 285; Fat: 8.7g; Sodium 605mg; Carbs: 35.6g; Fiber 1g; Sugars: 3.9g; Protein 16.8g

Savory Beef Borscht

Prep time: 10 minutes | Cook Time: 25 minutes | Serves: 4

1 large bunch red beets with greens, peeled and cut into ½-inch pieces
1¼ pounds beef chuck roast, trimmed and cut into ½-inch chunks
1 tablespoon extra-virgin olive oil
Salt and freshly ground black pepper
2½ cups store-bought beef broth,
or homemade
1 yellow onion, chopped
1 teaspoon caraway seeds
1 teaspoon dried dill
1 tablespoon balsamic or red wine vinegar
OPTIONAL GARNISH
¾ cup sour cream or plain Greek yogurt

1. Brush oil over the beef and generously rub with salt and pepper to season. 2. Set your Instant Pot to Sauté at More heat. 3. After 30 seconds, add the seasoned beef and sear for 4 minutes or until well browned, stirring from time to time. Then turn off the heat. 4. Place the broth, the remaining beef, beet stems, caraway, dill, onions, and beets to the inner pot. 5. Close the lid and turn the steam release handle to Sealing position. 6. Set your Instant Pot on Pressure Cook at High and adjust the cooking time to 15 minutes. 7. When cooked, naturally release the pressure for 10 minutes. Then release the remaining pressure carefully. 8. Then add beet greens and vinegar in the inner pot. 9. Set your Instant Pot on Sauté at More heat. 10. Simmer the sauce until thicken and the greens are tender, about 1 minute. 11. Turn off the heat. Add salt and pepper to season. Sprinkle the sour cream on the top to garnish. 12. Serve and enjoy!
Per Serving: Calories 492; Fat: 36.2g; Sodium 589mg; Carbs: 6.3g; Fiber 1g; Sugars: 3.1g; Protein 33.4g

Miso Pork Ramen

Prep time: 10 minutes | Cook Time: 40 minutes | Serves: 4

4 large eggs
1½ pounds pork shoulder, cut into 4 large pieces
Salt and freshly ground black pepper
1 tablespoon canola oil
6 cups store-bought chicken
broth, or homemade
4 green onions, thinly sliced, white and green parts separated
3 tablespoons red or white miso
2 (3-ounce) packages dried ramen noodles (seasoning packet discarded)
2 heads baby bok choy, split lengthwise
OPTIONAL GARNISHES
Nori seaweed sheets, crushed
Canned bamboo shoots, diced
Shichimi togarashi (spicy Japanese chile and sesame seed seasoning)

1. In the inner pot, pour a cup of cold water. Place the trivet in the pot and arrange eggs on. 2. Close the lid and turn the steam release handle to Sealing. 3. Set your Instant Pot on Pressure Cook at High and timer for 3 minutes. 4. When cooked, quick release the pressure and then bath the eggs in cold water to avoid overcooked. Peel the eggs and cut them in half lengthwise. Set it aside. 5. Rub salt and pepper over the pork to season and drizzle oil. 6. Set the Instant Pot on Sauté at Normal heat. 7. After 30 seconds, add the seasoned pork in the inner pot and cook about 6 minutes or until browned. Then turn off the heat. 8. Pour broth and add the white parts of the green onions. 9. Close the lid and turn the steam release handle to Sealing position. 10. Set your Instant Pot on Pressure Cook at High and timer for 35 minutes. 11. When cooked, quick release the pressure. Carefully remove the lid and transfer the pork to a cutting board. 12. Slice the pork against the grain into thin slices with a sharp carving knife. 13. Set your Instant Pot on Sauté at Normal heat. 14. Simmer the broth and skim some of the foam/fat. Whisk in the miso. 15. Arrange the bok choy and noodles in the pot and simmer about 3 minutes or until just tender. Turn off the heat. 16. Divide the meal among serving bowls. 17. Top them with the remaining ingredients, and enjoy with the eggs.
Per Serving: Calories 739; Fat: 39.4g; Sodium 2562mg; Carbs: 43.8g; Fiber 1g; Sugars: 11.3g; Protein 52.5g

Flavorful Beef Chili

Prep time: 10 minutes | Cook Time: 15 minutes | Serves: 4

1-pound ground beef
1 green bell pepper, seeded and finely chopped
1 medium onion, finely chopped
3 garlic cloves, minced
1½ tablespoons chili powder
2 teaspoons ground cumin
1 teaspoon salt
½ teaspoon freshly ground black pepper
½ teaspoon paprika
¼ cup beef broth
2 tablespoons tomato paste
2 (14.5-ounce) cans diced tomatoes

1. Set the Instant Pot on Sauté at More heat. 2. When heated, add bell pepper, ground beef, garlic, onion, chili powder, salt, cumin, paprika, and pepper in the inner pot and cook about 10 minutes or until the meat has browned, stirring from time to time. 3. Then pour the beef broth to the pot and scrape all the browned bits of the pot. 4. Add tomato paste and stir well. Then turn off the heat. 5. Add the diced tomatoes with juice and mix well. 6. Close the lid and turn the steam release handle to Sealing position. 7. Set the Instant Pot on Pressure Cook at High and timer for 15 minutes. 8. When cooked, naturally release the pressure about 10 minutes and the quick-release the remaining pressure. 9. Carefully remove the lid and stir the chili. 10. Serve and enjoy!
Per Serving: Calories: 244; Fat: 9g; Sodium: 765mg; Carbs: 17g; Fiber: 5g; Protein: 26g

Spicy Chicken Chili

Prep time: 2 minutes | Cook Time: 3 minutes | Serves: 4

½ cup diced chicken breast
1 tablespoon dried onion flakes
½ teaspoon minced garlic
1 (14-ounce) can great northern beans, drained and rinsed
1 cup chicken broth
1 tablespoon chopped green
chilies
¼ teaspoon salt
1/16 teaspoon crushed red pepper flakes
¼ teaspoon ground cumin
1 ½ tablespoons sour cream
¼ cup heavy cream

1. Add chicken breast, onion flakes, minced garlic, beans, the chicken broth, chopped green chilies, salt, red pepper flakes, and ground cumin in the inner pot. 2. Close the lid and turn the steam release handle to Sealing. 3. Set your Instant Pot on Pressure Cook at High and adjust the cooking time to 3 minutes. 4. When the cooking time is up, turn the handle from Sealing position to Venting position. 5. Then carefully remove the lid. 6. Add the sour cream and heavy cream in the pot and stir well. 7. Serve on a serving bowl.
Per Serving: Calories 419; Fat: 6.1g; Sodium 358mg; Carbs: 64.2g; Fiber 1g; Sugars: 3.1g; Protein 28.9g

Peanut Butter Sweet Potato and Kale Stew

Prep time: 10 minutes | Cook Time: 15 minutes | Serves: 4

1 medium onion, diced
4 garlic cloves, minced
1 (1-inch) knob ginger, peeled and grated
1 teaspoon ground turmeric
1 teaspoon ground cumin
2 (14-ounce) cans no-salt-added fire-roasted tomatoes
3 medium sweet potatoes, peeled and chopped into 1½-inch chunks
2 cups warm water
¾ cup unsalted smooth peanut butter
5 ounces kale, chopped
Freshly ground black pepper
Salt (optional)
¾ cup chopped unsalted peanuts

1. Set your Instant Pot on Sauté at More heat. Cook the onion in the inner pot about 3 to 5 minutes. Add turmeric, ginger, garlic, and cumin and cook until fragrant about 30 seconds. 2. Turn off the heat and add tomatoes. To deglaze, scrape all the browned bits off the pot. Add sweet potatoes. 3. Whisk together peanut butter and water and blend in a medium bowl. Stir into the pot. Arrange the kale on the top. 4. Close the lid and turn the steam release handle to Sealing. 5. Set your Instant Pot on Pressure Cook at High and timer for 10 minutes. 6. When cooked, naturally release the pressure and then quick-release the remaining pressure. Remove carefully the lid and add salt and pepper to season. 7. Add peanuts to garnish and serve. Enjoy! (Store leftovers in the fridge for up to 4 days in a covered container.)
Per Serving: Calories 326; Fat: 13.8g; Sodium 75mg; Carbs: 44g; Fiber 1g; Sugars: 3.3g; Protein 10.5g

Chicken-Potato Stew

Prep time: 10 minutes | Cook Time: 25 minutes | Serves: 6

¼ cup olive oil
4 to 6 bone-in, skin-on chicken breasts or thighs
½ cup dry white wine
3 tablespoons white vinegar
1 (8-ounce) can tomato sauce
1½ pounds potatoes, peeled and cut into 1-inch pieces
1 medium onion, chopped
¼ cup Spanish-style green olives stuffed with pimentos
6 garlic cloves, chopped
1 teaspoon capers
1½ teaspoons salt

1. Set the Instant Pot on Sauté at More heat. Add oil in the inner pot and heat. 2. Then add the chicken to pot and sauté for 8 minutes, flipping once halfway through cooking. Transfer to a plate. 3. Add vinegar and wine in the pot and scrape all the browned bits off the pot. Simmer about 3 minutes, stirring from time to time. Then turn off the heat. 4. Drizzle the tomato sauce in the inner pot and mix well. 5. Add onion, olives, capers, garlic, salt, and potatoes and stir well. 6. Return the chicken back to the pot and soak the chicken in the sauce. 7. Close the lid and turn the steam release handle to Sealing position. 8. Set the Instant Pot on Pressure Cook at High and timer for 10 minutes. 9. When cooked, naturally release the pressure about 5 minutes and then quick-release the remaining pressure. 10. Remove the lid and set the Instant Pot on Sauté at More heat. Simmer for 5 minutes to thicken, stirring from time to time. 11. Serve and enjoy!
Per Serving: Calories: 533; Fat: 20g; Sodium: 1347mg; Carbs: 38g; Fiber: 6g; Protein: 46g

Balsamic Barley, Mushroom, and Kale Stew

Prep time: 10 minutes | Cook Time: 25 minutes | Serves: 4

1 medium onion, diced
4 celery stalks, diced
1 pound cremini mushrooms, sliced
3 garlic cloves, minced
2 tablespoons tomato paste
1 tablespoon no-salt-added poultry seasoning
6 cups Easy Vegetable Broth, no-salt-added vegetable broth, or water
1 cup pearled barley
2 tablespoons balsamic vinegar
1 tablespoon chickpea miso paste
1 bunch kale, stemmed and chopped
Freshly ground black pepper
Salt (optional)

1. Set the Instant Pot on Sauté at More heat. 2. Add celery, mushrooms, and onion until the onion is translucent about 3 to 5 minutes. To avoid sticking, add one tablespoon of water at a time. 3. Then add tomato paste, poultry seasoning, and garlic and stir until fragrant, about 30 seconds. 4. Pour broth and add the vinegar, barley, and miso in the pot. Scrape all the browned bits off the pot to deglaze. 5. Arrange kale on the top. Turn off the heat. 6. Close the lid and turn the steam release handle to Sealing position. 7. Set the Instant Pot on Pressure Cook at High and timer for 20 minutes. 8. When cooked, naturally release the pressure about 10 minutes and then quick release the remaining pressure. 9. Remove the lid carefully. Stir to combine well and add salt and pepper to season as you like. 10. Serve and enjoy! (Store any leftovers in the fridge for up to 4 days in a covered container.)
Per Serving: Calories: 248; Fat: 1g; Carbs: 52g; Fiber: 11g; Sugar: 7g; Sodium: 196mg; Protein: 11g

Chickpea Stew

Prep time: 20 minutes | Cook time: 35 minutes | Serves: 4-6

2 tablespoons olive oil
1 large-sized leek, chopped
3 cloves garlic, pressed
3 potatoes, diced
2 carrots, diced
1 sweet pepper, seeded and chopped
1 jalapeno pepper, seeded and chopped
1 cup tomato puree
½ teaspoons cumin powder
½ teaspoons turmeric powder
1 teaspoon mustard seeds
2 cups roasted vegetable broth
1 ½ cups chickpeas, soaked overnight

1. Press the "Sauté" button twice to select "Normal" settings and heat the oil until sizzling. 2. Once hot, cook the leeks and garlic for 2 to 3 minutes or until they are just tender. 3. Add the remaining ingredients and stir to combine well. 4. Put on the pressure cooker's lid and turn the steam valve to "Sealing" position. 5. Set the Instant Pot to Pressure Cook. 6. Use the "+/-" keys on the control panel to set the cooking time to 35 minutes. 7. Press the Pressure Level button to adjust the pressure to "High". 8. Once the cooking cycle is completed, quick-release the steam. 9. When all the steam is released, remove the pressure lid from the top carefully. 10. Serve in individual bowls. 11. Bon appétit!
Per Serving: Calories 382; Fat 7.9g; Sodium 704mg; Carbs 6g; Fiber 3.6g; Sugar 6g; Protein 18g

Texas Beef Chili

Prep time: 10 minutes | Cook Time: 32 minutes | Serves: 4

2½ pounds boneless beef chuck; Fat trimmed, cut into 1- to 1½-inch chunks
1 tablespoon canola oil
Salt and freshly ground black pepper
¼ cup prepared mole paste (such as Doña Maria brand)
½ cup store-bought beef broth, or homemade
2 tablespoons chili powder
1 large onion, chopped, ½ cup set aside for garnish
1 (15-ounce) can fire-roasted diced tomatoes with green chilies, with juice
2 tablespoons masa harina (corn flour)
OPTIONAL GARNISHES
1 cup sour cream
Sliced pickled jalapeños

1. Toss the beef with oil on a foil-lined baking sheet. Rub salt and pepper over the beef and season generously. 2. Put the oven rack 3 to 4 inches below the broiler element and preheat the broiler. Then arrange the beef in the broiler and broil for about 6 minutes or until one side is well browned. 3. In the inner pot, add the beef and the juices. 4. Whisk the broth, chili powder, and mole paste in a small mixing bowl. In the inner pot, add onion, tomatoes with juice, and the broth mixture and stir until well combined. 5. Close the lid and turn the steam release handle to Sealing position. 6. Set the Instant Pot on Pressure Cook at High and adjust the cooking time to 25 minutes. 7. When cooked, naturally release the pressure about 10 minutes and then quick-release the remaining pressure. 8. In a small bowl, place the masa harina and whisk in a cup of the soup. Transfer the mixture to the pot and gently stir. 9. Set your Instant Pot on Sauté at Normal heat. Simmer about 1 minute or until bubbly and thickened, stirring often. Then turn off the heat. 10. Add salt and pepper to season the chili. 11. Garnish and serve, as you like.
Per Serving: Calories 414; Fat: 29.5g; Sodium 377mg; Carbs: 8.1g; Fiber 1g; Sugars: 1.3g; Protein 28.8g

Savory Black Bean and Quinoa Chili

Prep time: 10 minutes | Cook Time: 15 minutes | Serves: 6

1 large onion, diced
2 bell peppers, diced
4 garlic cloves, minced
1 tablespoon gluten-free chili powder
2 teaspoons ground cumin
2 cups water
2 (14.5-ounce) cans no-salt-added

black beans, drained and rinsed
1 (28-ounce) can no-salt-added diced tomatoes
½ cup red quinoa
1 tablespoon gluten-free vegan Worcestershire sauce
Freshly ground black pepper
Salt (optional)

1. Set the Instant Pot on Sauté at More heat. When heated, cook the onion and bell peppers for 3 to 5 minutes. Add water to avoid sticking, one tablespoon at a time. 2. Add the chili powder, cumin, and garlic in the pot and stir until fragrant, about 30 seconds. 3. Then add black beans, quinoa, tomatoes, and Worcestershire sauce to the pot and add salt and pepper to season. 4. Turn off the heat. Close the lid and turn the steam release handle to Sealing position. 5. Set the Instant Pot on Pressure Cook at High and timer for 7 minutes. 6. When cooked, naturally release the pressure about 10 minutes and quick release the remaining pressure. 7. Then carefully remove the lid. Stir and serve immediately. 8. Leftovers are reserved in the fridge for up to 4 days in a covered container.
Per Serving: Calories 569; Fat: 2.3g; Sodium 115mg; Carbs: 104.4g; Fiber 1g; Sugars: 7.3g; Protein 36.3g

Beef and Barley Stew with Mushrooms

Prep time: 10 minutes | Cook Time: 25 minutes | Serves: 6

2 tablespoons canola oil
2 pounds stewing beef (chuck, round, or rump roast), trimmed of fat and cut into 1-inch cubes
Kosher salt
Freshly ground black pepper
¼ cup all-purpose flour
1 onion, diced
8 ounces mushrooms, chopped
½ cup dry red wine

2 carrots, peeled and chopped
2 celery stalks, chopped
3 garlic cloves, minced
1 small fresh rosemary sprig
3 fresh thyme sprigs
1 bay leaf
3 cups beef broth
1 cup water
1 cup pearl barley

1. To season, rub salt and pepper over the beef and then coat the beef with the flour. Shake off excess. 2. Set your Instant Pot on Sauté and adjust the temperature setting to More. 3. Add oil in the inner pot. When the oil has heated, add half the seasoned beef in the pot and cook until lightly browned, about 4 minutes. Then stir mushrooms. Pour wine and scrape all the browned bits off the pot to deglaze. 4. Add celery, garlic, bay leaf, broth, barley, water, beef, carrots, broth, and rosemary in the pot. Then add salt and pepper to season. 5. Close the lid and turn the steam release handle to Sealing. 6. Set your Instant Pot on Pressure Cook at High and adjust the cooking time to 25 minutes. 7. When the cooking time is up, naturally release the pressure and carefully remove the lid. 8. Serve in bowls or on soup plates and enjoy!
Per Serving: Calories: 521; Fat: 15.4g; Sodium: 535mg; Carbs: 36.5g; Fiber 1g; Sugars: 3.3g; Protein 53.8g

Worcestershire Stout Beef Stew

Prep time: 10 minutes | Cook Time: 35 minutes | Serves: 6

1 tablespoon vegetable oil
2 pounds chuck roast, cut into bite-size pieces
2 cups beef broth
1 cup Irish stout beer (such as Guinness)
3 tablespoons tomato paste
1 tablespoon Worcestershire sauce
1½ teaspoons salt

1 teaspoon freshly ground black pepper
½ teaspoon garlic powder
1-pound potatoes, peeled and cut into 1-inch pieces
1 large onion, chopped
3 carrots, peeled and chopped into 2-inch pieces
Chopped fresh parsley, for garnish

1. Set the Instant Pot on Sauté at More heat. Add oil in the inner pot and heat. 2. Add beef in the inner pot and cook each side about 4 minutes or until browned. Turn off the heat. 3. Then add beer and the beef broth in the pot and scrape all the browned bits off the pot to deglaze. 4. Stir in salt, Worcestershire sauce, pepper, garlic powder, and tomato paste until no tomato chunks in the pot. 5. Then add onion, carrots, and potatoes and combine well. 6. Close the lid and turn the steam release handle to Sealing position. 7. Set the Instant Pot on Pressure Cook at High and timer for 35 minutes. 8. When cooked, naturally release the pressure about 10 minutes and then quick-release the remaining pressure. 9. Carefully remove the lid and stir the stew. Sprinkle the chopped fresh parsley on the top to garnish and serve.
Per Serving: Calories: 386; Fat: 18g; Sodium: 833mg; Carbs: 20g; Fiber: 4g; Protein: 33g

Mexican Chorizo Chili

Prep time: 10 minutes | Cook Time: 25 minutes | Serves: 8

2 tablespoons canola oil, divided
2 cups dried pinto beans, rinsed, picked over (discard any bad beans), and soaked overnight
6 cups water
8 ounces Mexican chorizo, without casing
12 ounces ground beef
1 large onion, chopped
1 large red bell pepper, chopped
1 large jalapeño, seeded and

minced
3 garlic cloves, minced
1 tablespoon unsweetened cocoa powder
2 teaspoons ground cumin
1½ teaspoons chili powder
1 teaspoon dried oregano
1 (14.5-ounce) can diced tomatoes with juice
Kosher salt
Freshly ground black pepper

1. In the inner pot, add the beans, 1 tablespoon of oil, and water. 2. Close the lid and turn the steam release handle to Sealing. 3. Set your Instant Pot on Pressure Cook at High and adjust the cooking time to 13 minutes. 4. When the cooking time is up, turn off the heat and naturally release the pressure. 5. Drain the beans and reserve 2 cups of the soup. Rinse and dry the pot. 6. Set the Instant Pot on Sauté and set the temperature to More. 7. Add the chorizo and beef and cook with a wooden spatula to broke the beef for 4 minutes or until the beef is mostly browned. Then add onion. Cook and stir for 2 minutes or more. 8. Then cook and stir the jalapeno, garlic, and the bell pepper together in the inner pot, about 2 minutes. Add cumin, chili powder, oregano, and cocoa in the inner pot and cook for 1 minute. 9. Add the beans, diced tomatoes with juice, and the reserved soup. Add salt and pepper and stir to evenly season the meal. 10. Close the lid and turn the steam release handle to Sealing. 11. Set your Instant Pot on Pressure Cook at High and adjust the cooking time to 10 minutes. 12. When the cooking time is up, turn off the heat and naturally release the pressure. 13. Carefully remove the lid and serve!
Per Serving: Calories: 540; Fat: 27.4g; Sodium 732mg; Carbs: 40.1g; Fiber 1g; Sugars: 4.1g; Protein 33.6g

Barley Pottage

Prep time: 20 minutes | Cook time: 20 minutes | Serves: 4-6

1 tablespoon olive oil
1 onion, chopped
2 cloves garlic, minced
1 red chili pepper, minced
2 sweet peppers, seeded and chopped
1½ cups pearled barley

2 cups water
4 cups vegetable broth
2 stalks celery, chopped
2 carrots, chopped
2 tomatoes, pureed
1 teaspoon red pepper flakes
Sea salt and black pepper, to taste

1. Press the "Sauté" button twice to select "Normal" settings and heat the olive oil. 2. Now, sauté the onion until tender and translucent. 3. Then, stir in the garlic and peppers and cook an additional 3 minutes. Stir in the pearled barley. 4. Pour in water and broth. 5. Add the remaining ingredients to the inner pot. 6. Put on the pressure cooker's lid and turn the steam valve to "Sealing" position. 7. Set the Instant Pot to Pressure Cook. 8. Use the "+/-" keys on the control panel to set the cooking time to 15 minutes. 9. Press the Pressure Level button to adjust the pressure to "High". 10. Once the cooking cycle is completed, quick-release the steam. 11. When all the steam is released, remove the pressure lid from the top carefully. 12. Bon appétit!
Per Serving: Calories: 405; Fat 10.9g; Sodium 454mg; Carbs 10g; Fiber 3.1g; Sugar 5.2g; Protein 20g

Sweet Potato Black Bean Chili with Cinnamon

Prep time: 15 minutes | Cook Time: 27 minutes | Serves: 6

½ pound dry black beans	1 teaspoon salt
1 tablespoon avocado oil	¼ teaspoon black pepper
1 medium onion, peeled and diced	¼ teaspoon smoked paprika
3 cloves garlic, minced	¼ teaspoon ground cinnamon
2 medium-large sweet potatoes, peeled and cut into 1" cubes	1 (28-ounce) can diced fire-roasted tomatoes
1½ tablespoons ancho chili powder	3 cups vegetable stock
2 teaspoons ground cumin powder	1 (6-ounce) can tomato paste

1. In a large bowl, add the dry beans and then pour 5 cups of water over the beans. Let the beans soak at room temperature about 4 to 8 hours. Then drain and set aside. 2. Set your Instant Pot on Sauté and adjust the temperature setting to More. 3. Drizzle the oil in the inner pot and add onion to sauté about 5 to 6 minutes or until softened. Then add garlic and cook for 30 more seconds. 4. In the pot, add sweet potato, chili powder, salt, cumin, paprika, cinnamon, tomatoes, tomato paste, the soaked beans, and stock and stir together to combine. Scrape all the browned bits off the pot to deglaze. 5. Close the lid and turn the steam release handle to Sealing. 6. Set your Instant Pot on Pressure Cook at High and adjust the cooking time to 20 minutes. 7. When the cooking time is up, naturally release the pressure about 10 minutes and then quick release the remaining pressure. 8. Carefully remove the lid. Serve and enjoy!
Per Serving: Calories 209; Fat 1g; Sodium 434mg; Carbs: 42.4g; Fiber 1g; Sugars: 7.4g; Protein 10.4g

Chicken and Shrimp Gumbo

Prep time: 20 minutes | Cook time: 7 minutes | Serves: 4-6

2 tablespoons olive oil	2 tomatoes, chopped
1 onion, diced	1 tablespoon Creole seasoning
1 teaspoon garlic, minced	Sea salt and black pepper, to taste
½ pound chicken breasts, boneless, skinless and cubed	1 teaspoon cayenne pepper
½ pound smoked chicken sausage, cut into slices	1 tablespoon oyster sauce
	1 bay leaf
2 sweet peppers, diced	1-pound shrimp, deveined
1 jalapeno pepper, minced	½ pound okra, frozen
1 celery stalk, diced	2 stalks green onions, sliced thinly
2 cups chicken bone broth	1 tablespoon fresh lemon juice

1. Press the "Sauté" button two times to select "Normal" settings and heat the oil. 2. Sweat the onion and garlic until tender and aromatic or about 3 minutes; reserve. 3. Then, heat the remaining tablespoon of olive oil and cook the chicken and sausage until no longer pink, about 4 minutes. 4. Make sure to stir periodically to ensure even cooking. 5. Stir in the peppers, celery, broth, tomatoes, Creole seasoning, salt, black pepper, cayenne pepper, oyster sauce, and bay leaf. Add the reserved onion mixture. 6. Put on the pressure cooker's lid and turn the steam valve to "Sealing" position. 7. Set the Instant Pot to Pressure Cook. 8. Press the Pressure Level button to adjust the pressure to "High". 9. Use the "+/-" keys on the control panel to set the cooking time to 7 minutes. 10. Once the cooking cycle is completed, allow the steam to release naturally. 11. When all the steam is released, remove the pressure lid from the top carefully. 12. Afterwards, stir in the shrimp and okra. 13. Set the Instant Pot on Pressure Cook. Cook for 3 minutes at High pressure. 14. Once cooking is complete, use a natural pressure release; carefully remove the lid. 15. Divide between individual bowls and garnish with green onions. 16. Drizzle lemon juice over each serving. Bon appétit!
Per Serving: Calories 419; Fat 14g; Sodium 791mg; Carbs 8.9g; Fiber 4.6g; Sugar 8g; Protein 3g

Bosnian Pot Stew

Prep time: 20 minutes | Cook time: 35 minutes | Serves: 4-6

2 tablespoons safflower oil	cubes
2-pound pork loin roast, cut into	2 garlic cloves, chopped

1 onion, chopped	2 tomatoes, pureed
2 carrots, cut into chunks	2 cups chicken bone broth
2 celery ribs, cut into chunks	½ pound green beans, cut into 1-inch pieces
1 pound potatoes, cut into chunks	
sea salt and black pepper, to taste	2 tablespoons fresh parsley leaves, roughly chopped
1 teaspoon paprika	

1. Press the "Sauté" button twice to select "Normal" settings and heat the oil until sizzling. 2. Once hot, cook the pork until it is no longer pink on all sides. 3. Add the garlic and onion and cook for a minute or so, stirring frequently. 4. Stir in the carrots, celery, potatoes, salt, black pepper, paprika, tomatoes, and chicken bone broth. 5. Put on the pressure cooker's lid and turn the steam valve to "Sealing" position. 6. Set the Instant Pot to "Meat/Stew". 7. Use the "+/-" keys on the control panel to set the cooking time to 35 minutes. 8. Press the Pressure Level button to adjust the pressure to "High". 9. Once the cooking cycle is completed, quick-release the steam. 10. When all the steam is released, remove the pressure lid from the top carefully. 11. Add the green beans to the inner pot. 12. Press the "Sauté" button twice to select "Normal" settings again and let it simmer for a few minutes. 13. Serve in individual bowls garnished with fresh parsley.
Per Serving: Calories 421; Fat 10.9g; Sodium 354mg; Carbs 10.5g; Fiber 4.1g; Sugar 8.2g; Protein 26g

Spanish Olla Podrida

Prep time: 20 minutes | Cook time: 20 minutes | Serves: 4-6

2½-pound meaty pork ribs in adobo	2 carrots, sliced
	2 garlic cloves, sliced
½ pound Spanish chorizo sausage, sliced	Salt and black pepper, to taste
	1 pound alubias de Ibeas beans, soaked overnight
1 tablespoon olive oil	
2 onions, chopped	

1. Place the pork and sausage in the inner pot; cover with water. 2. Add the other ingredients and stir to combine. 3. Put on the pressure cooker's lid and turn the steam valve to "Sealing" position. 4. Set the Instant Pot to Pressure Cook. 5. Use the "+/-" keys on the control panel to set the cooking time to 20 minutes. 6. Press the Pressure Level button to adjust the pressure to "High". 7. Once the cooking cycle is completed, quick-release the pressure. 8. When all the steam is released, remove the pressure lid from the top carefully. 9. Serve hot with corn tortilla if desired. 10. Enjoy!
Per Serving: Calories 492; Fat 7.9g; Sodium 704mg; Carbs 6g; Fiber 3.6g; Sugar 6g; Protein 18g

Tuscan Chicken and Beans Stew

Prep time: 10 minutes | Cook Time: 15 minutes | Serves: 4

2 tablespoons extra-virgin olive oil	beans, rinsed and drained
	1 cup chicken broth
1 onion, chopped	6 bone-in, skin-on chicken thighs and/or drumsticks
2 celery stalks, chopped	
2 carrots, peeled and chopped	1 teaspoon dried oregano
4 garlic cloves, minced	Large pinch red pepper flakes
1 pound small red or white potatoes, halved	Kosher salt
	Freshly ground black pepper
1 (14.5-ounce) can chopped or crushed tomatoes with juice	1 tablespoon balsamic vinegar
1 (15-ounce) can red kidney	2 tablespoons chopped fresh parsley leaves

1. Set your Instant Pot on Sauté and adjust the temperature setting to More. 2. After 30 seconds, add oil in the inner pot. Then stir in onion, carrots, and celery and sauté until the onion is translucent, about 5 minutes. 3. Then add garlic and cook for 1 minute or more. 4. Add tomatoes and potatoes with beans, chicken, red pepper flakes, oregano, and broth in the pot. Then add salt and pepper to season. Mix together gently. 5. Set your Instant Pot on Pressure Cook at High and adjust the cooking time to 10 minutes. 6. When the cooking time is up, naturally release the pressure about 10 to 15 minutes. 7. Then carefully remove the lid and pull off the bones from the meat. 8. Return the meat to the inner pot. Add vinegar and parsley. 9. Taste for seasoning. Serve and enjoy!
Per Serving: Calories 527; Fat: 8.3g; Sodium 49mg; Carbs: 90g; Fiber 1g; Sugars: 6.4g; Protein 26.7g

Mushroom-Cabbage Stew

Prep time: 10 minutes | Cook Time: 15 minutes | Serves: 4

1 medium onion, diced
8 ounces shiitake or cremini mushrooms, chopped
4 garlic cloves, minced
1 (1-inch) knob fresh ginger, peeled and grated, or 1 teaspoon dried ginger
3 large carrots, diced
2 or 3 medium yellow potatoes, chopped into 1-inch chunks

1 tablespoon gluten-free soy sauce
2½ to 3 cups Easy Vegetable Broth or no-salt-added vegetable broth
1 small head green or napa cabbage, sliced
1 (14-ounce) can full-; Fat coconut milk
Freshly ground black pepper

1. Set your Instant Pot on Sauté at More heat. 2. Add mushrooms and onions in the inner pot and cook for 3 to 5 minutes or until the onion is translucent. To avoid sticking, add one tablespoon of water at a time. 3. Add ginger and garlic. Cook and stir until fragrant, about 30 seconds. Turn off the heat. 4. Add potatoes, soy sauce, and carrots in the pot. Then pour 2½ cups of broth or more to just soak the vegetables 5. Arrange the cabbage on the top. Close the lid and turn the steam release handle to Sealing. 6. Set the Instant Pot on Pressure Cook at High and timer for 3 minutes. 7. When cooked, naturally release the pressure about 5 minutes and then quick release the remaining pressure. 8. Carefully remove the lid and stir in coconut milk until completely heated. 9. Season with salt and pepper. 10. Serve and enjoy!
Per Serving: Calories 301; Fat: 23.8g; Sodium 49mg; Carbs: 21.8g; Fiber 1g; Sugars: 6.2g; Protein 5.4g

French Vegetable Stew

Prep time: 10 minutes | Cook Time: 10 minutes | Serves: 4

4 tablespoons olive oil, divided
1 medium eggplant, quartered lengthwise and then cut crosswise into ½-inch slices
1 medium onion, cut into ½-inch slices
1 large or 2 small zucchinis, cut into ½-inch slices

1 yellow bell pepper, seeded and cut into 2-inch chunks
3 garlic cloves, chopped
1 (28-ounce) can whole peeled tomatoes
1 teaspoon dried summer savory
Coarse salt
Freshly ground black pepper

1. Set the Instant Pot to Sauté at Normal heat. Add 2 tablespoons of olive oil in the inner pot and heat. 2. Add onion and eggplant and cook about 2 minutes, stirring from time to time. 3. Drizzle the remaining olive oil in the pot. Add bell pepper, garlic, and zucchini and cook about 2 minutes. 4. Turn off the heat and stir in the canned tomatoes with juices. Scrape all the browned bits off the bottom of the pot. Then add the summer savory, salt, and pepper to season. Mix well until the vegetables are well seasoned. 5. Close the lid and turn the steam release handle to Sealing position. 6. Set the Instant Pot on Pressure Cook at High and timer for 6 minutes. 7. Then reduce the pressure to Low and cook for 12 minutes. 8. When cooked, quick release the pressure. 9. Carefully remove the lid and add salt and pepper as needed to season. 10. Serve and enjoy!
Per Serving: Calories: 205; Fat: 13g; Sodium: 411mg; Carbs: 21g; Fiber: 7g; Protein: 4g

White Chicken Chili

Prep time: 20 minutes | Cook time: 20 minutes | Serves: 8

2 large boneless, skinless chicken breasts
1 (15-ounce) can black beans, drained
1 (15-ounce) can white beans, drained
1 medium onion, chopped
2 cups frozen corn
1 (10-ounce) can diced tomatoes

and green chilies
1 cup chicken broth
1 teaspoon chili powder
1 teaspoon ground cumin
1 (0.4-ounce) packet ranch dressing mix
8 oz. cream cheese, cut into 6 pieces

1. Combine the chicken, black beans, white beans, onion, corn, tomatoes, and chicken broth in the inner pot. 2. Sprinkle with the chili powder, cumin, and ranch dressing mix and stir well. 3. Put on the pressure cooker's lid and turn the steam valve to "Sealing" position. 4. Set the Instant Pot to Pressure Cook. 5. Use the "+/-" keys on the control panel to set the cooking time to 20 minutes. 6. Press the Pressure Level button to adjust the pressure to "High". 7. Once the cooking cycle is completed, allow the steam to release naturally for 10 minutes and then quick-release the remaining pressure. 8. When all the steam is released, remove the pressure lid from the top carefully. 9. Transfer the chicken to a plate and shred it with a fork. 10. Add the cream cheese to the bean mixture and stir until the cheese is melted and combined. 11. Return the chicken to the pot and stir well.
Per Serving: Calories 472; Fat 10.9g; Sodium 454mg; Carbs 10g; Fiber 3.1g; Sugar 5.2g; Protein 20g

Beef Peas Stew

Prep time: 20 minutes | Cook time: 27 minutes | Serves: 4-6

2 tablespoons olive oil
1½-pound beef stew meat, cut bite-sized pieces
1 red onion, chopped
4 cloves garlic, minced
1 carrot, cut into rounds
1 parsnip, cut into rounds
2 stalks celery, diced

Sea salt and black pepper, to taste
1 teaspoon cayenne pepper
4 cups beef bone broth
½ cup tomato paste
1 tablespoon fish sauce
2 bay leaves
1 cup frozen green peas

1. Press the "Sauté" button twice to select "Normal" settings and heat the oil. 2. Once hot, brown the beef stew meat for 4 to 5 minutes; set aside. 3. Then, cook the onion in pan drippings until tender and translucent; stir in the garlic and cook for 30 seconds. 4. Add the carrots, parsnip, celery, salt, black pepper, cayenne pepper, beef broth, tomato paste, fish sauce, and bay leaves. 5. Stir in the reserved beef stew meat. 6. Put on the pressure cooker's lid and turn the steam valve to "Sealing" position. 7. Set the Instant Pot to "Meat/Stew". 8. Use the "+/-" keys on the control panel to set the cooking time to 20 minutes. 9. Press the Pressure Level button to adjust the pressure to "High". 10. Once the cooking cycle is completed, quick-release the steam. 11. When all the steam is released, remove the pressure lid from the top carefully. 12. Stir in the green peas, cover, and let it sit in for 5 to 7 minutes. 13. Serve and enjoy!
Per Serving: Calories 334; Fat 19g; Sodium 354mg; Carbs 15g; Fiber 5.1g; Sugar 8.2g; Protein 32g

Italian Beef Stew

Prep time: 20 minutes | Cook time: 20 minutes | Serves: 4-6

2-pound beef top round, cut into bite-sized chunks
¼ cup all-purpose flour
1 tablespoon Italian seasoning
Sea salt and black pepper, to taste
1 tablespoon lard, at room temperature
1 onion, chopped
4 cloves garlic, pressed
¼ cup cooking wine
¼ cup tomato paste

1 pound sweet potatoes, diced
½ pound carrots, sliced into rounds
2 bell peppers, deveined and sliced
1 teaspoon fish sauce
2 bay leaves
4 cups beef broth
2 tablespoons fresh Italian parsley, roughly chopped

1. Toss the beef chunks with the flour, Italian seasoning, salt, and pepper until well coated. 2. Press the "Sauté" button twice to select "Normal" settings and melt the lard. 3. Then, sauté the onion and garlic for a minute or so; add the wine and stir. Scrape up all the browned bits off the inner pot. 4. Brown the beef chunks on all sides, stirring frequently; reserve. 5. Add the beef back into the inner pot. Stir in the tomato paste, sweet potatoes, carrots, bell peppers, fish sauce, bay leaves, and beef broth. 6. Put on the pressure cooker's lid and turn the steam valve to "Sealing" position. 7. Set the Instant Pot to "Meat/Stew". 8. Use the "+/-" keys on the control panel to set the cooking time to 20 minutes. 9. Press the Pressure Level button to adjust the pressure to "High". 10. Once the cooking cycle is completed, allow the steam to release naturally for 10 minutes. 11. When all the steam is released, remove the pressure lid from the top carefully. 12. Serve garnished with Italian parsley.
Per Serving: Calories 344; Fat 7.9g; Sodium 704mg; Carbs 6g; Fiber 3.6g; Sugar 6g; Protein 18g

Sausage and Bean Stew

Prep time: 20 minutes | Cook time: 25 minutes | Serves: 4-6

1 tablespoon olive oil
10-ounce smoked beef sausage, sliced
2 carrots, chopped
1 onion, chopped
2 garlic cloves, minced
Sea salt and black pepper, to taste
½ teaspoons fresh rosemary, chopped
1 teaspoon fresh basil, chopped
1 cup canned tomatoes, crushed
1 cup chicken broth
20-ounce pinto beans, soaked overnight
6-ounce kale, torn into pieces

1. Press the "Sauté" button twice to select "Normal" settings and heat the oil. 2. Once hot, brown the sausage for 3 to 4 minutes. 3. Add the remaining ingredients, except for the kale, to the inner pot. 4. Put on the pressure cooker's lid and turn the steam valve to "Sealing" position. 5. Set the Instant Pot to Pressure Cook. 6. Use the "+/-" keys on the control panel to set the cooking time to 25 minutes. 7. Press the Pressure Level button to adjust the pressure to "High". 8. Once the cooking cycle is completed, quick-release the steam. 9. When all the steam is released, remove the pressure lid from the top carefully. 10. Next, stir in the kale and seal the lid. Let it sit for 5 minutes before serving. 11. Bon appétit!
Per Serving: Calories 421; Fat 7.9g; Sodium 704mg; Carbs 6g; Fiber 3.6g; Sugar 6g; Protein 18g

Thai Curry Stew

Prep time: 20 minutes | Cook time: 44 minutes | Serves: 4-6

2 tablespoons sesame oil
2-pound beef chuck, cubed
2 onions, thinly sliced
2 cloves garlic, pressed
1 (2-inch) galangal piece, peeled and sliced
1 Bird's eye chili pepper, seeded and minced
½ cup tomato paste
4 cups chicken bone broth
¼ cup Thai red curry paste
1 tablespoon soy sauce
½ teaspoons ground cloves
½ teaspoons cardamom
½ teaspoons cumin
1 cinnamon quill
Sea salt and ground white pepper, to taste
½ (15-ounce) can full-fat coconut milk
2 cups cauliflower florets
2 tablespoons fresh cilantro, roughly chopped

1. Press the "Sauté" button twice to select "Normal" settings and heat the sesame oil. 2. When the oil starts to sizzle, cook the meat until browned on all sides. 3. Add a splash of broth and use a spoon to scrape the brown bits from the bottom of the pot. 4. Next, stir in the onion, garlic, galangal, chili pepper, tomato paste, broth, curry paste, soy sauce, and spices. 5. Put on the pressure cooker's lid and turn the steam valve to "Sealing" position. 6. Set the Instant Pot on "Soup/Broth". 7. Use the "+/-" keys on the control panel to set the cooking time to 40 minutes. 8. Press the Pressure Level button to adjust the pressure to "High". 9. Once the cooking cycle is completed, quick-release the steam. 10. When all the steam is released, remove the pressure lid from the top carefully. 11. After that, add the coconut milk and cauliflower to the inner pot. 12. Set the Instant Pot on Pressure Cook again and cook for 4 minutes at High pressure. 13. Once cooking is complete, use a quick pressure release; carefully remove the lid. 14. Serve garnished with fresh cilantro. 15. Enjoy!
Per Serving: Calories 479; Fat 10g; Sodium 891mg; Carbs 22.9g; Fiber 4g; Sugar 4g; Protein 33g

Vegan Pottage Stew

Prep time: 20 minutes | Cook time: 15 minutes | Serves: 4-6

2 tablespoons olive oil
1 onion, chopped
2 garlic cloves, minced
2 carrots, diced
2 parsnips, diced
1 turnip, diced
4 cups vegetable broth
2 bay leaves
2 thyme sprigs
2 rosemary sprigs
Kosher salt and black pepper, to taste
¼ cup red wine
1 cup porridge oats

1. Press the "Sauté" button twice to select "Normal" settings and heat the olive oil until sizzling. 2. Now, sauté the onion and garlic until just tender and fragrant. 3. Add the remaining ingredients to the inner pot; stir to combine. 4. Put on the pressure cooker's lid and turn the steam valve to "Sealing" position. 5. Set the Instant Pot to Pressure Cook. 6. Use the "+/-" keys on the control panel to set the cooking time to 10 minutes. 7. Press the Pressure Level button to adjust the pressure to "High". 8. Once the cooking cycle is completed, quick-release the steam. 9. When all the steam is released, remove the pressure lid from the top carefully. 10. Ladle into individual bowls and serve immediately. 11. Bon appétit!
Per Serving: Calories 382; Fat 7.9g; Sodium 704mg; Carbs 6g; Fiber 3.6g; Sugar 6g; Protein 18g

Bœuf À La Bourguignonne

Prep time: 20 minutes | Cook time: 26 minutes | Serves: 4-6

4 thick slices bacon, diced
2-pound beef round roast, cut into 1-inch cubes
Sea salt and black pepper, to taste
1 cup red Burgundy wine
2 onions, thinly sliced
2 carrots, diced
2 celery stalks, diced
4 cloves garlic, minced
2 tablespoons tomato paste
2 thyme sprigs
2 bay leaves
2 cups beef broth
2 tablespoons bouquet garni, chopped

1. Press the "Sauté" button twice to select "Normal" settings. 2. Cook the bacon until it is golden-brown; reserve. 3. Add the beef to the inner pot; sear the beef until browned or about 3 minutes per side. 4. Stir in the other ingredients; stir to combine well. 5. Put on the pressure cooker's lid and turn the steam valve to "Sealing" position. 6. Set the Instant Pot to Pressure Cook. 7. Use the "+/-" keys on the control panel to set the cooking time to 20 minutes. 8. Press the Pressure Level button to adjust the pressure to "High". 9. Once the cooking cycle is completed, quick-release the steam. 10. When all the steam is released, remove the pressure lid from the top carefully. 11. Serve in individual bowls topped with the reserved bacon. Bon appétit!
Per Serving: Calories 489; Fat 11g; Sodium 501mg; Carbs 8.9g; Fiber 4.6g; Sugar 8g; Protein 26g

Steak Kidney Bean Chili

Prep time: 20 minutes | Cook time: 18 minutes | Serves: 4-6

2-pound beef steak, cut into bite-sized cubes
4 tablespoons all-purpose flour
2 tablespoons vegetable oil
1 onion, chopped
2 cloves garlic, minced
1 jalapeño pepper, seeded and minced
2 cups beef broth
Sea salt and black pepper, to taste
1 teaspoon paprika
1 teaspoon celery seeds
1 teaspoon mustard seeds
2 tablespoons ground cumin
1 tablespoon brown sugar
2 cups red kidney beans, soaked overnight and rinsed
1 cup tomato sauce
2 tablespoons cornstarch, mixed with 4 tablespoons of water

1. Toss the beef steak with the flour. 2. Press the "Sauté" button twice to select "Normal" settings and heat the oil until sizzling. 3. Now, cook the beef steak in batches until browned on all side. Reserve. 4. Then, cook the onion, garlic, and jalapeño until they soften. 5. Scrape the bottom of the pot with a splash of beef broth. 6. Add the beef broth, spices, sugar, beans, and tomato sauce to the inner pot; stir to combine well. 7. Put on the pressure cooker's lid and turn the steam valve to "Sealing" position. 8. Set the Instant Pot to Pressure Cook. 9. Use the "+/-" keys on the control panel to set the cooking time to 18 minutes. 10. Press the Pressure Level button to adjust the pressure to "High". 11. Once the cooking cycle is completed, allow the steam to release naturally. 12. When all the steam is released, remove the pressure lid from the top carefully. 12. Press the "Sauté" button twice to select "Normal" settings. 13. Stir in the cornstarch slurry; stir for a few minutes to thicken the cooking liquid. 14. Bon appétit!
Per Serving: Calories 479; Fat 10g; Sodium 891mg; Carbs 22.9g; Fiber 4g; Sugar 4g; Protein 33g

Hungarian Beef Goulash

Prep time: 20 minutes | Cook time: 20 minutes | Serves: 4-6

2 tablespoons olive oil	Sea salt and black pepper, to taste
2-pound beef chuck, cut into bite-sized pieces	1 tablespoon Hungarian paprika
¼ cup Hungarian red wine	1 beef stock cube
2 onions, sliced	2 cups water
2 garlic cloves, crushed	2 ripe tomatoes, puréed
1 red chili pepper, minced	2 bay leaves

1. Press the "Sauté" button twice to select "Normal" settings and heat the oil. 2. Once hot, cook the beef until no longer pink. 3. Add the red wine and stir with a wooden spoon. 4. Stir in the remaining ingredients. 5. Put on the pressure cooker's lid and turn the steam valve to "Sealing" position. 6. Set the Instant Pot to Pressure Cook. 7. Use the "+/-" keys on the control panel to set the cooking time to 20 minutes. 8. Press the Pressure Level button to adjust the pressure to "High". 9. Once the cooking cycle is completed, quick-release the steam. 10. When all the steam is released, remove the pressure lid from the top carefully. 11. Serve in individual bowls and enjoy!
Per Serving: Calories 521; Fat 10.9g; Sodium 354mg; Carbs 10.5g; Fiber 4.1g; Sugar 8.2g; Protein 26g

Beef Potato Stew

Prep time: 20 minutes | Cook time: 33 minutes | Serves: 8

3 tablespoons olive oil	4 cups halved baby potatoes
2½-pound beef chuck roast, cut into 1½-inch pieces	1½ cups peeled and chopped carrots
1 large onion, diced	2 teaspoons salt
1½ cups chopped celery	2 teaspoons black pepper
2 tablespoons minced garlic	1 teaspoon dried thyme
¼ cup balsamic vinegar	1 teaspoon dried rosemary
3 cups beef broth	1 teaspoon dried oregano
3 tablespoons tomato paste	

1. Turn on the Sauté function on Normal mode, and when the inner pot is hot, pour in the oil. 2. Add the meat, working in batches if necessary, and brown it 2 to 3 minutes on each side. 3. Add the onion and celery and cook until the onion is translucent, 3 to 4 minutes. 4. Add the garlic and cook until fragrant, about 1 minute. 5. Pour in the balsamic vinegar and deglaze the pot, stirring to scrape up the browned bits from the bottom. 6. Add the remaining ingredients. Put on the pressure cooker's lid and turn the steam valve to "Sealing" position. 7. Set the Instant Pot to Pressure Cook. 8. Press the Pressure Level button to adjust the pressure to "High". 9. Use the "+/-" keys on the control panel to set the cooking time to 30 minutes. 10. Once the cooking cycle is completed, allow the steam to release naturally for 10 minutes and then quick-release the remaining pressure. 11. When all the steam is released, remove the pressure lid from the top carefully. 12. Serve.
Per Serving: Calories 479; Fat 10g; Sodium 891mg; Carbs 22.9g; Fiber 4g; Sugar 4g; Protein 33g

Irish Bean Cabbage Stew

Prep time: 20 minutes | Cook time: 25 minutes | Serves: 4-6

2 cups white beans, soaked and rinsed	1-pound cabbage, chopped
½ cup pearled barley	½ pound potatoes, diced
4 cups roasted vegetable broth	2 bay leaves
1 shallot, chopped	½ teaspoons mustard seeds
2 carrots, chopped	½ teaspoons caraway seeds
2 ribs celery, chopped	1 teaspoon cayenne pepper
1 sweet pepper, chopped	Sea salt and black pepper, to taste
1 serrano pepper, chopped	1 (14½-ounce) can tomatoes, diced
4 cloves garlic, minced	

1. Place the white beans, barley, and vegetable broth in the inner pot. 2. Put on the pressure cooker's lid and turn the steam valve to "Sealing" position. 3. Set the Instant Pot to "Bean/Chili". 4. Use the "+/-" keys on the control panel to set the cooking time to 25 minutes. 5. Press the Pressure Level button to adjust the pressure to "High". 6. Once the cooking cycle is completed, quick-release the steam. 7. When all the steam is released, remove the pressure lid from the top carefully. 8. Add the remaining ingredients and stir to combine. 9. Set the Instant Pot to Pressure Cook and cook for 5 minutes at High pressure. 10. Once cooking is complete, use a quick pressure release; carefully remove the lid. 11. Serve in individual bowls and enjoy!
Per Serving: Calories 449; Fat 2.9g; Sodium 511mg; Carbs 12; Fiber 3g; Sugar 8g; Protein 28g

Traditional Polish Stew

Prep time: 20 minutes | Cook time: 15 minutes | Serves: 4-6

2 slices smoked bacon, diced	2 bay leaves
1-pound Kielbasa, sliced	1 tablespoon cayenne pepper
½ pound pork stew meat, cubed	1 teaspoon mustard seeds
1 onion, chopped	1 teaspoon caraway seeds, crushed
4 garlic cloves, sliced	
2 carrots, trimmed and diced	Sea salt, to taste
1-pound sauerkraut, drained	½ teaspoons black peppercorns
1-pound fresh cabbage, shredded	½ cup dry red wine
1 teaspoon dried thyme	2½ cups beef stock
1 teaspoon dried basil	½ cup tomato puree

1. Press the "Sauté" button twice to select "Normal" settings. 2. Now, cook the bacon, Kielbasa, and pork stew meat until the bacon is crisp; reserve. 3. Add the onion and garlic, and sauté them until they're softened and starting to brown. 4. Add the remaining ingredients to the inner pot, including the reserved meat mixture. 5. Put on the pressure cooker's lid and turn the steam valve to "Sealing" position. 6. Set the Instant Pot to Pressure Cook. 7. Use the "+/-" keys on the control panel to set the cooking time to 15 minutes. 8. Press the Pressure Level button to adjust the pressure to "High". 9. Once the cooking cycle is completed, quick-release the steam. 10. When all the steam is released, remove the pressure lid from the top carefully. 11. Ladle into individual bowls and serve warm.
Per Serving: Calories 584; Fat 15g; Sodium 441mg; Carbs 17g; Fiber 4.6g; Sugar 5g; Protein 29g

Healthy Chickpea, Tomato, and Farro Stew

Prep time: 10 minutes | Cook Time: 15 minutes | Serves: 4

1 medium onion, diced	diced tomatoes
5 garlic cloves, minced	1 (15-ounce) can no-salt-added chickpeas, drained and rinsed
1 tablespoon no-salt-added Italian seasoning	5 ounces baby spinach
¼ to ½ teaspoon red pepper flakes	Zest and juice of 1 lemon
3 cups Easy Vegetable Broth, no-salt-added vegetable broth, or water	Freshly ground black pepper
	Salt (optional)
1 cup pearled farro	Plant-based parmesan (optional), for serving
1 (28-ounce) can no-salt-added	

1. Set your Instant Pot on Sauté at More heat. 2. Add onion and cook for 3 to 5 minutes. To prevent from sticking, pour water as needed, a tablespoon at a time. 3. Add Italian seasoning, red pepper flakes, and garlic to season and stir until fragrant, about 30 seconds. 4. Turn off the heat and add farro, chickpeas, broth, and tomatoes. 5. Close the lid and turn the steam release handle to Sealing position. 6. Set the Instant Pot on Pressure Cook at High and timer for 10 minutes. 7. When cooked, naturally release the pressure about 10 minutes and then quick release the remaining pressure. Then carefully remove the lid. 8. Stir in lemon juice, lemon zest, and spinach in the pot until the spinach is wilted. 9. Add salt and pepper as you needed to season. 10. Sprinkle with plant-based parmesan and serve. (up to 4 days are the leftovers kept in the fridge in a covered container) 11. When the cook time is complete, let the pressure release naturally for 10 minutes; quick-release any remaining pressure and carefully remove the lid. Stir in the spinach and lemon zest and juice, allowing the residual heat from the stew to wilt the spinach. Season to taste with pepper and salt (if using). Serve immediately with a sprinkle of plant-based parmesan, if desired. Store any leftovers in the fridge for up to 4 days in a covered container.
Per Serving: Calories 445; Fat: 0.2g; Sodium 105mg; Carbs: 95.2g; Fiber 1g; Sugars: 1.4g; Protein 19.6g

Italian Beef Ragù

Prep time: 20 minutes | Cook time: 10 minutes | Serves: 4-6

2 tablespoons butter, melted	¼ cup tomato puree
1 medium leek, diced	2 cups chicken stock
2 carrots, diced	1 tablespoon Italian seasoning
1 stalk celery, diced	blend
5-ounce bacon, diced	½ teaspoons kosher salt
1-pound ground chuck	½ teaspoons black pepper
½ cup Italian red wine	

1. Press the "Sauté" button twice to select "Normal" settings and melt the butter. 2. Sauté the leek, carrot, celery and garlic for 2 to 3 minutes. 3. Add the bacon and ground beef to the inner pot; continue to cook an additional 3 minutes, stirring frequently. 4. Add the remaining ingredients to the inner pot. 5. Put on the pressure cooker's lid and turn the steam valve to "Sealing" position. 6. Set the Instant Pot to Pressure Cook. 7. Use the "+/-" keys on the control panel to set the cooking time to 5 minutes. 8. Press the Pressure Level button to adjust the pressure to "High". 9. Once the cooking cycle is completed, quick-release the steam. 10. When all the steam is released, remove the pressure lid from the top carefully. 11. Serve with hot pasta if desired. 12. Bon appétit!
Per Serving: Calories 449; Fat 2.9g; Sodium 511mg; Carbs 12g; Fiber 3g; Sugar 8g; Protein 28g

Marsala Fish Stew

Prep time: 20 minutes | Cook time: 5 minutes | Serves: 4-6

2 tablespoons canola oil	Sea salt and black pepper, to taste
1 onion, sliced	2 bay leaves
3 garlic cloves, sliced	1 teaspoon smoked paprika
½ cup Marsala wine	½ teaspoons hot sauce
1½ cups shellfish stock	2-pound halibut, cut into bite-sized pieces
1 cup water	
1 pound Yukon Gold potatoes, diced	2 tablespoons fresh cilantro, chopped
2 ripe tomatoes, pureed	

1. Press the "Sauté" button twice to select "Normal" settings and heat the oil. 2. Once hot, cook the onions until softened; stir in the garlic and continue to sauté an additional 30 seconds. 3. Add the wine to deglaze the bottom of the inner pot, scraping up any browned bits. 4. Add the shellfish stock, water, potatoes, tomatoes, salt, black pepper, bay leaves, paprika, hot sauce, and halibut to the inner pot. 5. Put on the pressure cooker's lid and turn the steam valve to "Sealing" position. 6. Set the Instant Pot to Pressure Cook. 7. Use the "+/-" keys on the control panel to set the cooking time to 5 minutes. 8. Press the Pressure Level button to adjust the pressure to "High". 9. Once the cooking cycle is completed, quick-release the steam. 10. When all the steam is released, remove the pressure lid from the top carefully. 11. Serve with fresh cilantro and enjoy!
Per Serving: Calories 492; Fat 12.9g; Sodium 414mg; Carbs 11g; Fiber 5g; Sugar 9g; Protein 31g

Pork Chile Verde

Prep time: 20 minutes | Cook time: 20 minutes | Serves: 4-6

1 pound tomatillos, halved	3-pound pork stew meat, cut into
4 garlic cloves, sliced	2-inch cubes
2 chili peppers, minced	1 onion, chopped
2 heaping tablespoons cilantro, chopped	1 bell pepper, deveined and sliced
2 tablespoons olive oil	Salt and black pepper, to taste
	2 cups vegetable broth

1. Place the tomatillos under a preheated broiler for about 6 minutes. Let cool enough to handle. 2. Purée the tomatillos with the garlic, chili peppers, and cilantro in your blender; process until chopped. 3. Press the "Sauté" button twice to select "Normal" settings and heat the oil. 4. Once hot, cook the pork until no longer pink. 5. Add the onion and cook for a few minutes more or until it is tender and translucent. 6.

Add the remaining ingredients, including tomatillo sauce, to the inner pot. 7. Put on the pressure cooker's lid and turn the steam valve to "Sealing" position. 8. Set the Instant Pot to "Meat/Stew". 9. Use the "+/-" keys on the control panel to set the cooking time to 20 minutes. 10. Press the Pressure Level button to adjust the pressure to "High". 11. Once the cooking cycle is completed, quick-release the steam. 12. When all the steam is released, remove the pressure lid from the top carefully. 13. Ladle into serving bowls and garnish with tortillas if desired. 14. Bon appétit!
Per Serving: Calories 412; Fat 20g; Sodium 491mg; Carbs 9g; Fiber 3g; Sugar 8g; Protein 31g

Chicken Stew with Apples

Prep time: 20 minutes | Cook time: 10 minutes | Serves: 4-6

2 tablespoons olive oil	1 tablespoon fresh sage, chopped
2-pound chicken thighs	1-pound winter squash, peeled and cubed
1 onion, chopped	2 carrots, trimmed and diced
2 garlic cloves, minced	1 cup apple cider
1 (1-inch) piece fresh ginger, peeled and minced	1 cup chicken stock
Kosher salt and black pepper, to taste	2 cups chopped peeled Granny Smith apple
1 teaspoon paprika	

1. Press the "Sauté" button twice to select "Normal" settings and heat the oil. 2. Once hot, sear the chicken thighs for about 2 minutes per side; reserve. 3. Add the onion, garlic, and ginger and sauté them for 2 to 3 minutes or until just tender. 4. Add the salt, pepper, paprika, sage, winter squash, carrots, apple cider, and chicken stock. 5. Add the reserved chicken thighs. 6. Put on the pressure cooker's lid and turn the steam valve to "Sealing" position. 7. Set the Instant Pot to Pressure Cook. 8. Use the "+/-" keys on the control panel to set the cooking time to 10 minutes. 9. Press the Pressure Level button to adjust the pressure to "High". 10. Once the cooking cycle is completed, allow the steam to release naturally for 10 minutes. 11. When all the steam is released, remove the pressure lid from the top carefully. 12. Remove the chicken thighs and shred with two forks; discard the bones. 13. Add the shredded chicken back into the inner pot. 14. Afterwards, stir in the apples; Press the "Sauté" button twice to select "Normal" settings and let it simmer for 10 to 12 minutes longer or until the apples are tender. 15. Serve.
Per Serving: Calories 584; Fat 15g; Sodium 441mg; Carbs 17g; Fiber 4.6g; Sugar 5g; Protein 29g

Brunswick Stew

Prep time: 20 minutes | Cook time: 12 minutes | Serves: 4-6

2 tablespoons lard, melted	diced
1 onion, diced	2 cups chicken broth
2 cloves garlic, minced	1 tablespoon Worcestershire sauce
1-pound chicken breast, cut into 1-inch cubes	1 teaspoon Creole seasoning
2 cups lima beans, soaked	Sea salt and black pepper, to taste
1 (14½-ounce) can tomatoes,	1 teaspoon hot sauce
	1 cup corn kernels

1. Press the "Sauté" button twice to select "Normal" settings and melt the lard. 2. Once hot, cook the onion and garlic until just tender and aromatic. 3. Now, add the chicken and cook an additional 3 minutes, stirring frequently. 4. Add the lima beans, tomatoes, broth, Worcestershire sauce, Creole seasoning, salt, black pepper, and hot sauce to the inner pot. 5. Put on the pressure cooker's lid and turn the steam valve to "Sealing" position. 6. Set the Instant Pot to Pressure Cook. 7. Use the "+/-" keys on the control panel to set the cooking time to 12 minutes. 8. Press the Pressure Level button to adjust the pressure to "High". 9. Once the cooking cycle is completed, allow the steam to release naturally. 10. When all the steam is released, remove the pressure lid from the top carefully. 11. Stir in the corn kernels and seal the lid. Let it sit in the residual heat until heated through. 12. Enjoy!
Per Serving: Calories 419; Fat 14g; Sodium 791mg; Carbs 8.9g; Fiber 4.6g; Sugar 8g; Protein 3g

Mulligan Stew

Prep time: 20 minutes | Cook time: 20 minutes | Serves: 8

1 tablespoon lard, melted
2-pound pork butt roast, cut into 2-inch pieces
2-pound beef stew meat, cut into 2-inch pieces
2 chicken thighs, boneless
2 bell peppers, chopped
1 red chili pepper, chopped
1 onion, chopped
2 carrots, chopped

4 garlic cloves, chopped
4 cups beef bone broth
1 cup beer
1 (28-ounce) can tomatoes, crushed
Sea salt and black pepper, to taste
1 pound frozen corn kernels
3 tablespoons Worcestershire sauce

1. Press the "Sauté" button twice to select "Normal" settings and melt the lard. Once hot, brown the meat in batches. Remove the browned meats to a bowl. 2. Then, sauté the peppers, onion, carrots for about 3 minutes or until tender and fragrant. Add the garlic and continue to cook for 30 seconds more. 3. Add the meat back to the Instant Pot. Stir in the remaining ingredients, except for the corn kernels. 4. Put on the pressure cooker's lid and turn the steam valve to "Sealing" position. 5. Set the Instant Pot to "Meat/Stew". 6. Use the "+/-" keys on the control panel to set the cooking time to 20 minutes. 7. Press the Pressure Level button to adjust the pressure to "High". 8. Once the cooking cycle is completed, allow the steam to release naturally. 9. When all the steam is released, quick-release the steam. 10. Lastly, stir in the corn and continue to cook for a few minutes more on the "Sauté" function. 11. Serve immediately.
Per Serving: Calories 334; Fat 10.9g; Sodium 454mg; Carbs 10g; Fiber 3.1g; Sugar 5.2g; Protein 20g

Mediterranean Chicken Stew

Prep time: 20 minutes | Cook time: 15 minutes | Serves: 4

2 tablespoons olive oil
1 onion, chopped
1 stalk celery, chopped
2 carrots, chopped
1 teaspoon garlic, minced
4 chicken legs, boneless skinless
¼ cup dry red wine
2 ripe tomatoes, pureed

2 cups chicken bone broth
2 bay leaves
Sea salt and black pepper, to taste
½ teaspoon dried basil
1 teaspoon dried oregano
½ cup Kalamata olives, pitted and sliced

1. Press the "Sauté" button twice to select "Normal" settings and heat the oil. 2. Now, sauté the onion, celery, and carrot for 4 to 5 minutes or until they are tender. 3. Add the other ingredients, except for the Kalamata olives, and stir to combine. 4. Put on the pressure cooker's lid and turn the steam valve to "Sealing" position. 5. Set the Instant Pot to Pressure Cook. 6. Use the "+/-" keys on the control panel to set the cooking time to 15 minutes. 7. Press the Pressure Level button to adjust the pressure to "High". 8. Once the cooking cycle is completed, allow the steam to release naturally. 9. When all the steam is released, remove the pressure lid from the top carefully. 10. Serve warm garnished with Kalamata olives. 11. Bon appétit!
Per Serving: Calories 479; Fat 10g; Sodium 891mg; Carbs 22.9g; Fiber 4g; Sugar 4g; Protein 33g

Hungarian Chicken Stew

Prep time: 20 minutes | Cook time: 15 minutes | Serves: 4-6

2 tablespoons lard, at room temperature
2-pound chicken, cut into pieces
2 onions, chopped
2 cloves garlic, minced
1 cup tomato puree
1 Hungarian pepper, diced

2 tablespoons Hungarian paprika
2 cups chicken stock
Kosher salt and cracked black pepper
3 tablespoons all-purpose flour
1 cup full-fat sour cream

1. Press the "Sauté" button twice to select "Normal" settings and melt the lard. 2. Once hot, cook the chicken for about 3 minutes or until no longer pink. 3. Add the onion to the inner pot; continue sautéing an additional 3 minutes. 4. Now, stir in the garlic and cook for 30 seconds

more. 5. Add the tomato puree, Hungarian pepper, paprika, chicken stock, salt, and black pepper to the inner pot. 6. Put on the pressure cooker's lid and turn the steam valve to "Sealing" position. 7. Set the Instant Pot to Pressure Cook. 8. Use the "+/-" keys on the control panel to set the cooking time to 15 minutes. 9. Press the Pressure Level button to adjust the pressure to "High". 10. Once the cooking cycle is completed, quick-release the steam. 11. When all the steam is released, remove the pressure lid from the top carefully. 12. Remove the chicken from the inner pot; shred the chicken and discard the bones. 13. In a mixing bowl, stir the flour into the sour cream. 14. Add the flour/cream mixture to the cooking liquid, stirring constantly with a wire whisk. 15. Let it simmer until the sauce is thickened. 16. Return the chicken to your paprika, stir and press the "Cancel" button. 17. Enjoy!
Per Serving: Calories 584; Fat 15g; Sodium 441mg; Carbs 17g; Fiber 4.6g; Sugar 5g; Protein 29g

French Pot-Au-Feu

Prep time: 20 minutes | Cook time: 20 minutes | Serves: 4-6

2 tablespoons olive oil
2-pound beef pot roast, cut into 2-inch pieces
1 onion, chopped
2 carrots, chopped
3 garlic cloves, pressed
2 tomatoes, pureed
1 cup dry red wine

3 cups beef broth
½ teaspoons marjoram
½ teaspoons sage
Sea salt and black pepper, to taste
1 shallot, sliced
1 pound cremini mushrooms, sliced
1 cup chèvres cheese, crumbled

1. Press the "Sauté" button twice to select "Normal" settings and heat the olive oil. 2. Cook the beef in batches and transfer to a bowl. 3. Then, cook the onion in pan drippings. 4. Stir in the carrots and garlic and continue to cook an additional 3 minutes. 5. Add the tomatoes, wine, broth, marjoram, sage, salt, and black pepper. Add the browned beef. 6. Put on the pressure cooker's lid and turn the steam valve to "Sealing" position. 7. Set the Instant Pot on "Meat/Stew". 8. Use the "+/-" keys on the control panel to set the cooking time to 45 minutes. 9. Press the Pressure Level button to adjust the pressure to "High". 10. Once the cooking cycle is completed, quick-release the pressure. 11. When all the steam is released, remove the pressure lid from the top carefully. 12. Now, add the shallot and mushrooms; continue to cook on the "Sauté" function for 10 minutes. 13. Transfer your stew to a lightly greased casserole dish. 14. Top with the cheese and place under a preheated broiler for 10 minutes or until the cheese melts. 15. Serve warm.
Per Serving: Calories 489; Fat 11g; Sodium 501mg; Carbs 8.9g; Fiber 4.6g; Sugar 8g; Protein 26g

Beef and Potato Stew

Prep time: 20 minutes | Cook time: 20 minutes | Serves: 4-6

1 tablespoon lard, melted
2-pound chuck roast, cut into 2-inch cubes
2 onions, chopped
2 cloves garlic, minced
2 tablespoons Hungarian paprika
4 bell peppers, deveined and chopped

1 chili pepper, chopped
1 cup tomato puree
4 potatoes, diced
4 cups beef broth
2 bay leaves
Seasoned salt and black pepper, to taste

1. Press the "Sauté" button twice to select "Normal" settings and melt the lard. 2. Once hot, cook the beef until no longer pink. 3. Add a splash of broth and stir with a wooden spoon, scraping up the browned bits on the bottom of the inner pot. 4. Add the onion to the inner pot; continue sautéing an additional 3 minutes. 5. Now, stir in the garlic and cook for 30 seconds more. 6. Stir in the remaining ingredients. 7. Put on the pressure cooker's lid and turn the steam valve to "Sealing" position. 8. Set the Instant Pot on "Meat/Stew". 9. Press the Pressure Level button to adjust the pressure to "High". 10. Use the "+/-" keys on the control panel to set the cooking time to 20 minutes. 11. Once the cooking cycle is completed, quick-release the steam. 12. When all the steam is released, remove the pressure lid from the top carefully. 13. Discard the bay leaves and serve in individual bowls. 14. Bon appétit!
Per Serving: Calories 492; Fat 12.9g; Sodium 414mg; Carbs 11g; Fiber 5g; Sugar 9g; Protein 31g

Rich Chicken Purloo

Prep time: 20 minutes | Cook time: 10 minutes | Serves: 8

1 tablespoon olive oil	2 bay leaves
1 onion, chopped	1 teaspoon mustard seeds
3-pound chicken legs, boneless and skinless	¼ teaspoon marjoram
2 garlic cloves, minced	Seasoned salt and black pepper, to taste
5 cups water	1 teaspoon cayenne pepper
2 carrots, diced	2 cups white long-grain rice
2 celery ribs, diced	

1. Press the "Sauté" button twice to select "Normal" settings and heat the olive oil. 2. Now, add the onion and chicken legs; cook until the onion is translucent or about 4 minutes. 3. Stir in the minced garlic and continue to cook for a minute more. Add the water. 4. Put on the pressure cooker's lid and turn the steam valve to "Sealing" position. 5. Set the Instant Pot to Pressure Cook. 6. Use the "+/-" keys on the control panel to set the cooking time to 10 minutes. 7. Press the Pressure Level button to adjust the pressure to "High". 8. Once the cooking cycle is completed, quick-release the steam. 9. When all the steam is released, remove the pressure lid from the top carefully. 10. Add the remaining ingredients. 11. Set the Instant Pot to Pressure Cook and cook for 5 minutes at High pressure. 12. Once cooking is complete, use a quick pressure release; carefully remove the lid. 13. Serve warm.
Per Serving: Calories 479; Fat 10g; Sodium 891mg; Carbs 22.9g; Fiber 4g; Sugar 4g; Protein 33g

Almond Lentil Vegetable Stew

Prep time: 20 minutes | Cook time: 10 minutes | Serves: 4-6

1 tablespoon olive oil	3 cups vegetable broth
1 onion, chopped	Seasoned salt and black pepper, to taste
1 teaspoon fresh garlic, minced	1 teaspoon cayenne pepper
1 dried chili pepper, crushed	½ cup almond butter
1 pound potatoes, cut into 1-inch pieces	2 heaping tablespoons cilantro, roughly chopped
1-pound cauliflower, broken into florets	1 heaping tablespoon parsley, roughly chopped
1 cup green lentils	
3 cups tomato juice	

1. Press the "Sauté" button twice to select "Normal" settings and heat the olive oil. 2. Now, sauté the onion until it is transparent. Add garlic and continue to sauté an additional minute. 3. Stir in the chili pepper, potatoes, cauliflower, lentils, tomato juice, vegetable broth, salt, black pepper, and cayenne pepper. 4. Put on the pressure cooker's lid and turn the steam valve to "Sealing" position. 5. Set the Instant Pot to Pressure Cook. 6. Use the "+/-" keys on the control panel to set the cooking time to 10 minutes. 7. Press the Pressure Level button to adjust the pressure to "High". 8. Once the cooking cycle is completed, quick-release the steam. 9. When all the steam is released, remove the pressure lid from the top carefully. 10. Stir in the almond butter. Press the "Sauté" button on "Less" settings. 11. And simmer for about 3 minutes. 12. Garnish with cilantro and parsley. 13. Bon appétit!
Per Serving: Calories 461; Fat 7.9g; Sodium 704mg; Carbs 6g; Fiber 3.6g; Sugar 6g; Protein 18g

Catalan Shellfish Stew

Prep time: 20 minutes | Cook time: 10 minutes | Serves: 4-6

4 tablespoons olive oil	1 laurel (bay leaf)
1 onion, chopped	Sea salt and black pepper, to taste
3 cloves garlic, minced	1 teaspoon guindilla (cayenne pepper)
4-ounce prosciutto, diced	1 teaspoon rosemary, chopped
1½-pound shrimp	1 teaspoon basil, chopped
1½-pound clams	2 tomatoes, pureed
1 Chile de Árbol, minced	1 fresh lemon, sliced
½ cup dry white wine	
4 cups clam juice	

1. Press the "Sauté" button two times to select "Normal" settings and heat the olive oil. 2. Now, sauté the onion until it is transparent. Add the garlic and continue to sauté an additional 1 minute. 3. Add the prosciutto and cook an additional 3 minutes. Add the remaining ingredients, except for the lemon. 4. Put on the pressure cooker's lid and turn the steam valve to "Sealing" position. 5. Set the Instant Pot to Pressure Cook. 6. Use the "+/-" keys on the control panel to set the cooking time to 10 minutes. 7. Press the Pressure Level button to adjust the pressure to "High". 8. Once the cooking cycle is completed, allow the steam to release naturally for 10 minutes. 9. When all the steam is released, remove the pressure lid from the top carefully. 10. Serve in individual bowls garnished with lemon slices. 11. Enjoy!
Per Serving: Calories 478; Fat 7.9g; Sodium 704mg; Carbs 6g; Fiber 3.6g; Sugar 6g; Protein 18g

Indian Bean Stew

Prep time: 20 minutes | Cook time: 26 minutes | Serves: 4-6

2 tablespoons sesame oil	5 cups vegetable broth
1 onion, sliced	1 teaspoon coriander seeds
4 cloves garlic, finely chopped	½ teaspoons cumin seeds
1 (1-inch) piece fresh ginger root, peeled and grated	¼ teaspoon ground cinnamon
2 cups red kidney beans, soaked overnight	Seasoned salt and black pepper, to taste
2 Bhut jolokia peppers, minced	2 tomatoes, pureed
1 teaspoon red curry paste	2 tablespoons fresh coriander, chopped

1. Press the "Sauté" button twice to select "Normal" settings and heat the oil. 2. Now, sauté the onion until it is transparent. 3. Add the garlic and ginger and continue to sauté an additional 1 minute. 4. Add the beans, peppers, curry paste, vegetable broth spices, and tomatoes. 5. Put on the pressure cooker's lid and turn the steam valve to "Sealing" position. 6. Set the Instant Pot to Pressure Cook. 7. Use the "+/-" keys on the control panel to set the cooking time to 25 minutes. 8. Press the Pressure Level button to adjust the pressure to "High". 9. Once the cooking cycle is completed, quick-release the pressure. 10. When all the steam is released, remove the pressure lid from the top carefully. 11. Serve in individual bowls garnished with fresh coriander. 12. Enjoy!
Per Serving: Calories 472; Fat 10.9g; Sodium 354mg; Carbs 10.5g; Fiber 4.1g; Sugar 8.2g; Protein 26g

Beef Burgundy

Prep time: 10 minutes | Cook Time: 35 minutes | Serves: 6

5 strips bacon, roughly chopped	into ½-inch-thick coins
3 pounds beef chuck, fat trimmed, cut into 2-inch chunks (see Tasty Tip, below)	¾ cup store-bought beef broth, or homemade (page 228)
Salt and freshly ground black pepper	¼ cup all-purpose flour
1 large yellow onion, chopped	OPTIONAL ADD-INS
½ cup Pinot Noir	5 (3-inch) sprigs fresh thyme, or 1 (3-inch) sprig rosemary
3 large carrots, peeled and cut	2 tablespoons tomato paste

1. Set your Instant Pot on Sauté at Normal heat. 2. Add the bacon in the inner pot and cook about 3 to 4 minutes or until crispy and browned, stirring from time to time. Then turn off the heat. 3. Transfer the crispy bacon onto a paper towel-lined plate. Then spoon about 1½ tablespoons of the drippings in the pot and discard. 4. Add ¾ teaspoon salt and several grinds of pepper to season the beef. 5. Set the Instant Pot on Sauté at More heat. Then add 6 or 7 pieces of the meat to the pot. Leave space among the pieces. Cook about 3 minutes or until one side is well browned. 6. Add wine and simmer for 2 minutes. Scrape all the browned bits off the pot. Turn off the heat. 7. Add the remaining bacon, beef, carrots, ½ cup of the broth, and the optional add-ins, as you desired. 8. Close the lid and turn the steam release handle to Sealing position. 9. Set your Instant Pot on Pressure Cook at High and adjust the cooking time to 25 minutes. 10. When cooked, naturally release the pressure about 10 minutes and then quick release the remaining pressure. 11. The herb sprigs should be discard while using the herbs. 12. In a small bowl, place the flour. Gradually add the remaining ¼ cup broth and whisk. Then transfer the flour mixture to the pot. 13. Set your Instant Pot on Normal heat. Simmer and stir gently from time to time about 2 minutes or until thickened and bubbly. 14. Add salt and pepper to season. Serve and enjoy!
Per Serving: Calories 555; Fat: 21g; Sodium 636mg; Carbs: 10.2g; Sugars: 2.9g; Protein 76.4g

Basque Squid Stew

Prep time: 20 minutes | Cook time: 10 minutes | Serves: 4-6

2 tablespoons olive oil
1 onion, finely diced
2 cloves garlic, minced
1 thyme sprig, chopped
1 rosemary sprig, chopped
1 serrano pepper, deseeded and chopped
2 tomatoes, pureed
½ cup clam juice
1 cup chicken stock
½ cup cooking sherry
1-pound fresh squid, cleaned and sliced into rings
Sea salt and black pepper, to taste
1 teaspoon cayenne pepper
1 bay leaf
¼ teaspoon saffron
1 lemon, cut into wedges

1. Press the "Sauté" button twice to select "Normal" settings and heat the oil. 2. Now, sauté the onion until tender and translucent. 3. Now, add the garlic and continue to sauté an additional minute. 4. Add the remaining ingredients, except for the lemon. 5. Put on the pressure cooker's lid and turn the steam valve to "Sealing" position. 6. Set the Instant Pot to Pressure Cook. 7. Use the "+/-" keys on the control panel to set the cooking time to 10 minutes. 8. Press the Pressure Level button to adjust the pressure to "High". 9. Once the cooking cycle is completed, quick-release the pressure. 10. When all the steam is released, remove the pressure lid from the top carefully. 11. Serve garnished with lemon wedges. 12. Bon appétit!
Per Serving: Calories 493; Fat 12.9g; Sodium 414mg; Carbs 11g; Fiber 5g; Sugar 9g; Protein 31g

Slumgullion Stew

Prep time: 20 minutes | Cook time: 10 minutes | Serves: 4-6

1 tablespoon canola oil
1 leek, chopped
2 garlic cloves, minced
2 carrots, chopped
½ (16-ounce) package macaroni
½ pound ground beef
½ pound pork sausage, crumbled
1½ cups tomato puree
1½ cups chicken broth
Seasoned salt and black pepper, to taste
1 (15-ounce) can stewed tomatoes
2 cups green beans, cut into thirds

1. Press the "Sauté" button twice to select "Normal" settings and heat the oil. 2. Now, sauté the leek, garlic and carrot until they have softened. 3. Then, add the macaroni, ground beef, sausage, tomato puree, chicken broth, salt, and black pepper to the inner pot. 4. Put on the pressure cooker's lid and turn the steam valve to "Sealing" position. 5. Set the Instant Pot to Pressure Cook. 6. Use the "+/-" keys on the control panel to set the cooking time to 10 minutes. 7. Press the Pressure Level button to adjust the pressure to "High". 8. Once the cooking cycle is completed, quick-release the pressure. 9. When all the steam is released, remove the pressure lid from the top carefully. 10. After that, add the canned tomatoes and green beans; let it simmer on the "Sauté" function for 2 to 3 minutes. 11. Bon appétit!
Per Serving: Calories 405; Fat 19g; Sodium 354mg; Carbs 15g; Fiber 5.1g; Sugar 8.2g; Protein 32g

Lentil Vegetable Hotpot

Prep time: 20 minutes | Cook time: 15 minutes | Serves: 4-6

1 tablespoon olive oil
1 onion, chopped
3 cloves garlic, minced
1 carrot, chopped
1 stalk celery, chopped
1 parsnip, chopped
2 cups brown lentils
2 tomatoes, pureed
1 sprig thyme, chopped
1 sprig rosemary, chopped
1 teaspoon basil
Kosher salt and black pepper, to taste
2 cups vegetable broth
3 cups Swiss chard, torn into pieces

1. Press the "Sauté" button twice to select "Normal" settings and heat the oil. 2. Sauté the onion until tender and translucent or about 4 minutes. 3. Then, stir in the garlic and cook an additional 30 seconds or until fragrant. 4. Now, stir in the carrot, celery, parsnip, lentils, tomatoes, spices, and broth. 5. Afterwards, add the Swiss chard to the inner pot. 6. Put on the pressure cooker's lid and turn the steam

valve to "Sealing" position. 7. Set the Instant Pot to Pressure Cook. 8. Use the "+/-" keys on the control panel to set the cooking time to 10 minutes. 9. Press the Pressure Level button to adjust the pressure to "High". 10. Once the cooking cycle is completed, quick-release the pressure. 11. When all the steam is released, remove the pressure lid from the top carefully. 12. Bon appétit!
Per Serving: Calories 419; Fat 14g; Sodium 791mg; Carbs 8.9g; Fiber 4.6g; Sugar 8g; Protein 3g

Seafood Vegetable Ragout

Prep time: 20 minutes | Cook time: 10 minutes | Serves: 4-6

2 tablespoons olive oil
1 shallot, diced
2 carrots, diced
1 parsnip, diced
1 teaspoon fresh garlic, minced
½ cup dry white wine
2 cups fish stock
1 tomato, pureed
1 bay leaf
1-pound shrimp, deveined
½ pound scallops
Seasoned salt and pepper, to taste
1 tablespoon paprika
2 tablespoons fresh parsley, chopped
1 lime, sliced

1. Press the "Sauté" button twice to select "Normal" settings and heat the oil. 2. Now, sauté the shallot, carrot, and parsnip for 4 to 5 minutes or until they are tender. 3. Stir in the garlic and continue to sauté an additional 30 second or until aromatic. 4. Stir in the white wine, stock, tomato, bay leaf, shrimp, scallops, salt, black pepper, and paprika. 5. Put on the pressure cooker's lid and turn the steam valve to "Sealing" position. 6. Set the Instant Pot to Pressure Cook. 7. Use the "+/-" keys on the control panel to set the cooking time to 5 minutes. 8. Press the Pressure Level button to adjust the pressure to "High". 9. Once the cooking cycle is completed, allow the steam to release naturally for 5 minutes. 10. When all the steam is released, remove the pressure lid from the top carefully. 11. Enjoy!
Per Serving: Calories 449; Fat 2.9g; Sodium 511mg; Carbs 12g; Fiber 3g; Sugar 8g; Protein 28g

Chicken Fricassee with Wine

Prep time: 20 minutes | Cook time: 15 minutes | Serves: 4-6

2 tablespoons canola oil
6 chicken wings
1 onion, chopped
2 garlic cloves, minced
Kosher salt and black pepper, to taste
1 teaspoon cayenne pepper
1 teaspoon celery seeds
½ teaspoon mustard powder
2 carrots, chopped
2 celery stalks, chopped
3 cups vegetable broth
½ cup cooking sherry
2 tablespoons all-purpose flour
1 cup double cream

1. Press the "Sauté" button twice to select "Normal" settings and heat 1 tablespoon of olive oil. 2. Now, cook the chicken wings for 2 to 3 minutes per side; set aside. 3. Add a splash of cooking sherry to deglaze the pot. 4. Then, heat the remaining tablespoon of olive oil; sauté the onion until just tender or about 3 minutes. 5. Stir in the garlic and continue to cook an additional minute, stirring frequently. 6. Add the reserved chicken, salt, black pepper, cayenne pepper, celery seeds, mustard powder, carrots, celery, broth, and sherry to the inner pot. 7. Put on the pressure cooker's lid and turn the steam valve to "Sealing" position. 8. Set the Instant Pot on "Poultry". 9. Use the "+/-" keys on the control panel to set the cooking time to 15 minutes. 10. Press the Pressure Level button to adjust the pressure to "High". 11. Once the cooking cycle is completed, quick-release the pressure. 12. When all the steam is released, remove the pressure lid from the top carefully. 13. Mix the flour with the double cream. 14. Add the flour mixture to the hot cooking liquid. 15. Seal the lid and let it sit in the residual heat until thoroughly warmed. 16. Ladle into individual bowls and serve. 17. Bon appétit!
Per Serving: Calories 334; Fat 7.9g; Sodium 704mg; Carbs 6g; Fiber 3.6g; Sugar 6g; Protein 18g

Hyderabadi- Lentil Stew

Prep time: 20 minutes | Cook time: 10 minutes | Serves: 4-6

2 tablespoons canola oil	½ teaspoons tamarind paste
1 teaspoon cumin seeds	½ teaspoons red chili powder
1 onion, chopped	10 curry leaves
1 teaspoon garlic paste	1 cup tomato sauce
2 cups yellow lentils, soaked for 30 minutes and rinsed	Kosher salt and white pepper, to taste

1. Press the "Sauté" button twice to select "Normal" settings and heat the oil. 2. Then, sauté the cumin seeds for 1 to 2 minutes, stirring frequently. 3. Then, add the onion and cook an additional 2 minutes. Stir in the remaining ingredients. 4. Put on the pressure cooker's lid and turn the steam valve to "Sealing" position. 5. Set the Instant Pot to Pressure Cook. 6. Use the "+/-" keys on the control panel to set the cooking time to 5 minutes. 7. Press the Pressure Level button to adjust the pressure to "High". 8. Once the cooking cycle is completed, allow the steam to release naturally for 10 minutes. 9. When all the steam is released, remove the pressure lid from the top carefully. 10. Ladle into individual bowls and serve immediately. 11. Bon appétit!
Per Serving: Calories 405; Fat 12.9g; Sodium 414mg; Carbs 11g; Fiber 5g; Sugar 9g; Protein 31g

Kentucky Burgoo

Prep time: 20 minutes | Cook time: 55 minutes | Serves: 8

2 tablespoons lard, melted	2 carrots, sliced thickly
2 onions, chopped	2 parsnips, sliced thickly
1-pound pork shank, cubed	1 celery rib, sliced thickly
2-pound beef shank, cubed	2 sweet peppers, seeded and sliced
1-pound chicken legs	1 jalapeno pepper, seeded and minced
½ cup Kentucky bourbon	
4 cups chicken broth	
2 cups dry lima beans, soaked	1 teaspoon dried sage, crushed
2 cups tomato puree	1 teaspoon dried basil, crushed
1 pound potatoes, diced	Salt and black pepper, to taste

1. Press the "Sauté" button two times to select "Normal" settings and melt 1 tablespoon of lard. 2. Once hot, sauté the onion until tender and translucent; reserve. 3. Add the remaining tablespoon of lard; brown the meat in batches until no longer pink or about 4 minutes. 4. Add a splash of Kentucky bourbon to deglaze the pot. Pour chicken broth into the inner pot. 5. Put on the pressure cooker's lid and turn the steam valve to "Sealing" position. 6. Set the Instant Pot on "Meat/Stew". 7. Use the "+/-" keys on the control panel to set the cooking time to 45 minutes. 8. Press the Pressure Level button to adjust the pressure to "High". 9. Once the cooking cycle is completed, quick-release the pressure. 10. When all the steam is released, remove the pressure lid from the top carefully. 11. Shred chicken meat and discard the bones; add the chicken back to the inner pot. 12. Next, stir in lima beans and tomato puree. 13. Set the Instant Pot on Pressure Cook. Cook for 5 minutes at High pressure. 14. Once cooking is complete, use a quick pressure release; carefully remove the lid. 15. Then, stir in the remaining ingredients, including the sautéed onion. 16. Set the Instant Pot on Pressure Cook again. Cook for 5 minutes at High pressure. 17. Once cooking is complete, use a quick pressure release; carefully remove the lid. 18. Serve with cornbread if desired.
Per Serving: Calories 382; Fat 7.9g; Sodium 704mg; Carbs 6g; Fiber 3.6g; Sugar 6g; Protein 18g

Oyster Stew with Chorizo

Prep time: 20 minutes | Cook time: 10 minutes | Serves: 4-6

2 tablespoons olive oil	½ teaspoons smoked paprika
8-ounce Spanish chorizo sausage, sliced	½ pound fresh oysters, cleaned
	Sea salt and black pepper, to taste
1 onion, chopped	3 cups chicken broth
1 teaspoon ginger-garlic paste	2 cups kale leaves, washed
½ teaspoons dried rosemary	1 cup heavy cream

1. Press the "Sauté" button twice to select "Normal" settings and heat the sesame oil. 2. When the oil starts to sizzle, cook the sausage until no longer pink. 3. Add the onion to the inner pot and continue to sauté for a further 3 minutes or until tender and translucent. 4. Now, stir in the ginger-garlic paste, rosemary, paprika, oysters, salt, pepper, and chicken broth. 5. Put on the pressure cooker's lid and turn the steam valve to "Sealing" position. 6. Set the Instant Pot to Pressure Cook. 7. Use the "+/-" keys on the control panel to set the cooking time to 6 minutes. 8. Press the Pressure Level button to adjust the pressure to "High". 9. Once the cooking cycle is completed, quick-release the steam. 10. When all the steam is released, remove the pressure lid from the top carefully. 11. Add the kale leaves and heavy cream, seal the lid again, and let it sit in the residual heat. 12. Serve warm and enjoy!
Per Serving: Calories 412; Fat 20g; Sodium 491mg; Carbs 9g; Fiber 3g; Sugar 8g; Protein 31g

Lentil Curry Stew

Prep time: 20 minutes | Cook time: 15 minutes | Serves: 4-6

Dahl:	4 cups vegetable broth
2 tablespoons butter	½ teaspoons turmeric powder
1 brown onion, chopped	Kosher salt and black pepper, to taste
4 garlic cloves, minced	
1 (1-inch) piece ginger, peeled and grated	Tadka (Tempering):
1 red chili pepper, deseeded and minced	1 tablespoon butter
	A pinch of asafetida
6 fresh curry leaves	½ teaspoons cumin seeds
2 tomatoes, chopped	1 teaspoon mustard seeds
½ teaspoons ground cumin	½ onion, sliced
¼ teaspoon ground cardamom	1 bay leaf
1½ cups dried chana dal, soaked	2 dried chili peppers, seeded and cut in half

1. Press the "Sauté" button twice to select "Normal" settings and melt 2 tablespoons of butter. 2. Once hot, cook the onion until tender and translucent or about 3 minutes. 3. Then, stir in the garlic and ginger; continue to cook an additional minute or until they are fragrant. 4. Add the remaining ingredients for the Dahl. 5. Put on the pressure cooker's lid and turn the steam valve to "Sealing" position. 6. Set the Instant Pot to Pressure Cook. 7. Use the "+/-" keys on the control panel to set the cooking time to 10 minutes. 8. Press the Pressure Level button to adjust the pressure to "High". 9. Once the cooking cycle is completed, quick-release the pressure. 10. When all the steam is released, remove the pressure lid from the top carefully. 11. Clean the inner pot and Press the "Sauté" button two times to select "Normal" settings again. 12. Melt 1 tablespoon of butter. 13. Now, add a pinch of asafetida, cumin seeds, mustard seeds, onion and bay leaf; sauté for a minute. 14. Stir in the dried chili peppers and cook for 30 seconds longer. 15. Pour the hot tadka over the hot dal and serve.
Per Serving: Calories 305; Fat 7.9g; Sodium 704mg; Carbs 6g; Fiber 3.6g; Sugar 6g; Protein 18g

Vegetarian Ratatouille

Prep time: 20 minutes | Cook time: 15 minutes | Serves: 4-6

1-pound eggplant, cut into rounds	minced
1 tablespoon sea salt	Sea salt and black pepper, to taste
3 tablespoons olive oil	1 teaspoon capers
1 red onion, sliced	½ teaspoons celery seeds
4 cloves garlic, minced	2 tomatoes, pureed
4 sweet peppers, seeded and chopped	1 cup roasted vegetable broth
1 red chili pepper, seeded and	2 tablespoons coriander, chopped

1. Toss the eggplant with 1 tablespoon of sea salt; allow it to drain in a colander. 2. Press the "Sauté" button twice to select "Normal" settings and heat the olive oil. 3. Sauté the onion until tender and translucent, about 4 minutes. 4. Add the garlic and continue to sauté for 30 seconds more or until fragrant. 5. Add the remaining ingredients to the inner pot, including the drained eggplant. 6. Press the "Sauté" button two times to select "Normal" setting and cook for 7 minutes. 7. Bon appétit!
Per Serving: Calories 584; Fat 15g; Sodium 441mg; Carbs 17g; Fiber 4.6g; Sugar 5g; Protein 29g

Chapter 6 Bean, Pasta and Grain Recipes

Garlic Risotto with Parmesan Cheese

Prep time: 10 minutes | Cook Time: 10 minutes | Serves: 6

5 tablespoons salted butter, divided
1 medium onion, diced
3 garlic cloves, minced
2 cups Arborio rice
½ cup white wine
4 cups chicken broth

1 tablespoon dried thyme
1 teaspoon salt
½ teaspoon freshly ground black pepper
½ cup freshly grated Parmesan cheese

1. Insert the pot into the Cooker Base without the lid. 2. Select Sauté mode and then press the same button again and then adjust the cooking temperature to Normal. 3. When the display switches On to Hot, melt 2 tablespoons of butter; add diced onion and cook for 3 minutes or until just softened; add the garlic and cook for 1 minute or until fragrant; add the Arborio rice and stir constantly for 3 minutes; lastly, stir in the wine and deglaze and scrape up the browned bits from the bottom. 4. After adding the chicken broth, thyme, salt and pepper and stirring well, place and close the lid in right way. 5. Select Pressure Cook mode. Press Pressure Cook button again to adjust the cooking time to 5 minutes; press Pressure Level to choose High Pressure. 6. When the time is up, quickly and carefully turn the steam release handle from the Sealing position to the Venting position. 7. When the float valve drops, open the lid; stir in the remaining butter and cheese, then season with additional salt and pepper. 8. Serve and enjoy.
Per Serving: Calories 285; Fat 9.8g; Sodium 639mg; Carbs 11.1g; Fiber 1.2g; Sugars 5.1g; Protein 27.8g

Pinto Beans in Tomato Sauce

Prep time: 10 minutes | Cook Time: 31 minutes | Serves: 8

2 cups (1 pound) dry pinto beans
2 tablespoons avocado oil
1 large yellow onion, peeled and diced
1 medium jalapeño, seeded and diced
2 teaspoons minced garlic
3½ cups chicken stock

1 (8-ounce) can tomato sauce
2 tablespoons chili powder
1 tablespoon yellow mustard
1 teaspoon dried oregano
1 teaspoon cumin
½ teaspoon black pepper
2 bay leaves
½ teaspoon salt

1. In a bowl, add the beans and 3" water; allow the beans soak 4 to 8 hours; drain them. 2. Insert the pot into the Cooker Base without the lid. 3. Select Sauté mode and then press the same button again and then adjust the cooking temperature to Normal. 4. When the display switches On to Hot, add and heat the oil for 1 minute; add the onion, jalapeño, garlic and cook for 5 minutes or until softened; add the soaked beans, stock, tomato sauce, chili powder, mustard, oregano, cumin, pepper, bay leaves and salt, stir well and scrape any brown bits from the bottom of the pot. 5. Press Cancel button to stop this cooking program; place and close the lid in right way. 6. Select Pressure Cook mode. Press Pressure Cook button again to adjust the cooking time to 25 minutes; press Pressure Level to choose High Pressure. 7. When the time is up, leave the steam release handle in the Sealing position. 8. When the float valve drops, open the lid and discard the bay leaves. 9. Serve and enjoy.
Per Serving: Calories: 289; Fat: 5g; Sodium: 516mg; Fiber: 10g; Carbs: 44g; Sugar: 5g; Protein: 16g

Black Beans in Vegetable Stock

Prep time: 5 minutes | Cook Time: 20 minutes | Serves: 6

½ pound dry black beans

1 (13.25-ounce) can unsweetened

full-fat coconut milk
3 cups vegetable stock
1 tablespoon chopped fresh,

peeled ginger
1 tablespoon red curry paste
½ teaspoon kosher salt

1. In a bowl, add the dry black beans and 3" water; allow the beans soak 4 to 8 hours; drain them. 2. In the Inner Pot, add and mix up the soaked beans, coconut milk, stock, ginger, curry paste, and salt. 3. Insert the pot into the Cooker Base and then close the lid rightly. 4. Select Pressure Cook mode. Press Pressure Cook button again to adjust the cooking time to 20 minutes; press Pressure Level to choose High Pressure. 5. When the time is up, quickly and carefully turn the steam release handle from the Sealing position to the Venting position. 6. When finished, serve and enjoy.
Per Serving: Calories: 263; Fat: 13g; Sodium: 705mg; Fiber: 6g; Carbs: 27g; Sugar: 1g; Protein: 11g

Tasty Shrimp Paella with Peas

Prep time: 10 minutes | Cook Time: 9 minutes | Serves: 4

4 tablespoons (½ stick) unsalted butter
1 medium red bell pepper, seeded and diced
4 garlic cloves, minced
1½ cups chicken broth
1 cup jasmine rice, rinsed
¼ cup chopped fresh flat-leaf parsley

1 teaspoon salt
¼ teaspoon freshly ground black pepper
¼ teaspoon red pepper flakes
Juice of 1 medium lemon
¼ teaspoon saffron
1-pound frozen wild shrimp (16–20 count), shells and tails on
½ cup frozen peas, thawed

1. Insert the pot into the Cooker Base without the lid. 2. Select Sauté mode and then press the same button again and then adjust the cooking temperature to Normal. 3. When the display switches On to Hot, melt the butter; add the garlic, diced bell pepper and cook for 4 minutes or until the peppers start to soften; add the right amount of broth to deglaze the pot, stir and scrap the browned bits from the bottom. 4. Add the rice, parsley, red pepper flakes, lemon juice, saffron, salt, black pepper and the remaining chicken broth without stirring them, then top with the shrimp. 5. Place and close the lid rightly. 6. Select Pressure Cook mode. Press Pressure Cook button again to adjust the cooking time to 5 minutes; press Pressure Level to choose High Pressure. 7. When the time is up, quickly and carefully turn the steam release handle from the Sealing position to the Venting position. 8. When released, carefully remove the cooked shrimp from the rice and then peel them; transfer them back to the rice and then stir in the peas. 9. Serve and enjoy.
Per Serving: Calories 254; Fat 28 g; Sodium 346mg; Carbs 12.3 g; Sugar 1g; Fiber 0.7g; Protein 24.3 g

Homemade Teff

Prep time: 1 minutes | Cook Time: 4 minutes | Serves: 4

1 cup dry teff
½ teaspoon salt

3 cups water

1. In the Inner Pot, add the teff, salt and water. 2. Insert the pot into the Cooker Base and then close the lid rightly. 3. Select Pressure Cook mode. Press Pressure Cook button again to adjust the cooking time to 4 minutes; press Pressure Level to choose High Pressure. 4. When the time is up, leave the steam release handle in the Sealing position. 5. When done, serve and enjoy.
Per Serving: Calories: 177; Fat: 1g; Sodium: 296mg; Fiber: 4g; Carbs: 35g; Sugar: 1g; Protein: 6g

Tuscan White Beans in Vegetable Broth

Prep time: 5 minutes | Cook Time: 28 minutes | Serves: 6

½ pound dry cannellini beans
1 tablespoon avocado oil
3 large cloves garlic, smashed

¼ teaspoon crushed red pepper flakes
3 cups vegetable broth

1. In a bowl, add the beans and 5 cups of water; allow the beans soak 4 to 8 hours; drain them. 2. Insert the pot into the Cooker Base without the lid. 3. Select Sauté mode and then press the same button again and then adjust the cooking temperature to Normal. 4. When the display switches On to Hot, add and heat the oil for 2 minute; add the garlic, red pepper flakes and cook them for 30 seconds. 5. Add the beans and broth, press Cancel button stop this cooking program; place and close the lid in right way. 6. Select Pressure Cook mode. Press Pressure Cook button again to adjust the cooking time to 25 minutes; press Pressure Level to choose High Pressure. 7. When the time is up, quickly and carefully turn the steam release handle from the Sealing position to the Venting position. 8. When finished, serve and enjoy.
Per Serving: Calories: 156; Fat: 3g; Sodium: 276mg; Fiber: 6g; Carbs: 25g; Sugar: 1g; Protein: 9g

Creamy and Cheesy Elbow Macaroni

Prep time: 10 minutes | Cook Time: 4 minutes | Serves: 6

2½ cups uncooked elbow macaroni
1 cup chicken broth
2 cups water
3 tablespoons unsalted butter, cubed
¼ teaspoon salt
¼ teaspoon freshly ground black

pepper
¼ teaspoon mustard powder
¼ teaspoon garlic powder
⅓ cup whole or 2 percent milk
⅓ cup heavy (whipping) cream
2 cups shredded sharp cheddar cheese

1. In the Inner Pot, mix up the macaroni, broth, water, butter, mustard powder, garlic powder, salt and black pepper. 2. Insert the pot into the Cooker Base and then close the lid rightly. 3. Select Pressure Cook mode. Press Pressure Cook button again to adjust the cooking time to 4 minutes; press Pressure Level to choose High Pressure. 4. When the time is up, quickly and carefully turn the steam release handle from the Sealing position to the Venting position. 5. When released, stir in the milk, cream and cheese until smooth and creamy. 6. Serve and enjoy.
Per Serving: Calories 305; Fat 15g; Sodium 548mg; Carbs 12g; Sugar 1.2g; Fiber 0.7g; Protein 29g

Simple Steamed Black Beans

Prep time: 5 minutes | Cook Time: 25 minutes | Serves: 8

1 pound dry black beans
6 cups water

2 teaspoons salt

1. In a bowl, add the dry black beans and 3" water; allow the beans soak 4 to 8 hours; drain them. 2. In the Inner Pot, add 6 cups of water and the soaked beans. 3. Insert the pot into the Cooker Base and then close the lid rightly. 4. Select Pressure Cook mode. Press Pressure Cook button again to adjust the cooking time to 25 minutes; press Pressure Level to choose High Pressure. 5. When the time is up, leave the steam release handle in the Sealing position for 10 minutes, then turn the steam release handle to the Venting position. 6. When the float valve drops, open the lid, add the salt and then transfer the beans to a bowl. 7. Serve and enjoy.
Per Serving: Calories: 192; Fat: 0g; Sodium: 586mg; Fiber: 9g; Carbs: 36g; Sugar: 1g; Protein: 12g

Nutritious White Bean Salad with Vegetables

Prep time: 10 minutes | Cook Time: 25 minutes | Serves: 4

1 cup dry cannellini beans
2 cups water
3 tablespoons extra-virgin olive oil
1 tablespoon lemon juice
1 clove garlic, minced
½ teaspoon coarse sea salt

¼ teaspoon black pepper
1 cup grape tomatoes, halved
1 large avocado, peeled, pitted, cut in half lengthwise, and sliced
1 cup packed basil leaves, chopped

1. In a suitable bowl, add the beans and cover with 3" water; allow the beans soak 4 to 8 hours; drain them. 2. In the Inner Pot, add the beans and 2 cups of water. 3. Insert the pot into the Cooker Base and then close the lid rightly. 4. Select Pressure Cook mode. Press Pressure Cook button again to adjust the cooking time to 25 minutes; press Pressure Level to choose High Pressure. 5. While cooking, prepare an airtight container, add the oil, lemon juice, garlic, salt and pepper and shake them until they are well combined; set aside for later use. 6. When the time is up, leave the steam release handle in the Sealing position. 7. When the float valve drops, open the lid and cool the beans. 8. In a large bowl, add the beans, tomatoes, avocado and basil; drizzle them with the dressing and stir gently to coat evenly. 9. Enjoy.
Per Serving: Calories: 336; Fat: 15g; Sodium: 205mg; Fiber: 16g; Carbs: 39g; Sugar: 1g; Protein: 13g

Easy-to-Make Chickpeas

Prep time: 10 minutes | Cook Time: 10 minutes | Serves: 8

2 cups (1 pound) dry chickpeas
6 cups water

2 teaspoons salt

1. In a large bowl, add the chickpeas and 3" water; allow the beans soak 4 to 8 hours; drain them. 2. In the Inner Pot, add chickpeas, salt and water. 3. Insert the pot into the Cooker Base and then close the lid rightly. 4. Select Pressure Cook mode. Press Pressure Cook button again to adjust the cooking time to 10 minutes; press Pressure Level to choose High Pressure. 5. When the time is up, leave the steam release handle in the Sealing position for 10 minutes, then turn it to the Venting position. 6. When finished, serve and enjoy.
Per Serving: Calories: 214; Fat: 3g; Sodium: 594mg; Fiber: 7g; Carbs: 36g; Sugar: 6g; Protein: 12g

Spiced Millet with Onion

Prep time: 5 minutes | Cook Time: 7 minutes | Serves: 6

1 tablespoon avocado oil
1 medium yellow onion, peeled and diced
¼ teaspoon ground cumin
¼ teaspoon ground cardamom

⅛ teaspoon ground cinnamon
1 bay leaf
2 cups millet
3 cups water

1. Insert the pot into the Cooker Base without the lid. 2. Select Sauté mode and then press the same button again and then adjust the cooking temperature to Normal. 3. When the display switches On to Hot, add and heat the oil for 1 minute; add the onion, cumin, cardamom, cinnamon, and bay leaf, stir constantly for 5 minutes. 4. Press the Cancel button to stop this cooking program. 5. Add the millet and water to the Inner Pot and combine well; scrape any brown bits that may be stuck to the bottom. 6. Insert the pot into the Cooker Base and then close the lid rightly. 7. Select Pressure Cook mode. Press Pressure Cook button again to adjust the cooking time to 1 minutes; press Pressure Level to choose High Pressure. 8. When the time is up, leave the steam release handle in the Sealing position. 9. When the float valve drops, open the lid, discard the bay leaf and the transfer the millet to a bowl. 10. Serve and enjoy.
Per Serving: Calories: 280; Fat: 5g; Sodium: 4mg; Fiber: 6g; Carbs: 50g; Sugar: 1g; Protein: 8g

Rice Pilaf in Chicken Broth

Prep time: 10 minutes | Cook Time: 10-15 minutes | Serves: 4

4 tablespoons (½ stick) unsalted butter
⅓ cup vermicelli, broken into ½-inch pieces
1 cup long-grain white rice
1½ cups chicken broth
1 teaspoon garlic powder

¾ teaspoon salt
¼ teaspoon freshly ground black pepper
½ teaspoon onion powder
¼ teaspoon paprika
1 teaspoon dried parsley

1. Insert the pot into the Cooker Base without the lid. 2. Select Sauté mode and then press the same button again and then adjust the cooking temperature to Normal. 3. When the display switches On to Hot, melt the butter; add the vermicelli and stir for 2 to 3 minutes or until browned; add the rice and cook for 3 to 4 minutes more or until the rice starts to toast; lastly, stir in the chicken broth and the remaining ingredients, scrap up any browned bits from the bottom of the pot. 4. Place and close the lid in right way. 5. Select Pressure Cook mode. Press Pressure Cook button again to adjust the cooking time to 3 minutes; press Pressure Level to choose High Pressure. 6. When the time is up, leave the steam release handle in the Sealing position for 10 minutes, then turn it to the Venting position. 7. When done, serve and enjoy.
Per Serving: Calories 361; Fat 10g; Sodium 218mg; Carbs 16g; Sugar 1.2g; Fiber 0.7g; Protein 24g

Healthier Refried Beans with Onion

Prep time: 11 minutes | Cook Time: 27 minutes | Serves: 12

2 cups (1 pound) dry pinto beans
1 tablespoon avocado oil
1 large yellow onion, peeled and diced
4 cloves garlic, minced

7 cups water
2 teaspoons chili powder
1 teaspoon ground cumin
2 teaspoons salt

1. In a bowl, add the beans and 2" water; allow the beans soak 4 to 8 hours at room temperature; rinse and then drain them. 2. Insert the pot into the Cooker Base without the lid. 3. Select Sauté mode and then press the same button again and then adjust the cooking temperature to Normal. 4. When the display switches On to Hot, add and heat the oil; add the onion and cook for 6 minutes or until softened; add the garlic and cook for 30 seconds more. 5. Press Cancel button to stop this cooking program. 6. Transfer the processed beans, chili powder, cumin, water and salt to the Inner Pot; place and close the lid in right way. 7. Select Pressure Cook mode. Press Pressure Cook button again to adjust the cooking time to 20 minutes; press Pressure Level to choose High Pressure. 8. When the time is up, leave the steam release handle in the Sealing position. 9. When the float valve drops, open the lid, drain the beans and reserve the liquid; place the drained beans back to the Inner Pot, then use an immersion blender or potato masher to mix or mash the beans to the consistency you want, adding any reserved liquid as needed. 10. When done, serve and enjoy. 11. Transfer the beans to a bowl for serving. Refried beans may be stored in the refrigerator for three to four days or the freezer up to three months.
Per Serving: Calories: 149; Fat: 2g; Sodium: 405mg; Fiber: 6g; Carbs: 25g; Sugar: 1g; Protein: 8g

Chicken Fried Rice with Peas

Prep time: 10 minutes | Cook Time: 11 minutes | Serves: 4

2 teaspoons vegetable oil, divided
2 eggs, whisked
3 garlic cloves, minced
1¼ cups chicken broth
1-pound boneless, skinless chicken breasts, cubed
1 cup peeled and diced carrots

1½ cups jasmine rice, rinsed
3 tablespoons soy sauce
½ teaspoon toasted sesame oil
½ cup frozen peas, thawed
Sesame seeds, for garnish (optional)

1. Insert the pot into the Cooker Base without the lid. 2. Select Sauté mode and then press the same button again and then adjust the cooking temperature to Normal. 3. When the display switches On to Hot, add and heat 1 teaspoon of the oil; add the eggs and use a spatula to push them around to scramble them until fully cooked, then arrange them to a plate and set aside for later use. 4. Add and heat the remaining oil; add the garlic and cook for 1 minute until fragrant. 5. Press Cancel button to stop this cooking program. 6. Still in the Inner Pot, add the chicken, carrot and rice without stirring them; press the rice down to submerge it 7. Place and close the lid rightly. 8. Select Pressure Cook mode. Press Pressure Cook button again to adjust the cooking time to 3 minutes; press Pressure Level to choose High Pressure. 9. When the time is up, leave the steam release handle in the Sealing position for 10 minutes, then turn it to the Venting position. 10. When released, open the lid; stir in the soy sauce and sesame oil until the rice is well coated; add the scrambled eggs and peas, stir well. 11. Close the lid again and Keep Warm the food for 5 minutes to warm the peas and eggs. 12. When done, toss with sesame seeds and serve.
Per Serving: Calories 285; Fat 9.8g; Sodium 639mg; Carbs 11.1g; Fiber 1.2g; Sugars 5.1g; Protein 27.8g

Ginger Chicken Porridge

Prep time: 10 minutes | Cook Time: 15 minutes | Serves: 6

¼ cup vegetable oil
2 thumbs fresh ginger, peeled and cut into matchsticks
3 garlic cloves, minced
1 large onion, chopped
3 carrots, peeled and cubed
3 celery stalks, sliced
2 tablespoons fish sauce
2 to 3 pounds boneless, skinless chicken thighs

1¼ cups jasmine rice, rinsed
1½ tablespoons salt
1½ teaspoons freshly ground black pepper
2 bay leaves
8 cups chicken broth
6 hard-boiled eggs, peeled, for serving (optional)
Lemon slices, for serving (optional)

1. Insert the pot into the Cooker Base without the lid. 2. Select Sauté mode and then press the same button again and then adjust the cooking temperature to Normal. 3. When the display switches On to Hot, add and heat the oil; add the ginger, garlic, carrot, onion and celery and cook for 5 minutes or until the celery starts to soften; stir in the fish sauce. 4. Add the chicken thighs, bay leaves, broth, rice, salt and pepper without stirring them. 5. Place and close the lid rightly. 6. Select Pressure Cook mode. Press Pressure Cook button again to adjust the cooking time to 10 minutes; press Pressure Level to choose High Pressure. 7. When the time is up, leave the steam release handle in the Sealing position for 10 minutes, then turn it to the Venting position. 8. When released, take out the chicken thighs and shred them, then arrange them back to the pot. 9. Discard the bay leaves. 10. Serve and enjoy with an egg and a slice of lemon.
Per Serving: Calories: 285; Fat 9.8g; Sodium 639mg; Carbs 11.1g; Fiber 1.2g; Sugars 5.1g; Protein 27.8g

Ginger Oregano Brown Lentils

Prep time: 2 minutes | Cook Time: 20 minutes | Serves: 6

1½ cups brown lentils
2 cups vegetable broth
2 tablespoons tomato paste
1 (15-ounce) can unsweetened full-; Fat coconut milk

2 teaspoons curry powder
½ teaspoon dried ginger
½ teaspoon dried oregano
¼ teaspoon garlic salt

1. In the Inner Pot, add and mix up all of the ingredients. 2. Insert the pot into the Cooker Base and then close the lid rightly. 3. Select Pressure Cook mode. Press Pressure Cook button again to adjust the cooking time to 20 minutes; press Pressure Level to choose High Pressure. 4. When the time is up, leave the steam release handle in the Sealing position; when the float valve drops, open the lid. 5. Stir well before serving.
Per Serving: Calories: 320; Fat: 15g; Sodium: 316mg; Fiber: 6g; Carbs: 35g; Sugar: 2g; Protein: 14g

Tomato Brown Lentils

Prep time: 2 minutes | Cook Time: 20 minutes | Serves: 6

1½ cups brown lentils
1 (15-ounce) can tomato sauce
2 tablespoons tomato paste
1 (15-ounce) can unsweetened full-; Fat coconut milk

⅓ cup water
1 teaspoon dried basil
1 teaspoon dried oregano
¼ teaspoon garlic salt

1. In the Inner Pot, add and mix up all of the ingredients. 2. Insert the pot into the Cooker Base and then close the lid rightly. 3. Select Pressure Cook mode. Press Pressure Cook button again to adjust the cooking time to 20 minutes; press Pressure Level to choose High Pressure. 4. When the time is up, leave the steam release handle in the Sealing position; when the float valve drops, open the lid. 5. Stir well before serving.
Per Serving: Calories: 330; Fat: 15g; Sodium: 471mg; Fiber: 7g; Carbs: 37g; Sugar: 4g; Protein: 14g

Coconut Rice in Chicken Broth

Prep time: 10 minutes | Cook Time: 5 minutes | Serves: 6

1½ cups jasmine rice, rinsed
1 (14-ounce) can unsweetened coconut milk

½ cup chicken broth
¼ teaspoon salt

1. In the Inner Pot, mix up the rice, coconut milk, chicken broth and salt. 2. Insert the pot into the Cooker Base and then close the lid rightly. 3. Select Pressure Cook mode. Press Pressure Cook button again to adjust the cooking time to 5 minutes; press Pressure Level to choose High Pressure. 4. When the time is up, leave the steam release handle in the Sealing position. 5.When done, use a fork to fluff the rice and serve.
Per Serving: Calories 236; Fat 13.9g; Sodium 451mg; Carbs 13.2g; Fiber 1.2g; Sugars 1.4g; Protein 14.3g

Parmesan Polenta

Prep time: 10 minutes | Cook Time: 9 minutes | Serves: 4

1 cup dry cornmeal
4 cups water
1 teaspoon salt
1 teaspoon freshly ground black

pepper
3 tablespoons unsalted butter
½ cup freshly grated Parmesan cheese

1. In the Inner Pot, mix up the dried cornmeal, water, salt and pepper. 2. Insert the pot into the Cooker Base and then close the lid rightly. 3. Select Pressure Cook mode. Press Pressure Cook button again to adjust the cooking time to 9 minutes; press Pressure Level to choose High Pressure. 4. When the time is up, leave the steam release handle in the Sealing position. 5. When the float valve drops, open the lid; stir with the butter and Parmesan cheese until well combined. 6. Season with additional salt the pepper, enjoy.
Per Serving: Calories 199; Fat 10.5g; Sodium 693mg; Carbs: 23.9g; Fiber 1g; Sugars: 0.2g; Protein 3.8g

Barley with Ham and Onion

Prep time: 10 minutes | Cook Time: 25 minutes | Serves: 4

1 tablespoon unsalted butter
1 cup hulled barley
¼ cup finely chopped onion
4 cups water

½ teaspoon salt
½ cup diced cooked ham
½ cup mustard greens
4 eggs, cooked to your preference

1. Insert the pot into the Cooker Base without the lid. 2. Select Sauté mode and then press the same button again and then adjust the cooking temperature to Normal. 3. When the display switches On to Hot, add and melt the butter; add the barley, onion and cook for 1 to 2 minutes until the barley starts to toast; add the salt and water and stir well. 4. Press Cancel button to stop this cooking program; place and close the lid in right way.

5. Select Pressure Cook mode. Press Pressure Cook button again to adjust the cooking time to 18 minutes; press Pressure Level to choose High Pressure. 6. When the time is up, quickly and carefully turn the steam release handle from the Sealing position to the Venting position. 7. Drain the remaining liquid as needed. 8. Press Cancel button to stop this cooking program. 9. Select Sauté mode and then press the same button again and then adjust the cooking temperature to Normal. 10. Add the ham, greens and cook for 5 minutes or until the greens are just wilted. 11. When done, scoop a quarter of the barley into each bowl and put an egg of your choice on top.
Per Serving: Calories 344; Fat 14.9g; Sodium 227mg; Carbs 14g; Fiber 1g; Sugars 1.4g; Protein 25.7g

Quinoa with Enchilada Sauce and Cheese

Prep time: 10 minutes | Cook Time: 1 minutes | Serves: 4

½ small onion, diced
1 (4.3-ounce) can mild green chilies
1 (10-ounce) bag frozen corn
1 (15-ounce) can black beans, drained and rinsed
1 cup chopped fresh tomatoes
1 teaspoon chili powder

½ teaspoon ground cumin
¼ teaspoon salt
1 cup uncooked quinoa, rinsed well
2 cups water
1 cup enchilada sauce
1 cup shredded Monterey Jack cheese

1. In the Inner Pot, mix up the onion, chilies, corn, beans, cumin, chopped tomatoes, quinoa, salt and water. 2. Insert the pot into the Cooker Base and then close the lid rightly. 3. Select Pressure Cook mode. Press Pressure Cook button again to adjust the cooking time to 1 minutes; press Pressure Level to choose High Pressure. 4. When the time is up, leave the steam release handle in the Sealing position. 5. With the enchilada sauce and cheese, serve and enjoy.
Per Serving: Calories 272; Fat 19g; Sodium 389mg; Carbs 10.4g; Fiber 0.7g; Sugars 1.1g; Protein 15.6g

Lime Black Beans with Cilantro

Prep time: 5 minutes | Cook Time: 10 minutes | Serves: 12

2 cups (1 pound) dry black beans
4 cups vegetable broth
1 tablespoon chili powder
1 teaspoon smoked paprika

¼ teaspoon salt
Juice from 1 large lime
½ cup chopped cilantro

1. In a bowl, add the beans and 3" water; allow the beans soak 4 to 8 hours at room temperature; rinse and then drain them. 2. In the Inner Pot, mix up the soaked beans, broth, paprika, chili powder and salt. 3. Insert the pot into the Cooker Base and then close the lid rightly. 4. Select Pressure Cook mode. Press Pressure Cook button again to adjust the cooking time to 10 minutes; press Pressure Level to choose High Pressure. 5. When the time is up, leave the steam release handle in the Sealing position. 6. When the float valve drops, open the lid, stir in the lime juice and cilantro. 7. Serve and enjoy.
Per Serving: Calories: 136; Fat: 0g; Sodium: 251mg; Fiber: 7g; Carbs: 26g; Sugar: 1g; Protein: 8g

Simple Quinoa

Prep time: 1 minutes | Cook Time: 1 minutes | Serves: 4

1 cup dry quinoa

1 cup water

1. In a fine-mesh strainer, add the quinoa and rinse them until the water doesn't become turbid anymore. 2. In the Inner Pot, add the clean quinoa and water. 3. Insert the pot into the Cooker Base and then close the lid rightly. 4. Select Pressure Cook mode. Press Pressure Cook button again to adjust the cooking time to 1 minutes; press Pressure Level to choose High Pressure. 5. When the time is up, leave the steam release handle in the Sealing position. 6. When the float valve drops, open the lid; use a fork to fluff the quinoa. 7. Serve and enjoy.
Per Serving: Calories: 156; Fat: 2g; Sodium: 2mg; Fiber: 3g; Carbs: 27g; Sugar: 0g; Protein: 6g

Garlic Shrimp Pasta with Thai Sweet Chili Sauce

Prep time: 10 minutes | Cook Time: 6 minutes | Serves: 4

2 tablespoons olive oil
3 garlic cloves, minced, divided
16 ounces spaghetti, broken in half
3 cups water
1-pound medium shrimp (36–40 count), shells and tails left on
1 teaspoon paprika
¾ tablespoon lime juice
½ cup mayonnaise
⅓ cup Thai sweet chili sauce
2 teaspoons sriracha
¼ teaspoon red pepper flakes

1. Insert the pot into the Cooker Base without the lid. 2. Select Sauté mode and then press the same button again and then adjust the cooking temperature to Normal. 3. When the display switches On to Hot, add and heat the oil; add the garlic and cook for 1 minute or until fragrant. 4. Layer the spaghetti in a crisscross pattern and add the water, then gently press the spaghetti down to submerge completely. 5. Prepare a piece of aluminum foil, put the shrimp in its middle and then sprinkle the paprika and lime juice over the shrimp; fold the foil into a parcel and arrange it to the top of the spaghetti. 6. Place and close the lid rightly. 7. Select Pressure Cook mode. Press Pressure Cook button again to adjust the cooking time to 5 minutes; press Pressure Level to choose High Pressure. 8. While cooking, mix up the mayonnaise, chili sauce, sriracha, and red pepper flakes in a suitable bowl. 9. When the time is up, quickly and carefully turn the steam release handle from the Sealing position to the Venting position. 10. When released, unfold the shrimp parcel and dump the juices into the pasta; peel the shrimp and place them on the pasta. 11. Break up any spaghetti clumps, then stir in the sauce until everything is well combined. 12. Serve and enjoy.
Per Serving: Calories 344; Fat 14.9g; Sodium 227mg; Carbs 14g; Fiber 1g; Sugars 1.4g; Protein 25.7g

Worcestershire Mushroom Brown Rice

Prep time: 10 minutes | Cook Time: 35 minutes | Serves: 4

3 tablespoons unsalted butter, divided
1 small onion, diced
3 garlic cloves, minced
1-pound baby bella mushrooms, sliced
2 teaspoons Worcestershire sauce
½ teaspoon dried thyme
1 cup long-grain brown rice
1¼ cups vegetable broth
Salt
Freshly ground black pepper

1. Insert the pot into the Cooker Base without the lid. 2. Select Sauté mode and then press the same button again and then adjust the cooking temperature to Normal. 3. When the display switches On to Hot, melt 1 tablespoon of the butter; add the onion and cook for 3 minutes or until just softened; add the garlic and cook for 1 minute or until fragrant; add the mushrooms, Worcestershire sauce, thyme and stir constantly for 5 to 6 minutes until the mushrooms reduce in size; lastly, stir in rice and broth. 4. Place and close the lid in right way. 5. Select Pressure Cook mode. Press Pressure Cook button again to adjust the cooking time to 25 minutes; press Pressure Level to choose High Pressure. 6. When the time is up, quickly and carefully turn the steam release handle from the Sealing position to the Venting position. 7. When released, add the remaining butter and stir well; season with salt and black pepper. 8. Enjoy.
Per Serving: Calories 249; Fat 13g; Sodium 556mg; Carbs 10g; Sugar 1.1g; Fiber 0.7g; Protein 31g

Long-Grain White Rice with Jalapeño

Prep time: 10 minutes | Cook Time: 17 minutes | Serves: 6

2 tablespoons olive oil
1 medium yellow onion, diced
1 medium carrot, peeled and diced
2 celery stalks, diced
1 small jalapeño, diced
3 garlic cloves, minced
1 tablespoon apple cider vinegar
6 thyme sprigs
1 bay leaf
1 cup long-grain white rice
2 teaspoons sea salt
2½ cups chicken or vegetable broth

28 ounces frozen black-eyed peas

1. Insert the pot into the Cooker Base without the lid. 2. Select Sauté mode and then press the same button again and then adjust the cooking temperature to Normal. 3. When the display switches On to Hot, add the onion, carrot, celery and jalapeño, stir constantly for 4 minutes or until they are fragrant; add the garlic, thyme, vinegar and bay leaf, cook for 1 more minute; lastly, stir in the rice, chicken broth, peas and salt. 4. Press Cancel button to stop this cooking program. 5. Place and close the lid rightly. 6. Select Pressure Cook mode. Press Pressure Cook button again to adjust the cooking time to 12 minutes; press Pressure Level to choose High Pressure. 7. When the time is up, leave the steam release handle in the Sealing position for 10 minutes, then turn it to the Venting position. 8. When done, remove the thyme sprigs and bay leaf. 9. Serve and enjoy.
Per Serving: Calories 336; Fat 17.3g; Sodium 281mg; Carbs 8.1g; Fiber 5.3g; Sugars 17.7g; Protein 32.3g

Chicken Burrito Bowls with Chunky Salsa

Prep time: 10 minutes | Cook Time: 15 minutes | Serves: 5

2 tablespoons olive oil
1 medium onion, diced
3 garlic cloves, minced
1½ tablespoons chili powder
1½ teaspoons ground cumin
1 cup chicken broth
Salt
Freshly ground black pepper
2 pounds boneless, skinless chicken thighs, cubed
1 (15-ounce) can black beans, drained and rinsed
1 cup frozen corn
1 (16-ounce) jar chunky salsa
1 cup long-grain white rice

1. Insert the pot into the Cooker Base without the lid. 2. Select Sauté mode and then press the same button again and then adjust the cooking temperature to Normal. 3. When the display switches On to Hot, add and heat the oil; add the onion, garlic and cook for 4 minutes or until the onion is translucent; add the cumin, chili powder and cook for 1 minute until fragrant; add the broth and stir to scrape the browned bits from the bottom. 4. Sprinkle salt and pepper over the chicken evenly and arrange it to the Inner Pot, then stir well with the beans, corn, salsa; sprinkle the rice and just use a spoon to press it down gently to submerge it. 5. Place and close the lid rightly. 6. Select Pressure Cook mode. Press Pressure Cook button again to adjust the cooking time to 10 minutes; press Pressure Level to choose High Pressure. 7. When the time is up, leave the steam release handle in the Sealing position. 8. Stir everything to combine before serving.
Per Serving: Calories 307; Fat 11g; Sodium 477mg; Carbs 14g; Fiber 1g; Sugars 1.4g; Protein 25.7g

Tomato Goulash

Prep time: 10 minutes | Cook Time: 12 minutes | Serves: 6

1 tablespoon oil
1-pound ground beef
1 large onion, chopped
3 garlic cloves, minced
2½ cups water
3 cups elbow noodles, uncooked
2 (15-ounce) cans diced tomatoes
2 (15-ounce) cans tomato sauce
3 tablespoons soy sauce
2 tablespoons Italian seasoning
3 bay leaves
Salt
Freshly ground black pepper

1. Insert the pot into the Cooker Base without the lid. 2. Sauté mode and then press the same button again and then adjust the cooking temperature to Normal. 3. When the display switches On to Hot, add and heat the oil; add the beef, onion, garlic and cook for 5 to 7 minutes until the meat is browned. 4. Drain the redundant fat, stir in water and scrape up any browned bits from the bottom; without stirring, add the noodles, diced tomatoes and their juices, tomato sauce, soy sauce, Italian seasoning, bay leaves, salt and black pepper in order. 5. Press Cancel button to stop this cooking program and close the lid in right way. 6. Select Pressure Cook mode. Press Pressure Cook button again to adjust the cooking time to 5 minutes; press Pressure Level to choose High Pressure. 7. When the time is up, still quickly and carefully turn the steam release handle from the Sealing position to the Venting position. 8. When done, stir well after discarding the bay leaves. 9. Serve and done.
Per Serving: Calories 254; Fat 28 g; Sodium 346mg; Carbs 12.3 g; Sugar 1g; Fiber 0.7g; Protein 24.3 g

Shrimp Scampi with Lemon Wedges

Prep time: 10 minutes | Cook Time: 10 minutes | Serves: 6

2 tablespoons olive oil
3 tablespoons unsalted butter
3 garlic cloves, minced
¼ cup finely chopped flat-leaf parsley
½ cup dry white wine (such as Pinot Grigio, Sauvignon Blanc, or Chardonnay)
½ teaspoon red pepper flakes
½ teaspoon salt

½ teaspoon freshly ground black pepper
1 (15-ounce) can chicken broth
Juice of ½ lemon
2 pounds frozen medium shrimp (36–40 count), peeled and deveined
12 ounces angel hair pasta
Lemon wedges, for serving (optional)

1. Insert the pot into the Cooker Base without the lid. 2. Select Sauté mode and then press the same button again and then adjust the cooking temperature to Normal. 3. When the display switches On to Hot, add the garlic, parsley and cook for 1 to 2 minutes; add the red pepper flakes, wine, salt and black pepper and cook for 3 minutes; stir in the broth and lemon juice and scrape up the browned bits from the bottom; add the shrimp. 4. Divide the pasta into two pieces and layer them on the top of the shrimp, make sure they are completely submerged in the liquid without stirring them. 5. Place and close the lid rightly. 6. Select Pressure Cook mode. Press Pressure Cook button again to adjust the cooking time to 5 minutes; press Pressure Level to choose High Pressure. 7. When the time is up, quickly and carefully turn the steam release handle from the Sealing position to the Venting position. 8. Stir well and serve with the lemon wedges.
Per Serving: Calories 336; Fat 17.3g; Sodium 281mg; Carbs 8.1g; Fiber 5.3g; Sugars 17.7g; Protein 32.3g

Cheesy Chicken Broccoli Rice Casserole

Prep time: 10 minutes | Cook Time: 15 minutes | Serves: 4

2 tablespoons unsalted butter
2 pounds boneless, skinless chicken breasts, cubed
1 small onion, diced
2 garlic cloves, minced
1⅓ cups chicken broth
1 teaspoon salt
¾ teaspoon freshly ground black

pepper
1 teaspoon garlic powder
1⅓ cups long-grain rice
½ cup whole milk
2 cups shredded mild cheddar cheese
2 cups frozen broccoli florets, thawed

1. Insert the pot into the Cooker Base without the lid. 2. Select Sauté mode and then press the same button again and then adjust the cooking temperature to Normal. 3. When the display switches On to Hot, melt the butter; add chicken and onion and cook for 5 minutes or until the onion starts to turn translucent; add the garlic and cook for 1 minutes until fragrant; stir in the broth, salt, pepper and garlic powder. 4. Add the rice without stirring, just press it down to submerge it. 5. Place and close the lid rightly. 6. Select Pressure Cook mode. Press Pressure Cook button again to adjust the cooking time to 5 minutes; press Pressure Level to choose High Pressure. 7. When the time is up, leave the steam release handle in the Sealing position. 8. When released, stir in the milk, cheese and broccoli; close the lid again and Keep Warm for 2 to 3 minutes to melt the cheese and heat the broccoli. 9. Serve and enjoy.
Per Serving: Calories 272; Fat 19g; Sodium 389mg; Carbs 10.4g; Fiber 0.7g; Sugars 1.1g; Protein 15.6g

Tuna Casserole with Noodles

Prep time: 10 minutes | Cook Time: 7 minutes | Serves: 8

3 tablespoons unsalted butter
1 small onion, diced
3 cups chicken broth
½ teaspoon salt
½ teaspoon freshly ground black pepper
2 garlic cloves, minced
1 teaspoon onion powder

1 cup whole milk
2 (6-ounce) cans chunk white tuna in water, drained
1 (12-ounce) bag frozen peas
12 ounces wide egg noodles, uncooked
2 (10.5-ounce) cans condensed cream of mushroom soup

2 cups shredded mild cheddar   cheese

1. Insert the pot into the Cooker Base without the lid. 2. Select Sauté mode and then press the same button again and then adjust the cooking temperature to Normal. 3. When the display switches On to Hot, melt the butter; add the onion and cook for 4 minutes or until translucent; stir in the broth, garlic, onion powder, salt and black pepper. 4. Add the tuna, peas, noodles and milk without stirring them, then spread the mushroom soup over the noodles evenly without stirring them. 5. Place and close the lid rightly. 6. Select Pressure Cook mode. Press Pressure Cook button again to adjust the cooking time to 3 minutes; press Pressure Level to choose High Pressure. 7. When the time is up, quickly and carefully turn the steam release handle from the Sealing position to the Venting position. 8. When released, stir in the cheese. 9. Serve and enjoy.
Per Serving: Calories 351; Fat 22g; Sodium 502mg; Carbs 15.2g; Sugar 1.1g; Fiber 0.7g; Protein 26.4g

"Dirty" Rice with Herbs

Prep time: 10 minutes | Cook Time: 12-18 minutes | Serves: 4

1-pound ground beef
½ cup chopped celery
1 small onion, chopped
½ cup chopped green bell pepper
1 cup beef broth
1 tablespoon Creole seasoning

1 teaspoon dried thyme
1 teaspoon dried oregano
Salt
Freshly ground black pepper
1 cup long-grain white rice

1. Insert the pot into the Cooker Base without the lid. 2. Select Sauté mode and then press the same button again and then adjust the cooking temperature to Normal. 3. When the display switches On to Hot, add the beef and cook for 5 to 7 minutes until brown, then breaking it into small pieces as needed. 4. Add the onion, celery and bell pepper, cook with the beef pieces for 3 to 5 minutes until softened. 5. Press Cancel button to stop this cooking program. 6. Add the beef broth, thyme, oregano, Creole seasoning, salt and black pepper, stir to scrape up the brown bits from the bottom; add rice and just press it down gently to submerge it. 7. Place and close the lid rightly. 8. Select Pressure Cook mode. Press Pressure Cook button again to adjust the cooking time to 6 minutes; press Pressure Level to choose High Pressure. 9. When the time is up, leave the steam release handle in the Sealing position for 10 minutes, then turn it to the Venting position. 10. When released, use a fork to fluff the rice. 11. Serve and enjoy.
Per Serving: Calories 249; Fat 13g; Sodium 556mg; Carbs 10g; Sugar 1.1g; Fiber 0.7g; Protein 31g

Chicken Pasta with Monterey Jack Cheese

Prep time: 10 minutes | Cook Time: 14 minutes | Serves: 6

1-pound boneless, skinless chicken breasts
4 tablespoons (½ stick) unsalted butter
1 cup hot sauce
4 cups water, divided

16 ounces' penne pasta
8 ounces' cream cheese, cubed
1 cup prepared ranch or blue cheese dressing
¾ cup shredded Monterey Jack cheese

1. In the Inner Pot, mix up the butter, hot sauce, chicken and 1 cup of water. 2. Insert the pot into the Cooker Base and then close the lid rightly. 3. Select Pressure Cook mode. Press Pressure Cook button again to adjust the cooking time to 10 minutes; press Pressure Level to choose High Pressure. 4. When the time is up, quickly and carefully turn the steam release handle from the Sealing position to the Venting position. 5. When released, open the lid, reserve the liquid; take out the chicken and shred it. 6. Still in the Inner Pot, add the pasta and lay the shredded chicken on the surface; add the cream cheese, dressing and the remaining water. 7. Place and close the lid again. 8. Select Pressure Cook mode. Press Pressure Cook button again to adjust the cooking time to 4 minutes; press Pressure Level to choose High Pressure. 9. When the time is up, still quickly and carefully turn the steam release handle from the Sealing position to the Venting position. 10. When done, serve and stir in the Monterey Jack cheese. Enjoy.
Per Serving: Calories 285; Fat 9.8g; Sodium 639mg; Carbs 11.1g; Fiber 1.2g; Sugars 5.1g; Protein 27.8g

Parmesan Spaghetti Meatballs

Prep time: 10 minutes | Cook Time: 3 minutes | Serves: 8

1 (26-ounce) bag Italian-style frozen meatballs
16 ounces' spaghetti, broken in half
1 (24-ounce) jar pasta sauce
1 cup water
½ cup finely grated Parmesan cheese

1. In the Inner Pot, add the frozen meatballs and then layer the spaghetti in a crisscross pattern over them; without stirring, add the sauce and water. 2. Place and close the lid rightly. 3. Select Pressure Cook mode. Press Pressure Cook button again to adjust the cooking time to 3 minutes; press Pressure Level to choose High Pressure. 4. When the time is up, leave the steam release handle in the Sealing position. 5. When released, open the lid and stir well. 6. With the Parmesan on the top, enjoy.
Per Serving: Calories 285; Fat 9.8g; Sodium 639mg; Carbs 11.1g; Fiber 1.2g; Sugars 5.1g; Protein 27.8g

Creamy Chicken Alfredo

Prep time: 10 minutes | Cook Time: 5 minutes | Serves: 4

1½ cups chicken broth
1½ cups heavy (whipping) cream
3 garlic cloves, minced
Salt
Freshly ground black pepper
8 ounces' linguine pasta, broken in half
5 chicken tenderloins
1 cup shredded Parmesan cheese

1. In the Inner Pot, mix up the broth, cream, garlic, salt and pepper in order; layer in the pasta and arrange it in a crisscross pattern to prevent clumping, do not stir but push the noodles down with the back of a spoon to make them covered by the liquids. 2. Arrange the chicken to the pasta, season with salt and pepper. 3. Place and close the lid rightly. 4. Select Pressure Cook mode. Press Pressure Cook button again to adjust the cooking time to 5 minutes; press Pressure Level to choose High Pressure. 5. When the time is up, leave the steam release handle in the Sealing position. 6. When released, remove the chicken, then slowly add the Parmesan and use a tong to stir the pasta around. 7. Dice the chicken and toss into the sauce. 8. Serve and enjoy.
Per Serving: Calories 272; Fat 19g; Sodium 389mg; Carbs 10.4g; Fiber 0.7g; Sugars 1.1g; Protein 15.6g

Spanish Rice with Tomato Paste

Prep time: 10 minutes | Cook Time: 15 minutes | Serves: 4

1 tablespoon unsalted butter
1 small red bell pepper, seeded and chopped
1 small onion, chopped
3 garlic cloves, minced
1 cup long-grain white rice
2 tablespoons tomato paste
1 tablespoon ground cumin
1 teaspoon paprika
½ jalapeño pepper, seeded and diced
1½ cups water
Salt
Freshly ground black pepper

1. Insert the pot into the Cooker Base without the lid. 2. Select Sauté mode and then press the same button again and then adjust the cooking temperature to Normal. 3. When the display switches On to Hot, melt the butter; add the onion and bell pepper and cook for 3 minutes or until they start to soften; add the garlic and cook for 1 minutes until fragrant. 4. Press the Cancel button to stop this cooking program. 5. In the Inner Pot, mix up the rice, cumin, paprika, tomato paste, jalapeño and water. 6. Place and close the lid rightly. 7. Select Pressure Cook mode. Press Pressure Cook button again to adjust the cooking time to 5 minutes; press Pressure Level to choose High Pressure. 8. When the time is up, leave the steam release handle in the Sealing position for 10 minutes, then turn it to the Venting position. 9. When done, use a fork to fluff the rice, season with salt and pepper. 10. Serve and enjoy.
Per Serving: Calories 285; Fat 9.8g; Sodium 639mg; Carbs 11.1g; Fiber 1.2g; Sugars 5.1g; Protein 27.8g

Chickpea Mushrooms

Prep time: 15 minutes | Cook time: 40 minutes | Serves: 8

2 cups dried chickpeas, soaked overnight and drained
½ teaspoon salt
9 cups water
½ pound fresh green beans, trimmed and cut into 1» pieces
4-ounce sliced button mushrooms
½ red bell pepper, seeded, thinly sliced, and cut into 1» pieces
½ medium red onion, peeled and diced
¼ cup chopped fresh flat-leaf
parsley
2 tablespoons chopped fresh chives
2 tablespoons chopped fresh tarragon
¼ cup olive oil
2 tablespoons red wine vinegar
1 teaspoon Dijon mustard
1 teaspoon honey
½ teaspoon black pepper
¼ teaspoon salt
¼ cup grated Parmesan cheese

1. Add chickpeas, salt, and 8 cups of water to the Inner Pot. 2. Select Pressure Cook mode, and then press the "Pressure Cook" button again to select "Normal" time option. 3. Use the "+" key to set the cooking time to 40 minutes. 4. Press the Pressure Level button to adjust the pressure to "Low Pressure." 5. Once the cooking cycle is completed, allow the steam to release naturally for 10 minutes, then turn the steam release handle to the Venting position. 6. Drain chickpeas, transfer them to a large bowl and cool to room temperature. 7. Add the remaining water to the Inner Pot. Place the Steam Rack in the Inner Pot. 8. Add the green beans to the steamer basket and put the basket on the rack. 9. Select Pressure Cook mode, and then press the "Pressure Cook" button again to select "Less" time option. 10. Use the "-" key to set the cooking time to 10 minutes. 11. Press the Pressure Level button to adjust the pressure to "High Pressure." 12. Once the cooking cycle is completed, allow the steam to release naturally. 13. Rinse the green beans with cool water and add to bowl with the chickpeas. 14. Add green bean to the mushrooms along bell pepper, red onion, parsley, chives, and tarragon, mix well. 15. In a small bowl, combine olive oil, vinegar, mustard, honey, black pepper, and salt. 16. Whisk to combine, then pour over chickpea and green bean mixture, and toss to coat. 17. Top the dish with cheese and serve immediately.
Per Serving: Calories 122; Fat 7.9g; Sodium 704mg; Carbs 6g; Fiber 3.6g; Sugar 6g; Protein 18g

Chickpea Salad

Prep time: 15 minutes | Cook time: 20 minutes | Serves: 12

1 pound dried chickpeas
1½ tablespoons plus ¼ cup olive oil
4 cups water
¾ teaspoon salt
4 scallions, sliced
1 medium red onion, peeled and diced
1 small green bell pepper, seeded and diced
1 small red bell pepper, seeded
and diced
½ cup minced fresh parsley
1 large carrot, peeled and grated
2 teaspoons lemon juice
2 teaspoons white wine vinegar
1 tablespoon olive oil mayonnaise
1 clove garlic, peeled and minced
⅛ teaspoon ground white pepper
½ teaspoon dried oregano
¼ cup grated Parmesan cheese

1. Place chickpeas in the Inner Pot along with 1½ tablespoons oil, 4 cups of water, and salt. 2. Put on the pressure cooker's lid and turn the steam valve to "Sealing" position. 3. Select Pressure Cook mode, and then press the "Pressure Cook" button again to select "Less" time option. 4. Press the Pressure Level button to adjust the pressure to "Low Pressure." 5. Once the cooking cycle is completed, allow the steam to release naturally. 6. When all the steam is released, remove the pressure lid from the top carefully. 7. Add scallions, onion, bell peppers, parsley, and carrot to chickpeas and toss to combine. 8. In a small bowl, combine remaining ¼ cup of oil, lemon juice, vinegar, mayonnaise, garlic, white pepper, and oregano, and whisk to mix. 9. Pour dressing over chickpea mixture and stir to combine. Sprinkle cheese on top. 10. Close lid and allow to stand on the Keep Warm setting for 10 minutes before serving.
Per Serving: Calories 221; Fat 19g; Sodium 354mg; Carbs 15g; Fiber 5.1g; Sugar 8.2g; Protein 12g

Homemade Three-Bean Salad

Prep time: 15 minutes | Cook time: 30 minutes | Serves: 8

¼ pound dried pinto beans, soaked overnight and drained
¼ pound dried black beans, soaked overnight and drained
¼ pound dried red beans, soaked overnight and drained
8 cups water
1 tablespoon light olive oil
1 stalk celery, chopped
½ medium red onion, peeled and chopped

½ medium green bell pepper, seeded and chopped
¼ cup minced fresh cilantro
¼ cup minced fresh flat-leaf parsley
3 tablespoons olive oil
3 tablespoons red wine vinegar
1 tablespoon honey
½ teaspoon black pepper
½ teaspoon sea salt

1. Place beans, water, and light olive oil in the Inner Pot. 2. Put on the pressure cooker's lid and turn the steam valve to "Sealing" position. 3. Press the "Bean/Chili" button twice to select "Normal" option. 4. Press the Pressure Level button to adjust the pressure to "Low Pressure." 5. Once the cooking cycle is completed, allow the steam to release naturally. 6. When all the steam is released, remove the pressure lid from the top carefully and drain the beans, set aside to cool to room temperature. 7. Transfer cooled beans to a large bowl. Add celery, onion, bell pepper, cilantro, and parsley. 8. Mix well. In a small bowl, whisk together olive oil, vinegar, honey, black pepper, and salt. 9. Pour dressing over bean mixture and toss to coat. Refrigerate for 4 hours before serving.
Per Serving: Calories 219; Fat 10g; Sodium 891mg; Carbs 22.9g; Fiber 4g; Sugar 4g; Protein 13g

Cannellini Bean Salads

Prep time: 15 minutes | Cook time: 40 minutes | Serves: 6

1 cup dried cannellini beans, soaked overnight and drained
4 cups water
4 cups vegetable stock
1 tablespoon olive oil
1 teaspoon salt

2 cloves garlic, peeled and minced
½ cup diced tomato
½ teaspoon dried sage
½ teaspoon black pepper

1. Add beans and water to the Inner Pot. 2. Put on the pressure cooker's lid and turn the steam valve to "Sealing" position. 3. Press the "Bean/Chili" button twice to select "Normal" option. 4. Press the Pressure Level button to adjust the pressure to "High Pressure." 5. Once the cooking cycle is completed, quickly and carefully turn the steam release handle from Sealing position to the Venting position. 6. When all the steam is released, remove the pressure lid from the top carefully. 7. Drain and rinse beans, and return to pot along with stock. Soak for 1 hour. 8. Add olive oil, salt, garlic, tomato, sage, and pepper to beans. 9. Put on the pressure cooker's lid and turn the steam valve to "Sealing" position. 10. Select Pressure Cook mode, and then press the "Pressure Cook" button again to select "Less" time option. 11. Use the "+/-" keys on the control panel to set the cooking time to 10 minutes. 12. Press the Pressure Level button to adjust the pressure to "Low Pressure." 13. Once the cooking cycle is completed, quickly and carefully turn the steam release handle from Sealing position to the Venting position. 14. When all the steam is released, remove the pressure lid from the top carefully. 15. Serve hot.
Per Serving: Calories 289; Fat 14g; Sodium 791mg; Carbs 18.9g; Fiber 4.6g; Sugar 8g; Protein 6g

Salty Edamame

Prep time: 10 minutes | Cook time: 25 minutes | Serves: 4

1 cup shelled edamame
8 cups water
1 tablespoon vegetable oil

1 teaspoon coarse sea salt
2 tablespoons soy sauce

1. Add edamame and 4 cups of water to the Inner Pot. 2. Put on the pressure cooker's lid and turn the steam valve to "Sealing" position. 3. Select Pressure Cook mode, and then press the "Pressure Cook" button

again to select "Less" time option. 4. Use the "+/-" keys on the control panel to set the cooking time to 1 minutes. 5. Press the Pressure Level button to adjust the pressure to "High Pressure." 6. Once the cooking cycle is completed, quickly and carefully turn the steam release handle from Sealing position to the Venting position. 7. When all the steam is released, remove the pressure lid from the top carefully. 8. Add the remaining 4 cups of water and resuming cooking on Pressure Cook mode for 11 minutes at High Pressure. 9. Once the cooking cycle is completed, allow the pressure release naturally. 10. When done, drain edamame and transfer to a serving bowl. 11. Sprinkle with salt and serve with soy sauce on the side for dipping.
Per Serving: Calories 334; Fat 7.9g; Sodium 704mg; Carbs 6g; Fiber 3.6g; Sugar 6g; Protein 18g

Dill Black-Eyed Peas

Prep time: 10 minutes | Cook time: 20 minutes | Serves: 8

¼ cup olive oil
4 sprigs oregano, leaves minced and stems reserved
2 sprigs thyme, leaves stripped and stems reserved
4 sprigs dill, fronds chopped and

stems reserved
1 pound dried black-eyed peas, soaked overnight and drained
¼ teaspoon salt
1 teaspoon black pepper
4 cups water

1. In a small bowl, combine oil, oregano leaves, thyme leaves, and dill fronds, and mix to combine. 2. Cover and set aside. Tie herb stems together with butcher's twine. 3. Add to the Inner Pot along with black-eyed peas, salt, pepper, and water. 4. Put on the pressure cooker's lid and turn the steam valve to "Sealing" position. 5. Select Pressure Cook mode, and then press the "Pressure Cook" button again to select "Less" time option. 6. Press the Pressure Level button to adjust the pressure to "Low Pressure." 7. Once the cooking cycle is completed, allow the steam to release naturally. 8. When all the steam is released, remove the pressure lid from the top carefully. 9. Remove and discard herb stem bundle, and drain off any excess liquid. 10. Stir in olive oil mixture. 11. Serve hot.
Per Serving: Calories 184; Fat 5g; Sodium 441mg; Carbs 17g; Fiber 4.6g; Sugar 5g; Protein 9g

Black Bean Sliders

Prep time: 10 minutes | Cook time: 55 minutes | Serves: 8

1 tablespoon olive oil
1 slice bacon
1 small red bell pepper, seeded and diced
2 cups vegetable broth
1 cup dried black beans, soaked overnight and drained
½ teaspoon garlic powder

¼ teaspoon coriander
½ teaspoon chili powder
½ teaspoon ground cumin
½ teaspoon sea salt
¼ cup chopped fresh cilantro
1 large egg
1 cup panko bread crumbs
16 slider buns

1. Press the "Sauté" button twice to select "Normal" and then heat oil. 2. Add bacon and bell pepper. Cook until bacon is cooked through, about 5 minutes. 3. Add broth and scrape bottom of pot to release browned bits. 4. Add beans, garlic powder, coriander, chili powder, cumin, salt, and cilantro. 5. Stir well, then press the Cancel button. 6. Put on the pressure cooker's lid and turn the steam valve to "Sealing" position. 7. Press the "Pressure Cook" button one time to select "Normal" option. 8. Use the "+/-" keys on the control panel to set the cooking time to 30 minutes. 9. Press the Pressure Level button to adjust the pressure to "Low Pressure." 10. Once the cooking cycle is completed, allow the steam to release naturally. 11. When all the steam is released, remove the pressure lid from the top carefully. 12. Remove and discard bacon. 13. Without the lid, press the Sauté button, press again to change the heat to Less, and simmer bean mixture for 10 minutes to thicken. 14. Transfer mixture to a large bowl. Once cool enough to handle, quickly mix in egg and bread crumbs. 15. Form into 16 equal-sized small patties. 16. Cook on stovetop in a skillet over medium heat for approximately 2–3 minutes per side until browned. 17. Remove from heat and add each patty to a bun. 18. Serve warm.
Per Serving: Calories 314; Fat 7.9g; Sodium 704mg; Carbs 6g; Fiber 3.6g; Sugar 6g; Protein 18g

Beans with Tomato and Parsley

Prep time: 10 minutes | Cook time: 60 minutes | Serves: 4

2 tablespoons light olive oil
1 medium white onion, peeled and chopped
2 cloves garlic, peeled and minced
1 pound dried giant beans, soaked overnight and drained
2 thyme sprigs
1 bay leaf
5 cups water

1 (15-ounce) can diced tomatoes, drained
1 (8-ounce) can tomato sauce
¼ cup chopped fresh flat-leaf parsley
2 tablespoons chopped fresh oregano
1 tablespoon chopped fresh dill
½ cup crumbled feta cheese
1 small lemon, cut into 8 wedges

1. Press the "Sauté" button twice to select the cooking mode and "Normal" cooking temperature, then add and heat oil. 2. Add onion and cook until tender, about 3 minutes. 3. Add garlic and cook until fragrant, about 30 seconds. Press the Cancel button. 4. Add beans, thyme, bay leaf, and water to the Inner Pot. 5. Put on the pressure cooker's lid and turn the steam valve to "Sealing" position. 6. Press the "Pressure Cook" button one time to select "More" option. 7. Use the "+/-" keys on the control panel to set the cooking time to 50 minutes. 8. Press the Pressure Level button to adjust the pressure to "Low Pressure." 9. Once the cooking cycle is completed, quickly and carefully turn the steam release handle from Sealing position to the Venting position. 10. When all the steam is released, remove the pressure lid from the top carefully. 11. Add diced tomatoes and tomato sauce. 12. Close lid and let stand on the Keep Warm setting for 10 minutes to heat through. 13. Remove and discard bay leaf. Stir in herbs and ladle into soup bowls. 14. Garnish with feta and lemon slices, and serve hot.
Per Serving: Calories 382; Fat 10.9g; Sodium 354mg; Carbs 20.5g; Fiber 4.1g; Sugar 8.2g; Protein 06g

Garlicky Black-Eyed Pea Soup

Prep time: 10 minutes | Cook time: 30 minutes | Serves: 8

2 tablespoons light olive oil
2 stalks celery, chopped
1 medium white onion, peeled and chopped
2 cloves garlic, peeled and minced
2 tablespoons chopped fresh oregano

1 teaspoon fresh thyme leaves
1 pound dried black-eyed peas, soaked overnight and drained
¼ teaspoon salt
1 teaspoon black pepper
4 cups water
1 (15-ounce) can diced tomatoes

1. Press the "Sauté" button two time to select "Normal" and then heat oil. 2. Add celery and onion, and cook for 5 minutes or until just tender. 3. Add garlic, oregano, and thyme, and cook until fragrant, about 30 seconds. 4. Press the Cancel button. 5. Add black-eyed peas, salt, pepper, water, and tomatoes to the Inner Pot and stir well. 6. Put on the pressure cooker's lid and turn the steam valve to "Sealing" position. 7. Select Pressure Cook mode, and then press the "Pressure Cook" button again to select "Less" time option. 8. Press the Pressure Level button to adjust the pressure to "Low Pressure." 9. Once the cooking cycle is completed, allow the steam to release naturally. 10. When all the steam is released, remove the pressure lid from the top carefully. 11. Stir well. Serve hot.
Per Serving: Calories 310; Fat 7.9g; Sodium 704mg; Carbs 6g; Fiber 3.6g; Sugar 6g; Protein 18g

Black Beans with Corn and Tomato Relish

Prep time: 10 minutes | Cook time: 30 minutes | Serves: 6

½ pound dried black beans, soaked overnight and drained
1 medium white onion, peeled and sliced in half
2 cloves garlic, peeled and lightly crushed

8 cups water
1 cup corn kernels
1 large tomato, seeded and chopped
½ medium red onion, peeled and chopped

¼ cup minced fresh cilantro
½ teaspoon ground cumin
¼ teaspoon smoked paprika
¼ teaspoon black pepper

¼ teaspoon salt
3 tablespoons olive oil
3 tablespoons lime juice

1. Add beans, white onion, garlic, and water to the Inner Pot. 2. Put on the pressure cooker's lid and turn the steam valve to "Sealing" position. 3. Press the "Bean/Chili" button twice to select "Normal" option. 4. Press the Pressure Level button to adjust the pressure to "High Pressure." 5. Once the cooking cycle is completed, allow the steam to release naturally. 6. When all the steam is released, remove the pressure lid from the top carefully. 7. Discard onion and garlic. Drain beans well and transfer to a medium bowl. 8. Cool to room temperature, about 30 minutes. 9. In a separate small bowl, combine corn, tomato, red onion, cilantro, cumin, paprika, pepper, and salt. 10. Toss to combine. Add to black beans and gently fold to mix. 11. Whisk together olive oil and lime juice in a small bowl and pour over black bean mixture. Gently toss to coat. 12. Serve at room temperature or refrigerate for at least 2 hours.
Per Serving: Calories 372; Fat 20g; Sodium 891mg; Carbs 29g; Fiber 3g; Sugar 8g; Protein 7g

White Bean Soup

Prep time: 10 minutes | Cook time: 30 minutes | Serves: 8

4 cups water
1 pound dried white kidney beans, soaked overnight and drained
2 medium carrots, peeled and sliced
2 medium onions, peeled and diced
2 stalks celery, thinly sliced
1 medium parsnip, peeled and thinly sliced

1 cup tomato sauce
1 tablespoon dried rosemary
1 tablespoon dried thyme
3 bay leaves
4 tablespoons minced fresh parsley
¼ cup olive oil
4 cloves garlic, peeled
¾ teaspoon salt
½ teaspoon black pepper

1. Place water, beans, carrots, onions, celery, parsnip, tomato sauce, rosemary, thyme, bay leaves, parsley, oil, and garlic in the Inner Pot. 2. Put on the pressure cooker's lid and turn the steam valve to "Sealing" position. 3. Press the "Bean/Chili" button twice to select "Normal" option. 4. Press the Pressure Level button to adjust the pressure to "Low Pressure." 5. Once the cooking cycle is completed, allow the steam to release naturally. 6. When all the steam is released, remove the pressure lid from the top carefully. 7. Discard bay leaves, and season with salt and pepper. 8. Serve hot.
Per Serving: Calories 349; Fat 2.9g; Sodium 511mg; Carbs 12g; Fiber 3g; Sugar 8g; Protein 7g

Creamy White Bean Soup

Prep time: 10 minutes | Cook time: 27 minutes | Serves: 6

1 tablespoon olive oil
1 medium white onion, peeled and chopped
1 medium carrot, peeled and chopped
1 stalk celery, chopped
2 cloves garlic, peeled and minced

1 cup dried cannellini beans, soaked overnight and drained
4 cups vegetable broth
1 (15-ounce) can diced tomatoes
1 teaspoon minced fresh sage
½ teaspoon black pepper
½ teaspoon sea salt

1. Press the "Sauté" button two time to select "Normal" and heat oil. 2. Add onion, carrot, and celery and sauté 5 minutes. 3. Add garlic and cook 30 seconds. Stir in beans. Press the Cancel button. 4. Add broth, tomatoes, sage, pepper, and salt and stir. 5. Put on the pressure cooker's lid and turn the steam valve to "Sealing" position. 6. Select Pressure Cook mode, and then press the "Pressure Cook" button again to select "Less" time option. 7. Press the Pressure Level button to adjust the pressure to "Low Pressure." 8. Once the cooking cycle is completed, quickly and carefully turn the steam release handle from Sealing position to the Venting position. 9. When all the steam is released, remove the pressure lid from the top carefully. 10. Remove 1 cup beans and mash until smooth. Stir back into pot. 11. Serve hot.
Per Serving: Calories 372; Fat 20g; Sodium 891mg; Carbs 29g; Fiber 3g; Sugar 8g; Protein 7g

Herbed Lima Beans

Prep time: 10 minutes | Cook time: 6 minutes | Serves: 6

1 pound frozen baby lima beans, thawed	2 tablespoons olive oil
2 cloves garlic, peeled and minced	3 cups water
2 thyme sprigs	1 tablespoon chopped fresh dill
1 bay leaf	1 tablespoon chopped fresh tarragon
	1 tablespoon chopped fresh mint

1. Add lima beans, garlic, thyme, bay leaf, oil, and water to the Inner Pot. 2. Put on the pressure cooker's lid and turn the steam valve to "Sealing" position. 3. Select Pressure Cook mode, and then press the "Pressure Cook" button again to select "Less" time option. 4. Use the "+/-" keys on the control panel to set the cooking time to 6 minutes. 5. Press the Pressure Level button to adjust the pressure to "High Pressure." 6. Once the cooking cycle is completed, quickly and carefully turn the steam release handle from Sealing position to the Venting position. 7. When all the steam is released, remove the pressure lid from the top carefully. 8. Discard thyme and bay leaf, and stir well. 9. Stir in dill, tarragon, and mint, and serve.
Per Serving: Calories 219; Fat 10g; Sodium 891mg; Carbs 22.9g; Fiber 4g; Sugar 4g; Protein 13g

Greek Navy Bean Soup

Prep time: 10 minutes | Cook time: 30 minutes | Serves: 8

1 cup small dried navy beans, soaked overnight and drained	½ cup tomato purée
1 large stalk celery, halved lengthwise and sliced into ½" pieces	½ cup olive oil
	2 bay leaves
1 large carrot, peeled, halved, and sliced into ½" pieces	1 medium chili pepper, stemmed and minced
2 medium onions, peeled and chopped	2 teaspoons smoked paprika
	8 cups water
	½ teaspoon salt

1. Add beans, celery, carrot, onions, tomato purée, oil, bay leaves, chili pepper, paprika, and water to the Inner Pot. 2. Put on the pressure cooker's lid and turn the steam valve to "Sealing" position. 3. Press the "Bean/Chili" button twice to select "Normal" option. 4. Press the Pressure Level button to adjust the pressure to "High Pressure." 5. Once the cooking cycle is completed, allow the steam to release naturally. 6. When all the steam is released, remove the pressure lid from the top carefully. 7. Season with salt. Remove and discard bay leaves. 8. Serve hot.
Per Serving: Calories 282; Fat 12.9g; Sodium 414mg; Carbs 11g; Fiber 5g; Sugar 9g; Protein 11g

Three-Bean Chili

Prep time: 10 minutes | Cook time: 40 minutes | Serves: 12

1 cup dried pinto beans, soaked overnight and drained	1 (28-ounce) can diced tomatoes
1 cup dried red beans, soaked overnight and drained	1 (15-ounce) can tomato sauce
	¼ cup chili powder
1 cup dried black beans, soaked overnight and drained	2 tablespoons smoked paprika
	1 teaspoon ground cumin
2 medium white onions, peeled and chopped	1 teaspoon ground coriander
	½ teaspoon salt
2 medium red bell peppers, seeded and chopped	½ teaspoon black pepper
	3 cups vegetable broth
2 stalks celery, chopped	1 cup water

1. Place all ingredients in the Inner Pot and stir to combine. 2. Put on the pressure cooker's lid and turn the steam valve to "Sealing" position. 3. Press the "Bean/Chili" button twice to select "Normal" option. 4. Press the Pressure Level button to adjust the pressure to "Low Pressure." 5. Once the cooking cycle is completed, quickly and carefully turn the steam release handle from Sealing position to the Venting position. 6. When all the steam is released, remove the

pressure lid from the top carefully. 7. Press Cancel button to stop this cooking program. 8. Press the "Sauté" button twice to select "Less" mode and let chili simmer, uncovered, until desired thickness is reached. 9. Serve warm.
Per Serving: Calories 289; Fat 14g; Sodium 791mg; Carbs 18.9g; Fiber 4.6g; Sugar 8g; Protein 6g

White Bean Barley Soup

Prep time: 10 minutes | Cook time: 37 minutes | Serves: 8

2 tablespoons light olive oil	½ teaspoon black pepper
½ medium onion, peeled and chopped	1 (14-ounce) can fire-roasted diced tomatoes, undrained
1 medium carrot, peeled and chopped	½ cup medium pearl barley, rinsed and drained
1 stalk celery, chopped	4 cups vegetable broth
2 cloves garlic, peeled and minced	2 cups water
	2 (15-ounce) cans Great Northern beans, drained
2 sprigs fresh thyme	½ teaspoon salt
1 bay leaf	

1. Press the "Sauté" button twice to select "Normal" and heat oil. 2. Add onion, carrot, and celery. Cook until just tender, about 5 minutes. 3. Add garlic, thyme, bay leaf, and pepper, and cook until fragrant, about 30 seconds. Press the Cancel button. 4. Add the tomatoes, barley, broth, and water. 5. Put on the pressure cooker's lid and turn the steam valve to "Sealing" position. 6. Press the "Soup" button one time to select "Less" option. 7. Press the Pressure Level button to adjust the pressure to "Low Pressure." 8. Once the cooking cycle is completed, allow the steam to release naturally. 9. When all the steam is released, remove the pressure lid from the top carefully. 10. Stir soup, then add beans and salt. Close lid and let stand on the Keep Warm setting for 10 minutes. 11. Remove and discard bay leaf. 12. Serve hot.
Per Serving: Calories 382; Fat 7.9g; Sodium 704mg; Carbs 6g; Fiber 3.6g; Sugar 6g; Protein 18g

Bean and Lentil Chili

Prep time: 10 minutes | Cook time: 25 minutes | Serves: 6

2 tablespoons vegetable oil	drained
1 large Spanish onion, peeled and diced	3 tablespoons chili powder
1 small jalapeño pepper, seeded and minced	1 tablespoon sweet paprika
	1 teaspoon dried oregano
1 clove garlic, peeled and minced	1 teaspoon ground cumin
1 cup dried brown or green lentils, rinsed and drained	1 (28-ounce) can diced tomatoes
	1 chipotle pepper in adobo sauce, minced
1 (15-ounce) can black beans, drained	6 cups vegetable broth
	½ teaspoon salt
1 cup pearl barley, rinsed and	¼ teaspoon black pepper

1. Press the "Sauté" button two time to select "Normal" and heat oil. 2. Add onion and cook until just tender, about 3 minutes. Stir in jalapeño and cook for 1 minute. 3. Add garlic and cook until fragrant, about 30 seconds. 4. Stir in lentils, black beans, barley, chili powder, paprika, oregano, cumin, tomatoes, chipotle pepper, and vegetable broth. 5. Put on the pressure cooker's lid and turn the steam valve to "Sealing" position. 6. Select Pressure Cook mode, and then press the "Pressure Cook" button again to select "Less" time option. 7. Use the "+/-" keys on the control panel to set the cooking time to 10 minutes. 8. Press the Pressure Level button to adjust the pressure to "Low Pressure." 9. Once the cooking cycle is completed, quickly and carefully turn the steam release handle from Sealing position to the Venting position. 10. When all the steam is released, remove the pressure lid from the top carefully. 11. Press the Cancel button, then press the Sauté button twice to choose "Less". 12. Bring to a simmer. Season with salt and black pepper, and simmer until slightly thickened, about 10 minutes. 13. Serve immediately.
Per Serving: Calories 450; Fat 7.9g; Sodium 704mg; Carbs 6g; Fiber 3.6g; Sugar 6g; Protein 18g

Pepper Couscous Salad

Prep time: 10 minutes | Cook time: 7 minutes | Serves: 4

1 cup couscous
2 cups water
½ cup chopped Kalamata olives
1 medium red bell pepper, seeded and diced

1 clove garlic, peeled and minced
1 teaspoon olive oil
1 teaspoon red wine vinegar
½ teaspoon salt

1. Stir couscous and water together in the Inner Pot. 2. Put on the pressure cooker's lid and turn the steam valve to "Sealing" position. 3. Select Pressure Cook mode, and then press the "Pressure Cook" button again to select "Less" time option. 4. Use the "+/-" keys on the control panel to set the cooking time to 7 minutes. 5. Press the Pressure Level button to adjust the pressure to "High Pressure." 6. Once the cooking cycle is completed, allow the steam to release naturally. 7. When all the steam is released, remove the pressure lid from the top carefully for 10 minutes, then turn the steam release handle to the Venting position. 8. Fluff couscous with a fork. Stir in olives, bell pepper, garlic, oil, vinegar, and salt. 9. Cover and refrigerate for 2 hours before serving.
Per Serving: Calories 382; Fat 7.9g; Sodium 704mg; Carbs 6g; Fiber 3.6g; Sugar 6g; Protein 18g

Vegetarian Loaf

Prep time: 10 minutes | Cook time: 50 minutes | Serves: 6

1 cup dried pinto beans, soaked overnight and drained
8 cups water
1 tablespoon vegetable oil
1 teaspoon salt
1 cup diced onion
1 cup chopped walnuts
½ cup rolled oats

1 large egg, beaten
¾ cup ketchup
1 teaspoon garlic powder
1 teaspoon dried basil
1 teaspoon dried parsley
½ teaspoon salt
½ teaspoon black pepper

1. Add beans and 4 cups of water to the Inner Pot. 2. Put on the pressure cooker's lid and turn the steam valve to "Sealing" position. 3. Select Pressure Cook mode, and then press the "Pressure Cook" button again to select "Less" time option. 4. Use the "+/-" keys on the control panel to set the cooking time to 1 minutes. 5. Press the Pressure Level button to adjust the pressure to "High Pressure." 6. Once the cooking cycle is completed, quickly and carefully turn the steam release handle from Sealing position to the Venting position. 7. When all the steam is released, remove the pressure lid from the top carefully; drain and rinse the beans and then return to the pot with the remaining 4 cups of water. Soak for 1 hour. 8. Still in the pot. Add the oil and salt. 9. Put on the pressure cooker's lid and turn the steam valve to "Sealing" position. 10. Select Pressure Cook mode, and then press the "Pressure Cook" button again to select "Less" time option. 11. Use the "+/-" keys on the control panel to set the cooking time to 11 minutes. 12. Press the Pressure Level button to adjust the pressure to "High Pressure." 13. Once the cooking cycle is completed, allow the pressure release naturally. 14. In a suitable bowl, stir in onion, walnuts, oats, egg, ketchup, garlic powder, basil, parsley, salt, and pepper. 15. Spread the mixture into a loaf pan and bake for 30–35 minutes in the preheated oven at 350 degrees F. 16. Cool for 20 minutes in pan before slicing and serving.
Per Serving: Calories 221; Fat 7.9g; Sodium 704mg; Carbs 6g; Fiber 3.6g; Sugar 6g; Protein 18g

Toasted Orzo Salad

Prep time: 10 minutes | Cook time: 10 minutes | Serves: 6

2 tablespoons light olive oil
1 clove garlic, peeled and crushed
2 cups orzo
3 cups vegetable broth
½ cup sliced black olives
3 scallions, thinly sliced
1 medium Roma tomato, seeded

and diced
1 medium red bell pepper, seeded and diced
¼ cup crumbled feta cheese
1 tablespoon olive oil
1 tablespoon red wine vinegar
½ teaspoon black pepper

¼ teaspoon salt

1. Press the "Sauté" button twice to select "Normal" and heat light olive oil. 2. Add garlic and orzo and cook, stirring frequently, until orzo is light golden brown, about 5 minutes. 3. Press Cancel button to stop this cooking program, add the broth and stir. 4. Put on the pressure cooker's lid and turn the steam valve to "Sealing" position. 5. Select Pressure Cook mode, and then press the "Pressure Cook" button again to select "Less" time option. 6. Use the "+/-" keys on the control panel to set the cooking time to 3 minutes. 7. Press the Pressure Level button to adjust the pressure to "Low Pressure." 8. Once the cooking cycle is completed, quickly and carefully turn the steam release handle from Sealing position to the Venting position. 9. When all the steam is released, remove the pressure lid from the top carefully. 10. Transfer orzo to a medium bowl, then set aside to cool to room temperature, about 30 minutes. 11. Add olives, scallions, tomato, bell pepper, feta, olive oil, vinegar, black pepper, and salt, and stir until combined. 12. Serve at room temperature or refrigerate for at least 2 hours.
Per Serving: Calories 282; Fat 12.9g; Sodium 414mg; Carbs 11g; Fiber 5g; Sugar 9g; Protein 11g

Israeli Pasta Salad

Prep time: 10 minutes | Cook time: 5 minutes | Serves: 6

½ pound whole-wheat penne pasta
4 cups water
1 tablespoon plus ¼ cup olive oil
1 cup quartered cherry tomatoes
½ English cucumber, chopped
½ medium orange bell pepper, seeded and chopped

½ medium red onion, peeled and chopped
½ cup crumbled feta cheese
1 teaspoon fresh thyme leaves
1 teaspoon chopped fresh oregano
½ teaspoon black pepper
¼ cup lemon juice

1. Add pasta, water, and 1 tablespoon oil to the Inner Pot. 2. Put on the pressure cooker's lid and turn the steam valve to "Sealing" position. 3. Select Pressure Cook mode, and then press the "Pressure Cook" button again to select "Less" time option. 4. Use the "+/-" keys on the control panel to set the cooking time to 4 minutes. 5. Press the Pressure Level button to adjust the pressure to "High Pressure." 6. Once the cooking cycle is completed, quickly and carefully turn the steam release handle from Sealing position to the Venting position. 7. When all the steam is released, remove the pressure lid from the top carefully. 8. Drain and set aside to cool for 30 minutes. 9. Stir in tomatoes, cucumber, bell pepper, onion, feta, thyme, oregano, black pepper, lemon juice, and remaining ¼ cup oil. 10. Serve.
Per Serving: Calories 334; Fat 7.9g; Sodium 704mg; Carbs 6g; Fiber 3.6g; Sugar 6g; Protein 18g

Chickpea Soup

Prep time: 10 minutes | Cook time: 25 minutes | Serves: 8

1 pound dried chickpeas
4 cups water
¾ teaspoon salt
½ teaspoon black pepper
10 strands saffron
2 medium onions, peeled and

diced
1 cup olive oil
1 teaspoon dried oregano
3 tablespoons lemon juice
2 tablespoons chopped fresh parsley

1. Add chickpeas, water, salt, pepper, saffron, onions, oil, and oregano to the Inner Pot and stir well. 2. Put on the pressure cooker's lid and turn the steam valve to "Sealing" position. 3. Press the "Bean/Chili" button one time to select "Less" option. 4. Press the Pressure Level button to adjust the pressure to "Low Pressure." 5. Once the cooking cycle is completed, allow the steam to release naturally. 6. When all the steam is released, remove the pressure lid from the top carefully. 7. Serve hot or cold, sprinkled with lemon juice. 8. Garnish with chopped parsley.
Per Serving: Calories 289; Fat 14g; Sodium 791mg; Carbs 18.9g; Fiber 4.6g; Sugar 8g; Protein 6g

White Bean Cassoulet

Prep time: 10 minutes | Cook time: 45 minutes | Serves: 8

1 tablespoon olive oil	chopped
1 medium onion, peeled and diced	½ teaspoon fennel seed
2 cups dried cannellini beans, soaked overnight and drained	¼ teaspoon ground nutmeg
	½ teaspoon garlic powder
1 medium parsnip, peeled and diced	1 teaspoon sea salt
	½ teaspoon black pepper
2 medium carrots, peeled and diced	2 cups vegetable broth
	1 (15-ounce) can diced tomatoes, including juice
2 stalks celery, diced	
1 medium zucchini, trimmed and	2 sprigs rosemary

1. Press the "Sauté" button two time to select "Normal" mode on the Inner Pot and heat oil. 2. Add onion and cook until translucent, about 5 minutes. Add beans and toss. 3. Add a layer of parsnip, then a layer of carrots, and next a layer of celery. 4. Finally, add a layer of zucchini. Sprinkle in fennel seed, nutmeg, garlic powder, salt, and pepper. 5. Press Cancel button to stop this cooking program. 6. Gently pour in broth and canned tomatoes. Top with rosemary. 7. Put on the pressure cooker's lid and turn the steam valve to "Sealing" position. 8. Press the "Pressure Cook" button one time to select "Normal" option. 9. Use the "+/-" keys on the control panel to set the cooking time to 30 minutes. 10. Press the Pressure Level button to adjust the pressure to "Low Pressure." 11. Once the cooking cycle is completed, allow the steam to release naturally for 10 minutes, then turn the steam release handle to the Venting position. 12. When all the steam is released, press Cancel button to stop this cooking program and remove the pressure lid from the top carefully. 13. Press the Sauté button twice to select the cooking mode and "Less" cooking temperature, and simmer bean mixture uncovered for 10 minutes to thicken. 14. Transfer to a serving bowl and carefully toss. 15. Remove and discard rosemary and serve.
Per Serving: Calories 220; Fat 10.9g; Sodium 354mg; Carbs 20.5g; Fiber 4.1g; Sugar 8.2g; Protein 06g

White Bean Soup with Kale

Prep time: 10 minutes | Cook time: 27 minutes | Serves: 8

1 tablespoon light olive oil	4 cups chopped kale
2 stalks celery, chopped	1 pound dried Great Northern beans, soaked overnight and drained
1 medium yellow onion, peeled and chopped	
2 cloves garlic, peeled and minced	8 cups vegetable broth
	¼ cup lemon juice
1 tablespoon chopped fresh oregano	1 tablespoon olive oil
	1 teaspoon black pepper

1. Press the "Sauté" button two time to select "Normal" mode and heat light olive oil. 2. Add celery and onion and cook 5 minutes. Add garlic and oregano and sauté 30 seconds. 3. Add kale and turn to coat, then cook until just starting to wilt, about 1 minute. 4. Press the Cancel button. 5. Add beans, broth, lemon juice, olive oil, and pepper to the Inner Pot and stir well. 6. Put on the pressure cooker's lid and turn the steam valve to "Sealing" position. 7. Select Pressure Cook mode, and then press the "Pressure Cook" button again to select "Less" time option. 8. Press the Pressure Level button to adjust the pressure to "Low Pressure." 9. Once the cooking cycle is completed, allow the steam to release naturally. 10. When all the steam is released, remove the pressure lid from the top carefully. 11. Serve hot.
Per Serving: Calories 450; Fat 7.9g; Sodium 704mg; Carbs 6g; Fiber 3.6g; Sugar 6g; Protein 18g

Beefsteak Tomatoes with Cheese

Prep time: 10 minutes | Cook time: 30 minutes | Serves: 4

½ cup orzo	minced
4 large beefsteak tomatoes	2 tablespoons minced fresh basil
1 cup shredded mozzarella cheese	2 tablespoons minced fresh parsley
2 cloves garlic, peeled and	

½ teaspoon salt
¼ teaspoon black pepper

2 tablespoons olive oil

1. Place orzo in the Inner Pot and add water just to cover. 2. Put on the pressure cooker's lid and turn the steam valve to "Sealing" position. 3. Select Pressure Cook mode, and then press the "Pressure Cook" button again to select "Less" time option. 4. Use the "+/-" keys on the control panel to set the cooking time to 3 minutes. 5. Press the Pressure Level button to adjust the pressure to "Low Pressure." 6. Once the cooking cycle is completed, quickly and carefully turn the steam release handle from Sealing position to the Venting position. 7. When all the steam is released, remove the pressure lid from the top carefully. 8. Drain orzo and set aside. Cut tops off tomatoes and scoop out seeds and pulp. 9. Place pulp in a medium bowl. Add orzo, cheese, garlic, basil, parsley, salt, and pepper. 10. Stuff tomatoes with orzo mixture and place on a baking sheet. 11. Drizzle oil over tomatoes and bake for 15–20 minutes at 350 degrees F in your preheated oven. 12. Serve hot.
Per Serving: Calories 289; Fat 14g; Sodium 791mg; Carbs 18.9g; Fiber 4.6g; Sugar 8g; Protein 6g

Pasta with Marinated Artichokes

Prep time: 10 minutes | Cook time: 10 minutes | Serves: 6

1-pound whole-wheat spaghetti, broken in half	hearts
	2 tablespoons chopped fresh oregano
3½ cups water	
4 tablespoons olive oil	2 tablespoons chopped fresh flat-leaf parsley
¼ teaspoon salt	
2 cups baby spinach	1 teaspoon black pepper
1 cup drained marinated artichoke	½ cup grated Parmesan cheese

1. Add pasta, water, 2 tablespoons oil, and salt to the Inner Pot. 2. Put on the pressure cooker's lid and turn the steam valve to "Sealing" position. 3. Select Pressure Cook mode, and then press the "Pressure Cook" button again to select "Less" time option. 4. Use the "+/-" keys on the control panel to set the cooking time to 5 minutes. 5. Press the Pressure Level button to adjust the pressure to "High Pressure." 6. Once the cooking cycle is completed, allow the steam to release naturally. 7. When all the steam is released, press Cancel button and remove the pressure lid from the top carefully. 8. Press the "Sauté" Button, two times to select "Normal" settings. 9. Stir in remaining 2 tablespoons oil and spinach. Toss until spinach is wilted. 10. Stir in artichokes, oregano, and parsley until well mixed. 11. Sprinkle with pepper and cheese, and serve immediately.
Per Serving: Calories 302; Fat 19g; Sodium 354mg; Carbs 15g; Fiber 5.1g; Sugar 8.2g; Protein 12g

Couscous with Tomatoes

Prep time: 10 minutes | Cook time: 3 minutes | Serves: 4

1 tablespoon tomato paste	2 tablespoons minced fresh oregano
2 cups vegetable broth	
1 cup couscous	2 tablespoons minced fresh chives
1 cup halved cherry tomatoes	1 tablespoon olive oil
½ cup halved mixed olives	1 tablespoon red wine vinegar
¼ cup minced fresh flat-leaf parsley	½ teaspoon black pepper

1. Pour tomato paste and broth into the Inner Pot and stir until completely dissolved. Stir in couscous. 2. Put on the pressure cooker's lid and turn the steam valve to "Sealing" position. 3. Select Pressure Cook mode, and then press the "Pressure Cook" button again to select "Less" time option. 4. Use the "+/-" keys on the control panel to set the cooking time to 3 minutes. 5. Press the Pressure Level button to adjust the pressure to "High Pressure." 6. Once the cooking cycle is completed, allow the steam to release naturally for 10 minutes, then turn the steam release handle to the Venting position. 7. When all the steam is released, remove the pressure lid from the top carefully. 8. Fluff couscous with a fork. 9. Add tomatoes, olives, parsley, oregano, chives, oil, vinegar, and pepper, and stir until combined. 10. Serve warm or at room temperature.
Per Serving: Calories 334; Fat 7.9g; Sodium 704mg; Carbs 6g; Fiber 3.6g; Sugar 6g; Protein 18g

Chili-Spiced Beans

Prep time: 10 minutes | Cook time: 40 minutes | Serves: 8

1 pound dried pinto beans, soaked overnight and drained	2 tablespoons smoked paprika
1 medium onion, peeled and chopped	1 teaspoon ground cumin
¼ cup chopped fresh cilantro	1 teaspoon ground coriander
1 (15-ounce) can tomato sauce	½ teaspoon black pepper
¼ cup chili powder	2 cups vegetable broth
	1 cup water

1. Place all ingredients in the Inner Pot and stir to combine. 2. Put on the pressure cooker's lid and turn the steam valve to "Sealing" position. 3. Press the "Bean/Chili" button one time to select "Normal" option. 4. Press the Pressure Level button to adjust the pressure to "Low Pressure." 5. Once the cooking cycle is completed, quickly and carefully turn the steam release handle from Sealing position to the Venting position. 6. When all the steam is released, remove the pressure lid from the top carefully. 7. Press Cancel button to stop this cooking program. 8. Press the "Sauté" button two time to select "Less" mode and let beans simmer, uncovered, until desired thickness is reached. 9. Serve warm.
Per Serving: Calories 334; Fat 7.9g; Sodium 704mg; Carbs 6g; Fiber 3.6g; Sugar 6g; Protein 18g

Toasted Couscous with Feta

Prep time: 10 minutes | Cook time: 10 minutes | Serves: 8

1 tablespoon plus ¼ cup light olive oil	1 medium red onion, peeled and chopped
2 cups Israeli couscous	½ cup crumbled feta cheese
3 cups vegetable broth	¼ cup red wine vinegar
2 large tomatoes, seeded and diced	½ teaspoon black pepper
1 large English cucumber, diced	¼ cup chopped flat-leaf parsley
	¼ cup chopped fresh basil

1. Press the "Sauté" Button two times to select "normal" settings and heat 1 tablespoon oil. 2. Add couscous and cook, stirring frequently, until couscous is light golden brown, about 7 minutes. 3. Press the Cancel button. Add broth and stir. 4. Put on the pressure cooker's lid and turn the steam valve to "Sealing" position. 5. Select Pressure Cook mode, and then press the "Pressure Cook" button again to select "Less" time option. 6. Use the "+/-" keys on the control panel to set the cooking time to 2 minutes. 7. Press the Pressure Level button to adjust the pressure to "Low Pressure." 8. Once the cooking cycle is completed, allow the steam to release naturally. 9. When all the steam is released, remove the pressure lid from the top carefully. 10. Fluff couscous with a fork, then transfer to a medium bowl and set aside to cool. 11. Add remaining ¼ cup oil, tomatoes, cucumber, onion, feta, vinegar, pepper, parsley, and basil, and stir until combined. 12. Serve.
Per Serving: Calories 302; Fat 12.9g; Sodium 414mg; Carbs 11g; Fiber 5g; Sugar 9g; Protein 11g

Pasta Primavera

Prep time: 10 minutes | Cook time: 20 minutes | Serves: 8

1-pound bowtie pasta	2 cloves garlic, peeled and chopped
4 cups water	1 cup white wine
2 tablespoons olive oil	2 tablespoons cold unsalted butter
1½ cups chopped summer squash	½ teaspoon salt
1½ cups chopped zucchini	¾ teaspoon black pepper
3 cups chopped broccoli	¼ cup chopped fresh basil
½ cup sun-dried tomatoes	

1. Place pasta, water, and 1 tablespoon oil in the Inner Pot. 2. Put on the pressure cooker's lid and turn the steam valve to "Sealing" position. 3. Select Pressure Cook mode, and then press the "Pressure Cook" button again to select "Less" time option. 4. Use the "+/-" keys on the control panel to set the cooking time to 4 minutes. 5. Press the Pressure Level button to adjust the pressure to "Low Pressure." 6. Once the cooking cycle is completed, quickly and carefully turn the steam release handle from Sealing position to the Venting position. 7. When all the steam is released, press Cancel button and remove the pressure lid from the top carefully. 8. Press the "Sauté" Button, two times to select "Normal" settings. 9. Heat remaining 1 tablespoon oil. 10. Add squash, zucchini, broccoli, and sun-dried tomatoes, and cook until very tender, about 10 minutes. 11. Add garlic and wine. Allow wine to reduce for about 2–3 minutes. 12. Add butter to pot, stirring constantly to create an emulsion. Season with salt and pepper. 13. Pour sauce and vegetables over pasta, and stir to coat. 14. Top with basil and enjoy.
Per Serving: Calories 361; Fat 7.9g; Sodium 704mg; Carbs 6g; Fiber 3.6g; Sugar 6g; Protein 18g

Tomato, Arugula and Feta Pasta Salad

Prep time: 10 minutes | Cook time: 5 minutes | Serves: 8

1-pound rotini	and diced
4 cups water	2 tablespoons white wine vinegar
3 tablespoons olive oil	5-ounce baby arugula
2 medium Roma tomatoes, diced	1 cup crumbled feta cheese
2 cloves garlic, peeled and minced	½ teaspoon salt
1 medium red bell pepper, seeded	½ teaspoon black pepper

1. Add pasta, water, and 1 tablespoon oil to the Inner Pot. 2. Put on the pressure cooker's lid and turn the steam valve to "Sealing" position. 3. Select Pressure Cook mode, and then press the "Pressure Cook" button again to select "Less" time option. 4. Use the "+/-" keys on the control panel to set the cooking time to 4 minutes. 5. Press the Pressure Level button to adjust the pressure to "High Pressure." 6. Once the cooking cycle is completed, quickly and carefully turn the steam release handle from Sealing position to the Venting position. 7. When all the steam is released, remove the pressure lid from the top carefully. 8. Drain pasta, then rinse with cold water. Set aside. 9. In a large bowl, mix the remaining oil, tomatoes, garlic, bell pepper, vinegar, arugula, and cheese. 10. Stir in pasta and season with salt and pepper. 11. Cover and refrigerate for 2 hours before serving.
Per Serving: Calories 289; Fat 14g; Sodium 791mg; Carbs 18.9g; Fiber 4.6g; Sugar 8g; Protein 6g

Dill Pasta Salad

Prep time: 10 minutes | Cook time: 5 minutes | Serves: 8

½ cup low-fat plain Greek yogurt	1 tablespoon olive oil
1 tablespoon apple cider vinegar	1 medium red bell pepper, seeded and chopped
2 tablespoons chopped fresh dill	1 medium sweet onion, peeled and diced
1 teaspoon honey	
1-pound whole-wheat elbow macaroni	1 stalk celery, diced
4 cups water	½ teaspoon black pepper

1. In a small bowl, combine yogurt and vinegar. 2. Add dill and honey, and mix well. Refrigerate until ready to use. 3. Place pasta, water, and olive oil to the Inner Pot. 4. Put on the pressure cooker's lid and turn the steam valve to "Sealing" position. 5. Select Pressure Cook mode, and then press the "Pressure Cook" button again to select "Less" time option. 6. Use the "+/-" keys on the control panel to set the cooking time to 4 minutes. 7. Press the Pressure Level button to adjust the pressure to "Low Pressure." 8. Once the cooking cycle is completed, quickly and carefully turn the steam release handle from Sealing position to the Venting position. 9. When all the steam is released, remove the pressure lid from the top carefully. 10. Drain off any excess liquid. Cool pasta to room temperature, about 30 minutes. 11. Add prepared dressing and toss until pasta is well coated. 12. Add bell pepper, onion, celery, and black pepper, and toss to coat. 13. Refrigerate for 2 hours. Stir well before serving.
Per Serving: Calories 382; Fat 7.9g; Sodium 704mg; Carbs 6g; Fiber 3.6g; Sugar 6g; Protein 18g

Lima Bean Soup

Prep time: 10 minutes | Cook time: 17 minutes | Serves: 6

1 tablespoon olive oil	2 cups dried lima beans, soaked
1 small onion, peeled and diced	overnight and drained
1 clove garlic, peeled and minced	½ teaspoon salt
2 cups vegetable stock	½ teaspoon black pepper
½ cup water	2 tablespoons thinly sliced chives

1. Press the "Sauté" button two time to select "Normal" mode on the Inner Pot and heat oil. 2. Add onion and cook until golden brown, about 10 minutes. 3. Add garlic and cook until fragrant, about 30 seconds. 4. Press the Cancel button. 5. Add stock, water, and lima beans. 6. Put on the pressure cooker's lid and turn the steam valve to "Sealing" position. 7. Select Pressure Cook mode, and then press the "Pressure Cook" button again to select "Less" time option. 8. Use the "+/-" keys on the control panel to set the cooking time to 6 minutes. 9. Press the Pressure Level button to adjust the pressure to "High Pressure." 10. Once the cooking cycle is completed, allow the steam to release naturally. 11. When all the steam is released, remove the pressure lid from the top carefully. 12. Purée soup with an immersion blender or in batches in a blender. 13. Season with salt and pepper, then sprinkle with chives before serving.
Per Serving: Calories 212; Fat 10.9g; Sodium 454mg; Carbs 10g; Fiber 3.1g; Sugar 5.2g; Protein 10g

Tahini Soup

Prep time: 10 minutes | Cook time: 5 minutes | Serves: 6

2 cups orzo	½ teaspoon black pepper
8 cups water	½ cup tahini
1 tablespoon olive oil	¼ cup lemon juice
1 teaspoon salt	

1. Add pasta, water, oil, salt, and pepper to the Inner Pot. 2. Put on the pressure cooker's lid and turn the steam valve to "Sealing" position. 3. Select Pressure Cook mode, and then press the "Pressure Cook" button again to select "Less" time option. 4. Use the "+/-" keys on the control panel to set the cooking time to 4 minutes. 5. Press the Pressure Level button to adjust the pressure to "High Pressure." 6. Once the cooking cycle is completed, quickly and carefully turn the steam release handle from Sealing position to the Venting position. 7. When all the steam is released, remove the pressure lid from the top carefully. 8. Add tahini to a small mixing bowl and slowly add lemon juice while whisking constantly. 9. Once lemon juice has been incorporated, take about ½ cup hot broth from the pot and slowly add to tahini mixture while whisking, until creamy smooth. 10. Pour mixture into the soup and mix well. 11. Serve immediately.
Per Serving: Calories 320; Fat 19g; Sodium 354mg; Carbs 15g; Fiber 5.1g; Sugar 8.2g; Protein 12g

Couscous with Crab

Prep time: 10 minutes | Cook time: 7 minutes | Serves: 4

1 cup couscous	1 tablespoon minced fresh dill
1 clove garlic, peeled and minced	8 oz. jumbo lump crabmeat
2 cups water	3 tablespoons lemon juice
3 tablespoons olive oil	½ teaspoon black pepper
¼ cup minced fresh flat-leaf parsley	¼ cup grated Parmesan cheese

1. Place couscous, garlic, water, and 1 tablespoon oil in the Inner Pot and stir well. 2. Put on the pressure cooker's lid and turn the steam valve to "Sealing" position. 3. Select Pressure Cook mode, and then press the "Pressure Cook" button again to select "Less" time option. 4. Use the "+/-" keys on the control panel to set the cooking time to 7 minutes. 5. Press the Pressure Level button to adjust the pressure to "Low Pressure." 6. Once the cooking cycle is completed, allow the steam to release naturally for 10 minutes, then turn the steam release handle to the Venting position. 7. When all the steam is released, remove the pressure lid from the top carefully. 8. Fluff couscous with a fork. 9. Add parsley, dill, crabmeat, lemon juice, pepper, and remaining 2 tablespoons oil, and stir until combined. 10. Top with cheese and serve immediately.
Per Serving: Calories 184; Fat 5g; Sodium 441mg; Carbs 17g; Fiber 4.6g; Sugar 5g; Protein 9g

Pasta with Chickpeas and Cabbage

Prep time: 10 minutes | Cook time: 30 minutes | Serves: 8

1-pound rotini pasta	⅔ cup dried chickpeas, soaked
8 cups water	overnight and drained
2 tablespoons olive oil	8 oz. button mushrooms, sliced
1 stalk celery, thinly sliced	½ teaspoon salt
1 medium red onion, peeled and	¾ teaspoon black pepper
sliced	½ cup grated Pecorino Romano
1 small head savoy cabbage,	cheese
cored and shredded	

1. Add pasta, 4 cups water, and 1 tablespoon oil to the Inner Pot. 2. Put on the pressure cooker's lid and turn the steam valve to "Sealing" position. 3. Select Pressure Cook mode, and then press the "Pressure Cook" button again to select "Less" time option. 4. Use the "+/-" keys on the control panel to set the cooking time to 4 minutes. 5. Press the Pressure Level button to adjust the pressure to "Low Pressure." 6. Once the cooking cycle is completed, quickly and carefully turn the steam release handle from Sealing position to the Venting position. 7. When all the steam is released, press the Cancel button and remove the pressure lid from the top carefully. 8. Press the "Sauté" Button, two times to select "normal" settings and heat remaining 1 tablespoon oil. 9. Add celery and onion, and cook until just tender, about 4 minutes. 10. Stir in cabbage and cook until wilted, about 2 minutes. 11. Add chickpeas, mushrooms, and remaining 4 cups water. Stir well, then press the Cancel button. 12. Put on the pressure cooker's lid and turn the steam valve to "Sealing" position. 13. Select Pressure Cook mode, and then press the "Pressure Cook" button again to select "Less" time option. 14. Press the Pressure Level button to adjust the pressure to "Low Pressure." 15. Once the cooking cycle is completed, allow the steam to release naturally. 16. When all the steam is released, remove the pressure lid from the top carefully. 17. Season with salt and pepper. Use a fork to mash some of the chickpeas to thicken sauce. 18. Pour sauce over pasta and top with cheese. 19. Serve hot.
Per Serving: Calories 184; Fat 5g; Sodium 441mg; Carbs 17g; Fiber 4.6g; Sugar 5g; Protein 9g

Rotini with Red Wine Marinara

Prep time: 10 minutes | Cook time: 25 minutes | Serves: 6

1-pound rotini	1 (15-ounce) can crushed
4 cups water	tomatoes
1 tablespoon olive oil	½ cup red wine
½ medium yellow onion, peeled	1 teaspoon sugar
and diced	2 tablespoons chopped fresh basil
3 cloves garlic, peeled and	½ teaspoon salt
minced	¼ teaspoon black pepper

1. Add pasta and water to the Inner Pot. 2. Put on the pressure cooker's lid and turn the steam valve to "Sealing" position. 3. Select Pressure Cook mode, and then press the "Pressure Cook" button again to select "Less" time option. 4. Use the "+/-" keys on the control panel to set the cooking time to 4 minutes. 5. Press the Pressure Level button to adjust the pressure to "Low Pressure." 6. Once the cooking cycle is completed, quickly and carefully turn the steam release handle from Sealing position to the Venting position. 7. When all the steam is released, press the Cancel button and remove the pressure lid from the top carefully. 8. Press the "Sauté" Button two times to select "Normal" settings and heat oil. 9. Add onion and cook until it begins to caramelize, about 10 minutes. Add garlic and cook 30 seconds. 10. Add tomatoes, red wine, and sugar, and simmer for 10 minutes. 11. Add basil, salt, pepper, and pasta. 12. Serve immediately.
Per Serving: Calories 212; Fat 7.9g; Sodium 704mg; Carbs 6g; Fiber 3.6g; Sugar 6g; Protein 18g

Couscous with Olives

Prep time: 10 minutes | Cook time: 7 minutes | Serves: 4

1 tablespoon tomato paste	¼ cup minced fresh flat-leaf
2 cups vegetable broth	parsley
1 cup couscous	2 tablespoons minced fresh
1 cup sliced cherry tomatoes	oregano
½ large English cucumber,	2 tablespoons minced fresh chives
chopped	1 tablespoon olive oil
½ cup pitted and chopped mixed	1 tablespoon red wine vinegar
olives	½ teaspoon black pepper

1. Stir together tomato paste and broth until completely dissolved. 2. Add to the Inner Pot with couscous and stir well. 3. Put on the pressure cooker's lid and turn the steam valve to "Sealing" position. 4. Select Pressure Cook mode, and then press the "Pressure Cook" button again to select "Less" time option. 5. Use the "+/-" keys on the control panel to set the cooking time to 7 minutes. 6. Press the Pressure Level button to adjust the pressure to "High Pressure." 7. Once the cooking cycle is completed, allow the steam to release naturally for 10 minutes, then turn the steam release handle to the Venting position. 8. When all the steam is released, remove the pressure lid from the top carefully. 9. Fluff couscous with a fork. Add all remaining ingredients and stir until combined. 10. Serve warm or at room temperature.
Per Serving: Calories 372; Fat 20g; Sodium 891mg; Carbs 29g; Fiber 3g; Sugar 8g; Protein 7g

Bowtie Pesto Pasta Salad

Prep time: 10 minutes | Cook time: 5 minutes | Serves: 8

1-pound whole-wheat bowtie	2 cups baby spinach
pasta	½ cup chopped fresh basil
4 cups water	½ cup prepared pesto
1 tablespoon olive oil	½ teaspoon black pepper
2 cups halved cherry tomatoes	½ cup grated Parmesan cheese

1. Add pasta, water, and olive oil to the Inner Pot. 2. Put on the pressure cooker's lid and turn the steam valve to "Sealing" position. 3. Select Pressure Cook mode, and then press the "Pressure Cook" button again to select "Less" time option. 4. Use the "+/-" keys on the control panel to set the cooking time to 4 minutes. 5. Press the Pressure Level button to adjust the pressure to "Low Pressure." 6. Once the cooking cycle is completed, quickly and carefully turn the steam release handle from Sealing position to the Venting position. 7. When all the steam is released, remove the pressure lid from the top carefully. 8. Drain off any excess liquid. Allow pasta to cool to room temperature, about 30 minutes. 9. Stir in tomatoes, spinach, basil, pesto, pepper, and cheese. 10. Refrigerate for 2 hours. Stir well before serving.
Per Serving: Calories 221; Fat 7.9g; Sodium 704mg; Carbs 6g; Fiber 3.6g; Sugar 6g; Protein 18g

Rotini with Walnut Pesto

Prep time: 10 minutes | Cook time: 4 minutes | Serves: 8

1 cup packed fresh basil leaves	¼ teaspoon salt
⅓ cup chopped walnuts	1-pound whole-wheat rotini pasta
¼ cup grated Parmesan cheese	4 cups water
¼ cup plus 1 tablespoon olive oil	1-pint cherry tomatoes
1 clove garlic, peeled	1 cup fresh or frozen green peas
1 tablespoon lemon juice	½ teaspoon black pepper

1. In a food processor, add basil and walnuts. 2. Pulse until finely chopped, about 12 pulses. 3. Add cheese, ¼ cup oil, garlic, lemon juice, and salt, and pulse until a rough paste forms, about 10 pulses. 4. Refrigerate until ready to use. 5. Add pasta, water, and remaining 1 tablespoon oil to the Inner Pot. 6. Put on the pressure cooker's lid and turn the steam valve to "Sealing" position. 7. Select Pressure Cook mode, and then press the "Pressure Cook" button again to select "Less" time option. 8. Use the "+/-" keys on the control panel to set the cooking time to 4 minutes. 9. Press the Pressure Level button to adjust the pressure to "High Pressure." 10. Once the cooking cycle is completed, quickly and carefully turn the steam release handle from Sealing position to the Venting position. 11. When all the steam is released, remove the pressure lid from the top carefully. 12. Drain off any excess liquid. Allow pasta to cool to room temperature, about 30 minutes. 13. Stir in basil mixture until pasta is well coated. Add tomatoes, peas, and pepper and toss to coat. 14. Refrigerate for 2 hours. Stir well before serving.
Per Serving: Calories 237; Fat 7.9g; Sodium 704mg; Carbs 6g; Fiber 3.6g; Sugar 6g; Protein 18g

Mixed Vegetable Couscous

Prep time: 10 minutes | Cook time: 10 minutes | Serves: 8

1 tablespoon light olive oil	2 tablespoons chopped fresh
1 medium zucchini, trimmed and	oregano
chopped	2 cups Israeli couscous
1 medium yellow squash,	3 cups vegetable broth
chopped	½ cup crumbled feta cheese
1 large red bell pepper, seeded	¼ cup red wine vinegar
and chopped	¼ cup olive oil
1 large orange bell pepper, seeded	½ teaspoon black pepper
and chopped	¼ cup chopped fresh basil

1. Press the "Sauté" Button two times to select "Normal" settings and heat light olive oil. 2. Add zucchini, squash, bell peppers, and oregano, and sauté 8 minutes. 3. Press the Cancel button. Transfer to a serving bowl and set aside to cool. 4. Add couscous and broth to the Inner Pot and stir well. 5. Put on the pressure cooker's lid and turn the steam valve to "Sealing" position. 6. Select Pressure Cook mode, and then press the "Pressure Cook" button again to select "Less" time option. 7. Use the "+/-" keys on the control panel to set the cooking time to 2 minutes. 8. Press the Pressure Level button to adjust the pressure to "High Pressure." 9. Once the cooking cycle is completed, allow the steam to release naturally. 10. When all the steam is released, remove the pressure lid from the top carefully. 11. Fluff with a fork and stir in cooked vegetables, cheese, vinegar, olive oil, black pepper, and basil. 12. Serve warm.
Per Serving: Calories 226; Fat 10.9g; Sodium 354mg; Carbs 20.5g; Fiber 4.1g; Sugar 8.2g; Protein 06g

Angel Hair Pasta with Spinach and White Wine

Prep time: 10 minutes | Cook time: 15 minutes | Serves: 6

1-pound angel hair pasta	½ cup white wine
4¼ cups water	1 tablespoon unsalted butter
2 tablespoons olive oil	1 tablespoon all-purpose flour
¼ medium yellow onion, peeled	½ teaspoon salt
and diced	¼ teaspoon black pepper
2 cloves garlic, peeled and	1 cup steamed spinach
minced	

1. Place pasta, 4 cups water, and 1 tablespoon oil in the Inner Pot. 2. Put on the pressure cooker's lid and turn the steam valve to "Sealing" position. 3. Select Pressure Cook mode, and then press the "Pressure Cook" button again to select "Less" time option. 4. Use the "+/-" keys on the control panel to set the cooking time to 4 minutes. 5. Press the Pressure Level button to adjust the pressure to "High Pressure." 6. Once the cooking cycle is completed, quickly and carefully turn the steam release handle from Sealing position to the Venting position. 7. When all the steam is released, press Cancel button and remove the pressure lid from the top carefully. 8. Press the "Sauté" Button two times to select "Normal" settings and heat remaining 1 tablespoon oil. 9. Add onion and garlic. Cook until onion is soft, about 5 minutes. 10. Add white wine and remaining ¼ cup water, then bring to a low simmer for about 10 minutes. 11. Add butter and flour, stirring until completely combined and sauce begins to thicken. 12. Season with salt and pepper. 13. In a large mixing bowl, combine spinach, pasta, and white wine sauce, then toss until the pasta is completely coated. 14. Serve immediately.
Per Serving: Calories 219; Fat 10g; Sodium 891mg; Carbs 22.9g; Fiber 4g; Sugar 4g; Protein 13g

Marinara Spaghetti with Mozzarella Cheese

Prep time: 10 minutes | Cook time: 5 minutes | Serves: 8

1-pound spaghetti	4 cups marinara sauce
4 cups water	1 cup shredded mozzarella cheese
1 tablespoon olive oil	2 tablespoons chopped fresh basil
4 cups cooked pinto beans	

1. Add pasta, water, and olive oil to the Inner Pot. 2. Put on the pressure cooker's lid and turn the steam valve to "Sealing" position. 3. Select Pressure Cook mode, and then press the "Pressure Cook" button again to select "Less" time option. 4. Use the "+/-" keys on the control panel to set the cooking time to 4 minutes. 5. Press the Pressure Level button to adjust the pressure to "High Pressure." 6. Once the cooking cycle is completed, quickly and carefully turn the steam release handle from Sealing position to the Venting position. 7. When all the steam is released, remove the pressure lid from the top carefully. 8. Add beans and marinara sauce, and stir well. 9. Top with cheese and basil and serve hot.
Per Serving: Calories 334; Fat 7.9g; Sodium 704mg; Carbs 6g; Fiber 3.6g; Sugar 6g; Protein 18g

Spaghetti with Meat Sauce

Prep time: 10 minutes | Cook time: 20 minutes | Serves: 6

1-pound spaghetti	¼ cup white wine
4 cups water	½ cup tomato sauce
3 tablespoons olive oil	1 (3") cinnamon stick
1 medium white onion, peeled and diced	2 bay leaves
½ pound lean ground veal	1 clove garlic, peeled
½ teaspoon salt	¼ cup grated aged mizithra or Parmesan cheese
¼ teaspoon black pepper	

1. Add pasta, water, and 1 tablespoon oil to the Inner Pot. 2. Put on the pressure cooker's lid and turn the steam valve to "Sealing" position. 3. Select Pressure Cook mode, and then press the "Pressure Cook" button again to select "Less" time option. 4. Use the "+/-" keys on the control panel to set the cooking time to 4 minutes. 5. Press the Pressure Level button to adjust the pressure to "High Pressure." 6. Once the cooking cycle is completed, quickly and carefully turn the steam release handle from Sealing position to the Venting position. 7. When all the steam is released, press Cancel button and remove the pressure lid from the top carefully. 8. Press the "Sauté" Button, two times to select "normal" settings and heat remaining 2 tablespoons oil. 9. Add onion and cook until soft, about 3 minutes. 10. Add veal and crumble well. Keep stirring until meat is browned, about 5 minutes. 11. Add salt, pepper, wine, and tomato sauce, and mix well. 12. 3 Stir in cinnamon stick, bay leaves, and garlic. Press the Cancel button. 13. Put on the pressure cooker's lid and turn the steam valve to "Sealing" position. 14. Select Pressure Cook mode, and then press the "Pressure Cook" button again to select "Less" time option. 15. Use the "+/-" keys on the control panel to set the cooking time to 5 minutes. 16. Press the Pressure Level button to adjust the pressure to "Low Pressure." 17. Once the cooking cycle is completed, quickly and carefully turn the steam release handle from Sealing position to the Venting position. 18. When all the steam is released, remove the pressure lid from the top carefully. 19. Remove and discard cinnamon stick and bay leaves. 20. Place pasta in a large bowl. Sprinkle with cheese and spoon meat sauce over top. 21. Serve immediately.
Per Serving: Calories 357; Fat 7.9g; Sodium 704mg; Carbs 6g; Fiber 3.6g; Sugar 6g; Protein 18g

Avgolemono

Prep time: 10 minutes | Cook time: 13 minutes | Serves: 6

6 cups chicken stock	½ teaspoon black pepper
½ cup orzo	¼ cup lemon juice
1 tablespoon olive oil	2 large eggs
12-ounce cooked chicken breast, shredded	2 tablespoons chopped fresh dill
½ teaspoon salt	1 tablespoon chopped fresh flat-leaf parsley

1. Add stock, orzo, and olive oil to the Inner Pot. 2. Put on the pressure cooker's lid and turn the steam valve to "Sealing" position. 3. Select Pressure Cook mode, and then press the "Pressure Cook" button again to select "Less" time option. 4. Use the "+/-" keys on the control panel to set the cooking time to 3 minutes. 5. Press the Pressure Level button to adjust the pressure to "High Pressure." 6. Once the cooking cycle is completed, quickly and carefully turn the steam release handle from Sealing position to the Venting position. 7. When all the steam is released, remove the pressure lid from the top carefully. 8. Stir in chicken, salt, and pepper. 9. In a medium bowl, combine lemon juice and eggs, then slowly whisk in hot cooking liquid. 10. Immediately add egg mixture to soup and stir well. 11. Let stand on the Keep Warm setting, stirring occasionally, for 10 minutes. 12. Add dill and parsley. Serve immediately.
Per Serving: Calories 349; Fat 2.9g; Sodium 511mg; Carbs 12g; Fiber 3g; Sugar 8g; Protein 7g

Zesty Couscous

Prep time: 10 minutes | Cook time: 5 minutes | Serves: 6

2 cups couscous	1 teaspoon salt
2½ cups water	1 tablespoon unsalted butter
1 cup low-sodium chicken broth	1 teaspoon grated lemon zest

1. Place all ingredients in the Inner Pot and stir to combine. 2. Put on the pressure cooker's lid and turn the steam valve to "Sealing" position. 3. Select Pressure Cook mode, and then press the "Pressure Cook" button again to select "Less" time option. 4. Use the "+/-" keys on the control panel to set the cooking time to 4 minutes. 5. Press the Pressure Level button to adjust the pressure to "High Pressure." 6. Once the cooking cycle is completed, quickly and carefully turn the steam release handle from Sealing position to the Venting position. 7. When all the steam is released, remove the pressure lid from the top carefully. 8. Stir well. Serve immediately.
Per Serving: Calories 351; Fat 10.9g; Sodium 454mg; Carbs 10g; Fiber 3.1g; Sugar 5.2g; Protein 10g

Chapter 7 Fish and Seafood Recipes

Linguine Clams with Parmesan Cheese

Prep time: 15 minutes | Cook Time: 10 minutes | Serves: 4

2 tablespoons olive oil
4 cups sliced mushrooms
1 medium yellow onion, peeled and diced
2 tablespoons chopped fresh oregano
3 cloves garlic, peeled and minced
¼ teaspoon salt
¼ teaspoon ground black pepper

½ cup white wine
1½ cups water
8 ounces' linguine, broken in half
1-pound fresh clams, rinsed and purged
3 tablespoons lemon juice
¼ cup grated Parmesan cheese
2 tablespoons chopped fresh parsley

1. Insert the pot into the Cooker Base without the lid. 2. Select Sauté mode and then press the same button again and then adjust the cooking temperature to Normal. 3. When the display switches On to Hot, add and heat the oil; add onion and mushrooms and cook for 5 minutes or until tender; add oregano, garlic, salt, and pepper and cook for 30 seconds or until very fragrant; add the water, wine and press the pasta down to submerge it. 4. Press Cancel button to stop this cooking program. 5. Top the clams over and pasta and sprinkle with lemon juice. 6. Place and close the lid rightly. 7. Select Pressure Cook mode. Press Pressure Cook button again to adjust the cooking time to 5 minutes; press Pressure Level to choose High Pressure. 8. When the time is up, quickly and carefully turn the steam release handle from the Sealing position to the Venting position. 9. When the float valve drops, open the lid, then serve the food on a suitable bowl. 10. Top with cheese and parsley before enjoying.
Per Serving: Calories:486; Fat:11g, Sodium:301mg, Fiber:5g, Carbs: 52g, Sugar: 12g, Protein:39g

Fresh Mixed Seafood Soup

Prep time: 15 minutes | Cook Time: 21 minutes | Serves: 8

2 tablespoons light olive oil
1 medium yellow onion, peeled and diced
1 medium red bell pepper, seeded and diced
3 cloves garlic, peeled and minced
1 tablespoon chopped fresh oregano
½ teaspoon Italian seasoning

½ teaspoon ground black pepper
2 tablespoons tomato paste
½ cup white wine
2 cups seafood stock
1 bay leaf
½ pound medium shrimp, peeled and deveined
½ pound fresh scallops
½ pound fresh calamari rings
1 tablespoon lemon juice

1. Insert the pot into the Cooker Base without the lid. 2. Select Sauté mode and then press the same button again and then adjust the cooking temperature to Normal. 3. When the display switches On to Hot, heat the oil; add the onion and bell pepper and cook for 5 minutes or until just tender; add the garlic, oregano, Italian seasoning, pepper and cook for 30 seconds until fragrant; add the tomato paste and cook for 1 minute; lastly, slowly pour in wine and scrape bottom of pot. 4. Press Cancel button to stop this cooking program. 5. Still in the Inner Pot, add the stock and bay leaf and stir well. 6. Place and close the lid in right way. 7. Select Pressure Cook mode. Press Pressure Cook button again to adjust the cooking time to 5 minutes; press Pressure Level to choose High Pressure. 8. When the time is up, quickly and carefully turn the steam release handle from the Sealing position to the Venting position. 9. When the float valve drops, open the lid, add in the shrimp, scallops, calamari rings, lemon juice and stir well. 10. Press Cancel button to stop this cooking program and remove the lid. 11. Allow soup to simmer for 10 minutes until seafood is cooked

through under the Sauté mode at Normal temperature. 12. When done, discard the bay leaf and serve.
Per Serving: Calories:172; Fat:7g, Sodium:481mg; Fiber:1g, Carbs: 9g, Sugar: 2g; Protein:15g

Simple Steamed Onion Clams

Prep time: 15 minutes | Cook Time: 10 minutes | Serves: 4

2 pounds' fresh clams, rinsed
1 tablespoon olive oil
1 small white onion, peeled and diced

1 clove garlic, peeled and quartered
½ cup Chardonnay
½ cup water

1. Insert the pot into the Cooker Base without the lid. 2. Select Sauté mode and then press the same button again and then adjust the cooking temperature to Normal. 3. When the display switches On to Hot, add the onion and cook for 3 minutes or until tender; add the garlic and cook for 30 seconds; pour in water and the Chardonnay. 4. Press Cancel button to stop this cooking program. 5. Place the clams on the Steam Rack and then arrange it to the Inner Pot. 6. Place and close the lid in right way. 7. Select Pressure Cook mode. Press Pressure Cook button again to adjust the cooking time to 4 minutes; press Pressure Level to choose High Pressure. 8. When the time is up, quickly and carefully turn the steam release handle from the Sealing position to the Venting position. 9. When done, place the clams in 4 bowls with a tablespoon of cooking sauce on top. 10. Enjoy.
Per Serving: Calories:205; Fat:6g, Sodium:135mg; Fiber:0g, Carbs: 7g, Sugar: 1g; Protein:30g

Tomato Mussels with Parsley

Prep time: 15 minutes | Cook Time: 12 minutes | Serves: 6

2 pounds' baby Yukon Gold potatoes, cut in half
½ cup water
2 tablespoons olive oil, divided
1 medium yellow onion, peeled and diced
1 tablespoon chopped fresh oregano
½ teaspoon paprika
4 cloves garlic, peeled and

minced
¼ teaspoon salt
¼ teaspoon ground black pepper
1 (15-ounce) can diced tomatoes
1½ cups water
2 pounds' mussels, scrubbed and beards removed
½ cup sliced green olives
2 tablespoons chopped fresh parsley

1. In the Inner Pot, add the potatoes, water, and 1 tablespoon oil. 2. Insert the pot into the Cooker Base and then close the lid rightly. 3. Select Pressure Cook mode. Press Pressure Cook button again to adjust the cooking time to 2 minutes; press Pressure Level to choose High Pressure. 4. When the time is up, leave the steam release handle in the Sealing position until the float valve drops. 5. Press Cancel button to stop this cooking program. 6. Without the lid, select Sauté mode and then press the same button again and then adjust the cooking temperature to Normal. 7. When the display switches On to Hot, add and heat the remaining oil; add onion and cook for 4 minutes or until tender; add the oregano, garlic, paprika, salt, black pepper and cook for 30 seconds or until very fragrant; stir in the tomatoes and water. 8. Press Cancel button to stop this cooking program, after stirring in the mussels, olives and potatoes, close the lid. 9. Select Pressure Cook mode again. Press Pressure Cook button again to adjust the cooking time to 5 minutes; press Pressure Level to choose High Pressure. 10. When the time is up, quickly and carefully turn the steam release handle from the Sealing position to the Venting position. 11. When released, discard the unopened mussels. 12. Serve with garnishing the parsley and enjoy.
Per Serving: Calories:272; Fat:8g, Sodium:560mg; Fiber:4g, Carbs: 35g, Sugar: 4g; Protein:15g

Steamed Calamari with Vegetables

Prep time: 15 minutes | Cook Time: 15 minutes | Serves: 6

2 tablespoons olive oil	1 (28-ounce) can diced tomatoes
1 small carrot, peeled and grated	½ cup white wine
1 stalk celery, finely diced	⅓ cup water
1 small white onion, peeled and diced	1 teaspoon dried parsley
3 cloves garlic, peeled and minced	1 teaspoon dried basil
	½ teaspoon salt
2½ pounds calamari	½ teaspoon ground black pepper

1. Insert the pot into the Cooker Base without the lid. 2. Select Sauté mode and then press the same button again and then adjust the cooking temperature to Normal. 3. When the display switches On to Hot, add and heat the oil; add the celery, carrot and cook for 2 minutes or until tender; add the onion and cook for 3 minutes or until tender; add the garlic and stir for 30 seconds or until fragrant. 4. Press Cancel button to stop this cooking program. 5. Still in the Inner Pot, add the calamari, tomatoes, wine, water, parsley, basil, salt and black pepper. 6. Place and close the lid in right way. 7. Select Pressure Cook mode. Press Pressure Cook button again to adjust the cooking time to 10 minutes; press Pressure Level to choose High Pressure. 8. When the time is up, quickly and carefully turn the steam release handle from the Sealing position to the Venting position. 9. When done, serve and enjoy.
Per Serving: Calories:394; Fat:7g, Sodium:505mg; Fiber:3g, Carbs: 12g, Sugar: 4g; Protein:62g

Italian Fish with Herbs

Prep time: 15 minutes | Cook Time: 3 minutes | Serves: 4

1 (14.5-ounce) can diced tomatoes	⅛ teaspoon dried lemon granules, crushed
¼ teaspoon dried minced onion	
¼ teaspoon onion powder	⅛ teaspoon chili powder
¼ teaspoon dried minced garlic	⅛ teaspoon dried red pepper flakes
¼ teaspoon garlic powder	
¼ teaspoon dried basil	1 tablespoon grated Parmesan cheese
¼ teaspoon dried parsley	
⅛ teaspoon dried oregano	4 (4-ounce) cod fillets, rinsed and patted dry
¼ teaspoon sugar	

1. In the Inner Pot, thoroughly mix up the tomatoes, minced onion, onion powder, minced garlic, garlic powder, basil, parsley, oregano, sugar, lemon granules, chili powder, red pepper flakes and cheese; arrange the fillets to this mixture, fold the thin tail ends under to give the fillets even thickness, then spoon some of the tomato mixture over the fillets. 2. Place and close the lid in right way. 3. Select Pressure Cook mode. Press Pressure Cook button again to adjust the cooking time to 3 minutes; press Pressure Level to choose High Pressure. 4. When the time is up, quickly and carefully turn the steam release handle from the Sealing position to the Venting position. 5. When done, serve and enjoy.
Per Serving: Calories:116; Fat:3g, Sodium:400mg; Fiber:2g, Carbs: 5g, Sugar: 3g; Protein:20g

Lemon Shrimp Scampi in White Wine

Prep time: 15 minutes | Cook Time: 5 minutes | Serves: 6

3 tablespoons unsalted butter	½ cup low-sodium chicken broth
3 tablespoons olive oil	2 pounds' tail-on shrimp (2½5 count)
3 cloves garlic, peeled and minced	
½ teaspoon salt	1 tablespoon lemon juice
½ teaspoon ground black pepper	2 tablespoons chopped fresh flat-leaf parsley
½ cup white wine	

1. Insert the pot into the Cooker Base without the lid. 2. Select Sauté mode and then press the same button again and then adjust the cooking temperature to Normal. 3. When the display switches On to Hot, heat the butter and olive oil; add the garlic, salt and black pepper and cook for 30 seconds; add the broth, white wine and stir quickly. 4. Press Cancel button to stop this cooking program. 5. Still in the Inner Pot, add the shrimp and let evenly coat with the garlic mixture. 6. Place and close the lid in right way. 7. Select Pressure Cook mode. Press Pressure Cook button again to adjust the cooking time to 1 minutes; press Pressure Level to choose High Pressure. 8. When the time is up, quickly and carefully turn the steam release handle from the Sealing position to the Venting position. 9. When done, add lemon juice and parsley. 10. Serve and enjoy.
Per Serving: Calories:326; Fat:25g, Sodium:1062mg; Fiber:0g, Carbs: 0g, Sugar: 0g; Protein:22g

Poached Garlic Octopus with Potatoes

Prep time: 15 minutes | Cook Time: 2 minutes | Serves: 8

2 pounds' potatoes (about 6 medium)	1 bay leaf
	2 teaspoons whole peppercorns
3 teaspoons salt, divided	½ cup olive oil
1 (2-pound) frozen octopus, thawed, cleaned, and rinsed	¼ cup white wine vinegar
	½ teaspoon ground black pepper
3 cloves garlic, peeled, divided	½ cup chopped fresh parsley

1. In the Inner Pot, add the potatoes and salt, then pour the water to just cover the potatoes halfway. 2. Insert the pot into the Cooker Base and then close the lid rightly. 3. Select Pressure Cook mode. Press Pressure Cook button again to adjust the cooking time to 6 minutes; press Pressure Level to choose High Pressure. 4. When the time is up, quickly and carefully turn the steam release handle from the Sealing position to the Venting position. 5. Press Cancel button to stop this cooking program. 6. With reserving the cooking water, use a tong to pick out the potatoes, peel them when they are just cool, dice and set aside for later use. 7. Still in the Inner Pot, add the octopus and more water if needed; add the bay leaf, peppercorns, and 1 garlic clove. 8. Close the lid and cook them under High Pressure for 10 minutes on Pressure Cook mode. 9. When the time is up, quickly and carefully turn the steam release handle from the Sealing position to the Venting position; when released, discard the bay leaf. 10. It is done if you can use a fork to sink the octopus easily into its thickest part; if not, you can cook 1 to 2 minutes more. 11. Drain the octopus, chop the head and tentacles into small, bite-sized chunks. 12. In a suitable container, crush the remaining garlic cloves, add olive oil, vinegar, the remaining salt and pepper, then cover lid and shake to combine well. 13. In your serving plate, mix up the potatoes and octopus, top with vinaigrette and sprinkle with parsley. Enjoy.
Per Serving: Calories:301; Fat:15g, Sodium:883mg; Fiber:2g, Carbs: 30g, Sugar: 1g; Protein:15g

Basil Cod Kebabs with Lemon Wedges

Prep time: 15 minutes | Cook Time: 2 minutes | Serves: 4

1 cup water	2 tablespoons extra-virgin olive oil
4 (4-ounce) cod or other white fish fillets, cut into 1" pieces	
	2 tablespoons chopped fresh basil
½ medium onion, peeled and cut into 1» pieces	½ teaspoon salt
	½ teaspoon ground black pepper
½ medium red bell pepper, seeded and cut into 1» pieces	1 small lemon, cut into wedges

1. Alternately thread the fish, onions, and bell peppers on four wooden skewers; brush each skewers with the olive oil, top with the basil, salt and black pepper, then place them on the Steam Rack. 2. In the Inner Pot, add water and place the Steam Rack. 3. Place and close the lid rightly. 4. Select Steam mode. Press Steam button again to adjust the cooking time to 2 minutes; press Pressure Level to choose High Pressure. 5. When the time is up, quickly and carefully turn the steam release handle from the Sealing position to the Venting position. 6. When done, serve and enjoy.
Per Serving: Calories:93; Fat:7g, Sodium:312mg; Fiber:1g, Carbs: 2g, Sugar: 1g; Protein:5g

Seafood Paella with Vegetables

Prep time: 15 minutes | Cook Time: 10 minutes | Serves: 4

½ teaspoon saffron threads
2 cups vegetable broth
2 tablespoons olive oil
1 medium yellow onion, peeled and diced
1 cup diced carrot
1 medium green bell pepper, seeded and diced
1 cup fresh or frozen green peas
2 cloves garlic, peeled and

minced
1 cup basmati rice
¼ cup chopped fresh flat-leaf parsley
½ pound medium shrimp, peeled and deveined
½ pound mussels, scrubbed and beards removed
½ pound clams, rinsed
¼ teaspoon ground black pepper

1. In a medium microwave-safe bowl, mix up the saffron and broth; microwave them for 30 seconds on High or the broth just starts to warm; set aside for later use. 2. Insert the pot into the Cooker Base without the lid. 3. Select Sauté mode and then press the same button again and then adjust the cooking temperature to Normal. 4. When the display switches On to Hot, heat the oil; add the onion, carrot, bell pepper, peas and cook for 5 minutes until they begin to soften; stir in the garlic and rice until well coated; add the saffron broth and parsley. 5. Press Cancel button to stop this cooking program. 6. Place and close the lid in right way. 7. Select Pressure Cook mode. Press Pressure Cook button again to adjust the cooking time to 5 minutes; press Pressure Level to choose High Pressure. 8. When the time is up, quickly and carefully turn the steam release handle from the Sealing position to the Venting position. 9. When released, stir well and top with shrimp, mussels, and clams. 10. Close the lid again and resume cook them on the Pressure Cook mode at High Pressure for 1 minutes. 11. When the time is up, leave the steam release handle in the Sealing position for 10 minutes, then turn it to the Venting position. 12. When done, discard the unopened mussels, season with black pepper. 13. Serve and enjoy.
Per Serving: Calories:555; Fat:12g, Sodium:1266mg; Fiber:3g, Carbs: 49g, Sugar: 6g; Protein:58g

Codfish with Scallions

Prep time: 15 minutes | Cook time: 3 minutes | Serves: 3

1 lemon, sliced
½ cup water
3 fillets smoked codfish

3 teaspoons butter
3 tablespoons scallions, chopped
Sea salt and black pepper, to taste

1. Place the lemon and water in the bottom of the Inner Pot. Place the steamer rack on top. 2. Place the cod fish fillets on the steamer rack. Add the butter, scallions, salt, and black pepper. 3. Put on the pressure cooker's lid and turn the steam valve to "Sealing" position. 4. Press the "Steam" button one time to select "Less" option. 5. Press the Pressure Level button to adjust the pressure to "Low Pressure." 6. Once the cooking cycle is completed, quickly and carefully turn the steam release handle from Sealing position to the Venting position. 7. When all the steam is released, remove the pressure lid from the top carefully. 8. Serve warm and enjoy!
Per Serving: Calories 461; Fat 7.9g; Sodium 704mg; Carbs 6g; Fiber 3.6g; Sugar 6g; Protein 18g

Teriyaki Fish Steaks

Prep time: 15 minutes | Cook time: 10 minutes | Serves: 4

2 tablespoons butter, melted
4 (6-ounce) salmon steaks
2 cloves garlic, smashed
1 (1-inch) piece fresh ginger, peeled and grated

⅓ cup soy sauce
½ cup water
2 tablespoons brown sugar
2 teaspoons wine vinegar
1 tablespoon cornstarch

1. Press the "Sauté" button two times to select "Normal" settings and then melt the butter. 2. Once hot, cook the salmon steaks for 2 minutes per side. 3. Add the garlic, ginger, soy sauce, water, sugar, and vinegar. 4. Put on the pressure cooker's lid and turn the steam valve to "Sealing" position. 5. Select Pressure Cook mode, and then press the "Pressure

Cook" button again to select "Less" time option. 6. Use the "+/-" keys on the control panel to set the cooking time to 5 minutes. 7. Press the Pressure Level button to adjust the pressure to "Low Pressure." 8. Once the cooking cycle is completed, quickly and carefully turn the steam release handle from Sealing position to the Venting position. 9. When all the steam is released, remove the pressure lid from the top carefully. 10. Reserve the fish steaks. 11. Mix the cornstarch with 2 tablespoons of cold water. 12. Add the slurry to the cooking liquid. Let it simmer until the sauce thickens. 13. Spoon the sauce over the fish steaks. 14. Bon appétit!
Per Serving: Calories 385; Fat 12.9g; Sodium 414mg; Carbs 11g; Fiber 5g; Sugar 9g; Protein 31g

Lemon Trout in Parsley Sauce

Prep time: 15 minutes | Cook Time: 3 minutes | Serves: 4

4 (½-pound) river trout, rinsed and patted dry
¾ teaspoon salt, divided
4 cups torn lettuce leaves, divided
1 teaspoon white wine vinegar
½ cup water
½ cup minced fresh flat-leaf parsley

1 small shallot, peeled and minced
2 tablespoons olive oil mayonnaise
½ teaspoon lemon juice
¼ teaspoon sugar
2 tablespoons toasted sliced almonds

1. Season the trout inside and out with ½ teaspoon of salt. 2. In the Inner Pot, put 3 cups of lettuce leaves on the bottom, then arrange the trout to the leaves and top with the remaining lettuce; stir in vinegar and water. 3. Place and close the lid in right way. 4. Select Pressure Cook mode. Press the button again to adjust the cooking time to 3 minutes; press Pressure Level to choose High Pressure. 5. When the time is up, quickly and carefully turn the steam release handle from the Sealing position to the Venting position. 6. Transfer the trout to a plate with a spatula, peel and discard the skin and heads. 7. In a small bowl, thoroughly mix up the parsley, shallot, mayonnaise, lemon juice, sugar, and remaining salt; evenly spread the mixture over the trout. 8. Sprinkle toasted almonds over the sauce and enjoy.
Per Serving: Calories:159; Fat:9g, Sodium:860mg; Fiber:1g, Carbs: 4g, Sugar: 0g; Protein:15g

Garlic Mussels with White Wine

Prep time: 15 minutes | Cook Time: 7 minutes | Serves: 6

2 tablespoons light olive oil
2 shallots, peeled and minced
4 cloves garlic, peeled and minced
½ teaspoon ground black pepper
3 pounds' mussels, scrubbed and

beards removed
2 cups white wine
¼ cup chopped fresh chives
¼ cup chopped fresh tarragon
2 tablespoons chopped fresh dill

1. Insert the pot into the Cooker Base without the lid. 2. Select Sauté mode and then press the same button again and then adjust the cooking temperature to Normal. 3. When the display switches On to Hot, heat the oil; add the shallots and cook for 1 minute until tender; add the garlic and pepper and cook for 30 seconds until fragrant. 4. Press Cancel button to stop this cooking program. 5. Still in the Inner Pot, stir in the mussels and wine, then place and close the lid in right way. 6. Select Pressure Cook mode. Press Pressure Cook button again to adjust the cooking time to 3 minutes; press Pressure Level to choose High Pressure. 7. When the time is up, quickly and carefully turn the steam release handle from the Sealing position to the Venting position. 8. When the float valve drops, open the lid and discard the unopened mussels; transfer mussels to a serving bowl but reserve the broth in the pot. 9. Press Cancel button to stop this cooking program. 10. Without the lid, select Sauté mode and then press the same button again and then adjust the cooking temperature to Normal. 11. Bring the broth to boil, add the chives, tarragon and dill and whisk for 3 minutes or until the broth has reduced slightly. 12. When cooked, pour the broth over the mussels and serve warm.
Per Serving: Calories:146; Fat:7g, Sodium:321mg; Fiber:0g, Carbs: 6g, Sugar: 0g; Protein:14g

Spiced Fish Potato Stew

Prep time: 15 minutes | Cook Time: 10 minutes | Serves: 4

3 tablespoons olive oil
2 stalks celery, sliced
2 medium carrots, peeled and sliced
1 medium onion, peeled and chopped
½ fennel bulb, trimmed and chopped
2 cloves garlic, peeled and minced
1 tablespoon chopped fresh oregano
3 sprigs fresh thyme
1 (14.5-ounce) can diced tomatoes
1½ cups vegetable broth
2 medium russet potatoes, peeled and diced
1-pound cod or other white fish fillets, cut into 1" pieces
¼ teaspoon ground black pepper
2 tablespoons chopped fresh parsley

1. Insert the pot into the Cooker Base without the lid. 2. Select Sauté mode and then press the same button again and then adjust the cooking temperature to Normal. 3. When the display switches On to Hot, add and heat the oil; add the celery, carrots, onion, fennel and cook for 8 minutes until vegetables are soft; add the garlic, oregano, thyme and cook for 30 seconds; lastly, stir in the tomatoes, potatoes and vegetable broth. 4. Press Cancel button to stop this cooking program and close the lid in right way. 5. Select Pressure Cook mode. Press the button again to adjust the cooking time to 4 minutes; press Pressure Level to choose High Pressure. 6. When the time is up, quickly and carefully turn the steam release handle from the Sealing position to the Venting position. 7. When released, stop this cooking mode by pressing Cancel button. 8. Still in the Inner Pot, add the fish, pepper and cook for 3 to 5 minutes on Sauté mode at Normal cooking temperature, until the fish is opaque. 9. When done, serve and sprinkle with parsley.
Per Serving: Calories:363; Fat:11g, Sodium:295mg; Fiber:6g, Carbs: 38g, Sugar: 11g; Protein:24g

Rosemary Salmon with Lemon Wedges

Prep time: 15 minutes | Cook Time: 5 minutes | Serves: 4

1 cup water
4 (4-ounce) salmon fillets
½ teaspoon salt
½ teaspoon ground black pepper
1 sprig rosemary, leaves stripped off and minced
2 tablespoons chopped fresh thyme
2 tablespoons extra-virgin olive oil
4 lemon wedges

1. Season the fillets with salt and pepper. 2. Prepare 4 pieces of large foil, lay the fillets on them separately; top them with rosemary, thyme and drizzle each with olive oil. 3. Carefully wrap fillet loosely in foil. 4. In the Inner Pot, place the Steam Rack and then place the foil pouches on the rack. 5. Select Steam mode. Press the button again to adjust the cooking time to 5 minutes; press Pressure Level to choose High Pressure. 6. When the time is up, quickly and carefully turn the steam release handle from the Sealing position to the Venting position. 7. When done, serve and enjoy with the lemon wedges.
Per Serving: Calories:160; Fat:8g, Sodium:445mg; Fiber:0g, Carbs: 0g, Sugar: 0g; Protein:24g

Garlic Shrimp with Parsley

Prep time: 15 minutes | Cook Time: 5 minutes | Serves: 6

2 tablespoons light olive oil
1 small shallot, peeled and minced
6 cloves garlic, peeled and thinly sliced
1 tablespoon chopped fresh dill
1 tablespoon chopped fresh chives
½ teaspoon ground black pepper
¼ teaspoon salt
¼ cup white wine
¼ cup low-sodium chicken broth
2 pounds' large tail-on shrimp
2 tablespoons lemon juice
2 tablespoons chopped fresh parsley

1. Insert the pot into the Cooker Base without the lid. 2. Select Sauté mode and then press the same button again and then adjust the cooking temperature to Normal. 3. When the display switches On to Hot, heat the oil; add the shallot and garlic and cook for 1 minute; add the dill, chives, pepper and salt and cook for 3 minutes; stir in wine and broth. 4. Press Cancel button to stop this cooking program. 5. Close the lid in right way. 6. Select Pressure Cook mode. Press Pressure Cook button again to adjust the cooking time to 1 minutes; press Pressure Level to choose High Pressure. 7. When the time is up, quickly and carefully turn the steam release handle from the Sealing position to the Venting position. 8. When done, add the lemon juice and parsley. 9. Serve and enjoy.
Per Serving: Calories:151; Fat:5g, Sodium:691mg; Fiber:0g, Carbs: 0g, Sugar: 0g; Protein:25g

Shrimp Risotto with Parmesan Cheese

Prep time: 15 minutes | Cook Time: 22 minutes | Serves: 6

4 tablespoons olive oil, divided
1 medium yellow onion, peeled and chopped
1 clove garlic, peeled and minced
1 teaspoon fresh thyme leaves
1½ cups Arborio rice
½ cup white wine
4 cups low-sodium chicken broth
1-pound medium shrimp, peeled and deveined
½ teaspoon ground black pepper
½ cup grated Parmesan cheese

1. Insert the pot into the Cooker Base without the lid. 2. Select Sauté mode and then press the same button again and then adjust the cooking temperature to Normal. 3. When the display switches On to Hot, heat 2 tablespoons of oil; add onion and cook for 3 minutes or until tender; add the garlic and thyme and cook for 30 seconds; add the rice and cook for 3 minutes, making sure the rice is thoroughly and evenly coated in fat. 4. Still in the Inner Pot, add the wine and stir constantly for 2 minutes until completely evaporated; add the broth, bring to boil, stir constantly for 3 minutes. 5. Press Cancel button to stop this cooking program. 6. Place and close the lid in right way. 7. Select Pressure Cook mode. Press Pressure Cook button again to adjust the cooking time to 6 minutes; press Pressure Level to choose High Pressure. 8. When the time is up, leave the steam release handle from the Sealing position. 9. When the float valve drops, press Cancel button to stop this cooking program and remove the lid. 10. Select Sauté mode and then press the same button again and then adjust the cooking temperature to Normal. 11. When the display switches On to Hot, stir in shrimp, pepper and cook for 4 minutes until they are pink and curled. 12. When done, place the risotto in 6 suitable bowls, top with cheese and the remaining oil. 13. Enjoy.
Per Serving: Calories:412; Fat:16g, Sodium:670mg; Fiber:4g, Carbs: 37g, Sugar: 2g; Protein:27g

Lemon Shrimp Pasta with Feta Cheese

Prep time: 15 minutes | Cook Time: 10 minutes | Serves: 6

3 tablespoons olive oil, divided
4 cloves garlic, peeled and minced
¼ teaspoon salt
¼ teaspoon ground black pepper
2 cups water
8 ounces' whole-wheat penne pasta
2 pounds' tail-on shrimp (3⅓5 count)
1 tablespoon lemon juice
1 teaspoon grated lemon zest
2 tablespoons chopped fresh basil
¼ cup crumbled feta cheese

1. Insert the pot into the Cooker Base without the lid. 2. Select Sauté mode and then press the same button again and then adjust the cooking temperature to Normal. 3. When the display switches On to Hot, add and heat 1 tablespoon oil; add the garlic, salt, black pepper and cook for 30 seconds or until fragrant; stir in the water and pasta. 4. Press Cancel button to stop this cooking program. 5. Place and close the lid in right way. 6. Select Pressure Cook mode. Press Pressure Cook button again to adjust the cooking time to 4 minutes; press Pressure Level to choose High Pressure. 7. When the time is up, quickly and carefully turn the steam release handle from the Sealing position to the Venting position. 8. When the float valve drops, open the lid; drain off any excess water before transferring the pasta to a serving bowl and covering with foil. 9. Press Cancel button to stop this cooking program. 10. After cleaning and drying the pot, insert it into the Cooker Base again. 11. Select Sauté mode and then press the same button again and then adjust the cooking temperature to Normal. 12. When the display switches On to Hot, heat the remaining oil; add shrimp and stir constantly for 2 minutes; add the lemon juice, lemon zest and basil and cook for 30 seconds. 13. When done, place the shrimp over the pasta and then top with feta. 14. Enjoy!
Per Serving: Calories:206; Fat:9g, Sodium:789mg; Fiber:2g, Carbs: 7g, Sugar: 0g; Protein:37g

Mediterranean Cod Fillets and Shrimp

Prep time: 15 minutes | Cook Time: 10 minutes | Serves: 6

2 tablespoons olive oil
1 medium yellow onion, peeled and chopped
1 stalk celery, chopped
1 medium carrot, peeled and chopped
3 cloves garlic, peeled and minced
1 tablespoon tomato paste
1 teaspoon fresh thyme leaves
1 teaspoon chopped fresh oregano
¼ teaspoon crushed red pepper

flakes
¼ teaspoon salt
¼ teaspoon ground black pepper
1 (28-ounce) can diced tomatoes
½ cup seafood stock
1-pound medium shrimp, peeled and deveined
8 ounces' cod fillets, cut into 1" pieces
2 cups cooked white rice
2 tablespoons chopped fresh parsley

1. Insert the pot into the Cooker Base without the lid. 2. Select Sauté mode and then press the same button again and then adjust the cooking temperature to Normal. 3. When the display switches On to Hot, add and heat the oil; add the celery, onion and carrot and cook for 5 minutes or until tender; add the garlic, tomato paste, thyme, oregano, red pepper flakes, salt and black pepper and cook for 30 seconds or until fragrant; lastly, add the tomatoes and stock and stir well. 4. Place and close the lid in right way. 5. Select Pressure Cook mode. Press Pressure Cook button again to adjust the cooking time to 5 minutes; press Pressure Level to choose High Pressure. 6. When the time is up, quickly and carefully turn the steam release handle from the Sealing position to the Venting position. 7. When released, open the lid and stir gently. 8. Serve with the rice and garnish with the parsley.
Per Serving: Calories:239; Fat:7g, Sodium:701mg; Fiber:3g, Carbs: 25g, Sugar: 5g; Protein:21g

Steamed Cayenne Dungeness Crab

Prep time: 15 minutes | Cook Time: 3 minutes | Serves: 2

1 tablespoon extra-virgin olive oil
½ teaspoon Old Bay seafood seasoning
½ teaspoon smoked paprika
¼ teaspoon cayenne pepper

2 cloves garlic, peeled and minced
2 (2-pound) Dungeness crabs
1 cup water

1. In a medium bowl, thoroughly mix up the oil, seafood seasoning, smoked paprika, cayenne pepper and garlic; coat the crabs with the mixture and then arrange them to the Steam Rack. 2. In the Inner Pot, add the water and place the Steam Rack, then close the lid in right way. 3. Select Pressure Cook mode. Press Pressure Cook button again to adjust the cooking time to 3 minutes; press Pressure Level to choose High Pressure. 4. When the time is up, quickly and carefully turn the steam release handle from the Sealing position to the Venting position. 5. When done, serve the crabs on a clean plate and enjoy.
Per Serving: Calories:185; Fat:8g, Sodium:434mg; Fiber:0g, Carbs: 1g, Sugar: 0g; Protein:25g

Oregano Mussels Saganaki with Feta Cheese

Prep time: 15 minutes | Cook Time: 6 minutes | Serves: 2

2 tablespoons extra-virgin olive oil
1 medium banana pepper, stemmed, seeded, and thinly sliced
2 medium tomatoes, chopped

½ teaspoon salt
1-pound mussels, scrubbed and beards removed
⅓ cup white wine
⅓ cup crumbled feta cheese
2 teaspoons dried oregano

1. Insert the pot into the Cooker Base without the lid. 2. Select Sauté mode and then press the same button again and then adjust the cooking temperature to Normal. 3. When the display switches On to Hot, heat the oil; add the pepper, tomatoes and salt and cook for 3 minutes until tender. 4. Press Cancel button to stop this cooking program. 5. Still in the Inner Pot, add the mussels and wine, then place and close the lid in right way. 6. Cook the food on Pressure Cook mode at High Pressure

for 3 minutes. 7. When the time is up, quickly and carefully turn the steam release handle from the Sealing position to the Venting position. 8. When done, discard the unopened mussels. 9. Add feta, oregano and stir them to combine well with the sauce. 10. Serve and enjoy.
Per Serving: Calories:250; Fat:21g, Sodium:1140mg; Fiber:1g, Carbs: 7g, Sugar: 2g; Protein:18g

Flavored Cioppino

Prep time: 15 minutes | Cook Time: 10 minutes | Serves: 6

3 tablespoons light olive oil
1 medium yellow onion, peeled and chopped
1 medium red bell pepper, seeded and chopped
2 cloves garlic, peeled and minced
1 (28-ounce) can crushed tomatoes
1 cup red wine

1 cup seafood stock
1 tablespoon lemon juice
1 bay leaf
¼ cup chopped fresh basil
½ teaspoon ground black pepper
1-pound fresh mussels, scrubbed and beards removed
1-pound large shrimp, peeled and deveined
1-pound clams, scrubbed

1. Insert the pot into the Cooker Base without the lid. 2. Select Sauté mode and then press the same button again and then adjust the cooking temperature to Normal. 3. When the display switches On to Hot, heat the oil; add the onion and bell pepper and cook for 3 minutes until just tender; add the garlic and cook for 30 seconds until fragrant; stir in the wine, tomatoes, stock, lemon juice, bay leaf, basil and black pepper. 4. Press Cancel button to stop this cooking program. 5. Place and close the lid in right way. 6. Select Pressure Cook mode. Press Pressure Cook button again to adjust the cooking time to 5 minutes; press Pressure Level to choose High Pressure. 7. When the time is up, quickly and carefully turn the steam release handle from the Sealing position to the Venting position. 8. When done, stop this cooking mode by pressing the Cancel button. 9. Open the lid, remove the bay leaf, add the mussels, shrimp and clams and cook for 3 minutes on Sauté mode at Normal temperature, until the shrimp are pink and shellfish have opened. 10. When cooked, discard the unopened mussels and serve.
Per Serving: Calories:384; Fat:11g, Sodium:671mg; Fiber:3g, Carbs: 14g, Sugar: 6g; Protein:47g

Spiced Salmon Poached in Red Wine

Prep time: 15 minutes | Cook Time: 16 minutes | Serves: 6

1 medium onion, peeled and quartered
2 cloves garlic, peeled and smashed
1 stalk celery, diced
1 bay leaf
½ teaspoon dried thyme
3½ cups water

2 cups dry red wine
2 tablespoons red wine vinegar
½ teaspoon salt
½ teaspoon black peppercorns
1 (2½-pound) center-cut salmon roast
1 medium lemon, cut into wedges

1. In the Inner Pot, add all ingredients except salmon and lemon. 2. Place and close the lid in right way. 3. Select Pressure Cook mode. Press the button again to adjust the cooking time to 10 minutes; press Pressure Level to choose High Pressure. 4. When the time is up, quickly and carefully turn the steam release handle from the Sealing position to the Venting position. 5. When released, stop this cooking mode by pressing Cancel button. 6. Still in the Inner Pot, place the Steam Rack and transfer a suitable steamer basket to the rack. 7. Wrap salmon in cheesecloth so that the ends are long enough to extend about 3 inches; use two sets of tongs to hold the 3-inch cheesecloth extension and then place the salmon on the rack. 8. Place and close the lid rightly. 9. Select Pressure Cook mode. Press the button again to adjust the cooking time to 6 minutes; press Pressure Level to choose High Pressure. 10. When the time is up, leave the steam release handle in the Sealing position. 11. When released, hold on to the 3-inch cheesecloth extensions to remove the salmon out of the pot with the tongs; drain away the extra moisture by setting in a colander. 12. Unwrap the cheesecloth after the salmon is cool enough to handle, then peel away and discard the skin. 13. Serve the salmon on a plate and garnish with lemon wedges.
Per Serving: Calories:435; Fat:24g, Sodium:213mg; Fiber:0g, Carbs: 4g, Sugar: 3g; Protein:43g

Vegetable Fish Soup

Prep time: 15 minutes | Cook Time: 20-25 minutes | Serves: 12

8 cups water
2 medium onions, peeled and diced
2 medium potatoes, cubed
2 stalks celery, diced
2 medium carrots, peeled and chopped
1 tablespoon dried marjoram
½ teaspoon salt
½ teaspoon ground black pepper
2 pounds' fresh cod, cut into pieces
2 pounds' fresh grey mullet, deboned and cut into pieces
1-pound mussels, scrubbed and beards removed
¼ cup chopped fresh parsley
¼ cup extra-virgin olive oil
2 tablespoons lemon juice

1. In the Inner Pot, add the water, onions, potatoes, celery, carrots, marjoram, salt and pepper. 2. Insert the pot into the Cooker Base and then close the lid rightly. 3. Select Pressure Cook mode. Press Pressure Cook button again to adjust the cooking time to 10 minutes; press Pressure Level to choose High Pressure. 4. When the time is up, quickly and carefully turn the steam release handle from the Sealing position to the Venting position. 5. Press Cancel button to stop this cooking program. 6. Still in the Inner Pot, add the cod, mullet, mussels and parsley; cook them under High Pressure for 4 minutes on Pressure Cook mode. 7. When the time is up, quickly and carefully turn the steam release handle from the Sealing position to the Venting position. 8. When released, discard the unopened mussels; serve the fish and mussels on a plate with a slotted spoon. 9. Filter the ingredients through a sieve; push softened vegetables through a sieve with a wooden spoon and then put the strained stock back to the pot. 10. Without the lid, select Sauté mode and then press the button again to adjust the cooking temperature to Normal. 11. When the display switches On to Hot, add the olive oil and lemon juice and bring them to simmer; add the fish and mussels and simmer for 3–5 minutes. 12. When done, serve and enjoy.
Per Serving: Calories:163; Fat:6g, Sodium:171mg; Fiber:2g, Carbs: 10g, Sugar: 3g; Protein:18g

Steamed Lemon Shrimp with Asparagus

Prep time: 15 minutes | Cook Time: 1 minutes | Serves: 4

1 cup water
1 bunch asparagus, trimmed
½ teaspoon salt, divided
1-pound shrimp (2½5 count), peeled and deveined
1½ tablespoons lemon juice
2 tablespoons olive oil

1. In the Inner Pot, add the water, put the Steam Rack in and place a suitable steamer basket on it. 2. Arrange the asparagus on steamer basket and sprinkle with ¼ teaspoon salt; add shrimp, drizzle with lemon juice, olive oil and sprinkle with remaining ¼ teaspoon salt. 3. Place and close the lid in right way. 4. Select Pressure Cook mode. Press Pressure Cook button again to adjust the cooking time to 1 minutes; press Pressure Level to choose High Pressure. 5. When the time is up, quickly and carefully turn the steam release handle from the Sealing position to the Venting position. 6. When the float valve drops, open the lid and serve the food on a plate. 7. Enjoy.
Per Serving: Calories:145; Fat:8g, Sodium:295mg; Fiber:0g, Carbs: 1g, Sugar: 1g; Protein:19g

Lobster Tails with Herbed Olive Oil

Prep time: 15 minutes | Cook Time: 3 minutes | Serves: 4

¼ cup extra-virgin olive oil
¼ teaspoon salt
¼ teaspoon ground black pepper
1 clove garlic, peeled and minced
1 tablespoon grated lemon zest
1 teaspoon chopped fresh tarragon
1 teaspoon chopped fresh dill
1 cup low-sodium chicken broth
2 tablespoons Old Bay seafood seasoning
2 pounds fresh cold-water lobster tails

1. In a skillet or saucepan, heat the oil, garlic, lemon zest, salt and pepper over low heat until oil is warm; after stirring in tarragon and dill, turn off the heat immediately; cover and set aside for later use. 2. In the Inner Pot, stir in the broth and seafood seasoning; place the Steam Rack in and then place the lobster tails shell side down on the rack. 3. Insert the pot into the Cooker Base and then close the lid rightly. 4. Select Pressure Cook mode. Press Pressure Cook button again to adjust the cooking time to 3 minutes; press Pressure Level to choose High Pressure. 5. When the time is up, quickly and carefully turn the steam release handle from the Sealing position to the Venting position. 6. When released, serve the lobster tails on a large plate; use the kitchen shears to carefully cut the bottom of each shell and pull tail meat out in one piece; slice into ½"-thick pieces. 7. With the herbed olive oil, serve and enjoy.
Per Serving: Calories:230; Fat:15g, Sodium:534mg; Fiber:0g, Carbs: 0g, Sugar: 0g; Protein:22g

Spiced Mussels with Tomatoes

Prep time: 15 minutes | Cook Time: 6 minutes | Serves: 6

2 tablespoons light olive oil
1 medium white onion, peeled and chopped
2 cloves garlic, peeled and minced
2 tablespoons chopped fresh dill
2 tablespoons chopped fresh tarragon
½ teaspoon ground fennel
½ teaspoon ground black pepper
3 pounds' mussels, scrubbed and beards removed
½ cup vegetable broth
1 (14.5-ounce) can diced tomatoes, drained

1. Insert the pot into the Cooker Base without the lid. 2. Select Sauté mode and then press the same button again and then adjust the cooking temperature to Normal. 3. When the display switches On to Hot, heat the oil; add the onion and cook for 3 minutes until tender; add the garlic, dill, tarragon, fennel and pepper and cook for 30 seconds until the garlic is fragrant. 4. Press Cancel button to stop this cooking program. 5. Still in the Inner Pot, stir in the mussels, tomatoes and broth, then place and close the lid in right way. 6. Select Pressure Cook mode. Press Pressure Cook button again to adjust the cooking time to 3 minutes; press Pressure Level to choose High Pressure. 7. When the time is up, quickly and carefully turn the steam release handle from the Sealing position to the Venting position. 8. When done, discard the unopened mussels. 9. Serve and enjoy.
Per Serving: Calories:162; Fat:7g, Sodium:435mg; Fiber:2g, Carbs: 10g, Sugar: 3g; Protein:14g

Thyme Cod Fillet Soup

Prep time: 15 minutes | Cook Time: 20 minutes | Serves: 6

3 tablespoons olive oil
1 fennel bulb, white part only, chopped
1 medium onion, peeled and chopped
1 medium zucchini, trimmed and chopped
4 cloves garlic, peeled and minced
1 tablespoon tomato paste
1 (14.5-ounce) can diced tomatoes
3 sprigs fresh thyme
1 tablespoon chopped fresh oregano
2 teaspoons grated orange zest
½ cup white wine
3 cups low-sodium chicken broth
1-pound russet potatoes, peeled and chopped
1-pound cod fillets, cut into 1" pieces
¼ cup chopped Kalamata olives
3 basil leaves, roughly torn

1. Insert the pot into the Cooker Base without the lid. 2. Select Sauté mode and then press the same button again and then adjust the cooking temperature to Normal. 3. When the display switches On to Hot, add and heat the oil; add the fennel and onion and cook for 8 minutes or until soft; add the zucchini, garlic and tomato paste and cook for 1 minute until fragrant; lastly, stir in the tomatoes, thyme, oregano and orange zest. 4. Press the Cancel button to stop this cooking program. 5. Still in the Inner Pot, add the potatoes, wine and broth, the close the lid in right way. 6. Select Pressure Cook mode. Press the button again to adjust the cooking time to 5 minutes; press Pressure Level to choose High Pressure. 7. When the time is up, quickly and carefully turn the steam release handle from the Sealing position to the Venting position. 8. When released, stop this cooking mode by pressing the Cancel button. 9. Add the fish and olives and cook for 3 to 5 minutes at Normal cooking temperature on Sauté mode, until the fish is opaque. 10. When done, top with the basil and serve warm.
Per Serving: Calories:198; Fat:10g, Sodium:279mg; Fiber:2g, Carbs: 17g, Sugar: 6g; Protein:9g

Steamed Halibut Fillets with Tomato

Prep time: 15 minutes | Cook Time: 7 minutes | Serves: 4

2 tablespoons olive oil
1 medium onion, peeled and chopped
2 cloves garlic, peeled and minced
1 tablespoon chopped fresh oregano
1 teaspoon fresh thyme leaves
½ teaspoon ground fennel
¼ teaspoon ground black pepper
¼ teaspoon crushed red pepper flakes
1 (14.5-ounce) can diced tomatoes
1 cup vegetable broth
1-pound halibut fillets
2 tablespoons chopped fresh parsley

1. Insert the pot into the Cooker Base without the lid. 2. Select Sauté mode and then press the same button again and then adjust the cooking temperature to Normal. 3. When the display switches On to Hot, and heat the oil; add the onion and cook for 4 minutes until soft; add the garlic, oregano, thyme, fennel and cook for 30 seconds until fragrant; add the black pepper, red pepper flakes, tomatoes and vegetable broth. 4. Press Cancel button to stop this cooking program and then close the lid in right way. 5. Select Pressure Cook mode. Press the button again to adjust the cooking time to 3 minutes; press Pressure Level to choose High Pressure. 6. When the time is up, quickly and carefully turn the steam release handle from the Sealing position to the Venting position. 7. When released, serve the fillets on a plate and spoon sauce over them, sprinkle with the parsley and serve.
Per Serving: Calories:212; Fat:8g, Sodium:449mg; Fiber:2g, Carbs: 10g, Sugar: 7g; Protein:24g

Citrus Fish Tacos

Prep time: 15 minutes | Cook Time: 3 minutes | Serves: 8

½ cup grated cabbage
1 large carrot, peeled and grated
1 small jicama, peeled and julienned
2 tablespoons lime juice, divided
2 tablespoons olive oil, divided
⅛ teaspoon hot sauce
¼ cup chopped fresh cilantro
½ teaspoon salt
1-pound cod, cut into 2" pieces
2 tablespoons orange juice
1 teaspoon garlic salt
1 teaspoon ground cumin
1 cup water
½ cup guacamole
½ cup diced tomatoes
8 (6") soft corn tortillas

1. In a medium bowl, mix up the cabbage, carrot, jicama, 1 tablespoon lime juice, hot sauce, cilantro, salt and 1 tablespoon of oil, then cover and refrigerate the mixture for 30 minutes or overnight. 2. In a large bowl, mix up the cod pieces, orange juice, garlic salt, cumin, the remaining lime juice and oil, then refrigerate for 15 minutes. 3. In the Inner Pot, add the water and place the Steam Rack, then put the suitable steamer basket on the rack. 4. Arrange the cod pieces to the basket and add the remaining marinade. 5. Place and close the lid in right way. 6. Select Pressure Cook mode. Press the button again to adjust the cooking time to 3 minutes; press Pressure Level to choose High Pressure. 7. When the time is up, quickly and carefully turn the steam release handle from the Sealing position to the Venting position. 8. When released, transfer the cod pieces to the serving bowl. 9. To make the cod tacos, add equal amounts of fish, slaw, guacamole, and tomatoes to each corn tortilla. 10. Enjoy.
Per Serving: Calories:240; Fat:8g, Sodium:564mg; Fiber:5g, Carbs: 25g, Sugar: 3g; Protein:14g

Cod Stew Vegetables

Prep time: 15 minutes | Cook Time: 10 minutes | Serves: 4

3 tablespoons olive oil
1 medium onion, peeled and diced
1 stalk celery, diced
1 medium carrot, peeled and chopped
2 cloves garlic, peeled and minced
1 tablespoon chopped fresh oregano
½ teaspoon ground fennel
1 sprig fresh thyme
1 (14.5-ounce) can diced tomatoes
1½ cups vegetable broth
1-pound cod fillets, cut into 1"

pieces
⅓ cup sliced green olives
¼ teaspoon ground black pepper
2 tablespoons chopped fresh dill

1. Insert the pot into the Cooker Base without the lid. 2. Select Sauté mode and then press the same button again and then adjust the cooking temperature to Normal. 3. When the display switches On to Hot, heat the oil; add the onion, celery, carrot and cook for 6 minutes until tender; add the garlic, oregano, fennel, thyme and cook for 30 seconds; lastly, stir in the tomatoes and vegetable broth. 4. Press Cancel button to stop this cooking program. 5. Place and close the lid in right way. 6. Select Pressure Cook mode. Press Pressure Cook button again to adjust the cooking time to 3 minutes; press Pressure Level to choose High Pressure. 7. When the time is up, quickly and carefully turn the steam release handle from the Sealing position to the Venting position. 8. When released, press Cancel button to stop this cooking program. 9. Still in the Inner Pot, add the fish, olives, pepper and cook for 3 to 5 minutes on Sauté mode at Normal cooking temperature. 10. When done, sprinkle with dill and serve.
Per Serving: Calories:200; Fat:16g, Sodium:379mg; Fiber:3g, Carbs: 14g, Sugar: 8g; Protein:7g

Spinach Fish Rice

Prep time: 15 minutes | Cook Time: 5 minutes | Serves: 4

1 cup water
1 cup white rice
1 tablespoon light olive oil
4 (4-ounce) cod or other white fish fillets
½ teaspoon salt
½ teaspoon ground black pepper
2 cups baby spinach
2 tablespoons extra-virgin olive oil
4 lemon wedges

1. Season the fillets with salt and pepper. 2. Prepare 4 pieces of large foil, lay the spinach and fillets on them separately; drizzle with extra-virgin olive oil and squeeze juice from lemon wedges. 3. Carefully wrap fillet loosely in foil. 4. In the Inner Pot, add the rice, light olive oil and water; place the Steam Rack in it and put the suitable steamer basket on the rack, then place the foil pouches on the basket. 5. Place and close the lid rightly. 6. Select Steam mode. Press the button again to adjust the cooking time to 5 minutes; press Pressure Level to choose High Pressure. 7. When the time is up, quickly and carefully turn the steam release handle from the Sealing position to the Venting position. 8. When released, carefully take out the pouches. 9. Divide rice into four servings, then enjoy with the fillets and spinach.
Per Serving: Calories:266; Fat:18g, Sodium:799mg; Fiber:1g, Carbs: 12g, Sugar: 0g; Protein:16g

Mediterranean Cod with Roma Tomato

Prep time: 15 minutes | Cook Time: 6 minutes | Serves: 2

1 cup water
2 (5-ounce) cod fillets
2 teaspoons olive oil
½ teaspoon salt
10 Kalamata olives, pitted and
halved
1 small Roma tomato, diced
3 tablespoons chopped fresh basil leaves, divided

1. Prepare a 10" × 10" square of aluminum foil and place each cod piece on it; drizzle each fillet with 1 teaspoon of oil and sprinkle with ¼ teaspoon of salt; top them 5 olives, half of the tomatoes and 1 tablespoon of basil; lift the sides of the foil and crimp on top to form a foil pouch. 2. In the Inner Pot, add the water and place the Steam Rack, then arrange the foil pouches to the rack. 3. Place and close the lid rightly. 4. Select Pressure Cook mode. Press the button again to adjust the cooking time to 6 minutes; press Pressure Level to choose High Pressure. 5. When the time is up, quickly and carefully turn the steam release handle from the Sealing position to the Venting position. 6. When released, remove the pouches out of the pot and transfer the fillets to 2 plates. 7. Enjoy with the remaining basil.
Per Serving: Calories:148; Fat:9g, Sodium:1202mg; Fiber:0g, Carbs: 1g, Sugar: 1g; Protein:18g

Spiced Salmon with Parsley

Prep time: 15 minutes | Cook Time: 3 minutes | Serves: 4

1 cup water
4 (4-ounce) skin-on salmon fillets
½ teaspoon salt
½ teaspoon ground black pepper
¼ cup chopped fresh dill
1 small lemon, thinly sliced
2 tablespoons extra-virgin olive oil
1 tablespoon chopped fresh parsley

1. Season the fish fillets with salt and pepper. 2. In the Inner Pot, add the water and place the Steam Rack. 3. Transfer the fish fillets to the rack, top them with the dill and 2-3 lemon slices. 4. Place and close the lid rightly. 5. Select Steam mode. Press Steam button again to adjust the cooking time to 3 minutes; press Pressure Level to choose High Pressure. 6. When the time is up, quickly and carefully turn the steam release handle from the Sealing position to the Venting position. 7. When released, serve the fillets on a plate; drizzle with the olive and garnish with the fresh parsley. 8. Enjoy.
Per Serving: Calories:160; Fat:9g, Sodium:545mg; Fiber:0g, Carbs: 0g, Sugar: 0g; Protein:19g

Simple and Delicious Halibut Fillets

Prep time: 15 minutes | Cook Time: 5 minutes | Serves: 2

1 cup chopped broccoli
1 large potato, peeled and diced
1 large carrot, peeled and grated
1 small zucchini, trimmed and grated
4 ounces' mushrooms, sliced
¼ teaspoon dried thyme
¼ teaspoon grated lemon zest
1 (½-pound) halibut fillet
½ cup white wine
½ cup lemon juice
1 teaspoon dried parsley
¼ teaspoon salt
¼ teaspoon ground black pepper
⅛ teaspoon ground nutmeg

1. In the Inner Pot, place the Steam Rack and then arrange the suitable steamer basket to the rack. 2. On the basket, place the broccoli, potato, carrot, zucchini, mushrooms and then sprinkle with the thyme and lemon zest. 3. Arrange the fillets over the vegetables, pour the lemon juice and wine, then sprinkle the parsley, salt and black pepper. 4. Place and close the lid rightly. 5. Select Pressure Cook mode. Press the button again to adjust the cooking time to 5 minutes; press Pressure Level to choose High Pressure. 6. When the time is up, quickly and carefully turn the steam release handle from the Sealing position to the Venting position. 7. When released, take out the food and divide them between 2 plates. 8. Sprinkle with the nutmeg and enjoy.
Per Serving: Calories:278; Fat:3g, Sodium:409mg; Fiber:5g, Carbs: 23g, Sugar: 4g; Protein:31g

Steamed Lemon Cod

Prep time: 15 minutes | Cook Time: 3 minutes | Serves: 4

1 cup water
4 (4-ounce) cod fillets, rinsed and patted dry
½ teaspoon ground black pepper
1 small lemon, thinly sliced
2 tablespoons extra-virgin olive oil
¼ cup chopped fresh parsley
2 tablespoons capers
1 tablespoon chopped fresh chives

1. Season the fish fillets with pepper and top each fillet with 3 lemon slices. 2. In the Inner Pot, add the water and place the Steam Rack, then arrange the fillets to the rack. 3. Place and close the lid rightly. 4. Select Steam mode. Press Steam button again to adjust the cooking time to 3 minutes; press Pressure Level to choose High Pressure. 5. While cooking, in a small bowl, thoroughly mix up the olive oil, parsley, capers and chives. 6. When the time is up, quickly and carefully turn the steam release handle from the Sealing position to the Venting position. 7. When done, transfer the fillets to a plate and discard the lemon slices. 8. Drizzle the fillets with the chives mixture and make sure each one is coated well. 9. Enjoy.
Per Serving: Calories:140; Fat:10g, Sodium:370mg; Fiber:0g, Carbs: 0g, Sugar: 0g; Protein:14g

Steamed Crabs in Sauce

Prep time: 15 minutes | Cook Time: 3 minutes | Serves: 2

2 tablespoons garlic chili sauce
1 tablespoon hoisin sauce
1 tablespoon minced fresh ginger
1 teaspoon fish sauce
2 cloves garlic, peeled and
minced
2 small bird's eye chilies, minced
2 (2-pound) Dungeness crabs
1 cup water

1. In a suitable bowl, thoroughly mix up the garlic chili sauce, hoisin sauce, ginger, fish sauce, garlic, and chilies; coat the crabs with mixture well and then arrange them to the Steam Rack. 2. In the Inner Pot, add the water and place the Steam Rack, then close the lid in right way 3. Select Pressure Cook mode. Press Pressure Cook button again to adjust the cooking time to 3 minutes; press Pressure Level to choose High Pressure. 4. When the time is up, quickly and carefully turn the steam release handle from the Sealing position to the Venting position. 5. When done, serve the crabs on a clean plate and enjoy.
Per Serving: Calories:128; Fat:1g, Sodium:619mg; Fiber:0g, Carbs: 1g, Sugar: 1g; Protein:25g

Dijon Halibut with Pistachio

Prep time: 15 minutes | Cook Time: 6 minutes | Serves: 2

1 tablespoon Dijon mustard
1 teaspoon lemon juice
2 tablespoons panko bread crumbs
¼ cup chopped unsalted
pistachios
¼ teaspoon salt
2 (5-ounce) halibut fillets
1 cup water

1. Prepare a baking sheet and line a piece of parchment paper on it. 2. In a suitable bowl, thoroughly mix up the mustard, lemon juice, bread crumbs, pistachios and salt to form a thick paste. 3. Use a paper towel to pat the fillets dry; rub the paste on the top of each fillet and place and then place them on the Steam Rack. 4. In the Inner Pot, add water and transfer the rack to it; place and close the lid rightly. 5. Select Pressure Cook mode. Press Pressure Cook button again to adjust the cooking time to 5 minutes; press Pressure Level to choose High Pressure. 6. While cooking, prepare a baking sheet and line a piece of parchment paper on it; preheat your broiler. 7. When the time is up, quickly and carefully turn the steam release handle from the Sealing position to the Venting position. 8. When released, transfer the fillets to the baking sheet; broil them in the broiler for 1 to 2 minutes until the tops are browned. 9. When done, serve and enjoy.
Per Serving: Calories:235; Fat:9g, Sodium:411mg; Fiber:2g, Carbs: 4g, Sugar: 1g; Protein:35g

Spiced Catfish with Tomatoes

Prep time: 15 minutes | Cook Time: 5 minutes | Serves: 4

1 (1½-pound) catfish fillet, rinsed in cold water, patted dry, cut into bite-sized pieces
1 (14.5-ounce) can diced tomatoes
2 teaspoons dried minced onion
¼ teaspoon onion powder
1 teaspoon dried minced garlic
¼ teaspoon garlic powder
1 teaspoon hot paprika
¼ teaspoon dried tarragon
1 medium green bell pepper, seeded and diced
1 stalk celery, finely diced
¼ teaspoon sugar
½ cup chili sauce
½ teaspoon salt
½ teaspoon ground black pepper

1. In the Inner Pot, mix up all of the ingredients. 2. Place and close the lid in right way. 3. Select Pressure Cook mode. Press the button again to adjust the cooking time to 5 minutes; press Pressure Level to choose High Pressure. 4. When the time is up, quickly and carefully turn the steam release handle from the Sealing position to the Venting position. 5. When released, stir gently; serve and enjoy.
Per Serving: Calories:284; Fat:9g, Sodium:696mg; Fiber:3g, Carbs: 7g, Sugar: 4g; Protein:31g

Lemon Crab Orzo with Parmesan Cheese

Prep time: 15 minutes | Cook Time: 5 minutes | Serves: 4

2 tablespoons light olive oil
1 medium shallot, peeled and minced
1 clove garlic, peeled and minced
¼ cup chopped fresh flat-leaf parsley
2 tablespoons chopped fresh basil
¼ teaspoon salt
¼ teaspoon ground black pepper
2 cups water
8 ounces' orzo
8 ounces' jumbo lump crabmeat
1 tablespoon lemon juice
¼ cup grated Parmesan cheese

1. Insert the pot into the Cooker Base without the lid. 2. Select Sauté mode and then press the same button again and then adjust the cooking temperature to Normal. 3. When the display switches On to Hot, heat the oil; add the shallot and garlic and cook for 1 minute until fragrant; stir in the parsley, basil, salt and pepper; add water and pasta. 4. Press Cancel button to stop this cooking program. 5. Place and close the lid in right way. 6. Select Pressure Cook mode. Press Pressure Cook button again to adjust the cooking time to 4 minutes; press Pressure Level to choose High Pressure. 7. When the time is up, quickly and carefully turn the steam release handle from the Sealing position to the Venting position. 8. When released, add the crab and lemon juice, stir lightly to combine. 9. Without the lid, Keep Warm the food for 10 minutes to heat the crab. 10. When done, top with the cheese and serve.
Per Serving: Calories:367; Fat:12g, Sodium:531mg; Fiber:3g, Carbs: 43g, Sugar: 1g; Protein:24g

Herbed River Trout

Prep time: 15 minutes | Cook Time: 3 minutes | Serves: 4

4 (½-pound) fresh river trout, rinsed and patted dry
1 teaspoon salt, divided
1 teaspoon white wine vinegar
½ cup water
½ cup minced fresh flat-leaf parsley
2 tablespoons chopped fresh oregano
1 teaspoon fresh thyme leaves
1 small shallot, peeled and minced
2 tablespoons olive oil
½ teaspoon lemon juice

1. Season the trout inside and out with ¾ teaspoon of salt. 2. In the Inner Pot, stir in the vinegar and water; place the Steam Rack and then arrange the trout to the rack. 3. Place and close the lid in right way. 4. Select Pressure Cook mode. Press the button again to adjust the cooking time to 3 minutes; press Pressure Level to choose High Pressure. 5. When the time is up, leave the steam release handle in the Sealing position. 6. Transfer the trout to a plate with a spatula, peel and discard the skin and heads. 7. In a small bowl, thoroughly mix up the parsley, oregano, thyme, shallot, olive oil, lemon juice and the remaining salt. 8. Pour the mixture over the trout and enjoy.
Per Serving: Calories:344; Fat:18g, Sodium:581mg; Fiber:0g, Carbs: 1g, Sugar: 0g; Protein:45g

Mustard Fish Fillets with Lemon Wedges

Prep time: 15 minutes | Cook Time: 3 minutes | Serves: 4

1 cup water
4 (4-ounce) cod or other white fish fillets
2 tablespoons Dijon mustard
2 tablespoons chopped fresh dill
2 tablespoons chopped fresh chives
½ teaspoon salt
½ teaspoon ground black pepper
1 small lemon, cut into wedges

1. In the Inner Pot, add the water and place the Steam Rack. 2. Brush the fish fillets with the Dijon mustard; sprinkle each fillet with dill, chives and season with salt and pepper, then arrange them to the rack. 3. Place and close the lid in right way. 4. Select Steam mode. Press the button again to adjust the cooking time to 3 minutes; press Pressure Level to choose High Pressure. 5. When the time is up, quickly and carefully turn the steam release handle from the Sealing position to the Venting position. 6. When released, take out the fillets. 7. With the lemon wedges, serve and enjoy.

Per Serving: Calories:80; Fat:3g, Sodium:765mg; Fiber:0g, Carbs: 0g, Sugar: 0g; Protein:14g

Delectable Orange Roughy Fillets

Prep time: 15 minutes | Cook Time: 5 minutes | Serves: 2

⅜ cup dry white wine
⅜ cup water
2 (8-ounce) orange roughy fillets, rinsed and patted dry
¼ teaspoon salt
4 thin slices white onion, divided
6 sprigs fresh dill, divided
3 tablespoons unsalted butter, melted
4 teaspoons lime juice
6 Kalamata olives, pitted and chopped

1. Sprinkle the fillets with salt 2. In the Inner Pot, add the water and place the Steam Rack; place 2 onion slices on the rack and top each slice with a dill sprig. 3. Arrange the fillets to the rack, top each fillet with a dill sprig and the remaining onion slices. 4. Place and close the lid rightly. 5. Select Pressure Cook mode. Press the button again to adjust the cooking time to 5 minutes; press Pressure Level to choose High Pressure. 6. When the time is up, quickly and carefully turn the steam release handle from the Sealing position to the Venting position. 7. In a small bowl, mix up the butter, lime juice, and ½ tablespoon cooking liquid from the fillet; stir in the olives. 8. Add the sauce over the fillets and garnish with the remaining dill sprigs; enjoy.
Per Serving: Calories:337; Fat:21g, Sodium:650mg; Fiber:0g, Carbs: 1g, Sugar: 0g; Protein:37g

Steamed Cilantro Lime Salmon

Prep time: 15 minutes | Cook Time: 3 minutes | Serves: 4

1 cup water
4 (4-ounce) skin-on salmon fillets, about 1 pound
¼ teaspoon ground cumin
¼ teaspoon smoked paprika
¼ teaspoon salt
¼ teaspoon ground black pepper
¼ cup chopped fresh cilantro
1 small lime, thinly sliced
2 tablespoons extra-virgin olive oil

1. Season the salmon fillets with the cumin, paprika, salt and black pepper; top each fillet with the cilantro and 2-3 lime slice. 2. In the Inner Pot, add the water and place the Steam Rack, then arrange the fillets to the rack. 3. Place and close the lid in right way. 4. Select Steam mode. Press the button again to adjust the cooking time to 3 minutes; press Pressure Level to choose High Pressure. 5. When the time is up, quickly and carefully turn the steam release handle from the Sealing position to the Venting position. 6. When released, serve and fillets on a plate and then drizzle with the olive oil. 7. Enjoy.
Per Serving: Calories:100; Fat:3g, Sodium:398mg; Fiber:0g, Carbs: 0g, Sugar: 0g; Protein:19g

Herbed Fish Packets

Prep time: 15 minutes | Cook Time: 5 minutes | Serves: 4

1 cup water
4 (4-ounce) halibut or other white fish fillets
½ teaspoon salt
½ teaspoon ground black pepper
1 small lemon, thinly sliced
¼ cup chopped fresh dill
¼ cup chopped fresh chives
2 tablespoons chopped fresh tarragon
2 tablespoons extra-virgin olive oil

1. Season the fillets with salt and pepper. 2. Prepare 4 pieces of large foil, lay the fillets on them separately; top the fillets with the lemon, dill, chives, and tarragon and drizzle each with olive oil. 3. Carefully wrap fillet loosely in foil. 4. In the Inner Pot, add the water and place the Steam Rack, then arrange the fillet pouches to the rack. 5. Place and close the lid rightly. 6. Select Steam mode. Press the button again to adjust the cooking time to 5 minutes; press Pressure Level to choose High Pressure. 7. When the time is up, quickly and carefully turn the steam release handle from the Sealing position to the Venting position. 8. When done, serve and enjoy.
Per Serving: Calories:185; Fat:9g, Sodium:355mg; Fiber:0g, Carbs: 0g, Sugar: 0g; Protein:23g

Calamari with Pimentos

Prep time: 20 minutes | Cook time: 25 minutes | Serves: 4

3 Pimentos, stem and core removed
2 tablespoons olive oil
½ cup leeks, chopped
2 cloves garlic chopped
1 ½ cups stock, preferably homemade
2 tablespoons fish sauce
⅓ cup dry sherry
Seas salt and black pepper, to taste
½ teaspoon red pepper flakes, crushed
1 teaspoon dried rosemary, chopped
1 teaspoon dried thyme, chopped
1½-pound frozen calamari, thawed and drained
2 tablespoons fresh chives, chopped

1. Split your Pimentos into halves and place them over the flame. 2. Cook, turning a couple of times, until the skin is blistering and blackened. 3. Allow them to stand for 30 minutes; peel your Pimentos and chop them. 4. Press the "Sauté" button two times to select "Normal" settings to heat up your Inner Pot; add olive oil. 5. Once hot, cook the leeks until tender and fragrant, about 4 minutes. 6. Now, stir in the garlic and cook an additional 30 seconds or until just browned and aromatic. 7. Add the stock, fish sauce, dry sherry, salt, pepper, red pepper flakes, rosemary, and thyme. 8. Add the roasted Pimentos. Lastly, place the calamari on top. Pour in 3 cups of water. 9. Put on the pressure cooker's lid and turn the steam valve to "Sealing" position. 10. Select Pressure Cook mode, and then press the "Pressure Cook" button again to select "Less" time option. 11. Use the "+/-" keys on the control panel to set the cooking time to 20 minutes. 12. Press the Pressure Level button to adjust the pressure to "High Pressure." 13. Once the cooking cycle is completed, quickly and carefully turn the steam release handle from Sealing position to the Venting position. 14. When all the steam is released, remove the pressure lid from the top carefully. 15. Serve warm garnished with fresh chopped chives. Enjoy!
Per Serving: Calories 412; Fat 20g; Sodium 491mg; Carbs 9g; Fiber 3g; Sugar 8g; Protein 31g

Curried Halibut Steaks

Prep time: 20 minutes | Cook time: 10 minutes | Serves: 4

1 tablespoon olive oil
1 cup scallions, chopped
½ cup beef bone broth
1-pound halibut steaks, rinsed and cubed
1 cup tomato purée
1 jalapeño pepper, seeded and
minced
1 teaspoon ginger garlic paste
1 tablespoon red curry paste
½ teaspoons ground cumin
1 cup coconut milk, unsweetened
Salt and black pepper, to taste

1. Press the "Sauté" button two times to select "Normal" settings 2. Now, heat the olive oil; cook the scallions until tender and fragrant. 3. Then, use the broth to deglaze the bottom of the Inner Pot. Stir in the remaining ingredients. 4. Put on the pressure cooker's lid and turn the steam valve to "Sealing" position. 5. Select Pressure Cook mode, and then press the "Pressure Cook" button again to select "Less" time option. 6. Use the "+/-" keys on the control panel to set the cooking time to 7 minutes. 7. Press the Pressure Level button to adjust the pressure to "High Pressure." 8. Once the cooking cycle is completed, quickly and carefully turn the steam release handle from Sealing position to the Venting position. 9. When all the steam is released, remove the pressure lid from the top carefully. 10. Taste, adjust the seasonings and serve right now.
Per Serving: Calories 334; Fat 7.9g; Sodium 704mg; Carbs 6g; Fiber 3.6g; Sugar 6g; Protein 18g

Carp Pilaf

Prep time: 20 minutes | Cook time: 6 minutes | Serves: 4

1 tablespoon olive oil
1 cup chicken stock
1 cup tomato paste
1 teaspoon dried rosemary, crushed
1 tablespoon dried parsley
½ teaspoons dried marjoram leaves
Sea salt and black pepper, to taste
½ teaspoons dried oregano leaves

1 cup Arborio rice
1-pound carp, chopped

1. Simply throw all of the above ingredients into your Inner Pot. 2. Put on the pressure cooker's lid and turn the steam valve to "Sealing" position. 3. Select Pressure Cook mode, and then press the "Pressure Cook" button again to select "Less" time option. 4. Use the "+/-" keys on the control panel to set the cooking time to 6 minutes. 5. Press the Pressure Level button to adjust the pressure to "High Pressure." 6. Once the cooking cycle is completed, quickly and carefully turn the steam release handle from Sealing position to the Venting position. 7. When all the steam is released, remove the pressure lid from the top carefully. 8. Serve in individual serving bowls, garnished with fresh lemon slices.
Per Serving: Calories 421; Fat 7.9g; Sodium 704mg; Carbs 6g; Fiber 3.6g; Sugar 6g; Protein 18g

Mediterranean Fish Stew with Hot Sauce

Prep time: 15 minutes | Cook Time: 12 minutes | Serves: 4

4 tablespoons olive oil
1 medium yellow onion, peeled and diced
2 cloves garlic, peeled and minced
½ teaspoon dried oregano leaves
½ teaspoon ground fennel
¼ teaspoon dried thyme leaves
1 (14.5-ounce) can diced tomatoes
1 cup seafood stock
½ cup white wine
1-pound white fish fillets, such as halibut or sea bass, cut into 2" pieces
¼ teaspoon salt
¼ teaspoon ground black pepper
½ teaspoon hot sauce

1. Insert the pot into the Cooker Base without the lid. 2. Select Sauté mode and then press the same button again and then adjust the cooking temperature to Normal. 3. When the display switches On to Hot, add and heat the oil; add the onion and cook for 4 minutes or until soft; add the garlic, oregano, fennel, thyme and cook for 30 seconds; lastly, stir in the tomatoes, seafood stock, and wine. 4. Press Cancel button to stop this cooking program. 5. Place and close the lid in right way. 6. Select Pressure Cook mode. Press Pressure Cook button again to adjust the cooking time to 3 minutes; press Pressure Level to choose High Pressure. 7. When the time is up, quickly and carefully turn the steam release handle from the Sealing position to the Venting position. 8. When released, press Cancel button to stop this cooking program. 9. Still in the Inner Pot, add fish and cook at Normal cooking temperature on Sauté for 5 minutes, until the fish is opaque. 10. When done, season with the salt and pepper; serve with the hot sauce.
Per Serving: Calories:282; Fat:15g, Sodium:456mg; Fiber:2g, Carbs: 8g, Sugar: 5g; Protein:26g

Tilapia Fillets with Mushrooms

Prep time: 20 minutes | Cook time: 10 minutes | Serves: 3

3 tilapia fillets
½ teaspoons sea salt
Black pepper, to taste
1 teaspoon cayenne pepper
1 cup Cremini mushrooms, thinly sliced
½ cup yellow onions, sliced
2 cloves garlic, peeled and minced
2 sprigs thyme, leaves picked
2 sprigs rosemary, leaves picked
2 tablespoons avocado oil

1. Season the tilapia fillets with salt, black pepper, and cayenne pepper on all sides. 2. Place the tilapia fillets in the steaming basket fitted for your Inner Pot. 3. Place the sliced mushroom and yellow onions on top of the fillets. 4. Add the garlic, thyme, and rosemary; drizzle avocado oil over everything. 5. Add 1 ½ cups of water to the base of your Inner Pot. 5. Add the steaming basket to the Inner Pot and Put on the pressure cooker's lid and turn the steam valve to "Sealing" position. 6. Select Pressure Cook mode, and then press the "Pressure Cook" button again to select "Less" time option. 7. Use the "+/-" keys on the control panel to set the cooking time to 8 minutes. 8. Press the Pressure Level button to adjust the pressure to "Low Pressure." 9. Once the cooking cycle is completed, quickly and carefully turn the steam release handle from Sealing position to the Venting position. 10. When all the steam is released, remove the pressure lid from the top carefully. 11. Serve immediately.
Per Serving: Calories 472; Fat 12.9g; Sodium 414mg; Carbs 11g; Fiber 5g; Sugar 9g; Protein 31g

Shrimp in Tomato Sauce

Prep time: 20 minutes | Cook time: 5 minutes | Serves: 4

1 tablespoon butter, at room temperature	deveined
1 cup green onion, chopped	1 tablespoon tamari sauce
1 teaspoon garlic, minced	1 sprig thyme
1½-pound shrimp, peeled and	1 sprig rosemary
	2 ripe tomatoes, chopped

1. Press the "Sauté" button two times to select "Normal" settings 2. Melt the butter and cook the green onions until they have softened. 3. Now, stir in the garlic and cook an additional 30 seconds or until it is aromatic. 4. Add the rest of the above ingredients. 5. Put on the pressure cooker's lid and turn the steam valve to "Sealing" position. 6. Select Pressure Cook mode, and then press the "Pressure Cook" button again to select "Less" time option. 7. Use the "+/-" keys on the control panel to set the cooking time to 3 minutes. 8. Press the Pressure Level button to adjust the pressure to "Low Pressure." 9. Once the cooking cycle is completed, allow the steam to release naturally. 10. When all the steam is released, remove the pressure lid from the top carefully. 11. Serve over hot jasmine rice and enjoy!
Per Serving: Calories 427; Fat 10.9g; Sodium 454mg; Carbs 10g; Fiber 3.1g; Sugar 5.2g; Protein 20g

Tuna Fillets with Eschalots

Prep time: 20 minutes | Cook time: 5 minutes | Serves: 4

2 lemons, 1 whole and 1 cutted	1 tablespoon dried parsley flakes
1-pound tuna fillets	2 tablespoons butter, melted
Sea salt and black pepper, to taste	2 eschalots, thinly sliced

1. Place 1 cup of water and lemon juice in the Inner Pot. Add a steamer basket too. 2. Place the tuna fillets in the steamer basket. 3. Sprinkle the salt, pepper, and parsley over the fish; drizzle with butter and top with thinly sliced eschalots. 4. Put on the pressure cooker's lid and turn the steam valve to "Sealing" position. 5. Press the "Steam" button one time to select "Less" option. 6. Use the "+/-" keys on the control panel to set the cooking time to 3 minutes. 7. Press the Pressure Level button to adjust the pressure to "High Pressure." 8. Once the cooking cycle is completed, quickly and carefully turn the steam release handle from Sealing position to the Venting position. 9. When all the steam is released, remove the pressure lid from the top carefully. 10. Serve immediately with lemon. Bon appétit!
Per Serving: Calories 219; Fat 10g; Sodium 891mg; Carbs 22.9g; Fiber 4g; Sugar 4g; Protein 23g

Chunky Tilapia Stew

Prep time: 20 minutes | Cook time: 10 minutes | Serves: 2

2 tablespoons sesame oil	to taste
1 cup scallions, chopped	1 teaspoon hot paprika
2 garlic cloves, minced	1-pound tilapia fillets, boneless,
⅓ cup dry vermouth	skinless and diced
1 cup shellfish stock	1 tablespoon fresh lime juice
2 cups water	1 teaspoon dried rosemary
2 ripe plum tomatoes, crushed	½ teaspoons dried oregano
Sea salt, to taste	½ teaspoons dried basil
¼ teaspoon black pepper, or more	

1. Press the "Sauté" button two times to select "Normal" settings. 2. Heat the oil and sauté the scallions and garlic until fragrant. 3. Add a splash of vermouth to deglaze the bottom of the Inner Pot. 4. Put on the pressure cooker's lid and turn the steam valve to "Sealing" position. 5. Select Pressure Cook mode, and then press the "Pressure Cook" button again to select "Less" time option. 6. Use the "+/-" keys on the control panel to set the cooking time to 5 minutes. 7. Press the Pressure Level button to adjust the pressure to "High Pressure." 8. Once the cooking cycle is completed, quickly and carefully turn the steam release handle from Sealing position to the Venting position. 9. When all the steam is released, remove the pressure lid from the top carefully. 10. Serve with some extra lime slices if desired. Bon appétit!
Per Serving: Calories 414; Fat 10.9g; Sodium 354mg; Carbs 10.5g;

Fiber 4.1g; Sugar 8.2g; Protein 26g

Cod Fish with Goat Cheese

Prep time: 20 minutes | Cook time: 5 minutes | Serves: 4

1-pound baby potatoes	2 tablespoons fresh Italian
2 tablespoons coconut oil, at room temperature	parsley, chopped
Sea salt and pepper, to taste	½ teaspoons fresh ginger, grated
1½-pound cod fish fillets	2 cloves garlic, minced
½ teaspoons smoked paprika	1 cup goat cheese, crumbled

1. Place the potatoes in the bottom of the Inner Pot. 2. Add 1 cup of water; then, add coconut oil, salt and pepper. Place the rack over the potatoes. 3. Place the cod fish fillets on the rack. Season the fillets with paprika and parsley. 4. Put on the pressure cooker's lid and turn the steam valve to "Sealing" position. 5. Press the "Steam" button two times to select "Less" option. 6. Press the Pressure Level button to adjust the pressure to "Low Pressure." 7. Once the cooking cycle is completed, quickly and carefully turn the steam release handle from Sealing position to the Venting position. 8. When all the steam is released, remove the pressure lid from the top carefully. 9. Continue to cook the potatoes until fork tender; add the ginger and garlic and cook for 2 minutes more. 10. Top with goat cheese and serve. Bon appétit!
Per Serving: Calories 449; Fat 2.9g; Sodium 511mg; Carbs 12g; Fiber 3g; Sugar 8g; Protein 27g

Tuna Fillets with Onions

Prep time: 20 minutes | Cook time: 5 minutes | Serves: 2

1 cup water	1 tablespoon butter, melted
A few sprigs of tarragon	Sea salt and black pepper, to taste
1 lemon, sliced	1 large onion, sliced into rings
1-pound tuna filets	

1. Put the water, herbs and lemon slices in the Inner Pot; now, place the steamer rack in the Inner Pot. 2. Lower the tuna fillets onto the rack. Add butter, salt, and pepper; top with onion slices. 3. Put on the pressure cooker's lid and turn the steam valve to "Sealing" position. 4. Press the "Steam" button two times to select "Less" option. 5. Press the Pressure Level button to adjust the pressure to "Low Pressure." 6. Once the cooking cycle is completed, quickly and carefully turn the steam release handle from Sealing position to the Venting position. 7. When all the steam is released, remove the pressure lid from the top carefully. 8. Serve immediately.
Per Serving: Calories 489; Fat 11g; Sodium 501mg; Carbs 8.9g; Fiber 4.6g; Sugar 8g; Protein 26g

Butter Grouper

Prep time: 20 minutes | Cook time: 5 minutes | Serves: 4

4 grouper fillets	½ teaspoons sweet paprika
4 tablespoons butter	½ teaspoons dried basil
2 tablespoons fresh lemon juice	Sea salt and black pepper, to taste
2 garlic cloves, smashed	

1. Add 1 ½ cups of water and steamer basket to the Inner Pot. 2. Then, place the fish fillets in the steamer basket. 3. Add the butter; drizzle with lemon juice; add the garlic, paprika, basil, salt, and black pepper. 4. Put on the pressure cooker's lid and turn the steam valve to "Sealing" position. 5. Select Pressure Cook mode, and then press the "Pressure Cook" button again to select "Less" time option. 6. Use the "+/-" keys on the control panel to set the cooking time to 4 minutes. 7. Press the Pressure Level button to adjust the pressure to "Low Pressure." 8. Once the cooking cycle is completed, quickly and carefully turn the steam release handle from Sealing position to the Venting position. 9. When all the steam is released, remove the pressure lid from the top carefully. 10. Serve immediately.
Per Serving: Calories 361; Fat 7.9g; Sodium 704mg; Carbs 6g; Fiber 3.6g; Sugar 6g; Protein 18g

Haddock Fillets with Black Beans

Prep time: 20 minutes | Cook time: 5 minutes | Serves: 2

1 cup water	½ teaspoons tarragon
2 haddock fillets	½ teaspoons paprika
2 teaspoons coconut butter, at room temperature	4 tomato slices
Salt and black pepper, to taste	2 tablespoons fresh cilantro, roughly chopped
2 sprigs thyme, chopped	1 can black beans, drained
¼ teaspoon caraway seeds	

1. Add 1 cup of water to the bottom of your Inner Pot. Add a steamer insert. 2. Brush the haddock fillets with coconut butter. Now, season the haddock fillets with salt and pepper. 3. Place the haddock fillets on top of the steamer insert. 4. Add thyme, caraway seeds, tarragon, and paprika. Place 2 tomato slices on top of each fillet. 5. Put on the pressure cooker's lid and turn the steam valve to "Sealing" position. 6. Select Pressure Cook mode, and then press the "Pressure Cook" button again to select "Less" time option. 7. Use the "+/-" keys on the control panel to set the cooking time to 3 minutes. 8. Press the Pressure Level button to adjust the pressure to "Low Pressure." 9. Once the cooking cycle is completed, allow the steam to release naturally. 10. When all the steam is released, remove the pressure lid from the top carefully. 11. Transfer the haddock fillets to serving plates. 12. Scatter chopped cilantro over each fillet and serve garnished with black beans. Bon appétit!
Per Serving: Calories 412; Fat 20g; Sodium 491mg; Carbs 9g; Fiber 3g; Sugar 8g; Protein 31g

Trout Salad

Prep time: 20 minutes | Cook time: 15 minutes | Serves: 4

2 tablespoons olive oil	Sea salt and black pepper, to taste
1 yellow onion, chopped	½ teaspoons sweet paprika
2 garlic cloves, minced	2 ripe Roma tomatoes, diced
1 green chili, seeded and minced	8-ounce dry egg noodles
2 pieces' ocean trout fillets, deboned and skinless	2 Lebanese cucumbers, chopped
1 cup water	½ bunch coriander, leaves picked, roughly chopped
½ cup dry vermouth	¼ cup lime juice

1. Press the "Sauté" button two times to select "Normal" settings 2. Now, heat the olive oil and sauté the onion until translucent. 3. Stir in the garlic and chili; continue to sauté until they are fragrant. 4. Add the fish, water, vermouth, salt, black pepper, sweet paprika, tomatoes, and noodles. 5. Put on the pressure cooker's lid and turn the steam valve to "Sealing" position. 6. Select Pressure Cook mode, and then press the "Pressure Cook" button again to select "Less" time option. 7. Use the "+/-" keys on the control panel to set the cooking time to 10 minutes. 8. Press the Pressure Level button to adjust the pressure to "Low Pressure." 9. Once the cooking cycle is completed, quickly and carefully turn the steam release handle from Sealing position to the Venting position. 10. When all the steam is released, remove the pressure lid from the top carefully. 11. Flake the fish and allow the mixture to cool completely. Add the cucumbers and coriander. 12. Drizzle fresh lime juice over the salad and serve. Bon appétit!
Per Serving: Calories 419; Fat 14g; Sodium 791mg; Carbs 8.9g; Fiber 4.6g; Sugar 8g; Protein 31g

Foil-Packet Fish with Aioli

Prep time: 20 minutes | Cook time: 15 minutes | Serves: 2

2 cod fish fillets	1 lemon, cut into slices
½ teaspoons seasoned salt	For Aioli:
¼ teaspoon black pepper, or more to taste	1 egg yolk
½ teaspoons mustard powder	A pinch of salt
½ teaspoons ancho chili powder	2 garlic cloves, minced
1 shallot, thinly sliced	2 teaspoons fresh lemon juice
	¼ cup olive oil

1. Prepare your Inner Pot by adding 1 ½ cups of water and steamer basket to the Inner Pot. 2. Place a fish fillet in the center of each piece of foil. 3. Season with salt, pepper, mustard powder, and chili powder. 4. Top with shallots and wrap tightly. 5. Put on the pressure cooker's lid and turn the steam valve to "Sealing" position. 6. Select Pressure Cook mode, and then press the "Pressure Cook" button again to select "Less" time option. 7. Use the "+/-" keys on the control panel to set the cooking time to 10 minutes. 8. Press the Pressure Level button to adjust the pressure to "High Pressure." 9. Once the cooking cycle is completed, allow the steam to release naturally. 10. When all the steam is released, remove the pressure lid from the top carefully. 11. In your food processor, mix the egg, salt, garlic, and lemon juice. 12. With the machine running, gradually and slowly add the olive oil. 13. Garnish the warm fish fillets with lemon slices; serve with aioli on the side. Bon appétit!
Per Serving: Calories 584; Fat 15g; Sodium 441mg; Carbs 17g; Fiber 4.6g; Sugar 5g; Protein 29g

Baked Fish with Parmesan

Prep time: 20 minutes | Cook time: 9 minutes | Serves: 2

2 ripe tomatoes, sliced	2 tablespoons butter, at room temperature
1 teaspoon dried rosemary	Sea salt and black pepper, to taste
1 teaspoon dried marjoram	8 oz. Parmesan cheese, freshly grated
½ teaspoons dried thyme	
4 mahi-mahi fillets	

1. Add 1 ½ cups of water and a rack to your Inner Pot. 2. Spritz a casserole dish with a nonstick cooking spray. 3. Arrange the slices of tomatoes on the bottom of the dish. Add the herbs. 4. Place the mahi-mahi fillets on the top; drizzle the melted butter over the fish. 5. Season it with salt and black pepper. Place the baking dish on the rack. 6. Put on the pressure cooker's lid and turn the steam valve to "Sealing" position. 7. Select Pressure Cook mode, and then press the "Pressure Cook" button again to select "Less" time option. 8. Use the "+/-" keys on the control panel to set the cooking time to 9 minutes. 9. Press the Pressure Level button to adjust the pressure to "Low Pressure." 10. Once the cooking cycle is completed, quickly and carefully turn the steam release handle from Sealing position to the Venting position. 11. When all the steam is released, remove the pressure lid from the top carefully. 12. Top with parmesan and seal the lid again; allow the cheese to melt and serve.
Per Serving: Calories 489; Fat 11g; Sodium 501mg; Carbs 8.9g; Fiber 4.6g; Sugar 8g; Protein 26g

Salmon Steaks with Kale Pesto Sauce

Prep time: 20 minutes | Cook time: 5 minutes | Serves: 4

1-pound salmon steaks	Kale Pesto Sauce:
1 shallot, peeled and sliced	1 avocado
½ cup Kalamata olives	1 teaspoon garlic, crushed
2 sprigs rosemary	2 tablespoons fresh parsley
2 tablespoons olive oil	1 cup kale
½ teaspoons whole mixed peppercorns	2 tablespoons fresh lemon juice
Sea salt, to taste	2 tablespoons olive oil

1. Prepare your Inner Pot by adding 1 ½ cups of water and a steamer basket to its bottom. 2. Place the salmon steaks in the steamer basket. 3. Add the shallots, olives, rosemary, olive oil, peppercorns, and salt. 4. Put on the pressure cooker's lid and turn the steam valve to "Sealing" position. 5. Press the "Steam" button two times to select "Less" option. 6. Use the "+/-" keys on the control panel to set the cooking time to 5 minutes. 7. Press the Pressure Level button to adjust the pressure to "High Pressure." 8. Once the cooking cycle is completed, quickly and carefully turn the steam release handle from Sealing position to the Venting position. 9. When all the steam is released, remove the pressure lid from the top carefully. 10. Add the avocado, garlic, parsley, kale, and lemon juice to your blender. 11. Then, mix on high until a loose paste forms. 12. Add the olive oil a little at a time and continue to blend. 13. Serve the fish fillets with the pesto on the side. Bon appétit!
Per Serving: Calories 424; Fat 7.9g; Sodium 704mg; Carbs 6g; Fiber 3.6g; Sugar 6g; Protein 18g

Tuna, Ham and Pea Chowder

Prep time: 20 minutes | Cook time: 6 minutes | Serves: 5

2 tablespoons olive oil	Sea salt and black pepper, to taste
4 slices ham, chopped	1 teaspoon cayenne pepper
1 cup shallots, chopped	½ teaspoons ground bay leaf
2 cloves garlic, minced	½ teaspoons mustard powder
2 carrots, chopped	1½ cups double cream
5 cups seafood stock	1½ cups frozen green peas
1¼-pound tuna steak, diced	

1. Press the "Sauté" button two times to select "Normal" settings. 2. Heat the oil and fry the ham until crispy. 3. Then, add the shallot and garlic; continue to cook an additional 2 minutes or until tender and fragrant. 4. Add the carrot, stock, tuna, salt, black pepper, cayenne pepper, ground bay leaf, and mustard powder. 5. Put on the pressure cooker's lid and turn the steam valve to "Sealing" position. 6. Select Pressure Cook mode, and then press the "Pressure Cook" button again to select "Less" time option. 7. Use the "+/-" keys on the control panel to set the cooking time to 6 minutes. 8. Press the Pressure Level button to adjust the pressure to "High Pressure." 9. Once the cooking cycle is completed, allow the steam to release naturally. 10. When all the steam is released, remove the pressure lid from the top carefully. 11. Add the double cream and frozen peas. 12. Press the "Sauté" button two times to select "Normal" settings again and cook for a couple of minutes more or until heated through. Bon appétit!
Per Serving: Calories 422; Fat 12.9g; Sodium 414mg; Carbs 11g; Fiber 5g; Sugar 9g; Protein 31g

Red Snapper in Mushroom Sauce

Prep time: 20 minutes | Cook time: 6 minutes | Serves: 4

½ stick butter, at room temperature	chopped
	2 tablespoons tomato ketchup
2 shallots, peeled and chopped	1 cup chicken stock, preferably
2 garlic cloves, minced	homemade
1 cup brown mushrooms, thinly sliced	1-pound red snapper, cut into bite-sized chunks
2 tablespoons coriander	Salt and black pepper, to taste
1 (11-ounce) can tomatillo,	

1. Press the "Sauté" button two times to select "Normal" settings. 2. Then, melt the butter. Once hot, cook the shallots with garlic until tender and aromatic. 3. Stir in the mushrooms; cook an additional 3 minutes or until they have softened. 4. Stir the remaining ingredients into your Inner Pot. 5. Put on the pressure cooker's lid and turn the steam valve to "Sealing" position. 6. Select Pressure Cook mode, and then press the "Pressure Cook" button again to select "Less" time option. 7. Use the "+/-" keys on the control panel to set the cooking time to 6 minutes. 8. Press the Pressure Level button to adjust the pressure to "High Pressure." 9. Once the cooking cycle is completed, quickly and carefully turn the steam release handle from Sealing position to the Venting position. 10. When all the steam is released, remove the pressure lid from the top carefully. 11. Serve over hot basmati rice if desired. Enjoy!
Per Serving: Calories 584; Fat 15g; Sodium 441mg; Carbs 17g; Fiber 4.6g; Sugar 5g; Protein 29g

Parmesan Cod with Basmati Rice

Prep time: 20 minutes | Cook time: 5 minutes | Serves: 4

2 cups basmati rice	1 teaspoon coriander
2 cups water	1 teaspoon lemon thyme
1 ¼-pound cod, slice into small pieces	2 tablespoons lemon juice
Salt and black pepper, to taste	½ cup heavy cream
1 teaspoon paprika	1 cup Parmesan cheese, freshly grated
2 bay leaves	

1. Put on the pressure cooker's lid and turn the steam valve to "Sealing" position. 2. Select Pressure Cook mode, and then press the "Pressure

Cook" button again to select "Less" time option. 3. Use the "+/-" keys on the control panel to set the cooking time to 4 minutes. 4. Press the Pressure Level button to adjust the pressure to "High Pressure." 5. Once the cooking cycle is completed, allow the steam to release naturally. 6. When all the steam is released, remove the pressure lid from the top carefully. 7. Press the Cancel button to stop this cooking program. 8. Press the "Sauté" button two times to select "Normal" settings. 9. Add the remaining ingredients and cook until the Parmesan has melted. 10. Serve the fish mixture over the hot basmati rice and enjoy!
Per Serving: Calories 521; Fat 7.9g; Sodium 704mg; Carbs 6g; Fiber 3.6g; Sugar 6g; Protein 18g

Indian Kulambu

Prep time: 20 minutes | Cook time: 2 minutes | Serves: 4

2 tablespoons butter	½ teaspoons turmeric powder
6 curry leaves	1 teaspoon ground coriander
1 onion, chopped	½ teaspoons ground cumin
2 cloves garlic, crushed	Kosher salt and black pepper, to
1 (1-inch) piece fresh ginger, grated	taste
	½ (14-ounce) can coconut milk
1 dried Kashmiri chili, minced	1-pound salmon fillets
1 cup canned tomatoes, crushed	1 tablespoon lemon juice

1. Press the "Sauté" button two times to select "Normal" settings and melt the butter. 2. Once hot, cook the curry leaves for about 30 seconds. 3. Stir in the onions, garlic, ginger and Kashmiri chili and cook for 2 minutes more or until they are fragrant. 4. Add the tomatoes, turmeric, coriander, cumin, salt, and black pepper. 5. Continue to sauté for 30 seconds more. Add the coconut milk and salmon. 6. Press the Cancel button to stop this cooking program. 7. Put on the pressure cooker's lid and turn the steam valve to "Sealing" position. 8. Select Pressure Cook mode, and then press the "Pressure Cook" button again to select "Less" time option. 9. Use the "+/-" keys on the control panel to set the cooking time to 2 minutes. 10. Press the Pressure Level button to adjust the pressure to "Low Pressure." 11. Once the cooking cycle is completed, quickly and carefully turn the steam release handle from Sealing position to the Venting position. 12. When all the steam is released, remove the pressure lid from the top carefully. 13. Spoon the fish curry into individual bowls. 14. Drizzle lemon juice over the fish curry and serve. 15. Enjoy!
Per Serving: Calories 479; Fat 10g; Sodium 891mg; Carbs 22.9g; Fiber 4g; Sugar 4g; Protein 23g

Ocean Trout Fillets

Prep time: 20 minutes | Cook time: 3 minutes | Serves: 4

1-pound ocean trout fillets	2 garlic cloves, minced
Sea salt, to taste	1 teaspoon mixed peppercorns
1 teaspoon caraway seeds	2 tablespoons champagne vinegar
½ teaspoons mustard seeds	1 tablespoon fish sauce
½ teaspoons paprika	2½ cups broth, preferably
½ cup spring onions, chopped	homemade

1. Place the steaming basket in your Inner Pot. 2. Sprinkle the ocean trout fillets with salt, caraway seeds, mustard seeds, and paprika. 3. Place the ocean trout fillet in the steaming basket. Add the other ingredients. 4. Put on the pressure cooker's lid and turn the steam valve to "Sealing" position. 5. Select Pressure Cook mode, and then press the "Pressure Cook" button again to select "Less" time option. 6. Use the "+/-" keys on the control panel to set the cooking time to 3 minutes. 7. Press the Pressure Level button to adjust the pressure to "Low Pressure." 8. Once the cooking cycle is completed, quickly and carefully turn the steam release handle from Sealing position to the Venting position. 9. When all the steam is released, remove the pressure lid from the top carefully. 10. Serve.
Per Serving: Calories 334; Fat 19g; Sodium 354mg; Carbs 15g; Fiber 5.1g; Sugar 8.2g; Protein 32g

Portuguese-Fish Medley

Prep time: 20 minutes | Cook time: 8 minutes | Serves: 4

1-pound fish, mixed pieces for fish soup, cut into bite-sized pieces	⅓ cup dry vermouth
1 yellow onion, chopped	2 fresh tomatoes, puréed
1 celery with leaves, chopped	1 tablespoon loosely packed saffron threads
2 carrots, chopped	Sea salt and black pepper, to taste
2 cloves garlic, minced	1 teaspoon Piri Piri
1 green bell pepper, thinly sliced	2 bay leaves
2 tablespoons peanut oil	¼ cup fresh cilantro, roughly chopped
1 ½ cups seafood stock	½ lemon, sliced

1. Simply throw all of the above ingredients, except for the cilantro and lemon, into your Inner Pot. 2. Put on the pressure cooker's lid and turn the steam valve to "Sealing" position. 3. Select Pressure Cook mode, and then press the "Pressure Cook" button again to select "Less" time option. 4. Use the "+/-" keys on the control panel to set the cooking time to 8 minutes. 5. Press the Pressure Level button to adjust the pressure to "Low Pressure." 6. Once the cooking cycle is completed, quickly and carefully turn the steam release handle from Sealing position to the Venting position. 7. When all the steam is released, remove the pressure lid from the top carefully. 8. Ladle the medley into individual bowls; serve with fresh cilantro and lemon. Enjoy!
Per Serving: Calories 349; Fat 2.9g; Sodium 511mg; Carbs 12g; Fiber 3g; Sugar 8g; Protein 7g

Prawns with Basmati Rice

Prep time: 20 minutes | Cook time: 5 minutes | Serves: 5

2 tablespoons olive oil	1 tablespoon tamari sauce
1 cup red onions, thinly sliced	1 pound prawns, peeled and deveined
2 cloves garlic, pressed	Sea salt and black pepper, to taste
2 bell peppers, seeded and thinly sliced	½ teaspoons sweet paprika
1 serrano pepper, seeded and thinly sliced	1 teaspoon dried rosemary
2 cups basmati rice	½ teaspoons dried oregano
1 (14-ounce) can tomatoes, diced	2 tablespoons fresh mint, roughly chopped
2½ cups vegetable stock	

1. Press the "Sauté" button two times to select "Normal" settings. 2. Then, heat the oil and sauté the onions until tender and translucent. 3. Stir in the garlic; continue to sauté until aromatic. 4. Add the rest of the above ingredients, except for the mint, to the Inner Pot. 5. Put on the pressure cooker's lid and turn the steam valve to "Sealing" position. 6. Select Pressure Cook mode, and then press the "Pressure Cook" button again to select "Less" time option. 7. Use the "+/-" keys on the control panel to set the cooking time to 3 minutes. 8. Press the Pressure Level button to adjust the pressure to "Low Pressure." 9. Once the cooking cycle is completed, allow the steam to release naturally. 10. When all the steam is released, remove the pressure lid from the top carefully. 11. Serve garnished with fresh mint leaves. Bon appétit!
Per Serving: Calories 382; Fat 10.9g; Sodium 454mg; Carbs 10g; Fiber 3.1g; Sugar 5.2g; Protein 20g

Haddock Fillets with Steamed Green Beans

Prep time: 20 minutes | Cook time: 6 minutes | Serves: 4

1 lime, cut into wedges	1 tablespoon fresh parsley
½ cup water	4 teaspoons ghee
4 haddock fillets	Sea salt and black pepper, to taste
1 rosemary sprig	2 cloves garlic, minced
2 thyme sprigs	4 cups green beans

1. Place the lime wedges and water in the Inner Pot. Add a steamer rack. 2. Lower the haddock fillets onto the rack; place the rosemary, thyme, parsley, and ghee on the haddock fillets. 3. Season with salt and pepper. 4. Then, add the garlic and green beans to the Inner Pot. 5. Put on the pressure cooker's lid and turn the steam valve to "Sealing" position. 6. Press the "Steam" button one time to select "Less" option. 7. Use the "+/-" keys on the control panel to set the cooking time to 6 minutes. 8. Press the Pressure Level button to adjust the pressure to "Low Pressure." 9. Once the cooking cycle is completed, quickly and carefully turn the steam release handle from Sealing position to the Venting position. 10. When all the steam is released, remove the pressure lid from the top carefully. 11. Serve the haddock fillets with green beans on the side. 12. Bon appétit!
Per Serving: Calories 219; Fat 10g; Sodium 891mg; Carbs 22.9g; Fiber 4g; Sugar 4g; Protein 23g

Greek-Shrimp with Feta Cheese

Prep time: 20 minutes | Cook time: 2 minutes | Serves: 4

1 pound frozen shrimp	tomatoes
1½ tablespoons olive oil	½ cup Kalamata olives
2 gloves garlic, minced	2-ounce feta cheese, crumbled
1 teaspoon basil	½ lemon, sliced
½ teaspoons dry dill weed	Chopped fresh mint leaves, for garnish
1 teaspoon oregano	
1 (26-ounce) canned diced	

1. Add the shrimp, olive oil, garlic, basil, dill, oregano, and tomatoes to the Inner Pot. 2. Put on the pressure cooker's lid and turn the steam valve to "Sealing" position. 3. Select Pressure Cook mode, and then press the "Pressure Cook" button again to select "Less" time option. 4. Use the "+/-" keys on the control panel to set the cooking time to 2 minutes. 5. Press the Pressure Level button to adjust the pressure to "Low Pressure." 6. Once the cooking cycle is completed, allow the steam to release naturally. 7. When all the steam is released, remove the pressure lid from the top carefully. 8. Top with Kalamata olives and feta cheese. Serve garnished with lemon and mint leaves. 9. Enjoy!
Per Serving: Calories 419; Fat 14g; Sodium 791mg; Carbs 8.9g; Fiber 4.6g; Sugar 8g; Protein 31g

Louisiana-Seafood Boil

Prep time: 15 minutes | Cook time: 10 minutes | Serves: 4

1 cup jasmine rice	4 cloves garlic, minced
1 tablespoon butter	1 cup chicken bone broth
1 tablespoon olive oil	2 bay leaves
½-pound chicken breasts, cubed	1 teaspoon oregano
1-pound shrimp	1 teaspoon sage
2 sweet peppers, deveined and sliced	1 teaspoon basil
1 habanero pepper, deveined and sliced	1 teaspoon paprika
1 onion, chopped	1 tablespoon fish sauce
	Sea salt and black pepper, to taste
	1 tablespoon cornstarch

1. Combine the rice, butter and 1 ½ cups of water in a pot and bring to a rapid boil. 2. Cover and let it simmer on low for 15 minutes. Fluff with a fork and reserve. 3. Press the "Sauté" button two times to select "Normal" settings and heat the oil. Once hot, cook the chicken breasts for 3 to 4 minutes. 4. Add the remaining ingredients, except for the cornstarch. 5. Put on the pressure cooker's lid and turn the steam valve to "Sealing" position. 6. Select Pressure Cook mode, and then press the "Pressure Cook" button again to select "Less" time option. 7. Use the "+/-" keys on the control panel to set the cooking time to 3 minutes. 8. Press the Pressure Level button to adjust the pressure to "Low Pressure." 9. Once the cooking cycle is completed, quickly and carefully turn the steam release handle from Sealing position to the Venting position. 10. When all the steam is released, remove the pressure lid from the top carefully. 11. Mix the cornstarch with 2 tablespoons of cold water. 12. Add the cornstarch slurry to the cooking liquid and stir at "Normal" cooking temperature on the "Sauté" mode until the sauce thickens. 13. Serve over hot jasmine rice. Bon appétit!
Per Serving: Calories 479; Fat 10g; Sodium 891mg; Carbs 22.9g; Fiber 4g; Sugar 4g; Protein 23g

Creole Gumbo

Prep time: 15 minutes | Cook time: 10 minutes | Serves: 4

2 tablespoons butter, melted	2 ripe tomatoes, pureed
1 shallot, diced	¼ cup ketchup
1 sweet pepper, sliced	1 bay leaf
1 jalapeno pepper, sliced	1 cup beef broth
1-pound tuna, cut into 2-inch chunks	2 tablespoons Worcestershire sauce
1 tablespoon Creole seasoning	1-pound raw shrimp, deveined
2 carrots, sliced	1 teaspoon filé powder
2 celery stalks, diced	Sea salt and black pepper, to taste

1. Press the "Sauté" button two times to select "Normal" settings and melt the butter. 2. Once hot, cook the shallot and peppers for about 3 minutes until just tender and fragrant. 3. Add the remaining ingredients; gently stir to combine. 4. Put on the pressure cooker's lid and turn the steam valve to "Sealing" position. 5. Select Pressure Cook mode, and then press the "Pressure Cook" button again to select "Less" time option. 6. Use the "+/-" keys on the control panel to set the cooking time to 5 minutes. 7. Press the Pressure Level button to adjust the pressure to "High Pressure." 8. Once the cooking cycle is completed, quickly and carefully turn the steam release handle from Sealing position to the Venting position. 9. When all the steam is released, remove the pressure lid from the top carefully. 10. Serve in individual bowls and enjoy!
Per Serving: Calories 489; Fat 11g; Sodium 501mg; Carbs 8.9g; Fiber 4.6g; Sugar 8g; Protein 26g

Blue Crabs with Wine and Herbs

Prep time: 15 minutes | Cook time: 5 minutes | Serves: 4

2-pound frozen blue crab	2 sprigs rosemary
½ cup water	2 sprigs thyme
½ cup dry white wine	1 lemon, cut into wedges
Sea salt and black pepper, to taste	

1. Add the frozen crab legs, water, wine, salt, black pepper, rosemary, and thyme to the Inner Pot. 2. Put on the pressure cooker's lid and turn the steam valve to "Sealing" position. 3. Select Pressure Cook mode, and then press the "Pressure Cook" button again to select "Less" time option. 4. Use the "+/-" keys on the control panel to set the cooking time to 3 minutes. 5. Press the Pressure Level button to adjust the pressure to "High Pressure." 6. Once the cooking cycle is completed, quickly and carefully turn the steam release handle from Sealing position to the Venting position. 7. When all the steam is released, remove the pressure lid from the top carefully. 8. Serve warm, garnished with fresh lemon wedges. Bon appétit!
Per Serving: Calories 478; Fat 7.9g; Sodium 704mg; Carbs 6g; Fiber 3.6g; Sugar 6g; Protein 18g

Sausage and Prawn Boil

Prep time: 15 minutes | Cook time: 10 minutes | Serves: 4

½-pound beef sausage, sliced	1 teaspoon Old Bay seasoning
4 baby potatoes	¼ teaspoon Tabasco sauce
1 cup fume (fish stock)	Sea salt and white pepper, to taste
¼ cup butter	1 pound prawns
2 cloves garlic, minced	1 fresh lemon, juiced

1. Place the sausage and potatoes in the Inner Pot; cover with the fish stock. 2. Put on the pressure cooker's lid and turn the steam valve to "Sealing" position. 3. Select Pressure Cook mode, and then press the "Pressure Cook" button again to select "Less" time option. 4. Use the "+/-" keys on the control panel to set the cooking time to 5 minutes. 5. Press the Pressure Level button to adjust the pressure to "High Pressure." 6. Once the cooking cycle is completed, allow the steam to release naturally. 7. When all the steam is released, remove the pressure lid from the top carefully. 8. Reserve. Clean the Inner Pot. 9. Press the "Sauté" button two times to select "Normal" settings and melt the butter. 10. Once hot, sauté the minced garlic until aromatic or about 1 minute. 11. Stir in the Old Bay seasoning, Tabasco, salt, and white pepper. Lastly, stir in the prawns. 12. Continue to simmer for 1 to 2 minutes or until the shrimp turn pink. 13. Press the "Cancel" button. 14. Add the sausages and potatoes, drizzle lemon juice over the top and serve warm.
Per Serving: Calories 422; Fat 12.9g; Sodium 414mg; Carbs 11g; Fiber 5g; Sugar 9g; Protein 31g

Sole Fillets with Vegetables

Prep time: 15 minutes | Cook time: 13 minutes | Serves: 4

2 tablespoons coconut oil	Salt and black pepper, to taste
1 small shallot, quartered	1-pound fennel, quartered
4 cloves garlic, sliced	1-pound sole fillets
1 cup beef stock	1 lemon, cut into wedges
1 ripe tomato, puréed	2 tablespoons fresh Italian parsley

1. Press the "Sauté" button two times to select "Normal" settings and heat the coconut oil. 2. Once hot, sauté the shallot and garlic until tender and aromatic. 3. Add the beef stock, tomato, salt, pepper, and fennel. 4. Press the Cancel button to stop this cooking program. 5. Put on the pressure cooker's lid and turn the steam valve to "Sealing" position. 6. Select Pressure Cook mode, and then press the "Pressure Cook" button again to select "Less" time option. 7. Use the "+/-" keys on the control panel to set the cooking time to 10 minutes. 8. Press the Pressure Level button to adjust the pressure to "High Pressure." 9. Once the cooking cycle is completed, quickly and carefully turn the steam release handle from Sealing position to the Venting position. 10. When all the steam is released, remove the pressure lid from the top carefully. 11. Then, remove all the vegetables with a slotted spoon and reserve, keeping them warm. 12. Add the sole fillets to the Inner Pot. 13. Choose the "Steam" mode and cook for 3 minutes at Low Pressure. 14. Once cooking is complete, quickly and carefully turn the steam release handle from Sealing position to the Venting position; carefully remove the lid. 15. Garnish the fish fillets with lemon and parsley. 16. With the reserved vegetables, serve and enjoy!
Per Serving: Calories 334; Fat 7.9g; Sodium 704mg; Carbs 6g; Fiber 3.6g; Sugar 6g; Protein 18g

Southern California Cioppino

Prep time: 15 minutes | Cook time: 30 minutes | Serves: 6

2 tablespoons coconut oil	1 teaspoon dried basil
1 onion, diced	1 teaspoon paprika
4 garlic cloves, minced	1 bay leaf
2 celery stalks, diced	Sea salt and black pepper, to taste
2 carrots, diced	1-pound halibut steaks, cubed
1 sweet pepper, diced	½-pound sea scallops, rinsed and drained
2 (14-ounce) cans of tomatoes, crushed	1-pound shrimp, peeled and deveined
1 cup clam juice	½-pound crab legs
1 teaspoon oyster sauce	¼ cup dry white wine
½ teaspoons dried parsley flakes	
1 teaspoon dried rosemary	

1. Press the "Sauté" button two times to select "Normal" settings to heat the coconut oil. 2. Once hot, sauté the onion, garlic, celery, carrots, and pepper for about 3 minutes or until they are just tender. 3. Add the canned tomatoes, clam juice, oyster sauce, parsley, rosemary, basil, paprika, bay leaf, salt, and black pepper to the Inner Pot. 4. Put on the pressure cooker's lid and turn the steam valve to "Sealing" position. 5. Press the "Soup/Broth" button one time to select "Normal" option. 6. Use the "+/-" keys on the control panel to set the cooking time to 30 minutes. 7. Press the Pressure Level button to adjust the pressure to "High Pressure." 8. Once the cooking cycle is completed, allow the steam to release naturally. 9. When all the steam is released, remove the pressure lid from the top carefully. 10. Add the seafood and wine. 11. Choose the "Steam" mode and cook for 3 minutes at Low Pressure. 12. Once cooking is complete, use a quick pressure release; carefully remove the lid. 13. Serve in individual bowls and enjoy!
Per Serving: Calories 412; Fat 20g; Sodium 491mg; Carbs 9g; Fiber 3g; Sugar 8g; Protein 31g

Fish and Vegetables

Prep time: 15 minutes | Cook time: 10 minutes | Serves: 4

12-ounce halibut steaks, cut into four pieces
1 red bell pepper, sliced
1 green bell pepper, sliced
1 onion, sliced
2 garlic cloves, minced
1 cup cherry tomatoes, halved
Sea salt and black pepper, to taste
1 teaspoon dried rosemary
1 teaspoon basil
½ teaspoons oregano
½ teaspoons paprika
4 teaspoons olive oil

1. Place 1 cup of water and a metal Steam Rack in the bottom of the Inner Pot. 2. Place 4 large sheets of heavy-duty foil on a flat surface. 3. Divide the ingredients between sheets of foil. Add a splash of water. 4. Bring the ends of the foil together; fold in the sides to seal. Place the fish packets on the Steam Rack. 5. Put on the pressure cooker's lid and turn the steam valve to "Sealing" position. 6. Press the "Steam" button one time to select "Normal" option. 7. Press the Pressure Level button to adjust the pressure to "High Pressure." 8. Once the cooking cycle is completed, quickly and carefully turn the steam release handle from Sealing position to the Venting position. 9. When all the steam is released, remove the pressure lid from the top carefully. 10. Bon appétit!
Per Serving: Calories 472; Fat 10.9g; Sodium 354mg; Carbs 10.5g; Fiber 4.1g; Sugar 8.2g; Protein 26g

Spinach-Stuffed Salmon

Prep time: 15 minutes | Cook time: 5 minutes | Serves: 3

3 (6-ounce) salmon fillets
Kosher salt and black pepper, to taste
½ teaspoons cayenne pepper
½ teaspoons celery seed, crushed
½ teaspoons dried basil
½ teaspoons dried marjoram
½ cup sour cream
½ cup mozzarella, shredded
1 cup frozen spinach, defrosted
2 cloves garlic, minced
1 tablespoon olive oil
1 lemon, cut into wedges

1. Add 1 cup of water and a steamer rack to the bottom of your Inner Pot. 2. Sprinkle your salmon with all spices. In a mixing bowl, thoroughly combine sour cream, mozzarella, spinach, and garlic. 3. Cut a pocket in each fillet to within ½-inch of the opposite side. 4. Stuff the pockets with the spinach/cheese mixture. Drizzle with olive oil. 5. Wrap the salmon fillets in foil and lower onto the rack. 6. Put on the pressure cooker's lid and turn the steam valve to "Sealing" position. 7. Select Pressure Cook mode, and then press the "Pressure Cook" button again to select "Less" time option. 8. Use the "+/-" keys on the control panel to set the cooking time to 4 minutes. 9. Press the Pressure Level button to adjust the pressure to "Low Pressure." 10. Once the cooking cycle is completed, quickly and carefully turn the steam release handle from Sealing position to the Venting position. 11. When all the steam is released, remove the pressure lid from the top carefully. 12. Garnish with lemon wedges and serve warm.
Per Serving: Calories 489; Fat 11g; Sodium 501mg; Carbs 8.9g; Fiber 4.6g; Sugar 8g; Protein 26g

Crab Dip

Prep time: 15 minutes | Cook time: 5 minutes | Serves: 10

1-pound lump crab meat
6-ounce Cottage cheese, at room temperature
½ cup Romano cheese, shredded
1 cup sour cream
Kosher salt and black pepper, to
taste
1 teaspoon smoked paprika
1½ cups Cheddar cheese, shredded
¼ cup fresh chives, chopped
2 tablespoons fresh lime juice

1. Place 1 cup of water and a metal Steam Rack in the Inner Pot. 2. Spritz a casserole dish with nonstick cooking spray. 3. Place the crab meat, Cottage cheese, Romano cheese and sour cream in the casserole dish. 4. Season with salt, black pepper, and smoked paprika. 5. Top with the Cheddar cheese. Lower the dish onto the Steam Rack. 6. Put on the pressure cooker's lid and turn the steam valve to "Sealing"

position. 7. Press the "Steam" button two times to select "Less" option. 8. Press the Pressure Level button to adjust the pressure to "Low Pressure." 9. Once the cooking cycle is completed, allow the steam to release naturally. 10. When all the steam is released, remove the pressure lid from the top carefully. 11. Scatter the chopped chives over the top and add a few drizzles of lime juice. 12. Serve warm or at room temperature. Enjoy!
Per Serving: Calories 584; Fat 15g; Sodium 441mg; Carbs 17g; Fiber 4.6g; Sugar 5g; Protein 29g

Spicy Thai Prawns

Prep time: 15 minutes | Cook time: 5 minutes | Serves: 4

2 tablespoons coconut oil
1 small white onion, chopped
2 cloves garlic, minced
1½-pound prawns, deveined
½ teaspoons red chili flakes
1 bell pepper, seeded and sliced
1 cup coconut milk
2 tablespoons fish sauce
2 tablespoons lime juice
1 tablespoon sugar
Kosher salt and white pepper, to your liking
½ teaspoons cayenne pepper
1 teaspoon fresh ginger, ground
2 tablespoons fresh cilantro, chopped

1. Press the "Sauté" button two times to select "Normal" settings and heat the coconut oil; once hot, sauté the onion and garlic until aromatic. 2. Add the prawns, red chili flakes, bell pepper, coconut milk, fish sauce, lime juice, sugar, salt, white pepper, cayenne pepper, and ginger. 3. Put on the pressure cooker's lid and turn the steam valve to "Sealing" position. 4. Select Pressure Cook mode, and then press the "Pressure Cook" button again to select "Less" time option. 5. Use the "+/-" keys on the control panel to set the cooking time to 3 minutes. 6. Press the Pressure Level button to adjust the pressure to "Low Pressure." 7. Once the cooking cycle is completed, quickly and carefully turn the steam release handle from Sealing position to the Venting position. 8. When all the steam is released, remove the pressure lid from the top carefully. 9. Divide between serving bowls and serve garnished with fresh cilantro. Enjoy!
Per Serving: Calories 390; Fat 10.9g; Sodium 454mg; Carbs 10g; Fiber 3.1g; Sugar 5.2g; Protein 20g

Spanish Paella

Prep time: 15 minutes | Cook time: 6 minutes | Serves: 5

2 tablespoons olive oil
2 links (6-ounce) Spanish chorizo sausage, cut into slices
1 yellow onion, chopped
3 cloves garlic, minced
2 sweet peppers, sliced
1 Chiles de Árbol, minced
1 cup Arborio rice, rinsed
1½-pound shrimp, deveined
1 cup chicken broth
1 cup water
⅓ cup white wine
½ teaspoons curry paste
Sea salt and white pepper, to taste
1 cup green peas, fresh or thawed
¼ cup fresh parsley leaves, roughly chopped

1. Press the "Sauté" button two times to select "Normal" settings and then heat the oil until sizzling. 2. Cook the sausage for 2 minutes, stirring continuously to ensure even cooking. 3. Stir in the onions and garlic; cook for about a minute longer, stirring frequently. 4. Add the peppers, rice, shrimp, broth, water, wine, curry paste, salt, and white pepper. 5. Put on the pressure cooker's lid and turn the steam valve to "Sealing" position. 6. Select Pressure Cook mode, and then press the "Pressure Cook" button again to select "Less" time option. 7. Use the "+/-" keys on the control panel to set the cooking time to 3 minutes. 8. Press the Pressure Level button to adjust the pressure to "High Pressure." 9. Once the cooking cycle is completed, quickly and carefully turn the steam release handle from Sealing position to the Venting position. 10. When all the steam is released, remove the pressure lid from the top carefully. 11. Add the green peas and seal the lid one more time; let it sit in the residual heat until warmed through. 12. Serve garnished with fresh parsley and enjoy!
Per Serving: Calories 397; Fat 7.9g; Sodium 704mg; Carbs 6g; Fiber 3.6g; Sugar 6g; Protein 18g

Haddock Curry

Prep time: 15 minutes | Cook time: 4 minutes | Serves: 2

2 tablespoons peanut oil	1 teaspoon mustard seeds
1 onion, chopped	1 teaspoon turmeric powder
2 garlic cloves, minced	1 teaspoon ground cumin
1 (1-inch) piece fresh root ginger, peeled and grated	Sea salt and black pepper
2 long red chilies, deseeded and minced	1 can reduced fat coconut milk
	1 cup chicken stock
2 tablespoons tamarind paste	1-pound haddock

1. Press the "Sauté" button two times to select "Normal" settings and heat the peanut oil. 2. once hot, sauté the onion, garlic, ginger, and chilies until aromatic. 3. Add the remaining ingredients and gently stir to combine. 4. Put on the pressure cooker's lid and turn the steam valve to "Sealing" position. 5. Select Pressure Cook mode, and then press the "Pressure Cook" button again to select "Less" time option. 6. Use the "+/-" keys on the control panel to set the cooking time to 4 minutes. 7. Press the Pressure Level button to adjust the pressure to "Low Pressure." 8. Once the cooking cycle is completed, quickly and carefully turn the steam release handle from Sealing position to the Venting position. 9. When all the steam is released, remove the pressure lid from the top carefully. 10. Divide between serving bowls and serve warm. Enjoy!
Per Serving: Calories 584; Fat 15g; Sodium 441mg; Carbs 17g; Fiber 4.6g; Sugar 5g; Protein 29g

Tuna and Asparagus Casserole

Prep time: 15 minutes | Cook time: 9 minutes | Serves: 4

1-pound tuna fillets	1 teaspoon paprika
1-pound asparagus, trimmed	A pinch of fresh thyme
2 ripe tomatoes, pureed	1 tablespoon dry white wine
Sea salt and black pepper, to taste	1 cup Cheddar cheese, grated

1. Place the tuna fillets in a lightly greased baking dish. 2. Add the asparagus, tomatoes, salt, black pepper, paprika, thyme, and wine. 3. Place a steamer rack inside the Inner Pot; add ½ cup of water. 4. Cut 1 sheet of heavy-duty foil and brush with cooking spray. 5. Top with the cheese. Cover with foil and lower the baking dish onto the rack. 6. Put on the pressure cooker's lid and turn the steam valve to "Sealing" position. 7. Select Pressure Cook mode, and then press the "Pressure Cook" button again to select "Less" time option. 8. Use the "+/-" keys on the control panel to set the cooking time to 9 minutes. 9. Press the Pressure Level button to adjust the pressure to "Low Pressure." 10. Once the cooking cycle is completed, quickly and carefully turn the steam release handle from Sealing position to the Venting position. 11. When all the steam is released, remove the pressure lid from the top carefully. 12. Place the baking dish on a cooling rack for a couple of minutes before slicing and serving. 13. Bon appétit!
Per Serving: Calories 361; Fat 19g; Sodium 354mg; Carbs 15g; Fiber 5.1g; Sugar 8.2g; Protein 32g

Steamed Tilapia with Spinach

Prep time: 15 minutes | Cook time: 12 minutes | Serves: 4

1 cup chicken broth	Salt and black pepper, to taste
2 cloves garlic, sliced	2 tablespoons butter, melted
1-pound tilapia, cut into 4 pieces	2 cups fresh spinach
1 tablespoon Worcestershire sauce	

1. Place the chicken broth and garlic in the Inner Pot. Place the Steam Rack on top. 2. Place the tilapia fillets on a sheet of foil; add Worcestershire sauce, salt, pepper, and butter. 3. Bring up all sides of the foil to create a packet around your fish. 4. Put on the pressure cooker's lid and turn the steam valve to "Sealing" position. 5. Press the "Steam" button two times to select "Normal" option. 6. Press the Pressure Level button to adjust the pressure to "Low Pressure." 7. Once the cooking cycle is completed, quickly and carefully turn the steam release handle from Sealing position to the Venting position.

8. When all the steam is released, remove the pressure lid from the top carefully. 9. Add the spinach leaves to the cooking liquid. 10. Press the Cancel button to stop this cooking program. 11. Press the "Sauté" function and let it simmer at "Less" cooking temperature for 1 to 2 minutes or until wilted. 12. Place the fish fillets on top of the wilted spinach, adjust the seasonings, and serve immediately. 13. Bon appétit!
Per Serving: Calories 419; Fat 14g; Sodium 791mg; Carbs 8.9g; Fiber 4.6g; Sugar 8g; Protein 31g

Fish Tacos

Prep time: 15 minutes | Cook time: 7 minutes | Serves: 4

1 lemon, sliced	1 tablespoon ancho chili powder
2 tablespoons olive oil	4 (6-inch) flour tortillas
1-pound haddock fillets	4 tablespoons mayonnaise
½ teaspoons ground cumin	4 tablespoons sour cream
½ teaspoons onion powder	2 tablespoons fresh cilantro, chopped
1 teaspoon garlic powder	
½ teaspoons paprika	Add ½ cup of water, ½ of lemon slices, and a steamer rack to the bottom of the Inner Pot.
Sea salt and black pepper, to taste	
1 teaspoon dried basil	

1. Press the "Sauté" button two times to select "Normal" settings and heat the olive oil until sizzling. 2. Now, sauté the haddock fillets for 1 to 2 minutes per side. 3. Season the fish fillets with all the spices and lower them onto the rack. 4. Put on the pressure cooker's lid and turn the steam valve to "Sealing" position. 5. Press the "Steam" button two times to select "Less" option. 6. Press the Pressure Level button to adjust the pressure to "Low Pressure." 7. Once the cooking cycle is completed, quickly and carefully turn the steam release handle from Sealing position to the Venting position. 8. When all the steam is released, remove the pressure lid from the top carefully. 9. Break the fish fillets into large bite-sized pieces and divide them between the tortillas. 10. Add the mayonnaise, sour cream and cilantro to each tortilla. 11. Garnish with the remaining lemon slices and enjoy!
Per Serving: Calories 397; Fat 7.9g; Sodium 704mg; Carbs 6g; Fiber 3.6g; Sugar 6g; Protein 18g

Fish and Couscous Pilaf

Prep time: 15 minutes | Cook time: 10 minutes | Serves: 4

2 tablespoons butter	2 ripe tomatoes, pureed
1 yellow onion, chopped	1½-pound halibut, cut into chunks
2 cups couscous	1 teaspoon coriander
2 cups water	1 teaspoon curry paste
1 cup vegetable broth	1 teaspoon ancho chili powder
1 cup coconut milk	2 bay leaves
Sea salt and black pepper, to taste	4 cardamom pods
1 teaspoon cayenne pepper	1 teaspoon garam masala
1 teaspoon dried basil	2 tablespoons almonds, slivered

1. Press the "Sauté" button two times to select "Normal" settings and melt the butter. 2. Once hot, cook the onions until tender and translucent. 3. Add the remaining ingredients, except for the slivered almonds, to the Inner Pot; stir to combine. 4. Put on the pressure cooker's lid and turn the steam valve to "Sealing" position. 5. Select Pressure Cook mode, and then press the "Pressure Cook" button again to select "Less" time option. 6. Use the "+/-" keys on the control panel to set the cooking time to 4 minutes. 7. Press the Pressure Level button to adjust the pressure to "High Pressure." 8. Once the cooking cycle is completed, quickly and carefully turn the steam release handle from Sealing position to the Venting position. 9. When all the steam is released, remove the pressure lid from the top carefully. 10. Serve garnished with almonds. 11. Bon appétit!
Per Serving: Calories 382; Fat 7.9g; Sodium 704mg; Carbs 6g; Fiber 3.6g; Sugar 6g; Protein 18g

Japanese Seafood Curry

Prep time: 15 minutes | Cook time: 5 minutes | Serves: 4

2 tablespoons butter, softened	½ pound shrimps, deveined
1 onion, chopped	2 tablespoons sesame oil
2 cloves garlic, minced	1 tablespoon garam masala
1 (1-inch) pieces fresh ginger, ground	1 teaspoon curry paste
1 red chili, deseeded and minced	1 (3-inch) kombu (dried kelp)
1 pound pollack, cut into large chunks	1 package Japanese curry roux
	2 tablespoons Shoyu sauce
	2 ripe tomatoes, pureed

1. Press the "Sauté" button two times to select "Normal" settings and melt the butter. 2. Cook the onion, garlic, ginger, and red chili until just tender and fragrant. 3. Add the pollack and shrimp and continue to sauté for a couple of minutes more. 4. Add the remaining ingredients. 5. Put on the pressure cooker's lid and turn the steam valve to "Sealing" position. 6. Select Pressure Cook mode, and then press the "Pressure Cook" button again to select "Less" time option. 7. Use the "+/-" keys on the control panel to set the cooking time to 5 minutes. 8. Press the Pressure Level button to adjust the pressure to "Low Pressure." 9. Once the cooking cycle is completed, quickly and carefully turn the steam release handle from Sealing position to the Venting position. 10. When all the steam is released, remove the pressure lid from the top carefully. 11. Serve your curry over hot steamed rice. Enjoy!
Per Serving: Calories 390; Fat 7.9g; Sodium 704mg; Carbs 6g; Fiber 3.6g; Sugar 6g; Protein 18g

Crabs with Garlic Sauce

Prep time: 15 minutes | Cook time: 6 minutes | Serves: 5

1½-pound crabs	1 teaspoon Old Bay seasoning
1 stick butter	1 lemon, sliced
2 cloves garlic, minced	

1. Place 1 cup water and a metal Steam Rack in the bottom of your Inner Pot. 2. Lower the crabs onto the Steam Rack. 3. Put on the pressure cooker's lid and turn the steam valve to "Sealing" position. 4. Press the "Steam" button two times to select "Less" option. 5. Press the Pressure Level button to adjust the pressure to "Low Pressure." 6. Once the cooking cycle is completed, quickly and carefully turn the steam release handle from Sealing position to the Venting position. 7. When all the steam is released, remove the pressure lid from the top carefully. 8. Empty the pot and keep the crab aside. 9. Press the "Sauté" button two times to select "Normal" settings and then melt butter. 10. Once hot, sauté the garlic and Old Bay seasoning for 2 to 3 minutes. 11. Add the cooked crabs and gently stir to combine. 12. Serve with lemon slices. 13. Bon appétit!
Per Serving: Calories 489; Fat 11g; Sodium 501mg; Carbs 8.9g; Fiber 4.6g; Sugar 8g; Protein 26g

Greek-Style Fish

Prep time: 15 minutes | Cook time: 3 minutes | Serves: 4

2 tablespoons olive oil	2 sprigs thyme, chopped
1½-pound cod fillets	1 bay leaf
1 pound tomatoes, chopped	2 cloves garlic, smashed
Sea salt and black pepper, to taste	½ cup Greek olives, pitted and sliced
2 sprigs rosemary, chopped	

1. Place 1 cup of water and a metal Steam Rack in the bottom of the Inner Pot. 2. Brush the sides and bottom of a casserole dish with olive oil. 3. Place the cod fillets in the greased casserole dish. 4. Add the tomatoes, salt, pepper, rosemary, thyme, bay leaf, and garlic. 5. Lower the dish onto the Steam Rack. 6. Put on the pressure cooker's lid and turn the steam valve to "Sealing" position. 7. Press the "Steam" button one time to select "Less" option. 8. Press the Pressure Level button to adjust the pressure to "Low Pressure." 9. Once the cooking cycle is completed, quickly and carefully turn the steam release handle from Sealing position to the Venting position. 10. When all the steam is released, remove the pressure lid from the top carefully. 11. Serve garnished with Greek olives and enjoy!

Per Serving: Calories 478; Fat 7.9g; Sodium 704mg; Carbs 6g; Fiber 3.6g; Sugar 6g; Protein 18g

French Fish En Papillote

Prep time: 15 minutes | Cook time: 3 minutes | Serves: 4

2 tablespoons olive oil	Sea salt and white pepper, to taste
4 (7-ounce) rainbow trout fillets	½-pound sugar snap peas, trimmed
1 tablespoon fresh chives, chopped	2 tomatillos, sliced
1 tablespoon fresh parsley, chopped	2 garlic cloves, minced

1. Place 1 cup of water and a metal rack in your Inner Pot. 2. Place all ingredients in a large sheet of foil. Fold up the sides of the foil to make a bowl-like shape. 3. Lower the fish packet onto the rack. 4. Put on the pressure cooker's lid and turn the steam valve to "Sealing" position. 5. Press the "Steam" button one time to select "Less" option. 6. Press the Pressure Level button to adjust the pressure to "Low Pressure." 7. Once the cooking cycle is completed, quickly and carefully turn the steam release handle from Sealing position to the Venting position. 8. When all the steam is released, remove the pressure lid from the top carefully. 9. Bon appétit!
Per Serving: Calories 584; Fat 15g; Sodium 441mg; Carbs 17g; Fiber 4.6g; Sugar 5g; Protein 29g

Prawn Dipping Sauce

Prep time: 15 minutes | Cook time: 3 minutes | Serves: 8

2 cups crabmeat, flaked	1½ tablespoons cornichon, finely chopped
1 onion, chopped	¼ cup tomato paste
2 cloves garlic, smashed	2 or so dashes of Tabasco
½ cup cream cheese, softened	½ cup fresh breadcrumbs
½ cup mayonnaise	
½ cup Parmesan cheese, grated	

1. Place all ingredients, except for the breadcrumbs, in a baking dish. 2. Stir until everything is well incorporated. 3. Top with breadcrumbs. 4. Put on the pressure cooker's lid and turn the steam valve to "Sealing" position. 5. Press the "Steam" button three times to select "Less" option. 6. Press the Pressure Level button to adjust the pressure to "Low Pressure." 7. Once the cooking cycle is completed, quickly and carefully turn the steam release handle from Sealing position to the Venting position. 8. When all the steam is released, remove the pressure lid from the top carefully. 9. Serve with raw vegetable sticks if desired. 10. Bon appétit!
Per Serving: Calories 449; Fat 2.9g; Sodium 511mg; Carbs 12g; Fiber 3g; Sugar 8g; Protein 27g

Mayo Shrimp Salad

Prep time: 15 minutes | Cook time: 2 minutes | Serves: 4

1-pound shrimp, deveined and peeled	1 stalk celery, chopped
Fresh juice of 2 lemons	1 tablespoon fresh dill, minced
Salt and black pepper, to taste	½ cup mayonnaise
1 red onion, chopped	1 teaspoon Dijon mustard

1. Prepare your Inner Pot by adding 1 cup of water and steamer basket to the Inner Pot. 2. Now, add the shrimp to the steamer basket. 3. Top with lemon slices. 4. Put on the pressure cooker's lid and turn the steam valve to "Sealing" position. 5. Select Pressure Cook mode, and then press the "Pressure Cook" button again to select "Less" time option. 6. Use the "+/-" keys on the control panel to set the cooking time to 2 minutes. 7. Press the Pressure Level button to adjust the pressure to "Low Pressure." 8. Once the cooking cycle is completed, quickly and carefully turn the steam release handle from Sealing position to the Venting position. 9. When all the steam is released, remove the pressure lid from the top carefully. 10. Add the remaining ingredients and toss to combine well. 11. Serve well chilled and enjoy!
Per Serving: Calories 489; Fat 11g; Sodium 501mg; Carbs 8.9g; Fiber 4.6g; Sugar 8g; Protein 26g

Halibut Steaks with Wild Rice

Prep time: 15 minutes | Cook time: 60 minutes | Serves: 6

1 cup wild rice, rinsed and drained	2 tablespoons olive oil
1 tablespoon butter	Sea salt and ground pepper, to your liking
½ teaspoons salt flakes	4 tablespoons cream cheese
½ teaspoons red pepper flakes, crushed	4 tablespoons mayonnaise
1½-pound halibut steaks	1 teaspoon stone-ground mustard
	2 cloves garlic, minced

1. In a saucepan, bring 3 cups of water and rice to a boil. 2. Reduce the heat to simmer; cover and let it simmer for 45 to 55 minutes. 3. Add the butter, salt, and red pepper; fluff with a fork. Cover and reserve, keeping your rice warm. 4. Cut 4 sheets of aluminum foil. Place the halibut steak in each sheet of foil. 5. Add the olive oil, salt, and black pepper to the top of the fish; close each packet and seal the cdgcs. 6. Add 1 cup of water and a steamer rack to the bottom of your Inner Pot. Lower the packets onto the rack. 7. Put on the pressure cooker's lid and turn the steam valve to "Sealing" position. 8. Press the "Steam" button one time to select "Less" option. 9. Press the Pressure Level button to adjust the pressure to "Low Pressure." 10. Once the cooking cycle is completed, allow the steam to release naturally. 11. When all the steam is released, remove the pressure lid from the top carefully. 12. Meanwhile, mix the cream cheese, mayonnaise, stone-ground mustard, and garlic until well combined. 13. Serve the steamed fish with the mayo sauce and wild rice on the side. Bon appétit!
Per Serving: Calories 482; Fat 7.9g; Sodium 704mg; Carbs 6g; Fiber 3.6g; Sugar 6g; Protein 18g

Tuna Steaks in Lime- Sauce

Prep time: 15 minutes | Cook time: 4 minutes | Serves: 3

3 tuna steaks	1 tablespoon fresh cilantro, chopped
1 ½ tablespoons sesame oil, melted	For the Sauce:
½ teaspoons salt	1 tablespoon butter, at room temperature
¼ teaspoon black pepper, to taste	
¼ teaspoon smoked paprika	1 tablespoon fresh lime juice
1 cup water	1 teaspoon Worcestershire sauce

1. Brush the tuna steaks with sesame oil. 2. Season the tuna steaks with salt, black pepper, and smoked paprika. 3. Place the fish in the steaming basket; transfer it to the Inner Pot. 4. Pour 1 cup of water into the base of your Inner Pot. 5. Put on the pressure cooker's lid and turn the steam valve to "Sealing" position. 6. Select Pressure Cook mode, and then press the "Pressure Cook" button again to select "Less" time option. 7. Use the "+/-" keys on the control panel to set the cooking time to 4 minutes. 8. Press the Pressure Level button to adjust the pressure to "Low Pressure." 9. Once the cooking cycle is completed, quickly and carefully turn the steam release handle from Sealing position to the Venting position. 10. When all the steam is released, remove the pressure lid from the top carefully. 11. Meanwhile, warm the butter over medium-low heat. 12. Add the lime juice and Worcestershire sauce; remove from the heat and stir. 13. Spoon the sauce over the tuna steaks, sprinkle with fresh cilantro leaves and serve. 14. Bon appétit!
Per Serving: Calories 471; Fat 10.9g; Sodium 454mg; Carbs 10g; Fiber 3.1g; Sugar 5.2g; Protein 20g

Vietnamese-Fish

Prep time: 15 minutes | Cook time: 10 minutes | Serves: 4

2 tablespoons coconut oil, melted	Sea salt and white pepper, to taste
¼ cup brown sugar	1 cup chicken broth
2 tablespoons fish sauce	4 (7-ounce) sea bass fillets
2 tablespoons soy sauce	2 tablespoons fresh chives, chopped
1 (1-inch) ginger root, grated	
Juice of ½ lime	

1. Press the "Sauté" button two times to select "Normal" settings and then heat the coconut oil. 2. Once hot, cook the brown sugar, fish sauce, soy sauce, ginger, lime, salt, white pepper, and broth. 3. Bring to a simmer and press the "Cancel" button. Add sea bass. 4. Put on the pressure cooker's lid and turn the steam valve to "Sealing" position. 5. Select Pressure Cook mode, and then press the "Pressure Cook" button again to select "Less" time option. 6. Use the "+/-" keys on the control panel to set the cooking time to 4 minutes. 7. Press the Pressure Level button to adjust the pressure to "High Pressure." 8. Once the cooking cycle is completed, quickly and carefully turn the steam release handle from Sealing position to the Venting position. 9. When all the steam is released, remove the pressure lid from the top carefully. 10. Remove the sea bass fillets from the cooking liquid. 11. Press the "Sauté" button two times to select "Normal" settings. 12. Reduce the sauce until it is thick and syrupy. 13. Spoon the sauce over the reserved sea bass fillets. 14. Garnish with fresh chives. 15. Bon appétit!
Per Serving: Calories 403; Fat 10.9g; Sodium 354mg; Carbs 10.5g; Fiber 4.1g; Sugar 8.2g; Protein 26g

Tilapia Fillets with Peppers

Prep time: 15 minutes | Cook time: 3 minutes | Serves: 4

1 lemon, sliced	1 tablespoon fresh tarragon, chopped
4 (6-ounce) tilapia fillets, skin on	
4 teaspoons olive oil	1 red onion, sliced into rings
Sea salt and white pepper, to taste	2 sweet peppers, julienned
1 tablespoon fresh parsley, chopped	4 tablespoons dry white wine

1. Place the lemon slices, 1 cup of water, and a metal Steam Rack in the bottom of the Inner Pot. 2. Place 4 large sheets of heavy-duty foil on a flat surface. 3. Divide the ingredients between the sheets of foil. 4. Bring the ends of the foil together; fold in the sides to seal. Place the fish packets on the Steam Rack. 5. Put on the pressure cooker's lid and turn the steam valve to "Sealing" position. 6. Press the "Steam" button one time to select "Less" option. 7. Press the Pressure Level button to adjust the pressure to "Low Pressure." 8. Once the cooking cycle is completed, quickly and carefully turn the steam release handle from Sealing position to the Venting position. 9. When all the steam is released, remove the pressure lid from the top carefully. 10. Bon appétit!
Per Serving: Calories 479; Fat 10g; Sodium 891mg; Carbs 22.9g; Fiber 4g; Sugar 4g; Protein 23g

Halibut Steaks with Tomatoes

Prep time: 15 minutes | Cook time: 5 minutes | Serves: 4

2 tablespoons Worcestershire sauce	4 halibut steaks
2 tablespoons oyster sauce	2 teaspoons olive oil
½ cup dry white wine	2 tomatoes, sliced
1 tablespoon Dijon mustard	2 spring onions, sliced
1 (1-inch) piece fresh ginger, grated	2 garlic cloves, crushed
	1 cup mixed salad greens, to serve

1. In a mixing bowl, whisk Worcestershire sauce, oyster sauce, white wine, mustard, and ginger. 2. Add the fish steaks and let them marinate for 30 minutes in your refrigerator. 3. Meanwhile, Press the "Sauté" button two times to select "Normal" settings on your Inner Pot. 4. Now, heat the olive oil and sauté the tomatoes with the spring onions and garlic until they are tender. 5. Add 2 cups of water to the base of your Inner Pot. Add the metal steamer insert to the Inner Pot. 6. Now, place the halibut steaks on top of the steamer insert. 7. Put on the pressure cooker's lid and turn the steam valve to "Sealing" position. 8. Select Pressure Cook mode, and then press the "Pressure Cook" button again to select "Less" time option. 9. Use the "+/-" keys on the control panel to set the cooking time to 5 minutes. 10. Press the Pressure Level button to adjust the pressure to "Low Pressure." 11. Once the cooking cycle is completed, quickly and carefully turn the steam release handle from Sealing position to the Venting position. 12. When all the steam is released, remove the pressure lid from the top carefully. 13. Serve the warm halibut steaks with the sautéed vegetables and mixed salad greens. 14. Enjoy!
Per Serving: Calories 334; Fat 7.9g; Sodium 704mg; Carbs 6g; Fiber 3.6g; Sugar 6g; Protein 18g

Shrimp Scampi with Carrots

Prep time: 15 minutes | Cook time: 6 minutes | Serves: 4

1 tablespoon olive oil
2 garlic cloves, sliced
1 bunch scallions, chopped
2 carrots, grated
1½-pound shrimp, deveined and rinsed
½ cup dry white wine see

½ cup cream of celery soup
Sea salt and freshly cracked black pepper, to taste
1 teaspoon cayenne pepper
½ teaspoon dried basil
1 teaspoon dried rosemary
½ teaspoons dried oregano

1. Press the "Sauté" button two times to select "Normal" settings and then heat the oil. 2. Once hot, cook the garlic, scallions, and carrots for 2 to 3 minutes. 3. Add a splash of wine to deglaze the Inner Pot. 4. Add the remaining ingredients. 5. Put on the pressure cooker's lid and turn the steam valve to "Sealing" position. 6. Press the "Pressure Cook" button three times to select "Less" option. 7. Use the "+/-" keys on the control panel to set the cooking time to 3 minutes. 8. Press the Pressure Level button to adjust the pressure to "Low Pressure." 9. Once the cooking cycle is completed, allow the steam to release naturally. 10. When all the steam is released, remove the pressure lid from the top carefully. 11. Divide between serving bowls and enjoy!
Per Serving: Calories 412; Fat 20g; Sodium 491mg; Carbs 9g; Fiber 3g; Sugar 8g; Protein 31g

Crab Sliders

Prep time: 15 minutes | Cook time: 3 minutes | Serves: 4

10-ounce crabmeat
4 heaping tablespoons fresh chives, chopped
2 garlic cloves, minced
½ cup mayonnaise
½ teaspoons hot sauce

1 teaspoon Old Bay seasoning
½ cup celery stalk, chopped
1 tablespoon fresh lime juice
8 mini slider rolls
2 cups Iceberg lettuce, torn into pieces

1. Add 1 cup of water, metal Steam Rack, and a steamer basket to your Inner Pot. 2. Place the crabmeat in the prepared steamer basket. 3. Put on the pressure cooker's lid and turn the steam valve to "Sealing" position. 4. Press the "Steam" button one time to select "Less" option. 5. Press the Pressure Level button to adjust the pressure to "Low Pressure." 6. Once the cooking cycle is completed, quickly and carefully turn the steam release handle from Sealing position to the Venting position. 7. When all the steam is released, remove the pressure lid from the top carefully. 8. Add the chives, garlic, mayo, hot sauce, Old Bay seasoning, celery, and lime juice; stir to combine well. 9. Divide the mixture between slider rolls and garnish with lettuce. 10. Serve and enjoy!
Per Serving: Calories 407; Fat 19g; Sodium 354mg; Carbs 15g; Fiber 5.1g; Sugar 8.2g; Protein 32g

Salmon on Croissants

Prep time: 15 minutes | Cook time: 3 minutes | Serves: 2

1½-pound salmon fillets
1 red onion, thinly sliced
¼ cup prepared horseradish, drained
¼ cup mayonnaise
2 tablespoons sour cream
Salt and white pepper, to taste
½ teaspoons red pepper flakes,

crushed
½ teaspoons dried rosemary, only leaves crushed
½ teaspoons dried oregano
1 cup cherry tomatoes, halved
2 cups Iceberg lettuce leaves, torn into pieces
6 croissants, split

1. Add 1 cup of water and metal Steam Rack to the Inner Pot. 2. Lower the salmon fillets onto the Steam Rack. 3. Put on the pressure cooker's lid and turn the steam valve to "Sealing" position. 4. Press the "Steam" button two times to select "Less" option. 5. Press the Pressure Level button to adjust the pressure to "Low Pressure." 6. Once the cooking cycle is completed, quickly and carefully turn the steam release handle from Sealing position to the Venting position. 7. When all the steam is released, remove the pressure lid from the top carefully. 8. Add the remaining ingredients and stir to combine well. 9. Place in your refrigerator until ready to serve. 10. Serve on croissants and enjoy!
Per Serving: Calories 412; Fat 20g; Sodium 491mg; Carbs 9g; Fiber 3g; Sugar 8g; Protein 31g

Fish Paprikash

Prep time: 15 minutes | Cook time: 7 minutes | Serves: 4

2 tablespoons butter, at room temperature
1 cup leeks, chopped
2 bell peppers, seeded and sliced
2 garlic cloves, minced
2 sprigs thyme
1 sprig rosemary
1 teaspoon sweet paprika
1 teaspoon hot paprika

Sea salt and black pepper, to taste
2 tomatoes, puréed
2 cups vegetable broth
2 cups water
1½-pound cod fish, cut into bite-sized chunks
2 tablespoons fresh cilantro, roughly chopped
1 cup sour cream, well-chilled

1. Press the "Sauté" button two times to select "Normal" settings. 2. Melt the butter and sauté the leeks until fragrant. 3. Then, stir in the peppers and garlic and continue to sauté an additional 40 seconds. 4. Add the thyme, rosemary, paprika, salt, black pepper, tomatoes, broth, water, and fish. 5. Put on the pressure cooker's lid and turn the steam valve to "Sealing" position. 6. Select Pressure Cook mode, and then press the "Pressure Cook" button again to select "Less" time option. 7. Use the "+/-" keys on the control panel to set the cooking time to 6 minutes. 8. Press the Pressure Level button to adjust the pressure to "High Pressure." 9. Once the cooking cycle is completed, quickly and carefully turn the steam release handle from Sealing position to the Venting position. 10. When all the steam is released, remove the pressure lid from the top carefully. 11. Ladle into individual bowls and serve garnished with fresh cilantro and well-chilled sour cream. 12. Bon appétit!
Per Serving: Calories 472; Fat 12.9g; Sodium 414mg; Carbs 11g; Fiber 5g; Sugar 9g; Protein 31g

Sole Fillets with Pickle

Prep time: 15 minutes | Cook time: 3 minutes | Serves: 4

1½-pound sole fillets
Sea salt and black pepper, to taste
1 teaspoon paprika

½ cup mayonnaise
1 tablespoon pickle juice
2 cloves garlic, smashed

1. Sprinkle the fillets with salt, black pepper, and paprika. 2. Add 1 ½ cups of water and a steamer basket to the Inner Pot. Place the fish in the steamer basket. 3. Put on the pressure cooker's lid and turn the steam valve to "Sealing" position. 4. Select Pressure Cook mode, and then press the "Pressure Cook" button again to select "Less" time option. 5. Use the "+/-" keys on the control panel to set the cooking time to 3 minutes. 6. Press the Pressure Level button to adjust the pressure to "Low Pressure." 7. Once the cooking cycle is completed, quickly and carefully turn the steam release handle from Sealing position to the Venting position. 8. When all the steam is released, remove the pressure lid from the top carefully. 9. Then, make the sauce by mixing the mayonnaise with the pickle juice and garlic. 10. Serve the fish fillets with the well-chilled sauce on the side. 11. Bon appétit!
Per Serving: Calories 382; Fat 7.9g; Sodium 704mg; Carbs 6g; Fiber 3.6g; Sugar 6g; Protein 18g

Butter dipped Lobster Tails

Prep time: 15 minutes | Cook time: 3 minutes | Serves: 4

1½-pound lobster tails, halved
½ stick butter, at room temperature

Sea salt and black pepper, to taste
½ teaspoon red pepper flakes

1. Add a metal Steam Rack, steamer basket, and 1 cup of water in your Inner Pot. 2. Place the lobster tails, shell side down, in the prepared steamer basket. 3. Put on the pressure cooker's lid and turn the steam valve to "Sealing" position. 4. Press the "Steam" button one time to select "Less" option. 5. Press the Pressure Level button to adjust the pressure to "Low Pressure." 6. Once the cooking cycle is completed, quickly and carefully turn the steam release handle from Sealing position to the Venting position. 7. When all the steam is released, remove the pressure lid from the top carefully. 8. Empty the pot and keep the crab aside. 9. Drizzle with butter. Season with salt, black pepper, and red pepper and serve immediately. 10. Enjoy!
Per Serving: Calories 397; Fat 12.9g; Sodium 414mg; Carbs 11g; Fiber 5g; Sugar 9g; Protein 31g

Orange Sea Bass

Prep time: 15 minutes | Cook time: 15 minutes | Serves: 4

1 tablespoon safflower oil
1-pound sea bass
Sea salt, to taste
¼ teaspoon white pepper
2 tablespoons tamari sauce

2 cloves garlic, minced
½ teaspoons dried dill weed
1 orange, juiced
1 tablespoon honey

1. Press the "Sauté" button two times to select "Normal" settings and heat the oil. 2. Now, cook the sea bass for 1 to 2 minutes per side. Season your fish with salt and pepper. 3. Add 1 cup of water and a steamer rack to the bottom of your Inner Pot. Lower the fish onto the rack. 4. Put on the pressure cooker's lid and turn the steam valve to "Sealing" position. 5. Press the "Steam" button three times to select "Normal" option. 6. Press the Pressure Level button to adjust the pressure to "Low Pressure." 7. Once the cooking cycle is completed, quickly and carefully turn the steam release handle from Sealing position to the Venting position. 8. When all the steam is released, remove the pressure lid from the top carefully. 9. Add the remaining ingredients to the cooking liquid and stir to combine well. 10. Press the "Sauté" button two times to select "Normal" settings again and let it simmer until the sauce thickens. 11. Spoon the sauce over the reserved fish. Bon appétit!
Per Serving: Calories 334; Fat 7.9g; Sodium 704mg; Carbs 6g; Fiber 3.6g; Sugar 6g; Protein 18g

Mussels in Scallion Sauce

Prep time: 15 minutes | Cook time: 5 minutes | Serves: 2

1 cup water
½ cup cooking wine
2 garlic cloves, sliced
1½-pound frozen mussels,

cleaned and debearded
2 tablespoons butter
1 bunch scallion, chopped

1. Add the water, wine, and garlic to the Inner Pot. Add a metal rack to the Inner Pot. 2. Put the mussels into the steamer basket; lower the steamer basket onto the rack. 3. Put on the pressure cooker's lid and turn the steam valve to "Sealing" position. 4. Press the "Steam" button two times to select "Less" option. 5. Press the Pressure Level button to adjust the pressure to "Low Pressure." 6. Once the cooking cycle is completed, quickly and carefully turn the steam release handle from Sealing position to the Venting position. 7. When all the steam is released, remove the pressure lid from the top carefully. 8. Press the "Sauté" button two times to select "Normal" settings and add butter and scallions; 9. let it cook until the sauce is thoroughly heated and slightly thickened. 10. Press the "Cancel" button and add the mussels. 11. Serve warm. Bon appétit!
Per Serving: Calories 419; Fat 14g; Sodium 791mg; Carbs 8.9g; Fiber 4.6g; Sugar 8g; Protein 31g

Risotto with Sea Bass

Prep time: 15 minutes | Cook time: 8 minutes | Serves: 4

2 tablespoons butter, melted
½ cup leeks, sliced
2 garlic cloves, minced
2 cups basmati rice
1½-pound sea bass fillets, diced

2 cups vegetable broth
1 cup water
Salt, to taste
½ teaspoon black pepper
1 teaspoon fresh ginger, grated

1. Press the "Sauté" button two times to select "Normal" settings. 2. Then, melt the butter and sweat the leeks for 2 to 3 minutes. 3. Stir in the garlic; continue to sauté an additional 40 seconds. Add the remaining ingredients. 4. Put on the pressure cooker's lid and turn the steam valve to "Sealing" position. 5. Select Pressure Cook mode, and then press the "Pressure Cook" button again to select "Less" time option. 6. Use the "+/-" keys on the control panel to set the cooking time to 4 minutes. 7. Press the Pressure Level button to adjust the pressure to "Low Pressure." 8. Once the cooking cycle is completed, quickly and carefully turn the steam release handle from Sealing position to the Venting position. 9. When all the steam is released, remove the pressure lid from the top carefully. 10. Serve warm in individual bowls and enjoy!
Per Serving: Calories 449; Fat 2.9g; Sodium 511mg; Carbs 12g; Fiber 3g; Sugar 8g; Protein 27g

Seafood Quiche with Colby Cheese

Prep time: 15 minutes | Cook time: 10 minutes | Serves: 4

6 eggs
½ cup cream cheese
½ cup Greek-style yogurt
Himalayan salt and black pepper, to taste
1 teaspoon cayenne pepper

1 teaspoon dried basil
1 teaspoon dried oregano
1-pound crab meat, chopped
½-pound raw shrimp, chopped
1 cup Colby cheese, shredded

1. In a mixing bowl, whisk the eggs with the cream cheese and yogurt. 2. Season with salt, black pepper, cayenne pepper, basil, and oregano. 3. Stir in the seafood; stir to combine and spoon the mixture into a lightly greased baking pan. 4. Lastly, top with the shredded cheese. 5. Cover with a piece of aluminum foil. 6. Put on the pressure cooker's lid and turn the steam valve to "Sealing" position. 7. Press the "Steam" button one time to select "Normal" option. 8. Press the Pressure Level button to adjust the pressure to "Low Pressure." 9. Once the cooking cycle is completed, quickly and carefully turn the steam release handle from Sealing position to the Venting position. 10. When all the steam is released, remove the pressure lid from the top carefully. 11. Bon appétit!
Per Serving: Calories 521; Fat 7.9g; Sodium 704mg; Carbs 6g; Fiber 3.6g; Sugar 6g;

Fish Burritos

Prep time: 15 minutes | Cook time: 10 minutes | Serves: 4

2 tablespoons olive oil
4 catfish fillets
Sea salt to taste
⅓ teaspoon black pepper, to taste
½ teaspoons cayenne pepper

½ teaspoons ground bay leaf
1 teaspoon dried thyme
4 burrito-sized tortillas
1 cup fresh salsa
1 large-sized tomato, sliced

1. Prepare your Inner Pot by adding 1 ½ cups of water and a metal rack to its bottom. 2. Place the fish fillets in the center of a foil sheet. 3. Drizzle olive oil over the fish. 4. Season with salt, black pepper, cayenne pepper, ground bay leaf and dried thyme. 5. Wrap tightly and lower it onto the rack. 6. Put on the pressure cooker's lid and turn the steam valve to "Sealing" position. 7. Select Pressure Cook mode, and then press the "Pressure Cook" button again to select "Less" time option. 8. Use the "+/-" keys on the control panel to set the cooking time to 10 minutes. 9. Press the Pressure Level button to adjust the pressure to "High Pressure." 10. Once the cooking cycle is completed, allow the steam to release naturally. 11. When all the steam is released, remove the pressure lid from the top carefully. 12. Divide the fish fillets among tortillas. 13. Top it with the salsa and tomatoes. 14. Roll each tortilla into a burrito and serve immediately.
Per Serving: Calories 380; Fat 7.9g; Sodium 704mg; Carbs 6g; Fiber 3.6g; Sugar 6g; Protein 18g

Shrimp Salad

Prep time: 15 minutes | Cook time: 3 minutes | Serves: 4

1-pound shrimp, deveined
Kosher salt and white pepper, to taste
1 onion, thinly sliced
1 sweet pepper, thinly sliced
1 jalapeno pepper, deseeded and minced

2 heaping tablespoons fresh parsley, chopped
1 head romaine lettuce, torn into pieces
4 tablespoons olive oil
1 lime, juiced and zested
1 tablespoon Dijon mustard

1. Add a metal Steam Rack and 1 cup of water to your Inner Pot. 2. Put the shrimp into the steamer basket. Lower the steamer basket onto the Steam Rack. 3. Put on the pressure cooker's lid and turn the steam valve to "Sealing" position. 4. Press the "Steam" button one time to select "Less" option. 5. Press the Pressure Level button to adjust the pressure to "Low Pressure." 6. Once the cooking cycle is completed, quickly and carefully turn the steam release handle from Sealing position to the Venting position. 7. When all the steam is released, remove the pressure lid from the top carefully. 8. Transfer steamed shrimp to a salad bowl; toss your shrimp with the remaining ingredients. 9. Serve well chilled. Bon appétit!
Per Serving: Calories 461; Fat 7.9g; Sodium 704mg; Carbs 6g; Fiber 3.6g; Sugar 6g; Protein 18g

Beer-Steamed Mussels

Prep time: 15 minutes | Cook time: 5 minutes | Serves: 4

1 tablespoon olive oil
½ cup scallions, chopped
2 cloves garlic, minced
2 medium-sized ripe tomatoes, puréed
1 (12-ounce) bottles lager beer
1 cup water
1 tablespoon fresh cilantro, chopped
Sea salt and black pepper, to taste
2 Thai chili peppers, stemmed and split
1 ½-pound mussels, cleaned and debearded

1. Press the "Sauté" button two times to select "Normal" settings. 2. Heat the oil and cook the scallions until tender and fragrant. 3. Then, stir in the garlic and cook an additional 30 seconds or until fragrant. 4. Add the remaining ingredients. 5. Put on the pressure cooker's lid and turn the steam valve to "Sealing" position. 6. Select Pressure Cook mode, and then press the "Pressure Cook" button again to select "Less" time option. 7. Use the "+/-" keys on the control panel to set the cooking time to 3 minutes. 8. Press the Pressure Level button to adjust the pressure to "Low Pressure." 9. Once the cooking cycle is completed, quickly and carefully turn the steam release handle from Sealing position to the Venting position. 10. When all the steam is released, remove the pressure lid from the top carefully. 11. Serve with garlic croutons. 12. Bon appétit!
Per Serving: Calories 384; Fat 7.9g; Sodium 704mg; Carbs 6g; Fiber 3.6g; Sugar 6g; Protein 18g

Fish Mélange

Prep time: 15 minutes | Cook time: 10 minutes | Serves: 4

1 tablespoon olive oil
2 shallots, diced
2 garlic cloves, smashed
2 carrots, diced
2 (6-ounce) cans crab, juice reserved
½-pound cod, cut into bite-sized chunks
Sea salt, to taste
½ teaspoons black pepper
2 bay leaves
1 tablespoon Creole seasoning
2 cups water
1 cup double cream
1 tablespoon lemon juice

1. Press the "Sauté" button two times to select "Normal" settings. 2. Then, heat the oil and sauté the shallots until tender. 3. Stir in the garlic and carrots; cook an additional minute or so. 4. Add the canned crab meat, cod, salt, black pepper, bay leaves, Creole seasoning, and water. 5. Put on the pressure cooker's lid and turn the steam valve to "Sealing" position. 6. Select Pressure Cook mode, and then press the "Pressure Cook" button again to select "Less" time option. 7. Use the "+/-" keys on the control panel to set the cooking time to 6 minutes. 8. Press the Pressure Level button to adjust the pressure to "High Pressure." 9. Once the cooking cycle is completed, quickly and carefully turn the steam release handle from Sealing position to the Venting position. 10. When all the steam is released, remove the pressure lid from the top carefully. 11. Lastly, stir in the double cream and lemon juice. 12. Press the "Sauté" button two times to select "Normal" settings; let it simmer until heated through. 13. Enjoy!
Per Serving: Calories 521; Fat 19g; Sodium 354mg; Carbs 15g; Fiber 5.1g; Sugar 8.2g; Protein 32g

Saucy Clams

Prep time: 15 minutes | Cook time: 10 minutes | Serves: 4

½ cup bacon, smoked and cubed
2 onions, chopped
3 garlic cloves, minced
1 sprig thyme
3 (5-ounce) cans clams, chopped
⅓ cup tarty white wine
⅓ cup water
½ cup clam juice
A pinch of cayenne pepper
1 bay leaf
5 lime juice
2 tablespoons fresh chives, roughly chopped

1. Press the "Sauté" button two times to select "Normal" settings. 2. Add the cubed bacon. Once your bacon releases its fat, add the onions, garlic, and thyme. 3. Cook for 3 minutes more or until the onion is transparent. 4. Add the clams, white wine, water, clam juice, cayenne pepper, and bay leaf. 5. Put on the pressure cooker's lid and turn the steam valve to "Sealing" position. 6. Select Pressure Cook mode, and then press the "Pressure Cook" button again to select "Less" time option. 7. Use the "+/-" keys on the control panel to set the cooking time to 4 minutes. 8. Press the Pressure Level button to adjust the pressure to "Low Pressure." 9. Once the cooking cycle is completed, allow the steam to release naturally. 10. When all the steam is released, remove the pressure lid from the top carefully. 11. Ladle into individual bowls and serve garnished with lime slices and fresh chives. 12. Bon appétit!
Per Serving: Calories 584; Fat 15g; Sodium 441mg; Carbs 17g; Fiber 4.6g; Sugar 5g; Protein 29g

Saucy Red Snapper

Prep time: 15 minutes | Cook time: 5 minutes | Serves: 4

1 tablespoon ghee, at room temperature
1 medium-sized leek, chopped
4 cloves garlic, minced
1 tablespoon capers
2 medium ripe tomatoes, chopped
1 cup chicken broth
1 red chili pepper, seeded and chopped
1 teaspoon basil
½ teaspoons oregano
½ teaspoons rosemary
3 (6-ounce) red snapper fillets
Coarse sea salt and black pepper, to taste
1 teaspoon Fish taco seasoning mix
1 lemon, cut into wedges

1. Press the "Sauté" button two times to select "Normal" settings and melt the ghee. 2. Once hot, sauté the leek and garlic until tender. 3. Add the remaining ingredients, except for the lemon wedges, to the Inner Pot. 4. Put on the pressure cooker's lid and turn the steam valve to "Sealing" position. 5. Select Pressure Cook mode, and then press the "Pressure Cook" button again to select "Less" time option. 6. Use the "+/-" keys on the control panel to set the cooking time to 4 minutes. 7. Press the Pressure Level button to adjust the pressure to "High Pressure." 8. Once the cooking cycle is completed, quickly and carefully turn the steam release handle from Sealing position to the Venting position. 9. When all the steam is released, remove the pressure lid from the top carefully. 10. Serve in individual bowls, garnished with lemon wedges. Enjoy!
Per Serving: Calories 472; Fat 7.9g; Sodium 704mg; Carbs 6g; Fiber 3.6g; Sugar 6g; Protein 18g

Mahi-Mahi Fish with Guacamole

Prep time: 15 minutes | Cook time: 5 minutes | Serves: 4

1 cup water
4 mahi-mahi fillets
2 tablespoons olive oil
Sea salt and black pepper, to taste
½ teaspoons red pepper flakes, crushed
½ cup shallots, sliced
2 tablespoons fresh lemon juice
1 teaspoon epazote
¼ cup fresh coriander, chopped
1 teaspoon dried sage
For Cumin Guacamole:
2 medium tomatoes, chopped
1 large avocado, peeled, pitted and mashed
2 tablespoons salsa Verde
1 clove garlic, minced
Fresh juice of 1 lime
Sea salt to taste

1. Pour 1 cup of water to the base of your Inner Pot. 2. Brush the mahi-mahi fillets with olive oil; then, sprinkle with salt, black pepper, and red pepper flakes. 3. Place the mahi-mahi fillets in the steaming basket; transfer it to the Inner Pot. 4. Add the shallots on top; add the lemon juice, epazote, coriander, and sage. 5. Put on the pressure cooker's lid and turn the steam valve to "Sealing" position. 6. Select Pressure Cook mode, and then press the "Pressure Cook" button again to select "Less" time option. 7. Use the "+/-" keys on the control panel to set the cooking time to 3 minutes. 8. Press the Pressure Level button to adjust the pressure to "Low Pressure." 9. Once the cooking cycle is completed, quickly and carefully turn the steam release handle from Sealing position to the Venting position. 10. When all the steam is released, remove the pressure lid from the top carefully. 11. Next, mix all ingredients for the cumin guacamole; place in your refrigerator for at least 20 minutes. 12. Serve the mahi-mahi fillets with fresh cumin guacamole on the side. 13. Bon appétit!
Per Serving: Calories 478; Fat 7.9g; Sodium 704mg; Carbs 6g; Fiber 3.6g; Sugar 6g; Protein 18g

Chapter 8 Chicken and Poultry Recipes

Chicken Pasta with Parmesan Cheese

Prep time: 5 minutes | Cook Time: 16 minutes | Serves: 1

1 tablespoon olive oil
1 tablespoon butter
1 cup diced chicken breast
1 teaspoon Cajun seasoning
1 cup chopped bell pepper, any color
½ tablespoon dried onion flakes
¾ cup chicken broth
½ cup heavy cream
1 tablespoon white wine
½ teaspoon minced garlic
½ tablespoon soy sauce
4 ounces uncooked linguine, broken in half
¾ cup diced tomatoes
1 tablespoon shredded Parmesan cheese

1. Toss the Cajun seasoning over the chicken in a medium bowl. 2. Set your Instant Pot on Sauté and adjust the temperature level to More. 3. After 10 seconds, add oil and butter in the inner pot. 4. When the butter has melted, add the chicken in the inner pot and sear the chicken for 5 minutes, flipping from time to time to evenly cook the chicken. 5. When cooked, remove the chicken. Place bell pepper and Sauté for 3 minutes. 6. Transfer the bell pepper to a small bowl and set aside. 7. Pour broth, wine, cream, and soy sauce with onion flakes and scrape all the browned bits off the pot to deglaze. 8. Turn off the heat and line noodles in a crisscross shape over the liquid to reduce clumping. 9. Pour the chicken together with the soup and pepper over the noodles. Add in the tomato. Do not stir the mixture. 10. Close the lid and turn the steam release handle to Sealing position. 11. Set your Instant Pot on Pressure Cook at High and adjust the cooking time to 8 minutes. 12. When cooked, quick release the pressure turning the handle from Sealing to Venting. 13. Remove the lid and stir. You can sauté for several minutes to thicken the sauce stirring from time to time if the sauce is too thin for your taste. 14. Transfer to a serving plate and top with Parmesan cheese. 15. Serve and enjoy!
Per Serving: Calories: 1,449; Fat: 72g; Sodium: 1,620mg; Carbs: 107g; Sugar: 18g; Protein: 75g

Lime Chicken Fajitas

Prep time: 7 minutes | Cook Time: 8 minutes | Serves: 1

1 tablespoon olive oil
½ teaspoon chili powder
½ teaspoon salt
½ teaspoon dried oregano
¼ teaspoon garlic powder
¼ teaspoon ground cumin
⅛ teaspoon crushed red pepper
flakes
1 cup diced chicken breast in 1" cubes
2 cups frozen bell pepper mix
⅓ cup water
1 tablespoon soy sauce
1 tablespoon lime juice

1. Set your Instant Pot on Sauté and adjust the temperature to More. 2. After 10 seconds, add oil in the inner pot. 3. Mix together salt, oregano, cumin, garlic powder, red pepper flakes, and chili powder in a small bowl. 4. Transfer half of the mixture to a second small bowl and reserve the rest half. Set aside. 5. Toss the chicken in the mixture and coat well. 6. Place the seasoned chicken in the heated inner pot and sear each side about 3 minutes or until browned without stirring. 7. Turn off the heat and add water, soy sauce, the reserved seasoning mixture, lime juice, and bell pepper in the inner pot. Scrape all the browned bits off the pot to deglaze. 8. Close the lid and turn the steam release handle to Sealing position. 9. Set your Instant Pot on Pressure Cook at High and adjust the cooking time to 2 minutes. 10. When cooked, quickly release the pressure turning the handle from Sealing to Venting. Remove the lid. 11. Transfer chicken and peppers to a serving plate with a tong. Serve and enjoy!
Per Serving: Calories: 476; Fat: 17g; Sodium: 2,194mg; Carbs: 17g; Sugar: 8g; Protein: 56g

Teriyaki Chicken Rice Bowl

Prep time: 5 minutes | Cook Time: 15 minutes | Serves: 1

Tzatziki Sauce
4 ½ tablespoons unsweetened plain Greek-style yogurt
3 tablespoons grated cucumber; liquid squeezed out
1 teaspoon lemon juice
⅛ teaspoon salt
1/16 teaspoon ground black pepper
¼ teaspoon dried dill
⅛ teaspoon minced garlic
1 teaspoon olive oil
Chicken Bowl
1 tablespoon olive oil
1 tablespoon butter
Juice and zest of 1 medium lemon
1 cup chicken broth
½ cup uncooked long-grain white
rice
1 teaspoon dried oregano
1 teaspoon minced garlic
¼ teaspoon salt
⅛ teaspoon ground black pepper
1 cup chopped chicken breast
1 teaspoon ground lemon pepper
Topping
2 tablespoons diced tomato
2 tablespoons diced red bell pepper
2 tablespoons crumbled feta cheese
2 tablespoons diced red onion
2 tablespoons diced cucumber
2 tablespoons chopped Kalamata olives

1. Combine all the sauce ingredients in a small jar or bowl and chill in refrigerator until ready to serve to make the Tzatziki sauce. 2. In the Instant Pot, add butter, oil, lime zest, lemon juice, rice, broth, salt, oregano, garlic, and black pepper and stir to combine to make the chicken bowl. 3. Toss the chicken with lemon pepper in a small bowl and then evenly spread the chicken over rice. 4. Close the lid and turn the steam release handle to Sealing position. 5. Set your Instant Pot on Pressure Cook at High and adjust cooking time to 10 minutes. 6. When cooked, naturally release the pressure about 5 minutes. Remove the lid. 7. Transfer the chicken and rice onto a serving bowl, and arrange bell pepper, feta cheese, cucumber, onion, olives, and tomato on the top. 8. Serve with the Tzatziki Sauce and enjoy!
Per Serving: Calories: 849; Fat: 44g; Sodium: 2,442mg; Carbs: 40g; Sugar: 7g; Protein: 64g

Ranch Chicken Lettuce Wraps

Prep time: 5 minutes | Cook Time: 15 minutes | Serves: 1

1 (8-ounce) boneless, skinless chicken breast, thinly sliced
1 cup water
1/16 teaspoon salt
1/16 teaspoon ground black pepper
1 teaspoon dry ranch seasoning
3 tablespoons buffalo sauce
1 tablespoon melted butter
½ tablespoon chopped green onion
2–4 leaves romaine lettuce
2 tablespoons shredded carrot
2 tablespoons crispy chow Mein noodles
2 tablespoons sweetened dried cranberries
2 tablespoons ranch dressing

1. With salt and pepper, season the chicken breast. 2. Then place the chicken thighs and water in the inner pot. 3. Close the pressure lid and turn the steam pressure knob to Sealing position. 4. Set your Instant Pot on Pressure Cook mode at High and adjust time to 10 minutes. 5. When cooked, naturally release the pressure about 5 minutes and remove the lid. 6. Transfer the cooked chicken in a small bowl and drip over with 1 tablespoon of cooking liquid. Shred the chicken with 2 forks. 7. Mix together with buffalo sauce, green onion, butter, and dry ranch seasoning. 8. Line a serving plate with the lettuce leaves. Evenly divide the chicken mixture onto the lettuce leaves and then add chow Mein noodles, ranch dressing, cranberries, and carrot over the chicken mixture. 9. Serve and enjoy!
Per Serving: Calories: 565; Fat: 30g; Sodium: 2,498mg; Carbs: 26g; Sugar: 13g; Protein: 48g

Sweet and Spicy Pineapple Chicken

Prep time: 7 minutes | Cook Time: 9 minutes | Serves: 1

1 tablespoon olive oil	¾ cup diced red bell pepper in 1
1 cup diced chicken breast in 1" cubes	½» pieces
⅛ teaspoon garlic powder	⅓ cup pineapple chunks
⅛ teaspoon salt	¼ cup chicken broth
⅛ teaspoon ground black pepper	1 tablespoon soy sauce
1/16 teaspoon ground ginger	¼ cup pineapple juice
⅛ teaspoon crushed red pepper flakes	1 tablespoon sweet chili sauce
	½ tablespoon cold water
	½ tablespoon cornstarch

1. Season the chicken with salt, black pepper, red pepper flakes, and ginger in a small bowl. 2. Set your Instant Pot on Sauté and adjust the temperature to More. 3. After 10 seconds, add oil. 4. Add the season chicken in the heated oil and sear each side of the chicken about 3 minutes or until browned without stirring. 5. Turn off the heat and add pineapple chunks, soy sauce, broth, pineapple juice, bell pepper, and chili sauce. Scrape all the browned bits off the pot to deglaze. 6. Close the lid and turn the steam release handle to Sealing position. 7. Set your Instant Pot on Pressure Cook at High and adjust the cooking time to 3 minutes. 8. When cooked, quickly release the pressure by turning the handle from Sealing to Venting. 9. Remove the lid and set the Instant Pot on Sauté and temperature at More. 10. Whisk water and cornstarch together in a cup. 11. Then drizzle the mixture slowly and stir in the inner pot. 12. Cook in the inner pot for about 3 minutes or until thickened. 13. Serve on a serving plate and enjoy!
Per Serving: Calories: 544; Fat: 17g; Sodium: 4,372mg; Carbs: 31g; Sugar: 20g; Protein: 58g

Barbecue Chicken and Veggies Bowl

Prep time: 5 minutes | Cook Time: 20 minutes | Serves: 1

1 tablespoon olive oil	2 tablespoons shredded Cheddar cheese
2 (4-ounce) boneless, skinless chicken thighs	2 tablespoons barbecue sauce
1 teaspoon barbecue dry rub	½ cup shredded lettuce
¾ cup chicken broth	¼ cup diced avocado
¼ cup uncooked long-grain white rice	2 tablespoons diced cherry tomatoes
¼ cup drained and rinsed canned black beans	1 tablespoon diced red onion
¼ cup corn	1 tablespoon chopped cilantro
	½ medium lime

1. Rub well the dry rub over the chicken. 2. Set your Instant Pot on Sauté and adjust the temperature level at More. 3. Wait for 10 seconds and add oil on the inner pot. 4. Place the seasoned chicken in the inner pot and cook about 8 minutes or until both sides are browned. Halfway through cooking, turn the chicken to the other side. 5. When cooked, remove the inner pot from the Instant Pot and turn off the heat. 6. Pour broth in the inner pot and scrape all the browned bits off the pot to deglaze. 7. Stir together corn, beans, and rice in the inner pot. Return the inner pot to the cooker base. 8. Then close the lid and turn the steam release handle to Sealing position. 9. Set your Instant Pot on Pressure cook at High and adjust the cooking time to 10 minutes. 10. When cooked, naturally release the pressure about 5 minutes. 11. Remove the lid and scoop the cooked chicken meal into a serving bowl. 12. Sprinkle barbecue sauce, lettuce, tomatoes, onion, lime, Cheddar, and lime on top. 13. Serve and enjoy!
Per Serving: Calories: 832; Fat: 36g; Sodium: 1,590mg; Carbs: 78g; Sugar: 16g; Protein: 42g

Lemony Chicken Thighs and Rice

Prep time: 5 minutes | Cook Time: 25 minutes | Serves: 1

1 tablespoon olive oil	Juice and zest of 1 medium lemon
1 tablespoon butter	1 cup chicken broth
2 (4-ounce) boneless, skinless chicken thighs	½ cup uncooked long-grain white rice
1 teaspoon ground lemon pepper	1 teaspoon Italian seasoning

1 teaspoon minced garlic	⅛ teaspoon ground black pepper
¼ teaspoon salt	1 tablespoon chopped parsley

1. Using lemon pepper, season all sides of the chicken thighs. 2. Set your Instant Pot on Sauté and adjust the temperature to More. 3. After 10 seconds, add oil and butter in the inner pot. Put the seasoned chicken inside and cook both sides for about 10 minutes to brown. 4. When cooked, turn off the machine and remove the inner pot from the cooker base. Add the lemon zest and juice in the inner pot, and then pour the broth. Scrape the browned bits off the inner pot to deglaze the pot. 5. Then add Italian seasoning, garlic, pepper, rice, and salt in the inner pot. 6. Return the inner pot back to the cooker base and close the lid. Then turn the steam release handle to the Sealing position. 7. Set the Instant Pot on Pressure Cook at High and adjust time to 10 minutes. 8. When cooked, naturally release the pressure about 5 minutes and then remove the lid. 9. Transfer the chicken and rice into a bowl and top with the chopped parsley. 10. Serve with a side of steamed broccoli or roasted vegetables.
Per Serving: Calories: 796; Fat: 34g; Sodium: 1,593mg; Carbs: 79g; Sugar: 2g; Protein: 36g

Sesame Teriyaki Chicken Thighs and Rice

Prep time: 5 minutes | Cook Time: 15 minutes | Serves: 1

2 (8-ounce) boneless, skinless chicken thighs	½ cup water
½ cup teriyaki sauce	½ tablespoon sesame seeds
½ cup uncooked long-grain white rice	½ tablespoon chopped green onion

1. Place the chicken thighs in the inner pot and pour the teriyaki sauce over the chicken. Place a trivet on the chicken. 2. Combine together water and rice in a suitable cake pan. Transfer onto the trivet. 3. Then close the lid and turn the steam release handle to Sealing position. 4. Set the Instant Pot on Pressure Cook at High and adjust the time to 10 minutes. 5. When cooked, naturally release the pressure about 5 minutes. 6. Remove the lid. Transfer the pan from the Instant Pot. Using a fork, fluff the rice. 7. Transfer the chicken on the rice and keep warm. 8. Sauté the remaining teriyaki sauce in the Instant Pot about 5 minutes until thicken. 9. Then pour the thickened teriyaki sauce over the chicken and rice. 10. Sprinkle the sesame seeds and onion on the top of the chicken and rice. 11. Serve and treat yourself now!
Per Serving: Calories: 704; Fat: 12g; Sodium: 5,605mg; Carbs: 98g; Sugar: 21g; Protein: 43g

Enticing Bruschetta Chicken

Prep time: 5 minutes | Cook Time: 15 minutes | Serves: 1

Chicken	⅓ cup diced tomatoes
1 cup water	½ tablespoon olive oil
1 (8-ounce) boneless, skinless chicken breast	¼ teaspoon balsamic glaze
⅛ teaspoon salt	¼ teaspoon minced garlic
⅛ teaspoon ground black pepper	1 teaspoon chopped fresh basil
¼ teaspoon Italian seasoning	1/16 teaspoon crushed red pepper flakes
2 (1-ounce) slices fresh mozzarella cheese	1/16 teaspoon ground black pepper
Bruschetta	1/16 teaspoon salt

1. In the inner pot, pour water and then place the trivet. 2. Rub the chicken with black pepper, Italian seasoning, and salt to season. Then place the seasoned chicken on the trivet. 3. Close the lid and turn the steam release handle to Sealing position. 4. Set your Instant Pot on Pressure Cook at High and adjust time to 15 minutes. 5. Meanwhile, to make the bruschetta, mix together the Bruschetta ingredients in a small bowl and then let it chill in refrigerator until ready to serve. 6. When cooked, naturally release the pressure about 5 minutes. Remove the lid and arrange mozzarella slices over the chicken. Close the lid and let it stand for 5 minutes or until the cheese has slightly melted. 7. When done, transfer to a serving plate and serve with Bruschetta on the top. 8. Enjoy!
Per Serving: Calories: 472; Fat: 22g; Sodium: 1,020mg; Carbs: 8g; Sugar: 4g; Protein: 60g

Barbecue Chicken Salad with Berries

Prep time: 10 minutes | Cook Time: 15 minutes | Serves: 1

1 (8-ounce) boneless, skinless chicken breast
1 cup water
1 teaspoon barbecue dry rub
3 tablespoons barbecue sauce
1 ½ cups chopped romaine lettuce
2 tablespoons drained and rinsed canned black beans
2 tablespoons sliced strawberries
1 ½ tablespoons packaged French fried onion
2 tablespoons sweetened dried cranberries
2 tablespoons corn
1 ½ tablespoons shredded smoked Gouda cheese
1 tablespoon bacon bits
¼ cup sliced avocado
2 tablespoons ranch dressing

1. In the inner pot, add chicken, water, and dry rub. 2. Close the lid and turn the steam release knob to Sealing position. 3. When cooked, naturally release the pressure and remove the lid. 4. Transfer the cooked chicken to a small bowl and add 1 tablespoon of cooking liquid. 5. Shred the chicken with 2 forks. 6. Mix in barbecue sauce thoroughly and cool slightly. 7. Meanwhile, toss together the beans, strawberries, French fried onions, corn, cranberries, Gouda, avocado, lettuce, and bacon bits in a medium bowl. 8. Arrange the shredded chicken on the top and sprinkle with ranch dressing. 9. Serve and enjoy!
Per Serving: Calories: 771; Fat: 35g; Sodium: 1,651mg; Carbs: 56g; Sugar: 32g; Protein: 60g

Mayonnaise Chicken Salad

Prep time: 15 minutes | Cook Time: 10 minutes | Serves: 1

1 cup water
1 (8-ounce) boneless, skinless chicken breast
⅛ teaspoon salt
⅛ teaspoon ground black pepper
4 ½ tablespoons mayonnaise
¼ teaspoon dried dill
⅛ teaspoon garlic powder
¼ teaspoon dried onion flakes
⅛ teaspoon dried basil
⅛ teaspoon seasoned salt
1 ½ tablespoons finely diced celery
8 grapes, quartered (about ¼ cup)
1 tablespoon cashew halves

1. Rub the chicken with salt and pepper to season. 2. Pour water inside the inner pot and then place the chicken inside. 3. Close the lid and turn the steam release knob to Sealing position. 4. Set your Instant Pot on Pressure Cook at high and adjust the cooking time to 10 minutes. 5. When cooked, naturally release the pressure about 10 minutes. 6. Remove the lid and transfer the chicken to a small bowl. 7. Dice the chicken into small pieces and cool in the refrigerator to get ready for serving. 8. Combine dill, onion flakes, basil, mayonnaise, garlic powder, seasoned salt, grapes, cashews, and celery in a separate bowl. 9. Mix together with the chicken slices and transfer to a serving plate. 10. Serve immediately or cool in the refrigerator to keep fresh.
Per Serving: Calories: 750; Fat: 55g; Sodium: 1,181mg; Carbs: 11g; Sugar: 7g; Protein: 51g

Savory Brown Butter Chicken Thighs

Prep time: 5 minutes | Cook Time: 27 minutes | Serves: 1

2 tablespoons butter
2 (6-ounce) bone-in chicken thighs
½ teaspoon garlic powder
½ teaspoon Italian seasoning
½ teaspoon salt
½ teaspoon ground black pepper
1 teaspoon minced garlic
½ cup chicken broth

1. Season both sides of the chicken with Italian seasoning, salt, pepper, and garlic powder. 2. Set your Instant Pot on Sauté and adjust the temperature to More. 3. After 10 seconds, add butter in the inner pot and Sauté for about 5 minutes or until browned. 4. Place the chicken in the pot, skin side down, and cook for 5 minutes with stirring. 5. When cooked, remove the chicken to a plate. 6. In the inner pot, add broth and the minced garlic. Turn off the heat and scrape all the browned bits off the pot to deglaze. 7. Close the lid and turn the steam release handle to Sealing position. 8. Set your Instant Pot to Pressure Cook

at High and adjust time to 12 minutes. 9. When cooked, naturally release the pressure about 5 minutes and remove the lid. 10. Serve on a serving plate and enjoy!
Per Serving: Calories: 1,074; Fat: 79g; Sodium: 1,938mg; Fiber: 0g; Carbs: 4g; Sugar: 1g; Protein: 65g

Delicious Chicken Drumsticks with Sweet Chili Sauce

Prep time: 5 minutes | Cook Time: 18 minutes | Serves: 1

1 cup water
4 (4-ounce) chicken drumsticks
¾ cup sweet chili sauce
1 tablespoon chopped green onion

1. Add the chicken drumsticks on a trivet. Pour water in the inner pot and place the trivet. 2. Close the lid and turn the steam release knob to Sealing position. 3. Set your Instant Pot on Pressure Cook at High and adjust the cooking time to 10 minutes for fresh chicken legs and 12 minutes for frozen chicken legs. 4. When cooked, quickly release the pressure, turning the knob from Sealing to the Venting position. 5. Line foil over a baking sheet and preheat an oven broiler to high. 6. Transfer the cooked chicken on the baking pan and brush chili sauce on the chicken. Broil for 4 minutes. 7. Again brush the other side and broil for 4 minutes or until browned and fluffy. 8. Transfer to a serving plate and baste with your favorite sauce. 9. Sprinkle green onion or your favorite seasoning blend on top to serve. 10. Enjoy!
Per Serving: Calories: 1,090; Fat: 29g; Sodium: 3,116mg; Carbs: 102g; Sugar: 84g; Protein: 88g

Garlic Turkey Sweet Potato Hash

Prep time: 10 minutes | Cook Time: 17 minutes | Serves: 4

1½ tablespoons avocado oil
1 medium yellow onion, peeled and diced
2 cloves garlic, minced
1 medium sweet potato, cut into
cubes (peeling not necessary)
½ pound lean ground turkey
½ teaspoon salt
1 teaspoon Italian seasoning blend

1. Set your Instant Pot on Sauté and adjust the temperature to More. 2. Add the oil in the inner pot and heat for 1 minute. 3. Then add onion and cook about 5 minutes or until transparent. Add garlic and cook for 30 seconds more. 4. Add the turkey, Italian seasoning, salt, and sweet potato in the inner pot and cook for another 5 minutes. 5. Turn off the heat and close the lid. 6. Set your Instant Pot on Pressure Cook at High and adjust the cooking time to 5 minutes. 7. When cooked, quick release the pressure until the float valve drops. 8. Carefully remove the lid and spoon onto serving plates. 9. Serve and enjoy!
Per Serving: Calories: 172; Fat: 9g; Sodium: 348mg; Carbs: 10g; Sugar: 3g; Protein: 12g

Lemon Whole "Roasted" Chicken

Prep time: 5 minutes | Cook Time: 28 minutes | Serves: 6

¾ cup water
1 medium lemon
1 (4-pound) whole chicken
1 tablespoon salt
2 teaspoons black pepper

1. In the inner pot, pour water. Cut the lemon into two. 2. Squeeze out juice from the lemon half and add salt and pepper to season. 3. Stuff the chicken with the rest half lemon. 4. Arrange the chicken in the inner pot with breast-side down. Close the lid. 5. Set your Instant Pot on Pressure Cook at High and adjust the cooking time to 28 minutes. 6. When cooked, naturally release the pressure. 7. Carefully remove the lid and then the chicken. On a cutting board, cut the cooled chicken into your desired size. 8. Serve and enjoy!
Per Serving: Calories: 341; Fat: 20g; Sodium: 1,249mg; Carbs: 1g; Sugar: 0g; Protein: 32g

Chicken and Broccoli with Honey-Sesame Sauce

Prep time: 2 minutes | Cook Time: 10 minutes | Serves: 1

¼ cup water
2 tablespoons honey
1 ½ tablespoons brown sugar
1 tablespoon soy sauce
1 tablespoon ketchup
½ tablespoon sriracha sauce
½ tablespoon sesame oil

½ teaspoon minced garlic
1 cup diced chicken breast in 1" pieces
1 ½ cups broccoli florets
½ teaspoon sesame seeds
1 cup cooked white rice

1. Whisk water, brown sugar, ketchup, oil, garlic, honey, and sriracha together in a small bowl. 2. Add the chicken to the inner pot and pour sauce over the chicken. 3. Close the lid and turn the steam release handle to Sealing. 4. Set your Instant Pot on Pressure Cook at High and adjust the cooking time to 2 minutes. 5. When cooked, quickly release the pressure by turning the handle from Sealing to Venting. 6. Remove the lid and set your Instant Pot on Sauté and adjust the temperature to More. 7. Place broccoli to the chicken and mix into sauce. Sauté for 6 to 8 minutes or until the broccoli is completely cooked and sauce is thickened and sticky. 8. Serve over rice with sesame seeds on top. Enjoy!
Per Serving: Calories: 830; Fat: 12g; Sodium: 1,336mg; Carbs: 116g; Sugar: 62g; Protein: 61g

Quick Balsamic Chicken

Prep time: 15 minutes | Cook Time: 20 minutes | Serves: 4

¼ cup Chicken Stock or store-bought low-sodium chicken stock
2 tablespoons balsamic vinegar
4 garlic cloves, minced
1½ pounds chicken tenderloins
1-pound baby red potatoes

8 carrots, peeled and cut into thirds
½ teaspoon cornstarch
¼ teaspoon kosher salt
¼ teaspoon freshly ground black pepper

1. Combine together the vinegar, garlic, and the stock in the inner pot. Then add the chicken, carrots, and potatoes in the pot. 2. Close the lid and turn the steam release handle to Sealing. 3. Set your Instant Pot on Pressure Cook at High and adjust the cooking time to 8 minutes. 4. When cooked, naturally release the pressure about 10 minutes and then quickly release the remaining pressure. 5. Remove the lid carefully and remove the chicken and vegetables to a serving bowl. Reserve the soup behind. 6. Set the Instant Pot on Sauté and adjust the temperature to More. 7. Whisk the cornstarch in the inner pot and simmer for 2 to 3 minutes or until the sauce is thickened. 8. To season, add salt and pepper. 9. Then carefully spoon the sauce over the chicken and vegetables. 10. Serve and enjoy!
Per Serving: Calories: 336; Fat: 3g; Carbs: 32g; Sugar: 8g; Sodium: 265mg; Protein: 43g

Turkey Carrot Taco Lettuce Boats

Prep time: 10 minutes | Cook Time: 24 minutes | Serves: 4

1 tablespoon avocado oil
1 medium onion, peeled and diced
2 large carrots, peeled and diced
2 medium stalks celery, ends removed and diced
2 cloves garlic, minced
1-pound lean ground turkey
1 teaspoon chili powder

1 teaspoon paprika
1 teaspoon cumin
½ teaspoon salt
¼ teaspoon black pepper
1 cup chipotle salsa
12 large romaine leaves
1 medium avocado, peeled, pitted, and sliced

1. Set your Instant Pot on Sauté and adjust the temperature to More. 2. Add the oil in the inner pot and heat 1 minute. Then add onion, celery, garlic, and carrots and cook about 5 minutes or until soften. 3. Add the turkey in the inner pot and cook about 3 minutes or until browned. 4. Stir in paprika, salt, cumin, chili powder, salsa, and pepper until well combined. 5. Turn off the heat and close the lid. 6. Set your Instant Pot on Pressure Cook at High and adjust the cooking time to 15 minutes. 7. When cooked, quick release the pressure until float valve drops. 8. Carefully remove the lid and spoon the taco meat into a romaine

lettuce leaf. 9. Then top with the avocado slices as you like. 10. Serve and enjoy!
Per Serving: Calories: 339; Fat: 18g; Sodium: 900mg; Carbs: 18g; Sugar: 8g; Protein: 27g

Chicken and Quinoa Bowl with Mushrooms

Prep time: 15 minutes | Cook Time: 5 minutes | Serves: 6

1 tablespoon avocado oil
1 small yellow onion, diced
6 cloves garlic, minced
1½ pounds boneless, skinless chicken thighs, cut into bite-sized pieces

2 (8-ounce) packages sliced white mushrooms
3 cups chicken stock
1½ cups quinoa, rinsed well
1 cup nondairy Greek-style yogurt

1. Set your Instant Pot on Sauté and adjust the temperature to More. 2. Add oil in the inner pot and heat for 1 minute. 3. Add onion and sauté about 5 minutes or until soften. Then add garlic and sauté for 30 seconds. 4. Turn off the heat. Add the mushrooms, quinoa, stock, yogurt, and chicken in the inner pot. Stir well. Close the lid and turn the steam release handle to Sealing. 5. Set your Instant Pot on Pressure Cook at High and adjust the cooking time to 3 minutes. 6. When cooked, quick release the pressure until the float valve drops. 7. Carefully remove the lid and spoon the chicken mixture onto a serving plate. 8. Serve and enjoy!
Per Serving: Calories: 397; Fat: 10g; Sodium: 294mg; Carbs: 37g; Sugar: 5g; Protein: 37g

Asian Noodle Bowls with Almonds

Prep time: 10 minutes | Cook Time: 3 minutes | Serves: 1

½ cup reduced sodium tamari
2 tablespoons rice vinegar
2 tablespoons almond butter
2 tablespoons erythritol
2 cups chicken broth
1 pound boneless, skinless chicken breast, cut into bite-sized

pieces
2 large carrots, peeled and thickly sliced (½") on the diagonal
8 ounces uncooked brown rice noodles
¼ cup sliced scallions
4 tablespoons chopped almonds

1. In the inner pot, add vinegar, erythritol, chicken pieces, carrots, broth, and almond butter. Sprinkle the noodles on the top. 2. Close the lid and turn the steam release handle to Sealing position. 3. Set your Instant Pot on Pressure Cook at High and adjust the cooking time to 3 minutes. 4. When cooked, quick release the pressure until the float valve drops. 5. Remove the lid and stir carefully the ingredients. 6. Divide the meal into four serving bowls. 7. Sprinkle the slices scallions and chopped almonds on the top to serve.
Per Serving: Calories: 482; Fat: 11g; Sodium: 1,392mg; Carbs: 62g; Sugar: 6g; Protein: 36g

Curried Chicken Tikka Masala

Prep time: 15 minutes | Cook Time: 15 minutes | Serves: 4

1-pound boneless, skinless chicken breast, cubed
1 cup tomato puree
¼ cup water
1 yellow onion, chopped
4 garlic cloves, minced
1 (1-inch) knob fresh ginger,

grated
1 tablespoon garam masala
¼ teaspoon kosher salt
¼ cup Homemade Yogurt or store-bought plain whole-milk yogurt
1 cup frozen peas

1. Combine the tomato sauce, onion, water, garlic, garam masala, salt, and chicken in the inner pot and close the lid. 2. Set your Instant Pot on Pressure Cook at High and adjust the cooking time to 13 minutes. 3. When cooked, naturally release the pressure about 10 minutes, and then quickly release the remaining pressure. 4. Remove the lid carefully. Add peas and yogurt and stir well. 5. Let it sit for 1 to 2 minutes or until the peas are thoroughly warmed. 6. Serve and enjoy!
Per Serving: Calories: 189; Fat: 3g; Carbs: 12g; Sugar: 6g; Sodium: 187mg; Protein: 29g

Greek-style Chicken and Quinoa with Olives

Prep time: 15 minutes | Cook Time: 10 minutes | Serves: 4

2 tablespoons olive oil
1 red onion, finely chopped
1 red bell pepper, seeded and finely chopped
1 cup Chicken Stock or store-bought low-sodium chicken stock
1½ pounds boneless, skinless chicken breast, cubed
¾ cup quinoa, rinsed well
1 teaspoon dried oregano
½ teaspoon kosher salt
½ teaspoon freshly ground black pepper
1 cup grape or cherry tomatoes, halved
½ cup pitted kalamata olives
¼ cup crumbled full-; Fat feta cheese
2 tablespoons freshly squeezed lemon juice

1. Set your Instant Pot on Sauté and adjust the temperature to More. Add the olive oil in the inner pot. 2. When the oil is heated, add bell pepper and onion. Sauté for 3 to 4 minutes or until softened, stirring from time to time. Turn off the heat. 3. Then add chicken, quinoa, oregano, black pepper, salt, and stock in the inner pot. Close the lid and turn the steam release handle to Sealing. 4. Set your Instant Pot on Pressure Cook at High and adjust the cooking time to 10 minutes. 5. When cooked, naturally release the pressure for 10 minutes, then quick release the remaining pressure. 6. Remove the lid carefully. Add olives, feta cheese, lemon juice, and tomatoes in the inner pot and stir well. 7. Serve and enjoy!
Per Serving: Calories: 454; Fat: 17g; Carbs: 28g; Sugar: 4g; Sodium: 437mg; Protein: 45g

Flavorful Turkey Lettuce Wraps

Prep time: 15 minutes | Cook Time: 15 minutes | Serves: 4

1 tablespoon olive oil
1 yellow onion, diced
2 garlic cloves, minced
1-pound lean (93 percent) ground turkey
⅓ cup water
2 tablespoons honey
2 tablespoons coconut aminos or tamari
1 tablespoon rice vinegar
1 (1-inch) knob fresh ginger, grated
1 (8-ounce) can water chestnuts, drained and diced
2 scallions, white and light green parts, thinly sliced
1 head butter lettuce

1. Set your Instant Pot on Sauté and adjust the temperature to More. 2. Add the olive oil in the inner pot. 3. When the oil has heated, add the garlic and onion and cook for 2 to 3 minutes or until softened, stirring from time to time. Turn off the heat. 4. Then add water, coconut aminos, honey, vinegar, ginger, and ground turkey in the inner pot and stir well to break up the turkey. 5. Close the lid and turn the steam release handle to Sealing position. 6. Set your Instant Pot on Pressure Cook at High and adjust the cooking time to 5 minutes. 7. When cooked, naturally release the pressure for 10 minutes and quick release the remaining pressure. 8. Remove the lid carefully. Then add water, scallions, and chestnuts and stir well. 9. If the sauce is too thin, simmer the sauce about 3 to 4 minutes to thicken. 10. Wrap the turkey mixture with lettuce to serve. Enjoy!
Per Serving: Calories: 355; Fat: 13g; Carbs: 35g; Sugar: 10g; Sodium: 488mg; Protein: 25g

Homemade Chicken and Vegetables

Prep time: 5 minutes | Cook Time: 15 minutes | Serves: 4

2 large bone-in chicken breasts (about 2 pounds)
1 teaspoon kosher salt, divided
½ teaspoon black pepper, divided
½ cup chicken stock
6 large carrots
8 medium whole new potatoes

1. To season, rub the chicken breasts with ½ teaspoon salt and ¼ teaspoon pepper. 2. In the inner pot, pour the stock and soak the chicken breasts in. 3. Arrange the potatoes and carrots over the chicken and add the rest of the salt and pepper to add taste. Close the lid and turn the steam release handle to Sealing. 4. Set your Instant Pot on Pressure Cook at High and adjust the cooking time to 15 minutes. 5.

When cooked, naturally release the pressure and carefully remove the lid. 6. Serve on a serving plate and spoon the soup over. 7. Enjoy!
Per Serving: Calories: 398; Fat: 5g; Sodium: 822mg; Carbs: 24g; Sugar: 6g; Protein: 58g

Chicken Dumplings

Prep time: 10 minutes | Cook time: 30 minutes | Serves: 8

For the chicken and broth
4 tablespoons butter
8 medium bone-in, skin-on chicken thighs
Kosher salt
Black pepper
½ cup all-purpose flour
4 celery stalks, chopped
3 carrots, peeled and chopped
2 onions, chopped
3½ cups chicken broth, preferably homemade (try the recipe here)
½ cup whole milk or half-and-half
2 tablespoons cornstarch
For the dumplings
1¾ cups all-purpose flour
¼ cup cornmeal
1 tablespoon baking powder
½ teaspoon kosher salt
¼ teaspoon black pepper
1 cup whole milk or half-and-half
3 tablespoons melted butter

1. Press the "Sauté" Button, two times to select "More" settings. 2. Add the butter. Season the chicken with salt and pepper and dredge in the flour, shaking off the excess. 3. Once the butter is sizzling and the pot is hot, add half of the chicken in one layer. 4. Brown on one side for 3 or 4 minutes, without moving, and flip and brown on the other side. 5. Remove and repeat with the remaining chicken. Set aside. 6. Add the celery, carrots, and onions to the pot. Sauté for 3 minutes, scraping the bottom of the pot. 7. Press Cancel button to stop this cooking program. 8. Add the chicken and broth. Season with salt and pepper. 9. Put on the pressure cooker's lid and turn the steam valve to "Sealing" position. 10. Select Pressure Cook mode, and then press the "Pressure Cook" button again to select "Less" time option. 11. Use the "+/-" keys on the control panel to set the cooking time to 11 minutes. 12. Press the Pressure Level button to adjust the pressure to "High Pressure." 13. Once the cooking cycle is completed, allow the steam to release naturally. 14. When all the steam is released, remove the pressure lid from the top carefully. 15. While the chicken is cooking, make the dumplings. 16. Mix together the flour, cornmeal, baking powder, salt, and pepper in a medium bowl. 17. Add the milk or half-and-half and melted butter, and stir just until incorporated (don't over-mix). Set aside. 18. Once cooking is complete, use a quick release. Remove the chicken and set aside. 19. Add the milk to the broth in the pot, mix, and season with salt and pepper. 20. In a small bowl, combine ½ cup of hot broth with the cornstarch and whisk well to combine. 21. Add back to the pot and stir. 22. Press the "Sauté" Button, two times to select "Normal" settings. 23. Once simmering, scoop heaping tablespoons of the dumpling mixture and drop them into the pot. 24. Reduce Sauté heat to low and cook for 12 to 15 minutes, loosely covered with the top without locking it, until the dumplings have doubled in size. 25. Meanwhile, bone the chicken, remove and discard the skin, and shred the meat. 26. Add back to the pot and serve in bowls.
Per Serving: Calories 334; Fat 7.9g; Sodium 704mg; Carbs 6g; Fiber 3.6g; Sugar 6g; Protein 18g

Classic Chicken Alfredo

Prep time: 5 minutes | Cook Time: 17 minutes | Serves: 1

1 tablespoon butter
¼ cup chicken broth
1 cup heavy cream
½ teaspoon minced garlic
4 ounces uncooked fettuccine, broken in half
1 cup diced chicken breast
¼ teaspoon salt
⅛ teaspoon ground black pepper
1 cup broccoli florets
¼ cup shredded Parmesan cheese

1. Add broth, garlic, butter, and cream in the inner pot. To reduce clumping, layer the noodles in a crisscross shape over the liquid. 2. Place the chicken over the noodles and season with salt and pepper. 3. Set your Instant Pot on Pressure Cook at High and adjust the cooking time to 7 minutes. 4. When cooked, quick release the pressure, turning from Sealing to Venting. 5. Remove the lid and stir for a while. Arrange the broccoli and close the lid. 6. Cook the broccoli for 8 to 10 minutes or until cooked completely. 7. Sprinkle Parmesan cheese on the top and stir well. 8. Serve and enjoy!
Per Serving: Calories: 1,732; Fat: 104g; Sodium: 1,379mg; Fiber: 6g; Carbs: 99g; Sugar: 12g; Protein: 81g

Kale Chicken Salad

Prep time: 20 minutes | Cook Time: 6 minutes | Serves: 4

1-pound boneless, skinless chicken breast	3 cups chopped cabbage
½ cup chicken stock	¼ cup pure sesame oil
2 bunches kale (about 12 ounces total), deveined and finely chopped	¼ cup almond butter
	¼ cup raw honey
1 medium red bell pepper, seeded and diced	Juice from 2 medium limes
	1 tablespoon reduced sodium tamari
1 cup diced carrot	¼ teaspoon minced garlic
	⅓ cup sesame seeds

1. In the inner pot, pour the stock and soak the chicken breast in. 2. Close the lid and turn the steam release handle to Sealing. 3. Set your Instant Pot on Pressure Cook at High and adjust the cooking time to 6 minutes. 4. When cooked, naturally release the pressure. 5. Carefully remove the lid. Transfer the chicken onto a cutting board. When it is completely cool, cut into your desired size. 6. Mix together the bell pepper, cabbage, carrots, chopped chicken, and kale in a large bowl. 7. Blend the almond butter, lime juice, garlic, tamari, and oil in a blender until smooth. 8. Then pour the almond butter mixture over the chicken mixture to make the salad. Toss well. 9. Sprinkle sesame seeds on the top and lightly toss. 10. Serve and enjoy!
Per Serving: Calories: 561; Fat: 30g; Sodium: 332mg; Carbs: 41g; Sugar: 25g; Protein: 36g

Tasty Lemon Chicken Thighs

Prep time: 10 minutes | Cook Time: 11 minutes | Serves: 4

1 tablespoon avocado oil	Juice and zest from 1 large lemon
1½ pounds boneless, skinless chicken thighs	1 tablespoon Italian seasoning blend
1 small onion, peeled and diced	⅓ cup chicken stock
1 tablespoon minced garlic	1 tablespoon arrowroot powder

1. Set your Instant Pot on Sauté and adjust the temperature to Normal. 2. Add oil onto the inner pot and heat for 2 minutes. 3. When the oil has heated, add the chicken thighs in the inner pot and cook each side for 2 minutes or until brown. 4. When cooked, remove the chicken thighs from the inner pot and set aside. 5. Sauté the onion in the inner pot for 2 minutes or until transparent. 6. Add garlic and cook for 30 seconds more. 7. Add the lemon zest, lemon juice, and Italian seasoning in the inner pot. To deglaze, scrape up all the brown bites off the pot. Turn off the heat. 8. Place the chicken thighs in the stock and close the lid. 9. Set your Instant Pot on Pressure Cook at High and adjust the cooking time to 7 minutes. 10. When cooked, naturally release the pressure until the float valve drops. 11. Remove the lid and transfer the chicken to a serving bowl. 12. Add the arrowroot powder in the sauce and stir well. 13. Pour the thickened sauce over the chicken thighs. 14. Serve and enjoy!
Per Serving: Calories: 262; Fat: 10g; Sodium: 190mg; Carbs: 6g; Sugar: 1g; Protein: 34g

Chili Chicken Thighs and Rice

Prep time: 5 minutes | Cook Time: 22 minutes | Serves: 1

½ tablespoon olive oil	2 (6–8-ounce) bone-in chicken thighs
1 teaspoon dried cilantro	
¼ teaspoon chili powder	½ cup uncooked long-grain white rice
¼ teaspoon ground cumin	
¼ teaspoon salt	½ cup chicken broth
¼ teaspoon garlic powder	1 medium lime, quartered

1. Combine together chili powder, salt, cumin, cilantro, and garlic powder in a small bowl. 2. Season each side of the chicken with ½ teaspoon of the mixture and reserve the remaining seasoning. 3. Set your Instant Pot on Sauté and adjust the temperature to More. 4. After 10 seconds, add oil in the inner pot and let it heat up until shiny. 5. Add the seasoned chicken in the inner pot, skin side down and sauté for 5 minutes or until the skin is golden and crispy. 6. Then add the

reserved mixture, broth, rice, and ¾ lime to the chicken. 7. Turn off the heat and scrape all the browned bits off the pot to deglaze. 8. Close the lid and turn the steam release handle to Sealing position. 9. Set your Instant Pot on Pressure Cook at High and adjust the cooking time to 12 minutes. 10. When cooked, naturally release the pressure about 5 minutes. 11. Remove the lid and transfer to a serving bowl and serve with the remaining lime on the top. Enjoy!
Per Serving: Calories: 1,261; Fat: 65g; Sodium: 1,378mg; Carbs: 77g; Sugar: 1g; Protein: 71g

Avocado Chicken Salad with Strawberries

Prep time: 10 minutes | Cook Time: 6 minutes | Serves: 4

1-pound boneless, skinless chicken breasts	⅛ teaspoon white pepper
	8 cups baby spinach
½ cup chicken stock	1 medium avocado, peeled, pitted, and cut into slices
13 large strawberries, hulled, divided	
	⅓ cup sliced almonds
2 tablespoons extra-virgin olive oil	½ teaspoon salt
	¼ teaspoon freshly ground black pepper
2 tablespoons fresh lemon juice	
¼ teaspoon ground ginger	

1. In the inner pot, add the chicken breasts and stock. 2. Close the lid and turn the steam release handle to Sealing. 3. Set your Instant Pot on Pressure Cook at High and adjust the cooking time to 6 minutes. 4. Place the hulled strawberries, lemon juice, ginger, white pepper, and oil in a blender and blend together until smooth. Set aside. 5. When cooked, naturally release the pressure until the float valve drops. 6. Carefully remove the lid and transfer the chicken onto a cutting board. 7. When cooled completely, cut the chicken into your desired size. 8. Add the avocado slices, almonds, strawberry slices, the chicken slices, and the baby spinach in a large serving bowl. 9. Drizzle the salad dressing over the chicken and fruit mixture. 10. Season with salt and pepper and toss well. 11. Serve and enjoy!
Per Serving: Calories: 333; Fat: 18g; Sodium: 392mg; Carbs: 12g; Sugar: 4g; Protein: 33g

Tuscan Chicken with Tomatoes and Kale

Prep time: 5 minutes | Cook Time: 14 minutes | Serves: 1

1 tablespoon olive oil	½ cup chicken broth
1 cup diced chicken breast in 1" cubes	¼ teaspoon soy sauce
	1 tablespoon chopped sun-dried tomatoes
¼ teaspoon Italian seasoning	
⅛ teaspoon garlic powder	½ cup sliced packed kale
⅛ teaspoon salt	¼ cup heavy cream
⅛ teaspoon ground black pepper	¼ cup shredded Parmesan cheese
½ teaspoon dried onion flakes	

1. Set your Instant Pot on Sauté and adjust the temperature level to More. 2. After 10 seconds, add oil. 3. Place the chicken in a small bowl. Then add garlic powder, pepper, salt, and Italian seasoning to coat the chicken. 4. Place the chicken in the inner pot and sear each side for about 3 minutes or until browned without stirring. 5. Turn off the heat and then add soy sauce, tomatoes, broth, and onion flakes. Scrape all the browned bits off the pot to deglaze. 6. Close the lid and turn the steam release handle to Sealing position. 7. Set your Instant Pot on Pressure Cook at High and adjust the cooking time to 3 minutes. 8. When cooked, quickly release the pressure turning the handle from Sealing to Venting. 9. Remove the lid. Add kale and stir. Close the lid and let it stand in the Instant Pot for about 5 minutes or until wilt down. 10. Then remove the lid. Add cream and Parmesan and stir well. 11. Transfer onto a serving plate and enjoy!
Per Serving: Calories: 704; Fat: 43g; Sodium: 1,300mg; Carbs: 7g; Sugar: 4g; Protein: 62g

Balsamic Chicken Cacciatore

Prep time: 15 minutes | Cook Time: 12 minutes | Serves: 6

6 bone-in chicken thighs, with skin
¼ teaspoon kosher salt
¼ teaspoon freshly ground black pepper
2 tablespoons olive oil
1 (28-ounce) can crushed tomatoes
2 green bell peppers, seeded and

diced
1 pint cremini mushrooms, halved lengthwise
½ cup pitted black olives
1 yellow onion, diced
1 teaspoon dried oregano
2 garlic cloves, minced
1 teaspoon balsamic vinegar

1. Toss the chicken with black pepper and salt to season. 2. Set your Instant Pot on Sauté and adjust the temperature to More. 3. After 10 seconds, pour olive oil in the inner pot. 4. When the oil has heated, place the chicken in the pot, with skin-side down. 5. Cook without stirring for 5 to 8 minutes or until the skin is golden brown. 6. Turn the chicken to skin-side up and turn off the heat. 7. Add bell peppers, onion, olives, garlic, oregano, balsamic vinegar, and tomatoes in the inner pot and close the lid. 8. Set your Instant Pot to Pressure Cook at High and adjust the cooking time to 12 minutes. 9. When cooked, naturally release the pressure about 10 minutes and quickly release the remaining pressure. 10. Transfer carefully the lid. 11. Serve and enjoy!
Per Serving: Calories: 520; Fat: 38g; Carbs: 10g; Sugar: 5g; Sodium: 446mg; Protein: 34g

Chicken Fajitas with Cilantro

Prep time: 15 minutes | Cook Time: 0 minutes | Serves: 4

2 red or yellow bell peppers, seeded and sliced
1 red onion, sliced
1 teaspoon olive oil
½ teaspoon chili powder

¼ teaspoon kosher salt
1¼ pounds boneless, skinless chicken breast, thinly sliced
12 cassava flour or corn tortillas

Combine onion, olive oil, bell pepper, salt, and chili powder
Per Serving: Calories: 367; Fat: 7g; Carbs: 38g; Sugar: 4g; Sodium: 187mg; Protein: 37g

Chicken and Rice Bowl with Cilantro

Prep time: 5 minutes | Cook Time: 5 minutes | Serves: 4

1 cup jasmine rice
1 (13.66-ounce) can unsweetened full-; Fat coconut milk
½ cup chicken stock
1¼ pounds boneless, skinless chicken breasts, cut into 1" cubes

1 teaspoon salt
½ teaspoon ground cumin
¼ teaspoon ground ginger
Juice from 1 medium lime
½ cup chopped cilantro leaves and stems

1. In the inner pot, add coconut milk, chicken, cumin, salt, ginger, stock, and rice and stir until well combined. Close the lid and turn the steam release handle to Sealing. 2. Set your Instant Pot on Pressure Cook at High and adjust the cooking time to 5 minutes. 3. When cooked, naturally release the pressure for 10 minutes and then quick release the remaining pressure. 4. Carefully remove the lid and add the lime juice and stir to mix well. 5. Divide the soup into four bowls and sprinkle with cilantro. 6. Serve and enjoy!
Per Serving: Calories: 527; Fat: 22g; Sodium: 702mg; Carbs: 38g; Sugar: 1g; Protein: 38g

Dijon Avocado Chicken Salad

Prep time: 10 minutes | Cook Time: 6 minutes | Serves: 4

1 pound boneless, skinless chicken breasts
½ cup chicken stock
1½ medium avocados, peeled,

pitted, and mashed (1 cup mashed)
1 medium stalk celery, ends removed and diced

1 scallion, thinly sliced
1 tablespoon lemon juice
1 tablespoon chopped fresh parsley
½ teaspoon dried dill weed

2 teaspoons Dijon mustard
½ teaspoon kosher salt
¼ teaspoon freshly ground black pepper

1. In the inner pot, pour the chicken stock and soak the chicken breasts in. 2. Close the lid and turn the steam release handle to Sealing. 3. Set your Instant Pot on Pressure Cook at High and adjust the cooking time to 6 minutes. 4. When cooked, naturally release the pressure and carefully remove the lid. 5. Transfer the chicken breasts onto a cutting board and let it cool completely. 6. Then cut the chicken into your desired size. 7. In a medium bowl, add the chopped chicken and the rest of the ingredients and stir until well tossed. 8. Serve and enjoy!
Per Serving: Calories: 230; Fat: 9g; Sodium: 421mg; Carbs: 6g; Sugar: 1g; Protein: 27g

Turkey with Butternut Squash and Carrots

Prep time: 15 minutes | Cook Time: 40 minutes | Serves: 4

1½ pounds turkey tenderloin
2 teaspoons olive oil, divided
½ teaspoon poultry seasoning
½ teaspoon kosher salt
¼ teaspoon freshly ground black

pepper
2 cups cubed butternut squash
4 celery stalks, sliced
4 carrots, peeled and sliced

1. Rub the 1 teaspoon of olive oil over the turkey. Then season with salt, pepper, and the poultry seasoning. Set the mixture aside. 2. On a piece of aluminum foil, add celery, carrots, and the squash. Foil the sides up together like a boat to contain the vegetables. Do not cover the top. 3. Drizzle the remaining olive oil over the vegetables and set aside. 4. In the inner pot, pour 1 cup of water. Place a trivet in the inner pot. Arrange the turkey on the trivet and then close the lid. 5. Turn the steam release handle to Sealing position. 6. Set your Instant Pot on Pressure Cook at High and adjust the cooking time to 20 minutes. 7. When cooked, quick release the pressure. 8. Remove the lid carefully and put the foil boat of vegetables directly on the turkey. 9. Close the lid and turn the steam release handle to Sealing position. 10. Set your Instant Pot on Pressure Cook at High and adjust the cooking time to 20 minutes. 11. When cooked, naturally release the pressure about 10 minutes, then quick release the remaining pressure. 12. Remove the lid carefully. Then transfer the foil boat of vegetables and set aside for serving. 13. Remove the turkey onto a cutting board and cut into your desired slices. 14. Serve alongside the vegetables and enjoy!
Per Serving: Calories: 281; Fat: 7g; Carbs: 16g; Sugar: 5g; Sodium: 367mg; Protein: 41g

Baked Chicken and Veggies

Prep time: 5 minutes | Cook Time: 5 minutes | Serves: 4

4 cups riced cauliflower
8 ounces white mushrooms, chopped
8 ounces shiitake mushrooms, stems removed and chopped
8 ounces oyster mushrooms, chopped
1½ pounds boneless, skinless

chicken breasts, cut into bite-sized pieces
¼ cup chicken stock
1 tablespoon minced garlic
1 teaspoon salt
1 teaspoon dried thyme
Juice from 1 large lemon

1. In the inner pot, add the mushrooms, chicken, and cauliflower. 2. Whisk the garlic, stock, salt, thyme, and lemon juice in a small bowl. 3. Pour the mixture over the chicken and vegetables and stir well. 4. Close the lid and turn the steam release handle to Sealing. 5. Set your Instant Pot on Pressure Cook at High and adjust the cooking time to 5 minutes. 6. When cooked, naturally release the pressure until the float valve drops. 7. Remove the lid. 8. Stir the mixture well. Serve and enjoy!
Per Serving: Calories: 432; Fat: 4g; Sodium: 428mg; Carbs: 54g; Sugar: 5g; Protein: 50g

Lemon Turkey Breast with Shallot

Prep time: 10 minutes | Cook Time: 17 minutes | Serves: 4

1 (1½-pound) boneless, skinless turkey breast	½ medium shallot, peeled and minced
2 tablespoons avocado oil, divided	1 large clove garlic, minced
Zest from ½ large lemon	½ teaspoon kosher salt
	¼ teaspoon black pepper

1. Using a towel, pat dry the turkey breast. Then cut the turkey breast into two. 2. Rub the 1 tablespoon of oil over the turkey breast. 3. Mix together the shallot, minced garlic, pepper, salt, and lemon zest in a small bowl. 4. Rub the turkey breast with mixture to season. 5. Set the Instant Pot on Sauté and adjust the temperature to More. 6. Add the remaining oil in the inner pot and heat about 2 minutes. 7. Add the turkey breast and sear each side about 3 minutes. Turn off the heat. 8. Set your Instant Pot on Pressure Cook at High and adjust the cooking time to 10 minutes. 9. When cooked, naturally release the pressure and carefully remove the lid. 10. Transfer the turkey breast onto a cutting board. When it is completely cool, cut into your desired slice. 11. Serve and enjoy!
Per Serving: Calories: 250; Fat: 9g; Sodium: 445mg; Carbs: 1g; Sugar: 0g; Protein: 40g

Thyme Turkey Breast

Prep time: 10 minutes | Cook Time: 18 minutes | Serves: 4

1½ pounds boneless, skinless turkey breast	1 teaspoon Italian seasoning blend
2 tablespoons avocado oil, divided	½ teaspoon kosher salt
1 teaspoon sweet paprika	½ teaspoon thyme
	¼ teaspoon garlic salt
	¼ teaspoon black pepper

1. Using a towel, pat dry the turkey breast. Then cut the turkey breast into two. 2. Rub 1 tablespoon of oil over the turkey breast. 3. Mix together Italian seasoning, thyme, kosher salt, garlic salt, pepper, and paprika in a small bowl. 4. Toss the chicken well with the mixture to season. 5. Set your Instant Pot on Sauté and adjust the temperature to More. Add the remaining oil and heat about 2 minutes. 6. Add the seasoned turkey breast and sear each side about 3 minutes. 7. Turn off the heat and transfer the turkey onto a serving plate. 8. Then pour 1 cup of water in the inner pot and scrape up all the brown bits off the pot with a spatula. 9. Place the steam rack with handles in the inner pot and top the turkey breast on the rack. 10. Close the lid and turn the steam release handle to Sealing. 11. When cooked, naturally release the pressure until the float valve drops. 12. Carefully remove onto a cutting board. When the meat is cool, cut into your desired slices. 13. Serve and enjoy!
Per Serving: Calories: 248; Fat: 9g; Sodium: 568mg; Carbs: 0g; Sugar: 0g; Protein: 40g

Savory Chicken Breasts with Veggies

Prep time: 10 minutes | Cook Time: 18 minutes | Serves: 4

2 tablespoons avocado oil	8 cups chopped green cabbage
1-pound sliced baby bella mushrooms	1½ teaspoons dried thyme
1½ teaspoons salt, divided	½ cup chicken stock
2 cloves garlic, minced	1½ pounds boneless, skinless chicken breasts

1. Set your Instant Pot on Sauté and adjust the temperature to More. 2. Add oil in the inner pot and heat about 1 minute. 3. Add the ¼ teaspoon salt and mushrooms in the inner pot and cook about 10 minutes or until their liquid evaporated. 4. Then add garlic and cook for 10 seconds more. Turn off the heat and close the lid. 5. Stir ¼ teaspoon salt, stock, thyme, and cabbage in the inner pot until well combined. 6. Close the lid and turn the steam release handle to Sealing. 7. Set your Instant Pot on Pressure Cook at High and adjust the cooking time to 6 minutes. 8. When cooked, naturally release the pressure for 10 minutes and quick release the remaining pressure. 9. Carefully remove the lid. 10. Serve on serving plates and drizzle the soup over.

Per Serving: Calories: 337; Fat: 10g; Sodium: 1,023mg; Carbs: 14g; Sugar: 2g; Protein: 44g

Spiced Chicken and Carrots

Prep time: 15 minutes | Cook Time: 15 minutes | Serves: 4

1 teaspoon dried thyme	(about 2 pounds)
¼ teaspoon ground ginger	½ cup chicken stock
¼ teaspoon ground allspice	2 medium onions, peeled and cut in fourths
1 teaspoon kosher salt	4 medium carrots
½ teaspoon black pepper	
2 large bone-in chicken breasts	

1. Mix together ginger, ground allspice, ginger, salt, thyme, and pepper in a small bowl. 2. Season the chicken breasts with half of the spice mixture. 3. In the inner pot, add the chicken stock and then place the chicken breasts. 4. Top the chicken with onions and carrots and add the remaining spice mixture. 5. Close the lid and turn the steam release handle to Sealing position. 6. Set your Instant Pot on Pressure Cook at High and adjust the cooking time to 15 minutes. 7. When cooked, naturally release the pressure. 8. Carefully remove the chicken and vegetables over rice or lentils to serve.
Per Serving: Calories: 337; Fat: 5g; Sodium: 755mg; Carbs: 12g; Sugar: 5g; Protein: 56g

Chicken and Fresh Green Beans

Prep time: 5 minutes | Cook Time: 7 minutes | Serves: 1

1 slice uncooked thick-cut bacon, chopped	½ tablespoon dried onion flakes
⅓ cup diced mushrooms	½ teaspoon minced garlic
1 cup diced chicken breast	¼ cup chicken broth
¼ teaspoon seasoned salt	1 teaspoon soy sauce
½ teaspoon Italian seasoning	5 ounces fresh green beans, trimmed

1. Set your Instant Pot to Sauté and adjust the temperature level to More. 2. Sauté the bacon in the inner pot for about 5 minutes or until crispy. 3. Then place onion flakes, soy sauce, chicken, salt, broth, garlic, Italian seasoning, and mushrooms in the inner pot. Turn off the heat and deglaze the pot by scraping the bottom of the pot with a wooden spoon. 4. Then stir in green beans. 5. Close the lid and turn the steam release handle to Sealing position. 6. Set your Instant Pot on Pressure Cook at High and adjust the cooking time to 2 minutes. 7. When cooked, naturally release the pressure about 5 minutes. 8. Remove the lid and serve on a serving bowl. 9. Enjoy!
Per Serving: Calories: 442; Fat: 12g; Sodium: 1,019mg; Carbs: 14g; Sugar: 6g; Protein: 63g

Dijon Chicken Tenders

Prep time: 5 minutes | Cook Time: 7 minutes | Serves: 4

1-pound chicken tenders	1 tablespoon avocado oil
1 tablespoon fresh thyme leaves	1 cup chicken stock
½ teaspoon salt	¼ cup Dijon mustard
¼ teaspoon black pepper	¼ cup raw honey

1. Using a towel, pat dry the chicken tender and rub with salt, pepper, and thyme to season. 2. Set your Instant Pot on Sauté and adjust the temperature to More. 3. Add the oil in the inner pot and heat for 2 minutes. 4. Add the chicken tenders and sear each side for 1 minute or until brown. Turn off the heat. 5. Carefully remove the chicken tenders and set aside. 6. Pour the stock in the inner pot and scrape up all the browned bits off the pot. 7. Place the steam rack with handles in the inner pot and arrange the chicken tender on top. 8. Close the lid and turn the steam release handle to Sealing. 9. Set your Instant Pot on Pressure Cook at High and adjust the cooking time to 3 minutes. 10. Combine the Dijon mustard and honey together in a small mixing bowl to make the honey mustard sauce. 11. When cooked, naturally release the pressure and carefully remove the lid. 12. Drizzle the honey mustard sauce over the chicken tenders. 13. Serve and enjoy!
Per Serving: Calories: 223; Fat: 5g; Sodium: 778mg; Carbs: 19g; Sugar: 18g; Protein: 22g

Coconut Chicken and Vegetables Bowl

Prep time: 15 minutes | Cook Time: 11 minutes | Serves: 4

1 tablespoon coconut oil	1 (13.66-ounce) can unsweetened full-; Fat coconut milk
1 small yellow onion, peeled and diced	1 cup chicken broth
2 heaping cups large cauliflower florets	Juice from 1 medium lime
1½ pounds boneless, skinless chicken breasts, cut into 1½" chunks	1 teaspoon kosher salt
	1 teaspoon ground cumin
	½ teaspoon ground ginger
	2 cups baby spinach leaves

1. Set your Instant Pot on Sauté and adjust the temperature to Normal. 2. Add the coconut oil in the inner pot, heat until the oil melts. 3. Then sauté the onion in the pot for 5 minutes, or until soften. 4. Stir in chicken, cauliflower, broth, coconut milk, lime juice, cumin, salt, and ginger until combined well. 5. Close the lid and turn the steam release handle to Sealing. 6. Set your Instant Pot on Pressure Cook at High and adjust the cooking time to 6 minutes. 7. When cooked, naturally release the pressure until the float valve drops. 8. Then remove the lid and add spinach in the inner pot. 9. Stir until wilted. 10. Serve and enjoy!
Per Serving: Calories: 457; Fat: 26g; Sodium: 931mg; Carbs: 9g; Sugar: 2g; Protein: 43g

Chicken and Green Beans with Basil

Prep time: 15 minutes | Cook Time: 10 minutes | Serves: 4

2 teaspoons olive oil	½ cup water
1½ pounds ground chicken	1 tablespoon coconut aminos or tamari
1 red bell pepper, seeded and sliced	1 tablespoon gluten-free fish sauce
1 shallot, finely chopped	½ pound fresh green beans
1 tablespoon all-natural Chile pepper paste	1 cup whole fresh basil leaves

1. Set your Instant Pot on Sauté and adjust the temperature to More. 2. Add olive oil in the inner pot. When the oil is heated, add the chicken and cook for 2 to 3 minutes or until brown. Stir from time to time to break up the chicken. Turn off the heat. 3. Sit in shallot, chile pepper paste, coconut aminos, fish sauce, water, and bell pepper to combine. 4. Close the lid and turn the steam release handle to Sealing position. 5. Set your Instant Pot on Pressure Cook at High and adjust the temperature to 2 minutes. Press Keep Warm. 6. When cooked, quick release the pressure. 7. Remove the lid carefully and add the green beans. 8. Let it sit in the pot for 5 minutes or until the green beans are steamed. 9. Remove the lid. Add basil in the pot and stir well. 10. Serve and enjoy!
Per Serving: Calories: 298; Fat: 16g; Carbs: 7g; Sugar: 4g; Sodium: 513mg; Protein: 32g

Tasty Turkey and Greens Meatloaf

Prep time: 15 minutes | Cook Time: 25 minutes | Serves: 4

1 tablespoon avocado oil	1-pound lean ground turkey
1 small onion, peeled and diced	¼ cup almond flour
2 cloves garlic, minced	1 large egg
3 cups mixed baby greens, finely chopped	¾ teaspoon salt
	½ teaspoon black pepper

1. Set your Instant Pot on Sauté and adjust the temperature to More. 2. Add oil in the inner pot and heat 1 minute. 3. Add the onion and sauté about 3 minutes or until soften. Add the garlic and greens and cook for 1 more minute. Turn off the heat. 4. Combine the flour, salt, egg, pepper, and turkey in a medium bowl. 5. Then stir the onion and greens mixture in the turkey mixture until well combined. 6. Rinse out the pot and pour in 2 cups of water. 7. Fold a large piece of foil in half and bend the edge upward to make an aluminum foil sling. 8. Make a rectangular loaf from the turkey mixture and place onto the aluminum sling. 9. Transfer the sling onto the steam rack with handles and lower into the pot. Close the lid. 10. Set the Instant Pot on Pressure Cook at High and adjust the cooking time to 20 minutes. 11. When cooked, quick release the pressure until the float valve drops. 12. Carefully remove the lid and transfer the meatloaf onto a cutting board. 13. When the meatloaf is completely cool, cut into your desired slices. 14. Serve and enjoy!
Per Serving: Calories: 271; Fat: 17g; Sodium: 406mg; Carbs: 5g; Sugar: 1g; Protein: 25g

Jerk Chicken with Mustard

Prep time: 15 minutes | Cook Time: 22 minutes | Serves: 8

1 large onion, peeled and cut into 8 pieces	1 teaspoon black pepper
1 tablespoon peeled and chopped fresh ginger	2 tablespoons red wine vinegar
3 much hot chili peppers, deveined and deseeded	2 tablespoons coconut aminos
½ teaspoon ground allspice	2 cloves garlic, minced
2 tablespoons dry mustard	½ cup chicken stock
	4 pounds boneless, skinless chicken breasts cut in 1" pieces

1. In a food processor, combine the onion, ginger, chili peppers, allspice, black pepper, red wine vinegar, coconut aminos, minced garlic, and chicken stock together. 2. Place the chicken in the inner pot and drizzle over with the sauce. Stir well. 3. Close the lid and turn the steam release handle to Sealing. 4. Set your Instant Pot on Pressure Cook at High and adjust the cooking time to 12 minutes. 5. When cooked, quick release the pressure. 6. Transfer the chicken onto a baking sheet lined with parchment paper or a silicone baking mat. 7. If you want it golden-browned, set your broiler to high and broil for 6 to 10 minutes or until the chicken is nicely browned, flipping once. 8. Pour the sauce over the chicken. 9. Serve and enjoy!
Per Serving: Calories: 306; Fat: 5g; Sodium: 210mg; Carbs: 6g; Sugar: 2g; Protein: 52g

Chicken Enchiladas

Prep time: 10 minutes | Cook time: 35 minutes | Serves: 4

3 medium boneless, skinless chicken breasts	2 (10-ounce) cans green enchilada sauce
Kosher salt	½ cup sour cream, plus more for serving
Black pepper	
1 cup chicken broth or water	10 to 12 corn tortillas
2 garlic cloves, minced	2 cups Monterey Jack cheese
½ onion, sliced	

1. Season the chicken with salt and pepper and place it in the Inner Pot, along with the broth, garlic, and onion. 2. Put on the pressure cooker's lid and turn the steam valve to "Sealing" position. 3. Select Pressure Cook mode, and then press the "Pressure Cook" button again to select "Less" time option. 4. Use the "+/-" keys on the control panel to set the cooking time to 7 minutes. 5. Press the Pressure Level button to adjust the pressure to "High Pressure." 6. Once the cooking cycle is completed, allow the steam to release naturally. 7. When all the steam is released, remove the pressure lid from the top carefully. 8. Heat your oven to 375 degrees F in advance. 9. Remove the chicken, shred it, and combine in a large bowl with ½ cup of enchilada sauce and the sour cream. Season with salt and pepper. 10. Spread another ½ cup of enchilada sauce into a 9-by-13-inch baking dish. 11. Warm the tortillas slightly in the oven, on the stove, or in the microwave to make them pliable. 12. Fill each with 2 to 3 tablespoons of the chicken mixture and a sprinkle of cheese. 13. Roll into cigar shapes and place, side-by-side and seam-side down, into the baking dish. 14. Top with the remaining sauce and cheese. Cover with foil. 15. Bake for 15 minutes. Remove the foil and bake for 5 to 10 minutes more, until the cheese is melted. 16. Serve hot.
Per Serving: Calories 382; Fat 7.9g; Sodium 704mg; Carbs 6g; Fiber 3.6g; Sugar 6g; Protein 18g

Chicken Pot Pie

Prep time: 10 minutes | Cook time: 25 minutes | Serves: 4-5

1 frozen puff pastry sheet	chicken breasts
1 tablespoon olive oil	1½ cups chicken broth
1 small onion, chopped	1 teaspoon kosher salt
2 medium carrots, peeled and chopped	2 tablespoons all-purpose flour
2 celery stalks, chopped	2 tablespoons cold butter
2 medium potatoes, cut into ¾-inch cubes	½ cup heavy cream or whole milk
3 medium bone-in, skin-on	1 cup frozen peas
	Black pepper

1. Thaw the puff pastry sheet on the counter for 30 minutes. 2. Press the "Sauté" Button, two times to select "Normal" settings and add the oil. 3. Add the onion, carrots, and celery. Stir and cook for 3 minutes. 4. Add the potatoes, chicken, broth, and salt. 5. Put on the pressure cooker's lid and turn the steam valve to "Sealing" position. 6. Select Pressure Cook mode, and then press the "Pressure Cook" button again to select "Less" time option. 7. Use the "+/-" keys on the control panel to set the cooking time to 7 minutes. 8. Press the Pressure Level button to adjust the pressure to "High Pressure." 9. Meanwhile, once the pastry sheet is pliable but still cold, lay it out on a baking sheet and cut into 4 even squares or rectangles. Bake for 15 minutes. 10. Remove the chicken and, once cool enough to handle, pull off the meat and discard the skin and bones. 11. Cut the meat into cubes. 12. Once the cooking cycle of Instant Pot is completed, allow the steam to release naturally. 13. When all the steam is released, press Cancel button and remove the pressure lid from the top carefully. 14. Press the "Sauté" Button, two times to select "Normal" settings 15. In a small bowl, combine the flour and butter into a smooth paste. 16. Add the paste to the simmering broth along with the cream or milk and peas. 17. Cook, stirring, until the paste has dissolved, 3 to 5 minutes. Add the chicken and season with salt and pepper. 18. To serve, spoon the stew into bowls and top with the puff pastry.
Per Serving: Calories 489; Fat 11g; Sodium 501mg; Carbs 8.9g; Fiber 4.6g; Sugar 8g; Protein 26g

Chicken with Potatoes and Peas

Prep time: 10 minutes | Cook time: 15 minutes | Serves: 4

4 small or 3 large bone-in, skin-on chicken breasts	1 teaspoon dried oregano
Kosher salt	Pinch red pepper flakes
Black pepper	1-pound large fingerling potatoes, washed and pricked with a knife
4 tablespoons olive oil, plus extra for garnish	2 cups chicken broth
3 garlic cloves, minced	1 cup frozen peas
1 fresh rosemary sprig, chopped (leaves only)	1 lemon
	½ cup olives

1. Season the chicken with salt and pepper. 2. In a large bowl, coat the chicken with 2 tablespoons of olive oil, the garlic, rosemary, oregano, and red pepper flakes. 3. Marinate for at least 30 minutes in the refrigerator. 4. Press the "Sauté" Button, two times to select "More" settings. 5. Add the remaining 2 tablespoons of olive oil and coat the bottom of the pot. 6. Add the chicken, skin-side down (reserving any marinade), and cook without moving for about 5 minutes, until the skin is crispy. 7. Remove the chicken and select Cancel. Add the potatoes and broth. 8. Place the chicken on top, skin-side up, and pour the reserved marinade on top. Season with salt and pepper. 9. Put on the pressure cooker's lid and turn the steam valve to "Sealing" position. 10. Select Pressure Cook mode, and then press the "Pressure Cook" button again to select "Less" time option. 11. Use the "+/-" keys on the control panel to set the cooking time to 7 minutes. 12. Press the Pressure Level button to adjust the pressure to "High Pressure." 13. Once the cooking cycle is completed, allow the steam to release naturally for 10 minutes, then turn the steam release handle to the Venting position. 14. When all the steam is released, remove the pressure lid from the top carefully. 15. Remove the chicken. Stir in the peas and cook until warmed. 16. Serve the potatoes and peas topped with the chicken. 17. Just before serving, add a squeeze of lemon, a drizzle of olive oil, and the olives.
Per Serving: Calories 221; Fat 7.9g; Sodium 704mg; Carbs 6g; Fiber

3.6g; Sugar 6g; Protein 18g

Chicken Wings

Prep time: 10 minutes | Cook time: 20 minutes | Serves: 4-5

3-pound chicken wings	Kosher salt
1 cup water	2 cups wing sauce

1. Add the chicken wings and water to the Inner Pot and season with salt. 2. Put on the pressure cooker's lid and turn the steam valve to "Sealing" position. 3. Select Pressure Cook mode, and then press the "Pressure Cook" button again to select "Less" time option. 4. Use the "+/-" keys on the control panel to set the cooking time to 10 minutes. 5. Press the Pressure Level button to adjust the pressure to "High Pressure." 6. Once the cooking cycle is completed, allow the steam to release naturally for 10 minutes, then turn the steam release handle to the Venting position. 7. When all the steam is released, remove the pressure lid from the top carefully. 8. Remove the wings to a cooling rack to drain. 9. In a large bowl, toss the wings in the sauce. 10. Place on a baking sheet and broil for about 5 minutes in your preheated oven, until crispy. Flip the wings and repeat. 11. Place the cooling rack with the wings on a baking sheet and refrigerate for 1 hour. 12. Heat the oil to 385 degrees F in your oven. Once hot, carefully lower 7 or 8 wings into the oil and fry for 3 minutes until crispy. Remove and place back on the rack. Repeat with the remaining wings. 13. Toss the wings in the sauce and serve immediately.
Per Serving: Calories 372; Fat 20g; Sodium 891mg; Carbs 29g; Fiber 3g; Sugar 8g; Protein 7g

Mushroom and Chicken Sausage Risotto

Prep time: 10 minutes | Cook time: 25 minutes | Serves: 4

2 tablespoons canola oil	Kosher salt
12-ounce fully cooked chicken sausage, cut into ¼-inch slices	Black pepper
3 tablespoons butter	1 tablespoon soy sauce
1 pound mushrooms (cremini, shiitake, oyster, or a mix), thinly sliced	½ cup dry white wine or red wine
1 medium yellow onion, chopped	4 cups good-quality chicken broth, preferably homemade (try the recipe here)
3 garlic cloves, minced	2 cups Arborio or Calrose rice
3 thyme sprigs, leaves only, plus more leaves for garnish	¼ cup finely grated Parmesan cheese

1. Press the "Sauté" Button, two times to select "More" settings. Add the oil. 2. Once hot, add the sausage and cook, stirring, for 5 minutes, until browned. Remove the sausage. 3. Reduce the heat to Normal. Melt the butter, then add the mushrooms and onion. 4. Cook, stirring, for 6 minutes until the onion is translucent and the mushrooms are cooked. 5. Add the garlic and cook for 1 minute more. Add the thyme and season with salt and pepper. 6. Add the soy sauce and wine. Cook, scraping up any brown bits off the bottom of the pot, for about 3 minutes, or until the alcohol smell has gone. 7. Add the broth and rice and stir. Press Cancel to stop this cooking program. 8. Put on the pressure cooker's lid and turn the steam valve to "Sealing" position. 9. Select Pressure Cook mode, and then press the "Pressure Cook" button again to select "Less" time option. 10. Use the "+/-" keys on the control panel to set the cooking time to 6 minutes. 11. Press the Pressure Level button to adjust the pressure to "High Pressure." 12. Once the cooking cycle is completed, quickly and carefully turn the steam release handle from Sealing position to the Venting position. 13. When all the steam is released, remove the pressure lid from the top carefully and stir. 14. If the risotto is too soupy, press the "Sauté" button two times to select "Normal" mode and cook, uncovered, for a few minutes. 15. Add the sausage and Parmesan. 16. Serve topped with thyme leaves.
Per Serving: Calories 289; Fat 14g; Sodium 791mg; Carbs 18.9g; Fiber 4.6g; Sugar 8g; Protein 6g

Chicken Tikka Masala

Prep time: 10 minutes | Cook time: 20 minutes | Serves: 4

2 tablespoons butter
1 small onion, chopped
3 garlic cloves, minced
1 (1-inch) piece ginger, peeled and grated
2 teaspoons ground cumin
2 teaspoons paprika
1 teaspoon ground turmeric
Big pinch cayenne
1 tablespoon sugar
1 (15-ounce) can diced or crushed tomatoes with juice
4 medium boneless, skinless chicken breasts
½ cup chicken broth
Kosher salt
Black pepper
¼ cup heavy cream
Juice of 1 lemon

1. Press the "Sauté" Button, two times to select "More" settings. Add the butter. 2. When the butter sizzles, add the onion, garlic, and ginger and stir. Cook for 3 to 4 minutes, stirring, until the onion is translucent. 3. Select Cancel and add the cumin, paprika, turmeric, and cayenne and stir, scraping the bottom. 4. Add the sugar and tomatoes with juice, stir, then add the chicken and broth. 5. Nestle the chicken in the mixture and season with salt and pepper. 6. Put on the pressure cooker's lid and turn the steam valve to "Sealing" position. 7. Select Pressure Cook mode, and then press the "Pressure Cook" button again to select "Less" time option. 8. Use the "+/-" keys on the control panel to set the cooking time to 7 minutes. 9. Press the Pressure Level button to adjust the pressure to "High Pressure." 10. Once the cooking cycle is completed, quickly and carefully turn the steam release handle from Sealing position to the Venting position. 11. When all the steam is released, remove the pressure lid from the top carefully. 12. Carefully remove the chicken and chop. 13. Press Cancel button. 14. Press the "Sauté" Button two times to select "normal" settings and simmer for 4 to 5 minutes until the liquid is reduced. 15. While simmering, add the cream and return the chicken to the pot. 16. Add the lemon juice and stir. Season as needed. 17. Serve and enjoy.
Per Serving: Calories 372; Fat 20g; Sodium 891mg; Carbs 29g; Fiber 3g; Sugar 8g; Protein 27g

Spiced Coconut Chicken

Prep time: 10 minutes | Cook time: 20 minutes | Serves: 4-5

1 tablespoon olive oil
1 onion, cut into ¼-inch slices
1 (1-inch) piece ginger, peeled and cut into ¼-inch slices
3 medium garlic cloves, minced
1 tablespoon curry powder
1 teaspoon ground turmeric
2-pound bone-in, skin-on chicken thighs
Kosher salt
Black pepper
1 (14-ounce) can light coconut milk
½ cup water
1⅓ cups jasmine rice, rinsed
2 tablespoons cilantro leaves plus stems, stems and leaves divided
1½ teaspoons sugar
1 lime, halved (one half cut into wedges, for serving)

1. Press the "Sauté" button two times to select "Normal" mode and add the oil. 2. Once hot, add the onion and ginger and sauté for 2 minutes. 3. Add the garlic, curry powder, and turmeric and cook, stirring, for 1 minute. 4. Press Cancel button. 5. Add the chicken and season with salt and pepper. Add the coconut milk and water. 6. Put on the pressure cooker's lid and turn the steam valve to "Sealing" position. 7. Press the "Pressure Cook" button two times to select "Normal" option. 8. Use the "+/-" keys on the control panel to set the cooking time to 13 minutes. 9. Press the Pressure Level button to adjust the pressure to "High Pressure." 10. Once the cooking cycle is completed, allow the steam to release naturally for 10 minutes, then turn the steam release handle to the Venting position. 11. When all the steam is released, remove the pressure lid from the top carefully. 12. Transfer the chicken to a platter. Add the rice, chopped cilantro stems, and sugar. 13. Select "Pressure Cook" and cook on High Pressure for 4 minutes. 14. Meanwhile, remove the skin and bones from the chicken and discard. 15. Select Cancel and let naturally release for 10 minutes. Release any remaining steam. 16. Add the chicken back to the pot and add the juice of half the lime. 17. Stir and season with salt and pepper. 18. Serve in bowls topped with cilantro leaves and lime wedges.
Per Serving: Calories 184; Fat 5g; Sodium 441mg; Carbs 17g; Fiber 4.6g; Sugar 5g; Protein 9g

Penne and Turkey Meatballs

Prep time: 10 minutes | Cook time: 6 minutes | Serves: 4

1-pound lean ground turkey
½ cup plain or panko breadcrumbs
3 tablespoons grated Parmesan cheese, plus extra for garnish
¼ yellow onion, finely chopped
2 garlic cloves, minced
1 tablespoon finely chopped fresh basil, plus more for garnish
1 egg, beaten
½ teaspoon kosher salt
¼ teaspoon black pepper
3 tablespoons olive oil
1 (15-ounce) can diced tomatoes with juice
1 (14- to 15-ounce) can tomato purée or sauce
½ cup water
8-ounce uncooked penne pasta

1. In a medium bowl, combine the turkey, breadcrumbs, Parmesan, onion, garlic, basil, egg, salt, and pepper. Mix well. 2. Form 1½-inch meatballs and place on a plate. 3. Press the "Sauté" button two times to select "More" mode. 4. Once hot, coat the bottom of the pot with the oil. 5. Add the meatballs, one at a time, in close proximity and, if possible, in one layer. Cook for 1 minute. 6. Add the tomatoes with juice, tomato purée or sauce, water, and pasta. 7. Carefully push the pasta down so that it's mostly submerged in the sauce. 8. Put on the pressure cooker's lid and turn the steam valve to "Sealing" position. 9. Select Pressure Cook mode, and then press the "Pressure Cook" button again to select "Less" time option. 10. Use the "+/-" keys on the control panel to set the cooking time to 5 minutes. 11. Press the Pressure Level button to adjust the pressure to "High Pressure." 12. Once the cooking cycle is completed, quickly and carefully turn the steam release handle from Sealing position to the Venting position. 13. When all the steam is released, remove the pressure lid from the top carefully. 14. Serve topped with more Parmesan and basil.
Per Serving: Calories 219; Fat 10g; Sodium 891mg; Carbs 22.9g; Fiber 4g; Sugar 4g; Protein 13g

Teriyaki Wing

Prep time: 10 minutes | Cook time: 15 minutes | Serves: 6

3-pound "party" chicken wings (separated at the joints)
½ cup plus 2 tablespoons low-sodium soy sauce
Salt and black pepper
⅓ cup packed brown sugar
2 tablespoons cider vinegar or
rice vinegar
4 teaspoons finely chopped fresh ginger
4 medium garlic cloves, finely chopped
1 tablespoon cornstarch

1. Pour 1½ cups water into the pot and place a Steam Rack or steamer basket inside. 2. In a large bowl, toss the wings with 2 tablespoons of the soy sauce and season with salt and pepper. 3. Place the wings on the Steam Rack or steamer basket. 4. Put on the pressure cooker's lid and turn the steam valve to "Sealing" position. 5. Press the "Pressure Cook" button three times to select "Less" option. 6. Use the "+/-" keys on the control panel to set the cooking time to 5 minutes. 7. Press the Pressure Level button to adjust the pressure to "High Pressure." 8. Once the cooking cycle is completed, allow the steam to release naturally. 9. When all the steam is released, remove the pressure lid from the top carefully. 10. Preheat the broiler and move an oven rack so that it is 4 inches below the broiler element. 11. Line a baking sheet with foil and spray it with cooking spray. 12. Transfer the wings to the prepared baking sheet. 13. Discard the cooking liquid and remove the Steam Rack or steaming basket from the pot. 14. Add the remaining ½ cup soy sauce, the brown sugar, vinegar, ginger, and garlic to the pot. 15. Press the "Sauté" button two times to select "Normal" mode. 16. Bring to a simmer and cook, stirring frequently, until the sugar has dissolved, 3 minutes. 17. In a small bowl, mix the cornstarch with 1 tablespoon water. 18. Add the cornstarch mixture to the pot and cook, stirring constantly, until the sauce has thickened, 1 minute. 19. Spoon the sauce over the wings, turning them so both sides are covered. 20. Broil the wings until browned and crispy on the edges, 3 minutes. 21. When done, serve and enjoy.
Per Serving: Calories 184; Fat 5g; Sodium 441mg; Carbs 17g; Fiber 4.6g; Sugar 5g; Protein 9g

Roasted Chicken with Tomatoes

Prep time: 10 minutes | Cook time: 25 minutes | Serves: 4

3 bacon slices, cut into ½-inch pieces
1 (3- to 4-pound) chicken, cut into 8 pieces
Kosher salt
Black pepper
1 tablespoon olive oil
1 onion, cut into ⅛-inch slices
4 garlic cloves, minced
8-ounce cremini mushrooms, chopped
¾ cup dry red wine
1 (15-ounce) can diced or crushed tomatoes with juice
1 bay leaf

1. Press the "Sauté" button two times to select "Normal" mode. 2. Once hot, add the bacon. Cook until lightly crisp, flipping as needed, and drain on a paper towel. 3. Season the chicken with salt and pepper. Turn the heat to More and add the olive oil. 4. Add the chicken, skin-side down, and cook for 5 minutes, or until browned. Transfer to a plate. 5. Add the onion and garlic and cook, stirring, for 2 minutes. 6. Add the mushrooms and cook, stirring, for 3 minutes more. 7. Add the wine and scrape the bottom of the pan to deglaze. Cook for 3 to 5 minutes. 8. Stir in the tomatoes with juice, bay leaf, and bacon. 9. Return the chicken to the pot, with the dark meat on the bottom and breasts on the top, skin-side up. 10. Put on the pressure cooker's lid and turn the steam valve to "Sealing" position. 11. Press the "Pressure Cook" button two times to select "Normal" option. 12. Use the "+/-" keys on the control panel to set the cooking time to 10 minutes. 13. Press the Pressure Level button to adjust the pressure to "High Pressure." 14. Once the cooking cycle is completed, quickly and carefully turn the steam release handle from Sealing position to the Venting position. 15. When all the steam is released, remove the pressure lid from the top carefully. 16. Remove the bay leaf and serve.
Per Serving: Calories 489; Fat 11g; Sodium 501mg; Carbs 8.9g; Fiber 4.6g; Sugar 8g; Protein 26g

Stuffed Turkey Breast

Prep time: 10 minutes | Cook time: 55 minutes | Serves: 6-8

5 tablespoons butter
1 large onion, chopped
2 celery stalks, chopped
¾ cup chopped mushrooms
2 garlic cloves, minced
2 tablespoons chopped fresh sage
1 heaping tablespoon chopped fresh parsley
¾ teaspoon kosher salt, plus more
for seasoning
¼ teaspoon black pepper, plus more for seasoning
2 cups plain breadcrumbs
3 cups chicken broth
1 (2- to 3-pound) boneless, skinless turkey breast, butterflied to an even thickness

1. Press the "Sauté" button two times to select "Normal" mode. 2. Once hot, add 3 tablespoons of butter. Once the butter is melted, add the onion and celery. 3. Stir and cook for 3 minutes until the onion is translucent. 4. Add the mushrooms and garlic. Stir and cook for 3 minutes more, or until the mushrooms are soft. 5. Press the Cancel button. 6. Transfer the vegetables and butter to a large bowl. 7. Add the sage, parsley, salt, pepper, and breadcrumbs and mix. 8. Add the broth, a bit at a time, and mix until you get a moist but crumbly texture, using ¾ to 1 cup of broth. 9. Lay the turkey breast top-side down on your work surface. 10. If it isn't an even thickness, pound the thick parts until it's mostly even. 11. Sprinkle with salt and pepper. Spread the stuffing mixture on the breast, making it about as thick as the turkey breast itself, and leaving at least 1 inch on each side. 12. Roll up tightly and secure with kitchen twine. Season the outside of the breast with salt and pepper. 13. Press the "Sauté" button two times to select "More" mode. 14. Once hot, add the remaining 2 tablespoons of butter. 15. Once melted, brown the stuffed turkey on all sides, about 3 minutes per side. 16. Finish with it lying seam-side down in the pot. 17. Press the Cancel button to stop this cooking program. 18. Add the remaining 2 cups of chicken broth and close the lid in right way. 19. Put on the pressure cooker's lid and turn the steam valve to "Sealing" position. 20. Select Pressure Cook mode, and then press the "Pressure Cook" button again to select "Less" time option. 21. Use the "+/-" keys on the control panel to set the cooking time to 25 minutes. 22. Press the Pressure Level button to adjust the pressure to "High Pressure." 23. Once the cooking cycle is completed, allow the steam to release naturally. 24. When all the steam is released, remove the pressure lid from the top carefully. 25. Remove the turkey and let it rest, tented with foil. 26. Press the "Sauté" button two times to select "More" mode. Reduce the cooking liquid for 10 to 15 minutes until concentrated. 27. Remove the kitchen twine from the turkey and spoon the gravy over the top. 28. Slice and serve.
Per Serving: Calories 237; Fat 10.9g; Sodium 354mg; Carbs 20.5g; Fiber 4.1g; Sugar 8.2g; Protein 06g

Duck with Vegetables

Prep time: 10 minutes | Cook time: 30 minutes | Serves: 4

2 tablespoons canola oil
4 duck legs
Kosher salt
Black pepper
8-ounce small Cipollini or pearl
onions
8-ounce sliced mushrooms
4 garlic cloves, minced
½ cup dry red wine
1 cup chicken broth

1. Press the "Sauté" button two times to select "More" mode and add the oil. 2. Dry the duck well and season with salt and pepper. 3. Place skin-side down in the pot and cook for about 5 minutes, or until nicely browned. Remove. 4. Turn the heat down to medium. Carefully discard all but 2 tablespoons of the fat and oil in the pot. 5. Add the onions and sauté until lightly browned, about 3 minutes. Add the mushrooms and garlic. 6. Cook, stirring, for 3 minutes more. 7. Add the wine and scrape up any brown bits off the bottom of the pot, cooking for 1 minute. 8. Add the broth and duck. 9. Put on the pressure cooker's lid and turn the steam valve to "Sealing" position. 10. Press the "Pressure Cook" button two times to select "Normal" option. 11. Use the "+/-" keys on the control panel to set the cooking time to 20 minutes. 12. Press the Pressure Level button to adjust the pressure to "High Pressure." 13. Once the cooking cycle is completed, quickly and carefully turn the steam release handle from Sealing position to the Venting position. 14. When all the steam is released, remove the pressure lid from the top carefully. 15. Serve the duck with the onions and mushrooms and spoon over some of the cooking liquid.
Per Serving: Calories 478; Fat 12.9g; Sodium 414mg; Carbs 11g; Fiber 5g; Sugar 9g; Protein 11g

Chicken Penne Puttanesca

Prep time: 15 minutes | Cook time: 11 minutes | Serves: 4

2 small (6- to 7-ounce) boneless, skinless chicken breasts
Salt and black pepper
2 tablespoons olive oil
12-ounce dry penne pasta
2½ cups store-bought chicken or vegetable broth, or homemade
1 (15-ounce) can diced tomatoes
with Italian herbs, with juices
½ cup oil-cured black or Kalamata olives
4 oil-packed rolled anchovies with capers, plus 1 tablespoon oil from the jar
Pinch of red pepper flakes

1. Pat the chicken dry with paper towels. Season the chicken all over with salt and several grinds of pepper. 2. Put the oil to the Instant pot. 3. Press the "Sauté" button two times to select "Normal" mode. 4. Add the chicken and cook until golden brown on one side, 3 minutes. 5. Add the penne, broth, tomatoes, olives, anchovies and oil, red pepper flakes, and several grinds of pepper. 6. Stir everything together and place the chicken breasts on top of the pasta mixture. 7. Put on the pressure cooker's lid and turn the steam valve to "Sealing" position. 8. Select Pressure Cook mode, and then press the "Pressure Cook" button again to select "Less" time option. 9. Use the "+/-" keys on the control panel to set the cooking time to 6 minutes. 10. Press the Pressure Level button to adjust the pressure to "Low Pressure." 11. Once the cooking cycle is completed, quickly and carefully turn the steam release handle from Sealing position to the Venting position. 12. When all the steam is released, remove the pressure lid from the top carefully. 13. Transfer the chicken to a cutting board and chop it into bite-size pieces. 14. Return the chicken to the pot and stir to combine. 15. Serve.
Per Serving: Calories 302; Fat 7.9g; Sodium 704mg; Carbs 6g; Fiber 3.6g; Sugar 6g; Protein 18g

Stuffed Chicken Parmesan

Prep time: 15 minutes | Cook time: 15 minutes | Serves: 4

1 slice sturdy sandwich bread, finely chopped
1 small (5-ounce) zucchini, grated
½ cup grated Italian cheese blend
1 teaspoon Italian seasoning
Salt and black pepper
4 medium (8-ounce) boneless, skinless chicken breasts
1 (24-ounce) jar thin marinara sauce (such as Rao's)

1. In a medium bowl, combine the breadcrumbs, zucchini, cheese, and Italian seasoning. 2. Season with salt and pepper. Cut a horizontal slit into each chicken breast to form a 5- to 6-inch-long pocket. 3. Stuff the chicken breasts with the breadcrumb mixture. Season the chicken with salt and pepper. 4. Pour the sauce into the pot. Add ¼ cup water to the marinara jar, screw on the lid, and shake. 5. Add the tomato-y water to the pot. Set a handled Steam Rack in the pot and place the chicken breasts on the Steam Rack. 6. Put on the pressure cooker's lid and turn the steam valve to "Sealing" position. 7. Press the "Pressure Cook" button two times to select "Normal" option. 8. Use the "+/-" keys on the control panel to set the cooking time to 8 minutes. 9. Press the Pressure Level button to adjust the pressure to "Low Pressure." 10. Once the cooking cycle is completed, allow the steam to release naturally. 11. When all the steam is released, remove the pressure lid from the top carefully. 12. Press the "Sauté" button two times to select "Less" mode. 13. Remove the Steam Rack, nestle the chicken into the sauce, and simmer a few minutes more. 14. Serve the chicken with the sauce.

Per Serving: Calories 584; Fat 15g; Sodium 441mg; Carbs 17g; Fiber 4.6g; Sugar 5g; Protein 29g

Mustard-Braised Chicken

Prep time: 15 minutes | Cook time: 35 minutes | Serves: 4

2 slices thick-cut bacon, chopped
8 bone-in chicken thighs, skin removed and fat trimmed
Salt and black pepper
4 cups quartered cremini mushrooms (8 oz.)
2 large shallots, thinly sliced (¾ cup)
1½ cups bottled hard apple cider (12 oz.)
2 tablespoons grainy mustard

1. Press the "Sauté" button two times to select "Normal" mode. 2. Add the bacon and cook, stirring occasionally, until the bacon is browned, 3 to 4 minutes. 3. Transfer to a bowl with a slotted spoon; leave the drippings in the pot. 4. Season the chicken all over with salt and pepper. 5. Add half the chicken to the pot and cook until browned on one side, 3 minutes. Transfer to a plate. 6. Add the mushrooms and shallots to the pot and sauté until the shallots are tender, 3 minutes. 7. Add the cider and mustard and bring to a simmer. 8. Add all the chicken, any accumulated juices, and the bacon to the pot. 9. Put on the pressure cooker's lid and turn the steam valve to "Sealing" position. 10. Select Pressure Cook mode, and then press the "Pressure Cook" button again to select "Less" time option. 11. Press the Pressure Level button to adjust the pressure to "High Pressure." 12. Once the cooking cycle is completed, quickly and carefully turn the steam release handle from Sealing position to the Venting position. 13. When all the steam is released, remove the pressure lid from the top carefully. 14. Transfer the chicken and vegetables to a serving dish with a slotted spoon. Cover with foil and set aside. 15. Press the "Sauté" button two times to select "More" mode, and bring to a simmer. 16. Using a ladle, skim any liquid fat that pools on top of the sauce and discard. 17. Cook until the sauce is reduced by half, 5 minutes. Press Cancel button. 18. Pour the sauce over the chicken and serve.

Per Serving: Calories 483; Fat 7.9g; Sodium 704mg; Carbs 6g; Fiber 3.6g; Sugar 6g; Protein 18g

Italian Sausage Ragu with Polenta

Prep time: 10 minutes | Cook time: 15 minutes | Serves: 4

2 tablespoons olive oil
8-ounce bulk spicy Italian sausage
1 medium yellow onion, chopped
1 red or green bell pepper, chopped
1 tablespoon balsamic vinegar
1 cup thin marinara sauce (such as Rao's or Trader Joe's Organic Marinara)
¼ cup store-bought chicken broth, or homemade
12-ounce boneless, skinless chicken thighs, fat trimmed, cut into 2-inch pieces
Salt and black pepper
¾ cup polenta (not quick-cooking)
OPTIONAL GARNISH
½ cup shaved Parmesan cheese curls

1. Put 1 tablespoon of the oil in the Instant pot. 2. Press the "Sauté" button two times to select "Normal" mode. 3. Add the sausage and cook, stirring occasionally, until browned, 3 minutes. 4. Add the onion and bell pepper and cook until tender, 4 minutes. Press Cancel. 5. Add the vinegar and scrape up the browned bits on the bottom of the pan. 6. Add the marinara sauce and broth and stir to combine. Season the chicken all over with salt and pepper. 7. Add it to the pot and stir to combine. 8. Place a tall Steam Rack in the pot over the chicken. 9. Place 2⅔ cups warm water, the remaining 1 tablespoon oil, and ½ teaspoon salt in a 7-inch round metal baking pan. 10. Gradually whisk in the polenta. Cover tightly with foil and place on the Steam Rack. 11. Put on the pressure cooker's lid and turn the steam valve to "Sealing" position. 12. Select Pressure Cook mode, and then press the "Pressure Cook" button again to select "Less" time option. 13. Use the "+/-" keys on the control panel to set the cooking time to 8 minutes. 14. Press the Pressure Level button to adjust the pressure to "High Pressure." 15. Once the cooking cycle is completed, allow the steam to release naturally for 10 minutes, then turn the steam release handle to the Venting position. 16. When all the steam is released, remove the pressure lid from the top carefully. 17. Remove the Steam Rack from the pot. 18. Serve the polenta in shallow bowls, topped with the chicken ragu and garnished with the cheese curls.

Per Serving: Calories 483; Fat 7.9g; Sodium 704mg; Carbs 6g; Fiber 3.6g; Sugar 6g; Protein 18g

Chicken Burrito Bowls

Prep time: 10 minutes | Cook time: 18 minutes | Serves: 4

2 teaspoons taco seasoning
6 to 8 boneless, skinless chicken thighs, fat trimmed
2 tablespoons olive oil
¾ cup fresh refrigerated tomato salsa
1 cup plus 1 tablespoon store-bought chicken
¾ cup red quinoa, rinsed
1 (15-ounce) can black beans, drained
Salt and black pepper
1 cup prepared guacamole

1. Rub the taco seasoning into the chicken. 2. Put the oil in the instant pot. Press the "Sauté" button two times to select "More" mode. 3. When the oil is hot, brown the chicken in batches on one side only until golden brown, 3 minutes per batch. 4. Drain off the fat in the pot and return the pot to the appliance. 5. Add ½ cup of the salsa and ¼ cup of the broth to the pot. 6. Add the chicken and any accumulated juices to the pot. 7. Spoon the remaining ¼ cup salsa over the chicken. 8. Place a tall Steam Rack in the pot over the chicken. 9. In a 7-inch metal baking pan, combine the quinoa and remaining ¾ cup plus 1 tablespoon broth. 10. Spoon the beans over the quinoa mixture, but don't stir them in. 11. Place the uncovered baking pan on the Steam Rack. 12. Put on the pressure cooker's lid and turn the steam valve to "Sealing" position. 13. Select Pressure Cook mode, and then press the "Pressure Cook" button again to select "Less" time option. 14. Use the "+/-" keys on the control panel to set the cooking time to 12 minutes. 15. Press the Pressure Level button to adjust the pressure to "High Pressure." 16. Once the cooking cycle is completed, allow the steam to release naturally. 17. When all the steam is released, remove the pressure lid from the top carefully. 18. Remove the baking pan and Steam Rack from the pot. 19. Fluff the quinoa-bean mixture with a fork and season with salt and pepper. 20. Divide the quinoa among bowls and top with the chicken and some of the cooking liquid from the pot. 21. Top with the guacamole. Sprinkle with the optional toppings, if using, and serve.

Per Serving: Calories 489; Fat 11g; Sodium 501mg; Carbs 8.9g; Fiber 4.6g; Sugar 8g; Protein 26g

Makhani Chicken

Prep time: 15 minutes | Cook time: 15 minutes | Serves: 4

3 tablespoons butter or ghee, at room temperature
1 medium yellow onion, halved and sliced through the root end
1 (10-ounce) can Ro-Tel tomatoes with green chilies, with juice
2 tablespoons mild Indian curry

paste (such as Patek's)
1½-pound boneless, skinless chicken thighs, fat trimmed, cut into 2- to 3-inch pieces
2 tablespoons all-purpose flour
Salt and black pepper

1. Put 1 tablespoon of the butter or ghee to the Instant pot 2. Press the "Sauté" button two times to select "Normal" mode. 3. Add the onion and cook, stirring frequently, until browned, 6 minutes. Press Cancel button. 4. Add the tomatoes to the pot, stir, and scrape up any browned bits on the bottom of the pot. 5. Add the curry paste and stir to combine. Nestle the chicken into the sauce. 6. Put on the pressure cooker's lid and turn the steam valve to "Sealing" position. 7. Press the "Pressure Cook" button two times to select "Normal" option. 8. Use the "+/-" keys on the control panel to set the cooking time to 8 minutes. 9. Press the Pressure Level button to adjust the pressure to "High Pressure." 10. Once the cooking cycle is completed, quickly and carefully turn the steam release handle from Sealing position to the Venting position. 11. When all the steam is released, remove the pressure lid from the top carefully. 12. Press the "Sauté" button two times to select "Normal" mode. 13. And add the flour mixture to the pot and cook until the sauce is thickened, 1 minute. 14. Season with salt and pepper and serve.
Per Serving: Calories 489; Fat 11g; Sodium 501mg; Carbs 8.9g; Fiber 4.6g; Sugar 8g; Protein 26g

Chicken–Stuffed Sweet Potatoes

Prep time: 15 minutes | Cook time: 18 minutes | Serves: 4

1 cup thin barbecue sauce
1 pound boneless, skinless chicken thighs, fat trimmed
4 small (8-ounce) sweet potatoes,

pricked with a fork
Salt and black pepper
1 cup sour cream
2 green onions, thinly sliced

1. Combine the barbecue sauce and chicken in the pot. 2. Place a tall Steam Rack over the chicken and arrange the sweet potatoes on top. 3. Put on the pressure cooker's lid and turn the steam valve to "Sealing" position. 4. Select Pressure Cook mode, and then press the "Pressure Cook" button again to select "Less" time option. 5. Use the "+/-" keys on the control panel to set the cooking time to 18 minutes. 6. Press the Pressure Level button to adjust the pressure to "High Pressure." 7. Once the cooking cycle is completed, allow the steam to release naturally for 10 minutes, then turn the steam release handle to the Venting position. 8. When all the steam is released, remove the pressure lid from the top carefully. 9. Split the sweet potatoes open lengthwise, season with salt and pepper, and set aside. 10. Remove the Steam Rack from the pot. Pull the chicken into shreds with two forks, return it to the sauce, and stir to combine. 11. Divide the chicken among the sweet potatoes; you may not need all of the sauce. 12. Top with dollops of sour cream and a sprinkle of the green onions and serve.
Per Serving: Calories 334; Fat 12.9g; Sodium 414mg; Carbs 11g; Fiber 5g; Sugar 9g; Protein 31g

Faux-Tesserae Chicken Dinner

Prep time: 10 minutes | Cook time: 45 minutes | Serves: 4-6

1 (4-pound) whole roasting chicken, neck and giblets in cavity removed and reserved
1 pound red potatoes, cut into 1¼-inch chunks
2 large carrots, peeled and cut into 1-inch pieces
2 tablespoons olive oil

4 teaspoons lemon pepper seasoning
OPTIONAL GRAVY
1½ tablespoons all-purpose flour
1½ tablespoons butter, at room temperature
Salt and black pepper

1. Place the Steam Rack with handles in the Instant pot and add 1 cup water. 2. Place the neck and giblets, if you have them, in the water. 3. Toss the vegetables with 1 tablespoon of the oil and 1 teaspoon of the lemon pepper seasoning. 4. Stuff about half the potatoes and carrots into the chicken cavity. 5. Tuck the wings behind the chicken's back and tie the drumsticks together with butcher's twine. 6. Season the outside of the chicken with the remaining lemon pepper seasoning. 7. Place the chicken breast-side up on the Steam Rack. 8. Place the remaining carrots and potatoes around the chicken. Drizzle with the remaining 1 tablespoon oil. 9. Put on the pressure cooker's lid and turn the steam valve to "Sealing" position. 10. Press the "Pressure Cook" button two times to select "Normal" option. 11. Use the "+/-" keys on the control panel to set the cooking time to 28 minutes. 12. Press the Pressure Level button to adjust the pressure to "High Pressure." 13. Once the cooking cycle is completed, quickly and carefully turn the steam release handle from Sealing position to the Venting position. 14. When all the steam is released, remove the pressure lid from the top carefully. 15. Press the "Sauté" button two times to select "Normal" mode for 5 minutes. 16. For crispy skin, preheat your oven and adjust the oven rack so that it is 8 inches below the broiler element. 17. Transfer the chicken on the Steam Rack to a foil-lined baking sheet. 18. Place the loose vegetables in a serving bowl and cover with foil. 19. Broil the chicken, rotating the pan once, until the skin on top is browned, about 6 minutes. 20. Carve the chicken and serve with the vegetables and a little of the cooking liquid. 21. If you want to make gravy and there is still cooking liquid in the pot, select Sauté and adjust to More. 22. When the liquid boils, the liquid fat will collect on the sides of the pot. 23. Skim fat with a spoon and then discard. 24. In a small bowl, whisk together butter and flour until smooth. Stir flour mixture into cooking liquid and simmer until thickened, 2 minutes. Press Cancel. 25. Serve with chicken.
Per Serving: Calories 334; Fat 19g; Sodium 354mg; Carbs 15g; Fiber 5.1g; Sugar 8.2g; Protein 12g

Quinoa-Stuffed Peppers

Prep time: 10 minutes | Cook time: 20 minutes | Serves: 4

⅔ cup dry quinoa, rinsed and drained
1¾ cups store-bought chicken broth, or homemade
Salt and black pepper
1-pound raw Italian chicken or turkey sausages, casings removed

½ cup chopped fresh basil
4 medium bell peppers, top ¼ inch of stem end removed, seeds discarded
1 cup thin jarred marinara sauce (such as Rao's)
1 cup grated mozzarella cheese

1. Place the quinoa, 1 cup of the broth, a pinch of salt, and a few grinds of pepper in the pot. 2. Put on the pressure cooker's lid and turn the steam valve to "Sealing" position. 3. Select Pressure Cook mode, and then press the "Pressure Cook" button again to select "Less" time option. 4. Use the "+/-" keys on the control panel to set the cooking time to 1 minute. 5. Press the Pressure Level button to adjust the pressure to "High Pressure." 6. Once the cooking cycle is completed, allow the steam to release naturally for 10 minutes, then turn the steam release handle to the Venting position. 7. When all the steam is released, remove the pressure lid from the top carefully. 8. Add the sausage and basil to the quinoa and mix well to combine. Stuff the quinoa mixture into the peppers. 9. In a small bowl, combine the remaining ¾ cup broth with the marinara sauce. 10. Pour 1¼ cups of the mixture into the pot. Place a Steam Rack with handles in the pot and set the peppers on top. Spoon the remaining sauce over the peppers and sprinkle with the cheese. 11. Put on the pressure cooker's lid and turn the steam valve to "Sealing" position. 12. Select Pressure Cook mode, and then press the "Pressure Cook" button again to select "Less" time option. 13. Use the "+/-" keys on the control panel to set the cooking time to 15 minutes. 14. Press the Pressure Level button to adjust the pressure to "High Pressure." 15. Once the cooking cycle is completed, allow the steam to release naturally. 16. When all the steam is released, remove the pressure lid from the top carefully. 17. Carefully lift the Steam Rack from the pot and transfer the peppers to dinner plates. 18. Spoon the sauce over the peppers.
Per Serving: Calories 382; Fat 12.9g; Sodium 414mg; Carbs 11g; Fiber 5g; Sugar 9g; Protein 31g

Chicken with Black Bean Garlic Sauce

Prep time: 10 minutes | Cook time: 10 minutes | Serves: 4

1½-pound boneless, skinless chicken thighs, fat trimmed, cut into 2-inch pieces
½ cup store-bought chicken broth, or homemade
3 tablespoons black bean garlic sauce (such as Lee Kum Kee brand)
1½ tablespoons julienned fresh ginger
1 tablespoon soy sauce
1 teaspoon balsamic vinegar
Black pepper
1½ cups long-grain white rice, rinsed
4 cups 1½-inch broccoli florets (10 oz.)
2 teaspoons cornstarch

1. Combine the chicken, broth, black bean garlic sauce, ginger, soy sauce, and vinegar in the Inner Pot. 2. Add several grinds of pepper. 3. Combine the rice with 1½ cups cold water in a 7 × 3-inch round metal baking pan. 4. Place the baking pan, uncovered, on a tall Steam Rack set over the chicken mixture. 5. Put on the pressure cooker's lid and turn the steam valve to "Sealing" position. 6. Press the "Pressure Cook" button three times to select "Less" option. 7. Use the "+/-" keys on the control panel to set the cooking time to 5 minutes. 8. Press the Pressure Level button to adjust the pressure to "High Pressure." 9. Once the cooking cycle is completed, quickly and carefully turn the steam release handle from Sealing position to the Venting position. 10. When all the steam is released, remove the pressure lid from the top carefully. 11. Remove the rice in the baking pan and the Steam Rack, if you used them, and set aside. 12. Add the broccoli to the pot, stir gently to combine, and place a regular pot lid on the Inner Pot. 13. Press the "Sauté" button two times to select "Normal" mode, and simmer for 3 minutes. 14. While the mixture is cooking, mix the cornstarch with 2 teaspoons of cold water. 15. Add to the pot, stir, and continue to cook until the sauce is thickened, 30 seconds. 16. Serve immediately with the rice.
Per Serving: Calories 372; Fat 20g; Sodium 891mg; Carbs 29g; Fiber 3g; Sugar 8g; Protein 27g

Game Hens with Garlic

Prep time: 10 minutes | Cook time: 20 minutes | Serves: 4

2 (24-ounce) Cornish game hens
1 tablespoon olive oil
2 teaspoons Herbes de Provence
Salt and black pepper
40 medium garlic cloves (about ¾ cup), peeled
¼ cup dry white wine
½ cup store-bought chicken broth, or homemade
1½ tablespoons all-purpose flour
1 tablespoon butter, at room temperature

1. Place the hens breast-side down on a clean cutting board. 2. Using kitchen shears, cut down the backbone of each bird. 3. Cut lengthwise through the breastbone to cleave the birds in half. 4. Add the oil to the Instant pot, Press the "Sauté" button two times to select "More" mode. 5. Rub the hens all over with the Herbes de Provence, salt, and pepper. 6. Brown the poultry skin-side down in batches until golden brown on one side, 4 minutes per batch. 7. Transfer to a plate. Adjust the cooking temperature to "Normal". 8. Add the garlic and cook, stirring frequently, until fragrant and browned in places, 1 minute. 9. Add the wine, scrape up any browned bits on the bottom of the pot, and simmer for 1 minute. 10. Add the broth and stir to combine. Place a Steam Rack with handles in the pot. 11. Place the hen halves skin-side up on the rack. You may have to stack them a bit, which is fine. 12. Put on the pressure cooker's lid and turn the steam valve to "Sealing" position. 13. Press the "Poultry" button three times to select "Less" option. 14. Use the "+/-" keys on the control panel to set the cooking time to 8 minutes. 15. Press the Pressure Level button to adjust the pressure to "High Pressure." 16. Once the cooking cycle is completed, allow the steam to release naturally for 10 minutes, then turn the steam release handle to the Venting position. 17. When all the steam is released, remove the pressure lid from the top carefully. 18. Transfer the hens to a serving plate, and cover loosely with foil. 19. In a small bowl, mix the flour and butter until smooth. 20 Press the "Sauté" button two times to select "Normal" mode. 21. Whisk the flour mixture into the liquid in the pot and simmer until the sauce has thickened, 1 minute. 22. Season the sauce with salt and pepper, spoon over the hens, and serve immediately.
Per Serving: Calories 471; Fat 7.9g; Sodium 704mg; Carbs 6g; Fiber 3.6g; Sugar 6g; Protein 18g

Wine Glazed Whole Chicken

Prep time: 10 minutes | Cook time: 18 minutes | Serves: 8

1 medium-sized, whole chicken (3-pound)
2 tablespoon sugar
2 teaspoons kosher salt
1 tablespoon onion powder
1 tablespoon garlic powder
1 tablespoon paprika
2 teaspoons black pepper
½ teaspoon cayenne pepper
1 cup water or chicken broth
1 tablespoon red wine
2 teaspoons soy sauce
1 minced green onion

1. In a medium bowl, combine the sugar, salt, onion powder, garlic powder, paprika, black pepper, and cayenne pepper. 2. Prepare the Inner Pot by adding the water to the pot and placing the steam rack in it. 3. Pour the wine and soy sauce into the pot. 4. Rub all sides of the chicken with the spice mix. 5. Place the chicken on the steam rack and 6. Put on the pressure cooker's lid and turn the steam valve to "Sealing" position. 7. Press the "Poultry" button three times to select "Normal" option. 8. Use the "+/-" keys on the control panel to set the cooking time to 18 minutes. 9. Press the Pressure Level button to adjust the pressure to "High Pressure." 10. Once the cooking cycle is completed, allow the steam to release naturally. 11. When all the steam is released, remove the pressure lid from the top carefully. 12. Top with minced green onion and serve.
Per Serving: Calories 289; Fat 14g; Sodium 791mg; Carbs 18.9g; Fiber 4.6g; Sugar 8g; Protein 6g

Seasoned Chicken

Prep time: 10 minutes | Cook time: 15 minutes | Serves: 6-8

5-pound chicken thighs
4 cloves garlic, minced
½ cup soy sauce
½ cup white vinegar
½ cup water
1 teaspoon black peppercorns
3 bay leaves
½ teaspoon salt
½ teaspoon black pepper

1. Add the garlic, soy sauce, vinegar, water, peppercorns, bay leaves, salt and pepper to the Inner Pot and stir well. 2. Add the chicken thighs. Stir to coat the chicken. 3. Put on the pressure cooker's lid and turn the steam valve to "Sealing" position. 4. Press the "Poultry" button three times to select "Less" option. 5. Use the "+/-" keys on the control panel to set the cooking time to 15 minutes. 6. Press the Pressure Level button to adjust the pressure to "High Pressure." 7. Once the cooking cycle is completed, allow the steam to release naturally. 8. When all the steam is released, remove the pressure lid from the top carefully. 9. Remove the bay leaves, stir and serve.
Per Serving: Calories 584; Fat 15g; Sodium 441mg; Carbs 17g; Fiber 4.6g; Sugar 5g; Protein 29g

Thai Chicken

Prep time: 10 minutes | Cook time: 10 minutes | Serves: 4

2-pound chicken thighs, boneless and skinless
1 cup lime juice
½ cup fish sauce
¼ cup olive oil
2 tablespoons coconut nectar
1 teaspoon ginger, grated
1 teaspoon mint, chopped
2 teaspoons cilantro, finely chopped

1. In a medium bowl, whisk together lime juice, fish sauce, olive oil, coconut nectar, ginger, mint and cilantro until combined. 2. Add the chicken thighs to the instant pot. 3. Pour the marinade on top. 4. Put on the pressure cooker's lid and turn the steam valve to "Sealing" position. 5. Select Pressure Cook mode, and then press the "Pressure Cook" button again to select "Less" time option. 6. Use the "+/-" keys on the control panel to set the cooking time to 10 minutes. 7. Press the Pressure Level button to adjust the pressure to "High Pressure." 8. Once the cooking cycle is completed, quickly and carefully turn the steam release handle from Sealing position to the Venting position. 9. When all the steam is released, remove the pressure lid from the top carefully. 10. Serve.
Per Serving: Calories 472; Fat 10.9g; Sodium 354mg; Carbs 10.5g; Fiber 4.1g; Sugar 8.2g; Protein 26g

Italian Chicken

Prep time: 10 minutes | Cook time: 15 minutes | Serves: 6

8 boneless, skinless chicken thighs
1 teaspoon kosher salt
½ teaspoon black pepper
1 tablespoon olive oil
2 medium-sized, chopped carrots
1 cup stemmed and quartered cremini mushrooms
1 chopped onion
3 cloves garlic, smashed
1 tablespoon tomato paste
2 cups cherry tomatoes, cut in half
½ cup pitted green olives
½ cup water
½ cup thinly-sliced fresh basil
¼ cup chopped fresh Italian parsley

1. Season the chicken thighs with ½ teaspoon salt and pepper. 2. Press the "Sauté" button two times to select "More" mode. 3. Wait 1 minute and add the oil to the bottom of the pot. 4. Add the carrots, mushrooms, onions, and ½ teaspoon salt and sauté for about 5 minutes until soft. 5. Add the garlic and tomato paste and cook for another 30 seconds. 6. Add the cherry tomatoes, chicken thighs, water and olives, stir well. 7. Put on the pressure cooker's lid and turn the steam valve to "Sealing" position. 8. Select Pressure Cook mode, and then press the "Pressure Cook" button again to select "Less" time option. 9. Use the "+/-" keys on the control panel to set the cooking time to 10 minutes. 10. Press the Pressure Level button to adjust the pressure to "High Pressure." 11. Once the cooking cycle is completed, quickly and carefully turn the steam release handle from Sealing position to the Venting position. 12. When all the steam is released, remove the pressure lid from the top carefully. 13. Top with fresh basil and parsley. 14. Serve and enjoy.
Per Serving: Calories 334; Fat 7.9g; Sodium 704mg; Carbs 6g; Fiber 3.6g; Sugar 6g; Protein 18g

Chicken Cacciatore

Prep time: 15 minutes | Cook time: 30 minutes | Serves: 4

4 chicken thighs, with the bone, skin removed
2 tablespoons olive oil
1 teaspoon kosher salt
1 teaspoon black pepper
½ cup diced green bell pepper
¼ cup diced red bell pepper
½ cup diced onion
½ (14-ounce) can crushed tomatoes
2 tablespoon chopped parsley or basil
½ teaspoon dried oregano
1 bay leaf

1. Press the "Sauté" button two times to select "More" mode. 2. Wait 1 minute and add 1 tablespoon of oil to the bottom of the pot. 3. Season the meat with salt and pepper. 4. Brown the meat for a few minutes on each side. Remove the chicken from the pot and set aside. 5. Pour another 1 tablespoon of oil into the pot. 6. Add bell peppers and onion and sauté for about 5 minutes or until soft and golden. 7. Put the chicken thighs in the Instant pot. Pour over the tomatoes. 8. Add the parsley, oregano and bay leaf, stir well. 9. Press the Cancel button to stop this cooking program and lock the lid in right way. 10. Put on the pressure cooker's lid and turn the steam valve to "Sealing" position. 11. Press the "Pressure Cook" button two times to select "Normal" option. 12. Use the "+/-" keys on the control panel to set the cooking time to 25 minutes. 13. Press the Pressure Level button to adjust the pressure to "High Pressure." 14. Once the cooking cycle is completed, allow the steam to release naturally. 15. When all the steam is released, remove the pressure lid from the top carefully. 16. Serve.
Per Serving: Calories 584; Fat 15g; Sodium 441mg; Carbs 17g; Fiber 4.6g; Sugar 5g; Protein 29g

Spicy Chicken Wings

Prep time: 10 minutes | Cook time: 10 minutes | Serves: 4

3-pound chicken wings
2 tablespoons olive oil
¼ cup light brown sugar
½ teaspoon garlic powder
½ teaspoon cayenne pepper
½ teaspoon black pepper
½ teaspoon paprika
½ teaspoon salt
1½ cups chicken broth or water

1. Rinse and dry the chicken wings with a paper towel. Put in the large bowl. 2. In a medium bowl, combine the olive oil, sugar, garlic powder, cayenne pepper, black pepper, paprika, and salt. Mix well. 3. Rub all sides of the chicken with the spice mix. 4. Pour the chicken broth into the Inner Pot and add the wings. 5. Put on the pressure cooker's lid and turn the steam valve to "Sealing" position. 6. Select Pressure Cook mode, and then press the "Pressure Cook" button again to select "Less" time option. 7. Use the "+/-" keys on the control panel to set the cooking time to 10 minutes. 8. Press the Pressure Level button to adjust the pressure to "High Pressure." 9. Once the cooking cycle is completed, quickly and carefully turn the steam release handle from Sealing position to the Venting position. 10. When all the steam is released, remove the pressure lid from the top carefully. 11. Serve.
Per Serving: Calories 489; Fat 11g; Sodium 501mg; Carbs 8.9g; Fiber 4.6g; Sugar 8g; Protein 26g

Hot Wings

Prep time: 10 minutes | Cook time: 20 minutes | Serves: 6

4-pound chicken wings, sectioned, frozen or fresh
½ cup cayenne pepper hot sauce
1 tablespoon Worcestershire sauce
½ cup butter
½ teaspoon kosher salt
1-2 tablespoon sugar, light brown
1½ cups water

1. Mix the hot sauce with the Worcestershire sauce, butter, salt, and brown sugar; microwave for 20 seconds or until the butter is melted. 2. Pour the water into the Inner Pot and place the Steam Rack. 3. Place chicken wings on the steam rack and lock the lid in right way. 4. Put on the pressure cooker's lid and turn the steam valve to "Sealing" position. 5. Select Pressure Cook mode, and then press the "Pressure Cook" button again to select "Less" time option. 6. Use the "+/-" keys on the control panel to set the cooking time to 10 minutes. 7. Press the Pressure Level button to adjust the pressure to "High Pressure." 8. Once the cooking cycle is completed, quickly and carefully turn the steam release handle from Sealing position to the Venting position. 9. When all the steam is released, remove the pressure lid from the top carefully. 10. Preheat the oven. 11. Carefully transfer the chicken wings to a baking sheet. 12. Brush the tops of the chicken wings with the sauce. 13. Place under the broiler for 4 to 5 minutes until browned. 14. Brush the other side with the remaining sauce and broil for another 4-5 minutes. 15. Serve.
Per Serving: Calories 521; Fat 7.9g; Sodium 704mg; Carbs 6g; Fiber 3.6g; Sugar 6g; Protein 18g

Chicken Puttanesca

Prep time: 15 minutes | Cook time: 25 minutes | Serves: 6

6 chicken thighs, skin on
2 tablespoons olive oil
1 cup water
14-ounce canned chopped tomatoes
2 cloves garlic, crushed
½ teaspoon red chili flakes or to
taste
6-ounce pitted black olives
1 tablespoon capers, rinsed and drained
1 tablespoon fresh basil, chopped
1 teaspoon kosher salt
1 teaspoon black pepper

1. Press the "Sauté" button two times to select "Normal" mode. and heat the oil. 2. Add the chicken thighs skin side down and Brown the meat for 4-6 minutes. 3. Transfer the meat to a bowl. 4. Add the water, tomatoes, garlic, chili flakes, black olives, capers, fresh basil, salt and pepper to the Inner Pot. Stir well and bring to a simmer. 5. Return the chicken to the pot. 6. Put on the pressure cooker's lid and turn the steam valve to "Sealing" position. 7. Select Pressure Cook mode, and then press the "Pressure Cook" button again to select "Less" time option. 8. Use the "+/-" keys on the control panel to set the cooking time to 16 minutes. 9. Press the Pressure Level button to adjust the pressure to "High Pressure." 10. Once the cooking cycle is completed, allow the steam to release naturally for 10 minutes, then turn the steam release handle to the Venting position. 11. When all the steam is released, remove the pressure lid from the top carefully. 12. Serve.
Per Serving: Calories 475; Fat 10.9g; Sodium 354mg; Carbs 10.5g; Fiber 4.1g; Sugar 8.2g; Protein 26g

BBQ Chicken with Potatoes

Prep time: 20 minutes | Cook time: 15 minutes | Serves: 4

2-pound chicken (breasts or thighs)	1 cup BBQ sauce
1 cup water	1 tablespoon Italian seasoning
3 large potatoes, unpeeled and quartered	1 tablespoon minced garlic
	1 large onion, sliced

1. Add the chicken, water, potatoes, BBQ sauce, Italian seasoning, garlic and onion to the Inner Pot. 2. Put on the pressure cooker's lid and turn the steam valve to "Sealing" position. 3. Select Pressure Cook mode, and then press the "Pressure Cook" button again to select "Less" time option. 4. Use the "+/-" keys on the control panel to set the cooking time to 15 minutes. 5. Press the Pressure Level button to adjust the pressure to "High Pressure." 6. Once the cooking cycle is completed, quickly and carefully turn the steam release handle from Sealing position to the Venting position. 7. When all the steam is released, remove the pressure lid from the top carefully. 8. Transfer the chicken to a plate and shred it. Return shredded chicken to the pot. 9. Stir well until fully coated with the sauce. 10. Serve and enjoy.
Per Serving: Calories 334; Fat 10.9g; Sodium 354mg; Carbs 10.5g; Fiber 4.1g; Sugar 8.2g; Protein 26g

Creamy Chicken with Bacon

Prep time: 20 minutes | Cook time: 20 minutes | Serves: 4

2-pound chicken breasts, skinless and boneless	1-ounce ranch seasoning
2 slices bacon, chopped	4-ounce cream cheese
1 cup chicken stock	Green onions, chopped for serving

1. Press the "Sauté" button two times to select "Normal" mode. 2. Add the button and sauté the bacon for 4-5 minutes. 3. Add the chicken, stock, and ranch seasoning. Stir well. 4. Put on the pressure cooker's lid and turn the steam valve to "Sealing" position. 5. Select Pressure Cook mode, and then press the "Pressure Cook" button again to select "Less" time option. 6. Use the "+/-" keys on the control panel to set the cooking time to 12 minutes. 7. Press the Pressure Level button to adjust the pressure to "High Pressure." 8. Once the cooking cycle is completed, allow the steam to release naturally. 9. When all the steam is released, remove the pressure lid from the top carefully. 10. Transfer the chicken to a plate and shred the meat. 11. Remove ⅔ cup of cooking liquid from the pot. 12. Add the cheese, Press the "Sauté" button two time to select "Normal" mode and continue to cook for 3 minutes. 13. Return chicken to pot and stir. 14. Press Cancel button to stop the cooking program. 15. Add green onions, stir and serve.
Per Serving: Calories 490; Fat 19g; Sodium 354mg; Carbs 15g; Fiber 5.1g; Sugar 8.2g; Protein 32g

Cajun Chicken with Rice

Prep time: 20 minutes | Cook time: 20 minutes | Serves: 4

1 tablespoon olive oil	1½ cups white rice, rinsed
1 onion, diced	1 bell pepper, chopped
3 cloves garlic, minced	Cajun spices:
1-pound chicken breasts, sliced	¼ teaspoon cayenne pepper
2 cups chicken broth	2 teaspoons dried thyme
1 tablespoon tomato paste	1 tablespoon paprika

1. Press the "Sauté" button two times to select "Normal" mode. and heat the oil. 2. Add the onion and garlic and cook until fragrant. 3. Add the chicken breasts and Cajun spices, stir well. Sauté for another 3 minutes. 4. Pour the broth and tomato paste into the pot. Stir to dissolve the tomato paste. 5. Add the rice and bell pepper, stir. 6. Put on the pressure cooker's lid and turn the steam valve to "Sealing" position. 7. Select Pressure Cook mode, and then press the "Pressure Cook" button again to select "Less" time option. 8. Press the Pressure Level button to adjust the pressure to "High Potatoes." 9. Once the cooking cycle is completed, allow the steam to release naturally for 10 minutes, then turn the steam release handle to the Venting position. 10. When all the steam is released, remove the pressure lid from the top

carefully. 11. Serve.
Per Serving: Calories 489; Fat 11g; Sodium 501mg; Carbs 8.9g; Fiber 4.6g; Sugar 8g; Protein 26g

Lime Chicken Wings

Prep time: 10 minutes | Cook time: 20 minutes | Serves: 4

2-pound chicken wings	1 small lime, juiced
3 tablespoon honey	½ teaspoon sea salt
2 tablespoon soy sauce	½ cup water

1. In a bowl, combine the soy sauce, lime juice, honey and salt. 2. Rinse and dry the chicken wings with a paper towel. 3. Add the chicken wings and honey mixture to a Ziploc bag and shake a couple of times. 4. Then refrigerate for 60 minutes. 5. Pour the water into the Inner Pot and add the chicken wings with marinade. 6. Put on the pressure cooker's lid and turn the steam valve to "Sealing" position. 7. Select Pressure Cook mode, and then press the "Pressure Cook" button again to select "Less" time option. 8. Use the "+/-" keys on the control panel to set the cooking time to 15 minutes. 9. Press the Pressure Level button to adjust the pressure to "High Pressure." 10. Once the cooking cycle is completed, allow the steam to release naturally for 10 minutes, then turn the steam release handle to the Venting position. 11. When all the steam is released, remove the pressure lid from the top carefully. 12. Press the "Sauté" button two times to select "Normal" mode and continue to cook until the sauce thickens. 13. Serve.
Per Serving: Calories 219; Fat 10g; Sodium 891mg; Carbs 22.9g; Fiber 4g; Sugar 4g; Protein 13g

Cream Cheese Chicken

Prep time: 20 minutes | Cook time: 20 minutes | Serves: 2

1-pound chicken breasts, boneless and skinless	drained
1 can (10-ounce) Rotel tomato, undrained	1-ounce dry ranch seasoning
1 can (15-ounce) corn, undrained	1½ teaspoon chili powder
1 can (15-ounce) black beans,	1½ teaspoon cumin
	8-ounce cream cheese
	¼ cup parsley

1. Combine all of the ingredients, except cheese, in the Inner Pot. 2. Put on the pressure cooker's lid and turn the steam valve to "Sealing" position. 3. Press the "Pressure Cook" button two times to select "Normal" option. 4. Use the "+/-" keys on the control panel to set the cooking time to 20 minutes. 5. Press the Pressure Level button to adjust the pressure to "High Pressure." 6. Once the cooking cycle is completed, allow the steam to release naturally for 10 minutes, then turn the steam release handle to the Venting position. 7. When all the steam is released, remove the pressure lid from the top carefully. 8. Transfer the chicken to a plate and shred the meat. 9. Add the cheese to the pot and stir well. Close the lid and let sit for 5 minutes, until cheese is melted. 10. Open the lid and return the chicken to the pot. Stir to combine. 11. Top with parsley and serve.
Per Serving: Calories 501; Fat 7.9g; Sodium 704mg; Carbs 6g; Fiber 3.6g; Sugar 6g; Protein 18g

Salsa Verde Chicken

Prep time: 10 minutes | Cook time: 20 minutes | Serves: 6

2½-pound boneless chicken breasts	1 teaspoon cumin
1 teaspoon smoked paprika	1 teaspoon salt
	2 cup (16-ounce) salsa Verde

1. Add the chicken breasts, paprika, cumin, and salt to the Inner Pot. 2. Pour the salsa Verde on top. 3. Put on the pressure cooker's lid and turn the steam valve to "Sealing" position. 4. Select Pressure Cook mode, and then press the "Pressure Cook" button again to select "Less" time option. 5. Press the Pressure Level button to adjust the pressure to "High Pressure." 6. Once the cooking cycle is completed, quickly and carefully turn the steam release handle from Sealing position to the Venting position. 7. When all the steam is released, remove the pressure lid from the top carefully. 8. Shred the meat, serve and enjoy.
Per Serving: Calories 382; Fat 7.9g; Sodium 704mg; Carbs 6g; Fiber 3.6g; Sugar 6g; Protein 18g

Chicken Drumsticks

Prep time: 15 minutes | Cook time: 20 minutes | Serves: 6

6 chicken drumsticks	½ cup + 2 tablespoons water
1 tablespoon olive oil	½ cup sugar-free barbecue sauce
1 onion, chopped	1½ tablespoons arrowroot
1 teaspoon garlic, minced	

1. Press the "Sauté" button two times to select "Normal" mode and then heat the oil. 2. Add the onion and sauté for about 3 minutes, until softened. 3. Add the garlic and cook for another 30 seconds. 4. Add ½ cup of water and barbecue sauce, stir well. 5. Add the chicken drumsticks to the pot. 6. Put on the pressure cooker's lid and turn the steam valve to "Sealing" position. 7. Select Pressure Cook mode, and then press the "Pressure Cook" button again to select "Less" time option. 8. Use the "+/-" keys on the control panel to set the cooking time to 10 minutes. 9. Press the Pressure Level button to adjust the pressure to "High Pressure." 10. Once the cooking cycle is completed, quickly and carefully turn the steam release handle from Sealing position to the Venting position. 11. When all the steam is released, remove the pressure lid from the top carefully. 12. In a cup, whisk together the remaining water and arrowroot until combined. Add to the pot. 13. Press the "Sauté" button two times to select "More" mode and cook for 5 minutes. 14. Serve the drumsticks with the sauce.
Per Serving: Calories 412; Fat 20g; Sodium 491mg; Carbs 9g; Fiber 3g; Sugar 8g; Protein 31g

Chicken Tomato Drumsticks

Prep time: 15 minutes | Cook time: 40 minutes | Serves: 6

6 chicken drumsticks (24 oz.), skin removed, on the bone	½ teaspoon black pepper
	1 teaspoon olive oil
1 tablespoon apple cider vinegar	1½ cups tomato sauce
1 teaspoon oregano, dried	1 jalapeno, seeded, cut in halves
½ teaspoon salt	¼ cup cilantro, chopped

1. In a medium bowl, combine the apple cider vinegar, oregano, salt and pepper. 2. Add the chicken to the bowl and coat it well with the marinade. 3. Press the "Sauté" button two times to select "Normal" mode, add the oil and heat it up. 4. Lower the chicken into the pot and sear for 5-8 minutes on each side, until nicely browned. 5. Add the tomato sauce, a half of the jalapeno and cilantro. 6. Put on the pressure cooker's lid and turn the steam valve to "Sealing" position. 7. Select Pressure Cook mode, and then press the "Pressure Cook" button again to select "Less" time option. 8. Press the Pressure Level button to adjust the pressure to "High Pressure." 9. Once the cooking cycle is completed, quickly and carefully turn the steam release handle from Sealing position to the Venting position. 10. When all the steam is released, remove the pressure lid from the top carefully. 11. Serve with the remaining cilantro and jalapeno.
Per Serving: Calories 334; Fat 7.9g; Sodium 704mg; Carbs 6g; Fiber 3.6g; Sugar 6g; Protein 18g

Chicken Piccata

Prep time: 15 minutes | Cook time: 15 minutes | Serves: 4

4 chicken breasts skinless, boneless, 1½ to 1¾ pounds	2 tablespoons butter
	2 tablespoons brined capers, drained
1 tablespoon olive oil	
¼ teaspoon black pepper	2 tablespoons flat-leaf fresh parsley, chopped
½ teaspoon salt	
1 cup chicken broth	Cooked rice or pasta
¼ cup fresh lemon juice	

1. Press the "Sauté" button two times to select "Normal" mode. 2. Wait 2 minutes and add the oil to the bottom of the Inner Pot. 3. Season the chicken with salt and pepper. 4. Add to the pot and brown the meat for 3 minutes on each side. Add the broth. 5. Put on the pressure cooker's lid and turn the steam valve to "Sealing" position. 6. Select Pressure Cook mode, and then press the "Pressure Cook" button again to select "Less" time option. 7. Use the "+/-" keys on the control panel to set the cooking time to 5 minutes. 8. Press the Pressure Level button to adjust the pressure to "High Pressure." 9. Once the cooking cycle is completed, quickly and carefully turn the steam release handle from Sealing position to the Venting position. 10. When all the steam is released, remove the pressure lid from the top carefully. 11. Remove the chicken from the pot to a serving bowl. 12. Press the "Sauté" button two times to select "Normal" mode and simmer for 5 minutes. 13. Add fresh lemon juice. 14. Add the butter. Once the butter is melted, add parsley and capers, stir. 15. Pour the sauce over chicken breasts. 16. Serve with rice or pasta.
Per Serving: Calories 349; Fat 2.9g; Sodium 511mg; Carbs 12g; Fiber 3g; Sugar 8g; Protein 7g

Chili Lime Chicken

Prep time: 20 minutes | Cook time: 10 minutes | Serves: 4

2-pound chicken breasts, bones removed	1 teaspoon onion powder
	6 cloves garlic, minced
¾ cup chicken broth or water	½ teaspoon liquid smoke
Juice of 2 medium limes	1 teaspoon kosher salt
1½ teaspoons chili powder	1 teaspoon black pepper
1 teaspoon cumin	

1. Dump all of the ingredients into the Inner Pot and give it a little stir to mix everything evenly. 2. Put on the pressure cooker's lid and turn the steam valve to "Sealing" position. 3. Select Pressure Cook mode, and then press the "Pressure Cook" button again to select "Less" time option. 4. Use the "+/-" keys on the control panel to set the cooking time to 10 minutes. 5. Press the Pressure Level button to adjust the pressure to "High Pressure." 6. Once the cooking cycle is completed, allow the steam to release naturally for 10 minutes, then turn the steam release handle to the Venting position. 7. When all the steam is released, remove the pressure lid from the top carefully. 8. Remove the chicken and shred it. 9. Serve with the remaining juice from the Inner Pot.
Per Serving: Calories 489; Fat 11g; Sodium 501mg; Carbs 8.9g; Fiber 4.6g; Sugar 8g; Protein 26g

Shredded Chicken with Marinara

Prep time: 20 minutes | Cook time: 25 minutes | Serves: 6

4-pound chicken breasts	1 teaspoon salt
½ cup chicken broth	2 cups marinara sauce
½ teaspoon black pepper	

1. Add the chicken breasts, broth, pepper, and salt to the Inner Pot, stir well. 2. Put on the pressure cooker's lid and turn the steam valve to "Sealing" position. 3. Select Pressure Cook mode, and then press the "Pressure Cook" button again to select "Less" time option. 4. Press the Pressure Level button to adjust the pressure to "High Pressure." 5. Once the cooking cycle is completed, quickly and carefully turn the steam release handle from Sealing position to the Venting position. 6. When all the steam is released, remove the pressure lid from the top carefully. 7. Shred the chicken in the pot. 8. Press the "Sauté" button two times to select "Normal" mode. 9. Add the marinara sauce and simmer for 5 minutes. 10. Serve with cooked rice, potato, peas or green salad.
Per Serving: Calories 419; Fat 14g; Sodium 791mg; Carbs 8.9g; Fiber 4.6g; Sugar 8g; Protein 31g

Chicken Coconut Curry

Prep time: 15 minutes | Cook time: 15 minutes | Serves: 4

2-pound chicken breast or thighs	1 cup onion, chopped or ¼ cup dry minced onion
16-ounce canned coconut milk	
16-ounce canned tomato sauce	2 tablespoons curry powder
6-ounce can tomato paste	3 tablespoons honey
2 cloves garlic, minced	1 teaspoon salt

1. Mix all of the ingredients in the Inner Pot and stir to combine. 2. Put on the pressure cooker's lid and turn the steam valve to "Sealing" position. 3. Select Pressure Cook mode, and then press the "Pressure Cook" button again to select "Less" time option. 4. Use the "+/-" keys on the control panel to set the cooking time to 15 minutes. 5. Press the Pressure Level button to adjust the pressure to "High Pressure." 6. Once the cooking cycle is completed, allow the steam to release naturally for 10 minutes, then turn the steam release handle to the Venting position. 7. When all the steam is released, remove the pressure lid from the top carefully. 8. Serve with cooked rice, potato or peas.
Per Serving: Calories 471; Fat 19g; Sodium 354mg; Carbs 15g; Fiber 5.1g; Sugar 8.2g; Protein 12g

8-Ingredient Chicken

Prep time: 10 minutes | Cook time: 25 minutes | Serves: 4

2-pound boneless chicken thighs
¼ cup soy sauce
3 tablespoons organic ketchup
¼ cup coconut oil

¼ cup honey
2 teaspoons garlic powder
½ teaspoon black pepper
1½ teaspoons sea salt

1. Combine the soy sauce, ketchup, coconut oil, honey, garlic powder, pepper, and salt in the Inner Pot. 2. Toss the chicken thighs in the mixture. 3. Put on the pressure cooker's lid and turn the steam valve to "Sealing" position. 4. Select Pressure Cook mode, and then press the "Pressure Cook" button again to select "Less" time option. 5. Use the "+/-" keys on the control panel to set the cooking time to 18 minutes. 6. Press the Pressure Level button to adjust the pressure to "High Pressure." 7. Once the cooking cycle is completed, quickly and carefully turn the steam release handle from Sealing position to the Venting position. 8. When all the steam is released, remove the pressure lid from the top carefully. 9. Press the "Sauté" button two times to select "Less" mode and simmer for 5 minutes. 10. Serve with vegetables.
Per Serving: Calories 361; Fat 7.9g; Sodium 704mg; Carbs 6g; Fiber 3.6g; Sugar 6g; Protein 18g

Chicken Congee

Prep time: 15 minutes | Cook time: 35 minutes | Serves: 6

6 chicken drumsticks
6 cups water
1 cup Jasmine rice
1 tablespoon fresh ginger

2 cloves garlic, crushed
Salt to taste
½ cup scallions, chopped
2 teaspoons sesame oil, optional

1. Add the chicken, rice, water, ginger and garlic to the Inner Pot. Stir well. 2. Put on the pressure cooker's lid and turn the steam valve to "Sealing" position. 3. Select Pressure Cook mode, and then press the "Pressure Cook" button again to select "Less" time option. 4. Use the "+/-" keys on the control panel to set the cooking time to 25 minutes. 5. Press the Pressure Level button to adjust the pressure to "High Pressure." 6. Once the cooking cycle is completed, allow the steam to release naturally for 10 minutes, then turn the steam release handle to the Venting position. 7. When all the steam is released, remove the pressure lid from the top carefully. 8. Take the chicken out from the pot, shred the meat and discard the bones. 9. Return the chicken meat to the pot. 10. Press the "Sauté" button two times to select "Normal" mode and cook for about 10 minutes. 11. Top with scallions and sesame oil. 12. Serve and enjoy.
Per Serving: Calories 478; Fat 19g; Sodium 354mg; Carbs 15g; Fiber 5.1g; Sugar 8.2g; Protein 32g

Chicken with Potatoes

Prep time: 15 minutes | Cook time: 21 minutes | Serves: 4

2-pound chicken thighs, skinless and boneless
2 tablespoons olive oil
¾ cup chicken stock
3 tablespoon Dijon mustard
¼ cup lemon juice

2 tablespoon Italian seasoning
2-pound red potatoes, peeled and cut into quarters
1 teaspoon salt
1 teaspoon black pepper

1. Press the "Sauté" button two times to select "Normal" mode. and heat the oil. 2. Season the chicken thighs with ½ teaspoon salt and ½ teaspoon pepper. 3. Add the chicken to the Inner Pot and brown the meat for 3 minutes on each side. 4. In a medium bowl, combine the stock, mustard, lemon juice and Italian seasoning. 5. Pour the mixture over the chicken. 6. Add the potatoes, ½ teaspoon salt and ½ teaspoon pepper. Stir. 7. Put on the pressure cooker's lid and turn the steam valve to "Sealing" position. 8. Select Pressure Cook mode, and then press the "Pressure Cook" button again to select "Less" time option. 9. Use the "+/-" keys on the control panel to set the cooking time to 15 minutes. 10. Press the Pressure Level button to adjust the pressure to "High Pressure." 11. Once the cooking cycle is completed, allow the steam to release naturally. 12. When all the steam is released, remove the pressure lid from the top carefully. 13. Serve.
Per Serving: Calories 382; Fat 7.9g; Sodium 704mg; Carbs 6g; Fiber 3.6g; Sugar 6g; Protein 18g

Chicken Adobo

Prep time: 15 minutes | Cook time: 30 minutes | Serves: 4

4 chicken drumsticks
½ teaspoon kosher salt
1 teaspoon black pepper
2 tablespoons olive oil
¼ cup white vinegar

⅓ cup soy sauce
¼ cup sugar
1 onion, chopped
5 cloves garlic, crushed
2 bay leaves

1. Press the "Sauté" button two times to select "More" mode. 2. Wait 1 minute and add the oil to the bottom of the pot. 3. Season the legs with salt and ½ teaspoon pepper. 4. Add the chicken drumsticks to the Inner Pot and brown for 4 minutes on each side. 5. Add the vinegar, soy sauce, sugar, onion, garlic, bay leaves and ½ teaspoon pepper. 6. Put on the pressure cooker's lid and turn the steam valve to "Sealing" position. 7. Select Pressure Cook mode, and then press the "Pressure Cook" button again to select "Less" time option. 8. Use the "+/-" keys on the control panel to set the cooking time to 10 minutes. 9. Press the Pressure Level button to adjust the pressure to "High Pressure." 10. Once the cooking cycle is completed, quickly and carefully turn the steam release handle from Sealing position to the Venting position. 11. When all the steam is released, remove the pressure lid from the top carefully. 12. Press the "Sauté" button two times to select "Less" mode and simmer for 10 minutes. 13. Remove the bay leaves. 14. Serve and enjoy.
Per Serving: Calories 489; Fat 11g; Sodium 501mg; Carbs 8.9g; Fiber 4.6g; Sugar 8g; Protein 26g

Orange Chicken

Prep time: 10 minutes | Cook time: 15 minutes | Serves: 4

4 chicken breasts
¼ cup water
¾ cup orange juice
¾ cup barbecue sauce
2 tablespoons soy sauce

1 tablespoon cornstarch + 2 tablespoons water
2 tablespoons green onions, chopped

1. Add the chicken breasts, ¼ cup of water, orange juice, barbecue sauce, and soy sauce to the Inner Pot. Stir well. 2. Put on the pressure cooker's lid and turn the steam valve to "Sealing" position. 3. Press the "Poultry" button three times to select "Normal" option. 4. Press the Pressure Level button to adjust the pressure to "High Pressure." 5. Once the cooking cycle is completed, quickly and carefully turn the steam release handle from Sealing position to the Venting position. 6. When all the steam is released, remove the pressure lid from the top carefully. 7. In a cup, combine the cornstarch and 2 tablespoons of water. 8. Press the "Sauté" button two times to select "Normal" mode and add the cornstarch slurry to the pot. 9. Simmer for 5 minutes or until the sauce has thickened. 10. Add green onions and serve.
Per Serving: Calories 458; Fat 12.9g; Sodium 414mg; Carbs 11g; Fiber 5g; Sugar 9g; Protein 31g

Teriyaki Chicken

Prep time: 15 minutes | Cook time: 15 minutes | Serves: 4

2-pound chicken breasts, skinless and boneless
⅔ cup teriyaki sauce
1 tablespoon honey

½ cup chicken stock
½ teaspoon salt
½ teaspoon black pepper
A handful green onions, chopped

1. Press the "Sauté" button two times to select "More" mode 2. Add the teriyaki sauce and honey, stir and simmer for 1 minute. 3. Add the chicken, stock, salt and pepper. Stir well. 4. Put on the pressure cooker's lid and turn the steam valve to "Sealing" position. 5. Select Pressure Cook mode, and then press the "Pressure Cook" button again to select "Less" time option. 6. Use the "+/-" keys on the control panel to set the cooking time to 12 minutes. 7. Press the Pressure Level button to adjust the pressure to "High Pressure." 8. Once the cooking cycle is completed, allow the steam to release naturally. 9. When all the steam is released, remove the pressure lid from the top carefully. 10. Transfer the chicken to a plate and shred the meat. 11. Remove ½ cup of cooking liquid and return shredded chicken to the pot. 12. Stir with the green onions and serve.
Per Serving: Calories 289; Fat 14g; Sodium 791mg; Carbs 18.9g; Fiber 4.6g; Sugar 8g; Protein 6g

Coca Cola Chicken

Prep time: 20 minutes | Cook time: 25 minutes | Serves: 4

4 chicken drumsticks
2 tablespoons olive oil
Salt and black pepper to taste
1 large finely onion, chopped
1 small chopped chili
1 tablespoon balsamic vinegar
17-ounce Coca Cola

1. Press the "Sauté" button two times to select "Normal" mode. 2. Wait 1 minute and add the oil to the bottom of the pot. 3. Season the chicken drumsticks with salt and pepper to taste. 4. Add the drumsticks to the Inner Pot and sear for 4 minutes on each side, until nicely browned. 5. Remove the chicken from the pot. Add the onions and sauté for about 3-5 minutes, until softened. 6. Then add the chili, balsamic vinegar and Coca-Cola, stir. 7. Return the drumsticks to the pot. 8. Put on the pressure cooker's lid and turn the steam valve to "Sealing" position. 9. Select Pressure Cook mode, and then press the "Pressure Cook" button again to select "Less" time option. 10. Use the "+/-" keys on the control panel to set the cooking time to 10 minutes. 11. Press the Pressure Level button to adjust the pressure to "High Pressure." 12. Once the cooking cycle is completed, allow the steam to release naturally for 10 minutes, then turn the steam release handle to the Venting position. 13. When all the steam is released, remove the pressure lid from the top carefully. 14. Serve.
Per Serving: Calories 521; Fat 12.9g; Sodium 414mg; Carbs 11g; Fiber 5g; Sugar 9g; Protein 31g

Buffalo Chicken

Prep time: 15 minutes | Cook time: 12 minutes | Serves: 4

2-pound chicken breasts, skinless, boneless and cut into thin strips
1 small yellow onion, chopped
½ cup celery, chopped
½ cup buffalo sauce
½ cup chicken stock
¼ cup bleu cheese, crumbled

1. Add the chicken breasts, onion, celery, buffalo sauce and stock to the Inner Pot. 2. Put on the pressure cooker's lid and turn the steam valve to "Sealing" position. 3. Select Pressure Cook mode, and then press the "Pressure Cook" button again to select "Less" time option. 4. Use the "+/-" keys on the control panel to set the cooking time to 12 minutes. 5. Press the Pressure Level button to adjust the pressure to "High Pressure." 6. Once the cooking cycle is completed, allow the steam to release naturally. 7. When all the steam is released, remove the pressure lid from the top carefully. 8. Remove ⅔ cup of cooking liquid. Add crumbled blue cheese to the pot and stir well. 9. Serve.
Per Serving: Calories 419; Fat 14g; Sodium 791mg; Carbs 8.9g; Fiber 4.6g; Sugar 8g; Protein 31g

Sesame Chicken

Prep time: 10 minutes | Cook time: 15 minutes | Serves: 6

6 boneless chicken thigh fillets
5 tablespoons sweet chili sauce
5 tablespoons hoisin sauce
1 chunk peeled, grated fresh ginger
4 peeled and crushed cloves garlic
1 tablespoon rice vinegar
1½ tablespoons sesame seeds
1 tablespoon soy sauce
½ cup chicken stock

1. In a medium bowl, whisk together the chili sauce, hoisin sauce, ginger, garlic, vinegar, sesame seeds, soy sauce, and chicken stock until combined. 2. Add the chicken thigh fillets to the Inner Pot and pour over the sauce mixture. 3. Put on the pressure cooker's lid and turn the steam valve to "Sealing" position. 4. Select Pressure Cook mode, and then press the "Pressure Cook" button again to select "Less" time option. 5. Use the "+/-" keys on the control panel to set the cooking time to 15 minutes. 6. Press the Pressure Level button to adjust the pressure to "High Pressure." 7. Once the cooking cycle is completed, allow the steam to release naturally for 10 minutes, then turn the steam release handle to the Venting position. 8. When all the steam is released, remove the pressure lid from the top carefully. 9. Serve with cooked rice, mashed potato or any other garnish.
Per Serving: Calories 219; Fat 10g; Sodium 891mg; Carbs 22.9g; Fiber 4g; Sugar 4g; Protein 23g

Shredded Chicken Breast

Prep time: 10 minutes | Cook time: 8 minutes | Serves: 4

5-2-pound boneless chicken breasts
½ teaspoon black pepper
½ teaspoon garlic salt
½ cup chicken broth

1. Season all sides of the chicken with the black pepper and salt. 2. Add the chicken breasts to the Inner Pot and pour the chicken broth. 3. Put on the pressure cooker's lid and turn the steam valve to "Sealing" position. 4. Select Pressure Cook mode, and then press the "Pressure Cook" button again to select "Less" time option. 5. Use the "+/-" keys on the control panel to set the cooking time to 8 minutes. 6. Press the Pressure Level button to adjust the pressure to "High Pressure." 7. Once the cooking cycle is completed, allow the steam to release naturally for 10 minutes, then turn the steam release handle to the Venting position. 8. When all the steam is released, remove the pressure lid from the top carefully. 9. Remove the chicken from the pot and shred it with 2 forks. 10. Serve and enjoy.
Per Serving: Calories 584; Fat 15g; Sodium 441mg; Carbs 17g; Fiber 4.6g; Sugar 5g; Protein 29g

Sriracha Chicken

Prep time: 10 minutes | Cook time: 15 minutes | Serves: 4

4 diced chicken breasts
5 tablespoons soy sauce
2-3 tablespoons honey
¼ cup sugar
4 tablespoons cold water
1 tablespoon minced garlic
2-3 tablespoons sriracha
2 tablespoons cornstarch

1. In the Inner Pot, whisk together soy sauce, honey, sugar, 2 tablespoons of water, garlic, and sriracha until combined. 2. Toss the chicken breasts in the mixture. 3. Put on the pressure cooker's lid and turn the steam valve to "Sealing" position. 4. Select Pressure Cook mode, and then press the "Pressure Cook" button again to select "Less" time option. 5. Use the "+/-" keys on the control panel to set the cooking time to 9 minutes. 6. Press the Pressure Level button to adjust the pressure to "High Pressure." 7. Once the cooking cycle is completed, quickly and carefully turn the steam release handle from Sealing position to the Venting position. 8. When all the steam is released, remove the pressure lid from the top carefully. 9. Meanwhile, in a small bowl combine 2 tablespoons of water and cornstarch. 10. Pour the cornstarch mixture into the pot. 11. Press the "Sauté" button two times to select "Less" mode, simmer and stir occasionally until the sauce begins to thicken. 12. Serve.
Per Serving: Calories 372; Fat 20g; Sodium 891mg; Carbs 29g; Fiber 3g; Sugar 8g; Protein 27g

Chicken Nachos

Prep time: 15 minutes | Cook time: 20 minutes | Serves: 6

2 pounds' chicken thighs, boneless, skinless
1 tablespoon olive oil
1 package (1 oz.) taco seasoning mix
⅔ cup mild red salsa
⅓ cup mild Herdez salsa Verde
½ cup water

1. Press the "Sauté" button two times to select "Normal" mode. and heat the oil. 2. Add the chicken thighs and brown the meat nicely for a few minutes on each side. 3. In a medium bowl, combine the taco seasoning and salsa. 4. Pour the mixture in the pot, add water and stir well. 5. Press the Cancel button to stop this cooking program and lock the lid in right way. 6. Put on the pressure cooker's lid and turn the steam valve to "Sealing" position. 7. Select Pressure Cook mode, and then press the "Pressure Cook" button again to select "Less" time option. 8. Use the "+/-" keys on the control panel to set the cooking time to 15 minutes. 9. Press the Pressure Level button to adjust the pressure to "High Pressure." 10. Once the cooking cycle is completed, allow the steam to release naturally for 10 minutes, then turn the steam release handle to the Venting position. 11. When all the steam is released, remove the pressure lid from the top carefully. 12. Shred the meat and serve with tortilla chips.
Per Serving: Calories 412; Fat 20g; Sodium 491mg; Carbs 9g; Fiber 3g; Sugar 8g; Protein 31g

Lemon Mustard Chicken with Potatoes

Prep time: 20 minutes | Cook time: 20 minutes | Serves: 6

2-pound chicken thighs	3 tablespoon Dijon mustard
2 tablespoons olive oil	1 cup chicken broth
3-pound red potatoes, peeled and quartered	¼ cup lemon juice
	1 teaspoon salt
2 tablespoon Italian seasoning	1 teaspoon black pepper

1. Press the "Sauté" button two times to select "Normal" mode. and heat the oil. 2. Add the chicken thighs to the pot and sauté for 2-3 minutes, until starting to brown. 3. Add the potatoes, Italian seasoning, and Dijon mustard. Cook for 2 minutes, stir occasionally. 4. Pour the broth and lemon juice into the pot, stir. Season with salt and pepper. 5. Put on the pressure cooker's lid and turn the steam valve to "Sealing" position. 6. Press the "Poultry" button three times to select "Normal" option. 7. Press the Pressure Level button to adjust the pressure to "High Pressure." 8. Once the cooking cycle is completed, allow the steam to release naturally for 10 minutes, then turn the steam release handle to the Venting position. 9. When all the steam is released, remove the pressure lid from the top carefully. 10. Serve.
Per Serving: Calories 472; Fat 7.9g; Sodium 704mg; Carbs 6g; Fiber 3.6g; Sugar 6g; Protein 18g

Olive Chicken

Prep time: 20 minutes | Cook time: 20 minutes | Serves: 4

4 chicken breasts, skinless and boneless	½ teaspoon black pepper
	Juice of 1 lemon
½ cup butter	1 cup chicken broth
½ teaspoon cumin	1 can pitted green olives
1 teaspoon salt	

1. Press the "Sauté" button two times to select "Normal" mode. 2. Once hot, add the butter and melt it. 3. Season the chicken breasts with cumin, salt, and pepper. 4. Put the breasts into the pot and sauté for 3-5 minutes on each side, until nicely browned. 5. Add the lemon juice, broth and olives, stir well. 6. Put on the pressure cooker's lid and turn the steam valve to "Sealing" position. 7. Select Pressure Cook mode, and then press the "Pressure Cook" button again to select "Less" time option. 8. Use the "+/-" keys on the control panel to set the cooking time to 10 minutes. 9. Press the Pressure Level button to adjust the pressure to "High Pressure." 10. Once the cooking cycle is completed, allow the steam to release naturally. 11. When all the steam is released, remove the pressure lid from the top carefully. 12. Serve.
Per Serving: Calories 584; Fat 15g; Sodium 441mg; Carbs 17g; Fiber 4.6g; Sugar 5g; Protein 29g

Pina Colada Chicken

Prep time: 10 minutes | Cook time: 20 minutes | Serves: 4

2-pound chicken thighs cut into 1-inch pieces	1 teaspoon cinnamon
	⅛ teaspoon salt
½ cup coconut cream, full fat	½ cup green onion, chopped
2 tablespoon soy sauce	1 teaspoon arrowroot starch
1 can (20-ounce) pineapple chunks	1 tablespoon water

1. Combine all of the ingredients, except arrowroot starch, water and green onion, in the Inner Pot and stir to combine. 2. Put on the pressure cooker's lid and turn the steam valve to "Sealing" position. 3. Press the "Poultry" button three times to select "Normal" option. 4. Press the Pressure Level button to adjust the pressure to "High Pressure." 5. Once the cooking cycle is completed, allow the steam to release naturally for 10 minutes, then turn the steam release handle to the Venting position. 6. When all the steam is released, remove the pressure lid from the top carefully. 7. Transfer the chicken to a serving bowl. 8. In a cup, combine the arrowroot starch and water. Mix well. 9. Add the mixture to the instant pot. 10. Press the "Sauté" button two times to select "Normal" mode and continue to cook, stirring occasionally, until the sauce begins to thicken. 11. Serve the chicken with green onion and sauce.
Per Serving: Calories 412; Fat 20g; Sodium 491mg; Carbs 9g; Fiber 3g; Sugar 8g; Protein 31g

Apricot Chicken

Prep time: 10 minutes | Cook time: 20 minutes | Serves: 4-6

2½ pounds chicken thighs, skinless	⅛ teaspoon allspice powder
	½ cup chicken broth
1 tablespoon vegetable oil	8-ounce canned apricots
1 teaspoon kosher salt	1 lb. canned tomatoes, diced
1 teaspoon black pepper	1 tablespoon fresh ginger, grated
3 cloves garlic, minced	½ teaspoon cinnamon, ground
1 large onion, chopped	Fresh parsley, chopped

1. Press the "Sauté" button two times to select "Normal" mode, add the oil and heat it up. 2. Season the chicken thighs with salt and pepper. 3. Add the chicken, garlic, and onion to the Instant pot. 4. Sprinkle with the allspice powder and cook for 5 minutes or until nicely browned. 5. Pour the broth. Add the apricots, tomatoes, fresh ginger, and cinnamon to the pot. Stir well. 6. Select Pressure Cook mode, and then press the "Pressure Cook" button again to select "Less" time option. 7. Use the "+/-" keys on the control panel to set the cooking time to 12 minutes. 8. Press the Pressure Level button to adjust the pressure to "High Pressure." 9. Once the cooking cycle is completed, quickly and carefully turn the steam release handle from Sealing position to the Venting position. 10. When all the steam is released, remove the pressure lid from the top carefully. 11. Transfer the dish to a serving bowl, top with parsley and serve.
Per Serving: Calories 219; Fat 10g; Sodium 891mg; Carbs 22.9g; Fiber 4g; Sugar 4g; Protein 23g

Salsa Chicken

Prep time: 20 minutes | Cook time: 25 minutes | Serves: 4

2-pound chicken breasts, skinless and boneless	2 teaspoons cumin
	2 cups chunky salsa, or your preference
1 teaspoon kosher salt	
1 teaspoon black pepper	½ cup water
A pinch of oregano	

1. Add the chicken breasts to the Inner Pot and season with salt and pepper. 2. Add the oregano, cumin, salsa and water, stir well. 3. Put on the pressure cooker's lid and turn the steam valve to "Sealing" position. 4. Press the "Poultry" button three times to select "More" option. 5. Use the "+/-" keys on the control panel to set the cooking time to 25 minutes. 6. Press the Pressure Level button to adjust the pressure to "High Pressure." 7. Once the cooking cycle is completed, quickly and carefully turn the steam release handle from Sealing position to the Venting position. 8. When all the steam is released, remove the pressure lid from the top carefully. 9. Remove the chicken and shred it. 10. Serve shredded chicken in the casseroles or add to corn tortillas with some avocado, cilantro.
Per Serving: Calories 419; Fat 14g; Sodium 791mg; Carbs 8.9g; Fiber 4.6g; Sugar 8g; Protein 31g

Ginger Chicken

Prep time: 20 minutes | Cook time: 15 minutes | Serves: 4-6

1 chicken cut into pieces	1-inch ginger, finely grated
2 tablespoons olive oil	¼ cup dry sherry
¼ cup soy sauce	¼ cup water
1 large onion, finely diced	Salt and black pepper to taste.

1. Press the "Sauté" button two times to select "Normal" mode. 2. Add and heat the oil. 3. Put the chicken in the Inner Pot and sauté until the chicken has turned light brown. 4. Add the soy sauce, onion, ginger, sherry, and water. Mix just until combined. 5. Put on the pressure cooker's lid and turn the steam valve to "Sealing" position. 6. Select Pressure Cook mode, and then press the "Pressure Cook" button again to select "Less" time option. 7. Use the "+/-" keys on the control panel to set the cooking time to 10 minutes. 8. Press the Pressure Level button to adjust the pressure to "High Pressure." 9. Once the cooking cycle is completed, allow the steam to release naturally. 10. When all the steam is released, remove the pressure lid from the top carefully. 11. Season with salt and pepper to taste. 12. Serve and enjoy.
Per Serving: Calories 478; Fat 7.9g; Sodium 704mg; Carbs 6g; Fiber 3.6g; Sugar 6g; Protein 18g

Crack Chicken

Prep time: 10 minutes | Cook time: 30 minutes | Serves: 4

2-pound chicken breast, boneless	1 cup water
8-ounce cream cheese	3 tablespoon cornstarch
1 (1-ounce) packet ranch seasoning	4-ounce cheddar cheese, shredded
	6-8 bacon slices, cooked

1. Add the chicken breasts and cream cheese to the Inner Pot. 2. Season with the ranch seasoning. Add 1 cup of water. 3. Put on the pressure cooker's lid and turn the steam valve to "Sealing" position. 4. Press the "Pressure Cook" button two times to select "Normal" option. 5. Use the "+/-" keys on the control panel to set the cooking time to 25 minutes. 6. Press the Pressure Level button to adjust the pressure to "High Pressure." 7. Once the cooking cycle is completed, quickly and carefully turn the steam release handle from Sealing position to the Venting position. 8. When all the steam is released, remove pressure lid from the top carefully. 9. Transfer the chicken to a plate and shred the meat. 10. Press the Cancel button to stop this cooking program. 11. Press the "Sauté" button two times to select "Normal" mode and add the cornstarch. Stir well. 12. Add shredded chicken, cheese and bacon to the pot, stir. Sauté for 3 minutes. 13. Serve.
Per Serving: Calories 489; Fat 11g; Sodium 501mg; Carbs 8.9g; Fiber 4.6g; Sugar 8g; Protein 26g

Hunter Chicken

Prep time: 20 minutes | Cook time: 25 minutes | Serves: 4

8 chicken drumsticks, bone in	1 teaspoon oregano, dried
1 yellow onion, chopped	1 bay leaf
1 cup chicken stock	1 teaspoon kosher salt
1 teaspoon garlic powder	½ cup black olives, pitted and sliced
28-ounce canned tomatoes and juice, crushed	

1. Press the "Sauté" button two times to select "Normal" mode 2. Add the onion and cook for 6 to 7 minutes, until the onion is translucent. 3. Add the stock, garlic powder, tomatoes, oregano, bay leaf and salt, stir well. 4. Put the chicken in the pot and stir. 5. Put on the pressure cooker's lid and turn the steam valve to "Sealing" position. 6. Select Pressure Cook mode, and then press the "Pressure Cook" button again to select "Less" time option. 7. Use the "+/-" keys on the control panel to set the cooking time to 15 minutes. 8. Press the Pressure Level button to adjust the pressure to "High Pressure." 9. Once the cooking cycle is completed, allow the steam to release naturally for 10 minutes, then turn the steam release handle to the Venting position. 10. When all the steam is released, remove the pressure lid from the top carefully. 11. Remove the bay leaf. Divide the dish among plates, top with olives and serve.
Per Serving: Calories 382; Fat 10.9g; Sodium 454mg; Carbs 10g; Fiber 3.1g; Sugar 5.2g; Protein 20g

Mojo Chicken Tacos

Prep time: 20 minutes | Cook time: 30 minutes | Serves: 4

4 skinless, boneless chicken breasts	2 teaspoons ground cumin
For the Mojo:	2 teaspoons Kosher salt
¼ cup olive oil	¼ teaspoon black pepper
⅔ cup fresh lime juice	¼ cup chopped fresh cilantro + more for garnishing
⅔ cup orange juice	To serve:
8 cloves garlic, minced	8–12 organic corn tortillas
1 tablespoon grated orange peel	½ cup red onion, finely diced
1 tablespoon dried oregano	1 avocado, sliced

1. Add the chicken breasts to the Inner Pot. 2. In a bowl, whisk together all mojo ingredients until combined. 3. Add this mixture to the pot. 4. Put on the pressure cooker's lid and turn the steam valve to "Sealing" position. 5. Press the "Poultry" button three times to select "Normal" option. 6. Use the "+/-" keys on the control panel to set the cooking time to 20 minutes. 7. Press the Pressure Level button to adjust the pressure to "High Pressure." 8. Once the cooking cycle is

completed, allow the steam to release naturally. 9. When all the steam is released, remove the pressure lid from the top carefully. 10. Transfer the chicken to a plate and shred it. Return the meat to the pot and stir. 11. Preheat the oven to broil. Transfer shredded chicken with the sauce to a baking sheet. 12. Place under the broiler for 5 to 8 minutes, or until the edges of the chicken are brown and crispy. 13. Top with cilantro. Serve in tacos with chopped onion and sliced avocado.
Per Serving: Calories 412; Fat 10.9g; Sodium 454mg; Carbs 10g; Fiber 3.1g; Sugar 5.2g; Protein 10g

Chicken Curry

Prep time: 15 minutes | Cook time: 15 minutes | Serves: 2

1-pound chicken breast, chopped	5-ounce canned coconut cream
1 tablespoon olive oil	6 potatoes, cut into halves
1 yellow onion, thinly sliced	½ cup water
1 bag (1-ounce) chicken curry base	½ bunch coriander, chopped

1. Press the "Sauté" button two times to select "Normal" mode. and heat the oil. 2. Add the chicken and sauté for 2 minutes, until the chicken starts to brown. 3. Add onion, stir and cook for 1 more minute. 4. Press Cancel button to stop this cooking program. 5. In a medium bowl, combine the chicken curry base and coconut cream, stir well. 6. Pour into the pot, add potatoes and stir. Add water. 7. Put on the pressure cooker's lid and turn the steam valve to "Sealing" position. 8. Select Pressure Cook mode, and then press the "Pressure Cook" button again to select "Less" time option. 9. Use the "+/-" keys on the control panel to set the cooking time to 15 minutes. 10. Press the Pressure Level button to adjust the pressure to "High Pressure." 11. Once the cooking cycle is completed, quickly and carefully turn the steam release handle from Sealing position to the Venting position. 12. When all the steam is released, remove the pressure lid from the top carefully. 13. Top with coriander and serve.
Per Serving: Calories 334; Fat 12.9g; Sodium 414mg; Carbs 11g; Fiber 5g; Sugar 9g; Protein 31g

Roasted Tandoori Chicken

Prep time: 20 minutes | Cook time: 15 minutes | Serves: 6

6 chicken thighs, bone in	1 teaspoon kosher salt
½ cup plain yogurt	1 teaspoon black pepper
1-2 tablespoon tandoori paste	½ cup water
1 tablespoon lemon juice	

1. In a large bowl, combine the yogurt, lemon juice, and tandoori paste. 2. Add the chicken to the bowl and coat it well with the marinade. 3. Marinate for at least 6 hours in the refrigerator. 4. Sprinkle the chicken with salt and pepper. 5. Place the chicken, marinade and water in the Inner Pot. 6. Put on the pressure cooker's lid and turn the steam valve to "Sealing" position. 7. Select Pressure Cook mode, and then press the "Pressure Cook" button again to select "Less" time option. 8. Use the "+/-" keys on the control panel to set the cooking time to 10 minutes. 9. Press the Pressure Level button to adjust the pressure to "High Pressure." 10. Once the cooking cycle is completed, allow the steam to release naturally. 11. When all the steam is released, remove the pressure lid from the top carefully. 12. Preheat the oven to broil. Place under the broiler for 3 to 5 minutes until browned. 13. When done, serve and enjoy.
Per Serving: Calories 412; Fat 20g; Sodium 491mg; Carbs 9g; Fiber 3g; Sugar 8g; Protein 31g

Chapter 9 Soup Recipes

Tasty Beef Soup

Prep time: 10 minutes | Cook Time: 20 minutes | Serves: 4-6

1 lb. beef meat, ground	15 oz. canned garbanzo beans,
1 tbsp. vegetable oil	rinsed
1 celery rib, chopped	14 oz. canned tomatoes, crushed
1 yellow onion, chopped	12 oz. spicy V8 juice
3 cloves garlic, minced	28 oz. canned beef stock
1 potato, cubed	Salt and black pepper to taste
2 carrots, thinly sliced	½ cup frozen peas
½ cup white rice	

1. Insert the inner pot into the cooker base. Do not use a lid. 2. Press Sauté to select the program and then press it again to choose the Normal temperature option. 3. After 10 seconds, the cooker displays On to indicate that it has begun heating. 4. When display switches from On to Hot, add the ground beef and cook, stirring, for 5 minutes, until browned. When cooking completes, transfer the meat to a bowl. 5. Add the oil, celery and onion, stirring for 5 minutes, and then add the garlic and sauté for another 1 minute. 6. Stir in the potato, carrots, rice, beans, tomatoes, spicy juice, stock, browned beef, salt and pepper. 7. Press the Cancel key to stop the Sauté function. 8. Lock the lid in right way and then resume cooking for 5 minutes on Pressure Cook mode at High Pressure. 9. When the time is up, use a quick release and then remove the lid carefully. 10. Stir in the peas and let sit for 5 minutes. 11. Serve and enjoy.
Per Serving: Calories 351; Fat 22g; Sodium 502mg; Carbs 15.2g; Sugar 1.1g; Fiber 0.7g; Protein 26.4g

Homemade Broccoli Cheddar Soup

Prep time: 10 minutes | Cook Time: 15 minutes | Serves: 4-6

1 tbsp. olive oil	4 cups chicken broth
½ onion, chopped	1 tsp garlic salt
2 carrots, chopped	1½ cups cheddar cheese, grated
6 cups broccoli, chopped	¼ cup heavy cream

1. Insert the inner pot into the cooker base. 2. Connect the power cord to a 120 V power source. The cooker goes to Standby mode and the display indicates OFF. 3. Press Sauté to select the program and then press it again to choose the Normal temperature option. 4. Pour the oil into the Inner Pot and heat it. 5. Add the onion and sauté for 3-4 minutes until translucent. 6. Add the carrots and broccoli and sauté for 2 minutes more. 7. Pour in the broth. Press the Cancel key to stop the Sauté function. 8. Close and lock the lid. Select the Pressure Cook on the panel. 9. Press the button Again to choose Less option; use the "-" button to adjust the cooking time to 5 minutes. 10. Press Pressure Level to choose High Pressure. 11. When the timer beeps, quickly and carefully turn the steam release handle from Sealing position to the Venting position. Uncover the lid carefully. 12. Let the dish chill for a while. 13. Blend the soup to your desired texture using an immersion blender. 14. Season with salt and add the cheese and heavy cream. Stir to mix up for 1-2 minutes until the cheese melts. 15. Serve.
Per Serving: Calories 236; Fat 13.9g; Sodium 451mg; Carbs 13.2g; Fiber 1.2g; Sugars 1.4g; Protein 14.3g

Wonderful Cauliflower Soup

Prep time: 15 minutes | Cook Time: 10 minutes | Serves: 4

1 tbsp. butter	1 medium cauliflower, chopped
1 large onion, chopped	Salt and ground black pepper to
3 cups chicken broth	taste

1. Insert the inner pot into the cooker base. 2. Connect the power cord to a 120 V power source. The cooker goes to Standby mode and the display indicates OFF. 3. Press Sauté to select the program and then press it again to choose the Normal temperature option. 4. Once hot, add the butter and melt it. 5. Add the onion and sauté for 4-5 minutes, until softened. 6. Add the broth, cauliflower, salt and pepper. Stir to mix up. Close and lock the lid. 7. Press the Cancel button to stop the Sauté function, then select the Pressure Cook on the panel. 8. Press the button Again to choose Less option; use the "–" button to adjust the cooking time to 5 minutes. 9. Press Pressure Level to choose High pressure. 10. Once timer beeps, quickly and carefully turn the steam release handle from Sealing position to the Venting position. Uncover the lid carefully. 11. Blend the soup to your desired texture using an immersion blender. 12. Serve and enjoy.
Per Serving: Calories 344; Fat 14.9g; Sodium 227mg; Carbs 14g; Fiber 1g; Sugars 1.4g; Protein 25.7g

Homemade Chicken Moringa Soup

Prep time: 15 minutes | Cook Time: 20 minutes | Serves: 6-8

1½ lbs. chicken breasts	1 thumb-size ginger
5 cups water	2 cups moringa leaves or kale
1 onion, chopped	leaves
2 cloves garlic, minced	Salt and ground black pepper to
1 cup tomatoes, chopped	taste

1. Combine all of the ingredients, except moringa leaves, in the Inner Pot and stir to mix up. 2. Close and lock the lid. Select the Poultry on the panel. 3. Press the button Again to choose Normal option. 4. When the timer beeps, leave the steam release handle in the Sealing position for 15 minutes, then release any remaining steam manually. Uncover the lid carefully. 5. Add the moringa leaves and stir. Press Sauté to select the program and then press it again to choose the Less temperature option and then simmer for 3 minutes. 6. Season by adding some salt and pepper. 7. Serve and enjoy.
Per Serving: Calories 249; Fat 13g; Sodium 556mg; Carbs 10g; Sugar 1.1g; Fiber 0.7g; Protein 31g

Homemade Pork Shank Soup

Prep time: 45 minutes Cook Time: 40 minutes | Serves: 4-6

1½ lbs. pork shank, cleaned and	1 small piece of chenpi (dried
trimmed of excess; Fat	mandarin peel)
2 carrots, cut into chunks	2 jujubes, dried (optional)
1 thin slice of ginger	4½ cups water
1 large green radish, cut into	Sea salt to taste
chunks	

1. Soak the chenpi in cold water for 20 minutes. 2. Put all the ingredients in the Inner Pot and stir to mix up. 3. Close and lock the lid. Select the Pressure Cook on the panel. 4. Press the button Again to choose Normal option. 5. Press Pressure Level to choose High Pressure. 6. When the cooking is finished, leave the steam release handle in the Sealing position for 20 minutes. Release any remaining steam manually. Open the lid carefully. 7. Press Sauté to select the program, press it again to choose the Less temperature option and then simmer for 20 minutes. 8. Season by adding some salt and pepper. 9. Serve.
Per Serving: Calories 254; Fat 28 g; Sodium 346mg; Carbs 12.3 g; Sugar 1g; Fiber 0.7g; Protein 24.3 g

Tasty Wild Rice and Chicken Soup

Prep time: 15 minutes | Cook Time: 15 minutes | Serves: 4-6

2 tbsp. butter
1 cup yellow onion, chopped
1 cup celery, chopped
1 cup carrots, chopped
6 oz. wild rice
2 chicken breasts, skinless and boneless and chopped
1 tbsp. parsley, dried
28 oz. chicken stock
A pinch of red pepper flakes
Salt and ground black pepper to taste
2 tbsp. cornstarch mixed with 2 tbsp. water
4 oz. cream cheese, cubed
1 cup milk
1 cup half and half

1. Insert the inner pot into the cooker base. Do not use a lid. 2. Connect the power cord to a 120 V power source. The cooker goes to Standby mode and the display indicates OFF. 3. Press Sauté to select the program and then press it again to choose the Normal temperature option. Once hot, add the butter and melt it. 4. Add the onion, celery, and carrot. Stir and sauté for 5 minutes. 5. Add the rice, chicken breasts, parsley, stock, red pepper, salt and black pepper. Stir to mix up. 6. Close and lock the lid. Press the Cancel button to stop the Sauté function, then select the Pressure Cook on the panel. 7. Press the button Again to choose Less option; use the "-" button to adjust the cooking time to 5 minutes. 8. Press Pressure Level to choose High pressure. 9. When the timer beeps, quickly and carefully turn the steam release handle from Sealing position to the Venting position. Uncover the lid carefully. 10. Add the cornstarch mixed with water and stir to mix up. 11. Add the cheese, milk, half and half and stir. 12. Press Sauté to select the program and then press it again to choose the Less temperature option and cook for 3 minutes. 13. Serve.
Per Serving: Calories 336; Fat 17.3g; Sodium 281mg; Carbs 8.1g; Fiber 5.3g; Sugars 17.7g; Protein 32.3g

Delicious Beef Barley Soup

Prep time: 20 minutes |Cook Time: 50 minutes | Serves: 6-8

2 tbsp. olive oil
2 lbs. beef chuck roast, cut into 1½ inch steaks
Salt and ground black pepper to taste
2 onions, chopped
4 cloves of garlic, sliced
4 large carrots, chopped
1 stalk of celery, chopped
1 cup pearl barley, rinsed
1 bay leaf
8 cups chicken stock
1 tbsp. fish sauce

1. Insert the inner pot into the cooker base. 2. Connect the power cord to a 120 V power source. The cooker goes to Standby mode and the display indicates OFF. 3. Press Sauté to select the program and then press it again to choose the Normal temperature option. 4. Pour the oil into the Inner Pot and heat it. Then Sprinkle the beef with salt and pepper. Put in the pot and brown for about 5 minutes. Turn and brown the other side. 5. Transfer the meat to a bowl. 6. Add the onion, garlic, carrots, and celery, stirring, for 6 minutes, and then return the beef to the pot. Add the pearl barley, bay leaf, chicken stock and fish sauce. Stir to mix up. 7. Close and lock the lid. Press the Cancel button to reset the cooking program, then select the Pressure Cook on the panel. 8. Press the Pressure Cook button Again to choose Normal option; use the "-" button to adjust the cooking time to 30 minutes. 9. Press Pressure Level to choose High Pressure. 10. Leave the steam release handle in the Sealing position for 10 minutes after cooking has completed, and then release any remaining pressure manually. Open the lid carefully. 11. Remove cloves garlic, large vegetable chunks and bay leaf. 12. Season by adding some salt and pepper.
Per Serving: Calories 285; Fat 9.8g; Sodium 639mg; Carbs 11.1g; Fiber 1.2g; Sugars 5.1g; Protein 27.8g

Fresh and Delicious Buffalo Chicken Soup

Prep time: 15 minutes | Cook Time: 10 minutes | Serves: 4

2 chicken breasts, boneless, skinless, frozen or fresh
1 clove garlic, chopped
¼ cup onion, diced
½ cup celery, diced
2 tbsp. butter
1 tbsp. ranch dressing mix
3 cups chicken broth
⅓ cup hot sauce
2 cups cheddar cheese, shredded
1 cup heavy cream

1. Put the chicken breasts, garlic, onion and celery into the Inner Pot and then add the butter, ranch dressing mix, broth, and hot sauce before mixing them up. 2. Close and lock the lid and turn the steam release handle to the Sealing position. 3. Select Pressure Cook mode. Press Pressure Cook button again to adjust the cooking time to 10 minutes. Press Pressure level to choose High Pressure. 4. Leave the steam release handle in the Sealing position for 10 minutes after cooking has completed, then turn the steam release handle to the Venting position. 5. Transfer the chicken to a plate and shred the meat. Return to the pot. 6. Add the cheese and heavy cream. Stir to mix up. 7. Let sit for 5 minutes and serve.
Per Serving: Calories 711; Fat 55g; Sodium 1462mg; Carb 5.5g; Fiber 1g; Sugar 3.3g; Protein 48.6g

Homemade Beef Borscht Soup

Prep time: 20 | Cook Time: 20 minutes | Serves: 4-6

2 lbs. ground beef
3 beets, peeled and diced
2 large carrots, diced
3 stalks of celery, diced
1 onion, diced
2 cloves garlic, diced
3 cups shredded cabbage
6 cups beef stock
½ tbsp. thyme
1 bay leaf
Salt and ground black pepper to taste

1. Insert the inner pot into the cooker base. Connect the power cord to a 120 V power source. The cooker goes to Standby mode and the display indicates OFF. 2. Press Sauté to select the program and then press it again to choose the Normal temperature option. 3. After 10 seconds, the cooker displays on to indicate that it has begun heating. 4. When display switches from On to Hot, add the ground beef and cook, stirring, for 5 minutes, until browned. 5. Add all the rest ingredients into the Inner Pot and stir to mix up. Close and lock the lid. 6. Press the Cancel key to stop the Sauté function. 7. Select the Pressure Cook on the panel. 8. Press the button Again to choose Less option; use the" – "button to adjust the cooking time to 15 minutes. 9. Press Pressure Level to choose High Pressure. 10. When cooking completes, leave the steam release handle in the Sealing position for 10 minutes after cooking has completed, and then release any remaining pressure manually. Open the lid carefully. 11. Let the dish sit for 5-10 minutes and serve.
Per Serving: Calories 305; Fat 15g; Sodium 548mg; Carbs 12g; Sugar 1.2g; Fiber 0.7g; Protein 29g

Egg Roll Soup Easy to Make

Prep time: 15 minutes | Cook Time: 35 minutes | Serves: 4-6

1 tbsp. olive oil
1 onion, cubed
1 lb. ground beef
½ head cabbage, chopped
2 cups carrots, shredded
1 tsp garlic powder
1 tsp onion powder
1 tsp ground ginger
⅔ cup coconut aminos or soy sauce
4 cups chicken broth
Salt and ground black pepper to taste

1. Insert the inner pot into the cooker base. 2. Connect the power cord to a 120 V power source. The cooker goes to Standby mode and the display indicates OFF. 3. Press Sauté to select the program and then press it again to choose the Normal temperature option. 4. Pour the oil into the Inner Pot and heat it. 5. Add the onion and ground beef. Cook for 4-5 minutes, stir now and then and browned all the meat. 6. Add the cabbage, carrots, garlic powder, onion powder, ginger, coconut aminos, and broth. stir to mix up. 7. Add some salt and pepper before stirring. Close and lock the lid. 8. Press the Cancel button to stop the Sauté function, then press Soup/Broth to select the program and then press it again to choose the Less temperature option, and use the "+" button to adjust the time to 25 minutes. 9. Once timer beeps, quickly and carefully turn the steam release handle from Sealing position to the Venting position. Uncover the lid carefully. 10. Let the soup sit for 5-10 minutes and serve.
Per Serving: Calories 285; Fat 9.8g; Sodium 639mg; Carbs 11.1g; Fiber 1.2g; Sugars 5.1g; Protein 27.8g

Delicious Chicken Noodle Soup

Prep time: 20 minutes | Cook Time: 10 minutes | Serves: 6

3 tbsps. butter	chicken breasts, cooked and
1 medium onion, diced	cubed
3 celery stalks, diced	8 cups chicken broth or vegetable
2 large carrots, diced	broth
5 cloves garlic, minced	8 oz. spaghetti noodles break in
1 tsp oregano	half
1 tsp basil, dried	2 cups spinach, chopped
1 tsp thyme, dried	Salt and ground black pepper to
2 cups skinless and boneless	taste

1. Insert the inner pot into the cooker base. Do not use a lid. 2. Connect the power cord to a 120 V power source. The cooker goes to Standby mode and the display indicates OFF. 3. Press Sauté to select the program and then press it again to choose the Normal temperature option Once hot, add the butter and melt it. 4. Add the onion, celery, carrot and a big pinch of salt. Stir and sauté for 5 minutes until they're soft. 5. Add the garlic, oregano, basil and thyme. stir to mix up and sauté for 1 minute more. 6. Add the chicken, broth and noodles. And then close and lock the lid. 7. Press the Cancel button to reset the cooking program, then select the Pressure Cook on the panel. 8. Press the button Again to choose Less option; use the "-" button to adjust the cooking time to 4 minutes. 9. Press Pressure Level to choose High Pressure. 10. When the timer beeps, quickly and carefully turn the steam release handle from Sealing position to the Venting position. Uncover the lid carefully. 11. Add the spinach and Add salt and pepper as you like. stir to mix up and enjoy it.
Per Serving: Calories 305; Fat 15g; Sodium 548mg; Carbs 12g; Sugar 1.2g; Fiber 0.7g; Protein 29g

Tomato and Basil Soup Easy to Make

Prep time: 20 minutes | Cook Time: 20 minutes | Serves: 8

2 tbsp. olive oil	¼ tsp red pepper flakes
1 medium yellow onion, diced	½ cup fresh basil leaves, chopped
2 large stalks celery, diced	2 cans whole Roma tomatoes
2 large carrots, diced	1 cup vegetable broth
Salt and ground black pepper to	2 bay leaves
taste	¾ cup heavy cream

1. Insert the inner pot into the cooker base. 2. Connect the power cord to a 120 V power source. The cooker goes to Standby mode and the display indicates OFF. 3. Press Sauté to select the program and then press it again to choose the Normal temperature option. 4. Pour the oil into the Inner Pot and heat it. Add the onion, celery, and carrot. Stir and sauté for 5-6 minutes, until softened. 5. Add the salt, black pepper, red pepper flakes and basil, and sauté for 1-2 minutes more. 6. Add remaining ingredients, except for the heavy cream, in the Inner Pot and stir to mix up. 7. Close and lock the lid. Select the Pressure Cook on the panel. 8. Press the button Again to choose Less option; use the "-" button to adjust the cooking time to 10 minutes. 9. Press Pressure Level to choose High Pressure. 10. When the timer beeps, quickly and carefully turn the steam release handle from Sealing position to the Venting position. Uncover the lid carefully. 11. Press the Cancel button to stop the Pressure Cook function, then select the Sauté on the panel. 12. Press the button Again to choose Less option and simmer for 2 minutes. 13. Press the Cancel key to stop the Sauté function. 14. Serve and enjoy.
Per Serving: Calories 305; Fat 15g; Sodium 548mg; Carbs 12g; Sugar 1.2g; Fiber 0.7g; Protein 29g

Homemade Sweet Potato Soup

Prep time: 15 minutes | Cook Time: 30 minutes | Serves: 4

2 tbsp. butter	and diced
1 whole onion, chopped	½ tsp thyme
4 cloves garlic, chopped	½ tsp ground sage
6 carrots, peeled and diced	1-quart vegetarian broth
4 large red sweet potatoes, peeled	Salt and ground black pepper to

taste

1. Press Sauté to select the program and then press it again to choose the Normal temperature option. 2. Once hot, add the butter and melt it. 3. Add the onion, garlic, and carrots and sauté for about 8 minutes, until the onion is translucent. 4. Add the sweet potatoes, thyme, sage and broth. Season by adding some salt and pepper. Close and lock the lid. 5. Press the Cancel button to stop the Sauté function, then select the Pressure Cook on the panel. 6. Press the button Again to choose Less option. 7. Press Pressure Level to choose High pressure. 8. Once timer beeps, quickly and carefully turn the steam release handle from Sealing position to the Venting position. Uncover the lid carefully. 9. Blend the soup to your desired texture using an immersion blender. Serve.
Per Serving: Calories 285; Fat 9.8g; Sodium 639mg; Carbs 11.1g; Fiber 1.2g; Sugars 5.1g; Protein 27.8g

Nutritious Multi-Bean Soup

Prep time: 15 minutes | Cook Time: 40 minutes | Serves: 8-10

1 tbsp. olive oil	(Hurst Beans brand)
1 onion, chopped	1 can tomatoes, crushed
3 cloves garlic, minced	3 sprigs fresh thyme
1 red bell pepper, chopped	1 bay leaf
2 carrots, peeled and chopped	8 cups vegetable stock
2 stalks celery, chopped	Salt and ground black pepper to
1 bag of 15-bean soup blend	taste

1. Insert the inner pot into the cooker base. 2. Connect the power cord to a 120 V power source. The cooker goes to Standby mode and the display indicates OFF. 3. Press Sauté to select the program and then press it again to choose the Normal temperature option. 4. Pour the oil into the Inner Pot and heat it. 5. Add the onion and garlic and sauté for 1-2 minutes until fragrant. 6. Add the bell pepper, carrot, and celery and sauté for another 6 minutes. 7. Add the beans, tomatoes, thyme, bay leaf and stock. Mix up well. 8. Add salt and pepper as you like. Close and lock the lid. 9. Press the Cancel button to reset the cooking program, then select the Pressure Cook on the panel. 10. Press the button Again to choose Normal option; use the "-" button to adjust the cooking time to 30 minutes. 11. Press Pressure Level to choose High pressure 12. When the cooking is finished, select Cancel and leave the steam release handle in the Sealing position for 10 minutes. Release any remaining steam manually. Open the lid carefully. 13. Stir and Serve.
Per Serving: Calories 254; Fat 28 g; Sodium 346mg; Carbs 12.3 g; Sugar 1g; Fiber 0.7g; Protein 24.3 g

Chicken Soup with Cannellini Beans

Prep time: 20 minutes | Cook Time: 45 minutes | Serves: 6

1 cup cannellini beans	1 cup fresh dill, chopped
1 lb. chicken fillet, cut into 1½	4 tbsp. salsa
inch strips	⅓ cup cream
7 cups water	1 tsp soy sauce
1 jalapeno pepper, chopped	2 tsp kosher salt
1 red bell pepper, sliced	1 tsp ground black pepper
1 white onion, sliced	

1. Put the cannellini beans and chicken in the Inner Pot. 2. Pour in the water and stir. Close and lock the lid. 3. Select the Pressure Cook on the panel, press the button again to adjust the cooking time to 30 minutes. 4. Press Pressure Level to choose High Pressure. 5. When the timer beeps, quickly and carefully turn the steam release handle from Sealing position to the Venting position. Uncover the lid carefully. 6. Add the jalapeno pepper, bell pepper, onion, and dill. Mix up well. 7. Close and lock the lid. Select the Soup/Broth on the panel. 8. Press the button Again to choose Less option; use the - button to adjust the cooking time to 15 minutes. 9. Press Pressure Level to choose High pressure. 10. When the timer beeps, quickly and carefully turn the steam release handle from Sealing position to the Venting position. Uncover the lid carefully. 11. Add the salsa, cream, soy sauce, salt and black pepper. Stir to mix up, close the lid and let the soup sit for 10 minutes. 12. Serve.
Per Serving: Calories 344; Fat 14.9g; Sodium 227mg; Carbs 14g; Fiber 1g; Sugars 1.4g; Protein 25.7g

Delicious Smoked Turkey Soup

Prep time: 15 minutes | Cook Time: 40 minutes | Serves: 8

½ tbsp. olive oil	10-12 oz. smoked turkey
1 medium-size onion, chopped	drumstick
1 celery stalk, chopped	2 cups black beans, dried
1 large carrot, chopped	1 tsp salt
½ cup parsley, chopped	¼ tsp ground black pepper
3 cloves garlic, pressed	2 bay leaves
6 cups water	

1. Insert the inner pot into the cooker base. 2. Connect the power cord to a 120 V power source. The cooker goes to Standby mode and the display indicates OFF. 3. Press Sauté to select the program and then press it again to choose the Less temperature option. 4. Pour the oil into the Inner Pot and heat it. 5. Put the onion, celery, carrots, and parsley in the pot. 6. Sauté for 8-10 minutes, until the veggies are softened. 7. Add the garlic and sauté for 1 minute more. 8. Pour in the water. Add the turkey, beans, salt, pepper and bay leaves, stir to mix up. 9. Bring to a boil, close and lock the lid. 10. Press the Cancel button to reset the cooking program, then select the Pressure Cook on the panel. 11. Press the button Again to choose Normal option; use the "-" button to adjust the cooking time to 30 minutes. 12. Press Pressure Level to choose High pressure 13. When the cooking is finished, leave the steam release handle in the Sealing position for 10 minutes. Release any remaining steam manually. Open the lid carefully. 14. Remove the bay leaves. Transfer the turkey drumstick to a plate. Shred the meat. 15. Blend the soup to your desired texture using an immersion blender. Return the meat to the pot and stir. 16. Serve and enjoy the delicious soup.
Per Serving: Calories 344; Fat 14.9g; Sodium 227mg; Carbs 14g; Fiber 1g; Sugars 1.4g; Protein 25.7g

Fresh Fish Soup

Prep time: 10 minutes | Cook Time: 10 minutes | Serves: 4-6

1 lb. white fish fillets, boneless,	1 carrot, chopped
skinless and cubed	4 cups chicken stock
1 cup bacon, chopped	2 cups heavy cream

1. In the Inner Pot, combine the fish, bacon, carrot, and stock. stir to mix up. 2. Close and lock the lid. Select the Pressure Cook on the panel. 3. Press the button Again to choose Less option; use the "-" button to adjust the cooking time to 5 minutes. 4. Press Pressure Level to choose High Pressure 5. When the timer beeps, quickly and carefully turn the steam release handle from Sealing position to the Venting position. Uncover the lid carefully. 6. Add the heavy cream and stir. 7. Press Sauté to select the program, press it again to choose the Less temperature option and then simmer for 3 minutes. 8. Serve.
Per Serving: Calories 305; Fat 15g; Sodium 548mg; Carbs 12g; Sugar 1.2g; Fiber 0.7g; Protein 29g

Meatball Soup

Prep time: 10 minutes | Cook Time: 30 minutes | Serves: 4-6

1 tbsp. olive oil	1 green bell pepper, chopped
1 onion, chopped	½ tsp cumin
2 cloves garlic, minced	1 tbsp. oregano
1 package prepared meatballs	Salt and ground black pepper to
1 cup carrots, chopped finely	taste
1 can diced tomatoes	1 egg, beaten
4 cups beef broth	

1. Insert the inner pot into the cooker base. 2. Connect the power cord to a 120 V power source. The cooker goes to Standby mode and the display indicates OFF. 3. Press Sauté to select the program and then press it again to choose the Normal temperature options. Pour the oil into the Inner Pot and heat it. 4. Add the onion and garlic, sauté for 1-2 minutes. 5. Add the meatballs and cook for 4-5 minutes and brown all the meatballs. 6. Combine the carrot, tomatoes, water, bell pepper, cumin, oregano, salt and black pepper, stir to mix up. 7. Close and

lock the lid. Press the Cancel button to stop the Sauté function, then press the Soup/Broth button on the panel. 8. Press the button Again to choose Less option; use the "-" button to adjust the cooking time to 15 minutes. 9. Press Pressure Level to choose High pressure 10. When the timer beeps, quickly and carefully turn the steam release handle from Sealing position to the Venting position. Uncover the lid carefully. 11. Press the Cancel button to stop the Soup function. 12. Cook the food for 3 to 4 minutes on Sauté mode at Less cooking temperature. 13. When done, serve and enjoy.
Per Serving: Calories 351; Fat 22g; Sodium 502mg; Carbs 15.2g; Sugar 1.1g; Fiber 0.7g; Protein 26.4g

Toscana Soup

Prep time: 5 minutes | Cook Time: 35 minutes | Serves: 4-6

2 tbsp. olive oil	¼ cup water
1 onion, diced	6 cups chicken broth
4 cloves garlic, minced	Salt and ground black pepper to
1 lb. Italian sausages, chopped	taste
3 large russet potatoes, unpeeled	2 cups kale, chopped
and sliced thickly	¾ cup heavy cream

1. Insert the inner pot into the cooker base. Do not use a lid. 2. Connect the power cord to a 120 V power source. The cooker goes to Standby mode and the display indicates OFF. 3. Press Sauté to select the program and then press it again to choose the Normal temperature option. Pour the oil into the Inner Pot and heat it. 4. Add the onion, garlic, and Italian sausages. Stir and sauté for 4-5 minutes, until the sausages have turned light brown. 5. Add the potatoes, water, and chicken broth and stir to mix up. 6. Sprinkle with salt and pepper. 7. Press the Cancel key to stop the Sauté function. 8. Close and lock the lid. Select the Pressure Cook on the panel. 9. Press the button Again to choose Less option 10. Press Pressure Level to choose High Pressure 11. When the timer beeps, quickly and carefully turn the steam release handle from Sealing position to the Venting position. Uncover the lid carefully. 12. Press the Cancel button to stop the Pressure Cook function, then Select the Sauté on the panel. 13. Press the button Again to choose Less option and simmer for 3-4 minutes. 14. Press the Cancel key and let it sit for 5 minutes. 15. Serve.
Per Serving: Calories 236; Fat 13.9g; Sodium 451mg; Carbs 13.2g; Fiber 1.2g; Sugars 1.4g; Protein 14.3g

Turkey Cabbage Soup Easy to Make

Prep time: 20 minutes | Cook Time: 15 minutes | Serves: 4-6

1 tbsp. olive oil	4 cups chicken broth
1 lb. ground turkey	2 cups water
2 cloves garlic, minced	1 head cabbage, chopped
1 pack frozen onion, cubed	Salt and ground black pepper to
1 pack cauliflower florets	taste
1 jar marinara sauce	

1. Insert the inner pot into the cooker base. 2. Connect the power cord to a 120 V power source. The cooker goes to Standby mode and the display indicates OFF. 3. Press Sauté to select the program and then press it again to choose the Normal temperature option. Pour the oil into the Inner Pot and heat it. 4. Add the ground turkey and garlic and sauté, stir now and then, for 5-6 minutes and browned all the meat. 5. Transfer the browned turkey to a bowl. 6. Press the Cancel key to stop the Sauté function. 7. Stir in the onion, cauliflower, marinara sauce, broth and water to the pot. 8. Put the cabbage on top. 9. Close and lock the lid. Select the Pressure Cook on the panel. 10. Press the button Again to choose Less option; use the "-" button to adjust the cooking time to 6 minutes. 11. Press Pressure Level to choose High Pressure 12. When the timer beeps, leave the steam release handle in the Sealing position. 13. Open the lid carefully. Return the meat to the pot and stir to mix up. 14. Add salt and pepper as you like. 15. Serve.
Per Serving: Calories 285; Fat 9.8g; Sodium 639mg; Carbs 11.1g; Fiber 1.2g; Sugars 5.1g; Protein 27.8g

Bacon Soup with Navy Bean and Spinach

Prep time: 20 minutes Cook Time: 30 minutes | Serves: 6

3 cans (15 oz. each) navy beans, rinsed and drained
1 cup water
4 slices bacon, chopped
1 onion, chopped
1 large carrot, chopped
1 large celery stalk, chopped
2 tbsp. tomato paste
1 sprig fresh rosemary
2 bay leaves
4 cups chicken broth
3 cups baby spinach
Salt and ground black pepper to taste

1. Combine the 1 can beans with 1 cup of water. 2. Blend the mixture with an immersion blender. 3. Insert the inner pot into the cooker base. 4. Connect the power cord to a 120 V power source. The cooker goes to Standby mode and the display indicates OFF. 5. Press Sauté to select the program and then press it again to choose the Normal temperature option. Add the bacon and sauté until crisp. 6. Transfer the bacon to a plate. 7. Add the onion, carrot, and celery to the pot and sauté for 5 minutes, until softened. 8. Add the tomato paste and stir well. 9. Add 2 cans beans, pureed beans, rosemary, bay leaves, and broth. Close and lock the lid. 10. Press the Cancel key to stop the Sauté function. 11. Close and lock the lid. Select the Pressure Cook on the panel. 12. Press the button Again to choose Less option; use the "-" button to adjust the cooking time to 15 minutes. 13. Press Pressure Level to choose High Pressure. 14. When the cooking is finished, leave the steam release handle in the Sealing position for 10 minutes. Release any remaining steam manually. Open the lid carefully. 15. Remove the rosemary and bay leaves. Add the spinach. Add some salt and pepper before stirring well. 16. Let the dish sit for 5 minutes. Serve.
Per Serving: Calories 236; Fat 13.9g; Sodium 451mg; Carbs 13.2g; Fiber 1.2g; Sugars 1.4g; Protein 14.3g

Tasty Ham and Potato Soup

Prep time: 10 minutes | Cook Time: 30 minutes | Serves: 4-6

2 tbsp. butter
8 cloves garlic, minced
1 onion, diced
2 lbs. Yukon Gold potatoes, cut into small chunks
A dash of cayenne pepper
1 cup cooked ham, diced
½ cup cheddar cheese, grated
4 cups chicken broth
Salt and ground black pepper to taste
2 tbsp. fried bacon bits

1. Insert the inner pot into the cooker base. Do not use a lid. 2. Connect the power cord to a 120 V power source. The cooker goes to Standby mode and the display indicates OFF. 3. To preheat the Inner Pot, press Sauté to select the program and then press it again to choose the Normal temperature option. 4. Once hot, add the butter and melt it. 5. Add the garlic and onion, sauté for 1-2 minutes, or until fragrant. 6. Add the potatoes and sauté for 3 minutes more. 7. Add the cayenne pepper, cooked ham, and cheese. Pour in the broth and stir. 8. Add salt and pepper as you like. Close and lock the lid. 9. Press the Cancel button to reset the cooking program. Select the Pressure Cook on the panel. 10. Press the button Again to choose Less option; use the "+" button to adjust the cooking time to 25 minutes. 11. Press Pressure Level to choose High pressure 12. Once timer beeps, quickly and carefully turn the steam release handle from Sealing position to the Venting position. Uncover the lid carefully. 13. Top with bacon bits and serve.
Per Serving: Calories 344; Fat 14.9g; Sodium 227mg; Carbs 14g; Fiber 1g; Sugars 1.4g; Protein 25.7g

Delicious Lentil Soup with Sweet Potato

Prep time: 20 minutes | Cook Time: 20 minutes | Serves: 6

2 tsp olive oil
½ yellow onion, chopped
1 large celery stalk, diced
4 cloves garlic, minced
1 tsp paprika
1 tsp ground cumin
½ tsp red pepper flakes
¾ lb. sweet potato, peeled and cut
into ½-inch dice
1 cup green lentils
1 can (14 oz.) petite diced tomatoes
1 cup water
3½ cups vegetable broth
Salt and ground black pepper to taste

4 oz. spinach leaves

1. Insert the inner pot into the cooker base. 2. Connect the power cord to a 120 V power source. The cooker goes to Standby mode and the display indicates OFF. 3. Press Sauté to select the program and then press it again to choose the Normal temperature option. 4. Pour the oil into the Inner Pot and heat it. 5. Add the onion and celery and sauté for 4-5 minutes, until softened. 6. Add the garlic, paprika, and red pepper flakes, stir to mix up. Sauté for 1 minute. 7. Add the sweet potato, lentil, tomatoes, water, and broth. Stir to mix up. 8. Add salt and pepper as you like. 9. Press the Cancel key to stop the Sauté function. 10. Close and lock the lid. Select the Pressure Cook on the panel. 11. Press the button Again to choose Less option; use the "-" button to adjust the cooking time to 12 minutes. 12. Press Pressure Level to choose High Pressure 13. Once timer beeps, wait for 10 minutes, and then quickly and carefully turn the steam release handle from Sealing position to the Venting position. Uncover the lid carefully. 14. Add the spinach and stir. Serve.
Per Serving: Calories 312; Fat 15g; Sodium 548mg; Carbs 12g; Sugar 1.2g; Fiber 0.7g; Protein 29g

Fragrant and Delicious Black Bean Soup

Prep time: 20 minutes | Cook Time: 50 minutes | Serves: 6

2 tbsp. olive oil
5 cloves garlic, minced
1 onion, chopped
1 red bell pepper, chopped
2 tsp. ground oregano
1 tsp. ground cumin
1 bay leaf
1 lb. dried black beans, soaked overnight
4 cups water
½ cup red wine
2 tbsp. sherry vinegar
Salt and ground black pepper to taste

1. Insert the inner pot into the cooker base. 2. Connect the power cord to a 120 V power source. The cooker goes to Standby mode and the display indicates OFF. 3. Press Sauté to select the program and then press it again to choose the Normal temperature option. 4. Pour the oil into the Inner Pot and heat it. Add the garlic and onion and sauté for 2 minutes, until fragrant. 5. Add the bell pepper, oregano, cumin, and bay leaf. Stir and sauté for 1 minute more. 6. Add the beans and pour the water, wine and vinegar. Stir to mix up. 7. Sprinkle with salt and pepper. Close and lock the lid. 8. Press the Cancel button to stop the Sauté function, then select the Bean/Chili on the panel. 9. Press the button Again to choose the More option. 10. Use the "+" button to adjust the cooking time to 45 minutes. 11. Press Pressure Level to choose High pressure. 12. When the timer beeps, quickly and carefully turn the steam release handle from Sealing position to the Venting position. Uncover the lid carefully. 13. Serve.
Per Serving: Calories 285; Fat 9.8g; Sodium 639mg; Carbs 11.1g; Fiber 1.2g; Sugars 5.1g; Protein 27.8g

Tasty Pomodoro Soup

Prep time: 15 minutes | Cook Time: 15 minutes | Serves: 8

3 tbsp. vegan butter
1 onion, diced
3 lbs. tomatoes, peeled and
quartered
3½ cups vegetable broth
1 cup coconut cream

1. Press Sauté to select the program and then press it again to choose the Normal temperature option. 2. Once hot, add the butter and melt it. 3. Add the onion and sauté for 5 minutes. 4. Add the tomatoes and sauté for another 2-3 minutes. 5. Pour in the broth, stir. Close and lock the lid. 6. Press the Cancel button to reset the cooking program, and then select the Soup/Broth on the panel. 7. Press the button Again to choose Less option; use the "-" button to adjust the cooking time to 6 minutes. 8. Press Pressure Level to choose High pressure. 9. When the timer beeps, quickly and carefully turn the steam release handle from Sealing position to the Venting position. Uncover the lid carefully. 10. Add the coconut cream and stir. 11. Press the Cancel button to reset the cooking program, and then press Sauté to select the program. 12. Press it again to choose the Less temperature option and cook for 1-2 minutes. 13. Blend the soup to your desired texture using an immersion blender. 14. Serve and enjoy.
Per Serving: Calories 285; Fat 9.8g; Sodium 639mg; Carbs 11.1g; Fiber 1.2g; Sugars 5.1g; Protein 27.8g

Delicious Bean and Ham Soup

Prep time: 20 minutes | Cook Time: 50 minutes | Serves: 6-8

1 leftover ham bone with meat	1 onion diced
1 lb. white beans, rinsed	1 tsp chili powder
1 can diced tomatoes	1 lemon, juiced
1 clove garlic, minced	8 cups chicken broth

1. Put all the ingredients in the Inner Pot and stir to mix up. 2. Close and lock the lid. Select the Bean/Chili on the panel. 3. Press the button Again to choose More option; use the "+" button to adjust the cooking time to 50 minutes. 4. Press Pressure Level to choose High pressure. 5. When the timer beeps, quickly and carefully turn the steam release handle from Sealing position to the Venting position. 6. Let the soup sit for 10 minutes. Uncover the lid carefully. 7. Serve.
Per Serving: Calories 336; Fat 17.3g; Sodium 281mg; Carbs 8.1g; Fiber 5.3g; Sugars 17.7g; Protein 32.3g

Chicken Barley Soup Simple and Quick to Make

Prep time: 15 minutes | Cook Time: 20 minutes | Serves: 6

½ cup pearl barley, rinsed and drained	¾ cup celery
2 cups chicken breasts, sliced	3 cups chicken stock
2 cups carrots, diced	2 cups water
1 cup red potatoes, peeled and diced	1 tbsp. oregano
1 cup onion, diced	1 bay leaf
	Salt and ground black pepper to taste

1. Put all of the ingredients into the Inner Pot and mix them up. 2. Close and lock the lid. Press the Pressure Cook on the panel. 3. Press the button Again to choose Less option. 4. Leave the steam release handle in the Sealing position for 5 minutes when the cooking is finished. Release any remaining steam manually before uncovering the pot. 5. Serve.
Per Serving: Calories 236; Fat 13.9g; Sodium 451mg; Carbs 13.2g; Fiber 1.2g; Sugars 1.4g; Protein 14.3g

Homemade Keto Low-Carb Soup

Prep time: 10 minutes | Cook Time: 25 minutes | Serves: 4-6

1 tbsp. olive oil	Salt and ground black pepper
2 cloves garlic, minced	1 tbsp. Dijon mustard
1 large yellow onion, diced	4 dashes hot pepper sauce
1 tbsp. onion powder	6 slices cooked turkey bacon, diced
1 head cauliflower, coarsely chopped	2 cups shredded Cheddar cheese
1 green bell pepper, chopped	1 cup half and half
32 oz. chicken stock	

1. Insert the inner pot into the cooker base. 2. Connect the power cord to a 120 V power source. The cooker goes to Standby mode and the display indicates OFF. 3. Press Sauté to select the program and then press it again to choose the Normal temperature option. 4. Pour the oil into the Inner Pot and heat it. 5. Add the garlic and onion and sauté for 3-4 minutes. 6. Add the onion powder, cauliflower, bell pepper, and stock. Add salt and pepper as you like. Stir to mix up. 7. Close and lock the lid. Press the Cancel button to stop the Sauté function, then select the Soup/Broth on the panel. 8. Press the button Again to choose Less option; use the "-" button to adjust the cooking time to 15 minutes. 9. Press Pressure Level to choose High pressure. 10. When the timer beeps, quickly and carefully turn the steam release handle from Sealing position to the Venting position. 11. Wait for 5 minutes and uncover the lid carefully. 12. Add the Dijon mustard, hot sauce, turkey bacon, cheddar cheese, and half and half. Mix up well. 13. Press the Cancel button to stop the Soup function. 14. Press Sauté to select the program and then press it again to choose the Less temperature option and simmer the soup for 4-5 minutes. 15. Serve.
Per Serving: Calories 351; Fat 22g; Sodium 502mg; Carbs 15.2g; Sugar 1.1g; Fiber 0.7g; Protein 26.4g

Homemade Chicken Soup

Prep time: 20 minutes | Cook Time: 25 minutes | Serves: 4

2 frozen, boneless chicken breasts	½ big onion, diced
4 medium-sized potatoes, cut into chunks	2 cups chicken stock
3 carrots, peeled and cut into chunks	2 cups water
	Salt and ground black pepper to taste

1. Put the chicken breasts, potatoes, carrots and onion into the Inner Pot and then add the stock, water, salt and pepper before mixing them up. 2. Close and lock the lid and turn the steam release handle to the Sealing position. 3. Select Pressure Cook and set the cooking time for 25 minutes at High Pressure. 4. When the timer beeps, leave the steam release handle in the Sealing position for 10 minutes. Do not unlock the lid until the remaining pressure are released. 5. Serve.
Per Serving: Calories: 285; Fat: 12.8 g; Sodium 345mg; Carbs: 3.7 g; Protein: 38.1 g

Delicious Pumpkin Soup

Prep time: 20 minutes | Cook Time: 15 minutes | Serves: 2-4

½ tbsp. butter	½ apple, peeled, cored and grated
½ brown onion, chopped	1 cup coconut milk
½ butternut pumpkin, chunks	2 bay leaves
½ red potato or radishes, diced	Salt and ground black pepper to taste
Pinch curry powder	
1½ cups chicken stock	

1. Insert the inner pot into the cooker base. 2. Connect the power cord to a 120 V power source. The cooker goes to Standby mode and the display indicates OFF. 3. Press Sauté to select the program and then press it again to choose the Normal temperature option. 4. Add the onion, pumpkin, potato, and curry powder. Stir and sauté for 7-9 minutes until the onion is browned. 5. Add the stock, apple, bay leaves, salt and black pepper, stir. Close and lock the lid. 6. Press the Cancel button to reset the cooking program, and then choose the Pressure Cook. 7. Press the button Again to choose Less option; use the "-" button to adjust the cooking time to 5 minutes. 8. Press Pressure Level to choose High pressure. 9. When the cooking is finished, select Cancel and leave the steam release handle in the Sealing position for 10 minutes. Uncover the lid carefully. 10. Remove the bay leaves. Add the milk and stir to mix up. 11. Blend the soup until smooth using an immersion blender. 12. Season by adding some salt and pepper. Serve.
Per Serving: Calories 336; Fat 17.3g; Sodium 281mg; Carbs 8.1g; Fiber 5.3g; Sugars 17.7g; Protein 32.3g

Duck Millet Soup

Prep time: 20 minutes | Cook time: 20 minutes | Serves: 4

2 tablespoons olive oil	granules
1-pound duck portions with bones	½ cup millet, rinsed
2 garlic cloves, minced	Salt and freshly cracked black pepper, to taste
4 cups water	
1 tablespoon chicken bouillon	¼ cup fresh scallions, chopped

1. Press the "Sauté" button two times to select "Normal" settings and heat the oil. 2. Once hot, brown your duck for 4 to 5 minutes; stir in the garlic and cook an additional 30 seconds. 3. Add the remaining ingredients. 4. Put on the pressure cooker's lid and turn the steam valve to "Sealing" position. 5. Select Pressure Cook mode, and then press the "Pressure Cook" button again to select "Less" time option. 6. Use the "+/-" keys on the control panel to set the cooking time to 12 minutes. 7. Press the Pressure Level button to adjust the pressure to "High Pressure." 8. Once the cooking cycle is completed, quickly and carefully turn the steam release handle from Sealing position to the Venting position. 9. When all the steam is released, remove the pressure lid from the top carefully. 10. Remove the cooked duck to a cutting board. Shred the meat and discard the bones. 11. Put your duck back into the inner pot. Stir and serve immediately. 12. Bon appétit!
Per Serving: Calories 489; Fat 11g; Sodium 501mg; Carbs 8.9g; Fiber 4.6g; Sugar 8g; Protein 26g

Easy Lentil Soup

Prep time: 15 minutes | Cook Time: 10 minutes | Serves: 6

2 tbsp. olive oil	1½ tsp cumin
1 medium onion, chopped	1 cup red lentils, rinsed
3 cloves garlic, minced	1 cup green or brown lentils,
2 carrots, sliced into ¼ inch	rinsed
pieces	8 cups water
1 lb. red bliss or Yukon gold	1 bunch rainbow chard or
potatoes	spinach, chopped
2 celery stalks, diced (optional)	Salt and ground black pepper to
1½ tsp smoked paprika	taste

1. Insert the inner pot into the cooker base. 2. Connect the power cord to a 120 V power source. The cooker goes to Standby mode and the display indicates OFF. 3. Press Sauté to select the program and then press it again to choose the Normal temperature option. 4. Pour the oil into the Inner Pot and heat it. 5. Add the onion, garlic, carrot, potatoes, celery, paprika, and cumin. Sauté for 5 minutes. 6. Add the lentils and water, stir to mix up. Close and lock the lid. 7. Press the Cancel button to stop the Sauté function, then select the Pressure Cook on the panel. 8. Press the button Again to choose Less option; use the "-" button to adjust the cooking time to 3 minutes. 9. Press Pressure Level to choose High pressure. 10. When the timer beeps, leave the steam release handle in the Sealing position for 10 minutes. Open the lid carefully. 11. Add the chard and sprinkle with salt and pepper. Stir to mix up. 12. Let the soup sit for 5 minutes and serve.
Per Serving: Calories 285; Fat 9.8g; Sodium 639mg; Carbs 11.1g; Fiber 1.2g; Sugars 5.1g; Protein 27.8g

Flavorful Turkish Soup

Prep time: 15 minutes | Cook Time: 15 minutes | Serves: 2-4

3 tsp olive oil	1 carrot, chopped
3 cloves garlic, minced	½ cup celery
1 onion, chopped	½ tsp coriander
1 cup red lentils	½ tsp paprika
1 tbsp. rice	3 cups water
1 potato, chopped	Salt to taste

1. Insert the inner pot into the cooker base. 2. Connect the power cord to a 120 V power source. The cooker goes to Standby mode and the display indicates OFF. 3. Press Sauté to select the program and then press it again to choose the Normal temperature option. 4. Pour the oil into the Inner Pot and heat it. 5. Add the garlic and onion and sauté for 2-3 minutes, until fragrant. 6. Add the lentils and rice and mix up well. 7. Add the potato, carrot, celery, coriander, paprika and water, stir to mix up. 8. Close and lock the lid. Press the Cancel button to reset the cooking program, press the Pressure Cook and then press the button Again to choose Less option; use the "-" button to adjust the cooking time to 10 minutes. 9. Press Pressure Level to choose High pressure. 10. When the timer beeps, leave the steam release handle in the Sealing position. Open the lid carefully. 11. Season by adding salt and mix up well. Let the mixture sit for 10 minutes and then puree in a blender. 12. Serve.
Per Serving: Calories 336; Fat 17.3g; Sodium 281mg; Carbs 8.1g; Fiber 5.3g; Sugars 17.7g; Protein 32.3g

Tasty Soup with Cheddar, Broccoli and Potato

Prep time: 30 minutes | Cook Time: 10 minutes | Serves: 4-6

2 tbsp. butter	1 cup half and half
2 cloves garlic, crushed	1 cup cheddar cheese, shredded
2 lbs. Yukon gold potatoes, peeled	Chives or green onion, chopped,
and cut into small chunks	for garnish
1 broccoli head, medium-sized,	Salt and ground black pepper to
broken into large florets	taste
4 cups vegetable broth	

1. To preheat the Inner Pot, press Sauté to select the program and then press it again to choose the Normal temperature option. Once hot, add the butter and melt it. 2. Add the garlic and sauté for 2-3 minutes, until browned. 3. Add the potato, broccoli, and broth into the Inner Pot. Add salt and pepper as you like. Stir to mix up. 4. Press the Cancel key to stop the Sauté function. 5. Close and lock the lid. Select the Pressure Cook on the panel. 6. Press the button Again to choose Less option; use the "-" button to adjust the cooking time to 5 minutes. 7. Press Pressure Level to choose High Pressure. 8. When the timer beeps, leave the steam release handle in the Sealing position for 10 minutes, then release any remaining steam manually. Uncover the lid carefully. 9. Add the half and half and ½ cup cheese into the Inner Pot. Blend with an immersion blender until smooth. 10. Season by adding some salt and pepper. 11. Add the remaining cheese and green onion on the top. 12. Serve and enjoy.
Per Serving: Calories 344; Fat 14.9g; Sodium 227mg; Carbs 14g; Fiber 1g; Sugars 1.4g; Protein 25.7g

Tomato Soup

Prep time: 15 minutes | Cook time: 25 minutes | Serves: 4

2 tablespoons olive oil	¾ cup vegetable or chicken broth
1 large red onion, chopped	Kosher salt
1 large carrot, peeled and chopped	Black pepper
3 garlic cloves, smashed	⅓ cup heavy cream
3-pound ripe tomatoes, chopped	Fresh basil, for garnish
1 teaspoon sugar	Parmesan cheese, for garnish
1 tablespoon tomato paste	

1. Press the "Sauté" button two times to select "Normal" mode. 2. Once hot, add the oil followed by the onion and carrot. 3. Cook for 6 to 7 minutes, until the onion is translucent. Add the garlic and cook for 2 minutes more. 4. Add the tomatoes, sugar, tomato paste, and broth. Season with salt and pepper. 5. Put on the pressure cooker's lid and turn the steam valve to "Sealing" position. 6. Select Pressure Cook mode, and then press the "Pressure Cook" button again to select "Less" time option. 7. Use the "+/-" keys on the control panel to set the cooking time to 15 minutes. 8. Press the Pressure Level button to adjust the pressure to "High Pressure." 9. Once the cooking cycle is completed, allow the steam to release naturally for 10 minutes, then turn the steam release handle to the Venting position. 10. When all the steam is released, remove the pressure lid from the top carefully. 11. Add the cream. Use an immersion blender to purée the soup or carefully purée in batches in a blender. 12. If there are chunks of peel and they bother you, strain the soup or run it through a food mill. 13. Add more broth if a thinner soup is desired. 14. Taste for seasoning. Serve topped with fresh basil and Parmesan.
Per Serving: Calories 479; Fat 10g; Sodium 891mg; Carbs 22.9g; Fiber 4g; Sugar 4g; Protein 23g

French Onion Chicken Soup

Prep time: 20 minutes | Cook Time: 20 minutes | Serves: 4-6

6 tbsp. butter	1 lb. cheese, grated
3 lbs. onions, chopped	3 cups chicken stock
1 tsp apple cider vinegar	Salt and ground black pepper to
1 tsp fish sauce (or soy sauce)	taste
½ cup dry sherry	8 slices bread, toasted
2 sprigs thyme	1 tbsp. chives for garnish
1 bay leaf	

1. Insert the inner pot into the cooker base. 2. Connect the power cord to a 120 V power source. The cooker goes to Standby mode and the display indicates OFF. 3. Preheat the Inner Pot and once hot, add the butter and melt it. 4. Press Sauté to select the program and then press it again to choose the Normal temperature option. 5. Add the onion and sauté for 10 minutes until caramelized, stirring now and then. 6. Add the vinegar, fish sauce, dry sherry, thyme, bay leaf, cheese and stock. 7. Add salt and pepper as you like. stir to mix up. 8. Place the bread slices on top. Close and lock the lid. 9. Press the Cancel key to stop the Sauté function. 10. Close and lock the lid. Select the Pressure Cook on the panel. 11. Press the button Again to choose Less option; use the "-" button to adjust the cooking time to 10 minutes. 12. Press Pressure Level to choose High Pressure 13. When the cooking is finished, leave the steam release handle in the Sealing position for 10 minutes. Release any remaining steam manually. Open the lid carefully. 14. Remove the sprigs thyme. 15. Top with chives and serve.
Per Serving: Calories 285; Fat 9.8g; Sodium 639mg; Carbs 11.1g; Fiber 1.2g; Sugars 5.1g; Protein 27.8g

Homemade Butternut Squash Curry Soup

Prep time: 15 minutes | Cook Time: 36 minutes | Serves: 4

1 tsp. olive oil	into 1-inch cubes
1 large onion, chopped	1½ tsp. salt
2 cloves garlic, minced	1 tbsp. curry powder
3 cups water	½ cup coconut milk
1 butternut squash, peeled and cut	

1. Insert the inner pot into the cooker base. 2. Connect the power cord to a 120 V power source. The cooker goes to Standby mode and the display indicates OFF. 3. Press Sauté to select the program and then press it again to choose the Normal temperature option. 4. Add the onion and sauté for about 5 minutes, until softened. 5. Add the garlic and cook for another 1 minute. 6. Press the Cancel key to stop the Sauté function. 7. Pour in the water and add the squash. Sprinkle with salt and curry powder and stir to mix up. 8. Close and lock the lid. Select the Soup/Broth on the panel. 9. Press the button Again to choose Normal option. 10. Press Pressure Level to choose High pressure. 11. When the timer beeps, quickly and carefully turn the steam release handle from Sealing position to the Venting position. Uncover the lid carefully. 12. Blend the soup until smooth using an immersion blender. 13. Pour in the coconut milk and stir well. 14. Serve with dried cranberries and pumpkin seeds.
Per Serving: Calories 305; Fat 15g; Sodium 548mg; Carbs 12g; Sugar 1.2g; Fiber 0.7g; Protein 29g

Acorn Squash Soup

Prep time: 20 minutes | Cook time: 15 minutes | Serves: 4

1 tablespoon butter, softened	2 cups vegetable broth
2 cloves garlic, sliced	2 cups water
1 medium-sized leek, chopped	½ teaspoon ground allspice
1 turnip, chopped	1 sprig fresh thyme
1 carrot, chopped	Himalayan salt and black pepper,
1½-pound acorn squash, chopped	to taste

1. Press the "Sauté" button two times to select "Normal" settings and melt the butter. 2. Once hot, cook the garlic and leek until just tender and fragrant. 3. Add the remaining ingredients to the inner pot. 4. Put on the pressure cooker's lid and turn the steam valve to "Sealing" position. 5. Select Pressure Cook mode, and then press the "Pressure Cook" button again to select "Less" time option. 6. Use the "+/-" keys on the control panel to set the cooking time to 10 minutes. 7. Press the Pressure Level button to adjust the pressure to "High Pressure." 8. Once the cooking cycle is completed, quickly and carefully turn the steam release handle from Sealing position to the Venting position. 9. When all the steam is released, remove the pressure lid from the top carefully. 10. Puree the soup in your blender until smooth and uniform. 11. Serve warm and enjoy!
Per Serving: Calories 334; Fat 7.9g; Sodium 704mg; Carbs 6g; Fiber 3.6g; Sugar 6g; Protein 18g

Noodle Soup

Prep time: 20 minutes | Cook time: 20 minutes | Serves: 6

2 tablespoons olive oil	1 bay leaf
2 carrots, diced	Salt and black pepper
2 parsnips, diced	2-pound chicken thighs drumettes
1 yellow onion, chopped	2 cups wide egg noodles
2 cloves garlic, minced	¼ cup fresh cilantro, roughly
6 cups chicken bone broth	chopped

1. Press the "Sauté" button two times to select "Normal" settings and heat the oil. 2. Once hot, cook the carrots, parsnips, and onions until they are just tender. 3. Add the minced garlic and continue to cook for a minute more. 4. Add the chicken bone broth, bay leaf, salt, black pepper, and chicken to the inner pot. 5. Put on the pressure cooker's lid and turn the steam valve to "Sealing" position. 6. Select Pressure Cook mode, and then press the "Pressure Cook" button again to select "Less" time option. 7. Use the "+/-" keys on the control panel to set the cooking time to 9 minutes. 8. Press the Pressure Level button to adjust the pressure to "High Pressure." 9. Once the cooking cycle is completed, quickly and carefully turn the steam release handle from Sealing

position to the Venting position. 10. When all the steam is released, remove the pressure lid from the top carefully. 11. Shred the cooked chicken and set aside. 12. Stir in noodles and press the "Sauté" button two times to select "Normal" settings. 13. Cook approximately 5 minutes or until thoroughly heated. 14. Afterwards, add the chicken back into the soup. Serve garnished with fresh cilantro. 15. Bon appétit!
Per Serving: Calories 419; Fat 14g; Sodium 791mg; Carbs 8.9g; Fiber 4.6g; Sugar 8g; Protein 3g

Delicious Split Pea Soup

Prep time: 30 minutes | Cook Time: 25 minutes | Serves: 6

2 tbsp. olive or coconut oil	½ tbsp. smoked paprika
1 yellow onion, diced	1 bay leaf
2 cloves garlic, minced	¼ tsp thyme
3 stalks celery, sliced	6 cups vegetable broth
3 carrots, sliced	Salt and fresh ground pepper
1 lb. split peas	

1. Insert the inner pot into the cooker base. 2. Connect the power cord to a 120 V power source. The cooker goes to Standby mode and the display indicates OFF. 3. Press Sauté to select the program and then press it again to choose the Normal temperature option. 4. Pour the oil into the Inner Pot and heat it. 5. Add the onion, garlic, celery, and carrot. Stir and sauté for 5-6 minutes. 6. Add the peas, smoked paprika, bay leaf, thyme, and broth. Mix up well. 7. Add salt and pepper as you like. Close and lock the lid. 8. Press the Cancel button to reset the cooking program, press the Pressure Cook and then press the button again to choose Less option; use the "-" button to adjust the cooking time to 15 minutes. 9. Press Pressure Level to choose High pressure. 10. When the cooking is finished, leave the steam release handle in the Sealing position for 10 minutes, then release any remaining pressure manually. Uncover the lid carefully. 11. Season by adding some salt and pepper. 12. Serve.
Per Serving: Calories 249; Fat 13g; Sodium 556mg; Carbs 10g; Sugar 1.1g; Fiber 0.7g; Protein 31g

Black Bean Soup with Avocado Salsa

Prep time: 15 minutes | Cook time: 35 minutes | Serves: 6-8

2 poblano peppers	1 bay leaf
2 tablespoons plus 1 teaspoon olive oil	7 cups vegetable broth (try the recipe here)
1 large yellow onion, finely diced, ¼ cup reserved	Kosher salt
1 bell pepper, finely diced	Black pepper
5 garlic cloves, minced	2 medium avocados, peeled, pitted, diced
2 teaspoons ground cumin	1 tablespoon lime juice
2 teaspoons chili powder	1 large tomato or 2 small tomatoes, chopped
1 teaspoon dried oregano	2 tablespoons chopped cilantro
1 pound dried black beans, rinsed and picked over (discard any bad beans)	1 lime, halved

1. Preheat the oven. 2. Rub the poblanos with 1 teaspoon of oil. Broil until blistered on all sides. 3. Once cool enough to handle, slide off any loose skin, remove the stem and seeds, and chop the poblanos. 4. Press the "Sauté" button two times to select "Normal" mode. 5. Once hot, add the remaining 2 tablespoons of oil followed by all but ¼ cup of the onion, the bell pepper, and the garlic. 6. Stir and cook for about 3 minutes, until the onion softens. 7. Add the roasted poblano, cumin, chili powder, and oregano. Stir and cook for 1 minute. 8. Add the beans, bay leaf, and broth, and season with salt and pepper. 9. Put on the pressure cooker's lid and turn the steam valve to "Sealing" position. 10. Press the "Pressure Cook" button two times to select "Normal" option. 11. Use the "+/-" keys on the control panel to set the cooking time to 30 minutes. 12. Press the Pressure Level button to adjust the pressure to "High Pressure." 13. Meanwhile, in a medium bowl, combine the avocados, tomato, the reserved ¼ cup of diced onion, the cilantro, and a squeeze of lime juice. Season with salt and pepper. 14. Once the cooking cycle is completed, allow the steam to release naturally. 15. When all the steam is released, remove the pressure lid from the top carefully. 16. Remove the bay leaf. 17. Add the remaining lime juice to the pot. The liquid will thicken upon standing. 18. If desired, purée up to half of the soup with an immersion blender or in a countertop blender. 19. Serve hot, topped with avocado salsa.
Per Serving: Calories 419; Fat 14g; Sodium 791mg; Carbs 8.9g; Fiber 4.6g; Sugar 8g; Protein 31g

Hang Wau Soup

Prep time: 15 minutes | Cook time: 55 minutes | Serves: 4

2-pound oxtails	2 potatoes, peeled and diced
4 cloves garlic, sliced	2 carrots, diced
2 bay leaves	1 parsnip, diced
1 thyme sprig	1 cup vegetable broth
2 rosemary sprigs	2 bird's eye chilies, pounded in a
1 tablespoon soy sauce	mortar and pestle
1 teaspoon cumin powder	2 star anis
1 teaspoon paprika	Sea salt and black pepper, to taste

1. Place the oxtails in the inner pot. Cover the oxtails with water. 2. Stir in the garlic, bay leaves, thyme, rosemary, soy sauce, cumin, and paprika. 3. Put on the pressure cooker's lid and turn the steam valve to "Sealing" position. 4. Press the "Pressure Cook" button two times to select "More" option. 5. Use the "+/-" keys on the control panel to set the cooking time to 50 minutes. 6. Press the Pressure Level button to adjust the pressure to "High Pressure." 7. Once the cooking cycle is completed, allow the steam to release naturally. 8. When all the steam is released, remove the pressure lid from the top carefully. 9. After that, add the other ingredients to the inner pot. 10. Choose the "Manual" mode and cook for 4 minutes at High Pressure. 11. Once cooking is complete, use a quick pressure release; carefully remove the lid. 12. Serve with crusty bread and enjoy!
Per Serving: Calories 478; Fat 7.9g; Sodium 704mg; Carbs 6g; Fiber 3.6g; Sugar 6g; Protein 18g

Healthy Veggie Cheese Soup

Prep time: 20 minutes | Cook Time: 10 minutes | Serves: 4-6

1 package vegetables, frozen	Salt and ground black pepper to
1 can cream mushroom soup	taste
1 jar (16 oz.) cheese sauce	Mozzarella cheese, shredded

1. Add the vegetables to the Inner Pot. 2. Pour in the mushroom soup and cheese sauce, stir to mix up. 3. Sprinkle with salt and pepper, stir. 4. Add Mozzarella cheese on the top. Close and lock the lid. 5. Select the Pressure Cook on the panel. 6. Press the button Again to choose Less option; use the "-" button to adjust the cooking time to 7 minutes. 7. Press Pressure Level to choose High Pressure. 8. Once timer beeps, leave the steam release handle in the Sealing position for 10 minutes, then release any remaining pressure manually. Open the lid carefully. 9. Serve.
Per Serving: Calories 254; Fat 28 g; Sodium 346mg; Carbs 12.3 g; Sugar 1g; Fiber 0.7g; Protein 24.3 g

Yummy Beef and Cabbage Soup

Prep time: 10 minutes | Cook Time: 25 minutes | Serves: 4-6

2 tbsp. coconut oil	undrained
1 onion, diced	4 cups water
1 clove garlic, minced	Salt and ground black pepper to
1 lb. ground beef	taste
14 oz. can dice tomatoes,	1 head cabbage, chopped

1. Insert the Inner Pot into the Cooker Base. 2. Connect the power cord to a 120 V power source. The cooker goes to Standby mode and the display indicates OFF. 3. Press Sauté to select the program and then press it again to choose the Normal temperature option. 4. Pour the oil into the Inner Pot and heat it. 5. Add the onion and garlic and sauté for 2 minutes. 6. Add the beef and cook, stirring, for 2-3 minutes until lightly brown. 7. Pour in the water and tomatoes. Taste for seasoning by adding some salt and pepper if needed. 8. Press the Cancel key to stop the Sauté function. 9. Close and lock the lid. Select the Pressure Cook on the panel. 10. Press the button Again to choose Less option; use the "- "button to adjust the cooking time to 12 minutes. 11. Press Pressure Level to choose High Pressure 12. When the timer beeps, quickly and carefully turn the steam release handle from Sealing position to the Venting position. Uncover the lid carefully. 13. Add the cabbage, press Sauté to select the program and then press it again to choose the Less temperature options and then simmer for 5 minutes. 14. When done, serve and enjoy.

Per Serving: Calories 336; Fat 17.3g; Sodium 281mg; Carbs 8.1g; Fiber 5.3g; Sugars 17.7g; Protein 32.3g

Homemade Green Split Pea Soup

Prep time: 20 minutes | Cook Time: 30 minutes | Serves: 6

1 tbsp. olive oil	1 cup leftover ham, chopped
1 clove garlic, minced	1 lb. green split peas
1 cup onion, chopped	6 cups beef broth
1 cup chopped celery	Salt and ground black pepper to
1 cup chopped carrots	taste

1. Insert the inner pot into the cooker base. 2. Connect the power cord to a 120 V power source. The cooker goes to Standby mode and the display indicates OFF. 3. Press Sauté to select the program and then press it again to choose the Normal temperature option. 4. Pour the oil into the Inner Pot and heat it. Add the garlic, onion, celery, and carrot. Stir and sauté for 5-6 minutes. 5. Add the leftover ham, peas, and broth. Mix up well. 6. Add salt and pepper as you like. Close and lock the lid. 7. Press the Cancel button to stop the Sauté function, then select the Bean/Chili and press the button again to choose the Less option. 8. Press the Pressure Level button to choose High Pressure. 9. When the timer beeps, leave the steam release handle in the Sealing position for 10 minutes, then release any remaining steam manually. Uncover the lid carefully. 10. Season by adding some salt and pepper. 11. Serve.
Per Serving: Calories 236; Fat 13.9g; Sodium 451mg; Carbs 13.2g; Fiber 1.2g; Sugars 1.4g; Protein 14.3g

Easy Garden Harvest Soup

Prep time: 20 minutes | Cook Time: 10 minutes | Serves: 6-8

10 cup packaged vegetables of	1 tsp. thyme
your choice	1 tsp. rosemary
1 can crushed tomatoes	6 cups bone broth
1 tsp. parsley	Salt and ground black pepper to
1 tsp. basil	taste

1. Put all the ingredients in the Inner Pot and stir to mix up. 2. Close and lock the lid. Select the Pressure Cook on the panel. 3. Press the button again to choose Less option; use the "-" button to adjust the cooking time to 10 minutes. 4. Press Pressure Level to choose High Pressure. 5. When the cooking is finished, leave the steam release handle in the Sealing position for 10 minutes. Release any remaining steam manually. 6. Open the lid carefully. 7. Season by adding some salt and pepper. 8. Serve and enjoy.
Per Serving: Calories 285; Fat 9.8g; Sodium 639mg; Carbs 11.1g; Fiber 1.2g; Sugars 5.1g; Protein 27.8g

Ham Bone Soup

Prep time: 20 minutes | Cook time: 25 minutes | Serves: 4

2 tablespoons olive oil	1 parsnip, diced
½ cup onion, chopped	1 ham bone
2 carrots, diced	5 cups chicken stock
1 rib celery, diced	Sea salt and black pepper, to taste

1. Press the "Sauté" button two times to select "Normal" settings and heat the olive oil until sizzling. 2. Then, sauté the onion, carrot, celery, and parsnip until tender. 3. Add the ham bone, chicken stock, salt, and black pepper to the inner pot. 4. Put on the pressure cooker's lid and turn the steam valve to "Sealing" position. 5. Select Pressure Cook mode, and then press the "Pressure Cook" button again to select "Less" time option. 6. Use the "+/-" keys on the control panel to set the cooking time to 15 minutes. 7. Press the Pressure Level button to adjust the pressure to "High Pressure." 8. Once the cooking cycle is completed, allow the steam to release naturally. 9. When all the steam is released, remove the pressure lid from the top carefully. 10. Remove the ham bone from the inner pot. Chop the meat from the bone; add back into the soup. 11. Serve in individual bowls and enjoy!
Per Serving: Calories 412; Fat 20g; Sodium 491mg; Carbs 9g; Fiber 3g; Sugar 8g; Protein 31g

Tasty Tofu and Miso Soup

Prep time: 15 minutes | Cook Time: 7 minutes | Serves: 4

1 cup silken tofu, cubed	4 cups water
½ onion, diced	1 tbsp. tamari sauce
1 carrot, chopped	2 tbsp. miso paste
2 celery stalks, chopped	Salt to taste

1. Combine all of the ingredients, except for the miso and salt, in the Inner Pot and stir to mix up. 2. Close and lock the lid. Select the Poultry on the panel. 3. Press the button Again to choose Less option. 4. Use the "+/-" button to adjust the cooking time to 7 minutes. 5. Press Pressure Level to choose High Pressure 6. When the timer beeps, quickly and carefully turn the steam release handle from Sealing position to the Venting position. Uncover the lid carefully. 7. Whisk together the miso paste with some of the soup. 8. Pour the mixture in the soup and stir. 9. Season by adding some salt. 10. Serve and enjoy.
Per Serving: Calories 344; Fat 14.9g; Sodium 227mg; Carbs 14g; Fiber 1g; Sugars 1.4g; Protein 25.7g

Delicious Minestrone Soup

Prep time: 15 minutes | Cook Time: 15 minutes | Serves: 4-6

2 tbsp. olive oil	½ cup fresh spinach or kale
1 large onion, diced	(without the stalks), chopped
3 cloves garlic, minced	1 cup elbow pasta
2 celery stalks, diced	4 cups bone broth or vegetable
1 large carrot, diced	broth
1 tsp dried basil	1 bay leaf
1 tsp dried oregano	15 oz. can (or about 2 cups) white
Salt and ground black pepper to	or cannellini beans, cooked and
taste	drained
28 oz. can tomatoes, diced	

1. Insert the inner pot into the cooker base. 2. Connect the power cord to a 120 V power source. The cooker goes to Standby mode and the display indicates OFF. 3. Press Sauté to select the program and then press it again to choose the Normal temperature option. 4. Pour the oil into the Inner Pot and heat it. Add the onion, garlic, celery, and carrot. Stir and sauté for 5-6 minutes, until softened. 5. Add the basil, oregano, salt and pepper, stir. 6. Add the tomatoes, spinach, pasta, broth, and bay leaf. Mix up well. 7. Press the Cancel key to stop the Sauté function. 8. Close and lock the lid. Select the Pressure Cook on the panel. 9. Press the button Again to choose Less option; use the "-" button to adjust the cooking time to 6 minutes. 10. Press Pressure Level to choose High Pressure 11. When the timer beeps, let sit the mixture for 2 minutes, then quickly and carefully turn the steam release handle from Sealing position to the Venting position. Uncover the lid carefully. 12. Add the kidney beans and stir. Serve.
Per Serving: Calories 351; Fat 22g; Sodium 502mg; Carbs 15.2g; Sugar 1.1g; Fiber 0.7g; Protein 26.4g

Broccoli and Leek Soup

Prep time: 15 minutes | Cook time: 15 minutes | Serves: 4

4 tablespoons butter	Kosher salt
2 large leeks, soaked, rinsed, and	Black pepper
chopped	2 pinches red pepper flakes
3 garlic cloves, smashed	3 tablespoons all-purpose flour
1½-pound broccoli, cut into	1 cup milk
florets	¼ cup grated Parmesan cheese,
3 cups vegetable or chicken broth	plus more for garnish

1. Press the "Sauté" button two times to select "Normal" mode 2. Once hot, add 1 tablespoon of butter. 3. Once melted, add the leeks and garlic and sauté for 5 minutes, or until the leeks are translucent. 4. Add the broccoli and broth, and season with salt and pepper. Add the red pepper flakes. 5. Put on the pressure cooker's lid and turn the steam valve to "Sealing" position. 6. Select Pressure Cook mode, and then press the "Pressure Cook" button again to select "Less" time option. 7. Use the "+/-" keys on the control panel to set the cooking time to 6 minutes. 8. Press the Pressure Level button to adjust the pressure to

"High Pressure." 9. Once the cooking cycle is completed, allow the steam to release naturally. 10. When all the steam is released, remove the pressure lid from the top carefully. 11. Meanwhile, in a small saucepan over medium-high heat, melt the remaining 3 tablespoons of butter on the stove. 12. Whisk in the flour, followed by the milk. Cook, stirring, until thick and bubbly. 13. Add the Parmesan. Purée the broccoli and broth using an immersion blender or countertop blender. 14. Return the broccoli mixture to the pot and add the milk mixture, stirring well. 15. Press the "Sauté" button two times to select "Normal" mode to reheat the soup. 16. Serve in bowls with a sprinkling of Parmesan on top.
Per Serving: Calories 380; Fat 10.9g; Sodium 454mg; Carbs 10g; Fiber 3.1g; Sugar 5.2g; Protein 20g

Matzo Ball Soup

Prep time: 15 minutes | Cook time: 25 minutes | Serves: 4

1 cup matzo meal	¼ cup canola or vegetable oil
⅛ teaspoon baking powder	1 bone-in, skin-on chicken breast
1½ teaspoons kosher salt, plus	1 bay leaf
more for seasoning	6 cups homemade chicken broth
¼ teaspoon black pepper, plus	(try the recipe here)
more for seasoning	1 large carrot, finely diced
Pinch ground nutmeg	2 celery stalks, finely diced
4 eggs	1 tablespoon chopped fresh dill
5¼ cups water	

1. In a small bowl, combine the matzo meal, baking powder, 1 teaspoon of salt, pepper, and nutmeg. 2. In a medium bowl, beat together the eggs, ¼ cup of water, and the oil. 3. Add the matzo mixture and mix well. 4. Add 1 tablespoon more matzo meal. Chill in the refrigerator for at least 30 minutes. 5. Meanwhile, add the chicken, 3 cups of water, the remaining ½ teaspoon salt, and the bay leaf to the Instant Pot. 6. Put on the pressure cooker's lid and turn the steam valve to "Sealing" position. 7. Select Pressure Cook mode, and then press the "Pressure Cook" button again to select "Less" time option. 8. Use the "+/-" keys on the control panel to set the cooking time to 10 minutes. 9. Press the Pressure Level button to adjust the pressure to "High Pressure." 10. Once the cooking cycle is completed, quickly and carefully turn the steam release handle from Sealing position to the Venting position. 11. When all the steam is released, remove the pressure lid from the top carefully. 12. Remove the chicken and set aside. Remove the bay leaf and discard. 13. Add water until the liquid in the Instant Pot reaches 5 cups (about 2 cups more water). 14. Using a spoon and wet hands, form the matzo ball mixture into walnut-size balls (about 2 tablespoons). 15. As you form them, set them on a plate. Once all of the balls are formed, add them to the pot. 16. Make sure the balls are all separated without disturbing them too much. 17. Select Pressure Cook and cook at High Pressure for 10 minutes. 18. Meanwhile, in a large pot on the stove, heat the broth to a low simmer. 19. Add the carrot and celery and cook for 5 minutes. Season with salt and pepper and turn the heat to low. 20. Bone the chicken and discard the skin. Shred the meat. 21. Once the pressure cooking is complete, release the pressure naturally. 22. Ladle the broth and veggies into bowls and add the chicken. 23. Add 2 to 3 matzo balls per bowl and top with fresh dill.
Per Serving: Calories 419; Fat 14g; Sodium 791mg; Carbs 8.9g; Fiber 4.6g; Sugar 8g; Protein 3g

Easy Beet Soup

Prep time: 15 minutes | Cook Time: 35 minutes | Serves: 4

¾ lb. beets, peeled and chopped	Salt and ground black pepper to
4 cups chicken broth	taste
1 onion, chopped	¼ cup fresh basil leaves, chopped

1. Put all the ingredients in the Inner Pot and stir to mix up. 2. Close and lock the lid. Select the Soup/Broth on the panel. 3. Press the button Again to choose Normal option; use the "+" button to adjust the cooking time to 35 minutes. 4. Press Pressure Level to choose High pressure. 5. When the timer beeps, leave the steam release handle in the Sealing position for 10 minutes, then release any remaining steam manually. 6. Uncover the lid carefully. 7. Blend with an immersion blender until smooth. 8. Season by adding some salt and pepper.
Per Serving: Calories 336; Fat 17.3g; Sodium 281mg; Carbs 8.1g; Fiber 5.3g; Sugars 17.7g; Protein 32.3g

Cauliflower and Potato Soup

Prep-time: 15 minutes | Cook time: 10 minutes | Serves: 4

1 tablespoon olive oil	4 cups vegetable or chicken broth
1 medium yellow onion, diced	Kosher salt
3 garlic cloves, smashed	Black pepper
1 medium cauliflower head, broken into large florets	1 cup whole milk or half-and-half
1 pound Yukon Gold potatoes, peeled and cut into ½-inch cubes	1 cup shredded sharp Cheddar cheese

1. Press the "Sauté" button two times to select "Normal" mode 2. Once hot, add the oil followed by the onion and garlic. 3. Stir and cook for about 3 minutes, until the onion begins to turn translucent. 4. Add the cauliflower, potatoes, and broth. Season with salt and pepper. 5. Put on the pressure cooker's lid and turn the steam valve to "Sealing" position. 6. Select Pressure Cook mode, and then press the "Pressure Cook" button again to select "Less" time option. 7. Use the "+/-" keys on the control panel to set the cooking time to 5 minutes. 8. Press the Pressure Level button to adjust the pressure to "High Pressure." 9. Once the cooking cycle is completed, allow the steam to release naturally for 10 minutes, then turn the steam release handle to the Venting position. 10. When all the steam is released, remove the pressure lid from the top carefully. 11. Add the milk or half-and-half and ½ cup of cheese. 12. Blend until smooth using an immersion blender. 13. Add more broth if you want a thinner soup. 14. Taste for seasoning. Serve topped with a sprinkle of the remaining Cheddar.
Per Serving: Calories 479; Fat 10g; Sodium 891mg; Carbs 22.9g; Fiber 4g; Sugar 4g; Protein 3g

Lentil and Tomato Soup

Prep time: 20 minutes | Cook time: 10 minutes | Serves: 4

2 tablespoons butter	1 cup yellow lentils
1 red onion, chopped	1 teaspoon dried parsley flakes
½ cup celery, chopped	2 cups roasted vegetable broth
1 teaspoon ground cumin	2 cups tomato puree
1 teaspoon ground coriander	2 green onions, sliced
1 teaspoon garlic powder	

1. Press the "Sauté" button two times to select "Normal" settings and melt the butter. 2. Once hot, cook the onion and celery until just tender. 3. Stir in the remaining ingredients, except for the green onions. 4. Put on the pressure cooker's lid and turn the steam valve to "Sealing" position. 5. Select Pressure Cook mode, and then press the "Pressure Cook" button again to select "Less" time option. 6. Use the "+/-" keys on the control panel to set the cooking time to 8 minutes. 7. Press the Pressure Level button to adjust the pressure to "High Pressure." 8. Once the cooking cycle is completed, quickly and carefully turn the steam release handle from Sealing position to the Venting position. 9. When all the steam is released, remove the pressure lid from the top carefully. 10. Serve warm garnished with green onions. Enjoy!
Per Serving: Calories 380; Fat 7.9g; Sodium 704mg; Carbs 6g; Fiber 3.6g; Sugar 6g; Protein 18g

Wonderful Orange, Sweet Potato and Chickpea Soup

Prep time: 35 minutes | Cook Time: 10 minutes | Serves: 4-6

½ tbsp. olive oil	8 oz. orange juice
2 onions, sliced	4 cups vegetable broth
1 lb. sweet potatoes, diced	Salt and ground black pepper to taste
30 oz. canned chickpeas	

1. Insert the inner pot into the cooker base. 2. Connect the power cord to a 120 V power source. The cooker goes to Standby mode and the display indicates OFF. 3. Press Sauté to select the program and then press it again to choose the Normal temperature option. 4. Pour the oil into the Inner Pot and heat it. 5. Add the onion and sauté for 4-5 minutes, until soft. 6. Add the potatoes, chickpeas, orange juice, and broth. Stir to mix up. 7. Press the Cancel key to stop the Sauté function. 8. Close and lock the lid. Select the Pressure Cook on the panel. 9. Press the button Again to choose

Less option; use the "-" button to adjust the cooking time to 5 minutes. 10. Press Pressure Level to choose High Pressure. 11. When the cooking is finished, leave the steam release handle in the Sealing position for 10 minutes. Release any remaining steam manually. Open the lid carefully. 12. Season with salt and pepper to taste. Serve.
Per Serving: Calories 285; Fat 9.8g; Sodium 639mg; Carbs 11.1g; Fiber 1.2g; Sugars 5.1g; Protein 27.8g

French Onion Soup

Prep time: 20 minutes | Cook time: 15 minutes | Serves: 4

5 tablespoons butter	½ cup dry white wine
2-pound yellow onions, cut into ⅛-inch slices	6 cups beef or chicken broth
Kosher salt	2 fresh thyme sprigs
Black pepper	1 loaf French bread, cut into ¾-inch slices and toasted
Pinch sugar	1 cup grated Gruyère cheese

1. Press the "Sauté" button two times to select "Normal" mode. 2. Add and heat the butter. 3. Once the butter has melted, add the onions and stir. 4. Cover loosely with the lid and cook, stirring occasionally, until translucent, about 15 minutes. 5. Lower the heat to low. Season with salt and pepper and add the sugar. 6. Cook, stirring frequently, until the onions turn golden brown and become translucent, about 10 minutes. 7. Raise the heat back to medium. Add the wine. 8. Add the broth and thyme and season with salt and pepper. 9. Put on the pressure cooker's lid and turn the steam valve to "Sealing" position. 10. Select Pressure Cook mode, and then press the "Pressure Cook" button again to select "Less" time option. 11. Use the "+/-" keys on the control panel to set the cooking time to 6 minutes. 12. Press the Pressure Level button to adjust the pressure to "High Pressure." 13. Once the cooking cycle is completed, quickly and carefully turn the steam release handle from Sealing position to the Venting position. 14. When all the steam is released, remove the pressure lid from the top carefully. 15. Preheat the oven. 16. Spoon the soup into ovenproof bowls and top with toasted bread. 17. Sprinkle the top with cheese and place under the broiler for 5 to 7 minutes until the cheese is bubbly.
Per Serving: Calories 479; Fat 10g; Sodium 891mg; Carbs 22.9g; Fiber 4g; Sugar 4g; Protein 3g

Butternut Squash Soup

Prep time: 20 minutes | Cook time: 21 minutes | Serves: 4

2 tablespoons olive oil	cubes (about 4 cups)
8 fresh sage leaves	2 cups chicken or vegetable broth, plus more as needed
10-ounce uncooked Italian-style pork or chicken sausage, without casing	½ teaspoon baking soda
½ large yellow onion, chopped	Kosher salt
2 small celery stalks, chopped	Black pepper
2 large garlic cloves, smashed	½ cup heavy cream or half-and-half
1 medium butternut squash, peeled, seeded, and cut into 1-inch	Pinch ground nutmeg

1. Press the "Sauté" button two times to select "More" mode. 2. Once hot, add the oil followed by the sage leaves. Fry for 2 to 3 minutes until crispy. 3. Remove and drain on a paper towel. 4. Add the sausage. Use a spoon or spatula to break up the sausage into small pieces as it cooks. 5. Continue until the sausage is cooked through. Use a slotted spoon to transfer the sausage to a plate. 6. Add the onion to the pot and cook for 1 minute. 7. Add the celery and garlic and cook, stirring occasionally, for about 3 minutes. 8. Add the squash, broth, and baking soda and stir. Season with salt and pepper. 9. Put on the pressure cooker's lid and turn the steam valve to "Sealing" position. 10. Select Pressure Cook mode, and then press the "Pressure Cook" button again to select "Less" time option. 11. Use the "+/-" keys on the control panel to set the cooking time to 15 minutes. 12. Press the Pressure Level button to adjust the pressure to "High Pressure." 13. Once the cooking cycle is completed, quickly and carefully turn the steam release handle from Sealing position to the Venting position. 14. When all the steam is released, remove the pressure lid from the top carefully. 15. Add the cream and nutmeg, and purée with an immersion blender. 16. Add more broth or cream if you want a thinner soup. Add the sausage, and taste for seasoning. 17. Serve in bowls topped with crispy sage.
Per Serving: Calories 489; Fat 11g; Sodium 501mg; Carbs 8.9g; Fiber 4.6g; Sugar 8g; Protein 26g

Beef Stroganoff Soup

Prep time: 15 minutes | Cook time: 50 minutes | Serves: 4

1-pound beef stew meat, cubed	1 teaspoon garlic powder
5 cups beef bone broth	Sea salt and black pepper, to taste
½ teaspoons dried basil	7-ounce button mushrooms, sliced
½ teaspoons dried oregano	½ cup sour cream
½ teaspoons dried rosemary	2 tablespoons potato starch,
1 teaspoon dried sage	mixed with 4 tablespoons of cold
1 teaspoon shallot powder	water
½ teaspoons porcini powder	

1. In the inner pot, place the stew meat, broth, and spices. 2. Put on the pressure cooker's lid and turn the steam valve to "Sealing" position. 3. Press the "Soup/Broth" button three times to select "Normal" option. 4. Use the "+/-" keys on the control panel to set the cooking time to 50 minutes. 5. Press the Pressure Level button to adjust the pressure to "High Pressure." 6. Once the cooking cycle is completed, allow the steam to release naturally. 7. When all the steam is released, remove the pressure lid from the top carefully. 8. Add the mushrooms and sour cream to the inner pot. 9. Bring to a boil and add the potato starch slurry. 10. Continue to simmer until the soup thickens. 11. Ladle into serving bowls and serve immediately. Bon appétit!
Per Serving: Calories 449; Fat 2.9g; Sodium 511mg; Carbs 12g; Fiber 3g; Sugar 8g; Protein 7g

Chicken Noodle Soup

Prep time: 15 minutes | Cook time: 20 minutes | Serves: 4

2 tablespoons canola oil	1 tablespoon sugar
2 medium yellow onions, halved	8 cups water
1 (2-inch) piece ginger, cut into	Kosher salt
¼-inch slices	Black pepper
1 tablespoon coriander seeds	4 servings rice noodles, cooked
3 star anise pods	Toppings
5 cloves	3 scallions, sliced
1 cinnamon stick	1 small handful fresh herbs,
3 cardamom pods, lightly	chopped
smashed	1 lime, cut into wedges
6 bone-in, skin-on chicken thighs	Handful of bean sprouts
3 tablespoons fish sauce	1 jalapeño, thinly sliced

1. Press the "Sauté" button two times to select "More" mode 2. Once hot, add the oil to the pot. Add the onions, cut-side down, and the ginger. 3. Cook, without moving, until charred for 4 minutes. 4. Add the coriander, star anise, cloves, cinnamon stick, and cardamom. 5. Stir and cook for 1 minute more. 6. Add the chicken, fish sauce, and sugar and immediately pour over the water. 7. Put on the pressure cooker's lid and turn the steam valve to "Sealing" position. 8. Select Pressure Cook mode, and then press the "Pressure Cook" button again to select "Less" time option. 9. Use the "+/-" keys on the control panel to set the cooking time to 15 minutes. 10. Press the Pressure Level button to adjust the pressure to "High Pressure." 11. Once the cooking cycle is completed, allow the steam to release naturally for 10 minutes, then turn the steam release handle to the Venting position. 12. When all the steam is released, remove the pressure lid from the top carefully. 13. Remove the chicken from the pot and carefully strain the broth. Season with salt and pepper as desired. 14. Place the cooked noodles in 4 bowls. 15. When the chicken is cool enough to handle, pick the meat off the bones and add to the bowls. 16. Pour over the broth and top with scallions, herbs, lime, and bean sprouts and jalapeño.
Per Serving: Calories 461; Fat 12.9g; Sodium 414mg; Carbs 11g; Fiber 5g; Sugar 9g; Protein 31g

Beef Soup with Vegetables

Prep time: 20 minutes | Cook time: 20 minutes | Serves: 4

2 tablespoons olive oil	2 celery stalks, chopped
1½-pound beef stew meat, cubed	2 carrots, chopped
Sea salt and black pepper, to taste	2 cloves garlic, chopped
1 onion, chopped	2 rosemary sprigs

2 thyme sprigs	2 ripe tomatoes, pureed
¼ cup tamari sauce	6-ounce green beans, fresh or
2 bay leaves	thawed
5 cups beef bone broth	

1. Press the "Sauté" button two times to select "Normal" settings and heat the oil until sizzling. 2. Now, brown the beef meat for 3 to 4 minutes, stirring frequently to ensure even cooking. 3. Add the remaining ingredients, except for the green beans. 4. Put on the pressure cooker's lid and turn the steam valve to "Sealing" position. 5. Select Pressure Cook mode, and then press the "Pressure Cook" button again to select "Less" time option. 6. Use the "+/-" keys on the control panel to set the cooking time to 13 minutes. 7. Press the Pressure Level button to adjust the pressure to "High Pressure." 8. Once the cooking cycle is completed, allow the steam to release naturally. 9. When all the steam is released, remove the pressure lid from the top carefully. 10. Add the green beans. 11. Choose the "Pressure Cook" mode and cook for 2 minutes at High pressure. 12. Once cooking is complete, use a quick pressure release; carefully remove the lid. 13. Bon appétit!
Per Serving: Calories 380; Fat 19g; Sodium 354mg; Carbs 15g; Fiber 5.1g; Sugar 8.2g; Protein 32g

Vegetable Wild Rice Soup

Prep time: 20 minutes | Cook time: 40 minutes | Serves: 4

3 carrots, chopped	10-ounce button mushrooms,
3 stalks celery, chopped	sliced
1 turnip, chopped	5 cups vegetable broth
1 shallot, chopped	1 teaspoon granulated garlic
1½ cups wild rice	Sea salt and red pepper, to taste

1. Place the ingredients in the inner pot; stir to combine. 2. Put on the pressure cooker's lid and turn the steam valve to "Sealing" position. 3. Press the "Soup/Broth" button two times to select "Normal" option. 4. Use the "+/-" keys on the control panel to set the cooking time to 40 minutes. 5. Press the Pressure Level button to adjust the pressure to "High Pressure." 6. Once the cooking cycle is completed, quickly and carefully turn the steam release handle from Sealing position to the Venting position. 7. When all the steam is released, remove the pressure lid from the top carefully. 8. Serve warm garnished with a few drizzles of olive oil if desired. 9. Bon appétit!
Per Serving: Calories 380; Fat 7.9g; Sodium 704mg; Carbs 6g; Fiber 3.6g; Sugar 6g; Protein 18g

Minestrone Soup

Prep time: 20 minutes | Cook time: 20 minutes | Serves: 4

2 tablespoons canola oil	1 cup pasta, uncooked
1 onion, chopped	2 teaspoons Italian seasoning
2 stalks celery, diced	Sea salt and black pepper, to taste
2 carrots, diced	½ cup fresh corn kernels
2 cloves garlic, pressed	2 cups cannellini beans, canned
2-pound tomatoes, pureed	and rinsed
2 cups chicken broth	6-ounce Parmesan cheese, grated

1. Press the "Sauté" button two times to select "Normal" settings and heat oil until sizzling, 2. Then, sauté the onion, celery, and carrots for 3 to 4 minutes or until tender. 3. Add the garlic, tomatoes, broth, pasta, Italian seasoning, salt, and black pepper. 4. Put on the pressure cooker's lid and turn the steam valve to "Sealing" position. 5. Select Pressure Cook mode, and then press the "Pressure Cook" button again to select "Less" time option. 6. Use the "+/-" keys on the control panel to set the cooking time to 5 minutes. 7. Press the Pressure Level button to adjust the pressure to "High Pressure." 8. Once the cooking cycle is completed, quickly and carefully turn the steam release handle from Sealing position to the Venting position. 9. When all the steam is released, remove the pressure lid from the top carefully. 10. Lastly, stir in the corn kernels and beans. 11. Seal the lid and let it sit in the residual heat for 5 to 8 minutes. 12. Ladle into individual bowls and serve topped with Parmesan cheese. 13. Bon appétit!
Per Serving: Calories 478; Fat 7.9g; Sodium 704mg; Carbs 6g; Fiber 3.6g; Sugar 6g; Protein 18g

Cod Tomato Soup

Prep time: 15 minutes | Cook time: 7 minutes | Serves: 4

½ stick butter, at room temperature
1 onion, chopped
2 garlic cloves, minced
2 ripe tomatoes, pureed
2 tablespoons tomato paste
1 cup shellfish stock
¼ cup cooking wine

1-pound cod fish, cut into bite-sized pieces
½ teaspoons basil
½ teaspoons dried dill weed
¼ teaspoon dried oregano
¼ teaspoon hot sauce
½ teaspoons paprika
Sea salt and black pepper, to taste

1. Press the "Sauté" button two times to select "Normal" settings. 2. And melt the butter; once hot, cook the onion and garlic for about 2 minutes. 3. Add the remaining ingredients. 4. Put on the pressure cooker's lid and turn the steam valve to "Sealing" position. 5. Select Pressure Cook mode, and then press the "Pressure Cook" button again to select "Less" time option. 6. Use the "+/-" keys on the control panel to set the cooking time to 5 minutes. 7. Press the Pressure Level button to adjust the pressure to "High Pressure." 8. Once the cooking cycle is completed, quickly and carefully turn the steam release handle from Sealing position to the Venting position. 9. When all the steam is released, remove the pressure lid from the top carefully. 10. Ladle into serving bowls and serve immediately.
Per Serving: Calories 382; Fat 10.9g; Sodium 354mg; Carbs 10.5g; Fiber 4.1g; Sugar 8.2g; Protein 26g

Chicken Tortilla Soup

Prep time: 20 minutes | Cook time: 8 minutes | Serves: 4

2 tablespoons olive oil
½ cup shallots, chopped
1 sweet pepper, chopped
1 Poblano chili pepper, chopped
½-pound chicken thighs, boneless and skinless
2 ripe tomatoes, chopped
1 can (10-ounce) red enchilada sauce
2 teaspoons ground cumin
1 teaspoon ground coriander

1 teaspoon chili powder
Seasoned salt and freshly cracked pepper, to taste
4 cups roasted vegetable broth
1 bay leaf
1 can (15-ounce) black beans, drained
4 (6-inch) corn tortillas, cut crosswise into ¼-inch strips
1 avocado, cut into ½-inch dice
1 cup cheddar cheese, shredded

1. Press the "Sauté" button two times to select "Normal" settings and heat the olive oil. 2. Once hot, sauté the shallots and peppers until tender and aromatic. 3. Add the chicken thighs, tomatoes, enchilada sauce, cumin, coriander, chili powder, salt, black pepper, vegetable broth, and bay leaf to the inner pot. 4. Put on the pressure cooker's lid and turn the steam valve to "Sealing" position. 5. Select Pressure Cook mode, and then press the "Pressure Cook" button again to select "Less" time option. 6. Use the "+/-" keys on the control panel to set the cooking time to 8 minutes. 7. Press the Pressure Level button to adjust the pressure to "High Pressure." 8. Once the cooking cycle is completed, allow the steam to release naturally. 9. When all the steam is released, remove the pressure lid from the top carefully. 10. Stir in the canned beans and seal the lid; let it sit in the residual heat until everything is heated through. 11. Divide your soup between individual bowls and serve garnished with tortilla strips, avocado, and cheddar cheese.
Per Serving: Calories 584; Fat 15g; Sodium 441mg; Carbs 17g; Fiber 4.6g; Sugar 5g; Protein 29g

Pinot Grigio Soup

Prep time: 15 minutes | Cook time: 15 minutes | Serves: 4

2 slices bacon, chopped
1 medium leek, chopped
1 celery stalk, chopped
2 carrots, chopped
2 parsnips, chopped
⅓ cup Pinot Grigio
3 cups chicken broth

⅓ cup whole milk
½ pound frozen corn kernels, thawed
1 serrano pepper, minced
1 teaspoon granulated garlic
Seas salt and black pepper, to taste

1-pound shrimp, deveined

1. Press the "Sauté" button two times to select "Normal" settings and cook the bacon until it is crisp. 2. Chop the bacon and set aside. 3. Then, sauté the leeks, celery, carrots, and parsnips in the bacon drippings. 4. Cook for about 4 minutes or until they have softened. Add a splash of wine to deglaze the pot. 5. Press the "Cancel" button. Stir in the broth, milk, corn, pepper, granulated garlic, salt, and black pepper. 6. Put on the pressure cooker's lid and turn the steam valve to "Sealing" position. 7. Select Pressure Cook mode, and then press the "Pressure Cook" button again to select "Less" time option. 8. Use the "+/-" keys on the control panel to set the cooking time to 2 minutes. 9. Press the Pressure Level button to adjust the pressure to "High Pressure." 10. Once the cooking cycle is completed, quickly and carefully turn the steam release handle from Sealing position to the Venting position. 11. When all the steam is released, remove the pressure lid from the top carefully. 12. Stir in the shrimp and seal the lid again; allow it to stand in the residual heat for 5 to 10 minutes. 13. Garnish with the reserved crumbled bacon. Bon appétit!
Per Serving: Calories 489; Fat 11g; Sodium 501mg; Carbs 8.9g; Fiber 4.6g; Sugar 8g; Protein 26g

Creamy Clam Chowder

Prep time: 15 minutes | Cook time: 15 minutes | Serves: 4

2 tablespoons butter
1 onion, chopped
1 garlic clove, minced
1 stalk celery, diced
1 carrot, diced
1 cup water
2 cups fish stock

Sea salt and white pepper, to taste
1-pound Russet potatoes, peeled and diced
1 teaspoon cayenne pepper
18-ounce canned clams, chopped with juice
1 cup heavy cream

1. Press the "Sauté" button two times to select "Normal" settings. 2. And melt the butter; once hot, cook the onion, garlic, celery, and carrot for 3 minutes. 3. Add the water, stock, salt, white pepper, potatoes, and cayenne pepper. 4. Put on the pressure cooker's lid and turn the steam valve to "Sealing" position. 5. Select Pressure Cook mode, and then press the "Pressure Cook" button again to select "Less" time option. 6. Use the "+/-" keys on the control panel to set the cooking time to 2 minutes. 7. Press the Pressure Level button to adjust the pressure to "High Pressure." 8. Once the cooking cycle is completed, quickly and carefully turn the steam release handle from Sealing position to the Venting position. 9. When all the steam is released, remove the pressure lid from the top carefully. 10. Press the "Sauté" button two times to select "Normal" settings and use the lowest setting. 11. Stir in the clams and heavy cream. 12. Let it simmer for about 5 minutes or until everything is thoroughly heated. 13. Bon appétit!
Per Serving: Calories 479; Fat 10g; Sodium 891mg; Carbs 22.9g; Fiber 4g; Sugar 4g; Protein 3g

Cheesy Broccoli Soup

Prep time: 15 minutes | Cook time: 5 minutes | Serves: 4

4 tablespoons butter
2 cloves garlic, pressed
1 teaspoon shallot powder
4 cups cream of celery soup
1-pound small broccoli florets
Sea salt and black pepper, to taste

½ teaspoon chili powder
2 cups half and half
2 cups sharp cheddar cheese, freshly grated
2 scallion stalks, chopped

1. Add the butter, garlic, shallot powder, cream of celery soup, broccoli, salt, black pepper, and chili powder to the inner pot. 2. Put on the pressure cooker's lid and turn the steam valve to "Sealing" position. 3. Select Pressure Cook mode, and then press the "Pressure Cook" button again to select "Less" time option. 4. Use the "+/-" keys on the control panel to set the cooking time to 2 minutes. 5. Press the Pressure Level button to adjust the pressure to "High Pressure." 6. Once the cooking cycle is completed, quickly and carefully turn the steam release handle from Sealing position to the Venting position. 7. When all the steam is released, remove the pressure lid from the top carefully. 8. Stir in the half and half and cheese. Let it simmer until everything is thoroughly heated. 9. Divide between serving bowls and serve garnished with chopped scallions. 10. Bon appétit!
Per Serving: Calories 352; Fat 12.9g; Sodium 414mg; Carbs 11g; Fiber 5g; Sugar 9g; Protein 31g

Sage Onion Soup

Prep time: 15 minutes | Cook time: 2 minutes | Serves: 4

4 tablespoons butter, melted	4 cups chicken bone broth
1 pound onions, thinly sliced	1 loaf French bread, sliced
Kosher salt and ground white pepper, to taste	1 cup mozzarella cheese, shredded
½ teaspoons dried sage	

1. Press the "Sauté" button two times to select "Normal" settings and melt the butter. 2. Once hot, cook the onions until golden and caramelized. 3. Add the salt, pepper, sage, and chicken bone broth. 4. Put on the pressure cooker's lid and turn the steam valve to "Sealing" position. 5. Select Pressure Cook mode, and then press the "Pressure Cook" button again to select "Less" time option. 6. Use the "+/-" keys on the control panel to set the cooking time to 2 minutes. 7. Press the Pressure Level button to adjust the pressure to "High Pressure." 8. Once the cooking cycle is completed, quickly and carefully turn the steam release handle from Sealing position to the Venting position. 9. When all the steam is released, remove the pressure lid from the top carefully. 10. Divide the soup between four oven safe bowls; top with the bread and shredded cheese. 11. Now, place the bowls under the broiler for about 4 minutes or until the cheese has melted. 12. Bon appétit!
Per Serving: Calories 472; Fat 10.9g; Sodium 454mg; Carbs 10g; Fiber 3.1g; Sugar 5.2g; Protein 20g

Meatball Noodle Soup

Prep time: 15 minutes | Cook time: 25 minutes | Serves: 4

Meatballs:	Soup:
½-pound ground beef	1 tablespoon olive oil
½-pound ground turkey	1 onion, chopped
½ cup panko crumbs	1 celery stalk, chopped
¼ cup Pecorino Romano cheese, grated	2 cloves garlic, minced
1 egg, beaten	2 tomatoes, crushed
2 cloves garlic, crushed	4 cups chicken broth
2 tablespoons cilantro, chopped	2 bay leaves
Sea salt and black pepper, to taste	6-ounce noodles

1. In a mixing bowl, thoroughly combine all ingredients for the meatballs. 2. Form the mixture into 20 meatballs. 3. Press the "Sauté" button two times to select "Normal" settings and heat the oil. 4. Now, brown the meatballs in batches; reserve. 5. Heat the olive oil; sauté the onion, celery, and garlic for 3 to 4 minutes or until they are fragrant. 6. Add the tomatoes, broth, and bay leaves to the inner pot. 7. Put on the pressure cooker's lid and turn the steam valve to "Sealing" position. 8. Select Pressure Cook mode, and then press the "Pressure Cook" button again to select "Less" time option. 9. Use the "+/-" keys on the control panel to set the cooking time to 12 minutes. 10. Press the Pressure Level button to adjust the pressure to "High Pressure." 11. Once the cooking cycle is completed, quickly and carefully turn the steam release handle from Sealing position to the Venting position. 12. When all the steam is released, remove the pressure lid from the top carefully. 13. Next, stir in the noodles and secure the lid again. 14. Choose the "Pressure Cook" mode and cook for 5 minutes at High Pressure. 15. Once cooking is complete, use a quick pressure release; carefully remove the lid. 16. Bon appétit!
Per Serving: Calories 584; Fat 15g; Sodium 441mg; Carbs 17g; Fiber 4.6g; Sugar 5g; Protein 29g

Chipotle Chili Soup

Prep time: 15 minutes | Cook time: 33 minutes | Serves: 4

1 tablespoon canola oil	diced
1-pound ground beef	2 cups vegetable broth
2 cloves garlic, smashed	16 oz. pinto beans, undrained
1 medium leek, chopped	½ teaspoons cumin powder
2 chipotle chilies in adobo sauce, roughly chopped	1 teaspoon stone-ground mustard
1 (14½ -ounce) can tomatoes,	1 teaspoon chili powder

1. Press the "Sauté" button two times to select "Normal" settings and heat the oil. 2. Brown the ground beef for 2 to 3 minutes, stirring frequently. 3. Add the remaining ingredients and stir to combine well. 4. Put on the pressure cooker's lid and turn the steam valve to "Sealing" position. 5. Press the "Bean/Chili" button two times to select "Normal" option. 6. Press the Pressure Level button to adjust the pressure to "High Pressure." 7. Once the cooking cycle is completed, allow the steam to release naturally. 8. When all the steam is released, remove the pressure lid from the top carefully. 9. Bon appétit!
Per Serving: Calories 419; Fat 14g; Sodium 791mg; Carbs 8.9g; Fiber 4.6g; Sugar 8g; Protein 3g

Corn and Chicken Soup

Prep time: 15 minutes | Cook time: 15 minutes | Serves: 4

1 tablespoon olive oil	boneless and diced
1 yellow onion, chopped	1 teaspoon garlic powder
1 celery stalk, diced	1 teaspoon mustard powder
1 carrot, finely diced	1 (15-ounce) can creamed corn
1 turnip, diced	4 large eggs, whisked
6 cups roasted vegetable broth	Kosher salt and black pepper, to taste
1-pound chicken breasts, skinless,	

1. Press the "Sauté" button two times to select "Normal" settings and heat the oil. 2. Now, sauté the onion until just tender and translucent. 3. Add the celery, carrot, turnip, vegetable broth, chicken, garlic powder, and mustard powder. 4. Put on the pressure cooker's lid and turn the steam valve to "Sealing" position. 5. Select Pressure Cook mode, and then press the "Pressure Cook" button again to select "Less" time option. 6. Use the "+/-" keys on the control panel to set the cooking time to 9 minutes. 7. Press the Pressure Level button to adjust the pressure to "High Pressure." 8. Once the cooking cycle is completed, quickly and carefully turn the steam release handle from Sealing position to the Venting position. 9. When all the steam is released, remove the pressure lid from the top carefully. 10. Press the "Sauté" button two times to select "Less" settings. 11. Stir in the creamed corn and eggs; let it simmer, stirring continuously for about 5 minutes. 12. Season with salt and pepper to taste and serve warm. 13. Bon appétit!
Per Serving: Calories 351; Fat 7.9g; Sodium 704mg; Carbs 6g; Fiber 3.6g; Sugar 6g; Protein 18g

Kidney Bean Chicken Soup

Prep time: 15 minutes | Cook time: 17 minutes | Serves: 4

2 tablespoons butter, softened	1 teaspoon dried oregano
1 onion, chopped	1 teaspoon cayenne pepper
1 sweet pepper, deseeded and chopped	4 cups vegetable broth
1 habanero pepper, deseeded and chopped	1-pound chicken thighs
2 cloves garlic, minced	2 cans (15-ounce) red kidney beans
Sea salt and black pepper, to taste	¼ cup fresh cilantro, chopped
1 teaspoon dried basil	½ cup tortilla chips

1. Press the "Sauté" button two times to select "Normal" settings and melt the butter. 2. Once hot, cook the onion until tender and translucent. 3. Stir in the peppers and sauté for a few minutes more. 4. Add the minced garlic and continue to sauté for another minute. 5. Add the spices, vegetable broth, and chicken thighs to the inner pot. 6. Put on the pressure cooker's lid and turn the steam valve to "Sealing" position. 7. Select Pressure Cook mode, and then press the "Pressure Cook" button again to select "Less" time option. 8. Use the "+/-" keys on the control panel to set the cooking time to 13 minutes. 9. Press the Pressure Level button to adjust the pressure to "High Pressure." 10. Once the cooking cycle is completed, quickly and carefully turn the steam release handle from Sealing position to the Venting position. 11. When all the steam is released, remove the pressure lid from the top carefully. 12. Remove the chicken to a cutting board. Add the kidney beans to the inner pot and seal the lid again. 13. Let it sit in the residual heat until thoroughly heated. 14. Shred the chicken and discard the bones; put it back into the soup. 15. Serve with fresh cilantro and tortilla chips. Enjoy!
Per Serving: Calories 479; Fat 10g; Sodium 891mg; Carbs 22.9g; Fiber 4g; Sugar 4g; Protein 3g

Sweet Potato Soup with Swiss Chard

Prep time: 15 minutes | Cook time: 10 minutes | Serves: 4

2 tablespoons butter, softened at room temperature	2 ripe tomatoes, pureed
1 white onion, chopped	2 cups chicken bone broth
1 sweet pepper, deveined and chopped	2 cups water
2 cloves garlic, pressed	Kosher salt and black pepper, to taste
1 pound sweet potatoes, peeled and diced	¼ cup peanut butter
	2 cups Swiss chard, torn into pieces

1. Press the "Sauté" button two times to select "Normal" settings and melt the butter. 2. Once hot, cook the onion, pepper, and garlic until tender and fragrant. 3. Add the sweet potatoes and continue to sauté for about 3 minutes longer. 4. Now, stir in the tomatoes, broth, water, salt, and black pepper. 5. Put on the pressure cooker's lid and turn the steam valve to "Sealing" position. 6. Select Pressure Cook mode, and then press the "Pressure Cook" button again to select "Less" time option. 7. Use the "+/-" keys on the control panel to set the cooking time to 4 minutes. 8. Press the Pressure Level button to adjust the pressure to "High Pressure." 9. Once the cooking cycle is completed, quickly and carefully turn the steam release handle from Sealing position to the Venting position. 10. When all the steam is released, remove the pressure lid from the top carefully. 11. Stir in the peanut butter and Swiss chard; seal the lid again and let it sit in the residual heat until your greens wilt. 12. Serve warm.
Per Serving: Calories 521; Fat 7.9g; Sodium 704mg; Carbs 6g; Fiber 3.6g; Sugar 6g; Protein 18g

Turkey and Basmati Rice Soup

Prep time: 15 minutes | Cook time: 15 minutes | Serves: 4

1 tablespoon sesame oil	5 cups chicken broth
1 onion, chopped	1 teaspoon garlic powder
1 large thumb-sized pieces' fresh ginger, peeled and grated	1 teaspoon cumin seeds
1-pound turkey breast, boneless and cut into chunks	1 teaspoon garam masala
2 carrots, sliced	1 teaspoon turmeric powder
1 celery stalk, sliced	1 cup basmati rice, rinsed
	1 small handful of fresh coriander, roughly chopped

1. Press the "Sauté" button two times to select "Normal" settings. 2. And heat the sesame oil until sizzling. Now, sauté the onion and ginger until tender and aromatic. 3. Add the turkey, carrot, and celery to the inner pot; continue to cook for 3 to 4 minutes. 4. Add the chicken broth and spices to the inner pot. 5. Put on the pressure cooker's lid and turn the steam valve to "Sealing" position. 6. Select Pressure Cook mode, and then press the "Pressure Cook" button again to select "Less" time option. 7. Use the "+/-" keys on the control panel to set the cooking time to 5 minutes. 8. Press the Pressure Level button to adjust the pressure to "High Pressure." 9. Once the cooking cycle is completed, quickly and carefully turn the steam release handle from Sealing position to the Venting position. 10. When all the steam is released, remove the pressure lid from the top carefully. 11. After that, stir in the basmati rice. 12. Choose the "Pressure Cook" mode and cook for 4 minutes at High Pressure. 13. Once cooking is complete, use a quick pressure release; carefully remove the lid. 14. Ladle into four serving bowls and serve with fresh coriander. Enjoy!
Per Serving: Calories 449; Fat 2.9g; Sodium 511mg; Carbs 12g; Fiber 3g; Sugar 8g; Protein 7g

Beef Barley Soup

Prep time: 15 minutes | Cook time: 25 minutes | Serves: 4

1 tablespoon canola oil	4 cups beef broth
2 shallots, chopped	1 cup pearl barley
2 garlic cloves, minced	2 sprigs thyme
2 celery stalks, chopped	Sea salt and white pepper, to taste
1 parsnip, chopped	1 teaspoon red pepper flakes, crushed
1 cup tomato puree	

1. Press the "Sauté" button two times to select "Normal" settings and heat

the canola oil. 2. Once hot, sauté the shallots, garlic, celery, and parsnip until tender and aromatic. 3. Add the remaining ingredients and stir to combine. 4. Put on the pressure cooker's lid and turn the steam valve to "Sealing" position. 5. Press the "Soup/Broth" button one time to select "Less" option. 6. Press the Pressure Level button to adjust the pressure to "High Pressure." 7. Once the cooking cycle is completed, quickly and carefully turn the steam release handle from Sealing position to the Venting position. 8. When all the steam is released, remove the pressure lid from the top carefully. 9. Serve in individual bowls. 10. Bon appétit!
Per Serving: Calories 382; Fat 7.9g; Sodium 704mg; Carbs 6g; Fiber 3.6g; Sugar 6g; Protein 18g

Lima Bean Mushroom Soup

Prep time: 15 minutes | Cook time: 15 minutes | Serves: 5

2 tablespoons sesame oil	½ teaspoons red curry paste
1 pound cremini mushrooms, thinly sliced	½ teaspoons cayenne pepper
1 large-sized eggplant, sliced into rounds	Sea salt and black pepper, to taste
1 red onion, chopped	2 sprigs thyme
2 garlic cloves, chopped	2 sprigs rosemary
2 carrots, sliced	2 medium-sized tomatoes, pureed
2 sweet potatoes, peeled and diced	5 cups roasted vegetable broth
	16-ounce lima beans, soaked overnight
	Juice of 1 fresh lemon

1. Press the "Sauté" button two times to select "Normal" settings and heat the oil until sizzling. 2. Now, cook the mushrooms, eggplant, onion, and garlic until just tender and fragrant. 3. Add the carrots, sweet potatoes, curry paste, spices, tomatoes, broth, and lima beans. 4. Put on the pressure cooker's lid and turn the steam valve to "Sealing" position. 5. Select Pressure Cook mode, and then press the "Pressure Cook" button again to select "Less" time option. 6. Use the "+/-" keys on the control panel to set the cooking time to 13 minutes. 7. Press the Pressure Level button to adjust the pressure to "High Pressure." 8. Once the cooking cycle is completed, quickly and carefully turn the steam release handle from Sealing position to the Venting position. 9. When all the steam is released, remove the pressure lid from the top carefully. 10. Divide your soup between individual bowls; add a few drizzles of lemon juice to each serving and enjoy!
Per Serving: Calories 461; Fat 12.9g; Sodium 414mg; Carbs 11g; Fiber 5g; Sugar 9g; Protein 31g

Lobster Bisque

Prep time: 15 minutes | Cook time: 5 minutes | Serves: 4

1-pound lump lobster meat	1 tomato, pureed
2 tablespoons olive oil	¼ cup cooking sherry
1 yellow onion, chopped	3 cups clam juice
1 celery stalk, diced	1 tablespoon soy sauce
1 carrot, diced	½ teaspoons smoked paprika
2 cloves garlic, minced	Sea salt and ground white pepper, to taste
1 teaspoon rosemary	
1 teaspoon basil	1 teaspoon Tabasco sauce
1 teaspoon thyme	1 cup heavy cream
½ teaspoons turmeric powder	

1. In the Inner Pot of your Instant Pot, place the lobster meat, olive oil, onion, celery, carrot, garlic, rosemary, basil, thyme, turmeric, tomato puree, cooking sherry, and clam juice. 2. Put on the pressure cooker's lid and turn the steam valve to "Sealing" position. 3. Select Pressure Cook mode, and then press the "Pressure Cook" button again to select "Less" time option. 4. Use the "+/-" keys on the control panel to set the cooking time to 4 minutes. 5. Press the Pressure Level button to adjust the pressure to "High Pressure." 6. Once the cooking cycle is completed, quickly and carefully turn the steam release handle from Sealing position to the Venting position. 7. When all the steam is released, remove the pressure lid from the top carefully. 8. Set the lobster meat aside and chop into small chunks. 9. Now, add in the soy sauce, smoked paprika, salt, white pepper, Tabasco sauce, and heavy cream. 10. Continue to stir and simmer until it's all blended together and heated through. 11. Put the lobster meat back into your bisque. 12. Serve in individual bowls and enjoy!
Per Serving: Calories 419; Fat 14g; Sodium 791mg; Carbs 8.9g; Fiber 4.6g; Sugar 8g; Protein 3g

Seafood Chowder with Bacon

Prep time: 15 minutes | Cook time: 10 minutes | Serves: 4

3 strips bacon, chopped
1 onion, chopped
2 carrots, diced
2 stalks celery, diced
2 cloves garlic, minced
1 tablespoon Creole seasoning
Sea salt and black pepper, to taste

3 cups seafood stock
2 ripe tomatoes, pureed
2 tablespoons tomato paste
2 bay leaves
1 pound clams, chopped
1½ tablespoons flaxseed meal

1. Press the "Sauté" button two times to select "Normal" settings. 2. Now, cook the bacon until it is crisp; crumble the bacon and set it aside. 3. Now, sauté the onion, carrot, celery, and garlic in bacon drippings. 4. Add the remaining ingredients, except for the chopped clams, to the inner pot. 5. Put on the pressure cooker's lid and turn the steam valve to "Sealing" position. 6. Select Pressure Cook mode, and then press the "Pressure Cook" button again to select "Less" time option. 7. Use the "+/-" keys on the control panel to set the cooking time to 4 minutes. 8. Press the Pressure Level button to adjust the pressure to "High Pressure." 9. Once the cooking cycle is completed, quickly and carefully turn the steam release handle from Sealing position to the Venting position. 10. When all the steam is released, remove the pressure lid from the top carefully. 11. Stir in the chopped clams and flaxseed meal. 12. Press the "Sauté" button two times to select "Normal" settings. 13. And let it simmer for 2 to 3 minutes longer or until everything is heated through. 14. Serve in individual bowls topped with the reserved bacon. 15. Bon appétit!
Per Serving: Calories 350; Fat 19g; Sodium 354mg; Carbs 15g; Fiber 5.1g; Sugar 8.2g; Protein 32g

Potato Chowder

Prep time: 15 minutes | Cook time: 15 minutes | Serves: 4

2 tablespoons butter
1 sweet onion, chopped
2 garlic cloves, minced
1 sweet pepper, deveined and sliced
1 jalapeno pepper, deveined and sliced
4 tablespoons all-purpose flour

4 cups vegetable broth
1 pound potatoes, cut into bite-sized pieces
3 cups creamed corn kernels
1 cup double cream
Kosher salt and black pepper, to taste
½ teaspoons cayenne pepper

1. Press the "Sauté" button two times to select "Normal" settings and melt the butter. 2. Once hot, sauté the sweet onions, garlic, and peppers for about 3 minutes. 3. Sprinkle the flour over the vegetables; continue stirring for 4 minutes. 4. Add the broth and potatoes and gently stir to combine. 5. Put on the pressure cooker's lid and turn the steam valve to "Sealing" position. 6. Select Pressure Cook mode, and then press the "Pressure Cook" button again to select "Less" time option. 7. Use the "+/-" keys on the control panel to set the cooking time to 5 minutes. 8. Press the Pressure Level button to adjust the pressure to "High Pressure." 9. Once the cooking cycle is completed, quickly and carefully turn the steam release handle from Sealing position to the Venting position. 10. When all the steam is released, remove the pressure lid from the top carefully. 11. Press the "Sauté" button two times to select "Normal" settings and use the lowest setting. 12. Stir in the creamed corn, double cream, salt, black pepper, and cayenne pepper. 13. Let it simmer, stirring continuously for about 5 minutes or until everything is thoroughly heated. 14. Taste and adjust the seasonings. 15. Bon appétit!
Per Serving: Calories 412; Fat 20g; Sodium 491mg; Carbs 9g; Fiber 3g; Sugar 8g; Protein 31g

Halibut Chowder

Prep time: 15 minutes | Cook time: 10 minutes | Serves: 5

2 tablespoons butter
1 medium-sized leek, sliced
1 carrot, shredded
1 celery stalk, shredded

2 cloves garlic, minced
5 cups chicken bone broth
2 ripe tomatoes, chopped
1½-pound halibut, cut into small

cubes
Kosher salt and cracked black pepper, to taste

1 cup milk
½ cup double cream
1 cup Swiss cheese, shredded

1. Press the "Sauté" button two times to select "Normal" settings and melt the butter. 2. Once hot, sauté the leeks, carrot, celery, and garlic until they are just tender and fragrant. 3. Then, add the chicken bone broth, tomatoes, halibut, salt, and black pepper. 4. Put on the pressure cooker's lid and turn the steam valve to "Sealing" position. 5. Select Pressure Cook mode, and then press the "Pressure Cook" button again to select "Less" time option. 6. Use the "+/-" keys on the control panel to set the cooking time to 5 minutes. 7. Press the Pressure Level button to adjust the pressure to "High Pressure." 8. Once the cooking cycle is completed, quickly and carefully turn the steam release handle from Sealing position to the Venting position. 9. When all the steam is released, remove the pressure lid from the top carefully. 10. Press the "Sauté" button two times to select "Less" setting. 11. Stir in the milk and double cream. Allow it to simmer for about 3 minutes or until heated through. 12. Ladle your chowder into five serving bowls; top with the shredded Swiss cheese and serve immediately.
Per Serving: Calories 479; Fat 10g; Sodium 891mg; Carbs 22.9g; Fiber 4g; Sugar 4g; Protein 3g

Red Lentil Spinach Soup

Prep time: 15 minutes | Cook time: 5 minutes | Serves: 5

2 cups red lentils, rinsed
1 onion, chopped
2 cloves garlic, minced
1 teaspoon cumin
1 teaspoon smoked paprika
Sea salt and black pepper, to taste

2 carrots, sliced
6 cups water
2 bay leaves
2 cups fresh spinach leaves, torn into small pieces

1. Place all ingredients, except for the fresh spinach, in the inner pot. 2. Put on the pressure cooker's lid and turn the steam valve to "Sealing" position. 3. Select Pressure Cook mode, and then press the "Pressure Cook" button again to select "Less" time option. 4. Use the "+/-" keys on the control panel to set the cooking time to 3 minutes. 5. Press the Pressure Level button to adjust the pressure to "High Pressure." 6. Once the cooking cycle is completed, quickly and carefully turn the steam release handle from Sealing position to the Venting position. 7. When all the steam is released, remove the pressure lid from the top carefully. 8. Stir in the spinach and seal the lid again; let it sit until the spinach just starts to wilt. 9. Serve in individual bowls and enjoy!
Per Serving: Calories 349; Fat 10.9g; Sodium 454mg; Carbs 10g; Fiber 3.1g; Sugar 5.2g; Protein 20g

Minty Asparagus Soup

Prep time: 15 minutes | Cook time: 10 minutes | Serves: 4

1 tablespoon butter
1 Asian shallot, chopped
2 garlic cloves, minced
2-pound asparagus stalks, trimmed and chopped
Kosher salt and black pepper, to

taste
3 cups chicken broth
1 cup yogurt
2 tablespoons fresh mint leaves, chopped

1. Press the "Sauté" button two times to select "Normal" settings and melt the butter. 2. Once hot, cook the Asian shallots and garlic until just tender and fragrant. 3. Add the asparagus, salt, pepper, and broth. 4. Put on the pressure cooker's lid and turn the steam valve to "Sealing" position. 5. Select Pressure Cook mode, and then press the "Pressure Cook" button again to select "Less" time option. 6. Use the "+/-" keys on the control panel to set the cooking time to 4 minutes. 7. Press the Pressure Level button to adjust the pressure to "High Pressure." 8. Once the cooking cycle is completed, quickly and carefully turn the steam release handle from Sealing position to the Venting position. 9. When all the steam is released, remove the pressure lid from the top carefully. 10. Add the yogurt and blend the soup until it is completely smooth. Taste and season with more salt if desired. 11. Ladle into individual bowls; then, top each bowl with fresh mint leaves and serve.
Per Serving: Calories 489; Fat 11g; Sodium 501mg; Carbs 8.9g; Fiber 4.6g; Sugar 8g; Protein 26g

Peppery Ground Pork Soup

Prep time: 15 minutes | Cook time: 13 minutes | Serves: 4

1-pound ground pork	sliced
1 teaspoon Italian seasoning	1 jalapeno pepper, seeded and
1 teaspoon garlic powder	minced
Sea salt and black pepper, to taste	2 ripe tomatoes, pureed
2 sweet peppers, seeded and	4 cups chicken stock

1. Press the "Sauté" button two times to select "Normal" settings. 2. Then, brown the ground pork until no longer pink or about 3 minutes. 3. Add the remaining ingredients to the inner pot and stir. 4. Put on the pressure cooker's lid and turn the steam valve to "Sealing" position. 5. Select Pressure Cook mode, and then press the "Pressure Cook" button again to select "Less" time option. 6. Use the "+/-" keys on the control panel to set the cooking time to 10 minutes. 7. Press the Pressure Level button to adjust the pressure to "Low Pressure." 8. Once the cooking cycle is completed, allow the steam to release naturally. 9. When all the steam is released, remove the pressure lid from the top carefully. 10. Serve warm. Bon appétit!
Per Serving: Calories 489; Fat 11g; Sodium 501mg; Carbs 8.9g; Fiber 4.6g; Sugar 8g; Protein 26g

Chicken Vegetable Soup

Prep time: 15 minutes | Cook time: 20 minutes | Serves: 3

2 tablespoons butter, melted	½ teaspoons dried sage
½-pound chicken legs, boneless and skinless	½ teaspoons dried thyme leaves
1 onion, diced	Sea salt and black pepper, to taste
1 teaspoon garlic, minced	2 tablespoons tamari sauce
1 teaspoon ginger, peeled and grated	2 carrots, diced
3 cups chicken stock	2 parsnips, diced
	2 cups cauliflower florets

1. Press the "Sauté" button two times to select "Normal" settings and melt the butter. 2. Once hot, sauté the chicken until golden brown; reserve. 3. Cook the onion, garlic, and ginger in pan drippings until just tender and aromatic. 4. Add the reserved chicken, stock, and spices. 5. Put on the pressure cooker's lid and turn the steam valve to "Sealing" position. 6. Select Pressure Cook mode, and then press the "Pressure Cook" button again to select "Less" time option. 7. Use the "+/-" keys on the control panel to set the cooking time to 13 minutes. 8. Press the Pressure Level button to adjust the pressure to "High Pressure." 9. Once the cooking cycle is completed, quickly and carefully turn the steam release handle from Sealing position to the Venting position. 10. When all the steam is released, remove the pressure lid from the top carefully. 11. Now, add the tamari sauce and vegetables to the inner pot. 12. Choose the "Manual" mode and cook for 5 minutes at High Pressure. 13. Once cooking is complete, use a quick pressure release; carefully remove the lid. 14. Serve immediately.
Per Serving: Calories 334; Fat 7.9g; Sodium 704mg; Carbs 6g; Fiber 3.6g; Sugar 6g; Protein 18g

Farmhouse Soup

Prep time: 15 minutes | Cook time: 10 minutes | Serves: 4

2 tablespoons canola oil	4-ounce frozen green peas
1 shallot, chopped	8-ounce frozen broccoli, chopped
2 garlic cloves, minced	4-ounce frozen green beans
½ teaspoons dried oregano	2 ripe tomatoes, pureed
½ teaspoons dried basil	4 cups vegetable broth
½ teaspoons dried rosemary	Sea salt and black pepper, to taste
4-ounce frozen carrots, chopped	½ teaspoons red pepper flakes

1. Press the "Sauté" button two times to select "Normal" settings and heat the oil. 2. Sauté the shallot until softened, approximately 4 minutes. Stir in the garlic and cook for 30 seconds more. 3. Add the dried herbs, frozen vegetables, tomatoes, vegetable broth, salt, and black pepper. 4. Put on the pressure cooker's lid and turn the steam valve to "Sealing" position. 5. Select Pressure Cook mode, and then press the "Pressure Cook" button again to select "Less" time option. 6. Use the "+/-" keys on the control panel to set the cooking time to 4 minutes. 7. Press the Pressure Level button to adjust the pressure to "High Pressure." 8. Once the cooking cycle is completed, quickly and carefully turn the steam release handle from Sealing position to the Venting position. 9. When all the steam is released, remove the pressure lid from the top carefully. 10. Divide between serving bowls and garnish with red pepper flakes. 11. Bon appétit!
Per Serving: Calories 382; Fat 7.9g; Sodium 704mg; Carbs 6g; Fiber 3.6g; Sugar 6g; Protein 18g

Tomato Vegetable Soup

Prep time: 15 minutes | Cook time: 10 minutes | Serves: 4

1 tablespoon olive oil	1 teaspoon fresh basil, chopped
1 cup green onions, chopped	1 teaspoon fresh rosemary, chopped
2 stalks green garlic, chopped	1 (28-ounce) can tomatoes, crushed
1 celery stalk, diced	½ cup double cream
2 carrots, diced	½ cup feta cheese, cubed
2 cups vegetable broth	1 tablespoon olive oil
Sea salt and black pepper, to your liking	
½ teaspoons cayenne pepper	

1. Press the "Sauté" button two times to select "Normal" settings 2. And heat 1 tablespoon of olive oil. Sauté the green onions, garlic, celery, and carrots until softened. 3. Add the vegetable broth, salt, black pepper, cayenne pepper, basil, rosemary, and tomatoes to the inner pot. 4. Put on the pressure cooker's lid and turn the steam valve to "Sealing" position. 5. Select Pressure Cook mode, and then press the "Pressure Cook" button again to select "Less" time option. 6. Use the "+/-" keys on the control panel to set the cooking time to 6 minutes. 7. Press the Pressure Level button to adjust the pressure to "High Pressure." 8. Once the cooking cycle is completed, allow the steam to release naturally. 9. When all the steam is released, remove the pressure lid from the top carefully. 10. Stir in the double cream and seal the lid again; let it sit for 10 minutes more. 11. Ladle into soup bowls; garnish with feta and 1 tablespoon of olive oil. 12. Bon appétit!
Per Serving: Calories 584; Fat 15g; Sodium 441mg; Carbs 17g; Fiber 4.6g; Sugar 5g; Protein 29g

Sausage and Cabbage Soup

Prep time: 20 minutes | Cook time: 15 minutes | Serves: 5

2 tablespoons olive oil	shredded into small pieces
1-pound beef sausage, thinly sliced	5 cups beef bone broth
1 onion, chopped	1 tablespoon Italia seasoning blend
3 cloves garlic. minced	1 teaspoon cayenne pepper
1 stalk celery, chopped	1 bay leaf
1 carrot, peeled and chopped	Salt and cracked black pepper, to taste
¼ cup Italian cooking wine	
1 (1-pound) head cabbage,	

1. Press the "Sauté" button two times to select "Normal" settings and heat the oil. 2. Once hot, cook the beef sausage until no longer pink. 3. Now, stir in the onion and garlic; continue to sauté until they are fragrant. 4. Add a splash of cooking wine, scraping up any browned bits from the bottom of the inner pot. 5. Add the remaining ingredients. 6. Put on the pressure cooker's lid and turn the steam valve to "Sealing" position. 7. Select Pressure Cook mode, and then press the "Pressure Cook" button again to select "Less" time option. 8. Use the "+/-" keys on the control panel to set the cooking time to 6 minutes. 9. Press the Pressure Level button to adjust the pressure to "High Pressure." 10. Once the cooking cycle is completed, quickly and carefully turn the steam release handle from Sealing position to the Venting position. 11. When all the steam is released, remove the pressure lid from the top carefully. 12. Choose the "Manual" mode and cook for 6 minutes at High Pressure. 13. Once cooking is complete, use a quick pressure release; carefully remove the lid. 14. Divide between soup bowls and serve immediately
Per Serving: Calories 479; Fat 10g; Sodium 891mg; Carbs 22.9g; Fiber 4g; Sugar 4g; Protein 3g

Zucchini Quinoa Soup

Prep time: 15 minutes | Cook time: 10 minutes | Serves: 4

2 tablespoons olive oil	1-pound zucchini, cut into rounds
1 shallot, diced	1 cup quinoa
1 teaspoon fresh garlic, minced	4 cups vegetable broth
Sea salt and black pepper, to your liking	2 tablespoons fresh parsley leaves

1. Press the "Sauté" button two times to select "Normal" settings and heat the oil. 2. Once hot, sweat the shallot for 2 to 3 minutes. 3. Stir in the garlic and continue to cook for another 30 seconds or until aromatic. 4. Stir in the salt, black pepper, zucchini, quinoa, and vegetable broth. 5. Put on the pressure cooker's lid and turn the steam valve to "Sealing" position. 6. Select Pressure Cook mode, and then press the "Pressure Cook" button again to select "Less" time option. 7. Use the "+/-" keys on the control panel to set the cooking time to 3 minutes. 8. Press the Pressure Level button to adjust the pressure to "High Pressure." 9. Once the cooking cycle is completed, quickly and carefully turn the steam release handle from Sealing position to the Venting position. 10. When all the steam is released, remove the pressure lid from the top carefully. 11. Ladle into soup bowls; serve garnished with fresh parsley leaves. 12. Enjoy!
Per Serving: Calories 449; Fat 2.9g; Sodium 511mg; Carbs 12g; Fiber 3g; Sugar 8g; Protein 28g

Shrimp Vegetable Bisque

Prep time: 15 minutes | Cook time: 10 minutes | Serves: 4

2 tablespoons butter	¼ cup sherry wine
½ cup white onion, chopped	Sea salt and black pepper
1 celery rib, chopped	1 cup tomato puree
1 parsnip, chopped	3 cups chicken bone broth
1 carrot, chopped	16-ounce shrimp, deveined
2 tablespoons all-purpose flour	1 cup heavy whipping cream

1. Press the "Sauté" button two times to select "Normal" settings and melt the butter. 2. Once hot, cook the onion, celery, parsnip, and carrot until softened. 3. Add the flour and cook for 3 minutes more or until everything is well coated. 4. Pour in sherry wine to deglaze the pot. 5. Now, add the salt, pepper, tomato puree, and broth. 6. Put on the pressure cooker's lid and turn the steam valve to "Sealing" position. 7. Select Pressure Cook mode, and then press the "Pressure Cook" button again to select "Less" time option. 8. Use the "+/-" keys on the control panel to set the cooking time to 5 minutes. 9. Press the Pressure Level button to adjust the pressure to "High Pressure." 10. Once the cooking cycle is completed, quickly and carefully turn the steam release handle from Sealing position to the Venting position. 11. When all the steam is released, remove the pressure lid from the top carefully. 12. Now, add the shrimp and heavy cream. 13. Cook on the "Sauté" function for a further 2 to 3 minutes or until everything is heated through 14. Bon appétit!
Per Serving: Calories 479; Fat 10g; Sodium 891mg; Carbs 22.9g; Fiber 4g; Sugar 4g; Protein 3g

Borscht Soup

Prep time: 15 minutes | Cook time: 15 minutes | Serves: 4

2 tablespoons safflower oil	½-pound red bee roots, grated
1 red onion, chopped	1 tablespoon cider vinegar
2 cloves garlic, minced	2 tablespoons tomato paste
1 pound Yukon potatoes, peeled and diced	Sea salt and black pepper, to taste
2 carrots, chopped	2 bay leaves
1 small red bell pepper, finely chopped	½ teaspoons ground cumin
	4 cups chicken stock

1. Press the "Sauté" button two times to select "Normal" settings and heat the oil. 2. Once hot, cook the onion for about 2 minutes or until softened. 3. Add the garlic, potatoes, carrots, bell pepper, and beets to the inner pot. 4. Add the remaining ingredients to the inner pot and stir until everything is well combined. 5. Put on the pressure cooker's lid and turn the steam valve to "Sealing" position. 6. Select Pressure Cook mode, and then press the "Pressure Cook" button again to select "Less" time option. 7. Use the "+/-" keys on the control panel to set the cooking time to 10 minutes. 8. Press the Pressure Level button to adjust the pressure to "High Pressure." 9. Once the cooking cycle is completed, allow the steam to release naturally. 10. When all the steam is released, remove the pressure lid from the top carefully. 11. To serve, add more salt and vinegar if desired. 12. Bon appétit!
Per Serving: Calories 419; Fat 14g; Sodium 791mg; Carbs 8.9g; Fiber 4.6g; Sugar 8g; Protein 3g

Alfredo Ditalini Soup

Prep time: 15 minutes | Cook time: 25 minutes | Serves: 4

2 tablespoons coconut oil, melted	¼ cup all-purpose flour
1-pound chicken breast, skinless and boneless	4 cups vegetable broth
1 white onion, chopped	2 cups cauliflower florets, frozen
2 cloves garlic, pressed	2 cups Ditalini pasta
12 serrano pepper, minced	1 cup heavy cream
	Sea salt and black pepper, to taste

1. Press the "Sauté" button two times to select "Normal" settings and heat the oil. 2. Once hot, brown the chicken for 3 to 4 minutes per side; set aside. 3. Then, sauté the onion, garlic, and serrano pepper in pan drippings. 4. Add the flour and continue to stir until your veggies are well coated. 5. Add the vegetable broth, cauliflower, and pasta to the inner pot; put the chicken back into the inner pot. 6. Put on the pressure cooker's lid and turn the steam valve to "Sealing" position. 7. Select Pressure Cook mode, and then press the "Pressure Cook" button again to select "Less" time option. 8. Use the "+/-" keys on the control panel to set the cooking time to 6 minutes. 9. Press the Pressure Level button to adjust the pressure to "High Pressure." 10. Once the cooking cycle is completed, quickly and carefully turn the steam release handle from Sealing position to the Venting position. 11. When all the steam is released, remove the pressure lid from the top carefully. 12. Stir in the cauliflower and Ditalini pasta. 13. Choose the "Manual" mode and cook for 5 minutes at High Pressure. 14. Once cooking is complete, use a quick pressure release; carefully remove the lid. 15. Shred the cooked chicken and add it back into the soup. 16. Afterwards, add the heavy cream, salt, and black pepper. 17. Seal the lid and let it sit in the residual heat for 5 minutes. 18. Bon appétit!
Per Serving: Calories 584; Fat 15g; Sodium 441mg; Carbs 17g; Fiber 4.6g; Sugar 5g; Protein 29g

Hamburger Soup

Prep time: 20 minutes | Cook time: 15 minutes | Serves: 5

1 tablespoon olive oil	1 teaspoon fish sauce
1-pound ground beef	1 teaspoon basil
1 leek, diced	½ teaspoons oregano
2 cloves garlic, sliced	2 bay leaves
2 tablespoons cooking sherry	¼ teaspoon paprika
4 cups beef broth	Sea salt and black pepper, to taste
1 can condensed tomato soup	

1. Press the "Sauté" button two times to select "Normal" settings and heat the oil. 2. Once hot, brown the ground beef for 2 to 3 minutes, stirring and crumbling with a wooden spoon. 3. Stir in the leeks and garlic; continue to sauté an additional 2 minutes, stirring continuously. 4. Add a splash of cooking sherry to deglaze the pot. Add the other ingredients to the inner pot. 5. Put on the pressure cooker's lid and turn the steam valve to "Sealing" position. 6. Select Pressure Cook mode, and then press the "Pressure Cook" button again to select "Less" time option. 7. Use the "+/-" keys on the control panel to set the cooking time to 10 minutes. 8. Press the Pressure Level button to adjust the pressure to "High Pressure." 9. Once the cooking cycle is completed, allow the steam to release naturally. 10. When all the steam is released, remove the pressure lid from the top carefully. 11. Serve warm with crusty bread, if desired. 12. Bon appétit!
Per Serving: Calories 449; Fat 2.9g; Sodium 511mg; Carbs 12g; Fiber 3g; Sugar 8g; Protein 28g

Chapter 10 Stock and Sauce Recipes

Homemade Chicken Stock

Prep time: 10 minutes | Cook Time: 40 minutes | Serves: 12 cups

3 pounds chicken wings	2 bay leaves
4 carrots, coarsely chopped	1 teaspoon whole black
4 celery stalks, coarsely chopped	peppercorns
1 yellow onion, skin on, quartered	12 cups water
4 garlic cloves, smashed	

1. In the Inner Pot, combine the chicken wings, carrots, celery, onion, garlic, bay leaves, peppercorns, and water. Cover the lid and lock it 2. Select the Pressure Cook on the panel. Press the button again to choose Normal option; use the "+" button to adjust the cooking time to 40 minutes. Press Pressure Level to choose High pressure. 3. Leave the steam release handle in the Sealing position for 15 minutes after cooking has completed, then quickly and carefully turn the steam release handle from the Sealing position to the Venting position. 4. Open the lid carefully and strain the stock, removing any solids. Put in an airtight container and refrigerate for up to 4 days or freeze it for up to 6 months.
Per Serving: Calories: 15; Fat: 0g; Carbs: 1g; Fiber: 0g; Sugar: 0g; Sodium: 9mg; Protein: 2g

Fresh and Delicious Vegetable Broth

Prep time: 5 minutes | Cook Time: 30 minutes | Serves: 12 cups

8 ounces white mushrooms	2 bay leaves
3 carrots, coarsely chopped	1 tablespoon kosher salt
2 celery stalks, coarsely chopped	½ teaspoon whole peppercorns
1 yellow onion, unpeeled and quartered	10 cups cold water

1. In the Inner Pot, combine the mushrooms, carrots, celery, onion, bay leaves, salt, peppercorns, and water. Cover the lid and lock it 2. Select the Pressure Cook on the panel. Press the button again to choose Normal option; use the "+/-" button to adjust the cooking time to 30 minutes. Press Pressure Level to choose High pressure. 3. When the cook time is complete, quickly and carefully turn the steam release handle from the Sealing position to the Venting position. 4. Open the lid carefully and strain the broth, removing the solids. Refrigerate the broth for up to 1 week or freeze it for up to 3 months.
Per Serving: Calories: 12; Fat: 0g; Carbs: 3g; Fiber: 0g; Sugar: 1g; Sodium: 290mg; Protein: 0g

Simple Meaty Spaghetti Sauce

Prep time: 10 minutes | Cook Time: 25 minutes | Serves: 6-8

1 pound ground beef	1 teaspoon dried basil
1 medium onion, chopped	1 teaspoon salt
4 garlic cloves, finely chopped	½ teaspoon dried oregano
¼ cup dry red wine	¼ teaspoon freshly ground black
10 to 12 tomatoes, chopped	pepper
¼ cup tomato paste	

1. Insert the inner pot into the cooker base. 2. Press Sauté to select the program and press again to choose Normal option. Sauté the ground beef and onion for 5 minutes. Add the garlic and sauté for 2 more minutes. 3. Pour the red wine into the pot and scrape the bottom of the pot with a wooden spoon to loosen any browned bits. Simmer for another 2 minutes. 4. Add the tomatoes, tomato paste, basil, salt, oregano, and pepper to the pot and stir well. 5. Press the Cancel button to stop this cooking program. 6. Put the lid in place and lock

it, and select the Pressure Cook on the panel. Press the button again to choose Less option; use the "-" button to adjust the cooking time to 15 minutes. Press Pressure Level to choose High pressure. 7. When the cooking time ends, leave the steam release handle in the Sealing position for 10 minutes and then quickly and carefully turn the steam release handle from Sealing position to the Venting position. 8. Remove the lid and stir the sauce.
Per Serving: Calories: 179; Fat: 6g; Sodium: 469mg; Carbs: 14g; Sugar: 1g; Fiber: 4g; Protein: 18g

Homemade Smoky Barbecue Sauce

Prep time: 5 minutes | Cook Time: 15 minutes | Serves: 12

1 tablespoon olive oil	⅓ cup water
½ red onion, finely chopped	⅓ cup pure maple syrup
2 garlic cloves, minced	¼ cup apple cider vinegar
1 cup Sugar-Free Ketchup or	2 teaspoons Dijon mustard
store-bought no-sugar-added	¼ teaspoon liquid smoke
ketchup	

1. Insert the inner pot into the cooker base. 2. Press Sauté to select the program and then press it again to choose the Normal temperature option. Pour the olive oil into the Inner Pot and heat it. When the oil is hot, add the onion and garlic. Cook for 3 to 4 minutes, stirring frequently, until softened. Press Cancel. 3. Add the ketchup, water, maple syrup, vinegar, mustard, and liquid smoke; stir to combine. Cover the lid and lock it 4. Select the Pressure Cook on the panel. Press the button again to choose Less option; use the "-" button to adjust the cooking time to 10 minutes. Press Pressure Level to choose High pressure. 5. When the cook time is complete, quickly and carefully turn the steam release handle from Sealing position to the Venting position. 6. Open the lid carefully and serve. Store leftovers in an airtight container in the refrigerator for about 1 week.
Per Serving: Calories: 42; Fat: 1g; Carbs: 8g; Fiber: 0g; Sugar: 6g; Sodium: 13mg; Protein: 0g

Homemade Country Sausage Gravy

Prep time: 5 minutes | Cook Time: 8 minutes | Serves: 6

1-pound pork breakfast sausage	½ teaspoon freshly ground black
¼ cup chicken broth, store-bought	pepper
or homemade (here)	¼ teaspoon garlic powder
½ cup all-purpose flour	¼ teaspoon onion powder
3 cups milk	⅛ teaspoon dried sage
1 teaspoon salt	

1. Insert the inner pot into the cooker base. 2. Press Sauté to select the program and press it again to choose Normal option. Pour the oil into the Inner Pot and heat it. Add the sausage to the pot and sauté for 5 minutes, stirring until evenly browned and crumbled. 3. Press the Cancel button. 4. Pour the chicken broth into the pot and scrape the bottom of the pot with a wooden spoon to loosen any browned bits. 5. Put the lid in place and lock it. 6. Select the Pressure Cook on the panel. Press the button again to choose Less option; use the "-" button to adjust the cooking time to 3 minutes. Press Pressure Level to choose High pressure. 7. When the cooking time ends, leave the steam release handle in the Sealing position for 10 minutes and then quickly and carefully turn the steam release handle from the Sealing position to the Venting position. 8. Open the lid, press Sauté to select the program and press again to choose Less option, and stir the flour into the sausage mixture. Stir in the milk, salt, pepper, garlic powder, onion powder, and sage. 9. Simmer and stir regularly for 5 minutes until the sauce thickens. 10. When done, serve and enjoy.
Per Serving: Calories: 288; Fat: 19g; Sodium: 743mg; Carbs: 15g; Sugar: 1g; Fiber: 0g; Protein: 17g

Tasty Salsa

Prep time: 5 minutes | Cook Time: 10 minutes | Serves: 4 cups

1 (28-ounce) can whole peeled tomatoes	1 bunch fresh cilantro, chopped
1 green bell pepper, seeded and chopped	1 tablespoon freshly squeezed lime juice
1 sweet onion, diced	1 teaspoon hot sauce
4 garlic cloves, minced	½ teaspoon kosher salt

1. In the Inner Pot, combine the tomatoes with their juices, bell pepper, onion, and garlic. Cover the lid and lock it 2. Select the Pressure Cook on the panel. Press the button again to choose Less option; use the "-" button to adjust the cooking time to 10 minutes. Press Pressure Level to choose High pressure. 3. When the cook time is complete, let the pressure release Leave the steam release handle in the Sealing position for 10 minutes, then quickly and carefully turn the steam release handle from Sealing position to the Venting position. 4. Open the lid carefully and stir in the cilantro, lime juice, hot sauce, and salt. Let the salsa cool for about 10 minutes, then refrigerate it for 1 hour before serving. 5. Refrigerate the leftovers in an airtight container for up to 5 days.

Per Serving: Calories: 18; Fat: 0g; Carbs: 4g; Fiber: 1g; Sugar: 3g; Sodium: 46mg; Protein: 1g

Delicious Chicken and Vegetable Stock

Prep time: 30 minutes | Cook Time: 40 minutes | Serves: 9

1 chicken carcass	1 teaspoon mixed peppercorns
2 carrots, cut into 2-inch pieces	1 bay leaf
1 celery rib, cut into 2-inch pieces	1 bunch parsley
1 large onion, quartered	9 cups cold water
Sea salt, to taste	

1. Place all ingredients in the inner pot. 2. Put the lid in place and lock it. Select the Soup/Broth on the panel. Press the button again to adjust the cooking time to 40 minutes. Press Pressure Level to choose High pressure. 3. Once cooking is complete, leave the steam release handle in the Sealing position; open the lid carefully. 4. Remove the bones and vegetables with a slotted spoon. Use immediately or store for later use.

Per Serving: Calories: 87; Fat: 0g; Sodium: 1mg; Carbs: 15g; Sugar: 1g; Fiber: 1g; Protein: 1g

Homemade Chipotle Barbecue Sauce

Prep time: 5 minutes | Cook Time: 12 minutes | Serves: 5 cups

½ medium onion, coarsely chopped	½ cup apple cider vinegar
4 canned chipotle chilies in adobo sauce	3 teaspoons ground mustard
3 garlic cloves, coarsely chopped	1 teaspoon salt
4 cups tomato sauce	½ teaspoon freshly ground black pepper
½ cup molasses	¼ teaspoon garlic powder
	¼ teaspoon onion powder

1. Purée the onion, chipotle chilies and garlic cloves in a food processor. Put the mixture into the Inner Pot. 2. Put the tomato sauce, molasses, and apple cider vinegar to the pot and stir well. 3. Stir in the ground mustard, salt, pepper, garlic powder, and onion powder. 4. Put the lid in place and lock it. Select the Pressure Cook on the panel. Press the button again to choose Less option; use the "-" button to adjust the cooking time to 12 minutes. Press Pressure Level to choose High pressure. 5. When the cooking time ends, leave the steam release handle in the Sealing position for about 30 minutes. 6. Recover the lid and sit to cool and then you can put it into jars and place them in the refrigerator.

Per Serving: Calories: 51; Fat: 0g; Sodium: 176mg; Carbs: 11g; Sugar: 1g; Fiber: 1g; Protein: 1g

Homemade Sugar-Free Ketchup

Prep time: 5 minutes | Cook Time: 20 minutes | Serves: 12

1 (28-ounce) can crushed tomatoes	¼ cup apple cider vinegar
1 yellow onion, quartered	¼ teaspoon paprika
4 pitted dates	¼ teaspoon garlic powder
	¼ teaspoon kosher salt

1. In the Inner Pot, combine the tomatoes, onion, dates, vinegar, paprika, garlic powder, and salt. Cover the lid and lock it 2. Select the Pressure Cook on the panel. Press the button again to choose Less option; use the "+/-" button to adjust the cooking time to 5 minutes. Press Pressure Level to choose High pressure. 3. When the cook time is complete, quickly and carefully turn the steam release handle from the Sealing position to the Venting position. Press Cancel. 4. Open the lid carefully and remove the onion. Insert the inner pot into the cooker base. 5. Press Sauté to select the program and press again to choose Less option. Simmer for 15 minutes, stirring now and then, until thickened. 6. Transfer the ketchup to an airtight container and refrigerate it for up to 2 weeks.

Per Serving: Calories: 33; Fat: 0g; Carbs: 8g; Fiber: 2g; Sugar: 5g; Sodium: 150mg; Protein: 1g

Simple Vegetable Broth

Prep time: 5 minutes | Cook Time: 40 minutes | Serves: 10 cups

About 8 cups mixed vegetable scraps	10 cups water

1. Put the vegetable scraps into the pressure cooker pot, then add some water to make sure the water does not exceed your pot's maximum fill line. 2. Put the lid in place and lock it. Select the Pressure Cook on the panel. Press the button again to choose Less option; use the "-" button to adjust the cooking time to 40 minutes. Press Pressure Level to choose High pressure. It will take 23 to 28 minutes for the pot to come to pressure before the cooking time begins. 3. Leave the steam release handle in the Sealing position for 5 minutes and then quickly and carefully turn the steam release handle from Sealing position to the Venting position. (which will take an additional 3 to 4 minutes). 4. Set a colander over a large bowl and pour in the contents of the pot. Remove the solids. 5. Let the Broth sit for about 20 minutes before putting it to the fridge to cool. Portion into glass jars or plastic freezer bags to refrigerate or freeze.

Per Serving: Calories: 20; Fat: 0g; Sodium: 42mg; Carbs: 2g; Sugar: 5g; Fiber: 0g; Protein: 2g

Delicious Chicken Broth

Prep time: 15 minutes | Cook Time: 40 minutes | Serves: 10 cups

2½ pounds bone-in, skin-on chicken parts	pieces
	½ teaspoon whole black peppercorns
1 onion, peeled and quartered	1 bay leaf
1 celery stalk, cut into 2-inch pieces	10 cups water
1 carrot, peeled and cut into 2-inch	

1. Put the chicken, onion, celery, carrots, peppercorns, and bay leaf in the pressure cooker pot, then add some water to make sure the water does not exceed your pot's maximum fill line. 2. Put the lid in place and lock it. Press the button again to choose Normal option; use the "+" button to adjust the cooking time to 40 minutes. Press Pressure Level to choose High pressure. 3. Leave the steam release handle in the Sealing position for about 30 minutes and then tap or lightly shake the pot before removing the lid. 4. Put a colander over a bowl and dump in the food the pot. Remove the solids. 5. Let the Broth sit for about 30 minutes, then skim and remove the layer of; Fat on the surface. Put into the refrigerator to cool. Portion into glass jars or plastic freezer bags to refrigerate or freeze.

Per Serving: Calories: 35; Fat: 1g; Sodium: 54mg; Carbs: 1g; Sugar: 5g; Fiber: 0g; Protein: 5g

Perfect French Brown Stock

Prep time: 15 minutes | Cook Time: 2 hours| Serves: 10

3 pounds meaty pork bones	2 brown onions, quartered
2 carrots, chopped	1 tablespoon olive oil
1 celery stalk, chopped	

1. Add all ingredients to the inner pot of your Inner Pot. 2. Put the lid in place and lock it. Select the Soup/Broth on the panel. Press the button again to adjust the cooking time to 120 minutes. Press Pressure Level to choose Low pressure. 3. Once cooking is complete, leave the steam release handle in the Sealing position for 10 minutes. Open the lid carefully. 4. Remove the bones and vegetables using a metal spoon with holes and discard. Pour the liquid through the sieve into the bowl. 5. Use immediately or store in your refrigerator.
Per Serving: Calories 13; Fat 2.3g; Sodium 95mg; Carbs 2.4g; Fiber 1g; Sugars 1.5g; Protein 1.4g

Basic and Delicious Beans

Prep time: 5 minutes | Cook Time: 35 minutes | Serves: 6 cups

1-pound dried beans	2 bay leaves
4 cups vegetable broth or store-bought low-sodium vegetable broth, or water	2 teaspoons olive oil
	½ teaspoon kosher salt

1. Combine the dried beans, broth, bay leaves, olive oil, and salt in the Inner Pot. Cover the lid and lock it 2. Select the Pressure Cook on the panel. Press the button again to choose Normal option. Press Pressure Level to choose High pressure. 3. Leave the steam release handle in the Sealing position for 15 minutes after cooking has completed, then turn the steam release handle to the Venting position. 4. Open the lid carefully and remove the bay leaves.
Per Serving: Calories: 133; Fat: 1g; Carbs: 23g; Fiber: 6g; Sugar: 1g; Sodium: 55mg; Protein: 9g

Perfect Chicken and Herb Broth

Prep time: 15 minutes | Cook Time: 2 hours| Serves: 10

Chicken bones from 3 pounds roast chicken	2 tablespoons fresh coriander
1 parsnip	1 teaspoon fresh dill
1 celery	2 tablespoons cider vinegar
2 tablespoons fresh parsley	1 teaspoon sea salt
1 tablespoon fresh thyme	1 teaspoon ground black pepper

1. Place all ingredients in the Inner Pot. Add cold water until the pot is ⅔ full. 2. Put the lid in place and lock it. Select the Soup/Broth on the panel. Press the button again to adjust the cooking time to 120 minutes. Press Pressure Level to choose Low pressure. 3. Once cooking is complete, leave the steam release handle in the Sealing position for 10 minutes; Open the lid carefully. 4. Remove the bones and vegetables using a metal spoon with holes and discard. Pour the liquid through the sieve into the bowl. 5. Use immediately or store in your refrigerator.
Per Serving: Calories 69; Fat 3g; Sodium 255mg; Carbs 8.4g; Fiber 1g; Sugars 1g; Protein 1g

Homemade Marinara Sauce

Prep time: 5 minutes | Cook Time: 24 minutes | Serves: 4 cups

1 tablespoon olive oil	½ cup Vegetable Broth or store-bought low-sodium vegetable broth
1 yellow onion, finely chopped	
5 garlic cloves, minced	
3 pounds plum tomatoes, quartered	2 tablespoons double concentrated tomato paste

1. Insert the inner pot into the cooker base. Connect the power cord to a 120 V power source. The cooker goes to Standby mode and the display indicates OFF. Press Sauté to select the program and then press it again to choose the Normal temperature option 2. Pour the olive oil into the Inner Pot and heat it. When the oil is hot, add the onion and garlic. Cook for 3 to 4 minutes, stirring now and then, until softened. Press Cancel. 3. Add the tomatoes, broth, and tomato paste. Cover the lid and lock it 4. Select the Pressure Cook on the panel. Press the button again to choose Less option. Press Pressure Level to choose High pressure. 5. When the cook time is complete, quickly and carefully turn the steam release handle from Sealing position to the Venting position. 6. Open the lid carefully and stir, pressing down on any large pieces of tomato to break them down. For a smoother sauce, use an immersion blender to blend to your desired consistency. Refrigerate the marinara sauce for up to 1 week or freeze it for up to 3 months.
Per Serving: Calories: 29; Fat: 1g; Carbs: 5g; Fiber: 1g; Sugar: 3g; Sodium: 6mg; Protein: 1g

Perfect Vegan Tikka Masala Sauce

Prep time: 15 minutes | Cook Time: 15 minutes | Serves: 4

2 teaspoons olive oil	to taste
1 onion, chopped	1 teaspoon cayenne pepper
4 cloves garlic, chopped	1 teaspoon coriander powder
1 (1-inch) piece fresh ginger, peeled and grated	½ teaspoon turmeric powder
1 bird's eye chili, minced	1 teaspoon Garam Masala
1 bell pepper, seeded and chopped	2 ripe tomatoes, pureed
Sea salt and ground black pepper,	1 cup vegetable broth
	1 cup plain coconut yogurt

1. Insert the inner pot into the cooker base. 2. Press Sauté to select the program and press it again to choose Normal option. Add the oil and sauté the onion for about 3 minutes or until tender and fragrant. 3. Now, add the garlic, ginger and peppers; continue to sauté an additional minute or until they are aromatic. 4. Add the spices, tomatoes, and broth. 5. Put the lid in place and lock it. Select the Pressure Cook on the panel. Press the button again to choose Less option; use the "+/-" button to adjust the cooking time to 11 minutes. Press Pressure Level to choose High pressure. 6. Once cooking is complete, leave the steam release handle in the Sealing position for 10 minutes. Open the lid carefully. 7. Afterwards, add the coconut yogurt to the inner pot and stir to combine. 8. Serve with chickpeas or roasted vegetables.
Per Serving: Calories 206; Fat 17.3g; Sodium 195mg; Carbs 12.4g; Fiber 1g; Sugars 6.5g; Protein 4g

Perfect Sicilian-Style Meat Sauce

Prep time: 15 minutes | Cook Time: 40 minutes | Serves: 10

2 tablespoons olive oil	2 tablespoons fresh cilantro, chopped
2 ½ pounds pork butt	
1 onion, chopped	1 teaspoon dried basil
4 garlic cloves, pressed	1 teaspoon dried rosemary
¼ cup Malvasia wine, or other Sicilian wine	½ teaspoon cayenne pepper
	½ teaspoon black pepper, freshly cracked
2 fresh tomatoes, pureed	
5 ounces tomato paste	½ teaspoon salt
2 bay leaves	1 cup chicken broth

1. Insert the inner pot into the cooker base. 2. Press Sauté to select the program and press it again to choose Normal option, then add and heat the oil. When the oil starts to sizzle, cook the pork until no longer pink. 3. Add the onion and garlic and continue to cook for a few minutes more or until they are tender. Add a splash of wine to deglaze the pot. 4. Stir in the other ingredients. 5. Put the lid in place and lock it. Select the Meat/Stew on the panel. Press the button again to choose Normal option. Press Pressure Level to choose High pressure. 6. Once cooking is complete, leave the steam release handle in the Sealing position for 15 minutes. Open the lid carefully. 7. Next, remove the meat from the inner pot; shred the meat, removing the bones. Return the meat to your sauce.
Per Serving: Calories 378; Fat 24.3g; Sodium 127mg; Carbs 4.4g; Fiber 1g; Sugars 1.1g; Protein 34g

Fresh and Delicious Berry Compote

Prep time: 5 minutes | Cook Time: 1 minutes | Serves: 2 cups

1-pound fresh blueberries, raspberries, blackberries, and/or sliced strawberries	¼ cup sugar 1 teaspoon grated lemon zest 2 tablespoons fresh lemon juice

1. Put the berries in the pressure cooker pot and sprinkle the sugar evenly over them. Let the food sit for 10 minutes. 2. Stir in the lemon zest and juice. 3. Put the lid in place and lock it, Select the Pressure Cook on the panel. Press the button Again to choose Less option; use the "-" button to adjust the cooking time to 1 minutes. Press Pressure Level to choose High pressure. 4. When the cooking time ends, leave the steam release handle in the Sealing position for 10 minutes and then quickly and carefully turn the steam release handle from Sealing position to the Venting position. 5. Remove the lid and stir the compote. Once cooled, it can be used immediately as a breakfast or dessert topping, or in a jar in the refrigerator if you plan to serve it later.
Per Serving: Calories: 57; Fat: 0g; Sodium: 1mg; Carbs: 15g; Sugar: 1g; Fiber: 1g; Protein: 1g

Homemade Shrimp Stock

Prep time: 15 minutes | Cook Time: 30 minutes | Serves: 8

Shrimp shells from 3 pounds shrimp 8 cups water ½ cup cilantro, chopped 2 celery stalks, diced 4 cloves garlic	1 onion, quartered 1 teaspoon mixed peppercorns 1 tablespoon sea salt 2 bay leaves 4 tablespoons olive oil

1. Add all ingredients to the inner pot. 2. Put the lid in place and lock it. Select the Soup/Broth on the panel. Press the button again to choose Less option and use the "+/-" buttons to adjust the cooking time to 30 minutes. Press Pressure Level to choose High pressure. 3. Once cooking is complete, leave the steam release handle in the Sealing position. Open the lid carefully. 4. Strain the shrimp shells and vegetables using a colander.
Per Serving: Calories 69; Fat 6.3g; Sodium 255mg; Carbs 1.4g; Fiber 1g; Sugars 0.5g; Protein 0.4g

Homemade Ketchup

Prep time: 20 minutes | Cook time: 15 minutes | Serves: 8

2 tablespoons olive oil 1 medium onion, finely chopped 4 garlic cloves, smashed 1 (28-ounce) can whole tomatoes with juice ½ cup red wine vinegar 1 tablespoon tomato paste	1 teaspoon Worcestershire sauce ⅓ cup packed brown sugar ½ teaspoon paprika ¼ teaspoon white pepper ⅛ teaspoon ground allspice Pinch kosher salt

1. Press the "Sauté" button twice to select "Normal" mode. 2. Once hot, add the oil followed by the onion. 3. Cook for 3 minutes until the onion is starting to turn translucent. Add the garlic and sauté 1 minute more. 4. Add the tomatoes with juice, crushing the tomatoes with your hand as you add them. 5. Add the vinegar, tomato paste, Worcestershire sauce, brown sugar, paprika, white pepper, and allspice and bring to a simmer. Add a pinch of salt. 6. Put on the pressure cooker's lid and turn the steam valve to "Sealing" position. 7. Set the Instant Pot to Pressure Cook. 8. Use the "+/-" keys on the control panel to set the cooking time to 15 minutes. 9. Press the Pressure Level button to adjust the pressure to "High". 10. Once the cooking cycle is completed, allow the steam to release naturally. 11. When all the steam is released, remove the pressure lid from the top carefully. 12. Remove the lid and stir. Taste for seasoning. 13. Press the "Sauté" button twice to select "Normal" mode and cook, for 15 to 20 minutes. 14. Use an immersion blender to blend until smooth, or blend in a food processor. 15. Let it cool and store it in the refrigerator for up to 1 month or the freezer for several months.

Per Serving: Calories 84; Fat 15g; Sodium 441mg; Carbs 17g; Fiber 4.6g; Sugar 5g; Protein 29g

Delicious Court Bouillon

Prep time: 15 minutes | Cook Time: 30 minutes | Serves: 8

1 tablespoon salt 1 teaspoon mixed peppercorns 1 cup white wine 2 onions, sliced 2 celery ribs, sliced 2 carrots, sliced	2 bay leaves 2 sprig fresh rosemary A bunch of fresh parsley 1 lemon, sliced 2 tablespoons olive oil

1. Add all ingredients to the inner pot of your Inner Pot. Add cold water until the inner pot is ⅔ full. 2. Put the lid in place and lock it. Select the Soup/Broth on the panel. Press the button again to choose Normal option. Press Pressure Level to choose High pressure. 3. Once cooking is complete, leave the steam release handle in the Sealing position. 10 minutes. Open the lid carefully. 4. Remove the vegetables.
Per Serving: Calories 55; Fat 3.3g; Sodium 205mg; Carbs 0.4g; Fiber 1g; Sugars 1.5g; Protein 0.6g

Delicious Roasted Vegetable Stock

Prep time: 10 minutes | Cook Time: 65 minutes | Serves: 10

4 carrots, cut into 2-inch pieces 4 medium celery ribs, cut into 2-inch pieces 2 onions, peeled and quartered 2 sprigs fresh rosemary 2 sprigs fresh thyme	3 tablespoons olive oil Kosher salt and black peppercorns, to taste 1 cup dry white wine 10 cups water

1. Start by preheating your oven to 400 degrees F. Grease a large roasting pan with cooking spray 2. Place carrots, celery, onions and herbs in prepared baking pan. Roast for 35 minutes, tossing halfway through the cooking time, until the vegetables are tender. 3. Transfer the vegetables to the inner pot. Put the remaining ingredients into the Inner Pot. 4. Put the lid in place and lock it. Select the Soup/Broth on the panel. Press the button again to choose Normal option. Press Pressure Level to choose High pressure. 5. Once cooking is complete, leave the steam release handle in the Sealing position for 10 minutes; Open the lid carefully. 6. Strain the broth through a fine-mesh sieve and remove the solids. 7. Let it cool completely before storing.
Per Serving: Calories 56; Fat 1.3g; Sodium 195mg; Carbs 4.4g; Fiber 1g; Sugars 3.5g; Protein 0.4g

Homemade Beef Bone Broth

Prep time: 15 minutes | Cook Time: 2 hours 50 minutes | Serves: 8

3 pounds frozen beef bones 2 onions, halved 2 stalks celery, chopped 2 carrots, chopped 4 cloves garlic, whole	2 bay leaves 2 tablespoons apple cider vinegar 1 teaspoon sea salt 1 teaspoon black pepper 8 cups water

1. Preheat your oven to 390 degrees F. Line a baking sheet with aluminum foil. 2. Place the beef bones, onions, celery, carrots, and garlic on the baking pan. Roast for 40 to 45 minutes. 3. Transfer the roasted beef bones and vegetables to the inner pot of your Inner Pot. Add the bay leaves, apple cider vinegar, sea salt, pepper, and boiling water to the inner pot. 4. Put the lid in place and lock it. Select the Pressure Cook on the panel. Press the button again to choose More option; use the "+/-" button to adjust the cooking time to 120 minutes. Press Pressure Level to choose High pressure. 5. Once cooking is complete, leave the steam release handle in the Sealing position for 20 minutes. Open the lid carefully. 6. Remove the beef bones and vegetables and discard. Pour the broth through a strainer. 7. Enjoy,
Per Serving: Calories 65; Fat 2.4g; Sodium 200mg; Carbs 6.7g; Fiber 1g; Sugars 1.5g; Protein 6.4g

White Chicken Stock

Prep time: 20 minutes | Cook Time: 40 minutes | Serves: 10

2 pounds chicken white meat
1 white onion, quartered
1 leek, white parts
2 parsnips, sliced thickly
1 celery rib, sliced thickly

2 bay leaves
2 stalks flat-leaf parsley
½ teaspoon dried dill weed
1 teaspoon mixed peppercorns

1. Add all ingredients to the inner pot. 2. Put the lid in place and lock it. Select the Soup/Broth on the panel. Press the button again to choose Normal option and use the "+/-" buttons to adjust the cooking time to 40 minutes. Press Pressure Level to choose High pressure. 3. Once cooking is complete, leave the steam release handle in the Sealing position for 20 minutes; open the lid carefully. 4. Remove the vegetables and bones; save the chicken meat for later use.
Per Serving: Calories 53; Fat 1g; Sodium 95mg; Carbs 1.4g; Fiber 1g; Sugars 1.5g; Protein 1.4g

Homemade Pork Stock

Prep time: 15 minutes | Cook Time: 55 minutes | Serves: 10

2 pounds pork bones
4 celery stalks, cut into large chunks
4 carrots, cut into large chunks
1 onion, quartered

3 garlic cloves, smashed
2 bay leaves
Sea salt and black peppercorns, to taste
10 cups water, divided in half

1. Preheat your oven to 400 degrees F. Coat a roasting pan with a piece of aluminum foil; brush with a little oil. 2. Arrange pork bones and vegetables on prepared baking sheet. Bake in preheated oven for 25 to 30 minutes. 3. Transfer the roasted pork bones and vegetables to the inner pot of your Inner Pot. Now, stir in the bay leaves, salt, black peppercorns, and water. 4. Put the lid in place and lock it. Select the Pressure Cook on the panel. Press the button again to choose Less option; use the "+/-" button to adjust the cooking time to 25 minutes. Press Pressure Level to choose High pressure. 5. Once cooking is complete, quickly and carefully turn the steam release handle from Sealing position to the Venting position. Open the lid carefully. 6. Strain the stock and remove the solids. 7. Keep in your refrigerator or freezer if desired.
Per Serving: Calories 91; Fat 4.3g; Sodium 157mg; Carbs 3.3g; Fiber 1g; Sugars 1.5g; Protein 9.9g

Homemade Spanish Chorizo Sauce

Prep time: 10 minutes | Cook Time: 10 minutes | Serves: 4

1 tablespoon olive oil
1-pound Chorizo sausage, sliced
1 onion, chopped
1 teaspoon garlic, minced
1 sweet pepper, seeded and finely chopped
1 habanero pepper, seeded and minced
2 tablespoons sugar

1 teaspoon dried basil
1 teaspoon dried rosemary
1 teaspoon red pepper flakes
Sea salt and freshly ground black pepper, to taste
1 (28-ounce) can diced tomatoes, with juice
1 cup chicken broth

1. Insert the inner pot into the cooker base. Connect the power cord to a 120 V power source. The cooker goes to Standby mode and the display indicates OFF. 2. Press Sauté to select the program and press it again to choose Normal option, then add and heat the oil. When the oil starts to sizzle, cook the Chorizo until no longer pink; crumble it with a wooden spatula. 3. Add the onion, garlic, and peppers and cook for a minute or so. Add a splash of chicken broth to deglaze the pan. 4. Stir in the remaining ingredients. 5. Put the lid in place and lock it. Select the Pressure Cook on the panel. Press the button again to choose Less option; use the "-" button to adjust the cooking time to 6 minutes. 6. Press Pressure Level to choose High pressure. Once cooking is complete, leave the steam release handle in the Sealing position for 10 minutes; Open the lid carefully. 7. Serve and enjoy.
Per Serving: Calories 385; Fat 24.3g; Sodium 124mg; Carbs 20.4g; Fiber 1g; Sugars 11.5g; Protein 21.4g

Delicious Herby Tomato Sauce

Prep time: 10 minutes | Cook Time: 45 minutes | Serves: 6

2 (28-ounce) cans tomatoes, crushed
3 tablespoons olive oil
3 cloves garlic, minced
½ teaspoon dried rosemary
½ teaspoon dried basil
½ tablespoon dried oregano

1 onion, quartered
Kosher salt and freshly ground black pepper, to taste
1 teaspoon tamari sauce
2 tablespoons fresh parsley leaves, finely chopped

1. Reserve 1 cup of the crushed tomatoes. 2. Insert the inner pot into the cooker base. 3. Press Sauté to select the program and press it again to choose Normal option, then add and heat olive oil. Once hot, cook the garlic for a minute or so or until it is fragrant but not browned. 4. Now, stir in the rosemary, basil, and oregano; continue to sauté for 30 seconds more. Stir in the tomatoes, onion, salt, and pepper. 5. Put the lid in place and lock it. Select the Soup/Broth on the panel. Press the button again to choose Normal option; use the "+/-" button to adjust the cooking time to 40 minutes. Press Pressure Level to choose High pressure. 6. Once cooking is complete, quickly and carefully turn the steam release handle from Sealing position to the Venting position. Open the lid carefully. 7. Add the reserved tomatoes, tamari sauce and parsley to your tomato sauce.
Per Serving: Calories 115; Fat 7.3g; Sodium 168mg; Carbs5.4g; Fiber 1g; Sugars 3.5g; Protein 2.4g

Perfect Mixed Berry Sauce

Prep time: 15 minutes | Cook Time: 10 minutes | Serves: 12

2 cups frozen blueberries, thawed
2 cups frozen raspberries, thawed
2 cups frozen strawberries, thawed
½ cup granulated sugar

1 teaspoon cornstarch
1 cup water
2 tablespoons orange juice
½ cup cream cheese, at room temperature

1. Add the berries, sugar, and cornstarch, and water to the Inner Pot; stir to combine. 2. Put the lid in place and lock it. Select the Pressure Cook on the panel. Press the button again to choose Less option; use the "-" button to adjust the cooking time to 10 minutes. Press Pressure Level to choose High pressure. 3. Once cooking is complete, leave the steam release handle in the Sealing position for 10 minutes. Open the lid carefully. 4. Stir in the orange juice and cream cheese; stir to combine and serve with waffles or pancakes.
Per Serving: Calories 117; Fat 3g; Sodium 115mg; Carbs 22.4g; Fiber 1g; Sugars 1.5g; Protein 17.4g

Simple Chicken Ragù

Prep time: 10 minutes | Cook Time: 10 minutes | Serves: 4

2 tablespoons olive oil
1-pound ground chicken
1 onion, chopped
2 cloves garlic, minced
¼ cup dry red wine
1 stalk celery, chopped
1 bell pepper, chopped
1 teaspoon fresh basil, chopped

1 teaspoon fresh rosemary, chopped
1 teaspoon cayenne pepper
Salt and fresh ground pepper to taste
2 cups tomato sauce
1 cup chicken bone broth

1. Insert the inner pot into the cooker base. 2. Press Sauté to select the program and press it again to choose Normal option, then add and heat the oil. When the oil starts to sizzle, cook the ground chicken until no longer pink; crumble it with a wooden spatula. 3. Add the onion and garlic to the browned chicken; let it cook for a minute or so. Add a splash of wine to deglaze the pan. 4. Stir in the remaining ingredients. 5. Put the lid in place and lock it. Select the Pressure Cook on the panel. Press the button again to choose Less option; use the "-" button to adjust the cooking time to 6 minutes. Press Pressure Level to choose High pressure. 6. Once cooking is complete, leave the steam release handle in the Sealing position for 10 minutes; Open the lid carefully. 7. Serve and enjoy.
Per Serving: Calories 431; Fat 18g; Sodium 152mg; Carbs 33.4g; Fiber 1g; Sugars 17.5g; Protein 27g

Simple Carolina-Style Sticky Barbecue Sauce

Prep time: 10 minutes | Cook Time: 10 minutes | Serves: 8

2 tablespoons butter
1 shallot, chopped
2 cloves garlic, minced
2 cups tomato sauce
½ cup cider vinegar
2 tablespoons coconut sugar
⅓ cup molasses
2 tablespoons Worcestershire

sauce
1 teaspoon yellow mustard
1 teaspoon hot sauce
Kosher salt and ground black pepper
½ teaspoon paprika
1 cup vegetable broth

1. Insert the inner pot into the cooker base. 2. Press Sauté to select the program and press it again to choose Normal option, then add and melt the butter. Sauté the shallot for 4 minutes until tender and translucent. Add the garlic and cook for a further 30 seconds. 3. Stir in the remaining ingredients. 4. Put the lid in place and lock it. Select the Pressure Cook on the panel. Press the button again to choose Less option; use the "+/-" button to adjust the cooking time to 5 minutes. Press Pressure Level to choose High pressure. 5. Once cooking is complete, leave the steam release handle in the Sealing position for 5 minutes; Open the lid carefully.
Per Serving: Calories 215; Fat 4.4g; Sodium 225mg; Carbs 37.4g; Fiber 1g; Sugars 37.5g; Protein 37.4g

Simple Cranberry Sauce

Prep time: 15 minutes | Cook Time: 5 minutes | Serves: 8

1 ½ pounds fresh cranberries, rinsed
2 blood oranges, juiced
1 tablespoon blood orange zest
¾ cup sugar

¼ cup golden cane syrup
2-3 cloves
1 cinnamon stick
1 teaspoon vanilla extract

1. Add the cranberries to the inner pot of your Inner Pot. 2. Put the remaining ingredients into the Inner Pot to the inner pot; stir to combine well. 3. Put the lid in place and lock it. Select the Pressure Cook on the panel. Press the button again to choose Less option; use the "+/-" button to adjust the cooking time to 3 minutes. Press Pressure Level to choose High pressure. 4. Once cooking is complete, leave the steam release handle in the Sealing position for 10 minutes; Open the lid carefully. 5. Let it cool. Serve your sauce chilled or at room temperature.
Per Serving: Calories 125; Fat 13g; Sodium 254mg; Carbs 24.4g; Fiber 1g; Sugars 3.5g; Protein 0.4g

Homemade Beef Bolognese Pasta Sauce

Prep time: 10 minutes | Cook Time: 10 minutes | Serves: 4

2 tablespoons olive oil
1-pound ground beef
1 onion, chopped
1 teaspoon fresh garlic, minced
Sea salt and ground black pepper, to taste
1 teaspoon brown sugar
½ teaspoon dried sage

1 teaspoon dried oregano
1 teaspoon dried basil
½ teaspoon cayenne pepper, or to taste
2 cups beef broth
2 ripe tomatoes, pureed
2 tablespoons tomato ketchup

1. Insert the inner pot into the cooker base. 2. Press Sauté to select the program and press it again to choose Normal option, then add and heat the oil. When the oil starts to sizzle, cook the ground beef until no longer pink; crumble it with a wooden spatula. 3. Add the onion and garlic and continue to cook for a few minutes more or until they are tender and fragrant. Add a splash of beef broth to deglaze the pot. 4. Stir in the remaining ingredients; stir to combine well. 5. Put the lid in place and lock it. Select the Pressure Cook on the panel. Press the button again to choose Less option; use the "-" button to adjust the cooking time to 6 minutes. Press Pressure Level to choose High pressure. Once cooking is complete, leave the steam release handle in the Sealing position. Open the

lid carefully. 6. Serve over pasta if desired.
Per Serving: Calories 358; Fat 20.3g; Sodium 522mg; Carbs 8.4g; Fiber 1g; Sugars 4.5g; Protein 24.4g

Homemade Fish Stock

Prep time: 15 minutes | Cook Time: 40 minutes | Serves: 8

2 pounds meaty bones and heads of halibut, washed
2 lemongrass stalks, chopped
2 carrots, chopped
1 parsnip, chopped

1 onion, quartered
2 sprigs rosemary
2 sprigs thyme
2 tablespoons olive oil

1. Place all ingredients in the inner pot. Add cold water until the pot is ⅔ full. 2. Put the lid in place and lock it. Select the Soup/Broth on the panel. Press the button again to choose Normal option and use the "+/-" buttons to adjust the cooking time to 40 minutes. Press Pressure Level to choose High pressure. 3. Once cooking is complete, leave the steam release handle in the Sealing position. Open the lid carefully. 4. Strain the vegetables and fish. 5. Serve and enjoy.
Per Serving: Calories 63; Fat 3g; Sodium 155mg; Carbs 4.9g; Fiber 1g; Sugars 1.5g; Protein 1.4g

Homemade Eggplant Light Sauce with Wine

Prep time: 5 minutes | Cook Time: 10 minutes | Serves: 6

2 tablespoons olive oil
1-pound eggplants, sliced
4 garlic cloves, minced
2 tomatoes, chopped
1 cup white wine
1 teaspoon oregano
½ teaspoon rosemary

1 teaspoon basil
Sea salt and ground black pepper, to taste
2 tablespoons tahini (sesame butter)
½ cup Romano cheese, freshly grated

1. Insert the inner pot into the cooker base without the lid. 2. Press Sauté to select the program and press it again to choose Normal option, then add and heat the olive oil. Then, cook the eggplant slices until they are charred at the bottom. Work with batches. 3. Add the garlic, tomatoes, wine, and spices. 4. Put the lid in place and lock it. Select the Bean/Chili Cook on the panel. Press the button again to choose Less option; use the "-" button to adjust the cooking time to 3 minutes. Press Pressure Level to choose High pressure. 5. Once cooking is complete, quickly and carefully turn the steam release handle from Sealing position to the Venting position; open the lid carefully. 6. Press the Cancel button to stop this cooking program. 7. Press Sauté to select the program and press it again to choose Normal option, then add to thicken the cooking liquid. Add the tahini paste and stir to combine. 8. Top with Romano cheese and serve.
Per Serving: Calories 147; Fat 10.3g; Sodium 118mg; Carbs 9.4g; Fiber 1g; Sugars 4.5g; Protein 5.4g

Easy Salsa

Prep time: 15 minutes | Cook Time: 25 minutes | Serves: 8

2 onions, chopped
2 garlic cloves, pressed
2 ripe tomatoes, crushed
12 ounces canned tomato paste
2 sweet peppers, chopped
2 chili peppers, chopped

½ cup rice vinegar
2 tablespoons brown sugar
Sea salt and red pepper, to taste
1 teaspoon dried Mexican oregano

1. Put all ingredients into the inner pot of your Inner Pot. 2. Put the lid in place and lock it. Select the Pressure Cook on the panel. Press the button again to choose Less option; use the "+" button to adjust the cooking time to 25 minutes. Press Pressure Level to choose High pressure. 3. Once cooking is complete, leave the steam release handle in the Sealing position for 10 minutes. Open the lid carefully. 4. Allow your salsa to cool completely; store in your refrigerator or freezer.
Per Serving: Calories 83; Fat 0.3g; Sodium 241mg; Carbs 18.4g; Fiber 1g; Sugars 10.5g; Protein 3.4g

Cheese and Bacon Sauce

Prep time: 5 minutes | Cook Time: 10 minutes | Serves: 10

4 ounces bacon, diced	½ teaspoon turmeric powder
1 onion, chopped	Kosher salt and ground black
1 red chili pepper, seeded and minced	pepper, to taste
2 cloves garlic, pressed	1 cup vegetable broth
2 ripe tomatoes, chopped	10 ounces Cottage cheese, at room temperature
½ teaspoon ground cumin	1 cup Pepper Jack cheese, grated

1. Insert the inner pot into the cooker base. 2. Press Sauté to select the program and press it again to choose Normal option, then add to preheat your Inner Pot. Then, cook the bacon for 2 to 3 minutes. Reserve. 3. Add the onion and pepper to the inner pot and continue to cook until they are fragrant. Stir in the garlic and continue to sauté for 30 seconds more. 4. Now, add the tomatoes, spices, and broth. 5. Put the lid in place and lock it. Select the Pressure Cook on the panel. Press the button again to choose Less option; use the "-" button to adjust the cooking time to 5 minutes. Press Pressure Level to choose High pressure. 6. Once cooking is complete, quickly and carefully turn the steam release handle from the Sealing position to the Venting position. Open the lid carefully. 7. Finally, add the cheese. Cover again and let sit in residual heat until cheese is melted. 8. Ladle into a nice serving bowl, top with the reserved bacon, and serve.
Per Serving: Calories 135; Fat 9.5g; Sodium 154mg; Carbs 8.4g; Fiber 1g; Sugars 2.5g; Protein 8.4g

Homemade Black Bean Sauce in Mexican Style

Prep time: 5 minutes | Cook Time: 30 minutes | Serves: 8

2 tablespoons olive oil	Sea salt and ground black pepper, to taste
1 brown onion, chopped	
3 garlic cloves, chopped	1 ½ cups black beans, rinsed, drained
1 jalapeño pepper, seeded and minced	
1 teaspoon dried Mexican oregano	1 ½ cups chicken broth
	¼ cup fresh cilantro, chopped
½ teaspoon ground cumin	½ cup Pico de Gallo

1. Insert the inner pot into the cooker base. 2. Press Sauté to select the program and press it again to choose Normal option, then add and heat the olive oil until sizzling. Once hot, cook the onion for 3 to 4 minutes or until tender and fragrant. 3. After that, stir in the garlic; continue sautéing an additional 30 to 40 seconds. 4. Add the jalapeño pepper, oregano, cumin, salt, black pepper, beans, and broth to the inner pot. 5. Put the lid in place and lock it. Select the Bean/Chili Cook on the panel. Press the button again to choose Less option; press Pressure Level to choose High pressure. Once cooking is complete, quickly and carefully turn the steam release handle from Sealing position to the Venting position. Open the lid carefully. 5. Then, mash your beans with potato masher or use your blender. 6. Serve garnished with cilantro and Pico de Gallo.
Per Serving: Calories 181; Fat 4.3g; Sodium 121mg; Carbs 27.4g; Fiber 1g; Sugars 3.5g; Protein 9.4g

Spinach and Artichoke Dipping Sauce

Prep time: 5 minutes | Cook Time: 10 minutes | Serves: 8

2 tablespoons butter	pepper, to taste
1 onion, chopped	1 teaspoon red pepper flakes
2 cloves garlic, minced	1 pound fresh or frozen spinach leaves
10 ounces artichoke hearts	
1 cup chicken broth	9 ounces cream cheese
Sea salt and freshly ground black	1 cup goat cheese, crumbled

1. Insert the inner pot into the cooker base. 2. Press Sauté to select the program and press it again to choose Normal option, then add and melt the butter. Sauté the onion and garlic until just tender and fragrant. 3. Then, add the artichoke hearts, broth, salt, black pepper,

and red pepper flakes. 4. Press the Cancel button to stop this cooking program. 5. Put the lid in place and lock it. Select the Pressure Cook on the panel. Press the button again to choose Less option; use the "-" button to adjust the cooking time to 5 minutes. Press Pressure Level to choose High pressure. 6. Once cooking is complete, quickly and carefully turn the steam release handle from Sealing position to the Venting position. Open the lid carefully. 7. Add the spinach and cheese to the inner pot; seal the lid and let it sit in the residual heat until thoroughly warmed.
Per Serving: Calories 222; Fat 17g; Sodium 275mg; Carbs 8.4g; Fiber 1g; Sugars 2.5g; Protein 9.4g

Homemade Gravy Sauce

Prep time: 15 minutes | Cook Time: 5 minutes | Serves: 6

3 cups pan juices	Salt and ground black pepper, to taste
⅓ cup cornstarch	
⅓ cup cold water	½ teaspoon cayenne pepper

1. Insert the inner pot into the cooker base. 2. Press Sauté to select the program to and press it again to choose Normal option; cook the pan juices for about 3 minutes, bringing it to a boil. Stir cornstarch with cold water until cornstarch dissolves; then stir cornstarch slurry into pot juices. Add the salt, black pepper, and cayenne pepper; continue cooking on the lowest setting until your sauce has reduced slightly and the flavors have concentrated. 3. Serve and enjoy.
Per Serving: Calories 80; Fat 0.3g; Sodium 254mg; Carbs 21.4g; Fiber 1g; Sugars 13.5g; Protein 0.2g

Delicious Hot Sauce

Prep time: 10 minutes | Cook Time: 30 minutes | Serves: 10

1 tablespoon butter, melted	2 tomatoes, chopped
1 banana shallot, chopped	1 cup white vinegar
1 teaspoon garlic, minced	1 cup water
5 jalapeño peppers, seeded and chopped	2 tablespoons white sugar
5 serrano peppers, seeded and chopped	Sea salt and ground black pepper, to taste

1. Insert the inner pot into the cooker base. 2. Press Sauté to select the program and press it again to choose Normal option, then add and melt the butter. Once hot, cook the shallot for 3 to 4 minute or until it is tender and fragrant. 3. Now, add the garlic and continue to cook an additional 30 seconds or until aromatic. 4. Put the remaining ingredients into the Inner Pot. 5. Put the lid in place and lock it. Select the Pressure Cook on the panel. Press the button again to choose Normal option; use the "-" button to adjust the cooking time to 25 minutes. Press Pressure Level to choose High pressure. 6. Once cooking is complete, leave the steam release handle in the Sealing position for 10 minutes. Open the lid carefully. 7. Let it cool. Serve your sauce hot or at room temperature.
Per Serving: Calories 33; Fat 1.3g; Sodium 195mg; Carbs 4.4g; Fiber 1g; Sugars 3.5g; Protein 0.4g

Simple Salted Caramel Sauce

Prep time: 10 minutes | Cook Time: 5 minutes | Serves:6

½ cup water	½ cup heavy whipping cream
1 ⅓ cups granulated sugar	½ teaspoon coarse sea salt
4 tablespoons butter, cut into small pieces	1 teaspoon vanilla
	A pinch of cardamom

1. Insert the inner pot into the cooker base. 2. Press Sauté to select the program and press it again to choose Normal option. Cook the sugar and water, stirring frequently, until the sugar has dissolved. 3. Let the mixture boiling until it turns an amber color. 4. Add the butter followed by the rest of the ingredients. 5. Allow your sauce to cool. It will thicken up once it's cooled in your refrigerator.
Per Serving: Calories 191; Fat 11.3g; Sodium 170mg; Carbs 22.4g; Fiber 1g; Sugars 22.5g; Protein 0.3g

Perfect Applesauce with Dates

Prep time: 15 minutes | Cook Time: 10 minutes | Serves: 8

6 Honeycrisp apples, peeled, cored and chopped
1 cup water
1 tablespoon fresh lemon juice
¼ teaspoon ground cloves
½ teaspoon cinnamon powder
10 dates, pitted and chopped

1. Add all ingredients to the inner pot; stir to combine. 2. Put the lid in place and lock it. Select the Pressure Cook on the panel. Press the button again to choose Less option; use the "+/-" button to adjust the cooking time to 10 minutes. Press Pressure Level to choose High pressure. 3. Once cooking is complete, leave the steam release handle in the Sealing position for 10 minutes. Open the lid carefully. 4. Mash the apple mixture to the desired consistency. Serve warm or cold.
Per Serving: Calories 97; Fat 12.3g; Sodium 255mg; Carbs 24.4g; Fiber 1g; Sugars 11.5g; Protein 2.4g

Broccoli Pesto

Prep time: 20 minutes | Cook time: 3 minutes | Serves: 8

1 bunch broccoli (about 1 pound), cut into florets (reserve stems for vegetable stock)
3 cups water
⅓ cup toasted walnuts
3 garlic cloves, minced
1 packed cup fresh basil leaves
¼ cup olive oil
2 tablespoons lemon juice
¼ cup grated Parmesan cheese
Kosher salt
Black pepper

1. Add the broccoli and water to the Instant Pot. 2. Put on the pressure cooker's lid and turn the steam valve to "Sealing" position. 3. Set the Instant Pot to Pressure Cook. 4. Press the Pressure Level button to adjust the pressure to "High". 5. Use the "+/-" keys on the control panel to set the cooking time to 3 minutes. 6. Once the cooking cycle is completed, quick-release pressure. 7. When all the steam is released, remove the pressure lid from the top carefully. 8. Meanwhile, combine the walnuts and garlic in a food processor. 9. Pulse several times until crumbly, but before the walnuts turn to butter. 10. Remove the broccoli and rinse with cold water. 11. Drain well and add to the food processor, along with the basil, oil, and lemon juice. 12. Pulse until well mixed. Add ¼ cup of cooking liquid and the Parmesan, and season with salt and pepper. 13. Process until smooth. Add more cooking liquid as needed.
Per Serving: Calories 49; Fat 11g; Sodium 501mg; Carbs 8.9g; Fiber 4.6g; Sugar 8g; Protein 26g

Raspberry Ginger Coulis

Prep time: 10 minutes | Cook Time: 5 minutes | Serves: 6

1 (12-ounce) bag fresh or frozen raspberries
1 cup brown sugar
1 cup water
½ cup fresh orange juice
1 tablespoon fresh ginger root, peeled and finely grated
Zest from 1 organic orange, finely grated

1. Add all the ingredients to the inner pot of your Inner Pot. 2. Put the lid in place and lock it. Select the Pressure Cook on the panel. Press the button again to choose Less option; use the "-" button to adjust the cooking time to 3 minutes. Press Pressure Level to choose High pressure. 3. Once cooking is complete, leave the steam release handle in the Sealing position for 10 minutes. Open the lid carefully. 4. Let it cool. Serve your sauce chilled or at room temperature.
Per Serving: Calories 134; Fat 0.3g; Sodium 145mg; Carbs 34.4g; Fiber 1g; Sugars 30.5g; Protein 0.5g

Chicken Onion Stock

Prep time: 20 minutes | Cook time: 60 minutes | Serves: 8

2-pound chicken bones and parts
1 yellow onion, quartered
1 large garlic clove, smashed
1 carrot, cut into large chunks
1 bay leaf
½ teaspoon kosher salt
1 teaspoon whole black peppercorns
8 cups water

1. Add the chicken, onion, garlic, carrot, bay leaf, salt, and peppercorns to the pot. Pour the water over. 2. Put on the pressure cooker's lid and turn the steam valve to "Sealing" position. 3. Set the Instant Pot to Pressure Cook. 4. Press the Pressure Level button to adjust the pressure to "High". 5. Use the "+/-" keys on the control panel to set the cooking time to 60 minutes. 6. Once the cooking cycle is completed, allow the steam to release naturally. 7. When all the steam is released, remove the pressure lid from the top carefully. 8. Carefully strain the broth through a fine-mesh strainer or cheesecloth. 9. Store the stock in the refrigerator for a few days or freeze for up to 3 months.
Per Serving: Calories 19; Fat 14g; Sodium 91mg; Carbs 8.9g; Fiber 4.6g; Sugar 8g; Protein 3g

Vegetable Stock

Prep time: 20 minutes | Cook time: 60minutes | Serves: 8

2 onions, quartered
2 celery stalks, quartered
2 carrots, cut into large chunks
10 button mushrooms
4 garlic cloves, smashed
1 small bunch fresh parsley
1 bay leaf
8 cups water
Kosher salt

1. Add the onions, celery, carrots, mushrooms, garlic, parsley, bay leaf, and water to the Instant Pot. 2. Put on the pressure cooker's lid and turn the steam valve to "Sealing" position. 3. Set the Instant Pot to Pressure Cook. 4. Press the Pressure Level button to adjust the pressure to "High". 5. Use the "+/-" keys on the control panel to set the cooking time to 60 minutes. 6. Once the cooking cycle is completed, allow the steam to release naturally. 7. When all the steam is released, remove the pressure lid from the top carefully. 8. Carefully strain the stock using a fine-mesh strainer or cheesecloth. Season with salt. 9. Store the stock in the refrigerator for a few days or freeze for up to 3 months.
Per Serving: Calories 54; Fat 7.9g; Sodium 704mg; Carbs 6g; Fiber 3.6g; Sugar 6g; Protein 18g

Puttanesca Sauce

Prep time: 20 minutes | Cook time: 20 minutes | Serves: 8

2 tablespoons olive oil
1 small onion, finely chopped
4 garlic cloves, minced
1 (28-ounce) can whole tomatoes with juice
½ cup chopped pitted Kalamata olives
4 anchovy fillets, drained and minced
1 tablespoon tomato paste
1 tablespoon drained capers
¼ teaspoon red pepper flakes
Kosher salt
Black pepper

1. Press the "Sauté" button two times to select "Normal" mode 2. Once hot, add the oil followed by the onion. Sauté for 3 minutes, then add the garlic. Sauté 1 minute more. 3. Add the tomatoes with juice, squishing each one with your hand as it goes into the pot. 4. Add the olives, anchovies, tomato paste, capers, and red pepper flakes. Season with salt and pepper. 5. Put on the pressure cooker's lid and turn the steam valve to "Sealing" position. 6. Set the Instant Pot to Pressure Cook. 7. Press the Pressure Level button to adjust the pressure to "High". 8. Use the "+/-" keys on the control panel to set the cooking time to 20 minutes. 9. Once the cooking cycle is completed, allow the steam to release naturally. 10. When all the steam is released, remove the pressure lid from the top carefully. 11. If a thicker sauce is desired, press the "Sauté" button twice to select "Normal" mode and simmer for 5 minutes. Serve over pasta.
Per Serving: Calories 41; Fat 10.9g; Sodium 454mg; Carbs 10g; Fiber 3.1g; Sugar 5.2g; Protein 05g

Beef Bone Broth

Prep time: 20 minutes | Cook time: 1 hr. 30 minutes | Serves: 8

2½-pound beef bones, including short ribs, knuckles, oxtails, and more
1 teaspoon olive oil
1 yellow onion, quartered
2 celery stalks, quartered

1 carrot, cut into large chunks
1 bay leaf
2 teaspoons apple cider vinegar
1 tablespoon fish sauce
8 cups water

1. Preheat the oven to 400°F. 2. Toss the bones with the oil on a baking sheet and roast for 30 minutes. 3. Once cool enough to handle, add the bones, onion, celery, carrot, bay leaf, vinegar, fish sauce, and water to the Instant Pot. 4. Put on the pressure cooker's lid and turn the steam valve to "Sealing" position. 5. Set the Instant Pot to Pressure Cook. 6. Use the "+/-" keys on the control panel to set the cooking time to 1 hour 30 minutes. 7. Press the Pressure Level button to adjust the pressure to "High". 8. Once the cooking cycle is completed, allow the steam to release naturally. 9. When all the steam is released, remove the pressure lid from the top carefully. 10. Skim any fat off the top of the stock, if desired. 11. Carefully strain the broth using a fine-mesh strainer or cheesecloth. 12. Store the broth in the refrigerator for a few days or freeze for up to 3 months.
Per Serving: Calories 79; Fat 10g; Sodium 891mg; Carbs 22.9g; Fiber 4g; Sugar 4g; Protein 33g

Spicy Chicken Bone Broth

Prep time: 20 minutes | Cook time: 1 hr. 30 minutes | Serves: 8

2½-pound mixed chicken bones and feet
1 yellow onion, quartered
1 celery stalk, quartered
1 carrot, cut into large chunks
1 (1½-inch) piece ginger, peeled

and cut into ¼-inch slices
1 teaspoon whole black peppercorns
1 tablespoon fish sauce
1 teaspoon apple cider vinegar
8 cups water

1. Add the bones, onion, celery, carrot, ginger, peppercorns, fish sauce, vinegar, and water to the Instant Pot. 2. Put on the pressure cooker's lid and turn the steam valve to "Sealing" position. 3. Set the Instant Pot to Pressure Cook. 4. Press the Pressure Level button to adjust the pressure to "High". 5. Use the "+/-" keys on the control panel to set the cooking time to 1 hour 30 minutes. 6. Once the cooking cycle is completed, allow the steam to release naturally. 7. When all the steam is released, remove the pressure lid from the top carefully. 8. Skim any fat off the top of the stock, if desired. Carefully strain the broth using a fine-mesh strainer or cheesecloth. 9. Store the broth in the refrigerator for a few days or freeze for up to 3 months.
Per Serving: Calories 78; Fat 19g; Sodium 354mg; Carbs 15g; Fiber 5.1g; Sugar 8.2g; Protein 32g

Sweet and Tangy Barbecue Sauce

Prep time: 20 minutes | Cook time: 15 minutes | Serves: 8

4 tablespoons butter
1 small onion, finely chopped
3 garlic cloves, minced
1 cup tomato sauce
½ cup ketchup
½ cup apple cider vinegar

½ cup brown sugar
3 tablespoons molasses
1 tablespoon Dijon mustard
1 teaspoon liquid smoke
¼ teaspoon cayenne
¼ teaspoon black pepper

1. Press the "Sauté" button two times to select "Normal" mode 2. Once hot, add the butter and let it melt. Add the onion and cook for 3 minutes until it is starting to turn translucent. Add the garlic and sauté 1 minute more. 3. Add the tomato sauce, ketchup, vinegar, brown sugar, molasses, mustard, liquid smoke, cayenne, and pepper. 4. Put on the pressure cooker's lid and turn the steam valve to "Sealing" position. 5. Set the Instant Pot to Pressure Cook. 6. Use the "+/-" keys on the control panel to set the cooking time to 15 minutes. 7. Press the Pressure Level button to adjust the pressure to "High". 8. Once the cooking cycle is completed, allow the steam to release naturally. 9. When all the steam is released, remove the pressure lid from the top carefully. 10. Stir and taste for seasoning. If a thicker sauce is desired. 11. Press the "Sauté" button two times to select "Normal" mode and

cook, stirring occasionally, for 10 to 15 minutes. 12. Let it cool and store it in the refrigerator for up to 2 weeks or the freezer for several months.
Per Serving: Calories 32; Fat 10.9g; Sodium 354mg; Carbs 10.5g; Fiber 4.1g; Sugar 8.2g; Protein 26g

Strawberry Compote

Prep time: 20 minutes | Cook time: 4 minutes | Serves: 8

4 cups frozen strawberries
¼ cup sugar

1 tablespoon lemon juice

1. In your Instant Pot, combine the strawberries, sugar, and lemon juice. Stir to coat the berries. 2. Put on the pressure cooker's lid and turn the steam valve to "Sealing" position. 3. Set the Instant Pot to Pressure Cook. 4. Press the Pressure Level button to adjust the pressure to "High". 5. Use the "+/-" keys on the control panel to set the cooking time to 4 minutes. 6. Once the cooking cycle is completed, allow the steam to release naturally for 10 minutes and then quick-release the remaining pressure. 7. When all the steam is released, remove the pressure lid from the top carefully. 8. Using a potato masher, mash the berries until they are broken down completely. 9. Pour into a container and chill. The compote will thicken as it cools. 10. Store in the fridge for up to 4 weeks in a covered container.
Per Serving: Calories 42; Fat 11g; Sodium 91mg; Carbs 4g; Fiber 3g; Sugar 8g; Protein 3g

Cinnamon Applesauce

Prep time: 20 minutes | Cook time: 4 minutes | Serves: 8

10 to 12 medium apples, peeled, cored, and diced
½ cup apple cider, apple juice, or water

1 cinnamon stick, broken in half
Up to ¼ cup honey
1 tablespoon lemon juice

1. Add the apples, cider or juice or water, and both halves of the cinnamon stick to the Instant Pot. 2. Put on the pressure cooker's lid and turn the steam valve to "Sealing" position. 3. Set the Instant Pot to Pressure Cook. 4. Press the Pressure Level button to adjust the pressure to "Low". 5. Use the "+/-" keys on the control panel to set the cooking time to 4 minutes. 6. Once the cooking cycle is completed, allow the steam to release naturally. 7. When all the steam is released, remove the pressure lid from the top carefully. 8. Stir and remove the cinnamon stick halves. If the applesauce isn't sweet enough, add honey. 9. Serve.
Per Serving: Calories 84; Fat 5g; Sodium 41mg; Carbs 7g; Fiber 7.6g; Sugar 5g; Protein 2g

Orange and Lemon Marmalade

Prep time: 20 minutes | Cook time: 14 minutes | Serves: 8

1½-pound sweet oranges
8 oz. lemons, such as Meyer lemons

1 cup water
3-pound sugar

1. Cut the oranges and lemons into ⅛-inch slices. 2. Discard the end pieces that are all peel or pith, and remove the seeds and set aside for use later. Cut the slices into 4 or 5 pieces. 3. Add the fruit and water to the Instant Pot. 4. Put on the pressure cooker's lid and turn the steam valve to "Sealing" position. 5. Set the Instant Pot to Pressure Cook. 6. Use the "+/-" keys on the control panel to set the cooking time to 14 minutes. 7. Press the Pressure Level button to adjust the pressure to "Low". 8. Once the cooking cycle is completed, allow the steam to release naturally. 9. When all the steam is released, remove the pressure lid from the top carefully. 10. Add the sugar and stir until dissolved. 11. Place the seeds in a tea bag or gauze packet, cinch, and place in the mixture. Taste for sweetness. 12. Press the "Sauté" button two times to select "More" mode and boil for about 5 minutes. 13. Pour into clean jars and let them sit at room temperature until totally cooled. 14. Store in jars in the refrigerator for up to 3 weeks or the freezer for several months.
Per Serving: Calories 19; Fat 14g; Sodium 791mg; Carbs 8.9g; Fiber 4.6g; Sugar 8g; Protein 3g

Onion Gravy

Prep time: 20 minutes | Cook time: 10 minutes | Serves: 8

3 tablespoons butter
1 large sweet onion, finely chopped
2 cups chicken broth (try the recipe here)

2 fresh thyme sprigs
1 bay leaf
2 tablespoons all-purpose flour
Kosher salt
Black pepper

1. Press the "Sauté" button twice to select "Normal" mode. 2. Once hot, add 1 tablespoon of butter followed by the onion. 3. Sauté for 6 minutes, until translucent and starting to brown. 4. Add the broth, thyme, and bay leaf. 5. Put on the pressure cooker's lid and turn the steam valve to "Sealing" position. 6. Set the Instant Pot to Pressure Cook. 7. Press the Pressure Level button to adjust the pressure to "High". 8. Use the "+/-" keys on the control panel to set the cooking time to 10 minutes. 9. Once the cooking cycle is completed, allow the steam to release naturally. 10. When all the steam is released, remove the pressure lid from the top carefully. 11. Press the "Sauté" button twice to select "Normal" mode. 12. In a small bowl, knead together the remaining 2 tablespoons of butter with the flour until a pasty ball forms. 13. Add to the simmering broth and stir until the paste is dissolved and the gravy is thick, about 5 minutes. 14. Season with salt and pepper as desired.
Per Serving: Calories 33; Fat 7.9g; Sodium 704mg; Carbs 6g; Fiber 3.6g; Sugar 6g; Protein 18g

Marinara Sauce

Prep time: 20 minutes | Cook time: 30 minutes | Serves: 8

2 tablespoons olive oil
1 medium onion, grated
1 large carrot, peeled and grated
5 garlic cloves, grated
1 (28-ounce) can crushed

tomatoes with juice
½ teaspoon dried oregano
Pinch sugar
Kosher salt
Black pepper

1. Press the "Sauté" button twice to select "Normal" mode. 2. Once hot, add the oil followed by the onion and carrot. 3. Sauté for 2 minutes until the onion is translucent. Add the garlic and cook for 30 seconds. 4. Add the tomatoes with juice and stir. Add the oregano. 5. Put on the pressure cooker's lid and turn the steam valve to "Sealing" position. 6. Set the Instant Pot to Pressure Cook. 7. Use the "+/-" keys on the control panel to set the cooking time to 30 minutes. 8. Press the Pressure Level button to adjust the pressure to "High". 9. Once the cooking cycle is completed, allow the steam to release naturally. 10. When all the steam is released, remove the pressure lid from the top carefully. 11. Stir and taste for seasoning. Add the sugar, and season with salt and pepper as desired. 12. Store for up to a week in the refrigerator or freezer for several months.
Per Serving: Calories 42; Fat 19g; Sodium 354mg; Carbs 15g; Fiber 5.1g; Sugar 8.2g; Protein 2g

Mango-Apple Chutney

Prep time: 20 minutes | Cook time: 11 minutes | Serves: 8

1 tablespoon canola oil
1 large red onion, finely chopped
1 heaping tablespoon grated fresh ginger
1 red Thai chile, cut into a few pieces
2 large mangos, peeled and diced
2 apples, cored, partially peeled, and diced

1 red bell pepper, diced
½ cup golden raisins
1¼ cups sugar
½ cup apple cider vinegar
1 teaspoon kosher salt
1½ teaspoons curry powder
½ teaspoon ground cinnamon
1 tablespoon lemon juice

1. Press the "Sauté" button twice to select "Normal" mode. Add the oil. 2. Once hot, add the onion and sauté for 3 minutes. Add the ginger and chile, and cook for 1 minute. 3. Add the mangos, apples, bell pepper, raisins, sugar, vinegar, salt, curry powder, and cinnamon. 4. Put on the pressure cooker's lid and turn the steam valve to "Sealing" position. 5. Set the Instant Pot to Pressure Cook. 6. Press the Pressure Level button to adjust the pressure to "High".

7. Use the "+/-" keys on the control panel to set the cooking time to 7 minutes. 8. Once the cooking cycle is completed, allow the steam to release naturally. 9. When all the steam is released, remove the pressure lid from the top carefully. 10. Press the "Sauté" button two times to select "Normal" mode and simmer for 10 minutes. 11. Add the lemon juice and stir. 12. Store in airtight containers in the refrigerator for up to a month or in the freezer for up to a year.
Per Serving: Calories 49; Fat 2.9g; Sodium 511mg; Carbs 12g; Fiber 3g; Sugar 8g; Protein 28g

Yummy Zesty Pear Sauce

Prep time: 15 minutes | Cook Time: 10 minutes | Serves: 8

1 ½ pounds cup pears, cored, peeled and chopped
2 teaspoons freshly squeezed lemon juice

½ cup sugar
1 teaspoon ground cinnamon
½ teaspoon ground cardamom
1 teaspoon vanilla essence

1. Add all ingredients to the inner pot; stir to combine. 2. Put the lid in place and lock it. Select the Pressure Cook on the panel. Press the button again to choose Less option; use the "-" button to adjust the cooking time to 10 minutes. Press Pressure Level to choose High pressure. 3. Once cooking is complete, leave the steam release handle in the Sealing position for10 minutes. Open the lid carefully. 4. Mash the pear mixture to the desired consistency. 5. Serve at room temperature or cold.
Per Serving: Calories 73; Fat 1.3g; Sodium 195mg; Carbs 4.4g; Fiber 1g; Sugars 3.5g; Protein 0.4g

Simple Marinara Sauce

Prep time: 10 minutes | Cook Time: 45 minutes | Serves: 8

4 tablespoons olive oil
4 garlic cloves, minced
4 tablespoons tomato paste
1 (28-ounce) can crushed tomatoes with juice

1 cup water
Sea salt to taste
2 tablespoons fresh basil, minced
1 tablespoon fresh parsley, minced

1. Insert the inner pot into the cooker base without the lid. 2. Press Sauté to select the program and press it again to choose Normal option, then add and heat olive oil. Once hot, cook the garlic for a minute or so or until it is fragrant but not browned. 3. Now, stir in the remaining ingredients. 4. Put the lid in place and lock it. Select the Soup/Broth on the panel. Press the button Again to choose Normal option; use the "+" button to adjust the cooking time to 40 minutes. Press Pressure Level to choose High pressure. 5. Once cooking is complete, quickly and carefully turn the steam release handle from the Sealing position to the Venting position. Open the lid carefully. 6. Serve and enjoy.
Per Serving: Calories 86; Fat 7g; Sodium 220mg; Carbs 5.4g; Fiber 1g; Sugars 3.5g; Protein 1.4g

Cranberry Sauce

Prep time: 20 minutes | Cook time: 15 minutes | Serves: 8

4 cups washed cranberries, fresh or frozen
1 (1-inch) piece ginger, peeled and cut into ⅛-inch slices

½ cup orange juice
Zest from ½ orange
Juice and zest from ½ lemon
1 cup sugar

1. Add the cranberries, ginger, orange juice, orange zest, lemon juice, lemon zest, and sugar to the Instant Pot. 2. Put on the pressure cooker's lid and turn the steam valve to "Sealing" position. 3. Set the Instant Pot to Pressure Cook. 4. Press the Pressure Level button to adjust the pressure to "Low". 5. Use the "+/-" keys on the control panel to set the cooking time to 15 minutes. 6. Once the cooking cycle is completed, allow the steam to release naturally. 7. When all the steam is released, remove the pressure lid from the top carefully. 8. Let cool and remove the ginger if desired. 9. Store the sauce in the refrigerator for up to 3 weeks.
Per Serving: Calories 51; Fat 12.9g; Sodium 414mg; Carbs 11g; Fiber 5g; Sugar 9g; Protein 31g

Triple-Berry Jam

Prep time: 20 minutes | Cook time: 11 minutes | Serves: 8

8-ounce fresh strawberries, hulled and halved	1 cup sugar
	2 teaspoons lemon juice
8-ounce fresh blueberries	1 teaspoon grated lemon zest
8-ounce fresh raspberries	Up to ¼ cup honey

1. Add the strawberries, blueberries, raspberries, and sugar to the Instant Pot and stir. 2. Let it sit for at least 15 minutes or up to 1 hour. 3. Press the "Sauté" button twice to select "Normal" mode and bring the mixture to a boil for 3 minutes. 4. Put on the pressure cooker's lid and turn the steam valve to "Sealing" position. 5. Set the Instant Pot to Pressure Cook. 6. Use the "+/-" keys on the control panel to set the cooking time to 8 minutes. 7. Press the Pressure Level button to adjust the pressure to "High". 8. Once the cooking cycle is completed, allow the steam to release naturally. 9. When all the steam is released, remove the pressure lid from the top carefully. 10. Remove the lid and Press the "Sauté" button two times to select "Normal" mode. 11. Add the lemon juice and zest. Carefully taste the jam and add honey if needed. 12. Boil for 3 to 4 minutes, stirring frequently, or until the gel point is reached. 13. Select Cancel. Mash the jam if a smoother texture is desired. 14. Carefully transfer to lidded containers, close, and let them cool. 15. The jam could be kept in the refrigerator for up to 3 weeks or the freezer for at least 6 months.
Per Serving: Calories 42; Fat 11g; Sodium 91mg; Carbs 4g; Fiber 3g; Sugar 8g; Protein 3g

Chicken Stock

Prep time: 20 minutes | Cook time: 60 minutes | Serves: 8

1 chicken carcass	2 bay leaves
10 cups water	2 tablespoons apple cider vinegar
1 onion, quartered	1 sprig thyme
2 large carrots, cut into chunks	Salt to taste
12 whole pieces' peppercorns	

1. Put all of the ingredients into the Instant Pot. 2. Put on the pressure cooker's lid and turn the steam valve to "Sealing" position. 3. Set the Instant Pot to Pressure Cook. 4. Press the Pressure Level button to adjust the pressure to "High". 5. Use the "+/-" keys on the control panel to set the cooking time to 60 minutes. 6. Once the cooking cycle is completed, allow the steam to release naturally. 7. When all the steam is released, remove the pressure lid from the top carefully. 8. Season with salt to taste. Strain the stock and pour into jars. 9. Store in the refrigerator or freeze.
Per Serving: Calories 84; Fat 5g; Sodium 41mg; Carbs 7g; Fiber 7.6g; Sugar 5g; Protein 2g

Apple Butter

Prep time: 20 minutes | Cook time: 30 minutes | Serves: 8

4-pound apples, peeled, cored, and roughly chopped	1 cup brown sugar
	1 teaspoon ground cinnamon
½ cup apple cider	Pinch ground cloves or nutmeg
1 tablespoon lemon juice	Pinch kosher salt

1. Add the apples and cider to the Instant Pot. 2. Put on the pressure cooker's lid and turn the steam valve to "Sealing" position. 3. Set the Instant Pot to Pressure Cook. 4. Use the "+/-" keys on the control panel to set the cooking time to 30 minutes. 5. Press the Pressure Level button to adjust the pressure to "High". 6. Once the cooking cycle is completed, allow the steam to release naturally. 7. When all the steam is released, remove the pressure lid from the top carefully. 8. Add the lemon juice, brown sugar, cinnamon, cloves or nutmeg, and salt and stir. 9. Press the "Sauté" button two times to select "Normal" mode and cook for about 30 minutes. 10. Store in an airtight container in the refrigerator for up to a week or in the freezer for up to 3 months.
Per Serving: Calories 79; Fat 10g; Sodium 891mg; Carbs 22.9g; Fiber 4g; Sugar 4g; Protein 33g

Vegetable Broth

Prep time: 20 minutes | Cook time: 40 minutes | Serves: 8

2 medium onions, halved	mushrooms, whole
2 celery stalks with leaves, roughly chopped	12 cups water
	1 head garlic, halved crosswise
2 large carrots, scrubbed and roughly chopped	1 bunch parsley stems
	2 bay leaves
8-ounce white button or cremini	5 to 7 whole black peppercorns

1. Press the "Sauté" button two time on the Instant pot to select "Normal" settings. 2. Sauté the onions, celery, carrots, and mushrooms for 3 to 5 minutes. 3. Add the water, garlic, parsley, bay leaves, and peppercorns. 4. Put on the pressure cooker's lid and turn the steam valve to "Sealing" position. 5. Set the Instant Pot to Pressure Cook. 6. Use the "+/-" keys on the control panel to set the cooking time to 40 minutes. 7. Press the Pressure Level button to adjust the pressure to "High". 8. Once the cooking cycle is completed, quick-release pressure. 9. When all the steam is released, remove the pressure lid from the top carefully. 10. When the cook time is complete, quick-release the pressure and carefully remove the lid. 11. Strain the broth through a fine-mesh sieve into a large bowl and discard the solids. 12. Store the broth in a covered container in the fridge for up to 4 days or in the freezer for up to 6 months.
Per Serving: Calories 61; Fat 7.9g; Sodium 704mg; Carbs 6g; Fiber 3.6g; Sugar 6g; Protein 18g

Hot Pepper Sauce

Prep time: 20 minutes | Cook time: 2 minutes | Serves: 8

12 to 16-ounce fresh hot red peppers, stems removed, halved	¼ cup apple cider vinegar
	3 garlic cloves, smashed
1 cup distilled white vinegar	

1. In your Instant Pot, stir together the peppers, white vinegar, cider vinegar, and garlic. 2. Put on the pressure cooker's lid and turn the steam valve to "Sealing" position. 3. Set the Instant Pot to Pressure Cook. 4. Use the "+/-" keys on the control panel to set the cooking time to 2 minutes. 5. Press the Pressure Level button to adjust the pressure to "High". 6. Once the cooking cycle is completed, allow the steam to release naturally. 7. When all the steam is released, remove the pressure lid from the top carefully. 8. Using an immersion blender, food processor, or blender, blend the sauce until smooth. 9. Strain through a fine-mesh sieve and store in glass bottles or jars at room temperature for up to 6 months.
Per Serving: Calories 78; Fat 10.9g; Sodium 454mg; Carbs 10g; Fiber 3.1g; Sugar 5.2g; Protein 05g

Strawberry Applesauce

Prep time: 15 minutes | Cook time: 5 minutes | Serves: 6

8 peeled apples, cored and sliced	2 tablespoons lemon juice
3 cups strawberries, hulled and chopped	¼ teaspoon cinnamon powder
	2 tablespoons sugar

1. Combine all of the ingredients in the Instant Pot and stir to mix. 2. Put on the pressure cooker's lid and turn the steam valve to "Sealing" position. 3. Set the Instant Pot to Pressure Cook. 4. Press the Pressure Level button to adjust the pressure to "High". 5. Use the "+/-" keys on the control panel to set the cooking time to 5 minutes. 6. Once the cooking cycle is completed, allow the steam to release naturally for 15 minutes and then release the remaining pressure manually. 7. When all the steam is released, remove the pressure lid from the top carefully. 8. Use a potato masher to mash the mixture and get the consistency you like.
Per Serving: Calories 32; Fat 2.9g; Sodium 41mg; Carbs 11g; Fiber 5g; Sugar 9g; Protein 31g

Fresh Tomato Ketchup

Prep time: 20 minutes | Cook time: 15 minutes | Serves: 8

2-pound plum tomatoes, roughly chopped
5 pitted dates
6 tablespoons distilled white vinegar
1 tablespoon gluten-free vegan Worcestershire sauce
1 tablespoon paprika
1 teaspoon onion powder

1 teaspoon salt
½ teaspoon mustard powder
¼ teaspoon celery seed
¼ teaspoon garlic powder
Pinch of ground cloves
2 tablespoons water
1 tablespoon arrowroot powder or cornstarch

1. In your Instant Pot, combine the tomatoes, dates, vinegar, Worcestershire sauce, paprika, onion powder, salt, mustard powder, celery seed, garlic powder, and cloves. 2. Using a potato masher, mash the tomatoes until they have released much of their liquid. 3. Put on the pressure cooker's lid and turn the steam valve to "Sealing" position. 4. Set the Instant Pot to Pressure Cook. 5. Use the "+/-" keys on the control panel to set the cooking time to 5 minutes. 6. Press the Pressure Level button to adjust the pressure to "High". 7. Once the cooking cycle is completed, quick-release pressure. 8. When all the steam is released, remove the pressure lid from the top carefully. 9. Select the Sauté function and simmer about 10 minutes, until reduced, stirring often. 10. In a small bowl, whisk together the water and arrowroot and add to the simmering ketchup for 2 to 4 minutes. 11. Strain the ketchup through a fine-mesh sieve. 12. Store in the fridge for up to 6 months in a covered container.
Per Serving: Calories 84; Fat 5g; Sodium 41mg; Carbs 7g; Fiber 7.6g; Sugar 5g; Protein 2g

Turkey Stock

Prep time: 20 minutes | Cook time: 45 minutes | Serves: 6

1 bag turkey giblet
6 cups water
1 stalk celery, cut in half
1 carrot, cut into chunks

1 onion, quartered
1 bay leaf
1 teaspoon whole black peppercorns

1. Put all of the ingredients into the Instant Pot. 2. Put on the pressure cooker's lid and turn the steam valve to "Sealing" position. 3. Set the Instant Pot to Pressure Cook. 4. Use the "+/-" keys on the control panel to set the cooking time to 45 minutes. 5. Press the Pressure Level button to adjust the pressure to "High". 6. Once the cooking cycle is completed, allow the steam to release naturally for 10 minutes and then release the remaining pressure manually. 7. When all the steam is released, remove the pressure lid from the top carefully. 8. Strain the stock and pour into jars. Store in the refrigerator or freeze.
Per Serving: Calories 42; Fat 11g; Sodium 91mg; Carbs 4g; Fiber 3g; Sugar 8g; Protein 3g

Herb Stock

Prep time: 20 minutes | Cook time: 15 minutes | Serves: 8

4 cups water
3 bay leaves
2 cloves garlic, crushed
1 teaspoon whole black

peppercorns
A handful of rosemary
2 sprigs parsley
½ teaspoon salt

1. Put all of the ingredients, except salt, into the Instant Pot. 2. Put on the pressure cooker's lid and turn the steam valve to "Sealing" position. 3. Set the Instant Pot to Pressure Cook. 4. Press the Pressure Level button to adjust the pressure to "High". 5. Use the "+/-" keys on the control panel to set the cooking time to 15 minutes. 6. Once the cooking cycle is completed, allow the steam to release naturally for 10 minutes and then release the remaining steam manually. 7. When all the steam is released, remove the pressure lid from the top carefully. 8. Season with salt to taste. 9. Strain the stock and pour into jars. Store in the refrigerator or freeze.
Per Serving: Calories 84; Fat 5g; Sodium 41mg; Carbs 7g; Fiber 7.6g; Sugar 5g; Protein 2g

Pork Broth

Prep time: 20 minutes | Cook time: 60 minutes | Serves: 8

3-pound pork bones
8 cups water
3 large carrots, cut into large chunks
3 large stalks celery, cut into large chunks

1 bay leaf
2 cloves garlic, sliced
1 tablespoon apple cider vinegar
1 teaspoon whole peppercorns
Salt to taste

1. Dump all of the ingredients into the Instant Pot and give it a little stir to mix everything evenly. 2. Put on the pressure cooker's lid and turn the steam valve to "Sealing" position. 3. Set the Instant Pot to Pressure Cook. 4. Use the "+/-" keys on the control panel to set the cooking time to 60 minutes. 5. Press the Pressure Level button to adjust the pressure to "High". 6. Once the cooking cycle is completed, allow the steam to release naturally. 7. When all the steam is released, remove the pressure lid from the top carefully. 8. Strain the broth and pour into jars. Store in the refrigerator or freeze.
Per Serving: Calories 61; Fat 7.9g; Sodium 704mg; Carbs 6g; Fiber 3.6g; Sugar 6g; Protein 18g

Oil-Free Marinara Sauce

Prep time: 20 minutes | Cook time: 12 minutes | Serves: 8

1 medium onion, diced
4 tablespoons water, as needed
4 garlic cloves, minced
1 tablespoon dried basil
1 tablespoon dried oregano
¼ to 1 teaspoon red pepper flakes

2 (28-ounce) cans no-salt-added crushed tomatoes
½ cup Easy Vegetable Broth or no-salt-added vegetable broth
Black pepper
Salt

1. Press the "Sauté" button twice on the Instant pot to select "Normal" settings. 2. Sauté the onion for 1 to 2 minutes, until slightly browned, adding water as needed to prevent sticking. 3. Add the garlic, basil, oregano, and red pepper flakes to taste and stir for 30 seconds, until fragrant. 4. Stir in the tomatoes and broth, scraping up any browned bits from the bottom of the pot. 5. Season to taste with black pepper and salt. 6. Put on the pressure cooker's lid and turn the steam valve to "Sealing" position. 7. Set the Instant Pot to Pressure Cook. 8. Use the "+/-" keys on the control panel to set the cooking time to 12 minutes. 9. Press the Pressure Level button to adjust the pressure to "High". 10. Once the cooking cycle is completed, allow the steam to release naturally. 11. When all the steam is released, remove the pressure lid from the top carefully. 12. Store in a covered container in the fridge for up to 4 weeks or in the freezer for up to 3 months.
Per Serving: Calories 54; Fat 10.9g; Sodium 354mg; Carbs 10.5g; Fiber 4.1g; Sugar 8.2g; Protein 26g

Maple Barbecue Sauce

Prep time: 20 minutes | Cook time: 6 minutes | Serves: 8

2 tablespoons minced onion
2 garlic cloves, minced
1 teaspoon smoked paprika
1 teaspoon ground allspice
1 cup water
1 (15-ounce) can no-salt-added

tomato sauce
¼ cup maple syrup
2 tablespoons stone-ground mustard
2 tablespoons apple cider vinegar
½ teaspoon salt

1. Press the "Sauté" button twice on the Instant pot to select "Normal" settings. Sauté the onion for 2 minutes. 2. Add the garlic, paprika, and allspice and stir for 30 seconds, until fragrant. 3. Stir in the water, scraping up any browned bits from the bottom of the pot. 4. Add the tomato sauce, maple syrup, mustard, vinegar, and salt. Whisk to combine. 5. Put on the pressure cooker's lid and turn the steam valve to "Sealing" position. 6. Set the Instant Pot to Pressure Cook. 7. Press the Pressure Level button to adjust the pressure to "High". 8. Use the "+/-" keys on the control panel to set the cooking time to 4 minutes. 9. Once the cooking cycle is completed, quick-release pressure. 10. When all the steam is released, remove the pressure lid from the top carefully. 11. Store in the refrigerator for up to 4 weeks in a covered container.
Per Serving: Calories 34; Fat 9g; Sodium 354mg; Carbs 5g; Fiber 5.1g; Sugar 8.2g; Protein 2g

Nut-Free Cheese Sauce

Prep time: 20 minutes | Cook time: 7 minutes | Serves: 8

3 medium yellow potatoes, cut into 1-inch chunks
1 large carrot, cut into 1-inch chunks
2 cups water
¼ cup nutritional yeast

2 tablespoons lemon juice
2 teaspoons chickpea miso paste
½ teaspoon onion powder
½ teaspoon garlic powder
½ teaspoon mustard powder
¼ teaspoon ground turmeric

1. In your Instant Pot, combine the potatoes, carrot, and water. 2. Put on the pressure cooker's lid and turn the steam valve to "Sealing" position. 3. Set the Instant Pot to Pressure Cook. 4. Press the Pressure Level button to adjust the pressure to "High". 5. Use the "+/-" keys on the control panel to set the cooking time to 7 minutes. 6. Once the cooking cycle is completed, allow the steam to release naturally for 10 minutes and then quick-release the remaining pressure. 7. When all the steam is released, remove the pressure lid from the top carefully. 8. Using a slotted spoon, remove the potatoes and carrots to a blender, then add ½ cup of the cooking water along with the nutritional yeast, lemon juice, miso, onion powder, garlic powder, mustard powder, and turmeric. 9. Blend until smooth and creamy, adding more cooking water as necessary to thin. 10. Store in the fridge for up to 4 days in a covered container.
Per Serving: Calories 32; Fat 9g; Sodium 34mg; Carbs 2g; Fiber 5.1g; Sugar 2g; Protein 2g

Applesauce

Prep time: 20 minutes | Cook time: 4 minutes | Serves: 8

3-pound apples, cored, cut into large chunks

⅓ cup water
1 tablespoon lemon juice

1. In your Instant Pot, combine the apples, water, and lemon juice. 2. Put on the pressure cooker's lid and turn the steam valve to "Sealing" position. 3. Set the Instant Pot to Pressure Cook. 4. Press the Pressure Level button to adjust the pressure to "High". 5. Use the "+/-" keys on the control panel to set the cooking time to 4 minutes. 6. Once the cooking cycle is completed, allow the steam to release naturally for 10 minutes and then quick-release the remaining pressure. 7. When all the steam is released, remove the pressure lid from the top carefully. 8. Using a potato masher, mash the apples to your desired chunkiness. 9. Using a pair of tongs or a fork, transfer the apple peels to a deep, narrow container and blend using an immersion blender. 10. Return to the pot and stir to combine. Store in the fridge for up to 4 weeks in a covered container.
Per Serving: Calories 34; Fat 19g; Sodium 354mg; Carbs 25g; Fiber 5.1g; Sugar 8.2g; Protein 2g

Bone Broth

Prep time: 20 minutes | Cook time: 120 minutes | Serves: 8

2-3-pound bones (2-3-pound beef, lamb, pork, or 1 carcass of chicken)
½ onion
3 carrots, cut into large chunks
2 stalks celery, cut into large

chunks
Fresh herbs
1 teaspoon sea salt
1-2 tablespoon apple cider vinegar
Water as needed

1. Add the bones to the Instant Pot. Add all of the veggies, herbs, salt and vinegar. 2. Pour in the water to fill the pot 2/3 full. 3. Put on the pressure cooker's lid and turn the steam valve to "Sealing" position. 4. Press the "Soup" button one time to select "Less" option. 5. Use the "+/-" keys on the control panel to set the cooking time to 120 minutes. 6. Once the cooking cycle is completed, allow the steam to release naturally. 7. When all the steam is released, remove the pressure lid from the top carefully. 8. Strain the broth and pour into jars. Store in the refrigerator or freeze.
Per Serving: Calories 79; Fat 10g; Sodium 891mg; Carbs 2.9g; Fiber 4g; Sugar 4g; Protein 3g

Mushroom Broth

Prep time: 20 minutes | Cook time: 15 minutes | Serves: 8

4-ounce dried mushrooms, soaked and rinsed
8 cups water
½ cup carrots, chopped
½ cup celery, chopped

1 onion, quartered
4 cloves garlic, crushed
4 bay leaves
Salt and black pepper to taste.

1. Put all of the ingredients into the Instant Pot. 2. Put on the pressure cooker's lid and turn the steam valve to "Sealing" position. 3. Set the Instant Pot to Pressure Cook. 4. Press the Pressure Level button to adjust the pressure to "High". 5. Use the "+/-" keys on the control panel to set the cooking time to 15 minutes. 6. Once the cooking cycle is completed, quick-release pressure. 7. When all the steam is released, remove the pressure lid from the top carefully. 8. Season with salt and pepper to taste. 9. Strain the broth and pour into jars. Store in the refrigerator or freeze.
Per Serving: Calories 34; Fat 12.9g; Sodium 44mg; Carbs 11g; Fiber 5g; Sugar 9g; Protein 31g

Chicken Feet Stock

Prep time: 20 minutes | Cook time: 60 minutes | Serves: 8

1½-pound chicken feet, cleaned and rinsed
8 cups water
2 carrots, cut into chunks

1 onion, quartered
2 stalks celery, cut in half
1 teaspoon black peppercorns
1 bay leaf

1. Put all of the ingredients into the Instant Pot. 2. Put on the pressure cooker's lid and turn the steam valve to "Sealing" position. 3. Set the Instant Pot to Pressure Cook. 4. Press the Pressure Level button to adjust the pressure to "High". 5. Use the "+/-" keys on the control panel to set the cooking time to 60 minutes. 6. Once the cooking cycle is completed, allow the steam to release naturally for 10 minutes and then release the remaining steam manually. 7. When all the steam is released, remove the pressure lid from the top carefully. 8. Strain the stock and pour into jars. Store in the refrigerator or freeze.
Per Serving: Calories 44; Fat 2.2g; Sodium 811mg; Carbs 12g; Fiber 3g; Sugar 8g; Protein 8g

Fish Stock

Prep time: 20 minutes | Cook time: 45 minutes | Serves: 10

2 salmon heads, large-sized, cut into quarters
1 tablespoon olive oil
2 lemongrass stalks, roughly chopped
1 cup carrots, roughly chopped

1 cup celery, roughly chopped
2 cloves garlic, sliced
Handful fresh thyme, including stems
Water as needed

1. Wash the fish heads and pat them dry. 2. Press the "Sauté" button two times to select "Normal" mode. Add and heat the oil. 3. Add the salmon heads and lightly sear the fish on both sides. 4. Put all of the ingredients into the Instant Pot and pour the water to cover mix. 5. Put on the pressure cooker's lid and turn the steam valve to "Sealing" position. 6. Set your Instant Pot to Soup/Broth. 7. Use the "+/-" keys on the control panel to set the cooking time to 45 minutes. 8. Press the Pressure Level button to adjust the pressure to "High". 9. Once the cooking cycle is completed, allow the steam to release naturally for 15 minutes and then release the remaining pressure manually. 10. When all the steam is released, remove the pressure lid from the top carefully. 11. Strain the stock and pour into jars. Store in the refrigerator or freeze.
Per Serving: Calories 72; Fat 9g; Sodium 354mg; Carbs 2g; Fiber 5.1g; Sugar 8.2g; Protein 2g

Seafood Soup Stock

Prep time: 20 minutes | Cook time: 30 minutes | Serves: 8

Shells and heads from ½ lb. prawns
8 cups water
4 onions, quartered
4 carrots, cut into chunks
3 cloves garlic, sliced
2 bay leaves
1 teaspoon whole black peppercorns

1. Put all of the ingredients into the Instant Pot. 2. Put on the pressure cooker's lid and turn the steam valve to "Sealing" position. 3. Set the Instant Pot to Pressure Cook. 4. Press the Pressure Level button to adjust the pressure to "High". 5. Use the "+/-" keys on the control panel to set the cooking time to 30 minutes. 6. Once the cooking cycle is completed, allow the steam to release naturally for 15 minutes and then release the remaining pressure manually. 7. When all the steam is released, remove the pressure lid from the top carefully. 8. Strain the stock and pour into jars. Store in the refrigerator or freeze.
Per Serving: Calories 89; Fat 11g; Sodium 51mg; Carbs 8.9g; Fiber 4.6g; Sugar 8g; Protein 26g

Homemade Salsa

Prep time: 20 minutes | Cook time: 30 minutes | Serves: 8

6 cups fresh tomatoes, diced, peeled and seeded
1½ green bell peppers, diced
2 yellow onions, diced
1 cup jalapeno peppers, seeded and chopped
1½ cans (6-ounce) tomato paste
¼ cup vinegar
1½ tablespoon sugar
½ tablespoon kosher salt
1 tablespoon garlic powder
1 tablespoon cayenne pepper

1. Put all of the ingredients into the Instant Pot. Stir well to combine. 2. Put on the pressure cooker's lid and turn the steam valve to "Sealing" position. 3. Set the Instant Pot to Pressure Cook. 4. Press the Pressure Level button to adjust the pressure to "High". 5. Use the "+/-" keys on the control panel to set the cooking time to 30 minutes. 6. Once the cooking cycle is completed, allow the steam to release naturally for 10 minutes and then release the remaining pressure manually. 7. When all the steam is released, remove the pressure lid from the top carefully. 8. Serve warm or cool.
Per Serving: Calories 34; Fat 10.9g; Sodium 354mg; Carbs 10.5g; Fiber 4.1g; Sugar 8.2g; Protein 26g

Bolognese Sauce

Prep time: 20 minutes | Cook time: 15 minutes | Serves: 4

½ tablespoon unsalted butter
2 teaspoons garlic, minced
1 carrot, chopped
1 stalk celery, chopped
1 lb. ground beef
1 can pasta sauce
1 tablespoon sugar
½ teaspoon kosher salt
¼ teaspoon black pepper
¼ teaspoon basil, dried
¼ cup half and half cream
⅛ cup parsley, chopped

1. Press the "Sauté" button two times to select "Normal" mode. Once hot, add the butter and melt it. 2. Add the garlic and sauté for 30 seconds. 3. Add the carrots and celery and sauté for 6-8 minutes, or until soft. 4. Add the ground beef and cook for another 4-5 minutes until browned, stirring occasionally. 5. Add the pasta sauce, sugar, salt, pepper, and basil. Stir well. 6. Put on the pressure cooker's lid and turn the steam valve to "Sealing" position. 7. Set the Instant Pot to Pressure Cook. 8. Press the Pressure Level button to adjust the pressure to "High". 9. Use the "+/-" keys on the control panel to set the cooking time to 15 minutes. 10. Once the cooking cycle is completed, allow the steam to release naturally for 10 minutes, and then release the remaining pressure manually. 11. When all the steam is released, remove the pressure lid from the top carefully. 12. Add the half and half to the pot. Stir to combine. 13. Top with parsley and serve.
Per Serving: Calories 42; Fat 11g; Sodium 91mg; Carbs 4g; Fiber 3g; Sugar 8g; Protein 3g

Cranberry Apple Sauce

Prep time: 20 minutes | Cook time: 5 minutes | Serves: 2

1-2 apples, peeled, cored, and then cut into chunks
10-ounce cranberries, frozen or fresh, preferably organic
1 teaspoon cinnamon
½ cup maple syrup or honey
¼ cup lemon juice
¼ teaspoon sea salt

1. Combine all of the ingredients in the Instant Pot. 2. Put on the pressure cooker's lid and turn the steam valve to "Sealing" position. 3. Set the Instant Pot to Pressure Cook. 4. Use the "+/-" keys on the control panel to set the cooking time to 1 minute. 5. Press the Pressure Level button to adjust the pressure to "High". 6. Once the cooking cycle is completed, allow the steam to release naturally for 15 minutes and then release the remaining pressure manually. 7. When all the steam is released, remove the pressure lid from the top carefully. 8. Using a wooden spoon, mash the fruit a bit. 9. Press the "Sauté" button twice to select "Normal" mode and simmer for 1-2 minutes to evaporate some water, stirring occasionally. 10. Once the sauce begins to thicken, press the CANCEL key to stop the SAUTÉ function. 11. Pour into clean jars and refrigerate.
Per Serving: Calories 82; Fat 10.9g; Sodium 454mg; Carbs 10g; Fiber 3.1g; Sugar 5.2g; Protein 05g

Tabasco Sauce

Prep time: 20 minutes | Cook time: 1 minutes | Serves: 8

18-ounce fresh hot peppers or any kind, stems removed, chopped
3 teaspoon smoked or plain salt
1¾ cups apple cider

1. Combine all of the ingredients in the Instant Pot. 2. Put on the pressure cooker's lid and turn the steam valve to "Sealing" position. 3. Set the Instant Pot to Pressure Cook. 4. Press the Pressure Level button to adjust the pressure to "High". 5. Use the "+/-" keys on the control panel to set the cooking time to 1 minute. 6. Once the cooking cycle is completed, allow the steam to release naturally for 15 minutes and then release the remaining pressure manually. 7. When all the steam is released, remove the pressure lid from the top carefully. 8. Using an immersion blender, puree the mixture. 9. Pour into clean and sterilized bottles and refrigerate.
Per Serving: Calories 51; Fat 10.9g; Sodium 354mg; Carbs 10.5g; Fiber 4.1g; Sugar 8.2g; Protein 6g

Vegan Alfredo Sauce

Prep time: 20 minutes | Cook time: 3 minutes | Serves: 8

1½ tablespoons olive oil
10 cloves garlic, minced
¾ cup raw cashews
6 cups cauliflower florets
2 cups asparagus
6 cups vegetable broth
½ teaspoon salt

1. Press the "Sauté" button twice to select "Normal" mode. and heat the oil. 2. Add the garlic and sauté for 1-2 minutes, until fragrant. 3. Add the cashews, cauliflower, asparagus, and broth. Press Cancel to stop heating. 4. Put on the pressure cooker's lid and turn the steam valve to "Sealing" position. 5. Set the Instant Pot to Pressure Cook. 6. Press the Pressure Level button to adjust the pressure to "High". 7. Use the "+/-" keys on the control panel to set the cooking time to 3 minutes. 8. Once the cooking cycle is completed, quick-release steam. 9. When all the steam is released, remove the pressure lid from the top carefully. 10. Transfer to a blender. Season with salt and blend until smooth. 11. Serve with pasta or brow rice.
Per Serving: Calories 84; Fat 5g; Sodium 41mg; Carbs 7g; Fiber 7.6g; Sugar 5g; Protein 2g

Tomato Basil Sauce

Prep time: 20 minutes | Cook time: 15 minutes | Serves: 4

1 tablespoon olive oil	½ cup chopped basil
3 cloves garlic, minced	¼ cup vegetable broth
2½-pound Roma tomatoes, diced	Salt to taste

1. Press the "Sauté" button twice to select "Normal" mode on the Instant Pot and heat the oil. 2. Add the garlic and sauté for 1 minute. 3. Add the tomatoes, basil, and broth. Mix well. 4. Put on the pressure cooker's lid and turn the steam valve to "Sealing" position. 5. Set the Instant Pot to Pressure Cook. 6. Use the "+/-" keys on the control panel to set the cooking time to 10 minutes. 7. Press the Pressure Level button to adjust the pressure to "High". 8. Once the cooking cycle is completed, quick-release steam. 9. When all the steam is released, remove the pressure lid from the top carefully. 10. Press the "Sauté" button twice to select "Normal" mode again and cook for 5 minutes more. Turn off heat. 11. Using an immersion blender, blend until smooth. 12. Taste and season with salt if necessary. Serve.
Per Serving: Calories 79; Fat 10g; Sodium 891mg; Carbs 22.9g; Fiber 4g; Sugar 4g; Protein 3g

Caramel Sauce

Prep time: 20 minutes | Cook time: 15 minutes | Serves: 4

1 cup sugar	⅓ cup condensed coconut milk
⅓ cup water	1 teaspoon vanilla extract
3 tablespoon coconut oil	

1. Press the "Sauté" button twice to select "Normal" mode. 2. In the Instant Pot, combine the sugar and water. Cook for 12 minutes. 3. Add the coconut oil, milk, and vanilla. Stir well. 4. Cook, stirring occasionally, until the mixture is smooth. 5. Press the CANCEL key to stop the SAUTÉ function. 6. Transfer to a heatproof container. 7. Let it cool and serve.
Per Serving: Calories 7; Fat 10g; Sodium 891mg; Carbs 22.9g; Fiber 4g; Sugar 4g; Protein 3g

Mushroom Gravy Sauce

Prep time: 20 minutes | Cook time: 3 minutes | Serves: 8

2 tablespoon butter	2 tablespoon flour
¼ cup shallots, chopped	¼ cup half and half
1 package button mushrooms, sliced	Salt to taste
2 cups beef broth	½ teaspoon black pepper

1. Press the "Sauté" button twice to select "Normal" mode 2. Once hot, add the butter and melt it. 3. Add the shallots and mushrooms. Cook until fragrant. 4. Whisk in the broth and flour. Whisk until smooth. 5. Simmer the mixture for 5 minutes. 6. Pour in half and half, stir well. Season with salt and pepper. 7. Put on the pressure cooker's lid and turn the steam valve to "Sealing" position. 8. Set the Instant Pot to Pressure Cook. 9. Use the "+/-" keys on the control panel to set the cooking time to 3 minutes. 10. Press the Pressure Level button to adjust the pressure to "High". 11. Once the cooking cycle is completed, allow the steam to release naturally for 10 minutes and then release the remaining pressure manually. 12. When all the steam is released, remove the pressure lid from the top carefully. 13. Serve.
Per Serving: Calories 72; Fat 10g; Sodium 891mg; Carbs 22.9g; Fiber 4g; Sugar 4g; Protein 3g

Chili Sauce

Prep time: 15 minutes | Cook time: 8 minutes | Serves: 4

4 medium-sized Ancho chili peppers	1½ teaspoons sugar
½ teaspoon cumin, ground	1½ cups water
½ teaspoon dried oregano, ground	2 tablespoon apple cider vinegar
2 teaspoons kosher salt	2 cloves garlic, crushed
	2 tablespoons heavy cream

1. Cut the peppers in half and remove the stems and seeds. Chop into small pieces. 2. Add the peppers, cumin, oregano, salt, and sugar to the Instant Pot. 3. Pour in the water and stir well. 4. Put on the pressure cooker's lid and turn the steam valve to "Sealing" position. 5. Set the Instant Pot to Pressure Cook. 6. Use the "+/-" keys on the control panel to set the cooking time to 8 minutes. 7. Press the Pressure Level button to adjust the pressure to "High". 8. Once the cooking cycle is completed, allow the steam to release naturally for 10 minutes and then release the remaining pressure manually. 9. When all the steam is released, remove the pressure lid from the top carefully. 10. Transfer the mixture to a food processor. 11. Add the vinegar, garlic, and heavy cream. Pulse until smooth and creamy. 12. Serve.
Per Serving: Calories 78; Fat 7.9g; Sodium 704mg; Carbs 6g; Fiber 3.6g; Sugar 6g; Protein 18g

White Sauce

Prep time: 15 minutes | Cook time: 3 minutes | Serves: 8

12-ounce cauliflower florets	½ cup water
2 tablespoons almond milk	¼ teaspoon pepper
¼ teaspoon garlic salt	

1. In the Instant Pot, combine the cauliflower florets, garlic salt, pepper, and water. 2. Put on the pressure cooker's lid and turn the steam valve to "Sealing" position. 3. Set the Instant Pot to Pressure Cook. 4. Use the "+/-" keys on the control panel to set the cooking time to 3 minutes. 5. Press the Pressure Level button to adjust the pressure to "High". 6. Once the cooking cycle is completed, quick-release the steam. 7. When all the steam is released, remove the pressure lid from the top carefully. 8. Using an immersion blender, blend until smooth. 9. Pour in the almond milk and mix well. 10. Serve.
Per Serving: Calories 84; Fat 5g; Sodium 41mg; Carbs 7g; Fiber 7.6g; Sugar 5g; Protein 2g

Chapter 11 Vegetable and Side Recipes

Steamed Artichokes Dip

Prep Time: 10 minutes | Cook Time: 15 minutes | Serves: 4

2 large artichokes
1 lemon, halved
1 cup water

3 tablespoons mayonnaise
1 teaspoon Dijon mustard
Pinch smoked paprika

1. Discard the damaged outer leaves of the artichokes, trim the bottoms flat and trim the tough ends of the leaves, then rub with 1 lemon half. 2. In the Inner Pot, add the water and place the Steam Rack; put the artichokes on the rack with the bloom facing up. 3. Place and lock the lid. 4. Select the Pressure Cook mode and press the button again to adjust the cooking time to 10 to 15 minutes (depending on the size of the artichokes, you can also cook a few minutes more); press the Pressure Level button to choose High Pressure. 5. While cooking, in a suitable bowl, thoroughly mix up the mayonnaise, mustard, paprika, and a generous squeeze of lemon juice. 6. When the time is up, leave the steam release handle from the Sealing position. 7. Uncover the lid, serve and enjoy the artichokes warm with the dipping sauce on the side.
Per Serving: Calories 344; Fat 14.9g; Sodium 227mg; Carbs 14g; Fiber 1g; Sugars 1.4g; Protein 25.7g

Delicious Cauliflower Queso

Prep Time: 5 minutes | Cook Time: 5 minutes | Serves: 2

1 head cauliflower cut into about 4 cups florets
2 cups water
1½ cups carrots, chopped into ½-inch-thick round pieces
½ cup raw cashews
1 (15-ounce) can no-salt-added diced tomatoes, divided

½ cup nutritional yeast
1 tablespoon white miso paste
2 teaspoons gluten-free chili powder
1 red bell pepper, diced
4 scallions, white and green parts, diced

1. In your inner pot, combine the cauliflower, water, carrots, and cashews. Lock the lid and turn the steam release handle to Sealing. 2. Select the Pressure Cook on the panel. Press the button again to choose Less option; use the "-" button to adjust the cooking time to 5 minutes. Press Pressure Level to choose High pressure. 3. After cooking has completed, quickly and carefully turn the steam release handle from Sealing position to the Venting position and uncover the lid carefully. 4. Drain and pour the mixture into a blender or food processor. Add the liquid from the can of tomatoes and put the drained tomatoes aside. Add the nutritional yeast, miso, and chili powder and stir well until it is very smooth. 5. Transfer to a medium bowl before stirring in the drained tomatoes, bell pepper, and scallions. 6. Serve right away. 7. If you haven't eaten up the dish, you can put the leftovers in a covered container and put them in the refrigerator for up to 4 days.
Per Serving: Calories: 77; Fat: 4g; Carbs: 10g; Fiber: 3g; Sugar: 4g; Sodium: 114mg; Protein: 3g

Lemon Beet Hummus

Prep Time: 10 minutes | Cook Time: 45 minutes | Serves: 6

3 cups water
1 cup dried chickpeas, rinsed and sorted
1 medium beet, peeled and quartered

½ cup tahini
2 tablespoons freshly squeezed lemon juice
4 garlic cloves, crushed
Salt (optional)

1. In the Inner Pot, add the chickpeas, beets and stir in water. 2. Place and lock the lid. 3. Select the Pressure Cook mode and press the button again to adjust the cooking time to 45 minutes; press the Pressure Level button to choose High Pressure. 4. While cooking, add the lemon juice, garlic and salt to the blender, do not blend. 5. When the time is up, leave the steam release handle from the Sealing position for 10 minutes, then turn it to the Venting position. 6. Uncover the lid and carefully transfer the chickpeas and beets to the blender, then blend well. 7. Chill until cool before serving; if the dip needs to be thinner, you can add the remaining liquid in the pot as needed.
Per Serving: Calories: 382; Fat: 19g; Carbs: 41g; Fiber: 10g; Sugar: 7g; Sodium: 63mg; Protein: 16g

Homemade Smoky "Baked" Beans

Prep Time: 15 minutes | Cook Time: 6 minutes | Serves: 4-6

2 cups dried great Northern beans, picked over and soaked overnight or quick-soaked
1 medium yellow onion, chopped
½ cup chopped dry-cured Spanish chorizo (2½ ounces; optional)

Salt and freshly ground black pepper
¼ cup ketchup
¼ cup lightly packed brown sugar
3 tablespoons molasses
2 tablespoons cider vinegar

1. Drain the beans and place them in the pot. Add 2¾ cups water (just enough to cover the beans), the onion, chorizo, 1 teaspoon salt, and several grinds of pepper. 2. Lock on the lid. Select the Pressure Cook on the panel. Press the button again to choose Less option; use the "-" button to adjust the cooking time to 6 minutes. Press Pressure Level to choose High pressure. Make sure the steam valve is in the "Sealing" position. 3. When the cooking time is up, leave the steam release handle in the Sealing position for about 20 minutes. Ladle off 1 cup of the cooking liquid and discard. 4. In a small bowl, mix the remaining ingredients and add to the beans. 5. Insert the inner pot into the cooker base. 6. Press Sauté to select the program and then press it again to choose the Normal heat. Simmer and stir constantly for 5 minutes, until the sauce has thickened, 5 minutes. 7. Press Cancel. 8. Season with salt and pepper and serve.
Per Serving: Calories 351; Fat 22g; Sodium 502mg; Carbs 15.2g; Sugar 1.1g; Fiber 0.7g; Protein 6.4g

Steamed Corn with Parsley

Prep Time: 10 minutes | Cook Time: 6 minutes | Serves: 4

4 cups water
4 ears corn, shucked and halved
½ teaspoon canola oil
1 tablespoon finely grated Parmesan cheese

Kosher salt
Freshly ground black pepper
⅛ teaspoon paprika
1 tablespoon finely chopped fresh parsley

1. In the Inner Pot, add the water and corn. 2. Place and lock the lid. 3. Select the Pressure Cook mode and press the button again to adjust the cooking time to 2 minutes; press the Pressure Level button to choose High Pressure. 4. When the time is up, quickly and carefully turn the steam release handle from the Sealing position to the Venting position. 5. Uncover the lid and transfer the corn to a prepared plate lined with paper towel, then carefully pour the hot water and dry the pot. 6. Without the lid, select Sauté mode and then press the same button again and then adjust the cooking temperature to Normal. 7. When the display switches On to Hot, add and heat the oil; add the corn and quickly toss with the oil, cook for 4 minutes without moving the corn or until charred, then rotate the corn and repeat twice until a few sided are charred. 8. Press the Cancel button to stop this cooking program, then transfer the corn to a platter, sprinkle with half of the Parmesan and season with the salt, pepper and a sprinkle of paprika on all sides. 9. Garnish with the parsley and enjoy.
Per Serving: Calories 254; Fat 28 g; Sodium 346mg; Carbs 12.3 g; Sugar 1g; Fiber 0.7g; Protein 24.3 g

Savory Mushroom Polenta

Prep Time: 10 minutes | Cook Time: 21 minutes | Serves: 6

1 medium onion, diced	3 tablespoons tomato paste
1⅓ cups Easy Vegetable Broth or no-salt-added vegetable broth, divided, plus more as needed	2 teaspoons dried thyme
	1 teaspoon balsamic vinegar
	Freshly ground black pepper
2 garlic cloves, minced	3 cups water
8 ounces white button mushrooms, sliced	1 cup polenta or coarsely ground cornmeal
8 ounces cremini mushrooms, sliced	1 cup milk

1. Insert the Inner Pot into the Cooker Base without the lid. 2. Select Sauté mode and then press the same button again and then adjust the cooking temperature to Normal. 3. When the display switches On to Hot, add the onion and cook for 3 to 5 minutes until translucent, adding water to prevent sticking; add the garlic and cook for 30 seconds until fragrant; add the mushroom and cook for 5 minutes or until softened; stir in the tomato paste, vinegar, thyme, pepper and ⅓ cup of the broth, cook for 3 minutes and scrape the browned bits from the bottom. 4. When done, transfer the mushroom mixture to a prepared bowl; rinse and then dry the Inner Pot. 5. Insert the Inner Pot into the Cooker Base again without the lid. 6. Select Sauté mode and then press the same button again and then adjust the cooking temperature to Normal. 7. When the display switches On to Hot, add the polenta, milk, water and the remaining broth and stir constantly for 5 minutes, until the mixture starts to simmer. 8. Press the Cancel button and lock the lid. 9. Select the Pressure Cook mode and press the button again to adjust the cooking time to 10 minutes; press the Pressure Level button to choose High Pressure. 10. When the time is up, quickly and carefully turn the steam release handle from the Sealing position to the Venting position. 11. Uncover the lid and serve the food on a plate, then top with the mushroom mixture. 12. Enjoy!
Per Serving: Calories: 221; Fat: 2g; Carbs: 43g; Fiber: 4g; Sugar: 7g; Sodium: 47mg; Protein: 9g

Egg Salad

Prep Time: 10 minutes | Cook Time: 7 minutes | Serves: 4

1 cup water	1 teaspoon Dijon or wholegrain mustard
6 eggs	
⅓ cup finely diced celery	1 teaspoon freshly squeezed lemon juice
¼ cup high-quality or homemade mayonnaise	
	Kosher salt
2 teaspoons minced fresh parsley	Freshly ground black pepper

1. In the Inner Pot, add the water and place the Steam Rack; put the eggs on the rack. 2. Place and lock the lid. 3. Select the Pressure Cook mode and press the button again to adjust the cooking time to 7 minutes; press the Pressure Level button to choose Low Pressure. 4. While cooking, thoroughly mix up the celery, mayonnaise, parsley, mustard, lemon juice, pepper and a sprinkle in a suitable bowl. 5. When the time is up, quickly and carefully turn the steam release handle from the Sealing position to the Venting position. 6. Uncover the lid and let the eggs cool for 30 seconds before rinsing them under the cold water. 7. In a prepared bowl, peel the eggs; use a fork to mash them for the desired consistency and mix with the mayonnaise mixture. 8. You can refrigerate this dish in an airtight container for up to 3 days.
Per Serving: Calories 305; Fat 15g; Sodium 548mg; Carbs 12g; Sugar 1.2g; Fiber 0.7g; Protein 29g

Fingerling Potatoes in Broth

Prep Time: 10 minutes | Cook Time: 17 minutes | Serves: 4

2 tablespoons butter	Kosher salt
1½ pounds small fingerling potatoes, each pricked twice with a small knife	Freshly ground black pepper
	1 fresh rosemary sprig (leaves only), minced
½ cup vegetable or chicken broth	

1. Insert the Inner Pot into the Cooker Base without the lid. 2. Select Sauté mode and then press the same button again and then adjust the cooking temperature to More. 3. When the display switches On to Hot, add and melt the butter; add the potatoes and stir regularly for 10 minutes to coat well, or until the skins start to get crispy and the butter is browned; pour in the broth. 4. Press the Cancel button and lock the lid. 5. Select the Pressure Cook mode and press the button again to adjust the cooking time to 7 minutes; press the Pressure Level button to choose High Pressure. 6. When the time is up, leave the steam release handle in the Sealing position for 10 minutes, then turn it to the Venting position. 7. Uncover the lid and serve the food on a plate. 8. Season with salt, pepper and top with the rosemary and enjoy.
Per Serving: Calories 344; Fat 14.9g; Sodium 227mg; Carbs 12g; Fiber 1.2g; Sugars 1g; Protein 27g

Homemade Jalapeño Popper Dip

Prep Time: 10 minutes | Cook Time: 30 minutes | Serves: 2

2 jalapeño peppers, divided	½ cup cashews
½ pound dried great northern beans, rinsed and sorted	¼ cup milk
	2 garlic cloves, crushed
½ medium onion, roughly chopped	2 tablespoons nutritional yeast
	1 tablespoon chickpea miso paste
4 cups water, divided	1 tablespoon apple cider vinegar

1. Slice 1 of the jalapeños in half lengthwise and remove the seeds. 2. In your Inner Pot, combine the halved pepper, beans, onion, and 3 cups of the water. Lock the lid and turn the steam release handle to Sealing. 3. Select the Pressure Cook on the panel. Press the button again to choose Normal option; use the "-" button to adjust the cooking time to 30 minutes. Press Pressure Level to choose High pressure. 4. Boil the remaining 1 cup of water and pour in a large bowl over cashews; soak for at least 30 minutes. Drain the soaking liquid before adding the cashews. 5. After cooking has completed, leave the steam release handle in the Sealing position for 10 minutes after cooking has completed, then turn the steam release handle to the Venting position; quick-release any remaining pressure and uncover the lid carefully. 6. Remove the jalapeño from the pot and then chop it. Finely chop the remaining raw jalapeño and remove the seed. Put both peppers aside. 7. Drain the beans and onion, then combine them in a blender with the cashews, milk, garlic, nutritional yeast, miso, and vinegar. Blend all of them until the mixture is creamy. Spoon into a medium mixing bowl and stir in the jalapeños. 8. Serve right away.
Per Serving: Calories: 314; Fat: 9g; Carbs: 44g; Fiber: 13g; Sugar: 4g; Sodium: 177mg; Protein: 17g

Faux Gratin Potatoes in Broth

Prep Time: 10 minutes | Cook Time: 50 minutes | Serves: 4

2 tablespoons butter	⅔ cup store-bought vegetable or chicken broth
2 medium garlic cloves, sliced	
2 pounds Yukon Gold potatoes, peeled and cut into ¼-inch-thick slices	1½ cups grated cheese of your choice (cheddar, Gruyère, or Swiss; 6 ounces)
Salt and freshly ground black pepper	¼ cup heavy cream, warmed

1. Insert the Inner Pot into the Cooker Base without the lid. 2. Select Sauté mode and then press the same button again and then adjust the cooking temperature to Normal. 3. When the display switches On to Hot, add and melt the butter; add the garlic and stir constantly for 45 seconds until fragrant 4. Press the Cancel button to stop this cooking program. 5. Still in the pot, add the potatoes, 1 teaspoon of salt and several grinds of pepper, then stir to coat the potatoes with the garlic mixture; pour in the broth and then lock the lid. 6. Select the Pressure Cook mode and press the button again to adjust the cooking time to 9 minutes; press the Pressure Level button to choose Low Pressure. 7. When the time is up, leave turn the steam release handle in the Sealing position for 1 minute, then turn it to the Venting position. 8. Preheat your oven with the suitable oven rack in it. 9. In the suitable baking dish, pour the potato mixture and use the spatula to gently fold in 1 cup of cheese and cream; top with the ½ cup of cheese and broil for 3 to 5 minutes until browned and bubbly. 10. When done, serve and enjoy.
Per Serving: Calories 236; Fat 13.9g; Sodium 451mg; Carbs 13.2g; Fiber 1.2g; Sugars 1.4g; Protein 14.3g

Fresh Steamed Artichokes with Lemon-Dijon Dipping Sauce

Prep Time: 10 minutes | Cook Time: 15 minutes | Serves: 4

4 (10-ounce) whole artichokes, rinsed and drained
½ cup (1 stick) unsalted butter, at room temperature
2 garlic cloves, chopped
2½ tablespoons fresh lemon juice
1 tablespoon Dijon mustard
Salt and freshly ground black pepper

1. Trim the artichoke stems to within 1 inch of the base. Place the Steam Rack in the pot and add 1½ cups warm water. Place the artichokes stem-side down on the rack. 2. Select the Pressure Cook on the panel. Press the button again to choose Less option; use the "-" button to adjust the cooking time to 10 minutes. Press Pressure Level to choose High pressure. Make sure the steam valve is in the "Sealing" position. 3. When the cooking time is up, quickly and carefully turn the steam release handle from Sealing position to the Venting position. 4. To test for doneness, pull a leaf from near the center of an artichoke and scrape the tender bottom of the leaf off with your teeth; the flesh should come away easily. If they're not done, lock on the lid and cook under High pressure for a minute or so more. 5. Transfer the artichokes to serving plates with tongs, cover loosely. Remove the rack from the pot and remove the cooking water. 6. Press the Cancel button to stop this cooking program. 7. Insert the inner pot into the cooker base without the lid. 8. Press Sauté to select the program and press it again to choose More option. Add the butter and garlic to the pot and cook for 1 minute until the garlic is sizzling and fragrant. 9. Press Cancel. 10. Whisk in the lemon juice and mustard. Add some salt and pepper to season as you like. 11. Pour the butter mixture into dipping bowls and serve with the artichokes.
Per Serving: Calories 336; Fat 17.3g; Sodium 281mg; Carbs 8.1g; Fiber 5.3g; Sugars 17.7g; Protein 3.3g

Bok Choy with Sesame Seeds

Prep Time: 10 minutes | Cook Time: 4 minutes | Serves: 4

1 cup water
1 medium head bok choy, leaves separated
1 teaspoon soy sauce
½ teaspoon sesame oil
2 teaspoons sesame seeds
Kosher salt
Freshly ground black pepper

1. In the Inner Pot, add the water and place the Steam Rack; put the bok choy on the rack with the thickest leaves facing down. 2. Place and lock the lid. 3. Select the Pressure Cook mode and press the button again to adjust the cooking time to 4 minutes; press the Pressure Level button to choose High Pressure. 4. When the time is up, quickly and carefully turn the steam release handle from the Sealing position to the Venting position. 5. Uncover the lid and carefully remove the bok choy to a prepared bowl, toss it with the soy sauce, sesame oil, sesame seeds and season with the salt and pepper. 6. Enjoy.
Per Serving: Calories 36; Fat 17.3g; Sodium 281mg; Carbs 8.1g; Fiber 5.3g; Sugars 17.7g; Protein 32.3g

Steamed Garlic Edamame

Prep Time: 10 minutes | Cook Time: 10 minutes | Serves: 4

1 cup water
2 cups fresh or frozen edamame, in their pods
1 teaspoon sesame oil or extra-
virgin olive oil
3 large garlic cloves, minced
1 tablespoon soy sauce
Sea salt

1. In the Inner Pot, add the water and place the Steam Rack; put the edamame on the rack. 2. Place and lock the lid. 3. Select the Steam mode and press the button again to adjust the cooking time to 3 minutes; press the Pressure Level button to choose High Pressure. 4. While cooking, heat the oil in a suitable skillet over medium heat, once hot, add the garlic and cook for 1 to 2 minutes until cooked but not brown; add the soy sauce and then turn off the heat. 5. When the time is up, quickly and carefully turn the steam release handle from the Sealing position to the Venting position. 6. Uncover the lid and serve the edamame in a prepared bowl, toss with the garlic mixture. 7. Season with salt and enjoy.
Per Serving: Calories 249; Fat 13g; Sodium 556mg; Carbs 10g; Sugar 1.1g; Fiber 0.7g; Protein 31g

Delicious Corn Pudding

Prep Time: 10 minutes | Cook Time: 30 minutes | Serves: 4

2 tablespoons butter
2 shallots, finely chopped
1 cup fresh corn, cut off the cob
¾ cup whole milk
¼ cup sour cream
3 tablespoons cornmeal
1 tablespoon sugar
2 eggs, beaten
½ teaspoon kosher salt
¼ teaspoon freshly ground black pepper
1½ cups water

1. In a suitable bowl, mix up the corn, milk, sour cream, cornmeal, sugar, eggs, salt, and pepper. 2. Insert the Inner Pot into the Cooker Base without the lid. 3. Select Sauté mode and then press the same button again and then adjust the cooking temperature to More. 4. When the display switches On to Hot, add and melt the butter; add the shallots and press the Cancel button, cook the shallots until the sizzling stops. 5. Add the butter and shallots to the corn mixture and stir well. 6. Oil a suitable round baking dish with the butter and pour the mixture into it, cover with foil. 7. Add the water to the pot and place the Steam Rack, then arrange the baking dish to the rack; place and lock the lid. 8. Select the Pressure Cook mode and press the button again to adjust the cooking time to 30 minutes; press the Pressure Level button to choose Low Pressure. 9. When the time is up, quickly and carefully turn the steam release handle from the Sealing position to the Venting position. 10. Uncover the lid and remove the dish, let it cool a few minutes before serving.
Per Serving: Calories 236; Fat 13.9g; Sodium 451mg; Carbs 13.2g; Fiber 1.2g; Sugars 1.4g; Protein 14.3g

Corn on the Cob

Prep Time: 10 minutes | Cook Time: 2 minutes | Serves: 4

For The Corn
4 ears corn, shucked
For Mexican Corn on The Cob
⅓ cup mayonnaise
¼ cup finely chopped fresh cilantro
2 teaspoons ground New Mexican chile powder
½ cup crumbled aged Cotija or feta cheese
For Maple-Barbecue Corn on The Cob
4 tablespoons (½ stick) room-temperature butter
2 tablespoons maple syrup
4 teaspoons thick barbecue sauce
Garlic salt
For Hot Wings–Style Corn On The Cob
4 tablespoons (½ stick) butter, at room temperature
2 tablespoons hot sauce
4 teaspoons honey
½ cup crumbled blue cheese
1¼ teaspoons celery salt
For French Corn on The Cob
½ cup soft herb and garlic cheese spread (such as Boursin), at room temperature
2 tablespoons finely chopped fresh chives
Freshly ground black pepper

1. In the Inner Pot, add 1½ cups of warm water and place the Steam Rack; put the corn on the rack. 2. Place and lock the lid. 3. Select the Pressure Cook mode and press the button again to adjust the cooking time to 2 minutes; press the Pressure Level button to choose High Pressure. 4. When the time is up, quickly and carefully turn the steam release handle from the Sealing position to the Venting position. 5. To make the Mexican Corn: Spread the mayonnaise on the corn, sprinkle with the cilantro, cheese and chili powder. 6. To make the Maple-Barbecue Corn: Mix up the butter, maple syrup, BBQ sauce in a suitable bowl then and spread on the corn; sprinkle with the garlic salt before serving. 7. To make the Hot Wings-Style Corn: Mix up the butter, hot sauce and honey in a suitable bowl, then spread on the corn; roll the cobs in the blue cheese and sprinkle with the celery salt. 8. To make the French Corn: Spread the cheese all over the cobs, roll in the chives and season with pepper.
Per Serving: Calories 285; Fat 9.8g; Sodium 639mg; Carbs 11.1g; Fiber 1.2g; Sugars 5.1g; Protein 7.8g

Parmesan Spaghetti Squash

Prep Time: 10 minutes | Cook Time: 11 minutes | Serves: 4

1 (2- to 4-pound) spaghetti squash, halved crosswise
1 cup water
⅓ cup pine nuts
2 tablespoons extra-virgin olive oil
3 garlic cloves, minced
Juice of ½ lemon
⅓ cup grated Parmesan cheese
Kosher salt
Freshly ground black pepper
2 tablespoons chopped fresh basil leaves

1. Set half of each squash aside. Scoop out all the seeds and sticky fibrous innards with a spoon, making the two halves hollow. 2. In the Inner Pot, add the water and set the squash inside with the cut-side up. 3. Place and lock the lid. 4. Select the Pressure Cook mode and press the button again to adjust the cooking time to 7 minutes; press the Pressure Level button to choose High Pressure. 5. While cooking, cook the pine nuts for 3 minutes in a sauté pan over medium-high heat until toasted, tossing every 30 seconds; when done, remove and set aside for later use. 6. Still in the sauté pan, heat the oil and cook the garlic for 1 minutes, until cooked but not brown; when done, turn off the heat. 7. When the time is up, quickly and carefully turn the steam release handle from the Sealing position to the Venting position. 8. Uncover the lid, take out the squash and drain any collected water. 9. Separate the strands from the peel with a fork, keeping the strands as long as possible. 10. In a suitable bowl, toss the strands with the lemon juice, most of the Parmesan, cooked oil and garlic mixture; season the strands with salt and pepper, and top them with the toasted pine nuts, more Parmesan and basil. 11. Serve.
Per Serving: Calories 305; Fat 15g; Sodium 548mg; Carbs 12g; Sugar 1.2g; Fiber 0.7g; Protein 29g

Honey Cayenne Carrots

Prep Time: 10 minutes | Cook Time: 2 minutes | Serves: 4

1 cup water
5 to 6 large carrots, peeled and cut into 1-inch chunks (about 3 cups)
1 tablespoon butter
¼ teaspoon ground cumin
¼ teaspoon cayenne
Kosher salt
Freshly ground black pepper
2 teaspoons honey

1. In the Inner Pot, add the water and place the Steam Rack; put the carrots on the rack. 2. Place and lock the lid. 3. Select the Steam mode and press the button again to adjust the cooking time to 2 minutes; press the Pressure Level button to choose High Pressure. 4. When the time is up, quickly and carefully turn the steam release handle from the Sealing position to the Venting position. 5. Uncover the lid and carefully take out the carrots and rack; pour the hot cooking water, clean and dry the pot. 6. Insert the Inner Pot into the Cooker Base without the lid. 7. Select Sauté mode and then press the same button again and then adjust the cooking temperature to Normal. 8. When the display switches On to Hot, add and melt the butter; put the carrots back to pot and stir until well coated; stir in the cumin, cayenne, salt and pepper. 9. Lastly, add the honey and press the Cancel button. 10. Stir until fully coated before serving.
Per Serving: Calories 344; Fat 14.9g; Sodium 227mg; Carbs 14g; Fiber 1g; Sugars 1.4g; Protein 25.7g

Butternut Squash and Parsnips

Prep Time: 10 minutes | Cook Time: 10 minutes | Serves: 4

2 tablespoons butter
1½ cups peeled butternut squash, cut into 1-inch cubes
1 cup peeled parsnips, cut into 1-inch cubes
1 cup peeled turnips, cut into 1-inch cubes
¾ cup vegetable or chicken broth
⅛ teaspoon sugar
¼ teaspoon baking soda
Kosher salt
Freshly ground black pepper
1 teaspoon finely chopped fresh rosemary

1. Insert the Inner Pot into the Cooker Base without the lid. 2. Select Sauté mode and then press the same button again and then adjust the cooking temperature to Normal. 3. When the display switches On to Hot, add and melt the butter; add the butternut squash cubes and stir regularly for 4 minutes; stir in the parsnips, turnips, broth, sugar, baking soda, salt and pepper. 4. Press the Cancel button and then lock the lid. 5. Select the Pressure Cook mode and press the button again to adjust the cooking time to 6 minutes; press the Pressure Level button to choose High Pressure. 6. When the time is up, quickly and carefully turn the steam release handle from the Sealing position to the Venting position. 7. Uncover the lid and drain off most of the liquid. 8. With the rosemary, serve and enjoy.
Per Serving: Calories 236; Fat 13.9g; Sodium 451mg; Carbs 13.2g; Fiber 1.2g; Sugars 1.4g; Protein 14.3g

Butter Mashed Potatoes

Prep Time: 10 minutes | Cook Time: 10 minutes | Serves: 8

4 pounds Yukon Gold potatoes, peeled and quartered
3 cups water
1 teaspoon kosher salt, plus more for seasoning
5 tablespoons butter
½ cup whole milk
1 cup sour cream
¼ cup drained prepared horseradish
Freshly ground black pepper

1. In the Inner Pot, add the potatoes, water and salt. 2. Place and lock the lid. 3. Select the Pressure Cook mode and press the button again to adjust the cooking time to 10 minutes; press the Pressure Level button to choose High Pressure. 4. While cooking, heat the butter and milk in a small saucepan over low heat until start to be very warm. 5. When the time is up, quickly and carefully turn the steam release handle from the Sealing position to the Venting position. 6. Uncover the lid and drain off the cooking liquid, reserving ½ cup. 7. Mash the potatoes with a masher until fluffy and all lumps are gone; add the sour cream, horseradish, warm milk and butter; season with the pepper and then mix them to combine well. 8. Serve and enjoy. 9. You can add the cooking liquid as needed if the potatoes are too thick.
Per Serving: Calories 351; Fat 22g; Sodium 502mg; Carbs 15.2g; Sugar 1.1g; Fiber 0.7g; Protein 6.4g

Tasty Indian-Style Spaghetti Squash

Prep Time: 10 minutes | Cook Time: 15 minutes | Serves: 4

1 medium (2½-pound) spaghetti squash, halved lengthwise and seeded
3 tablespoons unsalted butter or ghee
1½ teaspoons brown mustard
seeds
1 teaspoon cumin seeds
3 medium garlic cloves, chopped
1 medium tomato, chopped
Salt and freshly ground black pepper

1. Place a trivet in the bottom of the pot and add 1½ cups cold water. Place the squash halves cut-side up in the pot. Lock on the lid, select the Pressure Cook on the panel. Press the button again to choose Less option; use the "-" button to adjust the cooking time to 8 minutes. Press Pressure Level to choose High pressure. Make sure the steam valve is in the "Sealing" position. 2. When the cooking time is up, quickly and carefully turn the steam release handle from Sealing position to the Venting position. 3. Transfer the squash to a cutting board. Drag a fork crosswise over the squash to scrape out the flesh into strands; remove the skins. Place the squash in a large serving bowl and cover with foil. 4. Insert the inner pot into the cooker base. 5. Remove the steaming water, dry out the pot, and return it to the appliance. Press Sauté to select the program and then adjust to Normal heat. Add the butter and when the butter has melted, add the mustard seeds and cumin seeds and cook, stirring frequently, until the seeds begin to pop, 1 minute. Add the garlic and tomato and cook until fragrant, 1 minute. 6. Press the Cancel button. 7. Pour the butter mixture over the squash. Add some salt and pepper to taste and mix well with tongs.
Per Serving: Calories 344; Fat 14.9g; Sodium 227mg; Carbs 14g; Fiber 1g; Sugars 1.4g; Protein 2.7g

Braised Cabbage in Broth

Prep Time: 10 minutes | Cook Time: 8 minutes | Serves: 6

3 bacon slices
1 tablespoon butter
1 small head green cabbage, cored, quartered, and cut into

½-inch strips
1 cup vegetable or chicken broth
Kosher salt
Freshly ground pepper

1. Insert the Inner Pot into the Cooker Base without the lid. 2. Select Sauté mode and then press the same button again and then adjust the cooking temperature to Normal. 3. When the display switches On to Hot, add the bacon and cook for 5 minutes, flipping halfway through, then remove the bacon and cut into pieces; add and melt the butter; stir in the cabbage, bacon, broth, salt and pepper. 4. Press the Cancel button and lock the lid. 5. Select the Pressure Cook mode and press the button again to adjust the cooking time to 3 minutes; press the Pressure Level button to choose High Pressure. 6. When the time is up, quickly and carefully turn the steam release handle from the Sealing position to the Venting position. 7. Uncover the lid and enjoy.
Per Serving: Calories: 70; Fat: 2g; Sodium: 263mg; Carbs: 7g; Sugar: 3g; Protein: 4g

Creamy Parmesan Polenta

Prep Time: 10 minutes | Cook Time: 39 minutes | Serves: 4

2 tablespoons olive oil
2 medium garlic cloves, thinly sliced
4 cups store-bought chicken or vegetable broth, warmed

1 bay leaf
Salt and freshly ground black pepper
1 cup polenta (not quick-cooking)
½ cup grated Parmesan cheese

1. Insert the Inner Pot into the Cooker Base without the lid. 2.Select Sauté mode and then press the same button again and then adjust the cooking temperature to Normal. 3.When the display switches On to Hot, add and heat the oil; add the garlic and stir constantly for 30 seconds until fragrant; add the broth, bay leaf and ½ teaspoon of salt, when the liquid starts to simmer, gradually whisk in the polenta. 4.Press the Cancel button to stop this cooking program and lock the lid. 5.Select the Pressure Cook mode and press the button again to adjust the cooking time to 9 minutes; press the Pressure Level button to choose Low Pressure. 6.When the time is up, leave turn the steam release handle in the Sealing position for 10 minutes, then turn it to the Venting position. 7.Uncover the lid, wait for seconds until the food is thicken, then whisk in the cheese and season with the salt and pepper; discard the bay leaf. 8.Serve. 9.For solid polenta to pan-fry or broil, transfer the polenta to a container and refrigerate without covering for at least 2 hours. 10.For pan-fry, cut into cubes and pan-fry in a non-stick skillet with a few tablespoons of olive oil over medium heat for 10 minutes, flipping halfway through, until golden brown. 11. For broil, spread squares of polenta on a baking sheet lined with foil; drizzle with oil, sprinkle with a little Parmesan cheese, and broil 4 inches for 6 minutes from the broiler element until the cheese is bubbly.
Per Serving: Calories 305; Fat 15g; Sodium 548mg; Carbs 12g; Sugar 1.2g; Fiber 0.7g; Protein 2g

Lemon Beets with Goat Cheese

Prep Time: 10 minutes | Cook Time: 20 minutes | Serves: 4

1 cup water
4 medium beets
½ cup crumbled goat cheese
Juice of ½ lemon

Extra-virgin olive oil
Kosher salt
Freshly ground black pepper

1. Trim the beets in the sink after cleaning them. 2. In the Inner Pot, add the water and place the Steam Rack; put the beets on the rack. 3. Place and lock the lid. 4. Select the Pressure Cook mode and press the button again to adjust the cooking time to 20 minutes (you can cook for 5 minutes more if the beets don't reach the needed doneness); press the Pressure Level button to choose High Pressure. 5. When the time is up, quickly and carefully turn the steam release handle from the Sealing position to the Venting position. 6. Uncover the lid and carefully take out the beets and rack. 7. Cool the beets under cold water in the sink, then slide the skins off and slice them on a plate board. 8. Serve the beet slices on a prepared plate, top them with the goat cheese, lemon juice, a drizzle of olive oil and season with salt and pepper. 9. Enjoy.
Per Serving: Calories 285; Fat 9.8g; Sodium 639mg; Carbs 11.1g; Fiber 1.2g; Sugars 5.1g; Protein 27.8g

Butter Potatoes Mash

Prep Time: 10 minutes | Cook Time: 10 minutes | Serves: 6

4 medium russet potatoes (2 pounds), peeled and quartered
Salt
1 medium (8-ounce) bunch lacinato kale, tough center rib discarded, leaves chopped

4 tablespoons (½ stick) unsalted butter, at room temperature
4 green onions, thinly sliced
¼ to ½ cup whole milk or heavy cream

1. In the Inner Pot, add 1 cup of water and add the potatoes; sprinkle with ½ teaspoon of salt; top the potatoes with the kale. 2. Place and lock the lid. 3. Select the Pressure Cook mode and press the button again to adjust the cooking time to 8 minutes; press the Pressure Level button to choose High Pressure. 4. When the time is up, quickly and carefully turn the steam release handle from the Sealing position to the Venting position. 5. Uncover the lid, transfer the potatoes and kale to the colander in the sink and cool them for a few minutes; let the steam evaporate will make the potatoes fluffier when you mash them. 6. While cooling, insert the Inner Pot into the Cooker Base without the lid. 7. Select Sauté mode and then press the same button again and then adjust the cooking temperature to Normal. 8. When the display switches On to Hot, add and melt the butter; add the green onions and cook for 1 minutes until tender; add the milk or cream and cook for 1 minute to bring to a simmer. 9. When done, press the Cancel button to stop this cooking program, then transfer the cooled potatoes and kale back to the pot. 10. Use a potato masher to mash the potatoes until mostly smooth. 11. Season with salt and pepper before serving.
Per Serving: Calories 344; Fat 14.9g; Sodium 227mg; Carbs 14g; Fiber 1g; Sugars 1.4g; Protein 2.7g

Bacon Potatoes

Prep Time: 10 minutes | Cook Time: 15 minutes | Serves: 6

8 ounces applewood-smoked bacon, chopped
½ cup store-bought chicken broth, or homemade
6 tablespoons white wine vinegar
2½ tablespoons grainy mustard
2 tablespoons packed light brown sugar

2 teaspoons caraway seeds
½ teaspoon salt, plus more for seasoning
3 pounds small red potatoes, unpeeled, cut into ¾-inch chunks
½ cup finely chopped sweet onion (such as Walla Walla or Vidalia)
Freshly ground black pepper

1. Insert the Inner Pot into the Cooker Base without the lid. 2. Select Sauté mode and then press the same button again and then adjust the cooking temperature to Normal. 3. When the display switches On to Hot, add the bacon and stir constantly for 8 minutes until crisp and browned, then transfer the bacon to the plate lined with a paper towel. 4. Reserve 2 tablespoons of the drippings in a small bowl for the dressing and discard the remaining drippings. 5. Press the Cancel button to stop this cooking program. 6. Still in the Inner Pot, stir in the broth, vinegar, mustard, brown sugar, caraway seeds and ½ teaspoon salt; place the Steam Rack and put the potatoes on it. 7. Place and lock the lid. 8. Select the Pressure Cook mode and press the button again to adjust the cooking time to 7 minutes; press the Pressure Level button to choose High Pressure. 9. When the time is up, quickly and carefully turn the steam release handle from the Sealing position to the Venting position. 10. Uncover the lid, transfer the potatoes to a suitable bowl; take out the rack, pour the cooking liquid and reserved bacon drippings over the potatoes. 11. After adding the onion and seasoning with the salt and several grinds of pepper, gently use a spatula to toss them to combine well. Enjoy.
Per Serving: Calories 336; Fat 17.3g; Sodium 281mg; Carbs 8.1g; Fiber 5.3g; Sugars 17.7g; Protein 2.3g

Simple Zucchini Ratatouille

Prep Time: 10 minutes | Cook Time: 15 minutes | Serves: 4

1 tablespoon extra-virgin olive oil, plus extra for serving
1 medium yellow onion, finely chopped
1 large red bell pepper, finely chopped
2 garlic cloves, minced
4 medium zucchini, chopped into bite-size pieces
¼ cup dry white wine
2 large tomatoes, seeded and diced, or 2 handfuls large cherry tomatoes, halved
1 bay leaf
3 fresh thyme sprigs
Kosher salt
Freshly ground black pepper
2 tablespoons torn fresh basil

1. Insert the Inner Pot into the Cooker Base without the lid. 2. Select Sauté mode and then press the same button again and then adjust the cooking temperature to More. 3. When the display switches On to Hot, add the oil, onion, bell pepper, garlic in order and stir regularly for 2 minutes until the vegetables start to brown; add the zucchini and cook for 3 minutes until it starts to brown; stir in the wine and then scrape the brown bits from the bottom of the pot. 4. Press the Cancel button to stop this cooking program, add the tomatoes, bay leaf, thyme, salt and pepper, then place and lock the lid. 5. Select the Pressure Cook mode and press the button again to adjust the cooking time to 3 minutes; press the Pressure Level button to choose High Pressure. 6. When the time is up, quickly and carefully turn the steam release handle from the Sealing position to the Venting position. 7. Uncover the lid. To reduce the liquid, resume cooking the food for 2 to 3 minutes on Sauté mode at More temperature. 8. When done, remove and discard the bay leaf; wait for a few minutes before serving and topping with the fresh basil and a drizzle of olive oil.
Per Serving: Calories 285; Fat 9.8g; Sodium 639mg; Carbs 11.1g; Fiber 1.2g; Sugars 5.1g; Protein 27.8g

Delicious Smoky Collard Greens or Kale

Prep Time: 15 minutes | Cook Time: 15 minutes | Serves: 4

3 slices thick-cut pepper bacon, chopped
1 small yellow onion, chopped
3 medium garlic cloves, chopped
¾ cup store-bought chicken or vegetable broth, or homemade (page 227 or 226)
2 large (9-ounce) bunches collard
greens or kale, tough center stems discarded, leaves torn
2 tablespoons cider vinegar or red wine vinegar
1 teaspoon smoked paprika
Salt and freshly ground black pepper

1. Insert the inner pot into the cooker base. 2. Press Sauté to select the program and adjust to Normal heat. Add the bacon and onion and cook, stirring now and then, until the bacon is browned, 8 minutes. Add the garlic and sauté until fragrant, 45 seconds. 3. Press. Cancel. 4. Add the broth and scrape up the browned bits on the bottom of the pot. Add the greens, vinegar, paprika, ½ teaspoon salt, and several grinds of pepper and toss with tongs to coat the greens with the liquid. Lock on the lid, select the Pressure Cook on the panel. Press the button again to choose Less option; use the "-" button to adjust the cooking time to 5 minutes. Press Pressure Level to choose High pressure. Make sure the steam valve is in the "Sealing" position. 5. When the cooking time is up, leave the steam release handle in the Sealing position for 10 minutes and then quickly and carefully turn the steam release handle from Sealing position to the Venting position. Add some salt and pepper to season as you like. 6. Serve the greens immediately.
Per Serving: Calories 285; Fat 9.8g; Sodium 639mg; Carbs 11.1g; Fiber 1.2g; Sugars 5.1g; Protein 2.8g

Homemade Sweet-and-Sour Red Cabbage

Prep Time: 10 minutes | Cook Time: 10 minutes | Serves: 6

1 medium (2-pound) red cabbage
2 tablespoons olive oil
½ medium red onion, sliced
1½ teaspoons caraway seeds
½ teaspoon baking soda
3 tablespoons red wine vinegar
1 tablespoon brown sugar
Salt and freshly ground black pepper

1. Cut the cabbage into quarters. Cut out the hard, white core at the base of each quarter and discard. Shred the cabbage into ¼-inch-wide strips. Set aside. 2. Insert the inner pot into the cooker base without the lid. 3. Press Sauté to select the program and then press it again to choose the Less temperature options. Put the oil in the pot, when the oil is hot, add the onion, caraway seeds, and baking soda and cook until tender, 4 minutes. Add the vinegar and brown sugar and sauté. 4. Add the cabbage, ½ teaspoon salt, and several grinds of black pepper and toss to coat. 5. Lock on the lid, select the Pressure Cook on the panel. Press the button again to choose Less option; use the "-" button to adjust the cooking time to 5 minutes. Press Pressure Level to choose High pressure. Make sure the steam valve is in the "Sealing" position. 6. When the cooking time is up, quickly and carefully turn the steam release handle from Sealing position to the Venting position. Season with salt and pepper, and serve.
Per Serving: Calories 249; Fat 13g; Sodium 556mg; Carbs 10g; Sugar 1.1g; Fiber 0.7g; Protein 1g

Garlic Baby Potatoes with Herbs

Prep Time: 10 minutes | Cook Time: 7 minutes | Serves: 6

2 pounds baby red-skinned potatoes
1 cup water
3 tablespoons plant-based butter, melted, or extra-virgin olive oil
1 teaspoon garlic powder
1 teaspoon dried thyme
1 teaspoon dried rosemary, crushed
1 teaspoon salt
Freshly ground black pepper

1. Use a fork to pierce the potatoes. 2. In the Inner Pot, add the potatoes and water. 3. Place and lock the lid. 4. Select the Pressure Cook mode and press the button again to adjust the cooking time to 7 minutes; press the Pressure Level button to choose High Pressure. 5. When the time is up, quickly and carefully turn the steam release handle from the Sealing position to the Venting position. 6. Press the Cancel button and uncover the lid; drain the water and select the Sauté mode, press it again to choose Normal option. 7. Add the olive oil or butter, garlic powder, thyme, rosemary, salt and pepper in the pot, then cook the mixture for 3 to 4 minutes until the potatoes are slightly browned. 8. When done, serve and enjoy.
Per Serving: Calories: 251; Fat: 10g; Carbs: 37g; Fiber: 4g; Sugar: 3g; Sodium: 623mg; Protein: 4g

California Basmati Rice

Prep Time: 10 minutes | Cook Time: 6 minutes | Serves: 4

2 tablespoons canola oil
3 medium garlic cloves, finely chopped
1 tablespoon finely chopped fresh ginger
1½ cups California basmati rice (such as Lundberg brand), rinsed
and drained
1½ teaspoons garam masala or curry powder
½ teaspoon ground turmeric
Salt
1 cup frozen peas

1. Insert the Inner Pot into the Cooker Base without the lid. 2. Select Sauté mode and then press the same button again and then adjust the cooking temperature to Normal. 3. When the display switches On to Hot, add and heat the oil; add the ginger, garlic and stir constantly for 45 seconds until fragrant. 4. Press the Cancel button to stop this cooking program. 5. Still in the Inner Pot, add the rice, garam marsala and turmeric, 1½ cups of water and ¾ teaspoon of salt, stir to coat, then top the rice with the peas. 6. Place and lock the lid. 7. Select the Pressure Cook mode and press the button again to adjust the cooking time to 6 minutes; press the Pressure Level button to choose High Pressure. 8. When the time is up, leave turn the steam release handle in the Sealing position for 10 minutes, then turn it to the Venting position. 9. Uncover the lid and use a fork to fluff the rice. 10. Serve and enjoy.
Per Serving: Calories 225; Fat 16.47g; Sodium 43mg; Carbs 26.26g; Fiber 11g; Sugar 0.48g; Protein 7.23g

Long-Grain Rice in Tomato Sauce

Prep Time: 10 minutes | Cook Time: 13 minutes | Serves: 4

2 tablespoons olive oil	and drained
1 small onion, finely chopped	2 tablespoons taco seasoning
1 cup chopped green bell pepper	⅔ cup V8 tomato juice (1 small
1½ cups long-grain rice, rinsed	5.5-ounce can)

1. Insert the Inner Pot into the Cooker Base without the lid. 2. Select Sauté mode and then press the same button again and then adjust the cooking temperature to Normal. 3. When the display switches On to Hot, add and heat the oil; add the onion, bell pepper and stir constantly for 4 minutes until tender. 4. Press the Cancel button to stop this cooking program. 5. Stir in the rice and taco seasoning and coat the rice with the vegetables and oil. 6. Place and lock the lid. 7. Select the Pressure Cook mode and press the button again to adjust the cooking time to 4 minutes; press the Pressure Level button to choose High Pressure. 8. When the time is up, leave the steam release handle in the Sealing position for 5 minutes, then turn it to the Venting position. 9. Uncover the lid and use a fork to fluff the rice. 10. Serve and enjoy.
Per Serving: Calories 348; Fat 8.92g; Sodium 361mg; Carbs 60.16g; Fiber 4.2g; Sugar 3.39g; Protein 6.44g

Homemade Baba Ghanoush

Prep Time: 5 minutes | Cook Time: 12 minutes | Serves: 2

¼ to ½ cup Easy Vegetable Broth or no-salt-added vegetable broth, divided	2 tablespoons freshly squeezed lemon juice
1 medium eggplant, peeled and sliced into 1-inch-thick rounds	2 tablespoons tahini
1 cup water	1 tablespoon white miso paste
3 garlic cloves, unpeeled	½ teaspoon ground cumin, plus more for garnish

1. Insert the Inner Pot into the Cooker Base without the lid. 2. Press Sauté to select the program and then press it again to choose the Normal temperature option. 3. Pour in 2 tablespoons of the broth. Arrange some slices of eggplant in one layer on the bottom of the pot. Sauté for 2 minutes, and then flip. Pour in more broth when needed. 2 minutes later, pile the first batch of eggplant on one side of the Inner Pot and add the remaining eggplant. Sauté on each side for 2 minutes, adding broth as needed. 4. Add the water and garlic, then lock the lid and set the steam valve to Sealing. Select the Pressure Cook on the panel. Press the button again to choose Less option; use the "-" button to adjust the cooking time to 3 minutes. Press Pressure Level to choose High pressure. 5. After cooking has completed, quickly and carefully turn the steam release handle from the Sealing position to the Venting position and uncover the lid carefully. 6. Remove the garlic and take off the outer peel with a pair of tongs. In a blender, combine the garlic, eggplant, lemon juice, tahini, miso, and cumin. Blend until smooth. 7. Serve warm or cover, refrigerate, and serve cold. 8. If you haven't eaten up the dish, you can put the leftovers in a covered container and put them in the refrigerator for up to 4 days.
Per Serving: Calories: 62; Fat: 3g; Carbs: 8g; Fiber: 3g; Sugar: 4g; Sodium: 110mg; Protein: 2g

Delicious Scalloped Potatoes

Prep Time: 15 minutes | Cook Time: 27 minutes | Serves: 2

1 cup milk	1 teaspoon minced fresh rosemary
½ cup Easy Vegetable Broth or no-salt-added vegetable broth	1 teaspoon mustard powder
2 scallions, white and green parts, chopped	Freshly ground black pepper
2 tablespoons nutritional yeast	Salt (optional)
1 tablespoon arrowroot powder	1½ pounds russet potatoes (4 or 5 medium), peeled
1 teaspoon garlic powder	1 cup water

1. Whisk together the milk, broth, scallions, nutritional yeast, arrowroot powder, garlic powder, rosemary, and mustard powder in a large bowl. Add some pepper and salt as you like. 2. Slice the potatoes thinly and finely with a Mandoline, the slicing blade on a food processor, or the slicing side of a box grater. 3. Arrange a 1-inch layer of potatoes in an ovenproof baking plate, and then add some sauce to cover the potatoes. Continue layering until all the potatoes are submerged under the sauce in the dish. 4. Add the water into the inner pot and insert a trivet on which the dish is placed. Lock and seal the lid. Select the Pressure button again to choose Less option; use the "+" button to adjust the cooking time to 27 minutes. Press Pressure Level to choose High pressure. 5. After cooking has completed, quickly and carefully turn the steam release handle from the Sealing position to the Venting position and uncover the lid carefully and the dish. 6. Serve right away.
Per Serving: Calories: 172; Fat: 1g; Carbs: 36g; Fiber: 3g; Sugar: 3g; Sodium: 54mg; Protein: 6g

Great Pâté with Lentils and Walnuts

Prep Time: 10 minutes | Cook Time: 3-5 minutes | Serves: 2

¾ cup walnuts	2 garlic cloves, minced
2 cups water	2 tablespoons freshly squeezed
1 cup green or brown lentils	lemon juice
½ medium onion, roughly chopped	1 tablespoon white miso paste
	1 tablespoon apple cider vinegar
1 bay leaf	Freshly ground black pepper

1. Insert the inner pot into the cooker base. Connect the power cord to a 120 V power source. The cooker goes to Standby mode and the display indicates OFF. 2. Press Sauté to select the program and then press it again to choose the Normal temperature option. 3. Pour in the walnuts and sauté for 3 to 5 minutes, stirring now and then, until slightly darker in color and the oils begin to release. Remove from the inner pot and set aside. 4. In your inner pot, combine the water, lentils, onion, and bay leaf. Lock the lid and turn the steam release handle to Sealing. Select the Pressure Cook on the panel. Press the button again to choose Less option; use the "-" button to adjust the cooking time to 10 minutes. Press Pressure Level to choose High pressure. 5. After cooking has completed, leave the steam release handle in the Sealing position for 10 minutes after cooking has completed, then turn the steam release handle to the Venting position; quick-release any remaining pressure and uncover the lid carefully. 6. Discard the bay leaf; blend the lentils, onion, garlic, lemon juice, miso, vinegar, and pepper in a blender until creamy. 7. Serve immediately or serve as a warm dip.
Per Serving: Calories: 331; Fat: 15g; Carbs: 37g; Fiber: 7g; Sugar: 3g; Sodium: 163mg; Protein: 16g

Tasty Brussels Sprouts with Sweet Dijon Vinaigrette

Prep Time: 5 minutes | Cook Time: 1 minutes | Serves: 2

1-pound fresh Brussels sprouts	2 tablespoons Dijon mustard
1 cup water	1 tablespoon maple syrup
2 garlic cloves, smashed	Freshly ground black pepper
3 tablespoons apple cider vinegar	

1. In your inner pot, combine the Brussels sprouts, water, and garlic. Lock the lid and turn the steam release handle to Sealing. 2. Select the Pressure Cook on the panel. Press the button again to choose Less option; use the "-" button to adjust the cooking time to 1 minute. Press Pressure Level to choose High pressure. 3. While cooking, whisk together the vinegar, mustard, and maple syrup in a small bowl. 4. After cooking has completed, quickly and carefully turn the steam release handle from the Sealing position to the Venting position and uncover the lid carefully. 5. Drain the water and mince the garlic. Add the dressing to the sprouts and garlic and toss to coat. Add some pepper to season and serve right away.
Per Serving: Calories: 71; Fat: 1g; Carbs: 15g; Fiber: 5g; Sugar: 6g; Sodium: 116mg; Protein: 4g

Sweet Acorn Squash in Sriracha Hot Sauce

Prep Time: 10 minutes | Cook Time: 5 minutes | Serves: 4

2 tablespoons butter, at room temperature
2 tablespoons packed brown sugar
1 teaspoon to 1 tablespoon Sriracha hot sauce
1 medium (2-pound) acorn

squash, halved and seeded
Salt and freshly ground black pepper
½ cup chopped toasted pecans, for garnish (optional)

1. In a small bowl, mix up the butter, brown sugar and the Sriracha. 2. Use a fork to prick the inside of the squash halves, season with the salt and pepper, then smear the mixture in the bowl all over the inside of the squash. 3. In the Inner Pot, add 1½ cups of water and place the Steam Rack; carefully transfer the squash to the rack with the cut-side facing up. 4. Select the Pressure Cook mode and press the button again to adjust the cooking time to 5 minutes; press the Pressure Level button to choose High Pressure. 5. When the time is up, leave the steam release handle from the Sealing position for 10 minutes, then turn it to the Venting position. 6. Uncover the lid, serve the squash on a prepared plate, making sure not to spill the liquid in the center. 7. Cut each half into 2 wedges and you can serve with the pecans.
Per Serving: Calories 254; Fat 28 g; Sodium 346mg; Carbs 12.3 g; Sugar 1g; Fiber 0.7g; Protein 4.3 g

Mini Corn on the Cob

Prep Time: 10 minutes | Cook Time: 6 minutes | Serves: 6

1 cup water
4 to 6 frozen mini corncobs
1 (14-ounce) package silken tofu, drained
1 tablespoon freshly squeezed lemon juice

1 tablespoon apple cider vinegar
1 teaspoon ground cumin
Salt (optional)
1 lime, cut into wedges
1 tablespoon no-salt-added gluten-free chili powder

1. In the Inner Pot, add the water and place the Steam Rack; put the corn on the rack. 2. Place and lock the lid. 3. Select the Pressure Cook mode and press the button again to adjust the cooking time to 6 minutes; press the Pressure Level button to choose High Pressure. 4. While cooking, blend the tofu, lemon juice, vinegar, cumin and salt well in a blender; set aside for later use. 5. When the time is up, quickly and carefully turn the steam release handle from the Sealing position to the Venting position. 6. Uncover the lid, rub each cob with a lime wedge and then slather it with a generous amount of crema; sprinkle ¼ to ½ teaspoon chili powder on each cob. 7. Serve and enjoy. 8. You can refrigerate the leftovers in an airtight container for up to 4 days.
Per Serving: Calories: 103; Fat: 4g; Carbs: 12g; Fiber: 2g; Sugar: 2g; Sodium: 68mg; Protein: 8g

Healthy Broccoli with Lemon Garlic Dressing

Prep Time: 5 minutes | Cook Time: 10 minutes | Serves: 4

4 medium garlic cloves, unpeeled, left whole
1-pound broccoli, cut into 1- to 1½-inch florets, stems thinly sliced

2 tablespoons fresh lemon juice
1 teaspoon Dijon mustard
¼ cup olive oil
Salt and freshly ground black pepper

1. Place 1 cup warm water and the garlic in the pot. Set a steamer basket in the pot and place the broccoli in it. 2. Lock on the lid, select the Pressure Cook on the panel. Press the button again to choose Less option; use the "- button to adjust the cooking time to 10 minutes. Press Pressure Level to choose High pressure. Make sure the steam valve is in the "Sealing" position. 3. When the cooking time is up, quickly and carefully turn the steam release handle from Sealing position to the Venting position. Transfer the broccoli to a large serving bowl. Remove the steaming basket from the pot. 4. Transfer the garlic to a cutting board, remove the peels, and chop the cloves. Dump the garlic, lemon juice, and mustard into a medium bowl and combine them. Gradually whisk in the oil. 5. Season the broccoli and season with salt and pepper.
Per Serving: Calories 285; Fat 9.8g; Sodium 639mg; Carbs 11.1g; Fiber 1.2g; Sugars 5.1g; Protein 2.8g

Artichoke Soup

Prep time: 15 minutes | Cook time: 30 minutes | Serves: 8

18 large fresh artichokes, trimmed, halved, and chokes removed
1 medium lemon, halved
6 tablespoons lemon juice
2 tablespoons olive oil
6 medium leeks, trimmed, cut lengthwise, and sliced

¾ teaspoon salt
½ teaspoon pepper
3 large potatoes, peeled and quartered
10 cups vegetable stock
½ cup low-fat plain Greek yogurt
½ cup chopped fresh chives

1. Rinse artichokes under running water, making sure water runs between leaves to flush out any debris. 2. Rub all cut surfaces with lemon. In a large bowl, combine artichokes, enough water to cover them, and 3 tablespoons lemon juice. Set aside. 3. Press the "Sauté" button two time to select "Normal" temperature setting on the Instant Pot and heat oil. 4. Add leeks, ½ teaspoon salt, and ¼ teaspoon pepper. Cook for 10 minutes or until leeks are softened. 5. Drain artichokes and add to leeks along with potatoes and stock. Add remaining ¼ teaspoon each salt and pepper. 6. Put on the pressure cooker's lid and turn the steam valve to "Sealing" position. 7. Set the Instant Pot to Pressure Cook. 8. Use the "+/-" keys on the control panel to set the cooking time to 20 minutes. 9. Press the Pressure Level button to adjust the pressure to "Low". 10. Once the cooking cycle is completed, allow the steam to release naturally. 11. When all the steam is released, remove the pressure lid from the top carefully. 12. Using an immersion blender, or in batches in a regular blender, purée the soup until smooth. Stir in remaining 3 tablespoons lemon juice. 13. Serve soup with a dollop of yogurt and a sprinkle of chives.
Per Serving: Calories 361; Fat 19g; Sodium 354mg; Carbs 25g; Fiber 5.1g; Sugar 8.2g; Protein 2g

Creamed Spinach with Nutmeg

Prep Time: 10 minutes | Cook Time: 10 minutes | Serves: 6

½ medium onion, diced
4 garlic cloves, minced
1 (16-ounce) package frozen chopped spinach
1¾ cups milk, divided
1 cup water
¾ cup raw cashews

1 tablespoon freshly squeezed lemon juice
1 teaspoon chickpea miso paste
½ teaspoon ground or freshly grated nutmeg
Freshly ground black pepper

1. Insert the Inner Pot into the Cooker Base without the lid. 2. Select Sauté mode and then press the same button again and then adjust the cooking temperature to Normal. 3. When the display switches On to Hot, add the onion and cook for 3 to 5 minutes until translucent, adding water to prevent sticking; add the garlic and cook for 30 seconds or until fragrant. 4. Press the Cancel button; add the spinach and 1¼ cups of the milk, then lock the lid. 5. Select the Pressure Cook mode and press the button again to adjust the cooking time to 5 minutes; press the Pressure Level button to choose High Pressure. 6. While cooking, in a suitable bowl, add the cashews and the enough boiled water over them, let the cashews soak for at least 30 minutes; then drain them. 7. Blend the drained cashews, lemon juice, miso, nutmeg, pepper and the remaining milk in a blender, until smooth. 8. When the time is up, leave the steam release handle from the Sealing position for 5 minutes, then turn it to the Venting position. 9. Uncover the lid combine the food with the cashews mixture. 10. Serve and enjoy.
Per Serving: Calories: 237; Fat: 14g; Carbs: 19g; Fiber: 5g; Sugar: 6g; Sodium: 193mg; Protein: 13g

Red Pepper Eggplant Dip

Prep Time: 10 minutes | Cook Time: 15 minutes | Serves: 6

5 tablespoons extra-virgin olive oil, divided	¾ cup roasted red peppers, chopped
2 pounds eggplant, at least half peeled but leaving some skin, and cut into 1-inch chunks	3 tablespoons freshly squeezed lemon juice
4 garlic cloves, minced	1 tablespoon tahini
1 cup water	1 teaspoon ground cumin
1 teaspoon kosher salt	Freshly ground black pepper

1. Insert the Inner Pot into the Cooker Base without the lid. 2. Select Sauté mode and then press the same button again and then adjust the cooking temperature to Normal. 3. When the display switches On to Hot, add 3 tablespoons of oil and heat; add half of the eggplant and brown one side for 4 to 5 minutes; remove and add 1 tablespoon of oil, garlic and the remaining eggplant and cook for 1 minutes. 4. Put the first batch of eggplant back to the pot, add the salt and water, then lock the lid. 5. Select the Pressure Cook mode and press the button again to adjust the cooking time to 3 minutes; press the Pressure Level button to choose High Pressure. 6. When the time is up, quickly and carefully turn the steam release handle from the Sealing position to the Venting position. 7. Uncover the lid, stir in the roasted red peppers and then wait for 5 minutes. 8. Drain out the cooking liquid, add the remaining oil, lemon juice, tahini, cumin and lastly season with the pepper. 9. Blend the mixture in an immersion blender until smooth, serve with bread or pita for dipping.
Per Serving: Calories 336; Fat 17.3g; Sodium 281mg; Carbs 8.1g; Fiber 5.3g; Sugars 17.7g; Protein 32.3g

Braised Eggplant

Prep time: 15 minutes | Cook time: 25 minutes | Serves: 4

2 large eggplants, cut into 1" pieces	minced
1¾ teaspoons salt	2 cups diced fresh tomatoes
3 tablespoons olive oil	1 cup water
1 medium yellow onion, peeled and diced	1 tablespoon dried oregano
3 cloves garlic, peeled and	½ teaspoon black pepper
	2 tablespoons minced fresh basil

1. Place eggplant in a colander and sprinkle with 1½ teaspoons salt. 2. Place colander over a plate. Let stand 30 minutes to drain. 3. Press the "Sauté" button twice to select "Normal" temperature setting on the Instant Pot and heat 2 tablespoons oil. 4. Add onion and cook until soft, about 5 minutes. Add garlic and cook until fragrant, about 30 seconds. 5. Add tomatoes and water. Press the Cancel button. Rinse eggplant well and drain. Add to pot. 6. Put on the pressure cooker's lid and turn the steam valve to "Sealing" position. 7. Set the Instant Pot to Pressure Cook. 8. Use the "+/-" keys on the control panel to set the cooking time to 8 minutes. 9. Press the Pressure Level button to adjust the pressure to "Low". 10. Once the cooking cycle is completed, allow the steam to release quickly. 11. When all the steam is released, remove the pressure lid from the top carefully. 12. Add oregano, pepper, and remaining ¼ teaspoon salt. 13. Add remaining 1 tablespoon oil to pot and stir well. 14. Press the "Sauté" button twice to select "Normal" temperature setting and simmer for 15 minutes to thicken. 15. Add basil and serve hot.
Per Serving: Calories 334; Fat 7.9g; Sodium 704mg; Carbs 6g; Fiber 3.6g; Sugar 6g; Protein 18g

Roasted Spaghetti Squash

Prep time: 15 minutes | Cook time: 10 minutes | Serves: 4

1 bulb garlic, top sliced off

3 tablespoons olive oil	½ teaspoon black pepper
1 (3-pound) spaghetti squash	¼ cup chopped fresh flat-leaf parsley
1 cup water	
½ teaspoon salt	¼ cup grated Parmesan cheese

1. At 400 degrees F, preheat your oven. 2. Place garlic bulb on a sheet of aluminum foil. Drizzle with 1 tablespoon oil. 3. Wrap bulb tightly and roast directly on the oven rack for 30–40 minutes, or until bulb is tender. 4. Unwrap and let bulb rest while you prepare squash. 5. Slice spaghetti squash in half lengthwise. Scoop out seeds with a spoon and discard. 6. Place the rack in the Instant Pot, add water, and place spaghetti squash on rack. 7. Put on the pressure cooker's lid and turn the steam valve to "Sealing" position. 8. Set the Instant Pot to Pressure Cook. 9. Press the Pressure Level button to adjust the pressure to "Low". 10. Use the "+/-" keys on the control panel to set the cooking time to 7 minutes. 11. Once the cooking cycle is completed, allow the steam to release naturally. 12. When all the steam is released, remove the pressure lid from the top carefully. 13. Clean and dry pot. Press the "Sauté" button twice to select "Normal" temperature setting and heat remaining 2 tablespoons of oil. 14. Squeeze garlic into pot and cook for 30 seconds, then add squash, salt, and pepper and cook until squash is thoroughly coated in the garlic. 15. Transfer to a serving bowl and top with parsley and cheese. 16. Serve immediately.
Per Serving: Calories 442; Fat 11g; Sodium 91mg; Carbs 14g; Fiber 3g; Sugar 8g; Protein 13g

Tomato Basil Soup

Prep time: 15 minutes | Cook time: 12 minutes | Serves: 4

1 tablespoon olive oil	¼ cup julienned fresh basil
1 small onion, peeled and diced	½ teaspoon salt
1 stalk celery, sliced	3 cups low-sodium chicken broth
8 medium heirloom tomatoes, seeded and quartered	1 cup heavy cream
	1 teaspoon black pepper

1. Press the "Sauté" button twice to select "Normal" temperature setting on the Instant Pot and heat oil. 2. Add onion and celery and cook until translucent, about 5 minutes. 3. Add tomatoes and cook for 3 minutes, or until tomatoes are tender and start to break down. 4. Add basil, salt, and broth. Press the Cancel button. 5. Put on the pressure cooker's lid and turn the steam valve to "Sealing" position. 6. Set the Instant Pot to Pressure Cook. 7. Use the "+/-" keys on the control panel to set the cooking time to 7 minutes. 8. Press the Pressure Level button to adjust the pressure to "Low". 9. Once the cooking cycle is completed, allow the steam to release naturally. 10. When all the steam is released, remove the pressure lid from the top carefully. 11. Add cream and pepper. Purée soup with an immersion blender, or purée in batches in a blender. 12. Ladle into bowls and serve warm.
Per Serving: Calories 472; Fat 7.9g; Sodium 704mg; Carbs 6g; Fiber 3.6g; Sugar 6g; Protein 18g

Artichokes Provençal

Prep time: 15 minutes | Cook time: 7 minutes | Serves: 4

4 large artichokes	2 tablespoons chopped fresh basil
1 medium lemon, cut in half	2 sprigs fresh thyme
2 tablespoons olive oil	2 medium tomatoes, seeded and chopped
½ medium white onion, peeled and sliced	
4 cloves garlic, peeled and chopped	¼ cup chopped Kalamata olives
	¼ cup red wine
2 tablespoons chopped fresh oregano	¼ cup water
	¼ teaspoon salt
	¼ teaspoon black pepper

1. Run artichokes under running water, making sure water runs between leaves to flush out any debris. 2. Slice off top ⅓ of artichoke, trim stem, and pull away any tough outer leaves. 3. Rub all cut surfaces with lemon. 4. Press the "Sauté" button twice to select "Normal" temperature setting on the Instant Pot and heat oil. 5. Add onion and cook until just tender, about 2 minutes. Add garlic, oregano, basil, and thyme, and cook until fragrant, about 30 seconds. 6. Add tomatoes and olives and gently mix, then add wine and water and cook for 30 seconds. 7. Press the Cancel button, then add artichokes cut side down to the Instant Pot. 8. Put on the pressure cooker's lid and turn the steam valve to "Sealing" position. 9. Set the Instant Pot to Pressure Cook. 10. Use the "+/-" keys on the control panel to set the cooking time to 5 minutes. 11. Press the Pressure Level button to adjust the pressure to "Low". 12. Once the cooking cycle is completed, allow the steam to release quickly. 13. When all the steam is released, remove the pressure lid from the top carefully. 14. Pour sauce over top, then season with salt and pepper. Serve warm.
Per Serving: Calories 272; Fat 10g; Sodium 891mg; Carbs 22.9g; Fiber 4g; Sugar 4g; Protein 3g

Hearty Minestrone Soup

Prep time: 15 minutes | Cook time: 20 minutes | Serves: 4

2 cups dried Great Northern beans, soaked overnight and drained	1 medium onion, peeled and diced
1 cup orzo	1 teaspoon minced garlic
2 large carrots, peeled and diced	1 tablespoon Italian seasoning
1 bunch Swiss chard, ribs removed and roughly chopped	1 teaspoon salt
1 medium zucchini, trimmed and diced	½ teaspoon black pepper
2 stalks celery, diced	2 bay leaves
	1 (15-ounce) can diced tomatoes, including juice
	4 cups vegetable broth
	1 cup tomato juice

1. Place all ingredients in the Instant Pot and stir to combine. 2. Put on the pressure cooker's lid and turn the steam valve to "Sealing" position. 3. Set the Instant Pot to Pressure Cook. 4. Use the "+/-" keys on the control panel to set the cooking time to 20 minutes. 5. Press the Pressure Level button to adjust the pressure to "Low". 6. Once the cooking cycle is completed, allow the steam to release naturally for 10 minutes and then quick-release the remaining pressure. 7. When all the steam is released, remove the pressure lid from the top carefully. Remove and discard bay leaves. 8. Ladle into bowls and serve warm.
Per Serving: Calories 384; Fat 5g; Sodium 41mg; Carbs 7g; Fiber 7.6g; Sugar 5g; Protein 2g

Spaghetti Squash with Mushrooms

Prep time: 15 minutes | Cook time: 15 minutes | Serves: 4

1 (3-pound) spaghetti squash	oregano
1 cup water	1 tablespoon chopped fresh basil
2 tablespoons olive oil	¼ teaspoon crushed red pepper flakes
4 cups sliced button mushrooms	1 cup marinara sauce
2 cloves garlic, peeled and minced	½ cup shredded Parmesan cheese
1 tablespoon chopped fresh	

1. Slice spaghetti squash in half lengthwise. Scoop out seeds with a spoon and discard. 2. Place the rack in the Instant Pot, add water, and place spaghetti squash on rack. 3. Put on the pressure cooker's lid and turn the steam valve to "Sealing" position. 4. Set the Instant Pot to Pressure Cook. 5. Use the "+/-" keys on the control panel to set the cooking time to 7 minutes. 6. Press the Pressure Level button to adjust the pressure to "Low". 7. Once the cooking cycle is completed, allow the steam to release quickly. 8. When all the steam is released, remove the pressure lid from the top carefully. 9. Wash and dry pot. Press the "Sauté" button two time to select "Normal" temperature setting and heat oil. 10. Add mushrooms and cook until tender and any juices have evaporated, about 8 minutes. 11. Add garlic and cook until fragrant, about 30 seconds. 12. Add spaghetti squash to pot and toss to mix. Add oregano, basil, red pepper flakes, and marinara sauce and toss to coat. 13. Press the Cancel button. Top with cheese and close the lid. Let stand 5 minutes until cheese melts. Serve hot.
Per Serving: Calories 305; Fat 10.9g; Sodium 454mg; Carbs 10g; Fiber 3.1g; Sugar 5.2g; Protein 05g

Greek-Style Peas

Prep time: 15 minutes | Cook time: 9 minutes | Serves: 4

3 tablespoons olive oil	diced
1 large russet potato, peeled and cut into ½" pieces	1 clove garlic, peeled and minced
1 medium white onion, peeled and diced	1 pound fresh or frozen green peas
1 medium carrot, peeled and diced	¼ cup chopped fresh dill
3 medium tomatoes, seeded and	¼ teaspoon salt
	¼ teaspoon black pepper
	⅓ cup crumbled feta cheese

1. Press the "Sauté" button two time to select "Normal" temperature setting on the Instant Pot and heat oil. 2. Add potato, onion, and carrot, and cook until onion and carrot are tender, about 8 minutes. 3. Add tomatoes and garlic, and cook until garlic is fragrant, about 1 minute.

Add peas. 4. Put on the pressure cooker's lid and turn the steam valve to "Sealing" position. 5. Set the Instant Pot to Pressure Cook. 6. Use the "+/-" keys on the control panel to set the cooking time to 1 minute. 7. Press the Pressure Level button to adjust the pressure to "Low". 8. Once the cooking cycle is completed, allow the steam to release quickly. 9. When all the steam is released, remove the pressure lid from the top carefully. 10. Stir in dill, salt, and pepper. Top with feta and serve hot.
Per Serving: Calories 242; Fat 11g; Sodium 91mg; Carbs 4g; Fiber 3g; Sugar 8g; Protein 3g

Gingered Sweet Potatoes

Prep time: 15 minutes | Cook time: 10 minutes | Serves: 6

2½-pound sweet potatoes, peeled and chopped	½ teaspoon salt
2 cups water	1 tablespoon maple syrup
1 tablespoon minced fresh ginger	1 tablespoon unsalted butter
	¼ cup whole milk

1. Place sweet potatoes and water in the Instant Pot. 2. Put on the pressure cooker's lid and turn the steam valve to "Sealing" position. 3. Set the Instant Pot to Pressure Cook. 4. Use the "+/-" keys on the control panel to set the cooking time to 10 minutes. 5. Press the Pressure Level button to adjust the pressure to "Low". 6. Once the cooking cycle is completed, allow the steam to release naturally. 7. When all the steam is released, remove the pressure lid from the top carefully. 8. Drain water from the Instant Pot. Add ginger, salt, maple syrup, butter, and milk to sweet potatoes. 9. Using an immersion blender, cream the potatoes until desired consistency is reached. 10. Serve warm.
Per Serving: Calories 419; Fat 14g; Sodium 791mg; Carbs 8.9g; Fiber 4.6g; Sugar 8g; Protein 3g

Stuffed Acorn Squash

Prep time: 15 minutes | Cook time: 25 minutes | Serves: 2

1 cup water	1 teaspoon chopped fresh rosemary
1 (1-pound) acorn squash, halved and seeded	1 teaspoon fresh thyme leaves
2 tablespoons olive oil	¼ teaspoon salt
½ medium white onion, peeled and sliced	¼ teaspoon black pepper
1 stalk celery, sliced	½ cup wild rice
2 cloves garlic, peeled and chopped	¾ cup vegetable stock
1 tablespoon chopped fresh sage	¼ cup chopped toasted walnuts
1 tablespoon chopped fresh flat-leaf parsley	¼ cup golden raisins
	¼ cup dried cranberries
	¼ cup crumbled goat cheese

1. Place the rack in the Instant Pot and add water. 2. Place squash halves on the rack. 3. Put on the pressure cooker's lid and turn the steam valve to "Sealing" position. 4. Set the Instant Pot to Pressure Cook. 5. Use the "+/-" keys on the control panel to set the cooking time to 10 minutes. 6. Press the Pressure Level button to adjust the pressure to "Low". 7. Once the cooking cycle is completed, allow the steam to release naturally for 10 minutes and then quick-release the remaining pressure. 8. Insert a paring knife into the squash to check for doneness. Once it pierces easily, it is cooked. Then transfer the squash to a platter and cover with foil to keep warm. 9. Wash and dry the inner pot. Set your Instant Pot to Sauté on "Normal" temperature setting. Heat oil. 10. Add garlic, sage, parsley, rosemary, and thyme. Then cook until fragrant, about 30 seconds. 11. Add salt and pepper and stir well to season. Then add wild rice and stock. Press the Cancel button. 12. Close the lid and turn the handle to "Sealing" position. 13. Set your Instant Pot to Pressure Cook. 14. Use the "+/-" keys on the control panel to set the cooking time to 25 minutes. 15. Press the Pressure Level button to adjust the pressure to "Low". 16. Once the cooking cycle is completed, quick-release the pressure. 17. When all the steam is released, remove the pressure lid from the top carefully. 18. Add walnuts, raisins, and cranberries, and stir well. 19. Close lid and let stand on the Keep Warm setting for 10 minutes. 20. Spoon mixture into acorn squash halves and top with goat cheese. 21. Serve warm.
Per Serving: Calories 305; Fat 12.9g; Sodium 754mg; Carbs 21g; Fiber 6.1g; Sugar 4.2g; Protein 11g

Spicy Corn On the Cob

Prep time: 15 minutes | Cook time: 2 minutes | Serves: 4

2 tablespoons olive oil
¼ teaspoon smoked paprika
¼ teaspoon ground cumin
¼ teaspoon black pepper
⅛ teaspoon cayenne pepper

1 cup water
4 large ears corn, husk and silks removed
½ teaspoon flaky sea salt

1. In a small bowl, whisk together olive oil, paprika, cumin, black pepper, and cayenne pepper. Set aside. 2. Place the rack in the Instant Pot, pour in water, and place corn on the rack. 3. Put on the pressure cooker's lid and turn the steam valve to "Sealing" position. 4. Set the Instant Pot to Pressure Cook. 5. Use the "+/-" keys on the control panel to set the cooking time to 2 minutes. 6. Press the Pressure Level button to adjust the pressure to "Low". 7. Once the cooking cycle is completed, allow the steam to release naturally. 8. When all the steam is released, remove the pressure lid from the top carefully. 9. Carefully transfer corn to a platter and brush with spiced olive oil. 10. Serve immediately with sea salt.
Per Serving: Calories 242; Fat 11g; Sodium 91mg; Carbs 14g; Fiber 3g; Sugar 8g; Protein 13g

Pureed Cauliflower Soup

Prep time: 15 minutes | Cook time: 21 minutes | Serves: 6

2 tablespoons olive oil
1 medium onion, peeled and chopped
1 stalk celery, chopped
1 medium carrot, peeled and chopped
3 sprigs fresh thyme

4 cups cauliflower florets
2 cups vegetable stock
½ cup half-and-half
¼ cup low-fat plain Greek yogurt
2 tablespoons chopped fresh chives

1. Press the "Sauté" button twice to select "Normal" temperature setting on the Instant Pot and heat oil. 2. Add onion, celery, and carrot. Cook until just tender, about 6 minutes. 3. Add thyme, cauliflower, and stock. Stir well, then press the Cancel button. 4. Put on the pressure cooker's lid and turn the steam valve to "Sealing" position. 5. Set the Instant Pot to Pressure Cook. 6. Use the "+/-" keys on the control panel to set the cooking time to 5 minutes. 7. Press the Pressure Level button to adjust the pressure to "Low". 8. Once the cooking cycle is completed, allow the steam to release naturally. 9. When all the steam is released, remove the pressure lid from the top carefully. 10. Open lid, remove and discard thyme stems, and with an immersion blender, purée soup until smooth. 11. Stir in half-and-half and yogurt. Garnish with chives and serve immediately.
Per Serving: Calories 484; Fat 5g; Sodium 41mg; Carbs 7g; Fiber 7.6g; Sugar 5g; Protein 2g

Green Beans with Tomatoes and Potatoes

Prep time: 15 minutes | Cook time: 4 minutes | Serves: 8

1 pound small new potatoes
1 cup water
1 teaspoon salt
2-pound fresh green beans, trimmed
2 medium tomatoes, seeded and diced

2 tablespoons olive oil
1 tablespoon red wine vinegar
1 clove garlic, peeled and minced
½ teaspoon dry mustard powder
¼ teaspoon smoked paprika
¼ teaspoon black pepper

1. Place potatoes in a steamer basket. 2. Place the rack in the Instant Pot, add water, and then put with the steamer basket. 3. Put on the pressure cooker's lid and turn the steam valve to "Sealing" position. 4. Set the Instant Pot to Pressure Cook. 5. Use the "+/-" keys on the control panel to set the cooking time to 4 minutes. 6. Press the Pressure Level button to adjust the pressure to "Low". 7. Once the cooking cycle is completed, allow the steam to release quickly. 8. When all the steam is released, remove the pressure lid from the top carefully. 9. Add salt, green beans, and tomatoes to the Instant Pot.

10. Transfer mixture to a serving platter or large bowl. 11. In a small bowl, whisk oil, vinegar, garlic, mustard, paprika, and pepper. Pour dressing over vegetables and gently toss to coat. 12. Serve hot.
Per Serving: Calories 489; Fat 11g; Sodium 501mg; Carbs 8.9g; Fiber 4.6g; Sugar 8g; Protein 26g

Dandelion Greens

Prep time: 15 minutes | Cook time: 1 minutes | Serves: 8

4-pound dandelion greens, stalks cut and, and greens washed
½ cup water
¼ cup olive oil

¼ cup lemon juice
½ teaspoon salt
½ teaspoon black pepper

1. Add dandelion greens and water to the Instant Pot. 2. Put on the pressure cooker's lid and turn the steam valve to "Sealing" position. 3. Set the Instant Pot to Pressure Cook. 4. Press the Pressure Level button to adjust the pressure to "Low". 5. Use the "+/-" keys on the control panel to set the cooking time to 1 minute. 6. Once the cooking cycle is completed, allow the steam to release quickly. 7. When all the steam is released, remove the pressure lid from the top carefully. 8. Combine olive oil, lemon juice, salt, and pepper in a small bowl. 9. Pour over greens and toss to coat.
Per Serving: Calories 305; Fat 12.9g; Sodium 754mg; Carbs 21g; Fiber 6.1g; Sugar 4.2g; Protein 11g

Cinnamon Sweet Potatoes

Prep Time: 10 minutes | Cook Time: 15-23 minutes | Serves: 6

1 cup water
6 medium sweet potatoes, pricked a few times with a fork
4 tablespoons butter, cubed

½ cup brown sugar
¼ cup all-purpose flour
½ teaspoon ground cinnamon
Pinch kosher salt

1. In the Inner Pot, add the water and place the Steam Rack; put the sweet potatoes on the rack. 2. Place and lock the lid. 3. Select the Pressure Cook mode and press the button again to adjust the cooking time to 12 to 18 minutes (depending on the size of the sweet potatoes); press the Pressure Level button to choose High Pressure. 4. While cooking, in a suitable bowl, thoroughly mix up the butter, brown sugar, flour, cinnamon and salt, until a well-combined but crumbly mixture is formed. 5. When the time is up, leave the steam release handle from the Sealing position for 10 minutes, then turn it to the Venting position. 6. Preheat your oven and prepare a suitable baking sheet. 7. Transfer the sweet potatoes to the baking sheet, slice each in half lengthwise and lay side by side with cut-side up; sprinkle each half with 1 heaping tablespoon of the sugar mixture and broil for 3 to 5 minutes until lightly crispy. 8. When done, serve and enjoy.
Per Serving: Calories 285; Fat 9.8g; Sodium 639mg; Carbs 11.1g; Fiber 1.2g; Sugars 5.1g; Protein 7.8g

Steamed Broccoli

Prep time: 5 minutes | Cook time: 1 minutes | Serves: 6

6 cups broccoli florets

1. Pour 1½ cups water into the inner pot of the Instant Pot. Place a steam rack inside. 2. Place the broccoli florets inside a steamer basket and place the basket on the steam rack. 3. Put on the pressure cooker's lid and turn the steam valve to "Sealing" position. 4. Set the Instant Pot on "Steam". 5. Use the "+/-" keys on the control panel to set the cooking time to 1 minute. 6. Press the Pressure Level button to adjust the pressure to "Low". 7. Once the cooking cycle is completed, quick-release the pressure. 8. When all the steam is released, remove the pressure lid from the top carefully. 9. Remove the steamer basket and serve.
Per Serving: Calories 305; Fat 10.9g; Sodium 454mg; Carbs 10g; Fiber 3.1g; Sugar 5.2g; Protein 05g

Wild Mushroom Soup

Prep time: 15 minutes | Cook time: 10 minutes | Serves: 8

3 tablespoons olive oil
1 stalk celery, diced
1 medium carrot, peeled and diced
½ medium yellow onion, peeled and diced
1 clove garlic, peeled and minced
1 (8-ounce) container hen of the woods mushrooms, sliced
1 (8-ounce) container porcini or

chanterelle mushrooms, sliced
2 cups sliced shiitake mushrooms
2 tablespoons dry sherry
4 cups vegetable broth
2 cups water
1 tablespoon chopped fresh tarragon
½ teaspoon salt
½ teaspoon black pepper

1. Press the "Sauté" button twice to select "Normal" temperature setting on the Instant Pot and heat oil. 2. Add celery, carrot, and onion. Cook, stirring often, until softened, about 3 minutes. 3. Add garlic and cook 30 seconds until fragrant, then add mushrooms and cook for 5 minutes. 4. Add sherry, broth, water, tarragon, salt, and pepper to pot, and stir well. Press the Cancel button. 5. Put on the pressure cooker's lid and turn the steam valve to "Sealing" position. 6. Set the Instant Pot to Pressure Cook. 7. Use the "+/-" keys on the control panel to set the cooking time to 5 minutes. 8. Press the Pressure Level button to adjust the pressure to "Low". 9. Once the cooking cycle is completed, allow the steam to release naturally. 10. When all the steam is released, remove the pressure lid from the top carefully. 11. Serve hot.
Per Serving: Calories 199; Fat 5g; Sodium 41mg; Carbs 7g; Fiber 7.6g; Sugar 5g; Protein 2g

Cabbage Soup

Prep time: 15 minutes | Cook time: 20 minutes | Serves: 8

2 tablespoons olive oil
3 medium onions, peeled and chopped
1 large carrot, peeled, quartered, and sliced
1 stalk celery, chopped
3 bay leaves
1 teaspoon smoked paprika
3 cups sliced white cabbage
1 teaspoon fresh thyme leaves
3 cloves garlic, peeled and minced
½ cup chopped roasted red pepper

1 (15-ounce) can white navy beans, drained
1½ cups low-sodium vegetable cocktail beverage
7 cups low-sodium vegetable stock
1 dried chili pepper
2 medium zucchini, trimmed, halved lengthwise, and thinly sliced
1 teaspoon salt
½ teaspoon black pepper

1. Press the "Sauté" button two time to select "Normal" temperature setting on the Instant Pot and heat oil. 2. Add onions, carrot, celery, and bay leaves. Cook for 7–10 minutes or until vegetables are soft. 3. Add paprika, cabbage, thyme, garlic, roasted red pepper, and beans. 4. Stir to combine and cook for 2 minutes. Add vegetable cocktail beverage, stock, and chili pepper. 5. Put on the pressure cooker's lid and turn the steam valve to "Sealing" position. 6. Set the Instant Pot to Pressure Cook. 7. Use the "+/-" keys on the control panel to set the cooking time to 20 minutes. 8. Press the Pressure Level button to adjust the pressure to "Low". 9. Once the cooking cycle is completed, allow the steam to release quickly. 10. When all the steam is released, remove the pressure lid from the top carefully. 11. Remove and discard bay leaves. 12. Add zucchini, close lid, and let stand on the Keep Warm setting for 15 minutes. 13. Season with salt and pepper. 14. Serve hot.
Per Serving: Calories 374; Fat 5g; Sodium 41mg; Carbs 7g; Fiber 7.6g; Sugar 5g; Protein 2g

Eggplant Caponata

Prep time: 15 minutes | Cook time: 5 minutes | Serves: 8

¼ cup olive oil
¼ cup white wine
2 tablespoons red wine vinegar
1 teaspoon ground cinnamon

1 large eggplant, peeled and diced
1 medium onion, peeled and diced
1 medium green bell pepper, seeded and diced

1 medium red bell pepper, seeded and diced
2 cloves garlic, peeled and minced
1 (15-ounce) can diced tomatoes
3 stalks celery, diced

½ cup chopped oil-cured olives
½ cup golden raisins
2 tablespoons capers, rinsed and drained
½ teaspoon salt
½ teaspoon black pepper

1. Place all ingredients in the Instant Pot. Stir well to mix. 2. Put on the pressure cooker's lid and turn the steam valve to "Sealing" position. 3. Set the Instant Pot to Pressure Cook. 4. Use the "+/-" keys on the control panel to set the cooking time to 5 minutes. 5. Press the Pressure Level button to adjust the pressure to "Low". 6. Once the cooking cycle is completed, allow the steam to release quickly. 7. When all the steam is released, remove the pressure lid from the top carefully. 8. Serve warm.
Per Serving: Calories 478; Fat 7.9g; Sodium 704mg; Carbs 6g; Fiber 3.6g; Sugar 6g; Protein 18g

Zucchini Pomodoro

Prep time: 15 minutes | Cook time: 6 minutes | Serves: 4-6

1 tablespoon vegetable oil
1 large onion, peeled and diced
3 cloves garlic, peeled and minced
1 (28-ounce) can diced tomatoes, including juice

½ cup water
1 tablespoon Italian seasoning
½ teaspoon salt
½ teaspoon black pepper
2 medium zucchini, trimmed and spiralized

1. Press the "Sauté" button twice to select "Normal" temperature setting on the Instant Pot and heat oil. 2. Add onion and cook until translucent, about 5 minutes. Add garlic and cook for an additional 30 seconds. 3. Add tomatoes, water, Italian seasoning, salt, and pepper. Add zucchini and toss to combine. 4. Put on the pressure cooker's lid and turn the steam valve to "Sealing" position. 5. Set the Instant Pot to Pressure Cook. 6. Use the "+/-" keys on the control panel to set the cooking time to 1 minute. 7. Press the Pressure Level button to adjust the pressure to "Low". 8. Once the cooking cycle is completed, allow the steam to release naturally for 5 minutes and then quick-release the remaining pressure. 9. When all the steam is released, remove the pressure lid from the top carefully. 10. Transfer zucchini to four bowls. 11. Press the Sauté button, then adjust the temperature setting to Less, and simmer sauce in the Instant Pot uncovered for 5 minutes. 12. Ladle over zucchini and serve immediately.
Per Serving: Calories 272; Fat 10g; Sodium 891mg; Carbs 22.9g; Fiber 4g; Sugar 4g; Protein 3g

Burgundy Mushrooms

Prep time: 15 minutes | Cook time: 20 minutes | Serves: 8

¼ cup olive oil
3 cloves garlic, peeled and halved
16-ounce whole white mushrooms
16-ounce whole baby bella mushrooms
1½ cups dry red wine
1 teaspoon Worcestershire sauce

1 teaspoon dried thyme
1 tablespoon Dijon mustard
1 teaspoon ground celery seed
½ teaspoon black pepper
3 cups beef broth
2 slices bacon

1. Press the "Sauté" button twice to select "Normal" temperature setting on the Instant Pot and heat oil. 2. Add garlic and mushrooms, and cook until mushrooms start to get tender, about 3 minutes. 3. Add wine and simmer for 3 minutes. 4. Add Worcestershire sauce, thyme, mustard, celery seed, pepper, broth, and bacon to pot. 5. Put on the pressure cooker's lid and turn the steam valve to "Sealing" position. 6. Set the Instant Pot to Pressure Cook. 7. Press the Pressure Level button to adjust the pressure to "Low". 8. Use the "+/-" keys on the control panel to set the cooking time to 20 minutes. 9. Once the cooking cycle is completed, allow the steam to release naturally. 10. When all the steam is released, remove the pressure lid from the top carefully. 11. Remove and discard bacon and garlic halves. Transfer mushrooms to a serving bowl. 12. Serve warm.
Per Serving: Calories 484; Fat 5g; Sodium 41mg; Carbs 7g; Fiber 7.6g; Sugar 5g; Protein 2g

Herbed Potato Salad

Prep time: 15 minutes | Cook time: 25 minutes | Serves: 10

¼ cup olive oil
3 tablespoons red wine vinegar
¼ cup chopped fresh flat-leaf parsley
2 tablespoons chopped fresh dill
2 tablespoons chopped fresh chives

1 clove garlic, peeled and minced
½ teaspoon dry mustard powder
¼ teaspoon black pepper
2-pound baby Yukon Gold potatoes
1 cup water
1 teaspoon salt

1. Whisk together oil, vinegar, parsley, dill, chives, garlic, mustard, and pepper in a small bowl. Set aside. 2. Place potatoes in a steamer basket. 3. Place the rack in the Instant Pot, add water and salt, then top with the steamer basket. 4. Put on the pressure cooker's lid and turn the steam valve to "Sealing" position. 5. Set the Instant Pot to Pressure Cook. 6. Press the Pressure Level button to adjust the pressure to "Low". 7. Use the "+/-" keys on the control panel to set the cooking time to 4 minutes. 8. Once the cooking cycle is completed, allow the steam to quick-release pressure. 9. When all the steam is released, remove the pressure lid from the top carefully. 10. Transfer hot potatoes to a serving bowl. Pour dressing over potatoes and gently toss to coat. 11. Serve warm or at room temperature.
Per Serving: Calories 382; Fat 7.9g; Sodium 704mg; Carbs 6g; Fiber 3.6g; Sugar 6g; Protein 18g

Steamed Cauliflower with Herbs

Prep time: 15 minutes | Cook time: 10 minutes | Serves: 6

1 head cauliflower, cut into florets (about 6 cups)
1 cup water
4 tablespoons olive oil
1 clove garlic, peeled and minced
2 tablespoons chopped fresh

oregano
1 teaspoon chopped fresh thyme leaves
1 teaspoon chopped fresh sage
¼ teaspoon salt
¼ teaspoon black pepper

1. Place cauliflower florets in a steamer basket. 2. Place the rack in the Instant Pot, add water, then top with the steamer basket. 3. Put on the pressure cooker's lid and turn the steam valve to "Sealing" position. 4. Set the Instant Pot to Pressure Cook. 5. Press the Pressure Level button to adjust the pressure to "Low". 6. Use the "+/-" keys on the control panel to set the cooking time to 10 minute. 7. Once the cooking cycle is completed, quick-release the steam. 8. When all the steam is released, remove the pressure lid from the top carefully. 9. While cauliflower cooks, prepare the dressing. 10. Whisk together olive oil, garlic, oregano, thyme, sage, salt, and pepper. 11. Carefully transfer cauliflower to a serving bowl and immediately pour dressing over cauliflower. 12. Carefully toss to coat. Let stand for 5 minutes. Serve hot.
Per Serving: Calories 272; Fat 10g; Sodium 891mg; Carbs 22.9g; Fiber 4g; Sugar 4g; Protein 3g

Maple Dill Carrots

Prep time: 15 minutes | Cook time: 5 minutes | Serves: 6

1 pound carrots, peeled and cut into quarters, or whole baby carrots
1 tablespoon minced fresh dill

1 tablespoon maple syrup
1 tablespoon ghee
½ teaspoon salt
½ cup water

1. Place all ingredients in the Instant Pot. 2. Put on the pressure cooker's lid and turn the steam valve to "Sealing" position. 3. Set the Instant Pot to Pressure Cook. 4. Use the "+/-" keys on the control panel to set the cooking time to 5 minutes. 5. Press the Pressure Level button to adjust the pressure to "Low". 6. Once the cooking cycle is completed, let the steam release naturally for 5 minutes and then quick-release the remaining pressure. 7. When all the steam is released, remove the pressure lid from the top carefully. 8. Transfer to a serving dish and serve warm.
Per Serving: Calories 472; Fat 10.9g; Sodium 354mg; Carbs 10.5g; Fiber 4.1g; Sugar 8.2g; Protein 6g

Ratatouille

Prep time: 15 minutes | Cook time: 25 minutes | Serves: 8

1 medium eggplant, cut into 1" pieces
2 teaspoons salt
4 tablespoons olive oil
1 medium white onion, peeled and chopped
1 medium green bell pepper, seeded and chopped
1 medium red bell pepper, seeded and chopped
1 medium zucchini, trimmed and

chopped
1 medium yellow squash, chopped
4 cloves garlic, peeled and minced
4 large tomatoes, cut into 1" pieces
2 teaspoons Italian seasoning
¼ teaspoon crushed red pepper flakes
6 fresh basil leaves, thinly sliced

1. Place eggplant in a colander and sprinkle evenly with salt. 2. Let stand 30 minutes, then rinse and dry eggplant. Set aside. 3. Press the "Sauté" button twice to select "Normal" temperature setting on the Instant Pot and heat 1 tablespoon oil. 4. Add onion and bell peppers. Cook, stirring often, until vegetables are just tender, about 5 minutes. 5. Transfer to a large bowl and set aside. 6. Add 1 tablespoon oil to pot and heat for 30 seconds, then add zucchini and squash. 7. Cook, stirring constantly, until vegetables are tender, about 5 minutes. 8. Add garlic and cook until fragrant, about 30 seconds. Transfer to bowl with onion and peppers. 9. Add 1 tablespoon oil to pot and heat for 30 seconds. 10. Add eggplant and cook, stirring constantly, until eggplant is golden brown, about 8 minutes. 11. Add tomatoes and cook until they are tender and releasing juice, about 4 minutes. 12. Return reserved vegetables to pot and stir in Italian seasoning and red pepper flakes. 13. Put on the pressure cooker's lid and turn the steam valve to "Sealing" position. 14. Set the Instant Pot to Pressure Cook. 15. Use the "+/-" keys on the control panel to set the cooking time to 5 minutes. 16. Press the Pressure Level button to adjust the pressure to "Low". 17. Once the cooking cycle is completed, quick-release the steam. 18. When all the steam is released, remove the pressure lid from the top carefully. 19. Serve topped with basil and remaining 1 tablespoon oil.
Per Serving: Calories 334; Fat 10.9g; Sodium 354mg; Carbs 10.5g; Fiber 4.1g; Sugar 8.2g; Protein 6g

Spinach Salad with Quinoa

Prep time: 15 minutes | Cook time: 6 minutes | Serves: 6

¼ cup olive oil
2 tablespoons fresh lemon juice
¼ teaspoon pure stevia powder
1 teaspoon Dijon mustard
¼ teaspoon salt
⅛ teaspoon black pepper
1 tablespoon avocado oil
1 small yellow onion, peeled and

diced
1 large carrot, peeled and diced
1 medium stalk celery, ends removed and sliced
½ cup dry quinoa
1 cup vegetable broth
10-ounce baby spinach leaves

1. In a small bowl, whisk together the olive oil, lemon juice, stevia, mustard, salt, and pepper. Set aside. 2. Add the avocado oil to the inner pot of the Instant Pot and press the Sauté button. 3. Allow the oil to heat 1 minute and then add the onion, carrot, and celery. 4. Cook the vegetables until they are softened, about 5 minutes. 5. Rinse the quinoa in a fine-mesh strainer under water until the water runs clear. 6. Add the quinoa to the inner pot and stir to combine with the vegetables. Press the Cancel button. 7. Add the vegetable broth to the inner pot. 8. Put on the pressure cooker's lid and turn the steam valve to "Sealing" position. 9. Set the Instant Pot to Pressure Cook. 10. Use the "+/-" keys on the control panel to set the cooking time to 1 minute. 11. Press the Pressure Level button to adjust the pressure to "Low". 12. Once the cooking cycle is completed, quick-release pressure. 13. When all the steam is released, remove the pressure lid from the top carefully. 14. Place the spinach leaves in a large bowl and top with the quinoa mixture. 15. Drizzle with the dressing and toss to combine. Serve warm.
Per Serving: Calories 371; Fat 10.9g; Sodium 454mg; Carbs 10g; Fiber 3.1g; Sugar 5.2g; Protein 05g

Boiled Cabbage

Prep time: 15 minutes | Cook time: 5 minutes | Serves: 6

1 large head green cabbage, cored and chopped	1 teaspoon salt
3 cups vegetable broth	½ teaspoon black pepper

1. Place the cabbage, broth, salt, and pepper in the inner pot. 2. Put on the pressure cooker's lid and turn the steam valve to "Sealing" position. 3. Set the Instant Pot to Pressure Cook. 4. Press the Pressure Level button to adjust the pressure to "Low". 5. Use the "+/-" keys on the control panel to set the cooking time to 5 minutes. 6. Once the cooking cycle is completed, allow the steam to release naturally. 7. When all the steam is released, remove the pressure lid from the top carefully. 8. Serve the cabbage with a little of the cooking liquid.
Per Serving: Calories 199; Fat 5g; Sodium 41mg; Carbs 7g; Fiber 7.6g; Sugar 5g; Protein 2g

Purple Cabbage Salad

Prep time: 15 minutes | Cook time: 2 minutes | Serves: 8

½ cup dry quinoa	3 tablespoons toasted sesame seed oil
1 (10-ounce) bag frozen shelled edamame	½ teaspoon pure stevia powder
1 cup vegetable broth	1 head purple cabbage, cored and chopped
¼ cup reduced sodium tamari	
¼ cup natural almond butter	

1. Place the quinoa, edamame, and broth in the inner pot of your Instant Pot. 2. Put on the pressure cooker's lid and turn the steam valve to "Sealing" position. 3. Set the Instant Pot to Pressure Cook. 4. Use the "+/-" keys on the control panel to set the cooking time to 2 minutes. 5. Press the Pressure Level button to adjust the pressure to "Low". 6. Once the cooking cycle is completed, quick-release the pressure. 7. When all the steam is released, remove the pressure lid from the top carefully. 8. Meanwhile, in a small bowl, whisk together the tamari, almond butter, sesame seed oil, and stevia. Set aside. 9. Use a fork to fluff the quinoa, and then transfer the mixture to a large bowl. 10. Allow the quinoa and edamame to cool, and then add the purple cabbage to the bowl and toss to combine. 11. Add the dressing and toss again until everything is evenly coated. 12. Serve.
Per Serving: Calories 242; Fat 11g; Sodium 91mg; Carbs 14g; Fiber 3g; Sugar 8g; Protein 13g

Steamed Cauliflower

Prep time: 15 minutes | Cook time: 2 minutes | Serves: 6

1 large head cauliflower, cored   and cut into large florets

1. Pour 2 cups water into the inner pot of the Instant Pot. Place a steam rack inside. 2. Place the cauliflower florets inside a steamer basket and place the basket on the steam rack. 3. Put on the pressure cooker's lid and turn the steam valve to "Sealing" position. 4. Set the Instant Pot on "Steam". 5. Use the "+/-" keys on the control panel to set the cooking time to 2 minutes. 6. Press the Pressure Level button to adjust the pressure to "Low". 7. Once the cooking cycle is completed, allow the steam to release naturally. 8. When all the steam is released, remove the pressure lid from the top carefully. 9. Carefully remove the steamer basket and serve.
Per Serving: Calories 378; Fat 19g; Sodium 354mg; Carbs 25g; Fiber 5.1g; Sugar 8.2g; Protein 2g

Saucy Brussels Sprouts and Carrots

Prep time: 15 minutes | Cook time: 13 minutes | Serves: 4

1 tablespoon coconut oil	12-ounce carrots (about 4 medium), peeled, ends removed, and cut into 1" chunks
12-ounce Brussels sprouts, tough ends removed and cut in half	

¼ cup fresh lime juice	½ cup coconut aminos
¼ cup apple cider vinegar	¼ cup almond butter

1. Press the "Sauté" button twice to select "Normal" mode and melt the oil in the inner pot. 2. Add the Brussels sprouts and carrots and sauté until browned, about 5–7 minutes. 3. While the vegetables are browning, make the sauce. 4. In a small bowl, whisk together the lime juice, vinegar, coconut aminos, and almond butter. 5. Pour the sauce over the vegetables and press the Cancel button. 6. Put on the pressure cooker's lid and turn the steam valve to "Sealing" position. 7. Set the Instant Pot to Pressure Cook. 8. Press the Pressure Level button to adjust the pressure to "Low". 9. Use the "+/-" keys on the control panel to set the cooking time to 6 minutes. 10. Once the cooking cycle is completed, allow the steam to release quickly. 11. When all the steam is released, remove the pressure lid from the top carefully. 12. Serve.
Per Serving: Calories 272; Fat 10g; Sodium 891mg; Carbs 22.9g; Fiber 4g; Sugar 4g; Protein 3g

Lemony Cauliflower Rice

Prep time: 15 minutes | Cook time: 7 minutes | Serves: 4

1 tablespoon avocado oil	4 cups riced cauliflower
1 small yellow onion, peeled and diced	Juice from 1 small lemon
1 teaspoon minced garlic	½ teaspoon salt
	¼ teaspoon black pepper

1. Press the Sauté button, add the oil to the pot, and heat 1 minute. 2. Add the onion and sauté 5 minutes. 3. Add the garlic and sauté 1 more minute. Press the Cancel button. 4. Add the cauliflower rice, lemon juice, salt, and pepper and stir to combine. 5. Put on the pressure cooker's lid and turn the steam valve to "Sealing" position. 6. Set the Instant Pot to Pressure Cook. 7. Press the Pressure Level button to adjust the pressure to "Low". 8. Use the "+/-" keys on the control panel to set the cooking time to 1 minute. 9. Once the cooking cycle is completed, quick-release pressure. 10. When all the steam is released, remove the pressure lid from the top carefully. 11. Serve.
Per Serving: Calories 334; Fat 7.9g; Sodium 704mg; Carbs 6g; Fiber 3.6g; Sugar 6g; Protein 18g

Simple Beet Salad

Prep time: 15 minutes | Cook time: 5 minutes | Serves: 8

6 medium beets, peeled and cut into small cubes	¼ teaspoon pure stevia powder
1 cup water	½ teaspoon salt
¼ cup olive oil	¼ teaspoon black pepper
¼ cup apple cider vinegar	1 large shallot, peeled and diced
1 teaspoon Dijon mustard	1 large stalk celery, ends removed and thinly sliced

1. Place the beets into the steamer basket. 2. Pour 1 cup water into the inner pot and place the steam rack inside. 3. Place the steamer basket with the beets on top of the steam rack. 4. Meanwhile, in a small container or jar with a tight lid add the oil, vinegar, mustard, stevia, salt, and pepper and shake well to combine. Set aside. 5. Put on the pressure cooker's lid and turn the steam valve to "Sealing" position. 6. Set the Instant Pot to Pressure Cook. 7. Use the "+/-" keys on the control panel to set the cooking time to 5 minutes. 8. Press the Pressure Level button to adjust the pressure to "Low". 9. Once the cooking cycle is completed, allow the steam to release naturally. 10. When all the steam is released, remove the pressure lid from the top carefully. 11. Carefully remove the basket from the Instant Pot and let the beets cool completely. 12. Place the shallot and celery in a large bowl and then add the cooked, cooled beets. 13. Drizzle with the dressing and toss to coat.
Per Serving: Calories 203; Fat 2.2g; Sodium 811mg; Carbs 12g; Fiber 3g; Sugar 8g; Protein 8g

Mashed Cauliflower

Prep time: 15 minutes | Cook time: 3 minutes | Serves: 4

1 large cauliflower crown, core removed and roughly chopped	½ teaspoon salt
2 cups chicken stock	½ teaspoon garlic powder
2 tablespoons olive oil plus ½ teaspoon for serving	¾ cup nutritional yeast
	¼ teaspoon black pepper

1. Add the cauliflower and stock to the inner pot. 2. Put on the pressure cooker's lid and turn the steam valve to "Sealing" position. 3. Set the Instant Pot to Pressure Cook. 4. Press the Pressure Level button to adjust the pressure to "Low". 5. Use the "+/-" keys on the control panel to set the cooking time to 3 minutes. 6. Once the cooking cycle is completed, quick-release pressure. 7. When all the steam is released, remove the pressure lid from the top carefully. 8. Use a slotted spoon to transfer the cauliflower to a food processor. 9. Add the 2 tablespoons oil, salt, garlic powder, and nutritional yeast to the food processor and process until silky smooth. 10. Transfer to a medium bowl, drizzle with ½ teaspoon olive oil, sprinkle with the pepper, and serve.

Per Serving: Calories 216; Fat 10.9g; Sodium 354mg; Carbs 10.5g; Fiber 4.1g; Sugar 8.2g; Protein 6g

Curried Mustard Greens

Prep time: 15 minutes | Cook time: 10 minutes | Serves: 6

1 tablespoon avocado oil	½ teaspoon salt
1 medium white onion, peeled and chopped	¼ teaspoon black pepper
1 tablespoon peeled and chopped ginger	2 cups vegetable broth
3 cloves garlic, minced	½ cup coconut cream
2 tablespoons curry powder	1 large bunch mustard greens (about 1 pound), tough stems removed and roughly chopped

1. Add the oil to the inner pot. 2. Press the "Sauté" button two time to select "Normal" mode and heat the oil 2 minutes. 3. Add the onion and sauté until softened, about 5 minutes. 4. Add the ginger, garlic, curry, salt, and pepper and sauté 1 more minute. 5. Stir in the vegetable broth and coconut cream until combined and then allow it to come to a boil, about 2–3 minutes more. 6. Stir in the mustard greens until everything is well combined. 7. Put on the pressure cooker's lid and turn the steam valve to "Sealing" position. 8. Set the Instant Pot to Pressure Cook. 9. Press the Pressure Level button to adjust the pressure to "Low". 10. Use the "+/-" keys on the control panel to set the cooking time to 1 minute. 11. Once the cooking cycle is completed, quick-release pressure. 12. When all the steam is released, remove the pressure lid from the top carefully. 13. Transfer to a bowl and serve.

Per Serving: Calories 272; Fat 10g; Sodium 891mg; Carbs 22.9g; Fiber 4g; Sugar 4g; Protein 3g

Ginger Broccoli and Carrots

Prep time: 15 minutes | Cook time: 5 minutes | Serves: 6

1 tablespoon avocado oil	2 large carrots, peeled and thinly sliced
1" fresh ginger, peeled and thinly sliced	½ teaspoon kosher salt
1 clove garlic, minced	Juice from ½ large lemon
2 broccoli crowns, stems removed and cut into large florets	¼ cup water

1. Add the oil to the inner pot. 2. Press the "Sauté" button twice to select "Normal" mode and heat oil 2 minutes. 3. Add the ginger and garlic and sauté 1 minute. 4. Add the broccoli, carrots, and salt and stir to combine. Press the Cancel button. 5. Add the lemon juice and water and use a wooden spoon to scrape up any brown bits. 6. Put on the pressure cooker's lid and turn the steam valve to "Sealing" position. 7. Set the Instant Pot to Pressure Cook. 8. Press the Pressure Level button to adjust the pressure to "Low". 9. Use the "+/-" keys on the control panel to set the cooking time to 2 minutes. 10. Once the cooking cycle is completed, quick-release pressure. 11. When all the

steam is released, remove the pressure lid from the top carefully. 12. Serve immediately.

Per Serving: Calories 419; Fat 14g; Sodium 791mg; Carbs 28.9g; Fiber 4.6g; Sugar 8g; Protein 3g

Lemony Steamed Asparagus

Prep time: 15 minutes | Cook time: 1minutes | Serves: 4-6

1-pound asparagus, woody ends removed	Juice from ½ large lemon
	¼ teaspoon kosher salt

1. Add ½ cup water to the inner pot and add the steam rack. 2. Add the asparagus to the steamer basket and place the basket on top of the rack. 3. Put on the pressure cooker's lid and turn the steam valve to "Sealing" position. 4. Set the Instant Pot on "Steam". 5. Use the "+/-" keys on the control panel to set the cooking time to 1 minute. 6. Press the Pressure Level button to adjust the pressure to "Low". 7. Once the cooking cycle is completed, quick-release pressure. 8. When all the steam is released, remove the pressure lid from the top carefully. 9. Transfer the asparagus to a plate and top with lemon juice and salt.

Per Serving: Calories 44; Fat 2.2g; Sodium 811mg; Carbs 12g; Fiber 3g; Sugar 8g; Protein 8g

Vegetable Cheese Sauce

Prep time: 15 minutes | Cook time: 6 minutes | Serves: 6

1 small yellow onion, peeled and chopped	2¼ cups vegetable broth
1 medium zucchini, peeled and sliced	¼ teaspoon paprika
	1 medium sweet potato, peeled and chopped
6 cloves garlic, chopped	½ cup nutritional yeast

1. Place the onion, zucchini, garlic, and ¼ cup broth into the inner pot. 2. Press the "Sauté" button two time to select "Normal" mode and let the vegetables sauté until soft, 5 minutes. 3. Add the remaining 2 cups broth, paprika, and sweet potato. 4. Put on the pressure cooker's lid and turn the steam valve to "Sealing" position. 5. Set the Instant Pot to Pressure Cook. 6. Press the Pressure Level button to adjust the pressure to "Low". 7. Use the "+/-" keys on the control panel to set the cooking time to 6 minutes. 8. Once the cooking cycle is completed, quick-release the pressure. 9. When all the steam is released, remove the pressure lid from the top carefully. 10. Allow to cool for a few minutes and then transfer the mixture to a large blender. 11. Add the nutritional yeast to the blender with the other ingredients and blend on high until smooth. 12. Serve warm as a topping for the vegetables of your choice.

Per Serving: Calories 521; Fat 7.9g; Sodium 704mg; Carbs 6g; Fiber 3.6g; Sugar 6g; Protein 18g

Simple Spaghetti Squash

Prep time: 15 minutes | Cook time: 25 minutes | Serves: 4

1 medium spaghetti squash	⅛ teaspoon salt
2 tablespoons olive oil	⅛ teaspoon black pepper

1. Place 1½ cups water in the inner pot of your Instant Pot. Place the steam rack inside. 2. Wash squash with soap and water and dry it. 3. Place the whole uncut squash on top of the steam rack inside the inner pot. 4. Put on the pressure cooker's lid and turn the steam valve to "Sealing" position. 5. Set the Instant Pot to Pressure Cook. 6. Use the "+/-" keys on the control panel to set the cooking time to 25 minutes. 7. Press the Pressure Level button to adjust the pressure to "Low". 8. Once the cooking cycle is completed, quick-release the pressure. 9. When all the steam is released, remove the pressure lid from the top carefully. 10. Allow the squash to cool, and then carefully remove it from the pot. 11. Use a sharp knife to cut the squash in half lengthwise. 12. Spoon out the seeds and discard. Use a fork to scrape out the squash strands into a medium bowl. 13. Drizzle with the oil, add the salt and pepper, and serve.

Per Serving: Calories 382; Fat 19g; Sodium 354mg; Carbs 25g; Fiber 5.1g; Sugar 8.2g; Protein 2g

Baked Sweet Potatoes

Prep time: 15 minutes | Cook time: 18 minutes | Serves: 4

4 medium sweet potatoes
2 tablespoons coconut oil
½ teaspoon ground cinnamon

1. Pour 1½ cups water into the Instant Pot and place the steam rack inside. 2. Place the sweet potatoes on the rack. It's okay if they overlap. 3. Put on the pressure cooker's lid and turn the steam valve to "Sealing" position. 4. Set the Instant Pot to Pressure Cook. 5. Use the "+/-" keys on the control panel to set the cooking time to 18 minutes. 6. Press the Pressure Level button to adjust the pressure to "Low". 7. Once the cooking cycle is completed, quick-release pressure. 8. When all the steam is released, remove the pressure lid from the top carefully. 9. Carefully remove the sweet potatoes from the pot. 10. Use a knife to cut each sweet potato lengthwise and open the potato slightly. 11. Add ½ tablespoon coconut oil and ⅛ teaspoon cinnamon to each potato and serve.
Per Serving: Calories 199; Fat 5g; Sodium 41mg; Carbs 7g; Fiber 7.6g; Sugar 5g; Protein 2g

Lemon Garlic Red Chard

Prep time: 15 minutes | Cook time: 7 minutes | Serves: 4

1 tablespoon avocado oil
1 small yellow onion, peeled and diced
1 bunch red chard, leaves and stems chopped
3 cloves garlic, minced
¾ teaspoon salt
Juice from ½ medium lemon
1 teaspoon lemon zest

1. Add the oil to the inner pot of the Instant Pot and allow it to heat 1 minute. 2. Add the onion and chard stems and sauté 5 minutes. 3. Add the garlic and sauté another 30 seconds. 4. Add the chard leaves, salt, and lemon juice and stir to combine. Press the Cancel button. 5. Put on the pressure cooker's lid and turn the steam valve to "Sealing" position. 6. Set the Instant Pot to Pressure Cook. 7. Press the Pressure Level button to adjust the pressure to "Low". 8. Use the "+/-" keys on the control panel to set the cooking time to 1 minute. 9. Once the cooking cycle is completed, quick-release pressure. 10. When all the steam is released, remove the pressure lid from the top carefully. 11. Spoon the chard mixture into a serving bowl and top with lemon zest.
Per Serving: Calories 203; Fat 12.9g; Sodium 754mg; Carbs 21g; Fiber 6.1g; Sugar 4.2g; Protein 11g

Cheesy Brussels Sprouts and Carrots

Prep time: 15 minutes | Cook time: 10 minutes | Serves: 4

1 pound Brussels sprouts, tough ends removed and cut in half
1-pound baby carrots
1 cup chicken stock
2 tablespoons lemon juice
½ cup nutritional yeast
¼ teaspoon salt

1. Add the Brussels sprouts, carrots, stock, lemon juice, nutritional yeast, and salt to the inner pot of your Instant Pot. Stir well to combine. 2. Put on the pressure cooker's lid and turn the steam valve to "Sealing" position. 3. Set the Instant Pot to Pressure Cook. 4. Use the "+/-" keys on the control panel to set the cooking time to 10 minutes. 5. Press the Pressure Level button to adjust the pressure to "Low". 6. Once the cooking cycle is completed, quick-release pressure. 7. When all the steam is released, remove the pressure lid from the top carefully. 8. Transfer the vegetables and sauce to a bowl and serve.
Per Serving: Calories 382; Fat 19g; Sodium 354mg; Carbs 25g; Fiber 5.1g; Sugar 8.2g; Protein 2g

Garlic Green Beans

Prep time: 15 minutes | Cook time: 5 minutes | Serves: 4

12-ounce green beans, ends trimmed
4 cloves garlic, minced
1 tablespoon avocado oil
½ teaspoon salt
1 cup water

1. Place the green beans in a medium bowl and toss with the garlic, oil, and salt. 2. Transfer this mixture to the steamer basket. 3. Pour 1 cup water into the inner pot and place the steam rack inside. 4. Place the steamer basket with the green beans on top of the steam rack. 5. Put on the pressure cooker's lid and turn the steam valve to "Sealing" position. 6. Set the Instant Pot to Pressure Cook. 7. Use the "+/-" keys on the control panel to set the cooking time to 5 minutes. 8. Press the Pressure Level button to adjust the pressure to "Low". 9. Once the cooking cycle is completed, allow the steam to release naturally. 10. When all the steam is released, remove the pressure lid from the top carefully. 11. Transfer to a bowl for serving.
Per Serving: Calories 199; Fat 5g; Sodium 41mg; Carbs 7g; Fiber 7.6g; Sugar 5g; Protein 2g

Spinach Salad with Beets

Prep time: 15 minutes | Cook time: 5 minutes | Serves: 4

3 medium beets, peeled and cut into small cubes
1 cup water
½ small shallot, peeled and finely chopped
⅓ cup olive oil
2 tablespoons apple cider vinegar
2½ tablespoons fresh orange juice
¼ teaspoon orange zest
5-ounce baby spinach leaves
¼ cup sliced almonds
⅛ teaspoon coarse salt
⅛ teaspoon black pepper

1. Place the beets into the steamer basket. 2. Pour 1 cup water into the inner pot and place the steam rack inside. 3. Place the steamer basket with the beets on top of the steam rack. 4. Meanwhile, in a container or jar with a tight lid add the shallot, oil, vinegar, orange juice, and orange zest and shake well to combine. Set aside. 5. Put on the pressure cooker's lid and turn the steam valve to "Sealing" position. 6. Set the Instant Pot to Pressure Cook. 7. Use the "+/-" keys on the control panel to set the cooking time to 5 minutes. 8. Press the Pressure Level button to adjust the pressure to "Low". 9. Once the cooking cycle is completed, quick-release pressure. 10. When all the steam is released, remove the pressure lid from the top carefully. 11. Place the spinach and almonds in a large bowl and add the cooked beets. 12. Drizzle with the dressing and toss to coat. Top the salad with salt and pepper and serve.
Per Serving: Calories 216; Fat 7.9g; Sodium 704mg; Carbs 6g; Fiber 3.6g; Sugar 6g; Protein 18g

Mashed Sweet Potatoes

Prep time: 15 minutes | Cook time: 8 minutes | Serves: 6

1 cup water
3 large sweet potatoes, peeled and cut into cubes
2 tablespoons olive oil
1 teaspoon dried thyme
1 teaspoon dried rosemary, crushed
¼ teaspoon garlic salt

1. Pour 1 cup water into the inner pot of the Instant Pot and place a steam rack inside. 2. Place the sweet potato into a steamer basket and place it on top of the steam rack. 3. Put on the pressure cooker's lid and turn the steam valve to "Sealing" position. 4. Set the Instant Pot to Pressure Cook. 5. Use the "+/-" keys on the control panel to set the cooking time to 8 minutes. 6. Press the Pressure Level button to adjust the pressure to "Low". 7. Once the cooking cycle is completed, quick-release pressure. 8. When all the steam is released, remove the pressure lid from the top carefully. 9. Carefully remove the steamer basket from the inner pot and transfer the sweet potatoes to a large bowl. 10. Add the olive oil, thyme, rosemary, and garlic salt and use a potato masher to mash the potatoes. 11. Serve.
Per Serving: Calories 242; Fat 11g; Sodium 91mg; Carbs 14g; Fiber 3g; Sugar 8g; Protein 13g

Chapter 12 Dessert Recipes

Chocolate Oatmeal Bars with Cranberries

Prep time: 10 minutes | Cook Time: 12 minutes | Serves: 8

3 eggs, whisked
½ cup sour cream
¼ cup honey
2 teaspoons coconut oil, melted
½ teaspoon rum extract
½ teaspoon vanilla extract
¾ cup quick oats, pudding-y
⅓ cup all-purpose flour

1 teaspoon baking soda
1 teaspoon baking powder
½ teaspoon cardamom
½ teaspoon cinnamon
1 cup dark chocolate chips
A pinch of kosher salt
¾ cup cranberries

1. In the inner pot, pour a cup of water and arrange a trivet in the inner pot. 2. Spritz a nonstick cooking spray over a suitable baking pan. 3. Add honey, rum extract, vanilla extract, coconut oil, sour cream, and the beaten eggs in a mixing bowl. Mix together until well combined. 4. Then add the flour, baking soda, baking powder, cinnamon, salt, chocolate chips, and cardamom and stir until well incorporated to make a batter. Fold in the cranberries. Transfer the batter to the baking pan. 5. Close the lid and turn the steam release handle to Sealing position. 6. Set the Instant Pot on Pressure Cook at High and timer for 12 minutes. 7. When cooked, naturally release the pressure. Remove the lid carefully. 8. Chill and serve.
Per Serving: Calories:223; Fat 10.3g; Sodium 210mg; Carbs 30.1g; Fiber 1.4g; Sugars 17.3g; Protein 5.1g

Bread Pudding with Apricots

Prep time: 10 minutes | Cook Time: 15 minutes | Serves: 6

4 cups Italian bread, cubed
½ cup granulated sugar
2 tablespoons molasses
½ cup dried apricots, soaked and chopped
2 tablespoons coconut oil
1 teaspoon vanilla paste

A pinch of grated nutmeg
A pinch of salt
1 teaspoon cinnamon, ground
½ teaspoon star anise, ground
2 cups milk
4 eggs, whisked
1 ⅓ cups heavy cream

1. In the inner pot, pour 1 ½ cups of water and place the trivet over the water. 2. Spritz the nonstick cooking spray inside a baking dish. Then divide the bread cubes in the greased baking dish. 3. Combine together the remaining ingredients in a mixing bowl. Then sprinkle the mixture over the bread cubes. 4. Cover the baking dish with a foil sheet. 5. Close the lid and turn the steam release handle to Sealing position. 6. Set the Instant Pot to Porridge at High and adjust time to 15 minutes. 7. When cooked, quick-release the pressure and remove the lid carefully. 8. Serve and enjoy!
Per Serving: Calories:358; Fat 19.8g; Sodium 236mg; Carbs 38.5g; Fiber 1g; Sugars 25.7g; Protein 8.9g

Avocado Chocolate Delight

Prep time: 10 minutes | Cook Time: 15 minutes | Serves: 8

⅓ cup avocado, mashed
2 plantains
1 ½ tablespoons butter, softened
¼ cup agave syrup
4 tablespoons cocoa powder

½ cup coconut flakes
1 teaspoon baking soda
½ teaspoon vanilla paste
1 teaspoon star anise, ground
⅛ teaspoon cream of tartar

1. In the inner pot, pour a cup of water and arrange a trivet in the inner pot. 2. Brush the melted butter over a baking pan. 3. In a blender, mix all the ingredients to make a batter. 4. Then arrange the batter to the baking

pan. 5. Close the lid and turn the steam release handle to Sealing position. 6. Set the Instant Pot to Porridge at High and timer for 15 minutes. 7. When cooked, add some fresh or dried fruit as you needed. 8. Serve and enjoy!
Per Serving: Calories:142; Fat 5.6g; Sodium 185mg; Carbs 25.5Fiber 2.7g; Sugars 7.1g; Protein 1.4g

Chocolate Cheesecake with Coconut

Prep time: 10 minutes | Cook Time: 1 hour | Serves: 10

1 ½ cups vanilla sugar cookies, crumbled
½ stick butter, melted
For the Filling:
22 ounces' cream cheese, room temperature
¾ cup granulated sugar
1 ½ tablespoons cornstarch
2 eggs, room temperature

⅓ cup sour cream
½ teaspoon coconut extract
½ teaspoon pure anise extract
¼ teaspoon freshly grated nutmeg
6 ounces' semisweet chocolate chips
3 ounces sweetened shredded coconut

1. Brush a suitable baking pan in the Instant Pot and cover a baking paper over the bottom. 2. Combine the crumbled cookies with the melted butter thoroughly and then press the crust into the prepared pan. Transfer the pan into your freezer. 3. Using a mixer, beat the cream cheese at low speed. Add sugar and cornstarch in the cheese and stir well at low speed until uniform and smooth. 4. Fold in the eggs, one at a time. Beat again with the mixer. 5. Then add the sour cream, coconut extract, anise extract, and nutmeg in the mixture and stir with the mixer. 6. Microwave the chocolate chips about 1 minute, stirring once or twice while cooking. 7. Add the melted chocolate to the cheesecake batter and then sprinkle with the shredded coconut. Stir until well combined. 8. Drizzle the chocolate mixture over the crust. 9. Pour 1 cup of water in the inner pot and place the trivet. 10. Lower the baking pan onto the trivet and then close the lid. Then turn the steam release handle to the Sealing position. 11. Set the Instant Pot on Pressure Cook at High and adjust time to 40 minutes. 12. Once cooked, naturally release for 15 minutes. Carefully remove the lid. 13. Cool the cheesecake completely and then slice. 14. Serve and enjoy!
Per Serving: Calories:444; Fat 34.1g; Sodium 242mg; Carbs 30.5g; Fiber 0.9g; Sugars 24.5g; Protein 6.2g

Creamy Rum Cheesecake

Prep time: 10 minutes | Cook Time: 20 minutes | Serves: 6

14 ounces full-; Fat cream cheese
3 eggs, whisked
½ teaspoon vanilla extract
1 teaspoon rum extract
½ cup agave syrup
¼ teaspoon cardamom
¼ teaspoon ground cinnamon

Butter-Rum Sauce:
½ cup granulated sugar
½ stick butter
½ cup whipping cream
1 tablespoon dark rum
⅓ teaspoon nutmeg

1. In a blender or food processor, combine together the eggs, cream cheese, rum extract, cardamom, cinnamon, agave syrup, cream cheese, and vanilla to make the batter. 2. Remove the batter to a baking pan and then use a sheet of foil to cover. 3. Pour 1 ½ cups of water in the inner pot and a metal trivet to the Instant Pot. Lower the pan onto the trivet. 4. Secure the lid and turn the steam release handle to Sealing position. 5. Set the Instant Pot on Soup/Broth at High and adjust the time to 20 minutes. 6. When cooked, naturally release the pressure and then carefully remove the lid. 7. In a sauté pan over moderate heat, melt the sugar with butter. 8. Then add rum, nutmeg, and the whipping cream in the pan. 9. To serve, top the cooled cheesecake with the warm sauce. Enjoy!
Per Serving: Calories:342; Fat 13.9g; Sodium 468mg; Carbs 43.3g; Fiber 0.1g; Sugars 17.2g; Protein 12.6g

Double-Chocolate and Peanut Fudge

Prep time: 10 minutes | Cook Time: 5 minutes | Serves: 6

8 ounces' semisweet chocolate, chopped
2 ounces' milk chocolate, chopped
⅓ cup applesauce
1 egg, beaten
½ teaspoon vanilla extract
½ teaspoon almond extract
¼ teaspoon ground cinnamon
⅓ cup peanut butter
A pinch of coarse salt
¼ cup arrowroot powder

1. In the inner pot, pour 1½ cups of water and then place a metal trivet. 2. Set the Instant pot on "Sauté" at Normal and melt the chocolate in a heatproof bowl over the simmering water. Turn off the heat. 3. Combine the egg, vanilla, almond extract, cinnamon, salt, peanut butter and applesauce in a mixing bowl. 4. Stir in the arrowroot powder in the mixture. Then fold in the melted chocolate and mix well. 5. Spritz the nonstick cooking spray inside the 6 heatproof ramekins and then divide the batter in the ramekins. Cover with foil and then transfer in the inner pot on the trivet. 6. Close the lid and turn the steam release handle to the Sealing position. 7. Set the Instant Pot on Pressure Cook at High and adjust time to 5 minutes. 8. When cooked, quick-release the pressure and then carefully remove the lid. 9. Allow the dessert to cool on a wire rack. Serve and enjoy!
Per Serving: Calories:333; Fat 22.1g; Sodium 128mg; Carbs 34g; Fiber 3.6g; Sugars 28.3g; Protein 6.8g

Crispy Peach and Raisin

Prep time: 10 minutes | Cook Time: 10 minutes | Serves: 6

6 peaches, pitted and chopped
½ teaspoon ground cardamom
1 teaspoon ground cinnamon
1 teaspoon vanilla extract
⅓ cup orange juice
2 tablespoons honey
4 tablespoons raisins
4 tablespoons butter
1 cup rolled oats
4 tablespoons all-purpose flour
⅓ cup brown sugar
A pinch of grated nutmeg
A pinch of salt

1. In the inner pot, spread the peaches on the bottom. Then add cardamom, vanilla, and cinnamon and drizzle on the top with honey, raisins, and orange juice. 2. Whisk together the oats, flour, nutmeg, brown sugar, salt, and butter in a mixing bowl. 3. Close the lid and turn the steam release handle to Sealing position. 4. Set the Instant Pot on Pressure Cook at High and adjust time to 10 minutes. 5. When cooked, naturally release the pressure about 10 minutes and then carefully remove the lid. 6. Serve and enjoy!
Per Serving: Calories:278; Fat 9.1g; Sodium 86mg; Carbs 47.7g; Fiber 4.3g; Sugars 32.6g; Protein 4.2g

Cherry and Almond Crisp Pie with Cinnamon

Prep time: 10 minutes | Cook Time: 10 minutes | Serves: 4

1-pound sweet cherries, pitted
1 teaspoon ground cinnamon
⅓ teaspoon ground cardamom
1 teaspoon pure vanilla extract
⅓ cup water
⅓ cup honey
½ stick butter, at room
temperature
1 cup rolled oats
2 tablespoons all-purpose flour
¼ cup almonds, slivered
A pinch of salt
A pinch of grated nutmeg

1. In the inner pot, place the cherries and then top with cinnamon, vanilla, and cardamom. Then pour in water and honey. 2. Combine the oats, butter, and flour in a separate mixing bowl and then sprinkle on the top of the cherry mixture with almond and nutmeg evenly. 3. Close the lid and turn the steam release handle to Sealing position. 4. Set the Instant Pot on Pressure Cook at High and adjust time to 10 minutes. 5. When cooked, naturally release the steam and then carefully remove the lid. 6. Serve and enjoy!
Per Serving: Calories:449; Fat 15.9g; Sodium 144mg; Carbs 73.9g; Fiber 4g; Sugars 23.8g; Protein 5g

Coconut Mini Cheesecakes with Almond

Prep time: 10 minutes | Cook Time: 25 minutes | Serves: 4

½ cup almonds
½ cup sunflower kernels
6 dates, chopped
16 ounces' coconut milk
¾ cup coconut yogurt

1. Grease 4 ramekins with nonstick cooking spray. 2. In a blender, blend the almonds, dates, and sunflower kernels until sticky. 3. Divide the mixture into the prepared ramekins and press well. 4. Combine the yogurt and coconut milk thoroughly in a mixing bowl. Then pour the liquid mixture in the ramekins and cover with a foil sheet. 5. In the inner pot, pour 1 cup of water and place the trivet. Lower the ramekins onto the trivet. 6. Close the lid and turn the steam release handle to Sealing position. 7. Set the Instant Pot on Pressure Cook at High and adjust time to 25 minutes. 8. When cooked, naturally release the pressure about 15 minutes and remove the lid carefully. 9. Serve and enjoy!
Per Serving: Calories:423; Fat 36.9g; Sodium 50mg; Carbs 22.2g; Fiber 5.7g; Sugars 15g; Protein 7.8g

Chocolate Pumpkin Puddings with Cinnamon

Prep time: 10 minutes | Cook Time: 25 minutes | Serves: 4

½ cup half-and-half
1 cup pumpkin puree
⅓ cup Turbinado sugar
1 egg plus 1 egg yolk, beaten
⅓ teaspoon crystallized ginger
½ teaspoon ground cinnamon
¼ teaspoon ground nutmeg
A pinch of table salt
For the Chocolate Ganache:
½ cup chocolate chips
¼ cup double cream

1. Pour the water in the inner pot and place the trivet. 2. Grease the four ramekins with butter and set them aside. 3. Combine the half-and-half with the pumpkin puree and sugar in the mixing bowl. 4. Then fold gently in the eggs and mix well. Divide evenly the mixture into the greased ramekins and put on the trivet side by side. 5. Close the lid and turn the steam release handle to Sealing position. 6. Set the Instant Pot on Pressure Cook at High and adjust the time to 25 minutes. 7. When cooked, quick-release the pressure and remove the lid carefully. 8. Allow the pudding to cool about 2 hours. Meanwhile, microwave the chocolate until melt to make the chocolate ganache about 30 seconds. Then stir and microwave for another 15 seconds. 9. Stir in the double cream until well combined. 10. Pour the chocolate ganache over the pumpkin puddings and use a table knife to spread, letting the cream run over sides. 11. Cool in the refrigerator. Serve and enjoy!
Per Serving: Calories:269; Fat 14.4g; Sodium 99mg; Carbs 31.4g; Fiber 2.7g; Sugars 24.9g; Protein 4.9g

Chocolate Mug Cakes with Mango

Prep time: 10 minutes | Cook Time: 10 minutes | Serves: 2

½ cup coconut flour
2 eggs
2 tablespoons honey
1 teaspoon vanilla
¼ teaspoon grated nutmeg
1 tablespoon cocoa powder
1 medium-sized mango, peeled and diced

1. Lightly grease two mugs. Add the eggs, vanilla, cocoa powder, nutmeg, coconut flour, and honey and combine together. 2. In the inner pot, pour 1 cup of water and then place the trivet. Lower the mugs onto the trivet. 3. Close the lid and turn the steam release handle to Sealing position. 4. Set the Instant Pot on Pressure Cook at High and adjust time to 10 minutes. 5. When cooked, quick-release the pressure and then remove the lid carefully. 6. Sprinkle the diced mango on the top. Serve chilled.
Per Serving: Calories:205; Fat 5.5g; Sodium 64mg; Carbs 34.4g; Fiber 3.7g; Sugars 29.3g; Protein 7.3g

Carrot and Almond Pudding

Prep time: 10 minutes | Cook Time: 10 minutes | Serves: 4

1 ½ cups jasmine rice
1 ½ cups milk
½ cup water
2 large-sized carrots, shredded
¼ teaspoon kosher salt
⅓ cup granulated sugar
2 eggs, beaten

⅓ cup almonds, ground
¼ cup dried figs, chopped
½ teaspoon pure almond extract
½ teaspoon vanilla extract
⅓ teaspoon ground cardamom
½ teaspoon ground star anise

1. In the inner pot, add carrots, salt, and jasmine rice and pour water and milk. Stir until well combined. 2. Close the lid and turn the steam release handle to Sealing position. 3. Set the Instant Pot on Pressure Cook at High and adjust time to 10 minutes. 4. When cooked, naturally release the pressure and carefully remove the lid. 5. Set the Instant Pot to Sauté at Less and then add eggs, almonds, and sugar. Stir well. 6. Cook to bring a boil and then turn off the heat. 7. Add the rest ingredients in the inner pot and stir well. The pudding will thicken as it sits. 8. Serve and enjoy!
Per Serving: Calories:249; Fat 4.8g; Sodium 138mg; Carbs 45.6g; Fiber 3.4g; Sugars 15.7g; Protein 6.4g

Traditional Apple Cake

Prep time: 10 minutes | Cook Time: 55 minutes | Serves: 8

4 apples, peeled, cored and chopped
½ teaspoon ground cloves
½ teaspoon ground cardamom
1 teaspoon ground cinnamon
3 tablespoons sugar
1 ⅓ cups flour

1 teaspoon baking powder
A pinch of salt
1 stick butter, melted
½ cup honey
2 tablespoons orange juice
½ teaspoon vanilla paste

1. Lightly brush a cake pan with oil and set it aside. 2. Toss the ground cloves, cardamom, sugar, and cinnamon over the apples. 3. Combine together the baking powder, salt, and flour in a mixing bowl. 4. In a separate bowl, add orange juice, vanilla paste, honey, and butter and combine well. 5. Stir in together with the wet ingredients to make the batter. 6. Then spoon half to the prepared baking pan. 7. On top of the batter, spread half of the apples. Then add the remaining batter on the apple chunks. Place the rest apple chunks on the top. 8. Use paper towel to cover the cake pan. 9. In the inner pot, pour 1 cup of water and place trivet. Lower the cake pan onto the trivet. 10. Close the lid and turn the steam release handle to Sealing position. Set the Instant Pot on Pressure Cook at High and adjust time to 55 minutes. 11. When cooked, naturally release the pressure and then remove the lid carefully. 12. Allow the cake to cool on a rack and sit for about 15 minutes. 13. Slice into your desired size and serve.
Per Serving: Calories:427; Fat 15.9g; Sodium 140mg; Carbs 72.5g; Fiber 4.8g; Sugars 45.2g; Protein 3.6g

Rice Pudding with Raisin

Prep time: 10 minutes | Cook Time: 3 minutes | Serves: 4

1 ½ cups basmati rice
3 cups coconut milk
1 teaspoon rosewater
A pinch of coarse salt
¼ teaspoon saffron, crushed

4 tablespoons unsalted pistachios, minced
½ cup jaggery
½ cup raisins

1. In the inner pot, add the basmati rice, coconut milk, rosewater, salt, saffron, pistachios, and jaggery and stir well. 2. Close the lid and then turn the steam release handle to Sealing position. 3. Set the Instant Pot to Soup at High and adjust time to 3 minutes. 4. When cooked, naturally release the pressure and then carefully remove the lid. 5. Sprinkle the raisins on the top and serve.
Per Serving: Calories:362; Fat 21.8g; Sodium 60mg; Carbs 40.2g; Fiber 2.8g; Sugars 8.7g; Protein 4.8g

Classic Chocolate Pots de Crème

Prep time: 10 minutes | Cook Time: 7 minutes | Serves: 4

½ cup granulated sugar
⅓ cup cocoa powder
2 tablespoons carob powder
⅔ cup whipping cream
1 cup coconut milk
1 teaspoon vanilla

½ teaspoon hazelnut extract
5 eggs, well-beaten
¼ teaspoon nutmeg, preferably freshly grated
A pinch of coarse salt

1. Melt the sugar, milk, vanilla, hazelnut extract, cocoa powder, carob powder, and cream in a sauté pan over medium-low heat. 2. Whisk together until everything is well combined and melted. 3. Fold in the eggs and mix well. Then season with salt and nutmeg. 4. Divide the mixture among jars. 5. In the inner pot, pour 1 cup of water and place the trivet. 6. Close the lid and turn the steam release handle to Sealing position. 7. Set the Instant Pot on Pressure Cook at High and adjust time to 7 minutes. 8. When cooked, quick-release the pressure and then remove the lid carefully. 9. Cool in the refrigerator about 4 hours. Serve and enjoy!
Per Serving: Calories:311; Fat 21g; Sodium 113mg; Carbs 27.6g; Fiber 2.7g; Sugars 21.7g; Protein 7.5g

Maple Rice Pudding with Cranberry

Prep time: 10 minutes | Cook Time: 3 minutes | Serves: 4

1 cup white rice
1 ½ cups water
A pinch of salt
2 cups milk
⅓ cup maple syrup

2 eggs, beaten
1 teaspoon vanilla extract
¼ teaspoon cardamom
A pinch of grated nutmeg
½ cup dried cranberries

1. In the inner pot, add the salt, rice, and water. 2. Close the lid and turn the steam release handle to Sealing position. 3. Set the Instant Pot on Pressure Cook at High and adjust time to 3 minutes. 4. When cooked, naturally release the pressure and then carefully remove the lid. 5. Then stir in the maple syrup, eggs, vanilla extract, cardamom, nutmeg, and milk in the inner pot until well combined. 6. Set the Instant Pot to Sauté at Normal. Cook and stir from time to time until the pudding begins to boil. 7. Then turn off the heat. Add the dried cranberries and stir well. 8. Cool the pudding to let it thicken. Serve and enjoy!
Per Serving: Calories:341; Fat 5.1g; Sodium 135mg; Carbs 62.3g; Fiber 1.2g; Sugars 22g; Protein 10.1g

Walnut Monkey Bread

Prep time: 10 minutes | Cook Time: 25 minutes | Serves: 6

12 frozen egg dinner rolls, thawed
¼ cup brown sugar
1 teaspoon ground cinnamon
¼ cup walnuts, ground

¼ cup coconut oil, melted
⅓ cup powdered sugar
1 tablespoon coconut milk

1. In the inner pot, pour 1 cup of water and place trivet. Then spritz cooking spray over a Bundt pan. Set aside. 2. Cut each dinner roll in half. 3. Combine thoroughly the brown sugar, cinnamon, and walnuts in a mixing bowl. 4. In a separate bowl, add the melted coconut oil. Sink the rolls halves in the coconut oil and roll them in the brown sugar mixture to coat. 5. Spread the rolls in the prepared Bundt pan. Use a piece of aluminum foil over the pan and allow it to rise overnight at room temperature. 6. Then transfer to the trivet. 7. Close the lid and turn the steam release handle to Sealing position. 8. Set the Instant Pot on Pressure Cook at High and adjust time to 25 minutes. 9. When cooked, naturally release the pressure about 10 minutes and then remove the lid carefully. 10. Remove the bread onto serving plates. 11. Whisk the coconut milk and powdered sugar in a mixing bowl until smooth. 12. Then top with the mixture to glaze over the top and sides of the cake. 13. Serve and enjoy!
Per Serving: Calories:306; Fat 14.8g; Sodium 302mg; Carbs 41.5g; Fiber 2.6g; Sugars 14.5g; Protein 5.3g

Lemony Mixed Berry Jam

Prep time: 10 minutes | Cook Time: 7 minutes | Serves: 10

2 ½ pounds fresh mixed berries	2 tablespoons fresh lemon juice
1 ¼ cups granulated sugar	3 tablespoons cornstarch

1. In the inner pot, add the sugar, lemon juice, and the fresh mixed berries. 2. Close the lid and turn the steam release handle to Sealing position. 3. Set the Instant Pot on Pressure Cook at High and adjust time to 2 minutes. 4. When cooked, naturally release the pressure about 15 minutes and remove the lid carefully. 5. Whisk the cornstarch with 3 tablespoons of water and stir well. 6. Set the Instant Pot on Sauté at More. Cook to bring the mixture to a rolling boil. Boil for about 5 minutes to thicken the jam, stirring frequently. 7. Serve and enjoy!
Per Serving: Calories:168; Fat 0.4g; Sodium 1mg; Carbs 41g; Fiber 4.1g; Sugars 33.2g; Protein 0.8g

Honey-Yogurt Compote

Prep time: 10 minutes | Cook Time: 2 minutes | Serves: 4

1 cup rhubarb	1 vanilla bean
1 cup plums	1 cinnamon stick
1 cup apples	½ cup caster sugar
1 cup pears	1 cup Greek yoghurt
1 teaspoon ground ginger	4 tablespoons honey

1. In the inner pot, add gingers, vanilla, caster sugar, cinnamon, and the fruits. 2. Close the lid and turn the steam release handle to Sealing position. 3. Set the Instant Pot on Pressure Cook at High and adjust time to 2 minutes. 4. When cooked, naturally release the pressure about 10 minutes and then remove the lid carefully. 5. Meanwhile, whisk the yogurt with honey. 6. Transfer the compote in individual bowls and drizzle with a dollop of honeyed Greek yogurt. Serve and enjoy!
Per Serving: Calories:225; Fat 0.3g; Sodium 3mg; Carbs 59.8g; Fiber 3.5g; Sugars 54.1g; Protein 0.8g

Fresh Lemony Blueberry Butter

Prep time: 10 minutes | Cook Time: 2 minutes | Serves: 10

2 pounds' fresh blueberries	1 tablespoon freshly grated lemon
1-pound granulated sugar	zest
½ teaspoon vanilla extract	¼ cup fresh lemon juice

1. In the inner pot, add the sugar, vanilla, and blueberries. 2. Close the lid and turn the steam release handle to Sealing position. 3. Set the Instant Pot on Pressure Cook at High and adjust time to 2 minutes. 4. When cooked, naturally release the pressure about 15 minutes and then remove the lid carefully. 5. Add the lemon zest and lemon juice and stir well. 6. To store, puree in a food processor and strain and push the mixture through a sieve. 7. Serve and enjoy!
Per Serving: Calories:224; Fat 0.4g; Sodium 2mg; Carbs 58.8g; Fiber 2.3g; Sugars 54.6g; Protein 0.8g

Coffee Cake with Cinnamon

Prep time: 10 minutes | Cook Time: 25 minutes | Serves: 10

2 (16.3-ounce) cans refrigerated biscuits	freshly grated
	½ cup raisins, if desired
¾ cup granulated sugar	¾ cup butter, melted
1 tablespoon ground cinnamon	½ cup firmly packed brown sugar
¼ teaspoon nutmeg, preferably	

1. In the inner pot, pour 1 cup of water and place the trivet. 2. Grease lightly cooking spray over the 12-cup fluted tube pan. 3. Mix the granulated sugar, nutmeg, and cinnamon in a food bag. 4. Divide the dough into biscuits and then cut into quarters. Transfer to the food bag and coat well on all sides. 5. Add into the pan and sprinkle with raisins among the biscuit pieces. 6. Whisk the melted butter with brown sugar in a small mixing bowl. Then pour the butter mixture over the biscuit. 7. Close the lid and turn the steam release handle to Sealing position. 8. Set the Instant Pot on Pressure Cook at High and adjust time to 25 minutes. 9. When cooked, naturally release the pressure about 10 minutes and then remove the lid carefully. 10. Transfer to a serving plate. Serve warm and enjoy!
Per Serving: Calories:507; Fat 18.7g; Sodium 1442mg; Carbs 79.6g; Fiber 2.4g; Sugars 33.9g; Protein 7.6g

Creamy Carrot Soufflé

Prep time: 10 minutes | Cook Time: 45 minutes | Serves: 6

1 ½ pounds carrots, trimmed and cut into chunks	½ teaspoon ground cinnamon
	3 tablespoons flour
¾ cup sugar	3 eggs
1 teaspoon baking powder	⅓ cup cream cheese room
1 teaspoon vanilla paste	temperature
¼ teaspoon ground cardamom	1 stick butter, softened

1. In the inner pot, pour 1 cup of water and place a steamer basket on the bottom. Then spread the carrots in the steamer basket. 2. Close the lid and turn the steam release handle to Sealing position. 3. Set the Instant Pot on Steam at High and adjust time to 10 minutes. 4. When cooked, quick-release the pressure and remove the lid carefully. 5. In a food processor, stir together sugar, baking powder, vanilla, cardamom, cinnamon, flour, and the mashed carrot until creamy and smooth. 6. Fold in eggs one at a time and mix well. Then add butter and the cream cheese and stir well. 7. Lightly grease a baking pan. Then spoon the carrot batter inside the baking dish. 8. Transfer to the steamer basket. Close the lid and turn the steamer release handle to Sealing position. 9. Set the Instant Pot on Pressure Cook at High and adjust time to 35 minutes. 10. When cooked, naturally release the pressure about 10 minutes and then remove the lid carefully. 11. Serve and Enjoy!
Per Serving: Calories:353; Fat 21.6g; Sodium 240mg; Carbs 40.2g; Fiber 3g; Sugars 30.6g; Protein 2.9g

Honey Butter Cake

Prep time: 10 minutes | Cook Time: 15 minutes | Serves: 6

1 cup butter cookies, crumbled	1 (14-ounce) can sweetened
3 tablespoons butter, melted	condensed milk
1 egg	3 tablespoons honey
2 egg yolks	½ cup heavy cream
½ cup lemon juice	¼ cup sugar

1. In the inner pot, pour 1 cup of water and place the trivet. Spritz nonstick cooking spray over a baking pan. 2. Combine together butter and cookies. Then press the crust in the prepared baking pan. 3. Using a hand mixer, combine the lemon juice, condensed milk, and honey. 4. Drizzle the mixture on the top of the crust. Transfer the baking pan onto the trivet and cover with foil sheet. 5. Close the lid and turn the steam release handle to Sealing position. 6. Set the Instant Pot on Pressure Cook at High and adjust time to 15 minutes. 7. When cooked, naturally release the pressure about 15 minutes and then remove the lid carefully. 8. Whip together the heavy cream with sugar until the crema gets stiff. 9. Frost the cake and serve chilled.
Per Serving: Calories:488; Fat 22.3g; Sodium 223mg; Carbs 66.6g; Fiber 0.8g; Sugars 60.8g; Protein 8.9g

Yummy Dulce de Leche

Prep time: 10 minutes | Cook Time: 20 minutes | Serves: 2

1 can (14-ounce) sweetened	condensed milk

1. In the inner pot, place the trivet and a steamer basket on the bottom. Put the can of milk in the steamer basket. 2. Then pour water in until the can is covered. 3. Close the lid and turn the steam release handle to Sealing position. 4. Set the Instant Pot on Pressure Cook at High and adjust time to 20 minutes. 5. When cooked, naturally release the pressure and remove the lid carefully. 6. Serve and enjoy!
Per Serving: Calories:491; Fat 13.3g; Sodium 194mg; Carbs 83.2g; Fiber 0g; Sugars 83.2g; Protein 12.1g

Buttery Banana Bread

Prep time: 10 minutes | Cook Time: 45 minutes | Serves: 8

1 stick butter, melted	1 teaspoon baking soda
2 eggs	2 bananas, mashed
1 teaspoon vanilla extract	1 ½ cups all-purpose flour
¾ cup sugar	½ cup coconut flaked

1. In a mixing bowl, add all the ingredients and stir well to make the batter. 2. In the inner pot, pour 1 cup of water and place the trivet on the bottom. 3. Grease lightly a baking pan with nonstick cooking oil. 4. Then place the batter into the greased pan and then transfer to the trivet. 5. Close the lid and turn the steam release handle to Sealing position. 6. Set the Instant Pot on Pressure Cook at High and adjust time to 45 minutes. 7. When cooked, quick-release the pressure and then remove the lid carefully. 8. Cool the banana bread and then slice into your desired size. Serve and enjoy!
Per Serving: Calories:305; Fat 13.2g; Sodium 258mg; Carbs 43.9g; Fiber 1.5g; Sugars 22.9g; Protein 4.3g

Chocolate Mini Crepes with Cinnamon

Prep time: 10 minutes | Cook Time: 25 minutes | Serves: 6

½ cup all-purpose flour	2 tablespoons granulated sugar
½ cup rice flour	2 eggs, whisked
1 ½ teaspoons baking powder	1 cup milk
1 teaspoon vanilla paste	¼ cup coconut oil
¼ teaspoon ground cinnamon	1 cup chocolate syrup
A pinch of salt	

1. In the inner pot, pour 1 cup of water and place a metal rack at the bottom. 2. Lightly grease a mini muffin tin with shortening of choice. 3. Add the flour, vanilla, salt, cinnamon, eggs, sugar, milk, coconut oil, and baking powder in a mixing bowl and mix until completely combined and smooth. 4. Transfer the batter into the muffin tin and lower it onto the rack. 5. Close the lid and turn the steam release handle to Sealing position. 6. Set the Instant Pot on Pressure Cook at High and adjust time to 25 minutes. 7. When cooked, naturally release the pressure about 10 minutes and remove the lid carefully. 8. Drizzle chocolate syrup over the mini crepe and enjoy!
Per Serving: Calories:362; Fat 12.2g; Sodium 104mg; Carbs 57.8g; Fiber 2g; Sugars 30.8g; Protein 6.1g

Blood Orange Cake

Prep time: 10 minutes | Cook Time: 40 minutes | Serves: 8

Nonstick cooking spray	½ teaspoon ground cloves
3 teaspoons granulated sugar	¼ teaspoon ground cardamom
3 blood oranges, peeled and cut into slices	¼ teaspoon ginger flavoring
	2 tablespoons fresh orange juice
1 egg plus 1 egg yolk, beaten	1 ⅓ cups cake flour
1 cup sugar	1 ½ teaspoons baking powder
1 stick butter, at room temperature	A pinch of table salt
⅓ cup plain 2% yogurt	

1. Spritz nonstick cooking spray over a baking pan. 2. In the inner pot, spread the orange slices at the bottom. 3. Whisk the eggs in a mixing bowl until frothy. Then mix in sugar and then stir in butter. 4. Then add yogurt, fresh orange juice, ginger flavoring, cardamom, and cloves. 5. Combine together salt, baking powder, and the flour. 6. Then stir together the wet egg mixture with the flour mixture to make the batter. Pour the batter over the orange slices. 7. In the inner pot, pour 1 cup of water and place a metal trivet at the bottom. Then transfer the baking pan onto the trivet. 8. Close the lid and turn the steam release handle to Sealing position. 9. Then set the Instant Pot on Soup at High and adjust time to 40 minutes. 10. When cooked, quick-release the pressure and carefully remove the lid. 11. Place a platter on the cake and invert the baking pan, lifting it to reveal the oranges on top. 12. Serve and enjoy!
Per Serving: Calories:284; Fat 11.8g; Sodium 110mg; Carbs 42.2g; Fiber 2.3g; Sugars 23.7g; Protein 3.6g

Simple Almond Cheesecake

Prep time: 10 minutes | Cook Time: 25 minutes | Serves: 8

1 cup cookies, crushed	⅓ cup sour cream
3 tablespoons coconut oil, melted	¼ teaspoon grated nutmeg
18 ounces' cream cheese	½ teaspoon pure vanilla extract
1 cup granulated sugar	½ cup almonds, slivered
2 eggs	

1. In the inner pot, pour 1 cup of water and place the trivet. 2. Lightly grease a baking pan with nonstick cooking spray. 3. Then mix the coconut oil and cookies to make a sticky crust. Then press into the greased baking pan. 4. In a mixing bowl, combine together the sugar, eggs, nutmeg, vanilla extract, sour cream, and cream cheese. 5. Pour the mixture over the crust and use a foil sheet to cover. 6. Transfer the baking pan onto the trivet. 7. Close the lid and turn the steam release handle to Sealing position. 8. Set the Instant Pot on Pressure Cook at High and adjust time to 25 minutes. 9. When cooked, naturally release the pressure for 15 minutes and then remove the lid carefully. 10. Sprinkle on the top with slivered almonds. Serve and enjoy!
Per Serving: Calories:476; Fat 34.5g; Sodium 273mg; Carbs 36.6g; Fiber 1g; Sugars 28.8g; Protein 8.5g

Creamy Cupcakes

Prep time: 10 minutes | Cook Time: 25 minutes | Serves: 4

1 cup cake flour	1 egg
1 ½ teaspoons baking powder	½ cup honey
A pinch of salt	¼ almond milk
¼ teaspoon ground cardamom	4 ounces' cream cheese
¼ teaspoon ground cinnamon	⅓ cup powdered sugar
1 teaspoon vanilla extract	1 cup heavy cream, cold

1. Combine the baking powder, cardamom, cinnamon, vanilla, flour, and salt in a mixing bowl. 2. Add in the egg, milk, and honey and then mix well. Then spoon the batter into silicone cupcake liners and use foil sheet to cover. 3. In the inner pot, pour 1 cup of water and place the trivet. Then transfer the cupcakes to the trivet. 4. Close the lid and turn the steam release handle to Sealing position. 5. Set the Instant Pot on Pressure Cook at High and adjust time to 25 minutes. 6. When cooked, naturally release the pressure about 10 minutes and then remove the lid carefully. 7. Meanwhile, mix the remaining ingredients to make frost. 8. Frost the cupcakes and serve.
Per Serving: Calories:509; Fat 22.6g; Sodium 162mg; Carbs 72.1g; Fiber 1.1g; Sugars 45.4g; Protein 7.6g

Chocolate Lava Cakes

Prep time: 10 minutes | Cook Time: 15 minutes | Serves: 6

½ stick butter	1 ½ cups self-rising flour
1 cup sugar	2 tablespoons cocoa powder
2 eggs	1 tablespoon carob powder
3 tablespoons coconut milk	4 ounces' bittersweet chocolate
1 teaspoon vanilla	4 ounces' semisweet chocolate

1. In the inner pot, pour 1 cup of water and place the trivet. 2. Add butter inside the custard cups and set them aside. 3. Beat the butter and sugar until creamy and then fold with eggs, one at a time. Then mix well. 4. Mix in the milk and vanilla. Then add cocoa powder, carob powder, and the flour and stir well. 5. Fold in chocolate and stir until well combined. 6. Divide into the prepared custard cups. Transfer to the trivet. 7. Close the lid and turn the steam release handle to Sealing position. 8. Set the Instant Pot on Pressure Cook at High and adjust time to 15 minutes. 9. When cooked, naturally release the pressure about 10 minutes and then remove the lid carefully. 10. Serve and enjoy!
Per Serving: Calories:542; Fat 22.7g; Sodium 94mg; Carbs 82g; Fiber 3.3g; Sugars 53.9g; Protein 7.9g

Stuffed Apples with Walnuts

Prep time: 10 minutes | Cook Time: 15 minutes | Serves: 4

4 baking apples
⅓ cup granulated sugar
½ teaspoon cardamom
½ teaspoon cinnamon
⅓ cup walnuts, chopped
4 tablespoons currants
2 tablespoons coconut oil

1. In the inner pot, pour 1 ½ cups of water and place a metal rack at the bottom. 2. Core the apples and scoop out a bit of the flesh with a melon baller. Add in the remaining ingredients and mix together. Divide into the cored apples. 3. Close the lid and secure. 4. Set the Instant Pot on Steam at High and adjust time to 15 minutes. 5. When cooked, quick-release the pressure and remove the lid carefully. 6. Serve with ice cream as you like. Serve and enjoy!
Per Serving: Calories:307; Fat 13.4g; Sodium 2mg; Carbs 49.9g; Fiber 6.6g; Sugars 40.5g; Protein 3.3g

Simple Mexican Horchata

Prep time: 10 minutes | Cook Time: 5 minutes | Serves: 8

20 ounces' rice milk, unsweetened
8 ounces' almond milk, unsweetened
5 tablespoons agave syrup
1 cinnamon stick
1 vanilla bean

1. In the inner pot, add all the ingredients and combine well. 2. Close the lid and turn the steam release handle to Sealing position. 3. Set the Instant Pot on Pressure Cook at High and adjust time to 5 minutes. 4. When cooked, naturally release the pressure about 10 minutes and then carefully remove the lid. 5. Sprinkle the ground cinnamon to garnish as you desire. 6. Serve and enjoy!
Per Serving: Calories:140; Fat 7.3g; Sodium 38mg; Carbs 19.3g; Fiber 0.6g; Sugars 1g; Protein 0.8g

Classic Agua de Jamaica

Prep time: 10 minutes | Cook Time: 5 minutes | Serves: 4

4 cups water
½ cup dried hibiscus flowers
½ cup brown sugar
½ teaspoon fresh ginger, peeled and minced
2 tablespoons lime juice

1. In the inner pot, add water, the dried hibiscus flowers, brown sugar, and fresh ginger and combine well. 2. Close the lid and turn the steam release handle to Sealing position. 3. Set the Instant Pot on Pressure Cook at High and adjust time to 5 minutes. 4. When cooked, naturally release the pressure about 10 minutes and then remove the lid carefully. 5. Pour in the lime juice and stir well 6. Allow it to cool. Serve and enjoy!
Per Serving: Calories:70; Fat 0g; Sodium 12mg; Carbs 17.9g; Fiber 0g; Sugars 17.6g; Protein 0g

Yummy Arroz Con Leche

Prep time: 10 minutes | Cook Time: 10 minutes | Serves: 4

1 cup white pearl rice
1 cup water
A pinch of salt
2 ¼ cups milk
½ cup sugar
¼ teaspoon grated nutmeg
1 teaspoon vanilla extract
1 teaspoon cinnamon
Peel of ½ lemon

1. In the inner pot, add ice, water, and salt. 2. Close the lid and turn the steam release handle to Sealing position. 3. Set the Instant Pot on Pressure Cook at Low and adjust time to 10 minutes. 4. When cooked, naturally release the pressure about 10 minutes and then carefully remove the lid. 5. Set the Instant Pot on Sauté at Normal. Cook until the pudding starts to boil, stirring continuously. 6. Turn off the heat. Serve and enjoy!
Per Serving: Calories:228; Fat 3g; Sodium 105mg; Carbs 45.8g; Fiber 0.3g; Sugars 31.4g; Protein 5.6g

Spiced Apple Cider

Prep time: 10 minutes | Cook Time: 50 minutes | Serves: 6

6 apples, cored and diced
¾ cup brown sugar
2 cinnamon sticks
1 vanilla bean
1 teaspoon whole cloves
1 small naval orange
4 tablespoons rum
4 cups water

1. In the inner pot, add all the ingredients. 2. Close the lid and turn the steam release handle to Sealing position. 3. Set the Instant Pot on Pressure Cook at High and adjust time to 50 minutes. 4. When cooked, quick-release the pressure and then remove the lid carefully. 5. Using a fork or potato masher, mash the apples and pour over a mesh strainer. 6. Serve and enjoy!
Per Serving: Calories:215; Fat 0.5g; Sodium 13mg; Carbs 50.7g; Fiber 5.9g; Sugars 42.3g; Protein 0.8g

Honey-Glazed Apples

Prep time: 10 minutes | Cook Time: 2 minutes | Serves: 4

4 apples
1 teaspoon ground cinnamon
½ teaspoon ground cloves
2 tablespoons honey

1. In the inner pot, add all the ingredients and then pour ⅓ cup of water. 2. Close the lid and turn the steam release handle to Sealing position. 3. Set the Instant Pot on Pressure Cook at High and adjust time to 2 minutes. 4. When cooked, quick-release the pressure and carefully remove the lid. 5. Divide into serving bowls. Enjoy!
Per Serving: Calories:150; Fat 0.5g; Sodium 3mg; Carbs 40.1g; Fiber 5.8g; Sugars 31.8g; Protein 0.7g

Citrusy Berries Compote

Prep time: 10 minutes | Cook Time: 2 minutes | Serves: 4

1-pound blueberries
½ pound blackberries
½ pound strawberries
½ cup brown sugar
1 tablespoon orange juice
¼ teaspoon ground cloves
1 vanilla bean

1. In the inner pot, add all the berries. 2. Then add sugar and set aside for 15 minutes. Add ground cloves, vanilla bean, and orange juice. 3. Close the lid and turn the steam release handle to Sealing position. 4. Set the Instant Pot on Pressure Cook at High and adjust time to 2 minutes. 5. When cooked, naturally release the pressure about 10 minutes and then remove the lid carefully. 6. Let it cool to thicken Serve and enjoy!
Per Serving: Calories:178; Fat 0.9g; Sodium 7mg; Carbs 44.5g; Fiber 6.9g; Sugars 34.7g; Protein 2.1g

Chai White Hot Chocolate

Prep time: 10 minutes | Cook Time: 6 minutes | Serves: 5

4 cups whole milk
⅓ cup almond butter
4 tablespoons honey
2 tablespoons Masala Chai Syrup
1 teaspoon vanilla extract
A pinch of sea salt
A pinch of grated nutmeg
2 tablespoons gelatin

1. In the inner pot, add the almond butter, milk, Masala Chai Syrup, honey, sea salt, vanilla extract, sea salt, and grated nutmeg. 2. Close the lid and turn the steam release handle to Sealing position. 3. Set the Instant Pot on Pressure Cook at Low and adjust time to 6 minutes. 4. When cooked, quick-release the pressure and then remove the lid carefully. 5. Using an immersion blender, add the gelatin and mix well until the chocolate is smooth. 6. Serve and enjoy!
Per Serving: Calories:187; Fat 7g; Sodium 131mg; Carbs 23g; Fiber 0.2g; Sugars 24.3g; Protein 9g

Aranygaluska Cake

Prep time: 10 minutes | Cook Time: 25 minutes | Serves: 8

1 cup granulated sugar
4 ounces' walnuts, ground
1 tablespoon grated lemon peel
4 tablespoons butter, at room temperature
1 tablespoon fresh lemon juice
16 ounces refrigerated buttermilk biscuits
2 tablespoons cream cheese, at room temperature
½ cup powdered sugar
1 teaspoon vanilla extract

1. In the inner pot, pour 1 cup of water and place the trivet. 2. Mix the walnuts, lemon peel, and granulated sugar. 3. In another shallow bowl, mix the lemon juice and melted butter. 4. Cut the biscuits in half. Dip the biscuits in the butter mixture. Roll in the walnut/sugar mixture. 5. Transfer onto a loaf pan. 6. Close the lid and turn the steam release handle to Sealing position. 7. Set the Instant Pot on Pressure Cook at High and adjust time to 25 minutes. 8. When cooked, naturally release the pressure about 5 minutes and then remove the lid carefully. 9. Meanwhile, whip together the powdered sugar, cream cheese, and vanilla extract. 10. Drizzle the mixture over the hot cake. Serve and enjoy!
Per Serving: Calories:418; Fat 17.6g; Sodium 757mg; Carbs 61.2g; Fiber 1.9g; Sugars 36.6g; Protein 7.5g

Amazing Hot Mulled Apple Cider

Prep time: 10 minutes | Cook Time: 1 hour 30 minutes | Serves: 8

8 cups apple cider
1 (1-inch piece) fresh ginger, peeled and sliced
2 cinnamon sticks
2 vanilla beans
1 teaspoon whole cloves
1 teaspoon allspice berries
1 orange, sliced into thin rounds
½ cups brandy

1. In the inner pot, add apple cider, fresh ginger, cinnamon, vanilla beans, whole cloves, all spice berries, and orange rounds. 2. Close the lid and turn steam release handle to Venting position. 3. Set the Instant Pot on Slow Cook at Less and adjust time to 1 hour 30 minutes. 4. Strain the cider mixture and stir in the brandy. Serve and enjoy!
Per Serving: Calories:132; Fat 0.4g; Sodium 8mg; Carbs 32g; Fiber 0.9g; Sugars 29.2g; Protein 0.4g

Classical German Pancake

Prep time: 10 minutes | Cook Time: 30 minutes | Serves: 4

4 tablespoons butter, melted
5 eggs
1 ¼ cups milk
1 cup all-purpose flour
¼ teaspoon kosher salt
½ teaspoon cinnamon powder
½ teaspoon vanilla extract
1 cup canned blueberries with syrup

1. In the inner pot, pour 1 cup of water and place the trivet. Line the parchment paper over the bottom of a spring-form pan. 2. Then grease the melted butter in the bottom and sides. 3. Add in the milk, flour, salt, vanilla, cinnamon, and eggs and mix well to make the batter. Then spoon the batter into the greased pan. Transfer to the trivet. 4. Close the lid and turn the steam release handle to Sealing position. 5. Set the Instant Pot on Pressure Cook at High and adjust time to 30 minutes. 6. When cooked, quick-release the pressure and then remove the lid carefully. 7. Garnish with fresh blueberries. Serve and enjoy!
Per Serving: Calories:354; Fat 19g; Sodium 343mg; Carbs 33.4g; Fiber 1.7g; Sugars 7.7g; Protein 13.1g

Coconut Butternut Squash Pudding

Prep time: 10 minutes | Cook Time: 10 minutes | Serves: 6

2 pounds' butternut squash, peeled, seeded, and diced
1 cup coconut cream
½ cup maple syrup
A pinch of kosher salt
1 teaspoon pumpkin pie spice mix
6 tablespoons almond milk

1. In the inner pot, pour 1 cup of water and place a metal rack on the bottom. Place the squash in a steamer basket. Then transfer to the rack. 2. Close the lid and secure. 3. Set the Instant Pot on Steam at High and adjust time to 10 minutes. 4. When cooked, quick-release the pressure and remove the lid carefully. 5. Add the remaining ingredients in the cooked squash and stir well with a potato masher. 6. Then sauté at Normal about 4 minutes or until everything is heated completely. 7. Serve and enjoy!
Per Serving: Calories:289; Fat 12.2g; Sodium 182mg; Carbs 45.5g; Fiber 3.9g; Sugars 26.3g; Protein 3.4g

Enticing Caramel Croissant Pudding

Prep time: 10 minutes | Cook Time: 25 minutes | Serves: 6

6 stale croissants, cut into chunks
1 cup granulated sugar
4 tablespoons water
1 cup milk
1 cup heavy cream
3 tablespoons rum
¼ teaspoon ground cinnamon
3 eggs, whisked
Lightly grease a casserole dish.

1. In the inner pot, pour 1 cup of water and place the trivet. Place the croissants in the greased dish. 2. Set the Instant Pot on Sauté at Less. Cook the granulated sugar and water until brown. 3. Then add the heavy cream and milk. Cook until completely heated. Add the cinnamon, eggs, and rum and stir well. 4. Close the lid and turn the steam release handle to Sealing position. 5. Set the Instant Pot on Pressure Cook at High and adjust time to 25 minutes. 6. When cooked, naturally release the pressure about 10 minutes and then remove the lid carefully. 7. Serve and enjoy!
Per Serving: Calories:493; Fat 17.4g; Sodium 324mg; Carbs 62.1g; Fiber 1.6g; Sugars 41.4g; Protein 9.2g

Citrusy Cranberry Spritzer

Prep time: 10 minutes | Cook Time: 15 minutes | Serves: 8

12 ounces' fresh cranberries
½ cup granulated sugar
2 cups pulp-free orange juice
1 cup water

1. In the inner pot, add all the ingredients. 2. Close the lid and turn the steam release handle to Sealing position. 3. Set the Instant Pot on Pressure Cook at High and adjust time to 15 minutes. 4. When cooked, naturally release the pressure about 15 minutes and then remove the lid carefully. 5. Serve in eight glasses and add club soda. Enjoy!
Per Serving: Calories:98; Fat 0.1g; Sodium 1mg; Carbs 22.8g; Fiber 1.7g; Sugars 19.3g; Protein 0.4g

Peanut Butter Chocolate Fudge

Prep time: 10 minutes | Cook Time: 15 minutes | Serves: 12

16-ounce canned condensed milk
2 tablespoons peanut butter
½ teaspoon ground cardamom
½ teaspoon ground cinnamon
1 teaspoon vanilla extract
8 ounces' bittersweet chocolate chips
8 ounces' semisweet chocolate chips

1. Line a piece of foil at the bottom of a baking sheet. 2. In the inner pot, combine peanut butter, milk, cinnamon, vanilla, and cardamom until well incorporated. 3. Set the Instant Pot on Sauté at Less. 4. Cook until completely warmed. Fold in the chocolate chips and stir well. 5. Transfer onto the prepared baking sheet and chill in the refrigerator until solid. 6. Cut into squares and serve. Bon appétit!
Per Serving: Calories:333; Fat 15.6g; Sodium 75mg; Carbs 44.5g; Fiber 1.9g; Sugars 39.9g; Protein 5.1g

Honey Stewed Dried Fruits

Prep time: 10 minutes | Cook Time: 2 minutes | Serves: 8

½ cup dried figs
1 cup dried apricots
½ cup sultana raisins
1 cup prunes, pitted
1 cup almonds
1 cup sugar

1 cinnamon stick
1 vanilla bean
½ teaspoon whole cloves
½ teaspoon whole star anise
2 cups water
2 tablespoons Greek honey

1. In the inner pot, add all the ingredients. 2. Close the lid and turn the steam release handle to Sealing position. 3. Set the Instant Pot on Pressure Cook at High and adjust time to 2 minutes. 4. When cooked, naturally release the pressure about 10 minutes and then remove the lid carefully. 5. Pour Greek yogurt or ice cream on the top as you desire. 6. Serve and enjoy!
Per Serving: Calories:260; Fat 6.3g; Sodium 4mg; Carbs 52.9g; Fiber 4.7g; Sugars 42.8g; Protein 3.7g

Rican Pudding

Prep time: 10 minutes | Cook Time: 25 minutes | Serves: 8

1 pound Puerto Rican sweet bread, torn into pieces
1 cup water
1 teaspoon cinnamon powder
½ teaspoon ground cloves
1 teaspoon vanilla essence

1 cup brown sugar
4 cups coconut milk
2 tablespoons rum
4 eggs, beaten
A pinch of salt
½ stick butter, melted

1. In the inner pot, pour 1 cup of water and place a metal trivet at the bottom. 2. Lightly grease a casserole dish and place the sweet bread pieces inside. 3. Mix the rest ingredients in a mixing bowl until well combined. Pour over the bread pieces. Set it aside and let it stand for 20 minutes. Spread the mixture evenly over the bread. 4. Close the lid and turn the steam release handle to Sealing position. 5. Set the Instant Pot on Pressure Cook at High and adjust time to 25 minutes. 6. When cooked, naturally release the pressure about 10 minutes and remove the lid carefully. 7. Serve and enjoy!
Per Serving: Calories:467; Fat 36.6g; Sodium 305mg; Carbs 32.8g; Fiber 2.7g; Sugars 28.8g; Protein 5.6g

Chocolate Pudding with Apricots

Prep time: 10 minutes | Cook Time: 30 minutes | Serves: 10

4 ounces instant pudding mix
3 cups milk
1 package vanilla cake mix

½ cup peanut butter
1 ½ cups chocolate chips
½ cup dried apricots, chopped

1. Lightly grease the inner pot. 2. Combine together the milk and pudding mix in a mixing bowl. Then pour into the inner pot. 3. Follow the cake mix instruction to prepare the vanilla cake mix. Gradually add in the peanut butter. Then place the batter over the pudding. 4. Close the lid and turn the steam release handle to Sealing position. 5. Set the Instant Pot on Pressure Cook at High and adjust time to 30 minutes. 6. When cooked, naturally release the pressure about 10 minutes and then remove the lid carefully. 7. Top with chocolate chips and dried apricots. Close the lid and stand for 10 to 15 minutes or until the chocolate melts. 8. Serve and enjoy!
Per Serving: Calories:408; Fat 15.5g; Sodium 981mg; Carbs 60.5g; Fiber 3.5g; Sugars 20.2g; Protein 7.7g

Traditional Chewy Brownies

Prep time: 10 minutes | Cook Time: 20 minutes | Serves: 12

½ cup walnut butter
½ cup sunflower seed butter
1 cup coconut sugar
½ cup cocoa powder
2 eggs

A pinch of grated nutmeg
A pinch of salt
½ cardamom powder
½ teaspoon cinnamon powder
½ teaspoon baking soda

1 teaspoon vanilla extract
½ cup dark chocolate, cut into

chunks

1. In the inner pot, pour 1 cup of water and place a metal trivet at the bottom. 2. Spritz cooking spray over a baking pan. 3. Add all ingredients except the chocolate in a mixing bowl and mix well to make a thick batter 4. Spoon onto the greased pan and then sprinkle over with the chocolate chunks. Press gently into the batter. Transfer to the trivet. 5. Close the lid and turn the steam release handle to Sealing position. 6. Set the Instant Pot on Pressure Cook at High and adjust time to 20 minutes. 7. When cooked, naturally release the pressure about 10 minutes and then remove the lid carefully. 8. Allow the brownies to cool on a rack and slice into your desired size. 9. Serve and enjoy!
Per Serving: Calories:82; Fat 1.2g; Sodium 75mg; Carbs 18.8g; Fiber 1.1g; Sugars 16.8g; Protein 1.6g

Cinnamon Pear Pie with Pecans

Prep time: 10 minutes | Cook Time: 25 minutes | Serves: 8

2 cans (12-ounce) refrigerated cinnamon rolls
¼ cup all-purpose flour
¼ cup packed brown sugar

½ teaspoon cinnamon
2 tablespoons butter
⅓ cup pecans, chopped
5 pears, cored and sliced

1. Add all the ingredients except the pears in a large mixing bowl and mix together to make the dough. 2. Make 8 rolls from the dough and press the rolls into a lightly greased pie plate. Place the pear slices on the prepared cinnamon roll crust. Then spoon the streusel onto the pear slices. 3. In the inner pot, pour 1 cup of water and place a metal rack on the bottom. Transfer the pie plate on the rack. 4. Close the lid and turn the steam release handle to Sealing position. 5. Set the Instant Pot on Pressure Cook at High and adjust time to 25 minutes. 6. When cooked, naturally release about 5 minutes and remove the lid carefully. 7. Serve and enjoy!
Per Serving: Calories:185; Fat 8.4g; Sodium 23mg; Carbs 34.2g; Fiber 5.2g; Sugars 22.2g; Protein 1.9g

Bread Pudding with Rum Sauce

Prep time: 20 minutes | Cook time: 35 minutes | Serves: 1

Bread Pudding
1 large egg
¾ cup heavy cream
¼ cup granulated sugar
2 teaspoons vanilla extract
4 slices Texas Toast bread, dried overnight and diced into 1" cubes
⅛ teaspoon ground cinnamon
1 cup water

Buttered Rum Sauce
2 tablespoons granulated sugar
1 tablespoon apple juice
1 ½ tablespoons brown sugar
2 tablespoons heavy cream
¼ teaspoon rum extract
⅛ teaspoon vanilla extract
2 tablespoons butter

1. Grease a 6" cake pan. Set aside. 2. In a small saucepan over medium heat, whisk together egg, ¾ cup cream, and ¼ cup granulated sugar until mixture starts to bubble slightly on the sides and steam. 3. Add 2 teaspoons vanilla and remove from heat. 4. Arrange bread pieces in prepared cake pan, then pour cream mixture over the top and let soak 5 minutes. 5. Sprinkle cinnamon on top. Cover pan tightly with foil. 6. Pour water into Instant Pot and add the trivet. Place pan on trivet. 7. Put on the pressure cooker's lid and turn the steam valve to "Sealing" position. 8. Set the Instant Pot to Pressure Cook. Use the "+/-" keys on the control panel to set the cooking time to 35 minutes. 9. Press the Pressure Level button to adjust the pressure to "Low". 10. Once the cooking cycle is completed, allow the steam to release naturally. 11. When all the steam is released, remove the pressure lid from the top carefully. 12. Prepare the Buttered Rum Sauce: In a separate small saucepan over medium heat, combine 2 tablespoons granulated sugar, apple juice, brown sugar, and 2 tablespoons cream. 13. Boil 5 minutes. Remove from heat, then add rum extract, ⅛ teaspoon vanilla, and butter, whisking constantly. 14. Remove pan, remove foil, and serve immediately with Buttered Rum Sauce.
Per Serving: Calories 382; Fat 7.9g; Sodium 704mg; Carbs 6g; Fiber 3.6g; Sugar 6g; Protein 18g

Polynesian Hazelnut Cake

Prep time: 10 minutes | Cook Time: 25 minutes | Serves: 8

1 cup granulated sugar
4 tablespoons hazelnuts, ground
10 refrigerated biscuits
1 stick butter, melted
4 ounces' cream cheese, at room
temperature
¼ cup powdered sugar
2 tablespoons apple juice
1 teaspoon vanilla extract

1. In the inner pot, pour 1 cup of water and place the trivet. Using cooking spray, lightly grease a suitable fluted tube pan. 2. Mix 1 cup of granulated sugar and ground hazelnuts in a shallow bowl. 3. Cut the biscuits into half and then dip with melted butter. Roll in the hazelnut/sugar mixture and then arrange in the fluted tube pan. 4. Close the lid and turn the steam release handle to Sealing position. 5. Set the Instant Pot on Pressure Cook at High and adjust time to 25 minutes. 6. When cooked, naturally release the pressure about 5 minutes and then remove the lid carefully. 7. Meanwhile, whip together the cream cheese with vanilla extract, apple juice, and the powdered sugar. 8. Then pour over the hot cake. Serve and enjoy!
Per Serving: Calories:382; Fat 19.3g; Sodium 507mg; Carbs 51.1g; Fiber 0.9g; Sugars 37g; Protein 3.6g

Mango Sticky Rice

Prep time: 15 minutes | Cook time: 5 minutes | Serves: 4-6

Sticky Rice
½ cup uncooked jasmine rice
¾ cup canned unsweetened full-fat coconut milk
⅛ teaspoon salt
Coconut Sauce
½ cup canned unsweetened full-fat coconut milk
4 teaspoons sugar
1/16 teaspoon salt
½ tablespoon cornstarch
½ tablespoon cold water
For Serving
½ cup ripe mango slices, chilled
½ teaspoon toasted sesame seeds

1. To the Instant Pot, add all Sticky Rice ingredients. 2. Put on the pressure cooker's lid and turn the steam valve to "Sealing" position. 3. Set the Instant Pot to Pressure Cook. Use the "+/-" keys on the control panel to set the cooking time to 3 minutes. 4. Press the Pressure Level button to adjust the pressure to "Low". 5. Once the cooking cycle is completed, allow the steam to release naturally. 6. When all the steam is released, remove the pressure lid from the top carefully. 7. While the rice is cooking, make the Coconut Sauce. 8. In a small saucepan over medium heat, combine coconut milk, sugar, and salt. 9. In a small bowl, mix together cornstarch and cold water to make a slurry. 10. When coconut milk mixture comes to a boil, whisk in the slurry about 1–2 minutes until thickened. 11. Remove from heat and allow to cool to room temperature. 12. Add ¼ cup Coconut Sauce to the rice in the Instant Pot and stir to combine. 13. Replace the lid and let cool 10 minutes. 14. To serve, spoon rice into a bowl and arrange mango slices over rice. 15. Pour remaining coconut sauce over the top and sprinkle with sesame seeds. Serve.
Per Serving: Calories 489; Fat 11g; Sodium 501mg; Carbs 28.9g; Fiber 4.6g; Sugar 8g; Protein 6g

Berry Almond Crisp

Prep time: 15 minutes | Cook time: 25 minutes | Serves: 4-6

¾ cup frozen berry mix
½ teaspoon almond extract
2 tablespoons granulated sugar
½ tablespoon cornstarch
1 tablespoon cold butter, cut up
1 tablespoon brown sugar
1/16 teaspoon ground cinnamon
1/16 teaspoon nutmeg
1½ tablespoons all-purpose flour
1½ tablespoons rolled oats
1 cup water
¼ cup vanilla ice cream

1. In a small bowl, toss together berries, almond extract, granulated sugar, and cornstarch. 2. Pour into an 8-ounce ramekin. 3. In a separate small bowl, using a fork, combine butter, brown sugar, cinnamon, nutmeg, flour, and oats until mixture resembles large crumbs. 4. Crumble over berry mixture and cover with foil. 5. Pour water into Instant Pot and add the trivet. Place ramekin on trivet. 6. Put on the pressure cooker's lid and turn the steam valve to "Sealing" position. 7. Set the Instant Pot to Pressure Cook. Use the "+/-" keys on the control panel to set the cooking time to 25 minutes. 8. Press the Pressure

Level button to adjust the pressure to "Low". 9. Once the cooking cycle is completed, allow the steam to release naturally. 10. When all the steam is released, remove the pressure lid from the top carefully. 11. Carefully remove ramekin from the Instant Pot, then remove foil and let cool 5 minutes. 12. Top with ice cream and serve immediately.
Per Serving: Calories 199; Fat 5g; Sodium 41mg; Carbs 7g; Fiber 7.6g; Sugar 5g; Protein 2g

Romantic Pots de Crème

Prep time: 10 minutes | Cook Time: 6 minutes | Serves: 6

2 cups double cream
½ cup whole milk
4 egg yolks
⅓ cup sugar
1 teaspoon instant coffee
A pinch of pink salt
9 ounces' chocolate chips

1. In the inner pot, pour 1 cup of water and place the trivet. 2. Add cream and milk in a saucepan and simmer. 3. Then combine sugar, instant coffee, salt, and egg yolks thoroughly. Whisk in the how cream mixture slowly and gently. 4. Blend together with chocolate chips. Then pour into mason jars. Transfer to the trivet. 5. Close the lid and turn the steam release handle to Sealing position. 6. Set the Instant Pot on Pressure Cook at High and adjust time to 6 minutes. 7. When cooked, naturally release the pressure and then remove the lid carefully. 8. Serve and enjoy!
Per Serving: Calories 455; Fat 31.1g; Sodium 62mg; Carbs 38.8g; Fiber 1.5g; Sugars 34.2g; Protein 6.5g

Vanilla Crème Brulee

Prep time: 20 minutes | Cook time: 8 minutes | Serves: 1

½ cup heavy cream
½ teaspoon vanilla bean paste
2 large egg yolks
2 tablespoons sugar
1 cup water
3 whole raspberries

1. In a small saucepan over medium-high heat, combine cream and vanilla bean paste until steaming. Do not boil and then remove from heat. 2. In a small bowl, whisk egg yolks and 1 tablespoon sugar until light and smooth. 3. While whisking, slowly pour hot cream into egg yolks and whisk to combine. 4. Pour cream mixture through a fine-mesh strainer into an 8-ounce ramekin. Cover with foil. 5. Pour water into Instant Pot and add the trivet. Place ramekin on trivet. 6. Put on the pressure cooker's lid and turn the steam valve to "Sealing" position. 7. Set the Instant Pot to Pressure Cook. Use the "+/-" keys on the control panel to set the cooking time to 8 minutes. 8. Press the Pressure Level button to adjust the pressure to "Low". 9. Once the cooking cycle is completed, allow the steam to release naturally. 10. When all the steam is released, remove the pressure lid from the top carefully. 11. Remove ramekin to cooling rack. Let cool and then refrigerate 6–8 hours. 12. To serve, remove foil. Sprinkle remaining 1 tablespoon sugar over the top of the crème Brûlée. 13. Using a kitchen torch, quickly torch the sugar in small circles until sugar is completely caramelized. 14. Cool 1 minute, then top with raspberries and serve.
Per Serving: Calories 334; Fat 10.9g; Sodium 354mg; Carbs 25g; Fiber 4.1g; Sugar 8.2g; Protein 11g

Brown Butter–Cinnamon Rice Treat

Prep time: 20 minutes | Cook time: 4 minutes | Serves: 1

½ tablespoon butter
½ cup mini marshmallows
⅛ teaspoon vanilla extract
1/16 teaspoon ground cinnamon
1 cup crispy rice cereal
1/16 teaspoon coarse sea salt

1. Lightly grease a medium bowl or line a small baking sheet with waxed paper. 2. On the Instant Pot, press Sauté button and adjust to Normal. 3. Add butter and cook about 4 minutes until slightly golden and browned. 4. Adjust the Instant Pot Sauté setting to Low and add marshmallows. 5. When melted, press Cancel button to turn off the heat and add vanilla and cinnamon. 6. Stir to combine, then add cereal and mix until completely combined. 7. Scrape mixture into prepared bowl or onto lined baking sheet. Lightly pat down to shape. 8. Immediately sprinkle with salt, then cool at least 10 minutes and serve.
Per Serving: Calories 489; Fat 11g; Sodium 501mg; Carbs 28.9g; Fiber 4.6g; Sugar 8g; Protein 6g

Stuffed Baked Apple À La Mode

Prep time: 15 minutes | Cook time: 7 minutes | Serves: 1

1 medium Honeycrisp apple
1 tablespoon brown sugar
1 tablespoon butter
½ teaspoon ground cinnamon
1 tablespoon chopped pecans
1 tablespoon sweetened dried cranberries
1 cup water
¼ cup vanilla ice cream

1. Core apple and scrape out center to create a cavity in the middle about 1" in diameter. 2. In a small bowl, mix together brown sugar, butter, cinnamon, pecans, and cranberries into a paste. 3. Scoop paste into apple and cover the top with a small piece of foil. 4. Pour water into Instant Pot and add the trivet. Place apple on trivet. 5. Put on the pressure cooker's lid and turn the steam valve to "Sealing" position. 6. Set the Instant Pot to Pressure Cook. 7. Press the Pressure Level button to adjust the pressure to "Low". 8. Use the "+/-" keys on the control panel to set the cooking time to 7 minutes. 9. Once the cooking cycle is completed, allow the steam to release naturally. 10. When all the steam is released, remove the pressure lid from the top carefully. 11. Using tongs, carefully remove apple from the Instant Pot and transfer to a bowl. Let cool 5 minutes. 12. Top with ice cream and serve immediately.
Per Serving: Calories 334; Fat 10.9g; Sodium 354mg; Carbs 25g; Fiber 4.1g; Sugar 8.2g; Protein 6g

Key Lime Pie

Prep time: 20 minutes | Cook time: 10 minutes | Serves: 1

Crust
¼ cup graham cracker crumbs
½ tablespoon sugar
1 tablespoon butter, melted
1/16 teaspoon ground cinnamon
Filling
1 large egg yolk
½ cup sweetened condensed milk
2 tablespoons lime juice
½ teaspoon lime zest
1 cup water
For Serving
2 tablespoons sweetened whipped cream
¼ teaspoon lime zest

1. In a medium bowl, mix together all Crust ingredients and press into an 8-ounce ramekin. Set aside. 2. In a separate medium bowl, mix together all Filling ingredients (except water) and pour over crust. 3. Cover with foil. Pour water into Instant Pot and add the trivet. Place ramekin on trivet. 4. Put on the pressure cooker's lid and turn the steam valve to "Sealing" position. 5. Set the Instant Pot to Pressure Cook. Use the "+/-" keys on the control panel to set the cooking time to 10 minutes. 6. Press the Pressure Level button to adjust the pressure to "Low". 7. Once the cooking cycle is completed, allow the steam to release naturally. 8. When all the steam is released, remove the pressure lid from the top carefully. 9. Let pie cool to room temperature, then refrigerate at least 6–8 hours or overnight. 10. Serve garnished with whipped cream and ¼ teaspoon lime zest.
Per Serving: Calories 199; Fat 5g; Sodium 41mg; Carbs 7g; Fiber 7.6g; Sugar 5g; Protein 2g

Cinnamon-Vanilla Rice Pudding

Prep time: 20 minutes | Cook time: 8 minutes | Serves: 1

½ cup uncooked long-grain white rice
1 cup water
1/16 teaspoon salt
2 ½ tablespoons sugar
1 cup whole milk
1 large egg
½ tablespoon butter
½ tablespoon vanilla extract
2 tablespoons heavy cream
⅛ teaspoon ground cinnamon

1. To the Instant Pot, add rice, water, and salt. 2. Put on the pressure cooker's lid and turn the steam valve to "Sealing" position. 3. Set the Instant Pot to Pressure Cook. Use the "+/-" keys on the control panel to set the cooking time to 3 minutes. 4. Press the Pressure Level button to adjust the pressure to "Low". 5. Once the cooking cycle is completed, allow the steam to release naturally. 6. When all the steam is released, remove the pressure lid from the top carefully. 7. Fluff rice, then add sugar and stir to dissolve. 8. Press Sauté button and adjust to Less. Whisk in ½ cup milk and bring to a low simmer. 9. In a liquid measuring cup, measure remaining ½ cup milk and whisk together

with egg until completely combined. 10. While whisking, pour egg mixture into the pot until completely incorporated. 11. Whisk about 5 minutes until thickened. Press Cancel button to turn off the heat. 12. Stir in butter, vanilla, and cream. Scoop into a bowl and serve with a sprinkle of cinnamon.
Per Serving: Calories 199; Fat 5g; Sodium 41mg; Carbs 7g; Fiber 7.6g; Sugar 5g; Protein 2g

Carrot Cake with Cream Cheese Frosting

Prep time: 20 minutes | Cook time: 65 minutes | Serves: 1

Carrot Cake
¼ cup granulated sugar
¼ cup brown sugar
2 tablespoons canola oil
1 large egg, lightly beaten
1 teaspoon vanilla extract
½ cup all-purpose flour
¾ teaspoon ground cinnamon
⅛ teaspoon ground nutmeg
⅛ teaspoon ground cloves
½ teaspoon baking soda
1 cup shredded carrots
½ cup pecans
⅓ cup chopped pineapple
¼ cup sweetened shredded coconut
1 cup water
Cream Cheese Frosting
4 oz. cream cheese, softened
3 tablespoons butter
1 ½ teaspoons vanilla extract
1/16 teaspoon salt
2 cups confectioners' sugar

1. Grease a 6" cake pan. Set aside. 2. In a medium bowl, combine granulated sugar, brown sugar, and oil. 3. Add egg and vanilla and stir until combined. 4. Sift in flour, cinnamon, nutmeg, cloves, and baking soda. Stir to combine. 5. Add carrots, pecans, pineapple, and coconut. Stir well, then let rest 5 minutes to allow the moisture from the carrots and pineapple to soften the batter. 6. Pour batter into prepared cake pan and cover tightly with foil. 7. Pour water into Instant Pot and add the trivet. Place pan on trivet. 8. Put on the pressure cooker's lid and turn the steam valve to "Sealing" position. 9. Set the Instant Pot to Pressure Cook. Use the "+/-" keys on the control panel to set the cooking time to 60 minutes. 10. Press the Pressure Level button to adjust the pressure to "Low". 11. Once the cooking cycle is completed, allow the steam to release naturally. 12. When all the steam is released, remove the pressure lid from the top carefully. 13. Carefully remove pan and let cool 15 minutes before placing in the refrigerator at least 5 hours, preferably overnight. 14. To make the Cream Cheese Frosting, in a medium bowl, combine all ingredients except confectioners' sugar. Whisk together or blend using an electric mixer until smooth. 15. Add confectioners' sugar 1 cup at a time. Incorporate each cup before adding the next. 16. Remove cake from pan and frost with Cream Cheese Frosting. Serve.
Per Serving: Calories 322; Fat 11g; Sodium 491mg; Carbs 24g; Fiber 3g; Sugar 8g; Protein 3g

Pumpkin Pie Bites

Prep time: 5 minutes | Cook time: 20 minutes | Serves: 1

¼ cup pumpkin puree
3 tablespoons sugar
¼ cup heavy cream
1 large egg
¼ teaspoon pumpkin pie spice
1/16 teaspoon salt
1 cup water
2 tablespoons sweetened whipped cream

1. Grease three cups of a silicone egg bites mold. Set aside. 2. In a small bowl, whisk together pumpkin, sugar, heavy cream, egg, pumpkin pie spice, and salt until combined. 3. Equally divide the mixture among prepared egg bite mold cups. Cover tightly with foil. 4. Pour water into Instant Pot and add the trivet. 5. Place mold on trivet. Alternatively, place the mold on a silicone sling and lower into the Instant Pot. 6. Put on the pressure cooker's lid and turn the steam valve to "Sealing" position. 7. Set the Instant Pot to Pressure Cook. 8. Use the "+/-" keys on the control panel to set the timer to 20 minutes. 9. Press the Pressure Level button to adjust the pressure to "Low". 10. Once the cooking cycle is completed, allow the steam to release naturally. 11. When all the steam is released, remove the pressure lid from the top carefully. 12. Allow pie bites to cool to room temperature, then refrigerate 4–8 hours until set. 13. Remove foil, invert pie bites onto a plate, and enjoy with whipped cream.
Per Serving: Calories 334; Fat 10.9g; Sodium 454mg; Carbs 10g; Fiber 3.1g; Sugar 5.2g; Protein 05g

Crème Caramel (Purin)

Prep time: 20 minutes | Cook time: 9 minutes | Serves: 1

4 tablespoons sugar	½ teaspoon vanilla extract
1 cup plus 2 tablespoons and 1 teaspoon water	1 tablespoon sweetened whipped cream
½ cup whole milk	1 maraschino cherry
1 large egg yolk	

1. To a small saucepan over medium heat, add 3 tablespoons sugar and 2 tablespoons water. 2. Tilt the pot and swirl to combine the mixture—do not stir—and cook about 6 minutes until dark amber in color and caramelized. 3. Remove from heat and carefully add 1 teaspoon water to the caramel to thin. 4. Quickly and carefully pour the hot caramel into an 8-ounce ramekin and set aside. 5. In a separate small saucepan over medium heat, heat milk until steaming, then remove from heat. 6. In a small bowl, whisk egg yolk and remaining 1 tablespoon sugar until creamy. 7. Slowly pour hot milk mixture into egg yolk mixture while constantly whisking. 8. Whisk in vanilla, then pour mixture over caramel in the ramekin and cover with foil. 9. Pour remaining 1 cup water into Instant Pot and add the trivet. Place ramekin on trivet. 10. Put on the pressure cooker's lid and turn the steam valve to "Scaling" position. 11. Set the Instant Pot to Pressure Cook. Use the "+/-" keys on the control panel to set the cooking time to 9 minutes. 12. Press the Pressure Level button to adjust the pressure to "Low". 13. Once the cooking cycle is completed, allow the steam to release naturally. 14. When all the steam is released, remove the pressure lid from the top carefully. 15. Carefully remove ramekin from the Instant Pot and let cool to room temperature. 16. Then refrigerate 6–8 hours or overnight. 17. When ready to serve, slide a wet knife around the edges of custard, then invert onto a plate. 18. Serve with whipped cream and cherry.
Per Serving: Calories 272; Fat 10g; Sodium 891mg; Carbs 22.9g; Fiber 4g; Sugar 4g; Protein 3g

Molten Chocolate Lava Cake

Prep time: 20 minutes | Cook time: 7 minutes | Serves: 1

½ cup semisweet chocolate chips	¼ teaspoon vanilla extract
2 tablespoons butter	1 tablespoon all-purpose flour
½ cup confectioners' sugar	½ tablespoon cocoa powder
1 large egg	1 cup water

1. In a medium microwave-safe bowl, combine chocolate chips and butter. 2. Microwave in 10-second intervals until completely melted. 3. Add sugar and combine until smooth. 4. Add egg and beat until completely combined. Add vanilla, flour, and cocoa powder. 5. Stir to combine. Pour into a greased 8-ounce ramekin. 6. Pour water into Instant Pot and add the trivet. Place ramekin on trivet. 7. Put on the pressure cooker's lid and turn the steam valve to "Sealing" position. 8. Set the Instant Pot to Pressure Cook. Use the "+/-" keys on the control panel to set the cooking time to 7 minutes. 9. Press the Pressure Level button to adjust the pressure to "Low". 10. Once the cooking cycle is completed, allow the steam to release quickly. 11. When all the steam is released, remove the pressure lid from the top carefully. 12. Invert cake onto a plate and serve immediately.
Per Serving: Calories 272; Fat 10g; Sodium 891mg; Carbs 12.9g; Fiber 4g; Sugar 4g; Protein 3g

Gooey Chocolate Chip Cookie Sundae

Prep time: 5 minutes | Cook time: 20 minutes | Serves: 1

1½ tablespoons butter, melted	1/16 teaspoon salt
1 tablespoon brown sugar	1 tablespoon mini semisweet chocolate chips
1 tablespoon granulated sugar	
1 large egg yolk	1 cup water
½ teaspoon vanilla extract	¼ cup vanilla bean ice cream
⅓ cup all-purpose flour	1 tablespoon chopped pecans
⅛ teaspoon baking soda	1 tablespoon chocolate syrup

1. Grease an 8-ounce ramekin. Set aside. 2. In a small bowl, combine butter with brown sugar and granulated sugar until dissolved. 3. Add egg yolk and vanilla and mix until smooth. 4. Add flour, baking soda, and salt; combine to make a dough. Mix in chocolate chips. 5. Scrape dough into prepared ramekin and press into the bottom of the ramekin. Cover with foil. 6. Pour water into Instant Pot and add the trivet. Place ramekin on trivet. 7. Put on the pressure cooker's lid and turn the steam valve to "Sealing" position. 8. Set your Instant Pot on Pressure Cook. Use the "+/-" keys on the control panel to set the cooking time to 20 minutes. 9. Press the Pressure Level button to adjust the pressure to "Low". 10. Once the cooking cycle is completed, allow the steam to release naturally. 11. When all the steam is released, remove the pressure lid from the top carefully. 12. Carefully remove ramekin from the pot. Remove foil and cool 3–5 minutes. 13. Top warm cookie with ice cream, pecans, and chocolate syrup. Serve immediately.
Per Serving: Calories 489; Fat 11g; Sodium 501mg; Carbs 8.9g; Fiber 4.6g; Sugar 8g; Protein 26g

Cherry Cheesecake Bites

Prep time: 20 minutes | Cook time: 5 minutes | Serves: 1

Crust	5 tablespoons sugar
4 ½ tablespoons graham cracker crumbs	½ teaspoon vanilla extract
2 tablespoons butter, melted	1 large egg, lightly beaten
½ tablespoon all-purpose flour	1 tablespoon sour cream
⅛ teaspoon ground cinnamon	1 cup water
½ tablespoon sugar	Topping
Cheesecake Filling	2 tablespoons sour cream
8 oz. cream cheese, softened	6 tablespoons cherry pie filling

1. To make the Crust, in a medium bowl, combine all Crust ingredients. 2. Add ½ tablespoon mixture into each cup of a silicone egg bites mold. 3. To make the Filling, in a separate medium bowl, mix together cream cheese and sugar until sugar is completely dissolved. 4. Add vanilla, egg, and sour cream, and whisk until just combined. Do not overmix. 5. Pour filling evenly on top of crust. Place a paper towel on top of the mold, then cover tightly with foil. 6. Pour water into Instant Pot and add the trivet. Place mold on trivet. 7. Put on the pressure cooker's lid and turn the steam valve to "Sealing" position. 8. Set the Instant Pot to Pressure Cook. Use the "+/-" keys on the control panel to set the cooking time to 5 minutes. 9. Press the Pressure Level button to adjust the pressure to "Low". 10. Once the cooking cycle is completed, allow the steam to release naturally. 11. When all the steam is released, remove the pressure lid from the top carefully. 12. Remove foil and paper towel, and cool to room temperature 1–2 hours, then refrigerate overnight. 13. To serve, invert cheesecakes onto a plate or scoop them out with a large spoon and place on a plate. 14. Spread a thin layer of sour cream over each bite, and top with cherry pie filling. 15. Serve.
Per Serving: Calories 378; Fat 19g; Sodium 354mg; Carbs 21g; Fiber 5.1g; Sugar 8.2g; Protein 2g

Stuffed Apples

Prep time: 20 minutes | Cook time: 6 minutes | Serves: 4-6

¼ cup chopped walnuts	1 teaspoon ground cinnamon
¼ cup gluten-free rolled oats	⅛ teaspoon salt
3 teaspoons coconut oil	4 apples, cored
1 teaspoon maple syrup	

1. In a small bowl, combine the walnuts, oats, coconut oil, maple syrup, cinnamon, and salt. 2. Spoon the mixture into the cored apples. 3. Pour 1 cup of water into the Instant Pot and insert the trivet. Place the apples on the trivet. 4. Put on the pressure cooker's lid and turn the steam valve to "Sealing" position. 5. Set the Instant Pot to Pressure Cook. Use the "+/-" keys on the control panel to set the cooking time to 6 minutes. 6. Press the Pressure Level button to adjust the pressure to "High". 7. Once the cooking cycle is completed, allow the steam to release quickly. 8. When all the steam is released, remove the pressure lid from the top carefully. 9. Serve the apples warm.
Per Serving: Calories 199; Fat 5g; Sodium 41mg; Carbs 7g; Fiber 7.6g; Sugar 5g; Protein 2g

White Chocolate Crème Brûlée

Prep time: 20 minutes | Cook time: 16 minutes | Serves: 1

3 tablespoons white chocolate chips
½ cup heavy cream
2 large egg yolks

1 tablespoon sugar
1 cup water
1 tablespoon crushed candy cane, crushed into a fine powder

1. To a small bowl, add chocolate chips. In a small saucepan over medium-high heat, warm cream until steaming. 2. Do not boil. Remove from heat and pour over chocolate chips and stir until melted. 3. In a separate small bowl, whisk egg yolks and sugar until light and smooth. 4. While whisking, slowly pour hot cream into egg yolks to temper the eggs. Whisk until completely combined. 5. Pour cream mixture through a fine-mesh strainer into an 8-ounce ramekin. Cover with foil. 6. Pour water into Instant Pot and add the trivet. Place ramekin on trivet. 7. Put on the pressure cooker's lid and turn the steam valve to "Sealing" position. 8. Set the Instant Pot to Pressure Cook. Use the "+/-" keys on the control panel to set the cooking time to 16 minutes. 9. Press the Pressure Level button to adjust the pressure to "Low". 10. Once the cooking cycle is completed, allow the steam to release naturally. 11. When all the steam is released, remove the pressure lid from the top carefully. 12. Sprinkle peppermint candy evenly over the top of crème Brûlée and shake to distribute it evenly. 13. Using a kitchen torch, quickly torch candy in small circles until completely caramelized. 14. Keep the torch moving to evenly melt candy. 15. Cool 1 minute, then serve immediately.
Per Serving: Calories 361; Fat 12.9g; Sodium 754mg; Carbs 21g; Fiber 6.1g; Sugar 4.2g; Protein 11g

White Chocolate–Lemon Pie

Prep time: 20 minutes | Cook time: 10 minutes | Serves: 1

Crust
¼ cup graham cracker crumbs
½ tablespoon sugar
1 tablespoon butter, melted
Filling
2 tablespoons white chocolate

chips
¼ cup sweetened condensed milk
1 large egg yolk
2 tablespoons lemon juice
½ teaspoon lemon zest
1 cup water

1. To make Crust, in a small bowl, mix together all Crust ingredients and press into an 8-ounce ramekin. 2. To make Filling, in a separate small microwave-safe bowl, microwave chocolate chips in 15-second intervals until melted. 3. Whisk in condensed milk, egg yolk, lemon juice, and lemon zest. Pour over the crust. Cover with foil. 4. Pour water into Instant Pot and add the trivet. Place ramekin on trivet. 5. Put on the pressure cooker's lid and turn the steam valve to "Sealing" position. 6. Set the Instant Pot to Pressure Cook. Use the "+/-" keys on the control panel to set the cooking time to 10 minutes. 7. Press the Pressure Level button to adjust the pressure to "Low". 8. Once the cooking cycle is completed, allow the steam to release naturally. 9. When all the steam is released, remove the pressure lid from the top carefully. 10. Let pie cool to room temperature, then refrigerate at least 6–8 hours or overnight, and then serve.
Per Serving: Calories 372; Fat 20g; Sodium 891mg; Carbs 29g; Fiber 3g; Sugar 8g; Protein 10g

Chocolate Peanut Butter Popcorn

Prep time: 5 minutes | Cook time: 6 minutes | Serves: 4-6

1 tablespoon coconut oil
¼ cup popcorn kernels
1 tablespoon creamy peanut butter

2 tablespoons dairy-free dark chocolate chips

1. Press the "Sauté" button two times to select "Normal" temperature on the Instant Pot and pour in the coconut oil. 2. When the oil is hot, add the popcorn kernels. 3. Cook until the kernels stop popping on a regular basis about 5 to 6 minutes. 4. Remove the lid and stir in the peanut butter, using the heat of the pot to help it melt and coat the popcorn. 5. Stir in the chocolate chips. Serve warm or let the chocolate set at room temperature before eating.
Per Serving: Calories 472; Fat 7.9g; Sodium 704mg; Carbs 6g; Fiber 3.6g; Sugar 6g; Protein 18g

Vanilla Bean Custard

Prep time: 20 minutes | Cook time: 7 minutes | Serves: 4-6

4 large egg yolks
1 cup whole milk
2 tablespoons honey

1 vanilla bean, scraped, or ¼ teaspoon vanilla extract

1. In a medium bowl, whisk together the egg yolks, milk, honey, and vanilla until smooth. 2. Divide among four 4-ounce ramekins. Cover the tops with aluminum foil. 3. Pour 1 cup of water into the Instant Pot and insert the trivet. Place the ramekins on the trivet. 4. Put on the pressure cooker's lid and turn the steam valve to "Sealing" position. 5. Set the Instant Pot to Pressure Cook. Use the "+/-" keys on the control panel to set the cooking time to 7 minutes. 6. Press the Pressure Level button to adjust the pressure to "High". 7. Once the cooking cycle is completed, allow the steam to release naturally. 8. When all the steam is released, remove the pressure lid from the pot carefully. 9. Serve warm or chilled.
Per Serving: Calories 489; Fat 11g; Sodium 501mg; Carbs 28.9g; Fiber 4.6g; Sugar 8g; Protein 6g

Peach Cobbler

Prep time: 20 minutes | Cook time: 10 minutes | Serves: 4-6

1 cup spelt flour
1 tablespoon baking powder
2 teaspoons coconut sugar
⅛ teaspoon kosher salt
1 cup buttermilk

2-pound frozen sliced peaches
¼ cup water
½ teaspoon ground cinnamon
¼ teaspoon ground coriander

1. In a medium bowl, combine the flour, baking powder, coconut sugar, and salt. 2. Stir in the buttermilk to form a thick dough. 3. In the Instant Pot, combine the peaches, water, cinnamon, and coriander. 4. Drop the dough, a tablespoon at a time, on top of the peaches, being careful to not let the dough touch the bottom or sides of the pot. 5. Put on the pressure cooker's lid and turn the steam valve to "Sealing" position. 6. Set the Instant Pot to Pressure Cook. Use the "+/-" keys on the control panel to set the cooking time to 10 minutes. 7. Press the Pressure Level button to adjust the pressure to "High". 8. Once the cooking cycle is completed, allow the steam to release quickly. 9. When all the steam is released, remove the pressure lid from the top carefully. 10. Let the cobbler cool for 5 to 10 minutes before serving.
Per Serving: Calories 334; Fat 7.9g; Sodium 704mg; Carbs 6g; Fiber 3.6g; Sugar 6g; Protein 18g

Lemon Bars

Prep time: 20 minutes | Cook time: 12 minutes | Serves: 4-6

¾ cup gluten-free rolled oats
¾ cup almond flour
¼ cup melted coconut oil
2 tablespoons honey, plus ⅓ cup
1 teaspoon vanilla extract

¼ teaspoon kosher salt
2 large eggs, beaten
Zest and juice of 2 lemons
1 teaspoon arrowroot powder or cornstarch

1. Line a 6-inch square cake pan with aluminum foil. 2. In a medium bowl, combine the oats, almond flour, coconut oil, 2 tablespoons of honey, the vanilla, and ⅛ teaspoon of salt to form a stiff dough. 3. Press the dough into the bottom of the prepared pan. 4. In a separate bowl, whisk together the eggs, lemon zest and juice, arrowroot powder, ⅓ cup of honey, and the remaining ⅛ teaspoon of salt. 5. Pour the mixture over the crust. Cover the pan with foil. 6. Pour 1 cup of water into the Instant Pot and insert the trivet. 7. Place the pan on top of the trivet. 8. Put on the pressure cooker's lid and turn the steam valve to "Sealing" position. 9. Set the Instant Pot to Pressure Cook. Use the "+/-" keys on the control panel to set the cooking time to 12 minutes. 10. Press the Pressure Level button to adjust the pressure to "High". 11. Once the cooking cycle is completed, allow the steam to release naturally for 15 minutes and then quick release the remaining pressure. 12. When all the steam is released, remove the pressure lid from the top carefully. 13. Lift out the pan. Chill the lemon bars in the refrigerator for at least 2 hours before slicing them into six portions and serving.
Per Serving: Calories 389; Fat 11g; Sodium 501mg; Carbs 28.9g; Fiber 4.6g; Sugar 8g; Protein 6g

Carrot Date Cake

Prep time: 20 minutes | Cook time: 45 minutes | Serves: 4-6

Nonstick cooking spray
1 cup almond flour
2 teaspoons ground cinnamon
1 teaspoon baking soda
¼ teaspoon ground nutmeg
¼ teaspoon kosher salt
2 eggs, beaten

¼ cup pure maple syrup
½ teaspoon vanilla extract
1 cup (about 2 medium) shredded carrots
¼ cup (about 5) pitted and chopped dates

1. Grease a 6-inch cake pan with nonstick cooking spray. Set aside. 2. In a medium bowl, combine the almond flour, cinnamon, baking soda, nutmeg, and salt. 3. In a separate bowl, whisk together the eggs, maple syrup, and vanilla. 4. Pour the egg mixture into the flour mixture and combine to form a batter. Fold in the carrots and dates. 5. Pour the batter into the prepared cake pan. 6. Cover the pan with a paper towel and then cover the top of the pan with foil. 7. Pour 1 cup of water into the Instant Pot and insert the trivet. Place the cake pan on top of the trivet. 8. Put on the pressure cooker's lid and turn the steam valve to "Sealing" position. 9. Set the Instant Pot to Pressure Cook. Use the "+/-" keys on the control panel to set the cooking time to 45 minutes. 10. Press the Pressure Level button to adjust the pressure to "High". 11. Once the cooking cycle is completed, allow the steam to release naturally for 10 minutes and then quickly release the remaining pressure. 12. When all the steam is released, remove the pressure lid from the top carefully. 13. Lift out the cake pan. Remove the foil and paper towel and let the cake cool on the trivet for 1 hour. 14. Cut the cake into six slices and serve.
Per Serving: Calories 334; Fat 10.9g; Sodium 454mg; Carbs 20g; Fiber 3.1g; Sugar 5.2g; Protein 05g

Dairy-Free Rice Pudding

Prep time: 20 minutes | Cook time: 3 minutes | Serves: 1

½ cup uncooked long-grain white rice
1 cup water
1/16 teaspoon salt
2 tablespoons brown sugar
¼ cup cream of coconut
1 cup canned unsweetened full-

fat coconut milk
1 large egg
½ teaspoon vanilla extract
⅛ teaspoon ground cinnamon
½ tablespoon toasted shredded coconut

1. To the Instant Pot, add rice, water, and salt. 2. Put on the pressure cooker's lid and turn the steam valve to "Sealing" position. 3. Set the Instant Pot to Pressure Cook. Use the "+/-" keys on the control panel to set the cooking time to 3 minutes. 4. Press the Pressure Level button to adjust the pressure to "Low". 5. Once the cooking cycle is completed, allow the steam to release naturally. 6. When all the steam is released, remove the pressure lid from the top carefully. 7. Fluff rice, then add brown sugar and cream of coconut. Stir to dissolve. 8. Press Sauté button and adjust to Less. 9. Add ½ cup coconut milk and bring to a low simmer, whisking constantly. 10. In a liquid measuring cup, measure remaining ½ cup coconut milk and whisk together with egg. 11. While whisking, pour egg mixture into the pot until completely incorporated. 12. Whisk about 5 minutes until thickened. Press Cancel button to turn off heat. 13. Stir in vanilla. Scoop into a bowl and serve with a sprinkle of cinnamon and toasted coconut.
Per Serving: Calories 334; Fat 7.9g; Sodium 704mg; Carbs 6g; Fiber 3.6g; Sugar 6g; Protein 18g

Berry Almond Bundt Cake

Prep time: 1 hour 10 minutes | Cook time: 45 minutes | Serves: 4-6

Nonstick cooking spray
1½ cups almond flour, plus 1 tablespoon
1 teaspoon baking soda
¼ teaspoon kosher salt

2 eggs, beaten
½ cup buttermilk
¼ cup pure maple syrup
½ teaspoon pure almond extract
1 cup fresh berries

1. Grease a 7-inch Bundt pan with nonstick cooking spray. 2. In a medium bowl, combine 1½ cups of almond flour, the baking soda, and salt. 3. In a separate bowl, whisk together the eggs, buttermilk, maple syrup, and almond extract. 4. Pour the egg mixture into the flour mixture and combine to form a batter. 5. In a small bowl, mix the berries with 1 tablespoon of almond flour until thoroughly coated. 6. Fold the berry mixture into the batter. 7. Pour the batter into the prepared Bundt pan and cover the top with aluminum foil. 8. Pour 1 cup of water into the Instant Pot and insert the trivet. Place the Bundt pan on top of the trivet. 9. Put on the pressure cooker's lid and turn the steam valve to "Sealing" position. 10. Set the Instant Pot to Pressure Cook. Use the "+/-" keys on the control panel to set the cooking time to 45 minutes. 11. Press the Pressure Level button to adjust the pressure to "High". 12. Once the cooking cycle is completed, allow the steam to release naturally for 10 minutes and quickly release the remaining pressure. 13. When all the steam is released, remove the pressure lid from the top carefully. 14. Lift out the Bundt pan. Remove the foil and let the cake cool on the trivet for 1 hour. 15. Cut the cake into six slices and serve.
Per Serving: Calories 366; Fat 10.9g; Sodium 354mg; Carbs 25g; Fiber 4.1g; Sugar 8.2g; Protein 11g

Brownies

Prep time: 1 hour 10 minutes | Cook time: 45 minutes | Serves: 4-6

Nonstick cooking spray
1 large egg plus 1 egg yolk
⅓ cup maple syrup
½ teaspoon vanilla extract
⅓ cup coconut oil, at room temperature

⅔ cup almond flour
3 tablespoons unsweetened cocoa powder
¼ teaspoon baking powder
¼ teaspoon kosher salt

1. Line a 6-inch cake pan with aluminum foil and grease it with nonstick cooking spray. 2. In a medium bowl, whisk together the egg, egg yolk, maple syrup, and vanilla. 3. Mix in the coconut oil until smooth. Stir in the almond flour, cocoa powder, baking powder, and salt. 4. Pour the batter into the prepared cake pan and cover it loosely with foil. 5. Pour 1 cup of water into the Instant Pot and insert the trivet. Place the cake pan on top of the trivet. 6. Put on the pressure cooker's lid and turn the steam valve to "Sealing" position. 7. Set the Instant Pot to Pressure Cook. Use the "+/-" keys on the control panel to set the cooking time to 45 minutes. 8. Press the Pressure Level button to adjust the pressure to "High". 9. Once the cooking cycle is completed, allow the steam to release naturally for 15 minutes and then quick release the remaining pressure. 10. When all the steam is released, remove the pressure lid from the top carefully. 11. Lift out the pan. Remove the foil and let the brownies cool on the trivet for 1 hour. 12. Cut the brownies into six portions and serve.
Per Serving: Calories 371; Fat 7.9g; Sodium 704mg; Carbs 6g; Fiber 3.6g; Sugar 6g; Protein 18g

Coconut Cake

Prep time: 20 minutes | Cook time: 40 minutes | Serves: 4-6

1 cup almond flour
½ cup unsweetened shredded coconut
⅓ cup erythritol
1 teaspoon baking powder
1 teaspoon ground cinnamon

½ teaspoon ground ginger
2 large eggs lightly whisked
¼ cup coconut oil, melted
½ cup unsweetened full-fat canned coconut milk

1. In a large bowl, whisk together the flour, coconut, erythritol, baking powder, cinnamon, and ginger. 2. Add the eggs, coconut oil, and coconut milk and stir until well combined. 3. Spray a 6" springform pan with nonstick cooking spray. Pour the cake batter into the pan. 4. Add 2 cups water to the inner pot and place a steam rack inside. Place the pan on top of the steam rack. 5. Put on the pressure cooker's lid and turn the steam valve to "Sealing" position. 6. Set the Instant Pot to Pressure Cook. Use the "+/-" keys on the control panel to set the cooking time to 40 minutes. 7. Press the Pressure Level button to adjust the pressure to "Low". 8. Once the cooking cycle is completed, allow the steam to release naturally for 10 minutes and then quick release the remaining pressure. 9. When all the steam is released, remove the pressure lid from the top carefully. 10. Allow the cake to cool 5–10 minutes before slicing to serve.
Per Serving: Calories 199; Fat 5g; Sodium 41mg; Carbs 7g; Fiber 7.6g; Sugar 5g; Protein 2g

Apple Crisp

Prep time: 20 minutes | Cook time: 17 minutes | Serves: 4

For the Filling
4 large apples, peeled, cored, and cut into wedges
2 tablespoons lemon juice
¼ cup erythritol
¼ teaspoon ground cinnamon
1 teaspoon pure vanilla extract
2 tablespoons almond flour
For the Topping
1 cup almond flour
⅓ cup erythritol
1 cup old fashioned rolled oats
½ cup chopped pecans
¾ teaspoon ground cinnamon
1½ teaspoons vanilla extract
¼ cup coconut oil
2 tablespoons water

1. In a medium bowl, combine the filling ingredients: apples, lemon juice, erythritol, cinnamon, vanilla, and almond flour. 2. Transfer to a 6" cake pan and set aside. 3. In a large bowl, combine the topping ingredients: almond flour, erythritol, oats, pecans, cinnamon, vanilla extract, oil, and water. 4. Use your hands to incorporate the coconut oil into the rest of the ingredients evenly. 5. Pour the topping over the apple filling. 6. Pour 2 cups water into the inner pot and place the steam rack inside. 7. Put on the pressure cooker's lid and turn the steam valve to "Sealing" position. 8. Set the Instant Pot to Pressure Cook. Use the "+/-" keys on the control panel to set the cooking time to 17 minutes. 9. Press the Pressure Level button to adjust the pressure to "Low". 10. Once the cooking cycle is completed, allow the steam to release naturally. 11. When all the steam is released, remove the pressure lid from the top carefully. 12. Spoon into four bowls and serve.
Per Serving: Calories 389; Fat 11g; Sodium 501mg; Carbs 28.9g; Fiber 4.6g; Sugar 8g; Protein 6g

Orange Walnut Coffee Cake

Prep time: 20 minutes | Cook time: 40 minutes | Serves: 4

3 large eggs
4½ tablespoons pure maple syrup
Zest from 1 medium orange
1 tablespoon fresh orange juice
1 teaspoon pure vanilla extract
1⅓ cups almond flour
1 teaspoon baking powder
¾ teaspoon ground cinnamon
½ teaspoon salt
½ cup walnut pieces

1. In a medium bowl, whisk the eggs, 4 tablespoons maple syrup, orange zest, orange juice, and vanilla. 2. Add in the flour, baking powder, ½ teaspoon cinnamon, and salt. 3. Transfer the mixture to a 6" cake pan. 4. In a small bowl, mix together the walnuts, ¼ teaspoon cinnamon, and ½ tablespoon maple syrup. 5. Sprinkle on the top of the cake and cover it with aluminum foil. 6. Pour 1 cup water into the inner pot and place a steam rack inside. 7. Place the cake pan on top of the steam rack. 8. Put on the pressure cooker's lid and turn the steam valve to "Sealing" position. 9. Set the Instant Pot to Pressure Cook. 10. Use the "+/-" keys on the control panel to set the cooking time to 40 minutes. 11. Press the Pressure Level button to adjust the pressure to "Low". 12. Once the cooking cycle is completed, allow the steam to release quickly. 13. When all the steam is released, remove the pressure lid from the top carefully. 14. Allow the cake to cool completely before slicing.
Per Serving: Calories 378; Fat 10.9g; Sodium 354mg; Carbs 25g; Fiber 4.1g; Sugar 8.2g; Protein 11g

Banana Pudding Cake

Prep time: 20 minutes | Cook time: 20 minutes | Serves: 6

3 tablespoons ground golden flaxseed meal
10 tablespoons water
1¾ cups mashed banana (about 3 bananas)
¼ cup avocado oil
1 teaspoon pure vanilla extract
2 cups almond flour
½ cup erythritol
1 teaspoon baking powder
¼ teaspoon salt
½ cup chopped pecans
½ teaspoon ground cinnamon

1. In a small bowl, combine the flaxseed and 9 tablespoons water and give it time to gel. 2. In a large bowl, whisk together the flaxseed and water mixture, banana, oil, and vanilla. 3. Add the flour, erythritol, baking powder, and salt and stir to combine well. 4. Spray a 7" cake pan with nonstick cooking spray. Pour the batter into the pan. 5. In a small bowl, combine the chopped pecans, cinnamon, and 1 tablespoon water. 6. Sprinkle on top of the cake batter. 7. Pour 1 cup water into the inner pot and place a steam rack inside. Place the pan on top of the steam rack. 8. Put on the pressure cooker's lid and turn the steam valve to "Sealing" position. 9. Set the Instant Pot to Pressure Cook. Use the "+/-" keys on the control panel to set the cooking time to 20 minutes. 10. Press the Pressure Level button to adjust the pressure to "Low". 11. Once the cooking cycle is completed, allow the steam to release naturally. 12. When all the steam is released, remove the pressure lid from the top carefully. 13. Spoon into six bowls and serve.
Per Serving: Calories 372; Fat 20g; Sodium 891mg; Carbs 29g; Fiber 3g; Sugar 8g; Protein 10g

Banana Chocolate Chip Bundt Cake

Prep time: 20 minutes | Cook time: 55 minutes | Serves: 8

½ cup room temperature coconut oil
1 cup monk fruit sweetener
2 large eggs, room temperature
3 medium bananas, mashed
2 cups oat flour
1½ teaspoons baking soda
½ teaspoon salt
½ cup stevia-sweetened chocolate chips

1. In a large bowl of a stand mixer with a paddle attachment, add the oil, sweetener, and eggs and beat together on medium speed until well combined. 2. Add the mashed banana and beat until combined. 3. Add the flour, baking soda, and salt and beat again until combined. 4. Remove the paddle attachment and stir in the chocolate chips. 5. Spray a 6" Bundt cake pan with cooking oil. Transfer the batter into the pan. 6. Place a paper towel over the top of the pan and then cover with aluminum foil. 7. Add 1½ cups water to the Instant Pot inner pot and then place a steam rack inside. 8. Place the Bundt pan on the steam rack. 9. Put on the pressure cooker's lid and turn the steam valve to "Sealing" position. 10. Set the Instant Pot to Pressure Cook. 11. Use the "+/-" keys on the control panel to set the cooking time to 55 minutes. 12. Press the Pressure Level button to adjust the pressure to "Low". 13. Once the cooking cycle is completed, allow the steam to release naturally for 10 minutes and then quick release the remaining pressure. 14. When all the steam is released, remove the pressure lid from the top carefully. 15. Allow to cool completely before removing from pan and slicing to serve.
Per Serving: Calories 382; Fat 7.9g; Sodium 704mg; Carbs 6g; Fiber 3.6g; Sugar 6g; Protein 18g

Blueberry Crisp

Prep time: 20 minutes | Cook time: 17 minutes | Serves: 4

For the Filling
1 (10-ounce) bag frozen blueberries
2 tablespoons fresh orange juice
¼ cup erythritol
1 teaspoon pure vanilla extract
2 tablespoons almond flour
1 teaspoon orange zest
For the Topping
1 cup almond flour
⅓ cup erythritol
1 cup old fashioned rolled oats
½ cup sliced almonds
1½ teaspoons pure vanilla extract
¼ cup coconut oil
2 tablespoons fresh orange juice

1. In a medium bowl, combine the filling ingredients: the blueberries, orange juice, erythritol, vanilla, flour, and orange zest. Transfer to a 6" cake pan and set aside. 2. In another bowl, combine the topping ingredients: the flour, erythritol, oats, almonds, vanilla, oil, and orange juice. 3. Use your hands to incorporate the oil into the rest of the ingredients evenly. 4. Pour the topping over the blueberry filling. 5. Pour 2 cups water into the inner pot and place the steam rack inside. 6. Place the cake pan on top of the steam rack. 7. Put on the pressure cooker's lid and turn the steam valve to "Sealing" position. 8. Set the Instant Pot to Pressure Cook. 9. Use the "+/-" keys on the control panel to set the cooking time to 17 minutes. 10. Press the Pressure Level button to adjust the pressure to "Low". 11. Once the cooking cycle is completed, allow the steam to release naturally. 12. When all the steam is released, remove the pressure lid from the top carefully. 13. Spoon into four bowls and serve.
Per Serving: Calories 334; Fat 19g; Sodium 354mg; Carbs 21g; Fiber 5.1g; Sugar 8.2g; Protein 2g

Caramelized Plantains

Prep time: 20 minutes | Cook time: 10 minutes | Serves: 4-6

1 tablespoon coconut oil	1 teaspoon ground cinnamon
3 medium ripe plantains, peeled and sliced thickly on the diagonal	2 tablespoons pure maple syrup
¼ teaspoon salt	¼ cup water

1. Put the oil in the inner pot and press the Sauté button. Set the temperature to Normal setting. 2. Once the oil is melted, add the plantains, salt, and cinnamon. 3. Stir until the plantains are coated in the oil and cinnamon. Press the Cancel button. 4. Stir in the maple syrup and water. 5. Put on the pressure cooker's lid and turn the steam valve to "Sealing" position. 6. Set the Instant Pot to Pressure Cook. 7. Press the Pressure Level button to adjust the pressure to "Low". 8. Use the "+/-" keys on the control panel to set the cooking time to 10 minute. 9. Once the cooking cycle is completed, allow the steam to release naturally. 10. When all the steam is released, remove the pressure lid from the top carefully. 11. Transfer to bowls for serving.
Per Serving: Calories 334; Fat 10.9g; Sodium 454mg; Carbs 20g; Fiber 3.1g; Sugar 5.2g; Protein 05g

Pumpkin Pudding

Prep time: 20 minutes | Cook time: 5 minutes | Serves: 6

1 (13.66-ounce) can unsweetened full-fat coconut milk	½ cup pure maple syrup
1 large egg	1 tablespoon pure vanilla extract
½ cup canned pumpkin purée	2 teaspoons pumpkin pie spice
	2 teaspoons arrowroot powder

1. In a medium bowl, whisk together the coconut milk, egg, pumpkin purée, maple syrup, and vanilla until you have a very smooth mixture. 2. Stir in the pumpkin pie spice and arrowroot powder. 3. Transfer the mixture to a 6" cake pan. 4. Pour 2 cups water into the inner pot and place the steam rack inside. 5. Place the cake pan on top of the steam rack. 6. Put on the pressure cooker's lid and turn the steam valve to "Sealing" position. 7. Set the Instant Pot to Pressure Cook. 8. Use the "+/-" keys on the control panel to set the cooking time to 5 minutes. 9. Press the Pressure Level button to adjust the pressure to "Low". 10. Once the cooking cycle is completed, allow the steam to release naturally. 11. When all the steam is released, remove the pressure lid from the top carefully. 12. Stir the pudding and then transfer it to a glass container with a lid. 13. Chill in the refrigerator 1 hour or more before serving.
Per Serving: Calories 361; Fat 12.9g; Sodium 754mg; Carbs 21g; Fiber 6.1g; Sugar 4.2g; Protein 11g

Apple Bundt Cake

Prep time: 15 minutes | Cook time: 55 minutes | Serves: 4-6

½ cup room temperature coconut oil	1½ teaspoons baking soda
1 cup monk fruit sweetener	1 teaspoon ground cinnamon
2 large eggs, room temperature	½ teaspoon salt
1 cup unsweetened apple sauce	1 large apple, peeled, cored, and diced
2 cups oat flour	

1. In a large bowl of a stand mixer with a paddle attachment, beat together the oil, sweetener, and eggs on medium speed until well combined. 2. Add the applesauce and beat until combined. 3. Add the flour, baking soda, cinnamon, and salt and beat again until combined. 4. Remove the paddle attachment and stir in the diced apple. 5. Spray a 6" Bundt cake pan with cooking oil. Transfer the batter into the pan. 6. Place a paper towel over the top of the pan and then cover with aluminum foil. 7. Add 1½ cups water to the Instant Pot inner pot and then place a steam rack inside. 8. Place the Bundt pan on the steam rack. 9. Put on the pressure cooker's lid and turn the steam valve to "Sealing" position. 10. Set the Instant Pot to Pressure Cook. 11. Use the "+/-" keys on the control panel to set the cooking time to 55 minutes. 12. Press the Pressure Level button to adjust the pressure to "Low". 13. Once the cooking cycle

is completed, allow the steam to release naturally for 10 minutes and then quick-release the remaining pressure. 14. When all the steam is released, remove the pressure lid from the top carefully. 15. Allow to cool completely before removing from pan and slicing to serve.
Per Serving: Calories 389; Fat 5g; Sodium 41mg; Carbs 27g; Fiber 7.6g; Sugar 5g; Protein 2g

Red Velvet Cake

Prep time: 15 minutes | Cook time: 12 minutes | Serves: 4-6

Nonstick cooking spray	divided, at room temperature
1 cup water	1 large egg
1½ cups all-purpose flour	2 tablespoons plain unsweetened Greek yogurt
⅓ cup unsweetened cocoa powder	1 teaspoon red food coloring
1 teaspoon baking powder	1 cup confectioners' sugar
1 teaspoon baking soda	4 oz. cream cheese, at room temperature
¼ teaspoon salt	1 tablespoon heavy cream
¾ cup granulated sugar	¼ teaspoon vanilla extract
½ cup buttermilk	
4 tablespoons (½ stick) plus 2 tablespoons unsalted butter,	

1. Spray the cups of two silicone egg molds with nonstick cooking spray. 2. Pour the water into the pressure cooker pot and place a steamer rack trivet in the bottom. 3. In a medium bowl, whisk together the flour, cocoa powder, baking powder, baking soda, and salt. 4. In a large bowl, beat together the granulated sugar, buttermilk, 4 tablespoons of butter, egg, and yogurt with a hand mixer until smooth. 5. Add the dry ingredients to the wet ingredients and mix with the hand mixer until well combined. 6. Add the red food coloring and beat until the color is fully incorporated into the batter 7. Fill the cups of the egg molds halfway with batter. 8. Lay a paper towel over the top of each mold. 9. Then cover the paper towel and egg bite molds loosely with aluminum foil. 10. Stack the two molds on top of each other and place on the trivet inside the pot. 11. Put on the pressure cooker's lid and turn the steam valve to "Sealing" position. 12. Set the Instant Pot to Pressure Cook. 13. Use the "+/-" keys on the control panel to set the cooking time to 12 minutes. 14. Press the Pressure Level button to adjust the pressure to "High". 15. Once the cooking cycle is completed, allow the steam to release naturally. 16. When all the steam is released, remove the pressure lid from the top carefully. 17. Remove the molds from the pressure cooker and cool on a wire rack before using a spoon to remove the cake bites from the molds. 18. In a small bowl, whip the confectioners' sugar, cream cheese, remaining 2 tablespoons of butter, heavy cream, and vanilla together with the hand mixer until fluffy, about 1 minute. 19. Dip each cake bite halfway into the cream cheese frosting. 20. Serve.
Per Serving: Calories 334; Fat 10.9g; Sodium 454mg; Carbs 20g; Fiber 3.1g; Sugar 5.2g; Protein 05g

Cinnamon Apples

Prep time: 20 minutes | Cook time: 10 minutes | Serves: 4-6

1 tablespoon coconut oil	1½ teaspoons ground cinnamon
5 medium apples, peeled, cored, and cut into large chunks	1 tablespoon water
	1 tablespoon lemon juice

1. Press the "Sauté" button two time to select "Normal" mode and put the oil in the inner pot to melt. 2. Once the oil is melted, add the apples, cinnamon, water, and lemon juice and stir to combine. 3. Put on the pressure cooker's lid and turn the steam valve to "Sealing" position. 4. Set the Instant Pot to Pressure Cook. 5. Press the Pressure Level button to adjust the pressure to "Low". 6. Use the "+/-" keys on the control panel to set the cooking time to 10 minute. 7. Once the cooking cycle is completed, allow the steam to release naturally. 8. When all the steam is released, remove the pressure lid from the top carefully. 9. Serve warm.
Per Serving: Calories 389; Fat 5g; Sodium 41mg; Carbs 27g; Fiber 7.6g; Sugar 5g; Protein 2g

Blueberry Pudding Cake

Prep time: 20 minutes | Cook time: 20 minutes | Serves: 6

3 tablespoons ground golden flaxseed meal
9 tablespoons water
1¼ cups unsweetened cinnamon applesauce
¼ cup avocado oil
1 teaspoon pure vanilla extract

2¼ cups almond flour
¾ cup erythritol
1 teaspoon baking powder
¼ teaspoon salt
½ cup sliced almonds
½ teaspoon ground cinnamon
1½ cups blueberries

1. In a small bowl, combine the flaxseed and water and give it time to gel. 2. In a large bowl, whisk together the flaxseed and water mixture, applesauce, oil, and vanilla. 3. Add 2 cups flour, ½ cup erythritol, baking powder, and salt and stir to combine well. 4. Spray a 7" cake pan with nonstick cooking spray. Pour the batter into the pan. 5. In a small bowl, combine the almonds, cinnamon, blueberries, remaining ¼ cup flour, and ¼ cup erythritol. Sprinkle mixture on top of the cake batter. 6. Pour 1 cup water into the inner pot and place a steam rack inside. Place the pan on top of the steam rack. 7. Put on the pressure cooker's lid and turn the steam valve to "Sealing" position. 8. Set the Instant Pot to Pressure Cook. 9. Use the "+/-" keys on the control panel to set the cooking time to 20 minutes. 10. Press the Pressure Level button to adjust the pressure to "Low". 11. Once the cooking cycle is completed, allow the steam to release quickly. 12. When all the steam is released, remove the pressure lid from the top carefully. 13. Spoon into six bowls and serve.
Per Serving: Calories 366; Fat 7.9g; Sodium 704mg; Carbs 6g; Fiber 3.6g; Sugar 6g; Protein 18g

Peanut Butter Pudding

Prep time: 15 minutes | Cook time: 8 minutes | Serves: 4

1 cup milk
1 cup half-and-half
⅓ cup sugar
2 tablespoons cornstarch

¼ teaspoon salt
½ cup creamy peanut butter
1 teaspoon vanilla extract
1 cup water

1. Press the "Sauté" button two time on the Instant pot to select "Normal" temperature settings. 2. Whisk the milk, half-and-half, sugar, cornstarch, and salt together in the pressure cooker pot. Simmer, for 7 minutes. 3. Whisk in the peanut butter and vanilla until the peanut butter is melted and mixed in completely. 4. Press cancel or turn off the burner. Transfer the pudding to a heat-safe bowl and cover with aluminum foil. 5. When the pot is cool enough to handle, wash and dry it. 6. Pour the water into the pressure cooker pot and place a steamer rack trivet in the bottom. 7. Place the bowl of pudding on the trivet. 8. Put on the pressure cooker's lid and turn the steam valve to "Sealing" position. 9. Set the Instant Pot to Pressure Cook. 10. Use the "+/-" keys on the control panel to set the cooking time to 8 minutes. 11. Press the Pressure Level button to adjust the pressure to "High". 12. Once the cooking cycle is completed, allow the steam to release quickly. 13. When all the steam is released, remove the pressure lid from the top carefully. 14. Carefully remove the bowl from the pressure cooker and stir the pudding. 15. Let it cool on the counter, then serve.
Per Serving: Calories 472; Fat 12.9g; Sodium 754mg; Carbs 21g; Fiber 6.1g; Sugar 4.2g; Protein 11g

Blueberry Almond Cakes

Prep time: 15 minutes | Cook time: 15 minutes | Serves: 4

4 large eggs
2 teaspoons pure vanilla extract
1⅓ cups almond flour
¼ cup erythritol

1 teaspoon baking powder
¼ teaspoon salt
1 cup blueberries
¼ cup sliced almonds

1. In a medium bowl, whisk the eggs and vanilla. 2. Add the flour, erythritol, baking powder, and salt, and stir to combine. Fold in the blueberries. 3. Spray four (6-ounce) glass Mason jars with cooking oil. 4. Divide the batter into the jars, top each jar with some of the almonds, and cover them with aluminum foil. 5. Pour 1 cup water into the inner pot. Place the steam rack inside and place the Mason jars on the rack. 6. Put on the pressure cooker's lid and turn the steam valve to "Sealing" position. 7. Set the Instant Pot to Pressure Cook. 8. Use the "+/-" keys on the control panel to set the cooking time to 15 minutes. 9. Press the Pressure Level button to adjust the pressure to "Low". 10. Once the cooking cycle is completed, allow the steam to release quickly. 11. When all the steam is released, remove the pressure lid from the top carefully. 12. Carefully remove the Mason jars from the inner pot and allow to cool before serving.
Per Serving: Calories 419; Fat 14g; Sodium 791mg; Carbs 28.9g; Fiber 4.6g; Sugar 8g; Protein 3g

Chocolate Rice Pudding

Prep time: 15 minutes | Cook time: 8 minutes | Serves: 4-6

1 cup Arborio rice
1½ cups water
¼ teaspoon salt
2 cups unsweetened full-fat canned coconut milk

½ cup erythritol
2 large eggs
½ teaspoon pure vanilla extract
¾ cup stevia-sweetened chocolate chips

1. Add the rice, water, and salt to the inner pot. 2. Put on the pressure cooker's lid and turn the steam valve to "Sealing" position. 3. Set the Instant Pot to Pressure Cook. 4. Use the "+/-" keys on the control panel to set the cooking time to 3 minutes. 5. Press the Pressure Level button to adjust the pressure to "Low". 6. Once the cooking cycle is completed, allow the steam to release naturally. 7. When all the steam is released, remove the pressure lid from the top carefully. 8. Add 1½ cups coconut milk and erythritol to rice in the inner pot; stir to combine. 9. In a small bowl, whisk eggs with remaining ½ cup coconut milk, and vanilla. 10. Pour through a fine-mesh strainer into the inner pot. 11. Press the "Sauté" button two time to select "Normal" temperature setting and cook, for 5 minutes. Turn off the heat. 12. Stir in the chocolate chips and spoon into bowls.
Per Serving: Calories 371; Fat 19g; Sodium 354mg; Carbs 21g; Fiber 5.1g; Sugar 8.2g; Protein 2g

Walnut Brownies

Prep time: 15 minutes | Cook time: 50 minutes | Serves: 6

Nonstick cooking spray
1½ cups water
1 cup sugar
½ cup all-purpose flour
⅓ cup unsweetened cocoa powder
¼ teaspoon baking powder

8 tablespoons (1 stick) unsalted butter, melted
2 large eggs
½ teaspoon vanilla extract
½ cup chopped walnuts

1. Spray a heat-safe bowl with nonstick cooking spray. 2. Pour the water into the pressure cooker pot and place a steamer rack trivet in the bottom. 3. In a medium bowl, whisk together the sugar, flour, cocoa powder, and baking powder. 4. In a large bowl, whisk together the melted butter, eggs, and vanilla. 5. Add the dry ingredients to the wet ingredients and mix until well combined. Fold in the chopped walnuts. 6. Pour the batter into the prepared heat-safe bowl and smooth the top with a spatula. 7. Lay a paper towel over the top of the bowl, then cover the paper towel and bowl loosely with aluminum foil. 8. Place the bowl on the trivet inside the pot. 9. Put on the pressure cooker's lid and turn the steam valve to "Sealing" position. 10. Set the Instant Pot to Pressure Cook. 11. Use the "+/-" keys on the control panel to set the cooking time to 50 minutes. 12. Press the Pressure Level button to adjust the pressure to "High". 13. Once the cooking cycle is completed, allow the steam to release naturally for 10 minutes and then quick-release the remaining pressure. 14. When all the steam is released, remove the pressure lid from the top carefully. 15. Carefully remove the bowl from the pot and cool on a wire rack before slicing.
Per Serving: Calories 389; Fat 5g; Sodium 41mg; Carbs 27g; Fiber 7.6g; Sugar 5g; Protein 2g

Zucchini Cake

Prep time: 15 minutes | Cook time: 40 minutes | Serves: 4

½ cup almond flour	¾ teaspoon baking powder
¼ cup coconut flour	3 large eggs
⅓ cup erythritol	¼ cup avocado oil
¼ teaspoon salt	1 teaspoon pure vanilla extract
1 teaspoon ground cinnamon	½ cup shredded zucchini

1. In a medium bowl, whisk together the almond flour, coconut flour, erythritol, salt, cinnamon, and baking powder. 2. In a separate large bowl, whisk together the eggs, oil, and vanilla. 3. Add the dry ingredients to the wet ingredients and stir to combine. Fold in the zucchini. 4. Transfer the batter to a 6" cake pan and cover with aluminum foil. 5. Pour 1 cup water into the inner pot and add the steam rack inside. Place the cake pan on the rack. 6. Put on the pressure cooker's lid and turn the steam valve to "Sealing" position. 7. Set the Instant Pot to Pressure Cook. 8. Use the "+/-" keys on the control panel to set the cooking time to 40 minutes. 9. Press the Pressure Level button to adjust the pressure to "Low". 10. Once the cooking cycle is completed, allow the steam to release naturally. 11. When all the steam is released, remove the pressure lid from the top carefully. 12. Allow the cake to cool completely before slicing and serving.
Per Serving: Calories 334; Fat 7.9g; Sodium 704mg; Carbs 6g; Fiber 3.6g; Sugar 6g; Protein 18g

Banana Sundae with Strawberry Sauce

Prep time: 15 minutes | Cook time: 1 minutes | Serves: 6

1 pound strawberries, hulled and chopped	1 teaspoon arrowroot powder
2 tablespoons fresh lemon juice	½ teaspoon water
½ cup erythritol	6 large ripe bananas, sliced and frozen

1. Add the strawberries, lemon juice, and erythritol to the inner pot. 2. Put on the pressure cooker's lid and turn the steam valve to "Sealing" position. 3. Set the Instant Pot to Pressure Cook. 4. Use the "+/-" keys on the control panel to set the cooking time to 1 minute. 5. Press the Pressure Level button to adjust the pressure to "Low". 6. Once the cooking cycle is completed, allow the steam to release naturally for 5 minutes and then quick-release the remaining pressure. 7. When all the steam is released, remove the pressure lid from the top carefully. 8. In a small bowl, mix the arrowroot powder with water to create a slurry. 9. Allow the strawberries to sit 5 minutes, and then stir in the arrowroot slurry. 10. Meanwhile, remove the bananas from the freezer and place them in your food processor. 11. Process the bananas until you have a thick, creamy mixture. 12. Spoon the mixture into six bowls, and spoon some strawberry sauce on the top of each bowl.
Per Serving: Calories 366; Fat 10.9g; Sodium 354mg; Carbs 25g; Fiber 4.1g; Sugar 8.2g; Protein 11g

Maple Pecan Pears

Prep time: 15 minutes | Cook time: 10 minutes | Serves: 4-6

2 large ripe but firm d'Anjou pears	1 tablespoon pure maple syrup
1½ tablespoons coconut oil, melted	½ teaspoon ground cinnamon
	¼ cup chopped pecans

1. Peel the pears and cut them in half lengthwise. Carefully scoop out the core and seeds from each half. 2. Press the "Sauté" button two time to select "Normal" temperature setting and add the oil to the inner pot. 3. Once the oil melts, place the pears in the inner pot, cut side down, and cook them until they are starting to get browned, about 2–3 minutes. 4. Carefully transfer the pears to a steamer basket. 5. Add ½ cup water to the inner pot and use a spoon to scrape any brown bits. 6. Place the steam rack inside, and place the steamer basket with the pears on top. 7. Put on the pressure cooker's lid and turn the steam valve to "Sealing" position. 8. Set the Instant Pot to Pressure Cook. 9. Use the "+/-" keys on the control panel to set the cooking time to 10 minutes. 10. Press the Pressure Level button to adjust the pressure to "Low". 11. Once the cooking cycle is completed, allow the steam to release quickly. 12. When all the steam is released, remove the pressure lid from the top carefully. 13. Remove the water and dry the inner pot. 14. Press Sauté button and add the maple syrup and cinnamon. 15. Stir to combine and heat to warm, about 1 minute. 16. Drizzle the heated maple syrup and cinnamon onto the pears. 17. Then sprinkle with chopped pecans and serve.
Per Serving: Calories 372; Fat 20g; Sodium 891mg; Carbs 29g; Fiber 3g; Sugar 8g; Protein 10g

Cinnamon Pineapple

Prep time: 20 minutes | Cook time: 2 minutes | Serves: 6

2 tablespoons coconut oil	into 2" pieces
1 large pineapple, cored and cut	1½ teaspoons ground cinnamon

1. Press the "Sauté" button two time to select "Normal" mode and add the oil to the inner pot. 2. When the oil is melted, add the pineapple and cinnamon and stir to combine. 3. Put on the pressure cooker's lid and turn the steam valve to "Sealing" position. 4. Set the Instant Pot to Pressure Cook. 5. Use the "+/-" keys on the control panel to set the cooking time to 2 minutes. 6. Press the Pressure Level button to adjust the pressure to "Low". 7. Once the cooking cycle is completed, allow the steam to release naturally. 8. When all the steam is released, remove the pressure lid from the top carefully. 9. Serve.
Per Serving: Calories 322; Fat 11g; Sodium 491mg; Carbs 24g; Fiber 3g; Sugar 8g; Protein 3g

Warm Caramel Apple Dip

Prep time: 20 minutes | Cook time: 1 minutes | Serves: 10

2 cups pitted dates	¼ cup maple syrup
½ cup tahini	¼ cup water

1. Place the dates, tahini, maple syrup and ¼ cup water in the inner pot of the Instant Pot and stir to combine. 2. Put on the pressure cooker's lid and turn the steam valve to "Sealing" position. 3. Set the Instant Pot to Pressure Cook. Use the "+/-" keys on the control panel to set the cooking time to 1 minute. 4. Press the Pressure Level button to adjust the pressure to "Low". 5. Once the cooking cycle is completed, allow the steam to release quickly. 6. When all the steam is released, remove the pressure lid from the top carefully. 7. Allow the mixture to cool slightly, and then transfer to a blender. 8. Blend the mixture on high until super smooth, adding additional water as needed, 1 tablespoon at a time. 9. Serve.
Per Serving: Calories 334; Fat 7.9g; Sodium 704mg; Carbs 6g; Fiber 3.6g; Sugar 6g; Protein 18g

Strawberry Chocolate Chip Cakes

Prep time: 15 minutes | Cook time: 15 minutes | Serves: 4

4 large eggs	¼ teaspoon salt
2 teaspoons pure vanilla extract	1 cup strawberry chunks
1⅓ cups almond flour	½ cup stevia-sweetened chocolate chips
¼ cup erythritol	
1 teaspoon baking powder	

1. In a medium bowl, whisk the eggs and vanilla. 2. Add the flour, erythritol, baking powder, and salt, and stir to combine. 3. Fold in the strawberries and chocolate chips. 4. Spray four (6-ounce) glass Mason jars with cooking oil. 5. Divide the batter into the jars and cover them with aluminum foil. 6. Pour 1 cup water into the inner pot. Place the steam rack inside and place the Mason jars on the rack. 7. Put on the pressure cooker's lid and turn the steam valve to "Sealing" position. 8. Set the Instant Pot to Pressure Cook. 9. Use the "+/-" keys on the control panel to set the cooking time to 15 minutes. 10. Press the Pressure Level button to adjust the pressure to "Low". 11. Once the cooking cycle is completed, allow the steam to release quickly. 12. When all the steam is released, remove the pressure lid from the top carefully. 13. Carefully remove the Mason jars from the inner pot and allow to cool before serving.
Per Serving: Calories 389; Fat 11g; Sodium 501mg; Carbs 28.9g; Fiber 4.6g; Sugar 8g; Protein 6g

Conclusion

In this fast-moving world, everything is fast and you have to maintain your lifestyle accordingly. For this purpose, many cooking appliances have been introduced to lower time and effort in cooking and having a delicious, healthy, and nutritional meal. The Instant pot is one of the best appliances considered for this fast-moving world as it allows you to cook fast and cooks a nutritional meal that fulfills your dietary requirements as well as is not hard on your budget. This appliance allows you to cook, bake, slow cook, and steam your food very fast.

The Instant pot cookbook is the perfect guide that helps you to operate your appliance like a pro and provide you with nutritional, healthy, and delicious recipes in no time. You can manage your kitchen time with other work and at the end have an amazingly delicious meal with your family.

This amazing cookbook helps you to have a variety of meals from all over the world. You can cook your food easily without being a regular cook or professional. This amazing cookbook allows you to prepare and cook your meal like a professional, so guys let's get started on our instant pot journey and enjoy our fast-forward life with delicious food.

Appendix 1 Measurement Conversion Chart

VOLUME EQUIVALENTS (LIQUID)

US STANDARD	US STANDARD (OUNCES)	METRIC (APPROXIMATE)
2 tablespoons	1 fl.oz	30 mL
¼ cup	2 fl.oz	60 mL
½ cup	4 fl.oz	120 mL
1 cup	8 fl.oz	240 mL
1½ cup	12 fl.oz	355 mL
2 cups or 1 pint	16 fl.oz	475 mL
4 cups or 1 quart	32 fl.oz	1 L
1 gallon	128 fl.oz	4 L

VOLUME EQUIVALENTS (DRY)

US STANDARD	METRIC (APPROXIMATE)
⅛ teaspoon	0.5 mL
¼ teaspoon	1 mL
½ teaspoon	2 mL
¾ teaspoon	4 mL
1 teaspoon	5 mL
1 tablespoon	15 mL
¼ cup	59 mL
½ cup	118 mL
¾ cup	177 mL
1 cup	235 mL
2 cups	475 mL
3 cups	700 mL
4 cups	1 L

TEMPERATURES EQUIVALENTS

FAHRENHEIT(F)	CELSIUS(C) (APPROXIMATE)
225 °F	107 °C
250 °F	120 °C
275 °F	135 °C
300 °F	150 °C
325 °F	160 °C
350 °F	180 °C
375 °F	190 °C
400 °F	205 °C
425 °F	220 °C
450 °F	235 °C
475 °F	245 °C
500 °F	260 °C

WEIGHT EQUIVALENTS

US STANDARD	METRIC (APPROXINATE)
1 ounce	28 g
2 ounces	57 g
5 ounces	142 g
10 ounces	284 g
15 ounces	425 g
16 ounces (1 pound)	455 g
1.5pounds	680 g
2pounds	907 g

Appendix 2 Recipes Index

Printed in Great Britain
by Amazon